The Dynamics of International Organization

The Dynamics of

International Organization

THE MAKING OF WORLD ORDER

BY

PHILIP E. JACOB, A.M., Ph.D.

Professor of Political Science

AND

ALEXINE L. ATHERTON, A.B., Ph.D.

Assistant Professor of Political Science

BOTH OF THE UNIVERSITY OF PENNSYLVANIA

1965 · THE DORSEY PRESS · HOMEWOOD, ILLINOIS

BETTY MUTHER JACOB

crusader on the frontiers of international public service
whose belief in persons
penetrated the political processes of nations
and won action, through UNRRA and UNICEF,
to sustain the lives of children
and strengthen the bonds of world community

Foreword

In this book, aptly entitled *The Dynamics of International Organization: The Making of World Order,* the authors, Professors Philip E. Jacob and Alexine L. Atherton, analyze the problems of international organization and of the making of world order from the most meaningful angle.

The reader is not presented here with a picture of international organizations *per se* with their numerous conferences, assemblies, councils, committees, subcommittees and supporting staffs. The basic approach flows from the opposite pole—the analysis of major international problems of a character requiring the concerted efforts of international organization in their solution. For international organizations are not ends in themselves; they are means to ends—ends of high significance to humanity. This correlation of means and ends is elaborated with great clarity by the authors who contribute to a much needed increase of understanding of the nature and scope of the tasks and of the performance of international organizations in coping with them.

Current international organizations are sometimes regarded as too numerous, too clumsy, too complex, too overlapping in their legislative, administrative, and operational arrangements and could be streamlined and simplified in the general interest. Serious, well-considered, and objective proposals for improvement in the constitutional and administrative structure of international organizations should always be given the consideration that they deserve, primary concern being centered upon the relevance of such proposals to the increase of effectiveness in handling the problems within the area of their competence. Failures and frustrations in the work of international organization is more often chargeable to major conflicts of interest and of the sweep of powerful political forces impinging upon proposed action than to structural weakness. In this area, therefore, the desired approach is not to change the structure of the organization, but to deal with the political forces standing in the way of effective action. As Dag Hammarskjold used to say while handling serious crises, "We must elbow the Cold War out of this situation."

The serious financial crisis in the United Nations illustrates the impact of the deep political differences in the field of peace-keeping upon the structural character and the effective working capacity of the Organization. It has precipitated a major debate as to the relative competences of the General Assembly and the Security Council involving concerns for the preservation of the peace-keeping capacity of the United Nations as well as the role and voice of individual members and of the majority of members.

Despite all shortcomings, international organization has made great advances in the last twenty years. Again, to quote Dag Hammarskjold, "The problem is not to bring international organization up to the level of world public opinion; world public opinion must be brought up to the level of world organization." Stronger international organizations come into being only as governments and people support them, understand their implications and visualize the benefits to be derived from them.

Each year adds to the intensely internationalized character of the lives of nations and peoples. The old patterns of national separateness, of independent national sovereignties have been made meaningless through the changes wrought by modern communication and transportation, through education and travel, and commerce and trade, as well as through the revolution of rising expectations of large sections of humanity seeking a better way of life. The internationalized character of many contemporary problems, their scope and deep relevance to the human condition, is set forth in these pages.

An event of prime historical importance in our generation has been the liquidation of great empires and the emergence of more than a half hundred new nations. Their existence as new articulate communities and as members of the United Nations have provided new challenges in nation building and in the forging of new and stable relationships between themselves and the older communities. North-South problems now vie in importance and magnitude with the old and continuing East-West tensions. The greatly increased membership in the United Nations has placed new strains upon the organization as well as provided new opportunities for it.

Problems and tensions reflected within the halls of the United Nations are generally clear reflections of the world political picture.

In an age when thermonuclear might has changed the whole character of the issues of war and peace, the prevention of war becomes a matter of major concern. The pursuit of avenues for the achievement of disarmament remains imperative and the development and utilization of effective means and procedures to mediate, conciliate and settle disputes becomes a solid responsibility of the world community.

This book presents a clear and full account of the varied approaches of the United Nations in peace-keeping. They range from the collective use of force against aggression in Korea to the United Nations presence as expressed by a single representative of the Secretary-General stationed in some sensitive area of the world. In crises like the Suez, the Congo and Lebanon, effective combinations of intense diplomatic activity directed by the Secretary-General were combined with field operations involving as many as 18,000 troops in the Congo or several hundred observers in Lebanon. The tools of mediation and peaceful settlement must be as variable as crises are different and must always be adjusted to the nature of the crisis. An invaluable advance was made in the theory, practices and processes of mediation and peaceful settlement and of allaying tensions by Dag Hammarskjold during his eight and a half years as Secretary-General.

A major aspect of success in United Nations peace-keeping efforts is the degree to which the generality of the membership maintains a true third-party role and joins with the Secretary-General in bringing a crisis or dispute to an end. There was a time when the "parties directly concerned" and "third parties" had distinct and clearly differentiated meanings. In the last years the distinction has often been blurred. Members, other than those directly concerned in a conflict, sometimes claim a direct interest in support of one and against the other party while at the same time claiming the role of the "third party." This was particularly true in the Congo crisis. The restoration of a clean distinction between "third parties" and "parties directly concerned" will increase the effectiveness of United Nations peace-keeping efforts, but this will likely only happen when the hot political and ideological emotions that sweep the world begin to subside.

This would represent a restoration of multilateral diplomacy in its full force. The multilateral processes available within the framework of the United Nations are generally more acceptable to the parties and more effective in dealing with disputes than bilateral approaches. However, it is a part of the worth of the United Nations that within the framework of multilateralism there can be great flexibility in the use of individual members or groups of members in facilitating a settlement.

Although less publicized, the large percentage of the funds available to international organizations and a large majority of the staffs are devoted to programs promoting the economic welfare of the peoples of the world and in particular, those of the developing countries. The Technical Assistance and Special Fund projects of the United Nations and of the specialized agencies have made vital contributions to the development of national resources and economic growth. The multilateral character of these programs have provided for them a favorable reception in the recipient countries since these countries, as members of the United Nations, are parties to the creation of the policies from which they benefit. The central problem in many of the new countries is the early creation of a sufficiently large *cadre* of trained personnel to supervise the projects and direct further economic growth. Closely related is the great need of political stability which will preserve the gains already made. Sound national growth also requires mature public support which can only be gained by bringing the advantages of education to an ever larger proportion of the population.

In the world-wide spectrum of economic development, the vital questions of trade, commodity prices and agreements, the growth of common markets and related questions are all part and parcel of sound economic growth for both developed and developing countries. These questions are being given increasing consideration by the United Nations and some of the specialized agencies.

In the final section of this book, problems are discussed relating to the increase of the human potential. Attention is centered upon the definition of and the means of guaranteeing human rights. Great gains have been made in many parts of the world, but grave abuses of human rights still persist in some quarters. A noted writer has said that "justice is like a train that always arrives late." Man's inhumanity to man sometimes persists for long periods of time until the conscience of man is sufficiently aroused to erase the evil. The Universal Declaration of Human Rights and other activities by the United Nations have done much to arouse the world's conscience in this field. The power of government—the combined influence of the executive, legislative, and judicial branches—is often necessary to cut new paths away from bigotry and to erase injustices. When a government throws its influence against the scales of justice, the rights of the oppressed become a matter of concern to the world community.

The wide ranging and major world problems discussed in this book have one element in common. Without exception, they are the types of problems that require the constant vigilance of the organized world community and it is only through the existence of such mechanisms as are provided by world organization that adequate and proper attention can be brought to bear continuously upon the problems of peace and human welfare.

ANDREW W. CORDIER
DEAN, SCHOOL OF INTERNATIONAL AFFAIRS
COLUMBIA UNIVERSITY

Acknowledgements

This book is the product of mutual teaching and learning between the authors and students in "functional" courses on International Law and Organization at the University of Pennsylvania.

In the preparation of the book, Dr. Jacob was responsible for Chapters 1 to 15, and Dr. Atherton for Chapters 16 to 20. The entire work, however, reflects their joint analysis, and both generally share the conclusions reached.

The authors are grateful for a faculty research grant from the University of Pennsylvania which made possible the helpful research assistance of Miss Ellen Ellis, for a part of the study.

We are indebted also to Miss Margaret Galey and Mrs. Judith Gault for their editorial services and to Mrs. Lucy Daghlian for her painstaking reproduction of the manuscript.

Table of Contents

Abbreviations

IFC . . . . International Finance Corporation (IBRD)

ILC . . . . International Law Commission (UN)

ILO . . . . International Labor Organization

IMCO . . . . Intergovernmental Maritime Consultative Organization

IMF . . . . International Monetary Fund

INTERPOL . . . . International Police

IRO . . . . International Refugee Organization

IRU . . . . International Railway Union

ITO . . . . International Trade Organization

ITU . . . . International Telecommunication Union

LAFTA . . . . Latin American Free Trade Association

NATO . . . . North Atlantic Treaty Organization

OAS . . . . Organization of American States

OAU . . . . Organization of African Unity

OECD . . . . Organization for Economic Cooperation and Development

OEEC . . . . Organization for European Economic Cooperation

OIHP . . . . International Office of Public Health

ONUC . . . . United Nations Operations in the Congo

OPEX . . . . Operational, Executive and Administrative Personnel Service

PCA . . . . Permanent Court of Arbitration

PCIJ . . . . Permanent Court of International Justice

PCOB . . . . Permanent Central Opium Board

SACEUR . . . . Supreme Allied Commander in Europe (NATO)

SC . . . . Security Council (UN)

SEATO . . . . Southeast Asian Treaty Organization

SHAPE . . . . Supreme Headquarters Allied Powers in Europe

TAB . . . . Technical Assistance Board (ECOSOC)

UAR . . . . United Arab Republic

UK . . . . United Kingdom

UN . . . . United Nations

UNCTAD . . . . United Nations Conference on Trade and Development

UNCURK . . . . United Nations Commission for the Unification and Rehabilitation of Korea

UNEF . . . . United Nations Emergency Force

UNESCO . . . . United Nations Educational, Scientific and Cultural Organization

UNHCR . . . . United Nations High Commissioner for Refugees

UNICEF . . . . United Nations Children's Fund (ECOSOC)

UNRRA . . . . United Nations Relief and Rehabilitation Administration

UNRWA . . . . United Nations Relief and Works Agency for Palestine Refugees in the Near East

UNSCAT . . . . United Nations Conference on Science and Technology for the Benefit of the Less Developed Areas

UNTEA . . . . United Nations Temporary Executive Authority

US . . . . United States

USSR . . . . Union of Soviet Socialist Republics

WEU . . . . Western European Union

WHO . . . . World Health Organization

WMO . . . . World Meteorological Organization

WTO . . . . Warsaw Treaty Organization

Chapter 1

Foundations of International Society

This book concerns the efforts of men to organize themselves to survive in a world made physically interdependent by their technology but kept politically divided by the passion for independence and the hostilities engendered by their ideological, social and economic differences.

The facts of life now are that the conditions of life transcend the boundaries of nation-states, the prime political units through which the bulk of mankind currently functions to achieve its aspirations. No nation-state, however powerful, can today, on its own, "establish Justice, insure domestic Tranquillity, provide for the common defence, promote the general Welfare, and secure the Blessings of Liberty" for its citizens or its posterity, as so boldly proposed by the United States Constitution at the end of the 18th century. On the other hand, the actions of the smallest and weakest of states can, and do, jeopardize the lives and livelihood of everyone, so intertwined are the political and social relationships of people and governments the world over.

To cope with the critical problems precipitated by this anachronistic situation, statesmen have groped for means of developing effective *international* cooperation, devising institutions through which national governments can work out joint solutions to these problems, and establishing, in some instances, common rules to order their conduct.

Inadequate though these ties of international organization and international law still may be as a basis for durable world order, it is the thesis of this treatise that they provide the principal available insurance against war, economic chaos and social upheaval. In progress toward common principles, practices and institutions of international cooperation, rather than in the illusory pursuit of national power, lies the key to survival for nations and for people in this age.

THE METHOD OF ANALYSIS

The view of international organization developed in this book is derived from a "functional" analysis of the behavior of governments in their relations with one another. This approach seeks to uncover the dynamics of political and social behavior, that is, to understand *why* people act the way they do, not just how they act. Social events and the development of social institutions are explained in terms of specific *needs* which prompt human action. The fulfillment or frustration of these needs (or the expectation that they will be fulfilled or frustrated) is the driving force which moves persons to act. The ways in which they act are, of course, powerfully influenced by the physical and social environment around them.

Functional analysis tries to identify the needs, or problems, which trigger action; then attempts to trace the continuing chain of interactions between what people do to meet these needs, the responses of success or failure that they encounter, and the resulting adjustments they then make in their actions. Need→personal action→environmental response→adjusted action: this is the "model" of social dynamics which conforms most closely, we believe, to what is currently known about the motivation of human conduct. In our judgment, this justifies its adoption as the analytical framework for a study of international institutions, because these institutions are the product of human decisions, and adequate explanations of their operation, as of any social institutions, should be rooted in understanding of the psychological and sociological imperatives of human behavior generally.

"Functional analysis" as used here differs somewhat from the "structural-functional" approach applied by some leading social scientists in the study of social systems. Our focus is on human actors and their needs as the primary phenomena to be observed, rather than on *systems* (i.e. patterns of inter-relationship among mutually dependent organs or parts.) Structural-functional analysis also considers "needs" but these are conceived as prerequisites for the successful maintenance, growth and survival of the system, rather than as direct motivational forces operating to produce action by individuals. A human being can, of course, be conceived as a "system," and is so conceived by the systems theorists referred to. An analysis of needs might then correspond rather closely to what we are talking about.

The difference between the approaches is marked, however, when analysis is directed to the relationships among people and to the social institutions they create. The systems theorist treats the set of relationships as a whole system (or as a network of sub-systems) with an identity of its own, quite apart from the human beings that live and act within it. The term "needs" then refers to the needs of the system, not of the persons whose relationships compose it. By contrast, what we might call "psycho-functional analysis" —the approach taken in this study of international institutions—consistently looks on the dynamics of social systems and institutions as the product of the actions of people, and on needs as a requirement of *persons,* not of impersonal systems. A system is always viewed as a result or series of results of human actions and interactions, to be evaluated in terms of its capacity to meet *human* needs, not some assumed "intrinsic" needs of its own.

In the end, both kinds of functional analysis of social institutions often lead to similar conclusions, perhaps because it is human beings that do form the ultimate stuff that is being analyzed, whether they are being treated as components of a system or the operators of a system.[1]

Two further points should be emphasized about this functional method of analysis. It is strictly *empirical.* That is, it looks to actual experience as the source of knowledge and the test of what is so, or not so; what is proved or unproved.

On the other hand, it is also *phenomenological.* It looks to the state of mind, feeling and perception of human beings as a crucial aspect of the "real" world, even if a person's view of the facts may be completely distorted by ignorance, bias or illusion. For, from the standpoint of explaining and possibly predicting his actions, it is the world that a person *sees* and his actual disposition towards it, however irrationally determined, that counts.

This means that the value judgments expressed in this book—and there are many—are intended to represent either (1) conclusions about international institutions and policies based on appraisal of evidence available as to their effectiveness in meeting the needs which led to their adoption; or (2) ideals, principles and norms which appear to have influenced action because some people have in fact held to them, however unrighteous others

---

[1] See Morton A. Kaplan, *System and Process in International Politics* (New York: John Wiley and Sons, 1957) for a major demonstration of the application of systems analysis to the field of international relations, using the structural-functional approach as a basic point of departure. The general theoretical framework of this approach has been most fully elaborated by Talcott Parsons. See especially his *The Social System* (Glencoe, Illinois: The Free Press, 1951).

For a succinct critical appraisal of this approach see Stanley H. Hoffmann (ed.), *Contemporary Theory in International Relations* (Englewood Cliffs, N.J.: Prentice-Hall, 1960).

Functional analysis, as used in *this* study, is closely related, at least in terms of its application to political processes and institutions, to a "decision-making" frame of reference, along lines conceptualized by Richard C. Snyder and others. See Richard C. Snyder, H. W. Bruck, and Burton Sapin (eds.), *Foreign Policy Decision-Making* (New York: The Free Press of Glencoe, 1962).

See David Mitrany, *A Working Peace System* (London and New York: Royal Institute of International Affairs, 1946) for a pioneering exposition of the functional approach as applied to the analysis of international institutions. A searching critique of selected areas of international organization and law from a functional perspective is provided by Percy L. Corbett, *Law and Society in the Relations of States* (New York: Harcourt, Brace, 1951). See also Corbett's *The Individual and World Society* (Princeton, N.J.: Princeton University Center for Research on World Political Institutions, 1953).

may regard them, or unreasonable or wrong they may appear in the light of supposedly objective truth. Of course, the authors have their own strong biases and illusions which have undoubtedly distorted their clarity of vision and sullied the purity of their critiques.

THE POLITICAL SETTING

The world of international relations, viewed in the perspective of functional analysis, is a world of national governments, more or less controlling the actions of the inhabitants of an area, but themselves the creatures of demands pressed upon them by those that are governed, by other governments and the people to which they respond, and, of course, by those who do the governing as part of the "establishment."

The fluidity and variation in the actions of governments as they twist and turn to respond to these complex pressures and counter-pressures generated by human needs belies the impression of national unity and solidarity conveyed by the customary language of international politics, in such expressions as: "The United States will fulfill its solemn commitment to defend the free people of West Berlin" or "The Soviet Union reaffirmed the readiness to continue rendering all necessary assistance to the Democratic Republic of Viet Nam for the repulsion of aggression by the United States." In the real world of international relations, the sources of action have to be sought in the motivations and perceptions of the real people who hold the reins of public authority, or who in one way or another have the capacity to influence those who have such authority. The actors are not mystic super-beings—nation-states—but live people, making decisions (or avoiding them), using the instrumentalities of government to make their decisions effective upon others.

This palpably obvious point would not be belabored, except that the conduct of international relations, as well as its analysis, has been strongly conditioned by a tendency to think of nations *as* persons, having interests, exercising powers of decision, asserting rights and undertaking commitments as responsible entities in themselves, quite apart from the individuals who form the nation and govern it. Indeed, this fiction is reflected in the forms and language of diplomacy, in the precepts of international law and in the charters and processes of international organizations. Living with the fiction as they do, day in and day out, many officials, as well as some of the people they speak to and for, come to act as though the fiction were fact. Some have even gone the length of the German philosopher Hegel, propounding the belief that the state is a live collective being, an organic reality with a personality and will of its own.

The practical effects of such thinking are, at best, to obscure the real lines of human decision-making which lead to governmental action on behalf of the "state," and cause miscalculation of the determinants and outcomes of public policies, as leaders believe or pretend that they are manipulating collectivities—whole states—rather than millions of live human beings, on the chessboard of world politics. Far more serious is the shirking of personal responsibility for governmental action, which results when leaders identify their decisions as decisions of the nation as a whole, or claim immunity from accountability because they have acted "in the national interest." This removes policy formation from any effective means of social control. It hoodwinks people into believing they have no personal right or capacity to share in the determination of the most vital decisions affecting their lives. In effect, it dehumanizes the entire sphere of life encompassed by international relations.[2]

Accepting the humanistic view of the nature of the state and the sources of governmental action (because it is validated by empirical observation rather than metaphysical *mystique*) the political setting of international affairs appears extraordinarily *pluralistic,* in at least two respects.

First, as has been suggested, no nation-state is so totally integrated internally that its government can be truly monolithic, acting as a genuinely collective arm to carry out the will of the whole people. People's needs are diverse; what they think they need and want is even more diverse; the priorities they attach to different needs vary; and to satisfy the needs of one person may deny satisfaction to others, especially if resources are not enough to go around. The result is an inescapable pluralism of social efforts *within* states, with control of governmental action the constant object of intense political competition, even if the processes of such competition are not formal or constitutional. "Consensus" is the maximum realizable degree of public commitment to a government's decision, and although in times of extreme crisis this may approach unanimity for a highly nationalistic population, it is likely to be short-lived, as the consequences of a decision to go to war, for instance, begin to be felt and reappraised. Even

---

[2] See the trenchant observations on consequences of state personification by Harold and Margaret Sprout, *Foundations of International Politics* (Princeton, N.J.: D. Van Nostrand, 1962) pp. 76–79.

See also Chadwick F. Alger, "Comparison of Intranational and International Politics," *American Political Science Review,* June, 1963, for an effective critique of classic and contemporary conceptions of international relations as a system of relationships among "states" or "nations." Alger argues persuasively that actors in international relations be consistently identified as those officials, engaged in the process of governmental decision-making in different countries, who interact with each other in face-to-face contact. This is much in line with our view, though we would widen the body of "actors" to include persons influencing governmental decision-making as well as those participating immediately in it.

On this issue, see also Arnold Wolfers, "The Actors in International Politics," in W. T. R. Fox (ed.) *Theoretical Aspects of International Relations* (Notre Dame: Notre Dame University Press, 1959); and J. David Singer, "The Level of Analysis Problem in International Relations," *World Politics,* October, 1961.

consensus of more modest scope is by no means characteristic of a nation's normal disposition toward the acts of government, though it is probable that the conduct of foreign relations commands wider concurrence than do domestic policies, if for no other reason than that people generally have less information about it and feel they should acquiesce in the judgment of those who supposedly know more because they preside over the controls.[3]

On balance, then, internal consensus is not so great, even on matters which involve a country's international relations, to sustain the fiction of the identity of nation and government in the pursuit of a single, uniform, all-encompassing "national interest."

The second respect in which the world is politically pluralistic, is the more obvious and acknowledged fact that decision-making is dispersed among a multitude of governments, none of whom likes to concede that it is accountable to any other for its decisions. Granted that there are vast differences in the power that governments can mobilize to back up their decisions, none has been able to muster up enough to impose its say on all the others. And the trend seems to be in the direction of greater pluralism, rather than less. Not only has the sheer number of states increased three-fold in the generation since World War II, as colonial empires have been liquidated under the insistent demands for self-determination, but competition among the great powers has made them unusually solicitous of the support of the smaller ones; and the price of support has more often been deference and material aid by the great power than the exercise of coercion.

This trend was masked for a few years after the traumatic experience of the Second World War when the power of initiative seemed to be exercised so overwhelmingly by the victorious super-powers, particularly the U.S. and the U.S.S.R., and their struggle for paramountcy dominated the course of events. But the concentration of power in Moscow and Washington was never so complete or absolute as assumed by those who expounded "bipolarism" as a fundamental transformation of the inter-

---

[3] A classic study of the extent of consensus on foreign policy issues in an open society is Gabriel Almond, *The American People and Foreign Policy* (2d ed.; New York: Frederick A. Praeger, Inc., 1960).

Important evidence on the question of consensus, based on analysis of attitudinal survey data in several countries, is presented in W. Buchanan and H. Cantril, *How Nations See Each Other* (Urbana: University of Illinois Press, 1953).

The differential impact of socio-economic status on political attitudes and behavior in countries with differing political systems is searchingly analyzed by Seymour M. Lipset, in *Political Man* (Garden City, N.Y.: Doubleday, 1960).

The heterogeneity of political attitudes in Communist countries is emerging with increasing clarity as reliable survey data become available, and through systematic content analysis of official documents and professional journals. See for instance the revealing study of Soviet expatriates by Alex Inkeles and Raymond A. Bauer, *The Soviet Citizen* (Cambridge, Mass.: Harvard University Press, 1959), and the reports of the Public Opinion Research Center of the Polish Radio.

national system; and in any case, it was short-lived. Aside from the emergence of more and more states unwilling to align with either pole, centrifugal forces tore at the interior cohesion of the two blocs and undermined the directive omnipotence of the pivotal powers. The realistic conclusion reached by two experienced scholars is that "the early postwar bipolarism, which evolved from the pre-1939 polycentered balance-of-power system, seems to be only a passing phase in a continuing transformation, again towards a polycentered system."[4]

The consequence of pluralism in international affairs, as in other political environments, is that there is great diversity in the sources of political action as people and their governments insist on exercising independent judgment in determining what are their interests and how best to pursue them.

But given the objective conditions of world interdependence, such diversity unavoidably results in the actions of one impinging on the interests of others. It is impossible to satisfy most human needs within the confines of each territorial state, even if its leaders and people honor the injunction of not coveting their neighbors' goods. Thus the actions of governments become *trans-national* as they seek to meet trans-national needs. What may start as a modest, seemingly local concern—to have a market for one's products at a fair price, to have a steady job at a living wage and without discrimination, to secure a competent education, or just to be left alone in peace—causes an ever-widening set of repercussions which quickly spill over beyond the national frontiers because the actions of "foreigners" are found to be critical in deciding whether or not these goals can be achieved.[5]

This sets the stage for conflict as people strive for the same or contradictory ends. But it also stimulates international cooperation, as people and their governments recognize the mutuality of their interests, and their inability to satisfy needs without support and collaboration by others. Both conflict and cooperation represent alternative methods of satisfying needs. The choice of one or the other depends in part on which does in fact produce the desired result, that is the kind of response from others which satisfies the sought need. But the choice may also be determined by what

---

[4] Harold and Margaret Sprout, *op. cit.*, p. 104.

The evanescence of bipolarism is still not widely recognized in contemporary studies of international affairs. But note the perceptive reappraisal of "Bipolarity in a Revolutionary Age" by Morton A. Kaplan, one of those who did most a few years ago to elaborate bipolar models for the analysis of international relations. Chapter 12 in Morton A. Kaplan (ed.) *The Revolution in World Politics* (New York: John Wiley and Sons, 1962). He concludes that "the historical actuality is thus considerably different from the abstract model of the loose bipolar system," *ibid.*, p. 266.

[5] Philip E. Jessup, in *Transnational Law* (New Haven, Conn.: Yale University Press, 1956) provides an admirable exposition of this outlook, in describing the circumstances which have given rise to much of the body of contemporary international law.

people *expect,* or *imagine* the result may be, quite apart from whether experience bears out the expectation. People tend to act as much or more on the basis of what they expect, as on what has been demonstrated to be so; on what they *believe* to be true or likely as on what a rational and informed appraisal of previous experience indicates is true or probable. Even if the expectation turns out to be wrong, choices may still be made in terms of it, because the frustration or failure may be explained by some other equally illusory rationalization. (Persons may, for instance, find a scapegoat to blame for the misfire of their expectation, rather than admitting that they themselves had been mistaken.) In other words, there is usually a long lag before "learning by experience" catches up with and corrects the great range of human myths, and establishes some correspondence between what people think or imagine to be so, and what really *is* so.

Thus the choice of international conflict or cooperation as means to satisfy trans-national needs is influenced only in part by a rational calculation of what is likely to work. The play of the essentially irrational factors of belief and prejudice, stereotyped images of others, and ideas of their hostile or friendly intentions, and accompanying attitudes of suspicion or trust, fear or assurance, is usually even more determinative of a government's foreign policies; as are the loyalties which people have developed, especially loyalty to nation.[6]

This helps to explain why the course of conflict is so often chosen, when the objective conditions of the present world environment appear to support, on rational grounds, a steadfast commitment to cooperation (and as a corollary, the limitation and resolution of conflict) as the means most likely to secure satisfaction of most of the needs of most of the people in the world. Overwhelming and cumulative evidence points to the development of *integrative processes* among peoples and nations as the foundation of a viable society, and probably the very condition of survival. But both new nations and old continue to operate on the basis of illusions of what they can secure through conflict—power, security, freedom, even peace itself—and these illusions usually over-ride the imperatives for cooperation.

There are signs, however, that experience may be catching up with illusion, as awareness grows of the devastating implications of the technological revolution in means of destruction, as well as of the positive potentialities of international collaboration in productive human enterprise. The development of international organizations is a major demonstration of this shift in orientation and motivation. They are a new kind of political

---

[6] For a searching examination of the sources of national loyalty, and an understanding of approaches to the resolution of conflicts of loyalty, see Harold Guetzkow, *Multiple Loyalties: Theoretical Approach to a Problem in International Organization* (Princeton, N.J.: Princeton University Center for Research on World Political Institutions, 1955); also, Sprout and Sprout, *op. cit.,* chap. 18.

institution, specifically adapted to the promotion of inter-governmental co-operation in a pluralistic political environment.

Not all such institutions are purely instruments of cooperation, to be sure. Especially when viewed in global perspective, some regional organizations stand out as mobilizers for conflict. But the functional thrust of most international organizations is to engender processes of negotiation, bargaining, and the synthesizing of interests which lead to jointly agreed action on commonly sought needs.

It is the purpose of the chapters which follow to examine the growth of these institutions as they have attempted to cope with the great trans-national problems of this century; and to understand the conditions of their various successes and failures. Attention will center on three major problems, or clusters of problems: (1) the prevention of war and maintenance of peace, (2) the promotion of economic welfare, and (3) the nurture of social rights and human dignity. In each case, a range of differing approaches is reviewed and evaluated in terms, on the one hand, of the assumptions which led to their adoption, and, on the other, of the outcomes of their practice.

We turn first, however, to a general analysis of the basic characteristics of international institutions, which, as has been suggested, represent one of the great political innovations, corresponding, in this period of history, to the introduction of federalism as an instrument of political integration during the last two centuries.

Chapter 2

Instruments of
International Action

Government in the mid-twentieth century has become an international business. A vast and growing volume of international affairs preoccupies officials of each nation; and to coordinate their efforts, national governments have devised an intricate mechanism of international organizations, supplementing the normal channels of diplomacy. Through some 200 such instruments, states consult and act to promote commerce, protect health and safety, maintain communications, settle disputes, suppress international crimes, restrain aggression, encourage financial and economic stability and progress, exchange educational and scientific information, and enhance the social well-being of the world. International agencies lack the powers of real government. Nor do they enjoy the active participation and support of all countries. Yet these institutions are now indispensable in the conduct of international life, when individual nations insist on independence but are obliged to coexist in an interdependent world.

THE IMPETUS TO INTERNATIONAL
ORGANIZATION

International organization is a product of crisis and emergency in the political and economic life of the last hundred years. When national diplomacy has proven inadequate to cope with problems of modern international relations, governments have grudgingly and falteringly sought new and more effective methods of collaboration. They were not disposed, however, to undertake innovations except where dictated by absolute necessity; hence, the growth of international organizations has been piecemeal, each agency created for a specific and limited purpose, and, until recently, unrelated to other areas of international activity.

Crises in international communications and transportation gave the first major impetus to the formation of new organs of international cooperation. During the first half of the nineteenth century, for instance, the confusion and delay in moving a growing volume of international mail across frontiers, with separate national postal provisions, became an intolerable impediment to business. Each country charged rates on the basis of "what the traffic would bear," and could change them at will. At one time, the cost of a letter from the United States to Australia was 5 cents, 33 cents, 45 cents, 60 cents, or $1.02 per half-ounce, according to the route by which it was sent. Each letter, furthermore, was checked and weighed at each frontier. The payment of charges by one country to another was complicated and cumbersome. Insistent demands for simplified and uniform handling of foreign mail ultimately led in 1874 to organization of the Universal Postal Union. All members of the union agreed to adopt a single postage rate and a common unit of weight, and constituted themselves "one postal territory" under a central international administration with headquarters at Berne, Switzerland.

The exigencies of global warfare in the twentieth century have likewise forced states to organize for joint action. In the face of imminent defeat by the well-unified command of German forces and resources, the Allies in World War I and World War II forged progressively more centralized machinery for military directions and mobilization and allocation of supplies. The Combined Food Board planned and controlled the production and distribution of foodstuffs in the United States and the British Commonwealth from 1942 to 1945. All Allied shipping in the second world war was pooled, and its use and movements directed by the Combined Shipping Board, which followed a precedent already established in the first world war. Munitions production was also controlled by an inter-Allied agency. The unprecedented degree of authority over national action exercised by these international organizations did not last beyond the wartime emergency, but the experience paved the way for peacetime experiments in collaboration along new lines. In particular, the impact of mass warfare with its tremendous toll on lives and property caused statesmen and laymen alike to demand a general organization of nations that would effectively prevent war. To this end, the League of Nations and the United Nations were primarily dedicated.

The crisis of reconstruction in the aftermath of war furnished still another imperative for international organization. Sheer physical destruction was so great in many of the war-devastated areas that only the mobilization and judicious international distribution of resources from countries that had not suffered the direct effects of war could prevent outright starvation and make possible gradual rehabilitation of economic life. While private organizations, sometimes supported with government contributions, were able to meet the most serious needs after World War I, the problem of reconstruction after the second world war called forth an unprecedented international organization, equipped with major financial resources and a substantial administrative staff—the United Nations Relief and Rehabilitation Administration.

Though UNRRA was a temporary agency, designed to liquidate the emergency of postwar rehabilitation in three years, most of the world could not return so soon to "normalcy." Longer-range problems of reconstruction emerged: an almost irreducible core of displaced persons, severely dislocated channels of trade, lowered standards of living, impaired conditions of health, and sharply reduced production. Such critical conditions demanded further, more permanent international action. The United States initiated the European Recovery Program in cooperation with 16 countries in Western Europe, while other aspects of reconstruction were undertaken by the International Refugee Organization, the World Health Organization, and the United Nations itself.

The problems of recurring world economic crisis and depressed living standards have spurred international efforts, especially during the last 25 years, to achieve greater economic stability and security. The International Labor Organization was created at the end of World War I to promote better work conditions and to improve relations between labor and management. At the conclusion of the second world war, special international agencies were formed to study and take action on other major problems of international economic relations: the International Monetary Fund, charged with insuring currency stabilization; the International Bank for Reconstruction and Development, to supplement private capital in assisting technological and economic advancement; the Food and Agriculture Organization, to improve agricultural practices and marketing; and the prospective international trade organization, to remove trade barriers and facilitate a broad exchange of commodities between nations. In addition, the Economic and Social Council of the United Nations and, to a lesser extent, its predecessor, the Economic and Financial Organization of the League of Nations, have been held responsible for recommending policies to forestall economic crises and depression. The pressures of insecurity, like the ravages of war, have dictated resort to organized international action when national action and the processes of diplomacy have proved ineffective.

In fact, the cumbersomeness of diplomacy has become abundantly apparent when problems, such as those just mentioned, have required negotiation and agreement among many states. In the absence of international organization, diplomacy is bilateral; each country communicates separately with every other. To secure concerted action to which all are agreed may easily necessitate a long-drawn-out process of exchanging and reconciling different views. In 1927–28, negotiation of the Kellogg–Briand Pact to renounce war, which contained just two one-sentence articles of substance, took over sixteen months, during which notes moved back and forth among various governments, suggesting reservations and changes of text. Even then, no real unity of interpretation was achieved; Mr. Kellogg declared, in effect, that each state could interpret the agreement as it saw fit. Effective multilateral action to meet crises demands a swifter means of reaching decisions; and where problems call for day-to-day administration, as in a wartime supply operation or a program of international economic aid, diplomacy is totally inadequate. On the other hand, the absence of world government or of a disposition to create one makes impossible an attack on such problems by a central legislative or executive authority. International organization, therefore, has been tailor-made to facilitate multilateral consultation and joint action without surrender of national sovereignty. It is, in a sense, a hybrid of the two main and opposing forces in contemporary international affairs—interdependence and nationalism.

EVOLUTION OF INTERNATIONAL AGENCIES

Three main types of international organization have developed over the last hundred years. First, administrative agencies have been set up for specialized technical tasks, such as regulation of international means of communication. Second, machinery for adjudication or conciliation of international disputes was established. Third, general international organizations were created on either a regional or global basis to provide collective security and promote cooperative action on a broad range of other international problems.

International Administration

International administration started with private associations that attempted to advance their particular interests across national frontiers. The problems of international rail traffic led to organization of the International Railway Union, a body representing the individual railroad managements in Europe. The International Red Cross was created as a private effort to assist the wounded and ease the suffering of other war victims. Gradually, governments agreed to support or even participate in some private bodies; and, ultimately, a number of "public international unions," usually representing only governments, were formed to carry out administrative tasks that required public authority. In 1856, for instance, the Treaty of Paris created two international commissions to regulate and improve navigation on the Danube River. The Universal Postal Union, as mentioned above, was established in 1874, the first International Telegraphic Union in 1865, the International Commission for Air Navigation and the International Labor Organization at the Paris Peace Conference in 1919. The structure and powers of such bodies have changed from time to time. Some have merged into new and different organizations. But the machinery for international administration has expanded and become permanent. At the present time, at least intergovernmental administrative agencies are in operation, aside from a much larger number of private bodies. An attempt is now being made through the United Nations to draw these agencies into a systematic relationship with one another and to provide greater coordination between their manifold activities.

Adjudication and Conciliation

The First Hague Conference in 1899 took the lead in establishing definite machinery to facilitate the settlement of disputes among nations. It proposed that commissions of inquiry be set up by agreement among parties to a dispute to determine the facts in the case; and it created the Permanent Court of Arbitration, with prescribed rules of procedure and a panel of arbitrators available for service whenever states involved in a dispute so desired. Only limited use has been made of the Court, since separate tribunals are usually established before states have resorted to arbitration. Inter-American treaties gradually developed machinery specifically applicable to disputes in the Western hemisphere. The "Bryan Treaties" in 1913 established permanent Commissions of Inquiry to which all disputes among American states must be submitted unless they are arbitrated. The commissions were later authorized to exercise conciliatory functions as well. Following the First World War, an international judicial institution was created in conjunction with the League of Nations—the Permanent Court of International Justice. Though its authority was very limited, it did settle several disputes and gave rulings on important questions of international law. It has now been replaced by an almost identical International Court of Justice, formed in 1945 as an organ of the United Nations.

Regional Organizations

International organizations with a broader scope of functions have been formed to promote cooperation on matters of common interest to states in a particular region. Regional organization has been extensively developed in the Americas. In 1889, the first Conference of American States established the Pan-American Union, primarily to encourage inter-American trade and to plan for succeeding conferences. Its functions were gradually expanded, although hostility and suspicion between the Latin-American countries and the United States severely hampered even economic cooperation. By 1936, as a result of the new approach taken by the United States in the Good Neighbor Policy, relations had sufficiently improved so that the Buenos Aires Conference for the Maintenance of Peace could approve a large program to promote cultural relations among American states, including government-supported exchange of scholars and students. This added to the responsibilities of the union, which became the official inter-American clearinghouse. Under the shadow of the second world war, the American states went further, empowering a Council of Foreign Ministers to work out plans for their mutual security and to stand by for immediate consultation in case of threatened aggression. Organization for security was strengthened when the United States and other American states entered the war, and was made permanent by the Treaty of Rio de Janeiro in 1946. An Organ of Consultation is charged with implementing reciprocal assistance in case of attack from outside the Americas and with the pacific settlement of disputes among American states. Finally, the Tenth Conference of American States at Bogota, in 1948, coordinated the various inter-American agencies in an overall Organization of American States, with comprehensive responsibility for all phases of inter-American collaboration on economic, cultural, and security problems.

The most intensive development of regional organization has occurred in Western Europe, especially along functional lines of economic cooperation. Establishment of the six-nation European Coal and Steel Community in 1952 triggered processes of integration which shortly led to the creation of the European Economic Community (the "Common Market") encompassing the full range of these countries' economic interrelationships. The success of this association exercised a magnetic attraction for others, in part because it also posed a powerful competitive threat. But for reasons discussed later, full membership in the Community was kept restricted to the original pioneering Six. Within the Community, integration has reached the point where its common institutions have acquired powers more nearly supranational than those of any international organization in existence.

Meanwhile, the vast reconstruction needs of the European continent after World War II generated a more inclusive framework of international organization. Upon United States initiative, the Organization for European Economic Cooperation pulled together the efforts of sixteen countries in a gigantic recovery program, whose success stands as one of the landmarks of international endeavor. But as the tide of need receded so did the disposition of European governments to function closely together on a continental-wide basis.

On the political front, Europe has shown far less inclination to organize internationally, although strong pressure in this direction has been exerted by a segment of leadership (largely outside the governments in office) through the European Movement. The Council of Europe was formed in 1949, with a European Parliamentary Assembly composed of representatives from the various European legislatures, and a Council of Ministers representing the executive branches of government. The Council is primarily a consultative body though the Assembly has provided an official international loudspeaker through which advocates of greater European unification could make their voices heard, and the actions of governments could be reviewed and criticized by a group reflecting the spread of political opinion both within countries and cutting across national boundaries.

The development of regional organizations for security purposes in Europe and elsewhere, is a long though quite recent story (mainly since World War II). This is reviewed later in detail. Suffice it to say here, that the institutional character of these arrangements has varied, from nominal alliance commitments to one another in case of attack, to the highly structured system of joint military planning and mutual assistance which has emerged in the North Atlantic Treaty Organization. The effectiveness of these alternatives is still very much in dispute.

League of Nations

The League of Nations was the first attempt to develop a comprehensive global international organization to preserve peace. It was born a compromise between the vision of a world parliament championed by Woodrow Wilson and a pact among the victorious Allies to maintain the peace treaties as demanded by French leaders. It was designed, in part, to provide the machinery for mutual aid among its members if they were victims of attack. At the same time, it had a much broader group of functions aimed at *preventing* war. It had specific responsibilities for encouraging peaceful settlement of disputes, developing plans for limitation of armaments, and supervising administration of the former German and Turkish colonies. The League was furthermore entrusted with supervision over international agreements relating to traffic in drugs and women and children, collection of information in all matters of international interest, and direction of international bureaus. The organization, though far from a government, nevertheless had broad competence to care for the world's welfare, and it quickly came to occupy a position in international affairs far beyond the status of the more specialized agencies that had previously existed. It served at once as a world forum, an instrument for continuous diplomatic negotiation, an international civil service, and an organ of economic and social collaboration. The League could not fulfill its political role as custodian of international security in the face of the resurgent nationalism of the 1930's and, in particular, the aggressive policies of Nazi Germany, Fascist Italy, and Japan. The organization was also seriously weakened because the United States had failed to become a member; the U.S. Senate insisted on reservations to the Covenant that were unacceptable to President Wilson. But the League's economic, financial, statistical, and social services grew so significant that they were continued even during the second world war.

The United Nations System

The framework of international society was so badly shattered by the war that Britain, Russia, the United States, and China decided not to revive the

League but, instead, to build a new general international organization through which they could continue their wartime collaboration and attempt to assure a durable peace. Concrete proposals for the organization were worked out while the war was still in full progress, in joint discussions of the four powers at Dumbarton Oaks (an estate in Washington, D.C.) from August 21 to October 7, 1944. They placed primary emphasis on the security functions of the agency and provided for the big powers to assume major responsibility for the maintenance of peace. On the other hand, formation of the organization was divorced from the process of making the peace with the Axis so that it might be less hampered than the League by identification with the specific settlements imposed by the victors. The Dumbarton Oaks proposals were made public and were discussed intensively for over six months, particularly in the United States and Great Britain. Criticisms and suggestions were invited from other governments, from private organizations, and individuals. In April, 1945, 50 nations assembled at San Francisco for the United Nations Conference on International Organization, which reconsidered the proposals, modified and amended them in important respects, and finally, on June 26, signed the Charter of the United Nations. In time, 115 states were admitted to membership.

The new organization, as tailored by the smaller states, has broader functions and a more democratic division of responsibility than originally envisaged by the four sponsoring powers. It has fused the predominant power interests of the postwar world with the heritage of functional cooperation left by the League of Nations. As a matter of fact, its powers extend well beyond those of the League. In addition to providing for peaceful settlement of international disputes and for collective action to prevent or stop aggression, the Charter endowed the United Nations with very wide responsibility for promoting economic and social welfare, exercising trusteeship over the former mandates, and encouraging respect for human rights and fundamental freedoms. While five powers—Britain, the United States, U.S.S.R., France, and China—received special prerogatives, particularly in regard to peace and security, all members of the organization, large and small, were given equal voice in most of the other United Nations' activities. The United Nations has been from the beginning, therefore, more than a mere league of victors; it is, in fact, a comprehensive system for the conduct and oversight of the entire range of international affairs.

The basic organization established by the Charter includes six major organs: the General Assembly, the Security Council, the Economic and Social Council, the Trusteeship Council, the Secretariat, and the International Court of Justice. In addition, there is a vast network of subsidiary commissions, committees, and other bodies, some established by the Charter and others by the U.N. organs themselves in the course of their operations. Completing the United Nations "system" are a group of affiliated but autonomous "specialized agencies." The accompanying chart provides a partial view of the scope and interrelationships of this complex and far-flung institution. More detailed description of the U.N.'s organization is given in an appendix.

Under the United Nations, international organization has reached an unparalleled comprehensiveness and integration. Its present membership approaches universality, crossing all geographical political and ideological lines. (Though denial of representation to the People's Republic of China has had the practical effect of dissociating the U.N. from the world's most populous country.) Its functions cover virtually every major field of human endeavor. Separate and isolated agencies of international administration and adjudication have, to a large extent, been brought under one umbrella as part of a single system of international cooperation. Though coordination is far from complete, and the authority of each institution is limited, the United Nations provides the most extensive framework yet achieved for joint action on international problems.[1]

EARMARKS OF INTERNATIONAL INSTITUTIONS

International organizations are unique political institutions with certain distinctive features determined by the fact that they are, in reality, associations of sovereign states. They have governmental functions to perform, but they do not have the powers normally assumed by governments. From one standpoint, an international organization is no more than a tool used by governments to carry out joint tasks, and is entirely dependent on their discretion. Yet, in time, it appears to develop an identity of its own, and it acquires a degree of autonomy in representing the *common* interest of states that sets it apart from and beyond the whim or fancy of any particular state. International organization is thus both less and more than national government. It is, in words used by Secretary-General Dag Hammarskjöld to describe the United Nations, "an institutional system for coexistence."

The essential characteristics of international organizations are these:

1. They are composed of states and represent national governments.
2. All members are presumed equal.
3. The organizations do *not* exercise legislative or executive powers binding on the member states.
4. Their functions are primarily to engineer intergovernmental collaboration.[2]

---

[1] For a general historical review of the development of international organizations, see Gerard J. Mangone, *A Short History of International Organization* (New York: McGraw-Hill, 1954).

[2] Differences in the degree to which these generalizations apply to particular international institutions will be noted in due course. For instance, some institutions of the Western European Community do, in effect, exercise certain legislative and executive powers binding on the member states. See, particularly, Chapter 15, pp. 440. But on the whole, these four features do characterize the fundamental structure and operational processes of most international organizations.

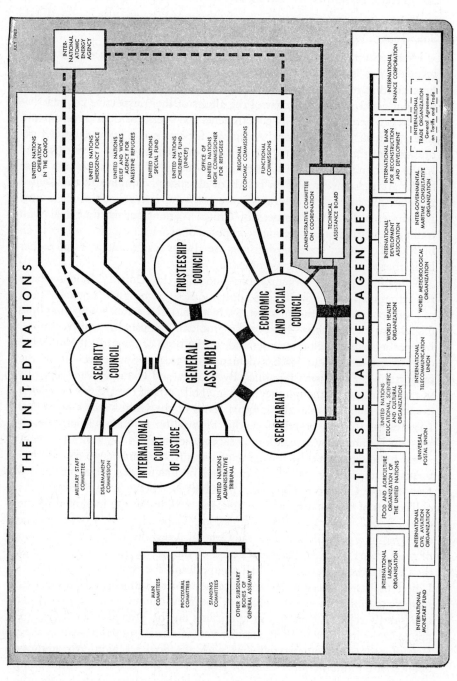

Source: *Yearbook of the United Nations, 1962*. Published by U.N. Department of Public Information.

The Governmental Basis of Participation

Membership in international organizations is usually open only to states recognized as "sovereign" by the governments of other states. This means, in practice, that representation in almost all international bodies is limited to national governments that control the affairs of their respective countries.

Delegates are appointed by governments and speak for their governments. In the United Nations General Assembly, for instance, a representative casts the vote "of the United States" or of the "government of the Soviet Union." In the Economic and Social Council or the Security Council, although these bodies are presumed to act on behalf of all states belonging to the United Nations, the individual delegates voice only the instructions of their own governments. Lesser committees of United Nations organs that deal with technical questions are sometimes composed of experts authorized to act in an individual capacity; but their decisions are always reviewable by some higher body that represents the governments.

Some international organizations—notably the United Nations—have run into unexpected difficulties in applying these seemingly elementary rules of participation. Even the question, "When is a state a state?"—and therefore eligible for membership—has posed a problem. The usual test of recognized independence was deliberately set aside at the birth of the United Nations in order to accommodate Stalin's demand for greater Soviet weight in the organization. Two Soviet republics, Byelorussia and Ukraine, were admitted as charter members, though they were integral parts of the U.S.S.R., enjoying even less autonomy than the internal states of the United States and other federations. (When Stalin made this proposition at Yalta, Roosevelt reportedly countered by demanding a seat for each of the 48 American states!)

Far more serious has been barring of states from membership for political reasons, though they are clearly qualified by independence. In the United Nations, the Charter requires that members be "peace-loving," accept the obligations of the Charter, and be able and willing "in the judgment of the organization" to carry out these obligations. To be admitted, a state must be approved by a two-thirds vote of the General Assembly, *on recommendation of the Security Council.* This gives each of the five permanent members of the Council the power to blackball an applicant. For many years, the Soviet Union and its Western adversaries used these provisions in an unrelenting struggle to limit each other's influence. The West commanded a majority that consistently rejected Communist applicants on the grounds that they were not peace-loving. The U.S.S.R. steadily vetoed others, sometimes citing their lack of proper diplomatic relations with the Soviet Union. An advisory opinion of the International Court of Justice held that states were justified in applying only the criteria explicitly set forth in the Charter when deciding on new members. But this changed nothing. In the end, the question was resolved by a set of purely political deals, admitting everybody who wanted in, except countries like Korea, Germany, and Vietnam which were splintered by ideological conflict. Paradoxically, political expediency has gone far toward establishing the principle of universality, making membership dependent on whether a state exists with a functioning government, able to conduct international relations, rather than on any particular political alignment. (Of course, in some international organizations membership is deliberately limited to states sharing particular regional, cultural, functional, or political affinities or common security interests.)

The knottiest problem of participation concerns representation of states in which two governments claim to rule. This confronts the organization with the necessity of choosing which to accept as spokesman in its deliberations and decisions. The usual procedure has been to recognize the government able to maintain effective control of the state's territory and, therefore, in a position to carry out commitments it undertakes (the "de facto" principle). If a revolt occurs, the organization waits to see who wins out, then accepts the credentials of whoever is appointed delegate by the regime in power, whatever the means it may have used to get power, or however antagonistic other governments may be toward it.

But in the case of China, a different approach has been taken. The legitimacy of the Communist government was challenged because it seized power by force; and its "peace-loving" disposition was disputed especially after its role in Korea. On these grounds, the United States succeeded in persuading a majority of members in each United Nations organ or agency to deny the government of the People's Republic the right to represent China; while, conversely, the Nationalist government has been seated, although unrecognized by many U.N. members and lacking control over the mainland. The U.S.S.R., leaving aside its ideological and political feud with the Chinese Communist leaders, has consistently contended that the People's Republic alone can rightfully represent China, and often insists that actions taken in its absence are illegal. This view is shared by many Asian and African countries and some Europeans, including France—a recent convert. Each organ or agency faces the question for itself at the opening of every session. This anomalous situation has, of course, cut both ways. While the Chinese Communists are barred from taking part in the United Nations, the United Nations cannot conduct direct relationships with the effective government of the world's most populous country. A suggestion to break the impasse by recognizing "two Chinas" and letting each government represent one has been flatly rejected by both.

With the exceptions noted, the effect of the membership and representation provisions of international organizations has been to insure that participation corresponds to governing authority in the associated countries. The constituencies of these organizations, unlike those of governments, *are* governments, not private persons or groups. Governments control what the organizations do. To a large extent, it is through the constituent governments that any decisions reached are carried out.[3]

"Sovereign Equality"

A second feature usually characteristic of international organization is the presumed equality of its members, regardless of size, population, wealth, or power. In principle, each member as a sovereign state is entitled to the same rights of participation in the work of the organization and the same benefits to be derived from it. In principle, each also shares the same obligations. Thus, in the United Nations, every member-state casts one vote, and every state is eligible for election to any organ.

The principle of equality is not applied universally, however. Five big powers have permanent seats on the Security Council and, unlike the other states, can veto action on matters of substance before the Council. The members do not contribute equally to the support of the United Nations; the budget is apportioned among them on an agreed scale, reflecting capacity to pay. In the International Monetary Fund and the International Bank, voting is weighted according to the shares of stock held by each country. Differences in power and wealth among nations are also acknowledged in the informal influence exerted by states on the conduct of the organization's business.

Nevertheless, the principle of "sovereign equality," as it is phrased by the United Nations Charter, still permeates the form and procedures of most international agencies. As a matter of fact, the United Nations has experienced a powerful push for greater recognition of equality among its members, gathering intensity as new members were admitted, most of them smaller states. This culminated in the unprecedented adoption by the General Assembly of two amendments to the Charter enlarging the Security Council (from 11 to 15 and its voting majority from 7 to 9) and the Economic and Social Council (from 18 to 27).[4]

Nonmandatory Powers

Another fundamental characteristic of international organization is its lack of legislative and executive powers. The range of action is usually confined

---

[3] A few organizations, notably the International Labor Organization, provide for functional representation of nongovernmental groups. See below, Chapter 17. But the basic pattern is the one described, with governments holding a monopoly on participation.

For a penetrating analysis of the problem of membership, see I. L. Claude, Jr., *Swords Into Plowshares* (3d ed.; New York: Random House, 1964), Chap. 5.

The membership of major international organizations is listed on the following pages: 115–17, 685–88.

[4] Under the amending procedures of the Charter, ratification is required by two-thirds of the Members, *including all the permanent Members of the Security Council.* Although the General Assembly adopted the amendments by overwhelming majorities far exceeding the two-thirds required, a threat of blockage was indicated by the fact that several permanent Members were either absent or abstained.

to matters prescribed quite explicitly by the charters. There is no general mandate to "provide for the general welfare" though the United Nations has been pressed from time to time to act on the basis that it did have a general responsibility to maintain peace and security, promote economic betterment and protect human rights by any or all means. This view can hardly be sustained, however, considering the self-interestedness of most of those who have advocated it: they use it when it suits their particular interest, and oppose the rationalization with equal vigor when it cuts against them.[5]

Furthermore, international agencies are often directly prohibited from interfering in matters which are considered within the "domestic jurisdiction" of a state. While these hands-off provisions have sometimes been loosened by interpretation to permit an international organ to override objections to its competence by affected states, they are nevertheless a standing reminder that the boundaries of international action are circumscribed.[6]

Even within their recognized jurisdiction, international agencies rarely have the authority or the means of compelling states to accept. They can recommend but cannot dictate to governments. They study, discuss, plan, and propose action, but do not legislate. The United Nations General Assembly may approve unanimously a program for technical assistance to underdeveloped areas or for rendering relief and medical aid to children, but these efforts can be effective only to the extent that each government individually agrees to support them. The International Labor Organization may propose a convention limiting the work of women in dangerous industries, but it can have no effect unless it is ratified and enforced by national governments. International organization does not have the power to tax individuals or governments to meet its budget, though in the United Nations and certain other bodies, failure to pay approved assessments may deprive a state of its vote in the organization. Generally, however, the international agency must rely either on the self-interest of states or the influence of public opinion to secure the execution of its recommendations.

There are a few notable exceptions. With respect to maintaining peace and security, the United Nations Security Council has been given authority to make decisions that are binding on all members of the United Nations, whether they have given their assent or not. The Organ of Consultation of the American States can similarly "legislate" action to be undertaken in defense of American security up to the point of, but not including, the use of armed force. The United Nations General Assembly was given specific authority in the Peace Treaty with Italy to determine the disposition of Italian colonies should the "big four" states fail to reach agreement on the

---

[5] The opportunism of advocates of this position in early United Nations debates is pointed out in Philip E. Jacob, "The Legality of United Nations Action," *University of Pittsburgh Law Review*, Fall, 1951.

[6] This issue is succinctly discussed in Claude *op. cit.*, Chapter 9, pp. 164–173.

issue; and in default of such agreement, the General Assembly did make the decision. Among the specialized agencies, the Universal Postal Union has, in effect, made decisions binding on national governments, for no country has been willing to incur the consequence of exclusion from the union for failure to carry out the prescribed regulations, however much it might dislike them. The International Monetary Fund and the International Bank also have a powerful sanction in the threat of denying the benefits of the organizations to a state that will not carry out action demanded by them. The exercise of mandatory supra-national powers is carried farthest by certain institutions of the (West) European Communities, most particularly by the High Authority of the Coal and Steel Community.

Such international authority is still the exception rather than the rule, however. The fact remains that international organizations can rarely apply compulsion to their members or bind them without their consent. The ultimate guarantee of the permissive character of these institutions is, of course, that membership is voluntary. A state can always withdraw—for any reason, or none.[7]

Collaborative Functions

The result is that the functions of international organization are almost exclusively collaborative. Their purpose, aptly expressed by the Charter of the United Nations, is *"harmonizing* the actions of states in the attainment of . . . common ends." (author's italics) Consultation and conference is, consequently, the dominant activity of international agencies. Modern international organization is a perpetual process of preparing for, holding, or reporting the result of world "town meetings." Depending as it does on voluntary cooperation to accomplish its ends, it must continuously seek through discussion and debate the reconciliation of differing national points of view and the widest possible area of final agreement among states.

Some international organizations have "operating" as well as conference functions, and directly undertake services, carry out regulations, and administer projects. Yet, these are also essentially collaborative activities, because an international body rather than a national government is the responsible administrative authority. For instance, a 26-nation Executive Board determines the basic policies and approves the programs of the United Nations International Children's Emergency Fund; and the 3-billion-dollar program of UNRRA—largest international operation in history—was supervised and

---

[7] The constitutions of international organizations usually specify formal procedures for withdrawal, requiring notification some time before the action legally goes into effect. In the case of the United Nations, however, the Charter contains no such provision and some authorities have maintained that this has the effect of prohibiting withdrawal. But such an interpretation did not prevail when Indonesia put the issue to the test in 1964–65. The Organization reluctantly acceded, after the Indonesian government formally and *in writing* confirmed Sukarno's angry pronouncement of secession.

controlled by a council of 44 nations, whose agreement was necessary for all major decisions in regard to the character, principles, and allocation of relief supplied to the war-devastated countries. These cooperative enterprises have demanded continuous collaboration and agreement among the participating nations. No single voice could command action.

THE PROCESSES OF INTERNATIONAL COLLABORATION

The organization and procedures of international agencies are particularly adapted to their functions of collaboration.

The "Conciliar" Pattern of Organization

The chief responsibility for policy-making rests with a group rather than a single person. Carrying out policy is also generally entrusted to corporate organs.

Typically, the final authority in an international organization is an assembly or conference in which every member state is represented. Active responsibility between meetings of the assembly is taken by a smaller council elected by the assembly. Each of these bodies meets and acts collectively, and each member participates in the deliberations as an equal. The president or chairman of the assembly or council has no more authority than any other delegate, and in no circumstances can he presume to act for the organ unless he is explicitly instructed to do so. He is not, in other words, a *prime* minister as in parliamentary governments.

Most international organizations do appoint a secretary-general or director-general as their chief administrative officer, and he has personal charge of the staff. But he is rarely given independent powers of policy determination, and even in administration he is constantly subject to check and direction by the council. He is certainly no presidential executive.

The conciliar structure of international organization insures that all important decisions shall be made by consultation and agreement among the members—an essential condition of effective collaboration among sovereign states, each of whom claims equal status with the others.

Respect for Equality

Respect for national equality is the keynote and major stumbling block of the international consultation process.

"Protocol" demands that in international organization each nation receive recognition equivalent to that accorded any other. Circular or semicircular seating arrangements are consequently preferred for meetings of the international bodies so that no state may have to take its place behind another. Where this is not possible, as in large meetings like the United Nations

General Assembly, the place of honor in the front row is determined by lot, and other delegations are seated in alphabetical order.

Every state is granted an extraordinary right to be heard, a right of which many delegates take full advantage. Equality in speech, in effect, means unlimited speech. Curtailment of a delegate's remarks might be interpreted as discrimination against his government, so others are reluctant to suggest limitations, however tedious or inconsequential the talk may be.

Chairmen and secretaries of committees are usually chosen so that every state may feel it has received a fair share of the positions of honor and responsibility. While the personal qualifications of a particular country's delegate are also taken into account, they are a secondary consideration,

The Organizational Pattern of International Agencies
(Compared with Governmental Organizations)

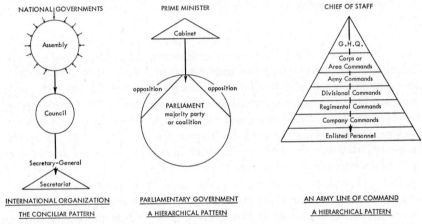

Diagrams illustrate the flow of responsibility in each type of organization, not necessarily the division of constitutional powers.

especially in regard to selection for posts of high prestige. Positions of responsibility are customarily rotated from session to session to afford the widest possible distribution among the member-states. In the Security Council of the United Nations, the chairmanship rotates every month according to an alphabetical order, so that each state occupies it at least once a year.

Recognition of Power

Despite these tokens of respect for equality, the facts of national power crop out in the procedure of international collaboration, particularly where political and security issues are at stake.

The most marked evidence of this is the veto that each of the five major powers can exercise in the Security Council. No action of "substance" can be taken by the Council without the affirmative vote of the permanent members, and a decision as to what is "substantive" or "procedural" likewise requires the approval of all five. Unanimous approval by the permanent members of the Security Council is also required before any amendment of the Charter can go into effect, although such approval is not necessary for calling a general conference to consider and propose revisions of the Charter.

A more subtle recognition of power in the United Nations is the custom of electing the large states continuously to *all* organs, giving them, in effect, permanent seats even though the procedure laid down in the Charter requires it only on the Security Council. There has also been a growing tendency to suspend formal discussion of difficult or highly controversial questions while an attempt is made informally, in subcommittee or in the lobbies, to iron out differences between the major powers. For example, the deadlocked discussions in the Atomic Energy Commission, on which all members of the Security Council were represented, were laid aside pending direct (and confidential) negotiations among the five permanent members and Canada.

Power has also intruded on the procedures of the specialized agencies. In such an innocuous organization as the Universal Postal Union, the larger states have demanded and gained more influence than the one vote to which they are presumably entitled. Colonial postal administrations have been admitted as full-fledged members of the union, and their votes are, of course, controlled by the "mother countries."

The councils (or executive committees) of several of the specialized agencies must include those states of primary importance in the field of activity with which the organization is concerned. On the International Civil Aviation Organization Council, states of "chief importance in air transport" or those that "make the largest contribution to the provision of facilities for international civil air navigation" must receive "adequate" representation. Of the sixteen persons representing governments on the Governing Body of the International Labor Organization, eight are appointed by the states of "chief industrial importance." Of the twelve executive directors of the International Bank, five are appointed by the states that have the largest number of shares (i.e., are the wealthiest member-states). In the Intergovernmental Maritime Consultative Organization, states with the largest registered tonnage have the right to sit on the executive board. (Ironically, this includes Panama and Liberia, whose wholesale issuance of "flags of convenience" entitles them, according to an advisory opinion of the International Court of Justice, to be considered great maritime powers, even though the ships are actually owned by nationals of other countries.)

In the specialized agencies—particularly in the "operating" programs— the United States as chief financial contributor has usually exercised extraordinary influence over the character and continuance of the programs. U.S. opposition killed two projects proposed for the Food and Agriculture

Organization which were approved by most of the other members—a world food board and a surplus commodity exchange board. The U.S. was primarily responsible for termination of UNRRA in 1946, at a time when almost all other participating nations wished it to continue. The United States government also served notice that it did not intend to support the U.N. International Children's Emergency Fund beyond June, 1950, though the program was unanimously commended by the General Assembly and its continuance generally advocated.

Notwithstanding the special privileges and influence they enjoy, the powerful states want more. They uniformly object to the "one nation–one vote" practice where it is in effect, and argue for the kind of weighted voting that prevails in such organizations as the International Bank and some other specialized agencies. The majority of states, not unnaturally, resist such preferential treatment, and their view tends to prevail except when the moneyed or the powerful threaten boycott if they are not granted a preponderant say.[8]

Regionalism and Bloc Voting

Parallel to the recognition of power, the procedures of international organization have been devised and manipulated to give expression to regional concerns.

A balanced geographical representation is required on many international organs, and states from the same region have shown a strong inclination to vote together as a "bloc" on many issues, particularly in the United Nations. As a matter of fact, bloc voting has become so well established that the United Nations, to a large extent, has been transformed from an association of individual sovereign states into an association of regions. The net effect has been to strengthen the influence of smaller states, which when banded together have in many situations forced consideration of their wishes as the price of cooperation on the interests of the larger powers. Regional blocs have often been willing to bargain and "trade" with each other in order to increase their weight and join their ends.

Five or possibly six regional groupings have crystallized in the operation of the United Nations. The twenty Latin-American republics, the nine Arab states, the Soviet bloc, a group of five to eight Asiatic countries, a varying combination of African and Asian countries, and some of the commonwealth often act together on many of the key issues before the General Assembly and in the election of members and officers of U.N. organs. Except for the Soviet bloc, regional voting is not completely consistent but appears at those points where the regional group considers it has a particular common interest. On other matters, states revert to independent decision. Formal as well as

---

[8] A competent study of the issue and practice of weighted voting, particularly as it has been faced in European regional organizations, is: Bora Ljubisavljevic, *Les Problèmes de la Pondération dans les Institutions Européennes,* (Leyde: A. W. Sythoff, 1959).

informal caucusing takes place within most of these groups throughout sessions of the United Nations.[9]

There is growing evidence, however, that voting in the United Nations is strongly influenced by groupings of interest along lines much broader than geographical regional association. In addition to the familiar East-West political division, a North-South split has now emerged, corresponding roughly to the have nations *vs.* the have-nots—poorer, less-developed—in the tropical and subtropical zones.[10]

Regional concerns are particularly evident in the choice of members of the U.N. councils and officers of U.N. organs. Though neither the Charter nor the rules of procedure specify criteria to govern the General Assembly in its elections, it has customarily followed a regional distribution. The six nonpermanent members of the Security Council, for example, consisted at first of two Latin-American states, a British dominion, an Eastern European state, an Arab state, and a Western European state. The blocs have usually come to a common understanding on which of their number should be chosen at a given time, and until the fourth session of the General Assembly, these selections had not been seriously contested. However, the self-announced and ultimately successful candidacy of Yugoslavia for a seat on the Security Council, in opposition to Soviet-backed Czechoslovakia, broke the precedent after bitter controversy. Significantly, many non-Communist states voted for Czechoslovakia on the grounds that the procedure of regional representation would be undermined if the choice of the region, however arrived at, was not scrupulously respected. Since then, the distribution has become quite fluid, with Asian and African countries insisting on specific representation as their numbers increased. The Charter amendments adopted by the General Assembly (see p. 22) provide, however, for an absolutely rigid geographical apportionment of seats in both the enlarged Security Council and the Economic and Social Council.

The Decision-making Process—Unanimity *vs.* Majority Rule

A peculiarly difficult problem for international organization has been to determine a satisfactory method of reaching decisions. If full regard were

---

[9] Several detailed studies of bloc voting practices have now been made. See, in particular, Thomas Hovet, Jr., *Bloc Politics in the United Nations* (Cambridge, Mass.: Harvard University Press, 1960); and his *Africa in the United Nations* (Evanston, Ill.: Northwestern University Press, 1963); also, Sydney D. Bailey, *The General Assembly* (New York: Praeger, 1960), Chap. 2. For a methodological critique of these studies, see Arend Lijphart, "The Analysis of Bloc Voting in the General Assembly," *American Political Science Review,* December, 1963.

[10] See the interesting results of Hayward Alker's study of "Dimensions of Conflict in the General Assembly," in which he applied the statistical technique of factor analysis to determine the degree of convergence of states voting on 70 roll calls in the Sixteenth General Assembly, then followed up with correlation and regression analysis to assess the relative importance of various determinants of voting behavior. Paper delivered at the American Political Science Association Annual Meeting, 1963.

maintained for the sovereignty of states, any action taken by an international body would require the unanimous consent of the members; in fact, the "unanimity rule" was the characteristic voting procedure in pre-World War II international organizations and is still widely followed. The League of Nations Council and Assembly could act on most questions only by agreement of all their members. An important exception was that in a dispute brought before the League, action did *not* require concurrence of parties to the dispute. At the present time, several commissions of the United Nations, such as the Economic Commission for Europe, conduct their business by unanimous agreement; and the Council of Europe is also restricted to action approved by all members of its committee of ministers, which assures that every participating government must consent.

On the other hand, the rule of unanimity has been increasingly forsaken in international bodies in favor of the greater flexibility of majority decision. From its beginning, the Universal Postal Union has set regulations by a two-thirds majority of its conference. In most other international unions or specialized agencies, a two-thirds or even a simple majority of the members present has been sufficient for action on most questions. The following voting arrangements are typical:

International Labor Organization Conference:	Simple majority of delegates present (except for budgetary arrangements, which are decided by two-thirds of delegates present; and new members, who are admitted by two-thirds of delegates present, including two-thirds of the government delegates present and voting).
UNESCO General Conference:	Simple majority (except for proposed amendments to the constitution and admission of new members, which require two-thirds' approval).
International Civil Aviation Organization Assembly:	Majority of votes cast.
Council:	Majority of all the members (except new members, admitted by four fifths of the assembly; and amendments, approved by two-thirds).
International Bank Board of Governors	Majority of votes cast (voting power determined by the shares of stock held by each member). (A number of exceptions on specific matters require a majority of the governors exercising a majority of total voting power.)

In the United Nations, a unique compromise has retained the principle of unanimity for the five major powers in the Security Council but has abandoned it for the rest of the organization. Decisions in the General Assembly require a two-thirds' vote; in the Economic and Social Council and the Trusteeship Council, a simple majority of those voting is sufficient. The votes of all members have equal weight. But in the Security Council, on all questions of substance a vote of seven of the eleven members is required for action, and, as mentioned above, all five permanent members must concur (except for parties to a dispute before the Council). Noting that the Security Council, in addition to concerning itself with the preservation of peace and security, also recommends the admission of new members and nominates the Secretary-General; this rule of great power unanimity (the so-called "veto") has seemed to have far-reaching effect.

The Veto. The Soviet Union has made the veto infamous by using it over 100 times (as of 1962), mostly to block applications for membership, but on several critical occasions to prevent action favored by the majority in regard to international conflicts.[11] Each of the other permanent members has also indulged in the veto at least once, and threatened its use more than once, when it considered its vital interests at stake, as in the 1956 Suez crisis when France and Britain both stood in the way of Security Council action to restrain their attack on Egypt. In fact, the full significance of the unanimity rule is missed by the customary manner of tallying vetoes"; a negative vote is counted only if it nullifies an otherwise effective majority. Every no vote by a permanent member is really a veto, having the same automatic power to cut off action whether the majority is on one side or the other. The ability of the Western powers to recruit majorities for their positions through most of the Security Council's history has hidden the large number of times when one or all of them were really responsible for failure of the Council to act. (For instance, the Western powers contributed to the membership impasse fully as much as the U.S.S.R. by refusing to approve admission of Communist states; but they do not consider their votes as vetoes, because there were enough other noes to prevent a favorable majority. The same thing happens regularly when the issue of Chinese representation arises; the U.S. and Nationalist China, usually joined by Britain and France, vote against the Soviet resolution; but so far a full seven-vote majority has not materialized in favor of seating the Chinese Communist government, and so the potential vetoing effect of the negative votes is ignored.)

From one point of view, the unanimity rule has tremendously complicated and obstructed Security Council operations, rendering what was confidently expected to be the most influential and expeditious of the United Nations organs virtually impotent in the face of controversy among the great powers. On the other hand, it should be recognized that the veto was *deliberately* inserted in the Charter by the great powers—and universally accepted by the

---

[11] The U.S.S.R. cast its 102nd veto on September 17, 1964, to block a resolution deploring an attack on Malaysia by Indonesia-based paratroops. Often, however, the point of the Soviet veto was that the action proposed was too weak rather than too strong.

others—as an automatic switchoff, to *prevent* the Security Council (and through it, all members of the U.N.) from becoming involved in a great-power showdown. In this respect, it has accomplished exactly what was intended. And no government has seriously urged that the veto be abolished in regard to actions involving the use of force.

Official proposals to modify the veto provision would limit its use in regard to such matters as the admission of members and recommendations for peaceful settlement of disputes; but there is no practical possibility of making such changes so long as any of the great powers (including the U.S.) fears this would enable others to override what it considers to be vital interests. (The veto, as previously noted, applies to any amendment of the Charter.) Earlier U.S. enthusiasm for restricting the use of the veto has cooled notice-ably as it has lost its capacity to win Council majorities.

With all the agonizing over the Council's paralysis as a result of the veto, a dispassionate appraisal finds that it has not been

the constantly growing, indefinitely expansible, cancerous factor in life of the organization which has sometimes been supposed. The striking thing about the list of vetoes, which have been cast in the Security Council is how little they have finally mattered.

[What does matter is that the veto functions] to inspire a sober recognition of the implications of the cleavage between East and West. . . . Viewed in this way, the veto is not so much an obstacle to be circumvented, or a defect to be remedied, as a salutary reminder of facts that must be acknowledged and of realities that must be respected. It is a safety valve—and the problem is not to shut it off, but to cope with the situation which is signaled by its operation.[12]

Majority Rule in the General Assembly.   Whether the "unanimity rule" in the Security Council be condemned or justified, its net effect has been to transfer increasing responsibility for action to the General Assembly, where the rule does not apply. The United Nations is, therefore, becoming more and more an instrument of majority decision. While this widens the range of definitive action, it has also proved dangerous. Given the authority to reach decisions by even a two-thirds majority, the General Assembly is sometimes tempted to disregard the determined opposition of a minority and to adopt proposals as though it were a governing legislature. Such was the case when the Assembly voted in favor of the partition of Palestine; and it was so again in regard to Palestine when at the Fourth Session a proposal to internationalize Jerusalem was approved despite vehement warning from both the Transjordan and Israel authorities that they would not yield their own control of the city. Such action puts the General Assembly in the unenviable position of having made a decision it has neither the power nor the authority to enforce as law on states that object. In exercising the greater

---

[12] Claude, *op. cit.,* pp. 140, 143, 146.

flexibility permitted by a voting procedure that does not require unanimity, an international organization is prone to forget that its essential role is still one of harmonizing the interests of nations rather than of regulating them.[13]

Open Diplomacy

The procedures of international organization are almost universally designed to assure the practice of open diplomacy. Meetings of the main organs and even of committees and commissions are usually public. Special facilities are arranged to accommodate the press, and in the United Nations many of the meetings are broadcast and televised. Verbatim records are kept of plenary sessions; summaries are sometimes considered sufficient for committee sessions. These documents are published, often in several languages, and a staggering quantity of paper flows from international agencies in all directions. At some sessions of the General Assembly, over a million sheets of mimeographed material a day have been prepared. The United Nations has been at pains to facilitate visitors at its sessions; its Department of Public Information sometimes receives as many as 4,500 persons on a single day. A substantial amount of publicity is prepared by international agencies in an attempt to acquaint students, educators, and private organizations and individuals everywhere with the work of the organization. Modern international organization is, indeed, so "public relations conscious" that it is used by governments as a most important medium for propagandizing their national policies.

Some delegates complain, however, that the limelight of publicity handicaps negotiations on difficult and explosive questions. In speaking "for the record," representatives of national governments tend to stake out extreme positions and defend them stubbornly, vehemently, and often vituperatively. Though the diplomacy is "open," it is not conciliatory. Passions are aroused among the public, and personal feelings among the delegates are ruffled. Reasonable compromise becomes difficult, if not impossible.

For such reasons, some questions—especially those involving vital issues of security or prestige, or essentially technical problems—have been shunted off the public platform into closed committees. For instance, Subcommittees of the General Assembly, and its Advisory Committee on Budget and Finance, and several of the bodies concerned with disarmament negotiations, deliberate in private, and report in public only when concrete decisions have been reached. This procedure reserves "open diplomacy" for the final

---

[13] See Claude, *ibid.,* Chap. 7, for a trenchant critique of international majoritarianism. The decision-making procedures of the General Assembly are thoroughly examined by Bailey, *op. cit.,* see especially Chapter 7. A close case study and appraisal of decision-making in the United Nations is John G. Hadwen and Johan Kaufmann, *How United Nations Decisions Are Made* (2nd rev. ed., New York: Oceana Publications, 1962).

review and debate, while permitting the delegates to explore differences and seek grounds for agreement without having to calculate at every moment the immediate public consequences of each word spoken.

THE ROLE OF THE INTERNATIONAL SECRETARIAT

The gradual development of secretariats of international agencies into functioning "international civil services" is among the most significant factors contributing to effective collaboration among nations. This core of persons, with its growing experience in the techniques of international administration, its relative permanence and continuity, and its sense of direct responsibility for the various agencies' operations, knits the organizations together and furnishes constant impetus to accomplishment of their objectives.

The secretariat is the truly international part of international organization. Each member of the staff, from the secretary-general or director-general to the janitor and clerk, undertakes to serve no authority other than the organization. Regulations of the United Nations prescribe that "their responsibilities are not national but exclusively international." Each employee, on accepting appointment, solemnly swears or declares

> to exercise in all loyalty, discretion and conscience the functions entrusted to me as a member of the international service of the United Nations, to discharge those functions and regulate my conduct with the interests of the United Nations only in view, and not to seek or accept instructions in regard to the performance of my duties from any government or other authority external to the Organization.

A similar requirement governs the staffs of the other international agencies. The staff is specifically warned to

> avoid any action, and in particular any kind of public pronouncement or activity which may adversely reflect on their position as international civil servants. They are not expected to give up their national sentiments or their political and religious convictions; but they shall at all times bear in mind the reserve and tact incumbent upon them by reason of their international status.

To maintain the international character of a secretariat, personnel is deliberately recruited from a large number of countries. Wide geographical distribution, indeed, is one of the basic criteria of employment laid down by the United Nations Charter and the constitutions of many other agencies. This requirement makes it almost impossible for United States citizens to secure positions with the United Nations at the present time because of the disproportion of Americans on the staff (60 to 70 per cent). Many Americans were hired when the United Nations was originally established, and since headquarters are in New York a large percentage of the maintenance and secretarial staff, recruited locally, are also American nationals. The General Assembly has instructed the Secretary-General to reduce the percentage of United States citizens on the staff so that it may correspond more nearly to the proportion of the budget contributed by the U.S. (approximately one-third); this not only limits the appointment of Americans to new positions, but means that posts held by Americans gradually are filled by nationals of other countries.

As international officials, members of secretariats are granted special privileges and immunities to facilitate their work. These generally resemble the diplomatic immunities established by international comity. In addition, the international official is presumably protected against pressure or influence from his own or other national governments in the discharge of his responsibilities. This immunity from national influence has generally been respected, though in the League of Nations the Nazi and Italian governments attempted to control their nationals on the secretariat even to the extent of organizing them into "cells" accountable to the top German or Italian official in the League.

The United Nations Secretary-General has diligently insisted on the prerogatives of his staff, while making it clear that he would cooperate fully with national authorities on matters of law enforcement not involving the work of the United Nations. He has, for instance, waived the immunity of his staff from prosecution for violations of New York State traffic laws, and of some persons explicitly accused of espionage by the United States government. On the other hand, he protested vigorously against charges made during a Congressional hearing that the United Nations Secretariat was infested with spies, claiming that such action amounted to legislative interference with the work of the organization. The United States government agreed and promptly denounced the action as an infringement of the obligations of the Charter. On another occasion, the Secretary-General refused to surrender for interrogation and trial a Czech on the staff of the United Nations Information Center in Prague, until the Czechoslovak government had given explicit assurances that its accusations in no way concerned his work with the United Nations. A United Nations representative was permitted to be present during the trial to make sure this understanding was observed.

The status of Soviet nationals on the United Nations staff is equivocal. Most of them are designated in the first place by the Soviet government; few Soviet citizens apply directly to the United Nations for appointment. Once on the staff, their official status and line of responsibility are the same as anyone else's. They are under obligation to serve the United Nations organ to which they are assigned without regard to possible contradiction between its decisions and Soviet policy. Apparently, this relationship is understood and accepted both by the Soviet government and the Soviet members of the U.N.

staff. The Assistant Secretary-General for Security Affairs has always been a Soviet citizen, yet he has carried out security responsibilities entrusted to the Secretariat by the General Assembly or the Security Council, even when the U.S.S.R. has opposed the action as contrary to the Charter. On the other hand, the Soviet government has exercised unique authority in regard to terminating the services of its nationals on the U.N. staff; whereas tenure in the Secretariat is usually subject only to regulations laid down by the General Assembly, the U.S.S.R. instructs its citizens when to give up their jobs and return home. Neither the individuals concerned nor the Secretary-General has contested this procedure. The Soviet government appears to consider these people as part of its own diplomatic corps, even though for a time they may be seconded to the United Nations. Their service for the U.N. is, therefore, a matter of discretion with the government, and the Soviet national cannot enjoy the full extent of the U.N. staff's immunity from government control.

On the whole, the secretariats of international agencies are expected to perform a service, not an executive or policy-making function. They gather information, plan for the sessions of the various organs, make reports to them, keep records, translate documents, and publicize the work of the organization. In a more responsible capacity, international officials make studies of problems with which the agency is concerned and advise with the representatives of national governments in regard to methods of meeting them. Some services are of a highly technical nature. The World Health Organization furnishes teams of medical experts to work with governments in developing their public health programs; the Food and Agriculture Organization sends its trained staff to plan with national agricultural leaders for the introduction of improved methods of conservation or production; the staff of the International Monetary Fund counsels governments on their fiscal policies. In international operating programs, the secretariat has been charged with large-scale administration and field services of extraordinary responsibility and complexity. For instance, the UNRRA staff of over 3,000, purchased supplies, arranged for shipment, and supervised distribution, and also directed camps for displaced persons, health and welfare services, agricultural rehabilitation programs, and others.

The role of international secretariats has grown in importance since the war, and, directly or indirectly, they are exercising an increased influence on the policies of their organizations. The United Nations Secretary-General in addition to fulfilling his function as chief administrative officer of the organization has, in effect, assumed the prerogative of acting as its chief executive and responsible spokesman. The Charter gives the Secretary-General one explicit executive function: he may "bring to the attention of the Security Council any matter which in his opinion may threaten the maintenance of international peace and security" (Art. 99). But all the incumbents of this post have stretched their powers well beyond this point. Under the guise of reporting to the General Assembly, Trygve Lie, for instance, bluntly warned member-states to live up to their obligations under the Charter. With the Assembly President, he personally intervened in the crisis over the Berlin blockade, appealing to the four major powers involved to compromise their disagreements. While the Security Council was considering the Iranian dispute in 1946 he astonished it with an opinion questioning the legality of the discussion because Iran had formally withdrawn its appeal. He was widely criticized but did not incur formal censure of the organization when he publicly expressed doubt that the proposed North Atlantic Treaty was compatible with the Charter.

Beyond such bold moves on specific issues, the Secretariat has exerted a pervading influence at all levels of policy-making and deliberation. Responsible officials attached to each organ and committee and equipped with a broad grasp of the subjects under consideration as well as of United Nations procedures have not hesitated to suggest to chairmen, rapporteurs, and other delegates ways of handling the problems before them. Delegates have increasingly turned to the Secretariat not only for information but for advice, recommendations, and even drafting of resolutions and conventions. The Secretariat is thus emerging as the real custodian of international organization, not just its clerk.

This growing influence of the Secretariat, and particularly the vigorous diplomatic initiative of the Secretary-General as exercised by Dag Hammarskjöld, was ultimately challenged head on by the Soviet Union. A dramatic confrontation was precipitated when the organization and direction of the United Nations peace-keeping operation in the Congo effectively excluded Soviet intervention and influence. Mr. Khrushchev personally led the attack. At the General Assembly on October 3, 1960, he accused Hammarskjöld of individual bias and demanded his resignation. But he went much farther and denounced the basic concept of a single Secretary-General accountable only to the United Nations as a whole. No one man, he insisted, could "interpret and execute decisions of the Assembly and of the Security Council, taking into account the interests of the countries of monopolistic capital and the interests of the Socialist countries and the interests of the neutralist countries. . . . Let those who believe in the existence of saints remain with their opinion, but we do not believe in these fairy tales." He called for a total and fundamental reorganization of the Secretariat, replacing the Secretary-General with a troika: an executive body of three persons of equal responsibility, representing each of the three "camps"—socialist, capitalist, and neutralist. Only in this way would the United Nations machinery "reflect the actual situation in the world" and take into account the interests of all groups of states on a footing of equality. "We are not seeking any privilege for ourselves, but we do not want others to have privileges over us. What we want is equality for all."

In an immediate, historic rejoinder, Hammarskjöld refused to resign, professing his "responsibility to all those states members for which the organization is of decisive importance, a responsibility which overrides all other considerations." The Soviet would make it impossible, he declared, to maintain an effective executive, and "a weak or nonexistent executive would mean that the United Nations would no longer be able to serve as an effective instrument for active protection of the interests of those many members who need such protection."

This shrewd appeal to the lesser nations to identify a *collectively* responsible Secretariat as the essential guardian of their interests in the midst of the pulls and counterpulls of the great powers succeeded in rallying a substantial majority to repel the bitterly pressed Soviet onslaught. Several judicious concessions were quietly made to reassure the doubtful that the Secretary-General would indeed follow agreed policy, not make it on his own; and that the advice he would hear and heed would come mainly from the great middle of the organization, rather than from either side of the cold war. Changes of personnel, rank, and procedures of consultation at the top level of the Secretariat made the entourage of the Secretary-General heavily non-European. On the Congo operation in particular, Hammarskjöld huddled even more closely than before with an advisory group of African delegates. But on the essential issue, which, as Hammarskjöld put it, was not "of a man but of an institution," the integrity of the Secretary-General's office was preserved.[14]

WEAKNESSES OF INTERNATIONAL ORGANIZATION

Despite its remarkable growth and the extent of its functions, international organization suffers from several critical weaknesses.

---

[14] For further reference concerning the nature, functions and problems of international secretariats, see: Claude, *op. cit.,* chapter 10; the detailed analysis of League of Nations experience by Egon F. Ranshoffen-Wertheimer, *The International Secretariat: A Great Experiment in International Administration* (Washington, D.C.: Carnegie Endowment for International Peace, 1945); and Sydney D. Bailey, *The Secretariat of the United Nations* (New York: Carnegie Endowment for International Peace, 1962).

For specific consideration of the role of Secretary-General, see: *The U.N. Secretary-General: His Role in World Politics* (New York: Commission to Study the Organization of Peace, 1961); Stephen M. Schwebel, *The Secretary-General of the United Nations* (Cambridge, Mass.: Harvard University Press, 1952); and, Wilder Foote (ed.), *Dag Hammarskjold: Servant of Peace* (New York: Harper and Row, 1962); also the definitive study of the pioneering Director-General of the International Labor Organization by E. J. Phelan, *Yes and Albert Thomas* (New York: Columbia University Press, 1949).

The mechanics of international cooperation involve serious practical problems that have not yet been effectively overcome. The conduct of business is complicated and cumbersome, the result, in part, of states' reluctance to delegate to others the shaping of policies affecting their interests. While international agencies have evolved a system of committees to facilitate discussion of their agenda, many of the committees include the full membership of the organization. This means in the United Nations General Assembly, for instance, that every state has the opportunity to debate every issue at least twice—in committee and before the plenary session of the Assembly—and the opportunity is often used to the full. With 112 states in the organization and as many as 70 items on the agenda, the machinery of the General Assembly grinds slowly and tediously. The liberal rules of debate mentioned above add to the harassment of chairmen or members of the Secretariat who want to get things done with dispatch.

Another mechanical problem, less serious now, is the necessity for interpretation and translation. It has not been possible for international organization to agree on a single language for working purposes. Considerations of prestige as well as many delegates' unfamiliarity with any one language have blocked such a procedure. Debate and discussion must therefore be conducted bi- or trilingually, with every remark meticulously translated into the other working languages. In the past, this has naturally consumed a great amount of time and has given rise to occasional misunderstandings. Fortunately, perfection of a device for simultaneous translation has almost entirely eliminated the time problem, and the skill of translators has reduced misinterpretations to a minimum. A new mechanical voting system in the General Assembly is further expediting business. Furthermore, English is more and more commonly used throughout international organization for both formal presentation and informal consultation.

The proliferation of international agencies and expansion of their functions have created a very difficult problem of coordination, both within and among the different bodies. Increasingly, the tasks of one overlap or duplicate the projects of another. The problem of coordination is particularly acute among the specialized agencies, for the United Nations does not have final authority to control their programs. This problem has been attacked by creation of a coordinating committee representing the specialized agencies and the United Nations. While in many ways this device has provided effective clearance on policies, it has developed in the specialized agencies a dangerous tendency to join together to defend their own separate programs as against the United Nations proper. The United Nations organization itself has become so complex and diffused that coordination is very difficult; neither the Secretary-General nor the General Assembly is quite able to keep in touch with all phases of the work and to achieve a thorough integration of the manifold activities.

The personnel of international agencies is another source of weakness. Able and devoted persons have joined the secretariats, but few of them have been drawn from the highest calibre of government, industrial, labor, or professional leadership. The demand for national representativeness has interfered with recruitment on the basis of sheer competence or experience; on the other hand, national governments have been loath to surrender their best personnel to international agencies. Unfortunately also, international organization has attracted and tolerated some people who want a sinecure with relatively good pay for a minimum amount of effort. The adoption of liberal personnel policies governing tenure and promotions in most international bodies has had the effect of affording job security for the unqualified as well as the qualified.

These problems are overshadowed by others more fundamental and less susceptible to change. The jurisdiction of international organizations is still highly restricted. They are authorized to act only within well-defined limits, and when they are disposed to go beyond in an effort to become more effective, they are sharply hauled back by states that wish to exercise an independent initiative.

Furthermore, as has been pointed out, international organization in the last analysis must depend on national governments to implement its decisions. It can rarely carry through a program under its own administration. Such dependence on national discretion makes the execution of international programs uncertain, uneven, and often ineffective.

The basic problem of international institutions is that they lack a solid foundation of loyalty and support either among governments or peoples. Loyalties are still essentially national. In the process of international collaboration, the interests and prestige of nations are paramount as against a more general concern for the welfare of the world community. When the interests of nations converge, international organization can function effectively. But if they conflict, the international body can as yet appeal to no higher loyalty that will insist that national governments yield their own immediate stakes in favor of the broader purposes of the organization.[15]

THE FINANCING PROBLEM

The following figures indicate the nature and dimensions of the problem that, more than any other, constricts international organizations. They are denied adequate financial support to carry out the tasks they are assigned, even though they spend but a tiny fraction of the world's governmental outlays.

---

[15] For a probing analysis of this problem, see Harold Guetzkow, *Multiple Loyalties: Theoretical Approach to a Problem in International Organization* (Princeton, N.J.: Princeton University Center for Research on World Political Institutions, 1955).

The U.N.'s budget for regular operations in 1964 was $95,498,780.

Nine specialized agencies budgeted $110,204,306.

Peace-keeping operations (Congo and UNEF) in the last half of 1963 were running at a rate of about $7 million a month (with the U.N.'s Congo force due to disband June 30, 1964).

For the various U.N. programs of technical and social assistance, governments pledged additional contributions of about $185 million for 1963.[16]

Total for all U.N. related agencies, all purposes was less than $500 million.

U.S. government budget, 1964, $96 billion.

United Nations deficit, June 30, 1964, $111,700,000 (difference between cash resources and current liabilities).

Accumulated arrears (unpaid assessments and pledges due), June 30, 1964, $123,100,000.[17]

In short, the United Nations is bankrupt. It has been spending more than it gets from members. It has borrowed money it cannot repay. The Secretary-General estimated that by the beginning of 1964 cash resources would be less than enough to pay the current month's bills.

This state of affairs is not the result of loose accounting or sloppy budgeting, although some countries make a habit of sniping at the "extravagance" of the Secretariat's estimates and expenditures. Quite the opposite. The U.N.'s budget process insures that every item will be repeatedly scrutinized by each of its 114 parsimonious members. In barest outline, the laborious procedure of authorizing the U.N. to pay the Secretary-General's salary or to print the General Assembly proceedings is as follows:

On notice from the Secretary-General, each department of the Secretariat submits an estimate of expenses needed to carry out the jobs assigned to it under resolutions of the various U.N. organs. No money can be budgeted except to carry out programs specifically authorized by a policy-making body.

These estimates are examined by the Budget Division; revisions are suggested and negotiated; the estimates are collated and transmitted to the Controller, together with any departmental protests against the Budget Division's recommendations; and unresolved differences (within the Secretariat) are settled. After final review by the Secretary-General and his executive assistant, the budget emerges as a unified and integrated report to the General Assembly, complete with information annexes documenting the need for each item. At this stage, the Secretary-General's budget reflects his judgment of the organization's overall requirements to fulfill prescribed tasks.

Now occurs a step peculiar to the United Nations, inherited from the League. The entire budget is examined by a special Advisory Committee on Administrative and Budgetary Questions, appointed by the General Assembly. It is *not*

---

[16] These figures do not take account of lending by such agencies as the International Bank, nor of the expenses of regional organizations and others unrelated to the U.N.

[17] The figures for deficit and arrears relate just to the United Nations organization itself, not to the specialized agencies.

composed of governmental representatives but of individuals who serve, usually for long terms, in a personal technical capacity. It answers only to the General Assembly and has acquired a substantial influence which it exercises, in extended hearings, to challenge the Secretariat's estimates and to recommend cuts. It is not in the habit of justifying increases. The Secretariat shows little relish for this exercise in running the gauntlet, especially as they must run it again in the Fifth Committee of the General Assembly, itself composed of representatives of all the national governments. (One particular cause for complaint is the two hats worn by some members of the Advisory Committee who also double as government representatives on the Fifth Committee. Budget officers feel they face prosecutor and judge in the same person.)

The General Assembly Fifth, or Administrative and Budgetary, Committee, 114 strong, looks at the Secretary-General's budget, compares the report of the Advisory Committee, and vigorously debates not only the amount of appropriation but also the substantive policies that the funds are to implement—matters presumably settled previously by other U.N. bodies and outside the competence of the Fifth Committee. Inevitably, the major political controversies of the organization erupt during the budget debates, in addition to fundamental and perennial disagreements over administrative and budgetary policies. The Secretariat is vilified in general and particular; its performance is condemned and, on occasion, praised. The proceedings are enlivened and often embittered by a running exchange between the Secretary-General and the long-ensconced Chairman of the Advisory Committee, Mr. Aghnides, who delights in these, his finest hours. This relationship has varied with personalities, of course, and was eased by Mr. Hammarskjöld's well-known diplomatic finesse. All this ends with votes on the appropriations—usually following the Advisory Committee's recommendations—and the Fifth Committee then passes the ball on to the General Assembly in plenary session.

The General Assembly is the only body authorized to make appropriations for the entire United Nations organization, and it requires a two-thirds vote to pass the budget. In practice, it has accepted the Fifth Committee's recommendations, though these need only to have been adopted by a simple majority.

Criticisms of this process are many: time-consuming, irrelevant, and inappropriate debate; an Advisory Committee that substitutes badgering for true fiscal expertise in reviewing the Secretariat's estimates, and whose members "tend to conceive of themselves as defenders of a specific national or regional interest rather than the inter-national, or organizational, interest"; an "alarming lack of both foresight and coordination" in the Fifth Committee, "manifested in the almost overwhelming desire to reduce or eliminate proposed expenditures not directly beneficial to the immediate country or region of the delegate." [18] Surely it cannot be said that the United Nations' financial difficulties stem from cavalier budgeting or an uncontrolled disposition to

---

[18] These conclusions as well as much of the previous description are drawn from J. David Singer's meticulous and penetrating study of the United Nations budget process, *Financing International Organization* (The Hague: Martinus Nijhoff, 1961). See especially pp. 173–179.

throw money around. According to an evaluation by a United States Senate subcommittee, "rarely have so many important people taken so much time to spend so little." [19] The problem lies in four interrelated aspects of the organization's *funding* process, not in its spending process:

First, the United Nations, like most international organizations, does not have the power to tax. It "assesses" *governments,* but not individuals, for its regular budget and some other purposes, and it has no means to enforce collections from governments (except to deprive a state of voting if it has not paid its assessment for two years.)

Second, many members of the U.N. insist they have no obligation to support programs of which they do not approve, or for which they do not themselves voluntarily assume a financial obligation. Were it otherwise, they maintain, the U.N. would, indeed, wield a taxing power. They claim the right to exercise a financial veto over every action outside the regular budget, at least to the extent of their own nonpayment.

Third, others hold, on the contrary, that membership in the U.N. carries with it a general obligation to support the organization, and this means to pay a reasonable share of the expense for *all* activities duly authorized by any of its organs—even those to which a particular country may object.

Fourth, and most basic, few governments have shown an inclination to be generous in their support of the United Nations when it comes to paying its bills, even for programs they do strongly advocate. The richer complain of being overburdened, the poorer plead inability to pay as both haggle over the scale of assessment or recriminate over the paucity of each other's voluntary contributions. (No nation pays as much as .5 percent of its gross national product; most U.N. members pay from .005 and .035 percent.) [20]

The practical effect of these contradictions has been to put the United Nations into a bind. Positive majorities commit the organization to expensive undertakings, such as the peace-keeping operations, without insuring the ways and means of paying for them. Opposing minorities refuse to pay any part of the resulting bill, while supporters refuse to pay any more than "their share." The financial crisis has reached its present acute proportions because the most costly United Nations programs have also been its most politically controversial. The issue of members' financial obligations, neatly bypassed in the early life of the organization, has now come to a showdown, and with it the basic question of whether the essential character of international organization shall be changed. For, at heart, the financial crisis is the outcome of an effort, indirect and not entirely self-conscious, to transform the United Nations into a body that *can* legislate binding decisions. Even if its general

---

[19] Subcommittee on the U.N. Charter, *Budgetary and Financial Problems of the United Nations* (Staff Study No. 6, 1954), p. 9, as quoted in *ibid.,* p. 177.

[20] See John G. Stoessinger and Associates, *Financing the United Nations System* (Washington, D.C.: Brookings Institution, 1964). This thorough study provides a penetrating analysis of the background and context of the U.N.'s financial crisis.

powers remain permissive—that is, as noted, to make recommendations rather than to order states to act—the power of assessment would give a United Nations organ the capacity to compel all states to support its decisions by the purse if not otherwise (or else lose their vote or get out). This is why the Soviet Union, and quite a company of non-Communist states, are so adamant in their resistance to every proposal to solve the U.N.'s fiscal problems by some kind of required payment. In the concrete instance of the U.N.'s Congo operation—the most costly and least supported of the actions—the Soviet Union asks why it should be expected to pay for an action it has denounced as illegal (and was designed, at least in part, to keep it out of the Congo).

The advocates of an obligatory basis for U.N. financing have scored several points; however.

1. From the beginning, the regular operating budget has been assessed against the members on a scale set by the General Assembly on recommendation of a Committee on Contributions. (It is significant that the term "contributions" is applied even to these assessments, keeping the formal record clear that the governments are giving rather than being taxed.) Supposedly based on the criterion of "capacity to pay" (measured by estimates of per capita income), the assessments have actually been reached through a delicate process of negotiation and compromise in which other factors have figured. A flat minimum was set for countries with smallest incomes (0.04); a maximum of 39.89 per cent for the U.S. was gradually reduced to 32.51 per cent by 1961 as membership increased and the U.S. insistently protested that other countries were greatly improving their relative financial positions. As might be expected, complaints have been numerous and persistent, especially from wealthier countries, as the ever-larger majority of poorer countries has tilted the scales against them. The U.S.S.R. has been saddled with the largest upward adjustment of its share, coinciding with its economic recovery and advance after the war (from 6.62 in 1946 to 15.08 in 1955, dropping back to 13.62 in 1959–61 after new members took up some of the load). But despite the complaints, all members have agreed to this process of assessment and have acknowledged their obligation to pay the assessment—*for the regular budget*. Some states make a practice of being in arrears, but none has forfeited its vote by failing to pay at least a portion of its assessment within two years.

2. A Working Capital Fund was established (consisting of assessed advances on the same scale as the budget) from which the Secretary-General is authorized to draw pending receipt of the revenues and also to cover unforeseen and emergency expenses. The emergency provision was first used to extend the principle of assessment to finance projects beyond the operating budget. The Secretary-General drew on this fund for the heavy expenses of the peace-keeping operations even before special appropriations were passed.

such as international postal and telecommunications, exploiting submarine resources under the high seas, licensing international civil aviation or maritime commerce, or servicing international tourism. The implication of giving the international organization even a limited right to levy taxes on individuals or corporations engaged in international transactions is repugnant. (The U.S. government even objected for a while to the raising of private *voluntary* contributions for UNICEF through the sale of Christmas cards and "trick or treat" solicitations by children at Halloween, though these efforts are now acceptable and worldwide in scope, netting over a million dollars annually. There are, however, definite limits to the amount and certainty of what can be raised from private sources.) Another idea—exploitation of resources in unoccupied areas (Antarctica, outer space) under U.N. auspices—has little prospect of return commensurate with development costs in the foreseeable future, even were the concerned governments amenable.

As things now stand, the problem of financing international organizations will have to be resolved principally by *voluntary* responses from national governments, based on a conviction that their own interest is deeply engaged in the operation. In other words, the pattern of financing must be consistent with the fundamental nature of international organizations as institutions of collaboration. If there is disagreement over a program, let those who agree with it support it rather than trying to extract a toll from those who wish to have no part of it. In general, this *is* the basis on which most effective action has so far been based. For instance, the United Nations decided early to approach the financing of refugee relief, children's welfare, technical assistance, and a wide range of economic development programs by soliciting voluntary contributions from governments that cared. Though the responses have rarely been equivalent to estimated basic needs, they have sustained substantial operations over a long period. Several U.N. programs now coordinate their fund-raising efforts, which head up into an annual pledging conference where governments announce their contributions in public and often egg on one another by making their pledges contingent on what others do. This seems to be the sound, long-range approach, given international organizations —and national governments—as they are.

THE EFFECTIVENESS OF INTERNATIONAL ORGANIZATIONS

Despite the weaknesses just outlined, international organizations are demonstrating a growing effectiveness. The record of their achievements in peaceful settlement of international disputes, in economic and social cooperation, in protection of human rights, and in other tasks for which they are responsible is, of course, the final test of effectiveness. These accomplishments are reviewed in succeeding chapters.

Along with the positive results of international cooperation, marked improvement has taken place in the day-to-day operation of international agencies. The process of consultation is smoother and more expeditious. The General Assembly usually goes through its invariably long agenda in less than three months. The mechanics of administration has been modified in most agencies so that the staffs function with reasonable efficiency. The organizations' tasks have become more settled, and though new and unexpected assignments continuously appear, the basic framework of international organization is now defined and the terms of reference fairly well understood.

Above all, there is some evidence of growing respect for the authority and the programs of international organizations, both among governments and peoples. The expanding role of the United Nations General Assembly is significant in this regard. Serious problems of postwar political and economic international relations have been placed before it, and top political and diplomatic leaders have participated in its deliberations. Though action on many issues has been inconclusive, the fact remains that governments have attached much importance to presentation of their policies before the Assembly and have indicated considerable concern about its ultimate verdict. The tangible results of international functional activities have also added substantially to the prestige of international organization. People have been able to *see* it in terms of concrete benefits—food, medicine, economic rehabilitation, seeds for new crops, safety measures in civil aviation—and this has bred confidence that international organization can act as well as talk. Such respect and confidence is both a sign and a condition of effectiveness.

Strong evidence supports the appraisal of the United Nations and its related agencies made by the first Secretary-General, Trygve Lie, who observed that they have shown remarkable adaptability to present world conditions, and that under such conditions these organizations represent the most effective instruments available for the achievement of world peace and welfare.

. . . the United Nations has become the chief force that holds the world together against all the conflicting strains and stresses that are pulling it apart. The United Nations has interposed law and human decency and the processes of conciliation and co-operation between the world's peoples and the naked, lawless use of power. The United Nations has continued to stand for brotherhood in the midst of all the voices that talk of national policy in terms of military strategy and tactics.

. . . the United Nations has been designed above all for a changing world. It has been so framed and so constructed that change can be brought about peacefully instead of by force of arms. It has been so built that the old nationalisms of the western world and the rising new nationalisms of Asia and the Far East can adjust themselves peacefully to each other. It has been built to contain within peaceful bounds any kind of ideological competition among capitalists, communist socialists, social democrats, or adherents to any other economic or political faith, provided that one group does not attempt to impose its will upon the others by the threat or use of force.

PART I

THE STRUGGLE FOR PEACE AND SECURITY

The supreme task expected of international organization in the 20th century is the prevention of war among nations. Almost all of the efforts to develop an organized society of states have originated in the hope that in one way or another they would provide a substitute for the violence which has marked the conduct of international relations. This aspiration as poignantly expressed in the leadline of the United Nations Charter which declared the dominant determination of "we the peoples of the United Nations" is to "save succeeding generations from the scourge of war."

At the same time, governments have insisted that the pursuit of peace should not impair the continued independence of the states they govern. Whatever might be done to prevent war must simultaneously insure the security of individual nations. When world political behavior is dictated essentially by the struggle for self-centered national interests, the pursuit of international peace is so intertwined with the achievement of national security as to make it almost a twin objective.

The result has been a persistent ambivalent outlook toward the problem of preventing war. The practice of war in the pursuit of national interest is now almost universally regarded as repugnant to the public international interest. Its prevention, and the devising of alternative means of resolving international conflict, are considered matters of grave concern to everyone, transcending the private interest of the particular states involved in a controversy.

On the other hand, most states continue to insist that the problem is pre-eminently theirs. Each reserves to itself the right ultimately to decide on the basis of immediate national interest whether to make or refrain from war. This inability fully to internationalize the problem of war constantly bedevils the efforts to forge a reliable peace system.

The organization of such a system is necessarily limited by the contemporary policies of national governments which accept as inviolable the separate identity of states and expect their freedom to be subject to no authority other than their own governments. This automatically rules out any idea of world government, whatever its theoretical merits as a means of preserving peace, for that would require a surrender of the control of policy which nations consistently regard as the essence of their "security."

Nevertheless, the advancing technology of military annihilation has brought most states to the point of admitting that the independent use of force in the pursuit of their interests, as traditionally practiced in international relations, can produce neither security nor peace. There appears a greater readiness than formerly to base national policy on the premise that resort to war must be subjected to the sanction of international authority except in extreme cases of need for self-defense. At least the internationalization of the problem of war has gone far enough to sustain a wide range of international efforts to deal with it—short of the establishment of full supra-national government.

Given a split world, international organization has become in the words of the late Secretary-General of the United Nations, Dag Hammarskjold, "the embodiment of an ideal and the symbol of an approach to international life which recognizes the common interest of all in the rejection of the use of force, in any form, as a means for settling international disputes and in adherence to the principles of law, justice, and human rights." *

* (From the Introduction to the Fifteenth Annual Report of the Secretary-General to the General Assembly, August 31, 1960.)

Chapter 3

Peace Enforcement:
The Collective Security System

The concept of collective security, embodied in somewhat different forms in the organization of both the League of Nations and the United Nations, has been for half a century the cornerstone of international efforts to establish a peaceful order within the pluralistic society of sovereign states. This ingenious approach has aimed to assure the security of each state through the collective action of most of the others, functioning through a settled framework of international institutions in fulfillment of voluntarily assumed obligations. It is an innovation, virtually without precedent in practical political experience, devised to restrain the hostile impulses inherent in relations among independent nations.

The essence of the idea is a mutual insurance contract among the states. Each state undertakes to guarantee the security of all the others, and for this premium presumably receives coverage for its own security through the commitments made by the others.

This assumes that the maintenance of peace and security is a legitimate common interest, and will be accepted as a fundamental common responsibility, of all states. Collective security further assumes that peace must be enforced and aggression restrained by bringing overwhelming power to bear on a violator. It expects that this can be done by the rest of the community of states voluntarily pooling their power and organizing collective sanctions.

Collective security thus repudiates the attempt, traditional with international diplomacy, to attain security through the contrivance of a perpetual *balancing* of power by a half hundred or more political entities varying in power, aspirations, and types of governments. It insists on the necessity of a preponderance of power in the hands of the body of states committed to the preservation of peace.

Yet, collective security shuns establishment of a centralized monopoly of force which would characterize a truly governmental approach to security. It leaves the effective control of force to national governments, banking on their readiness to join forces in face of a violent threat to the international order.

Collective security is sometimes held to involve much more than the enforcement of peace. One leading authority considers that enforcement measures are only one of three elements in the system, inseparable from provisions for the peaceful settlement of disputes and provisions for disarmament.[1] In practice, however, international organizations have generally kept these functions separate, treating them as complementary, but not necessarily interdependent, methods of preserving peace. The task of enforcement has nearly always been emphasized as the crucial element of a collective security system.

The term "collective security" has also come to be applied indiscriminately to arrangements that do not adhere to the principle that all states must share responsibility for the organization of peace.

NATO and other so-called regional pacts for collective self-defense are more aptly identified as examples of a *selective* approach to the general problem of war prevention. The allies purposely do not bind themselves to protect everyone's security, but only their own. They do not expect others to share their responsibilities. Indeed, they exclude others from their councils—their spotted enemies in particular. The perspective is so radically different from the view of the security problem from a global angle that to use the label "collective security" to describe both approaches produces nothing but confusion. The genius of collective security historically has been its insistence that the collectivity of states must include the whole world, not just part of it, in order to make security effective.[2]

The appropriate objectives of the system also have sometimes been misconstrued. International organizations, especially the United Nations, have been pressured to make a particular state accept international decisions of the justice and lawfulness of its conduct. Collective security has thus been called on to function as the general policing arm for the world community, responsible for enforcement of law as well as order. This goes far beyond the basic intent of the system. Collective security in the classic concept is designed only to guarantee conditions of peace, not to assure justice in all the relations of states. Enforcement, in this view, should be strictly limited to one task, that of preventing states from using force contrary to their international

---

[1] See Andrew Martin, *Collective Security* (Paris: UNESCO, 1952).

[2] See the clear-headed analysis of this distinction in Inis L. Claude, Jr., *Swords Into Plowshares* (3rd ed.; New York: Random House, 1959), p. 275.

obligations. Failure to recognize this restricted purpose of the system has caused many to become disillusioned when international organizations have been unwilling to compel states to submit to majority judgment concerning their rights and interests.

Much in the 50 years' experience with collective security casts doubt on its underlying assumptions and, hence, on the capacity of international organizations to use this approach effectively to fulfill their peace and security missions. The fact is that many states have failed to base their national policies on the expectation that collective security will succeed. By simultaneously pursuing their own separate devices to achieve security, they have prevented realization of the conditions necessary for success of the collective system. Yet, the idea still has allure, and most national governments voice at least nominal allegiance to it.

Meanwhile, the practical experience of the United Nations in seeking the preservation of peace has produced what promises to be an alternative to collective security, more appropriate to the contemporary conditions of international conflict. The United Nations Emergency Force, improvised in the white heat of the Suez crisis in 1956, expresses the moral authority, rather than the compulsive enforcement power, of the international community. The limitations of such a police force, measured by the yardstick of power, are obvious. But the truly effective function of international police in maintenance of peace and security has perhaps just been discovered to require little power. Restraint of aggression or the forestalling of hostilities may depend more on the live demonstration of the international community's immediate concern and the patrol of tense areas by a disinterested "peace force."

THE PRINCIPLE OF COLLECTIVE RESPONSIBILITY

The principle that maintenance of peace is a legitimate common interest, not simply a matter within the discretion of the individual states, was considered by the designers of collective security to be the practical consequence of modern conditions of international relations. Peace had become "indivisible," to use the expression widely current in both the League of Nations and the United Nations. A war anywhere in the world could easily spread to engulf states everywhere, because national interests were now far-flung, and one state's actions impinged on what others felt to be their vital rights. If Sarajevo and the Nazi attack on Poland could trigger chain reactions to launch two world-encompassing wars, then an equally global sweep was required for the statecraft of preventing war. The facts of international life dictated that the effects of *irresponsible* national policy would be unlimited. Hence, *responsible* national policy would have to recognize an unlimited range of actions with which states throughout the world might properly be concerned as threats to their security and to peace. This has been the pragmatic basis for the principle of collective responsibility.

The principle has now acquired a substantial legal basis as well. First through the Covenant of the League of Nations, then more comprehensively through the United Nations Charter, states undertook self-restraining obligations to refrain from actions which threatened international peace and security, and they asserted the unlawfulness of such actions. They simultaneously made a positive declaration that any such actions were of concern to all, and proclaimed the competence of international authority to take concerted countermeasures.

The League's Limited Peace Commitments

The positive expression of collective responsibility, as put by the Covenant of the League of Nations, declared any war or threat of war, whether immediately affecting members of the League or not, "a matter of concern to the whole League." The League, as a body, was given the broad mandate to "take any action that may be deemed wise and effectual to safeguard the peace of nations." (Art. 11, par. 1.) Should a member of the League go to war in disregard of the Covenant, it would be considered to have committed an act of war against all other members. (Art. 16.) The Covenant explicitly recognized a "friendly right" of each member to notify the Assembly or Council of the League of circumstances it felt threatened to disturb international peace. Thus it denied the validity of a frequently asserted claim that what a state did was no one else's business and that any interference by another state could be considered an unfriendly act justifying reprisal.

Collective responsibility, defined in terms of what states should *not* do, bound members of the League simply to respect the territorial integrity and political independence of the other members of the League. (Art. 10.)

The League Covenant, as might be expected with the pioneer move in a novel political experiment, had to compromise with traditional habits and did not erect a complete legal framework for the principle of collective responsibility. There were two main shortcomings.

First, members of the League strictly limited the circumstances in which they would consider forceful action by a state a violation of the Covenant and, hence, unlawful. This left large areas of permissible hostility, extending to full-scale war, for which the League of Nations had no responsibility. Analysis of Articles 12 and 15 from the standpoint of obligations *not* imposed on members shows that they remained free to take any action they wanted, including the use of force, in at least the following contingencies.

1. Should the League Council fail to agree *unanimously* on a report of the facts in a dispute, and just and proper recommendations for a settlement.
2. Should a majority of the League Assembly, including all the states that

are members of the Council, fail to reach agreement on what to do about a dispute.

3. Should the other party to a dispute not comply with the recommendations made by the Council or the Assembly.

4. Should the Council fail to make its report within six months after submission of the dispute.

5. Should the League member be embroiled with a state outside the League.

6. Once three months had elapsed after a decision proposing a peaceful settlement (whatever it might be—arbitral award, judicial settlement, or League report), all obligations lapsed. Thus, a state was really obligated only to observe a cooling-off period, not to abjure force as such.

7. Should the dispute be found by the League Council to arise out of a matter which was considered by international law solely within the domestic jurisdiction of the state.

The second fissure in the League's legal foundations for collective responsibility was a lack of clear authority to undertake enforcement action until an act of war, violating the Covenant, had actually occurred. To be sure, Article 10 provided in case of a threat of aggression that the Council should advise members how they should fulfill the obligation to preserve the security of the other members. But this was advice, not commitment. The responsibility of invoking real sanctions under Article 16 arose only after an act of war had breached the specific commitments in the Covenant to seek peaceful settlement.[3]

The states joining the League obviously were not prepared to shoulder the indeterminate burdens of full collective responsibility. The Covenant was deliberately drafted so as to limit the occasions when states would have to make major sacrifices in the common interest to situations where the common danger was unusually clear. Furthermore, the Covenant's gingerly approach left the League powerless to move forcefully to prevent the outbreak of war before it occurred.

The United Nations' Encompassing Security Commitments

The United Nations' system largely closed these gaps, insofar as formal commitments to collective responsibility were concerned.

The members' obligation to refrain from aggressive action is unlimited. It covers any threat or use of force against the integrity or independence of *any* state, or in *any* manner inconsistent with the purposes of the United Nations.

The Charter prescribes that members shall "refrain in their international relations from the threat or use of force against the territorial integrity or political independence of any State, or in any other manner inconsistent with

---

[3] If a state that was not a member of the League went to war with a League member after refusing an invitation to accept the obligations of League membership for the purpose of settling the dispute peacefully, it was subject to the sanctions of Article 16 just as though it had been a member who had breached the Covenant (Art. 17).

the Purposes of the United Nations." (Art. 2, par. 4.) They must refrain from giving assistance to any state against which the United Nations is taking preventive or enforcement action. (Art. 2, par. 5.) The obligation thus covers the full range of a member's international relations, whether the other countries involved are in the United Nations or not. It prohibits both the threat and the use of force.

The members' pledge of collective assistance is also nominally unlimited. They promise to give the United Nations *every* assistance in *any* action it takes in accordance with the Charter (Art. 2, par. 5) and to accept the decisions of the Security Council designed to maintain international peace and security.

Further, the Charter authorizes virtually unlimited preventive powers. Collective measures may be recommended (or, in the case of the Security Council, prescribed) to prevent an aggravation of a situation, or to counter any "threat to the peace" whether or not an outright act of aggression or war is involved, and quite apart from whether a specific provision of the Charter has been violated. (Arts. 39, 40.)

Finally, action may be directed against any state, inside or outside the United Nations, as the Charter vigorously asserts the responsibility of the organization to "ensure that States which are not Members of the United Nations act in accordance with these Principles so far as may be necessary for the maintenance of international peace and security." (Art. 2, par. 6.)

Some international lawyers still find this last proposition hard to digest. States traditionally deny the validity of obligations which they have not individually assumed; yet, here is a body of states asserting their collective authority to apply principles of international conduct to the entire world. By joining the United Nations, most states in the world have implied their acceptance of this novel doctrine in international relations: the right, under the principle of collective responsibility, for the organized community of states to force those outside the organization to comply with its decisions, at least in regard to the conditions necessary to maintain peace and security. The issue is not really settled, however, with such important countries as Communist China and Germany still outside and insistent that actions of the United Nations are inapplicable to them without their express consent.

An Exception for Neutrals

Another troublesome problem arising from the assertion of complete collective responsibility for peace is the status of neutrals. Neutrality in regard to any international controversy has in the past been considered an entirely proper and, indeed, honorable policy for countries to adopt. Neutrals have sought to maintain normal relations with both sides, and their right to do so was generally conceded, within the limits permitted by belligerents under recognized rules of warfare.

The collective security system, however, presumes the obligation of all states to support action to suppress an unlawful threat or use of force, and, of course, to refrain from any action that aids a state threatening peace and security. There is no place in the system for neutrality between an aggressor on the one hand and the law enforcing international body on the other. Logically, one must either be counted among the collectively responsible or stand as a subverter of the peaceful order. The United Nations' obligations, strictly interpreted, deny the option of neutrality to its members just as much as they deny the right to commit aggression.

Because of this implication, Switzerland, a state with a deep commitment to a policy of neutrality, has stayed out of the United Nations, even though it has cooperated in some of the economic and social activities of the organization and has housed many of its organs and conferences.

Others, such as Sweden, have felt they could join the United Nations on the basis of an understanding of the Charter which allows them considerable flexibility in determining the nature of their responsibilities should the organization get involved in enforcement action. It is now widely conceded that states may remain members of the United Nations in good standing, even though they quietly refrain from joining in the positive measures the organization applies to enforce the peace. To this extent, the idea of collective responsibility for peace, as expressed in the United Nations Charter, has been modified to accommodate the practice of neutrality.

The Exception of Self-Defense

The principle of collective responsibility for the use of force has also had to be squared with the most elemental of national rights—the right of self-defense.

In an ultimate sense, the two are mutually exclusive. For if each state may legitimately decide for itself when self-defense justifies resort to force, by what authority can the collective body of states decide that an act of force is unlawful and should be prevented? Although one state's claim to be acting in self-defense may appear unwarranted to others and even cloak an intent of aggression, its right to decide and to act on the basis of its decision is unchallengeable if, as is usually conceded, the right of self-defense inheres in national sovereignty.

The alternative—that the international community assume unequivocal responsibility for determining when a state is or is not acting in legitimate self-defense—would really do away with the right altogether. States would, in effect, have to yield this most precious of all decisions to others, trusting in the impartiality of the international body and in its capacity to guarantee the execution of its collective decisions. This they show little disposition to do at present.

The collective security system has had to straddle the issue of self-defense. For instance, the United Nations Charter, in Article 51, recognizes an "inherent right of individual or collective self-defense," but attempts to circumscribe its exercise. States may invoke it to justify action on their own only if an *armed* attack occurs against a member of the United Nations and only until the Security Council acts to maintain peace and security. In the meantime, states invoking the right must report to the Security Council the measures they are taking.

However, all provisions of the Charter expressing the principle of collective responsibility for the use of force are inapplicable—unless the Security Council takes "necessary" measures. More is involved in this formula than a short delay before the right of self-defense yields to the assertion of collective responsibility. The Security Council may never be able to act, dependent as it is on the concurrence of the five permanent members and two others. This has so continuously been the case in the course of the cold war that the United Nations has lost most of its potential control over national actions undertaken in the name of self-defense. Article 51 has proved the Achilles' heel in the seemingly firm legal basis of collective responsibility in the Charter.

THE ORGANIZATION OF COLLECTIVE DECISIONS

The collective responsibility of states for the maintenance of peace and security is expressed not only in legal commitments but also through common organs for decision-making.

It is essential in a system of collective security to have international institutions determine on behalf of the whole body of states when an occasion threatens the common security and what kind of joint action should be undertaken to cope with it. Without an adequate organizational basis, collective responsibility might be dissipated in uncoordinated, and perhaps even contradictory, actions as states decided separately on the implications of a crisis.

Three main problems have arisen in connection with the organization of responsibility for collective security: (1) Should the responsibility for decision be delegated to a representative organ or assumed by the entire body of states associated in the system? (2) Should the more powerful states have more say than the less powerful? (3) Should the decision-making organs have wide discretion, or should their decisions be guided by quite specific definitions—in advance—of the circumstances in which states should engage in collective enforcement action?

From Representation to Town Meeting?

In both the League of Nations and the United Nations, member states originally agreed to entrust the primary consideration of common enforcement action to international organs of a representative character. They generally believed that effective responsibility and the compactness of the decision-making organ went hand in hand.

The Council of the League, which included the "great" powers in the League plus four to ten others elected by the Assembly, had the duty of recommending the forces that members should contribute to protect the covenants of the League, as well as the task of advising generally on how states should fulfill their obligations in case of aggression, war, or threats thereof—this in addition to broad responsibilities for attempting the peaceful settlement of disputes.

The Charter of the United Nations placed primary responsibility for determining the occasions and measures of collective action on the eleven-member Security Council—five permanent and six elected. Its mandate, as put comprehensively in Article 39, was to "determine the existence of any threat to the peace, breach of the peace, or act of aggression" and to "make recommendations, or decide what measures shall be taken in accordance with Articles 41 and 42, to maintain or restore international peace and security."

After a while, both the League and the United Nations experienced a decided shift of opinion in favor of a broader base for decisions on security questions than had been originally intended. The repeated failure of the two Councils to act decisively led to exploration of the Assemblies as instruments of collective responsibility.

The Councils bogged down, in part, because they could not secure among their members the consensus required for action. The advantages of their compactness were more than offset by their voting procedures. League Council decisions had to be unanimous except for states that were parties to the controversy; the United Nations Security Council can act substantively only if the five permanent members and at least two others concur. In practice, divergent interests and outright conflict among the members made such agreement a rarity.

In the case of Korea, the Security Council did act despite sharp opposition from the Soviet Union. But this was recognized by all to be a fluke, made possible because the Soviet Union was momentarily boycotting the Security Council as a protest against the representation of Nationalist China and because the Council blandly accepted a most remarkable reinterpretation of the voting rules. It decided that a member forfeited its right to vote on a question by being absent and that, hence, only the concurring votes of *present* members need be secured.[4] In any case, it was abundantly clear that

---

[4] The Charter really does not permit of such equivocation. The debates at San Francisco, leading to the adoption of the veto provision, and the language of the article, especially in the equally official French version, leave no doubt that the concurrence of *all* permanent members is always required for substantive decisions. See the searching critique of "Voting Rules and Practice in the United Nations Security Council" by Julius Stone, in his *Legal Controls of International Conflict* (New York: Rinehart, 1954), Chapter 8. Stone contends, however, that the Security Council's action *was* legal, despite Soviet absence, because it represented *voluntary* action by members under the "license" of the Charter; that is, it was legal because it was not prohibited.

such an eventuality would not likely arise again, Council members having learned the lesson that they should always be on hand for crucial votes, whatever their pique over the proceedings.

In addition to the discomfiture of the Councils, a growing desire to mobilize the "opinion of mankind" as a moral sanction to restrain states from unlawful acts led to the involvement of the Assemblies in the consideration of security questions.

For the League, a shift to the broader arena of responsibility posed no great problem. The Covenant had provided that the Assembly could deal with "any matter within the sphere of action of the League or affecting the peace of the world." Consequently, states could freely choose where to appeal for decisions, and often went both to the Council and to the Assembly. A gentlemen's agreement usually kept one organ from acting while the other was taking the lead in a matter, but sometimes both went to work simultaneously.

The General Assembly Assumes a Security Role. Assumption by the United Nations General Assembly of responsibility for peace and security problems caused a major constitutional controversy. But it now appears to have firmly established its prerogative to consider and to *recommend* action, though not to reach decisions that would bind states to take action.

The crucial move to bring the General Assembly into the security field was the Assembly's passage, on November 3, 1950, of the Uniting for Peace Resolution. This was introduced by the United States on the assumption that in the future a Soviet veto in the Security Council would surely block any action similar to that taken in Korea. An alternative was for the Assembly to assert its authority to take over a crisis whenever the Council proved unable to act. This it did, in terms which provided that

> . . . if the Security Council, because of lack of unanimity of the permanent members, fails to exercise its primary responsibility for the maintenance of international peace and security in any case where there appears to be a threat to the peace, breach of the peace, or act of aggression, the General Assembly shall consider the matter immediately with a view to making appropriate recommendations to Members for collective measures, including in the case of breach of the peace or act of aggression the use of armed force when necessary, to maintain or restore international peace and security.[5]

The Security Council could drop a question from its agenda by a procedural vote (to which the veto would not apply). Then, the Assembly could take it up. This was designed to meet the requirement in Article 12 that the General Assembly refrain from recommendations on a matter while the Security Council was acting on it.

---

[5] From Section A, Resolution 377 (V), "Uniting for Peace" (Official Records, Supplement No. 20, U.N. General Assembly, 5th sess.), p. 10. Other parts of this important resolution are considered later.

The Uniting for Peace Resolution was adopted only after vehement challenge by the Soviet Union and strong reservations by others on grounds that it contradicted the Charter's clear assignment of responsibility to the Security Council. The Security Council alone was named in Chapter VII, it was pointed out, to determine the occasions and the measures of United Nations enforcement action. Even more explicit was the provision in Article 11, requiring the General Assembly either before or after discussion to refer to the Security Council any question relating to peace and security "on which action is necessary." This implied, said opponents of the resolution, that the General Assembly could take no action on such questions—action was reserved to the Security Council. "Action" referred to every aspect of the enforcement proceedings spelled out in Chapter VII—from the initial determination that a threat or breach of the peace or act of aggression had occurred, to the extreme military measures which the Council could invoke. There was a clear separation of functions between the two organs, according to this argument, with the Assembly limited to discussion and recommendations directed at the peaceful settlement of a dispute, and the Council's having exclusive control over collective enforcement measures.

The General Assembly's competence was justified, countered the uniters for peace, by a look at Article 10's broad proviso, authorizing it to discuss and make recommendations directly to members of the United Nations as well as the Security Council concerning "any" matters within the scope of the Charter. This, they said, meant *any* matters, including problems calling for enforcement action. No limit was placed on either the subject or the nature of the recommendations the General Assembly could make—granted that they could not be made while the Security Council was actively functioning on a question. The intention of Article 11 was to reserve to the Security Council the making of binding decisions—this was what "action" meant. So long as the Assembly limited itself to recommendations, as provided in the resolution, it was fully within its mandate.[6]

Whatever the respective merits of the legal arguments, the United Nations has confirmed by practice the General Assembly's extended role. Even the Soviet Union was able to reconcile its legal qualms with support of Assembly action when British and French vetoes stymied the Security Council in the Suez crisis in 1956.

The General Assembly has actually gone farther in assuming responsibility—even greater than implied in the Uniting for Peace Resolution—by rendering a categorical verdict of guilty against the Chinese People's Republic for aggression in Korea. This verdict is repeatedly cited as

---

[6] For further elaboration of the legal and other implications of the "Uniting for Peace Resolution," see Stone, *op. cit.*, pp. 266–84; Claude, *op. cit.*, pp. 245–48; and Leland M. Goodrich and Anne P. Simons, *The United Nations and the Maintenance of International Peace and Security* (Washington, D.C.: The Brookings Institution, 1955), pp. 406–14.

a bar to Chinese Communist participation in the United Nations and as the basis for economic sanctions against China. The Assembly itself acted as the conclusive judging agent for the United Nations. It did not *propose* to the states that they consider China an aggressor; it *resolved* that China was such.

The General Assembly has, therefore, become the ultimate custodian of collective responsibility for the United Nations. By the voice of two-thirds of the members, with or without agreement of any or all of the five big powers, the United Nations can now determine when a danger to their peace and security has arisen, and who is at fault, and can recommend what joint measures they should take to counter the threat.

The United Nations has thus reverted to the precedent of the League, where responsibility rested on *both* a smaller representative organ and the entire body of states in the organization, whichever was able to function most effectively.

There are these differences, however, dictated by the respective terms of Covenant and Charter. The General Assembly has to concede to the Security Council the right to act first, if it is able to do so. And the Security Council nominally has the power to peremptory action which the General Assembly has not—that is, deciding rather than merely recommending what measures states should take. In the League, the competence of both organs was the same; either could act at any time, and neither could order states to act. But the most important difference between the two arrangements is the ability of the General Assembly to act for the entire organization, even in the face of a recalcitrant minority. Two-thirds of the community of states may speak and act for the whole, unlike the League Assembly which was bound by a rule of unanimity (excepting the parties to the dispute). The United Nations has accepted the unprecedented position of majoritarian responsibility for peace and security. Whether this strengthens the organization is debatable, and will be examined later in the light of recent experiences. But the effect is to broaden the base of active responsibility for security in the United Nations and, because of the majoritarian principle, to increase the flexibility of the organization in moving against widely felt threats to peace and security.

The Rule of Power

Probably the most critical problem in the organization of collective responsibility has concerned the role of the most powerful states, and the extent to which their policies should be decisive in determining the collective action.

From the standpoint of the basic principle of collective responsibility, states may properly claim that the business of providing for security is of equal concern to all, that each should have the same say as the others in making collective decisions, and that each should share in the contributions required to an equally sacrificial degree—though because of great differences in national resources, obviously not in equal amounts. This point of view banked heavily on the proposition that a state's size or power has nothing to do with the devotion of its people to its security or the stake they feel in the maintenance of peace. In fact, a small state might have a much more acute sense of the common responsibility than a more powerful one, because its dependence for security on collective effort rather than independent action would be so much greater. This was confirmed in the experience of both the League of Nations and the United Nations, where some of the smaller states provided the most consistent and insistent support for vigorous collective measures.

The states with the most power took a different slant. The success or failure of any collective effort depended on their support. The physical basis of enforcement—whether in military, economic, or diplomatic terms—required a heavy commitment of their resources, which would far exceed that of the majority of states. They would be reluctant to put their power behind an effort they did not directly determine to be in line with their national interests. They would certainly not wish to have others governing the commitment and disposition of their power in a joint operation, however sympathetic they might be to the organization of the effort. Power entails responsibility and, conversely, responsibility for the use of power properly belongs to the powerful. The organization of collective security should be designed, so the great powers stated with one voice, to distinguish between the beneficiaries of the system and the operators. The beneficiaries' responsibility would be to express their opinions and lend such support as they might with their limited resources. The operators would have to be entrusted with the major responsibility for the vital decisions on when and how to act.

The evolution of the League and the United Nations security organization has witnessed a continual tugging between the yen for equality of responsibility and acquiescence to the terms of power.

Leadership without Power—The League's Experience. In the League's experience, the role of the powerful gradually diminished, relative to lesser states.

This was partly due to accident. The self-isolation of the United States and the long ostracism of the Soviet Union removed two of the powerful from the deliberations at the outset. Another factor was the tendency of some of the powerful to misbehave. Japan, Italy, Germany, and finally Russia flouted the organization and either pulled out or were expelled. The other powerful ones—Britain and France—provided strong leadership only at times, beset as they were by domestic and foreign pressures which caused their policies to vacillate. Meanwhile, remarkably able and strong statesmanship emerged from the leaders of a group of "middle states."

The changing membership of the League Council reflected the shifting balance of influence away from the great powers. Intended at first to provide a permanent great power majority of five to four, the Council soon included more elected members from outside the ranks of the great, and, ultimately, ten were so chosen. Simultaneously, the number of powers with permanent seats shrank. After 1931, there were never more than four, and at the end only Britain and France remained. Of course, this preponderance of smaller states did not affect the actual power over collective decisions. Because of the rule of unanimity, the great powers still effectually controlled what happened. The League could take no action at all without their consent and the consent of all other Council members.

Power and Frustration in the United Nations.   To the founders of the United Nations, the League's experience spelled the ultimate in futility, and they therefore designed the organization to insure special prerogatives for the powerful, with particular emphasis on their role in the procedures for collective enforcement.

By conferring on five states almost the entire responsibility for organizing and directing the forceful actions of the United Nations, the members, in effect, yielded to an ultimatum. This was the price, stated the major powers, for any renewal of the collective security experiment. One must admit that most states appeared quite willing to accede. At San Francisco, virtually no argument was raised against the principle of great power responsibility as applied to the enforcement machinery. Nor was there dispute over the much more questionable requirement that this responsibility be discharged only through unanimous agreement of the five. But responsibility, hitched to a unilateral veto, became irresponsibility, and rule by the powerful proved no less futile than the League's attempt to enforce security by the influence of the less powerful.

The Charter provided that the five permanent members of the Security Council should have the following responsibilities, or, put negatively, that each could veto measures to discharge those responsibilities concerned with enforcement of collective security:

1. To determine if there was a threat to the peace, breach of the peace, or act of aggression.
2. To recommend or decide what provisional measures should be taken to prevent an aggravation of the situation.
3. To recommend or decide what measures, military or nonmilitary, members of the United Nations should apply to maintain or restore peace and security.
4. To make special agreements with members for contributions of armed forces, assistance, and facilities to be made available to the Security Council on its call.
5. To make special agreements with members to hold immediately available national air force contingents for urgent combined international enforcement action.

6. To compose the Military Staff Committee (consisting of the five powers' chiefs of staff or their representatives)—this Committee to be responsible for the strategic command of armed forces put at the disposal of the Security Council and for advising the Council on all questions relating to military measures of enforcement.

Smaller powers might be permitted to share in some of these responsibilities, provided they happened to be elected to the Security Council or called on to contribute their support to the enforcement measures. But their role was completely conditioned on the initiative of the Big Five, whose unanimous assent was essential before any of these responsibilities could become operative.

The requirement of unanimity made a dead letter of most of these provisions, and gradually the exalted position of the powerful gave way before their own inability to agree on almost any collective security question. The demise of the powerful has not been so obvious in the United Nations as it was in the League, but their contribution to the maintenance of collective security is almost as inconsequential, despite rigging of the machinery to afford them a predominant role.

As the General Assembly has taken on itself some of the security business of the United Nations, the voices of the less powerful have been heard more frequently and vigorously, and the major powers have found themselves in the position of bidding for support rather than commanding it. A veteran small power delegate concluded that it was not the Great Powers which maintained peace among the little states; it was the little states which reminded the Great Powers of their promises of cooperation, who urged them to get along together, who tried to reconcile them: the system in other words was functioning backwards from what had been postulated by the assumptions of the Charter.[7] The function of the Security Council has become increasingly that of registering disagreement among its permanent members, thereby providing public notice that they shall default on their collective responsibilities for security. They have on no occasion engineered the requisite unanimity among themselves to enable the Security Council to use the measures so meticulously designed in Chapter VII of the Charter for the restraint of war and aggression.[8]

Yardsticks for Action—the Test of Aggression

The third organizational issue that has bothered the designers of the collective security system has been whether those responsible for collective

---

[7] Fernand Van Langenhove, *La Crise du Système de Securité Collective des Nations Unies, 1946–57* (La Haye: Nijhoff, 1958), p. 80.

[8] In the case of Korea, the Council called on U.N. members—but did not decide to *direct* members—to take some of the actions anticipated by the Charter. But even this was possible only because the Soviet Union was absent when the Council decided and, hence, was not in accord with the original prescription for great power control.

decisions should have wide discretion or should be guided by specific, formal directions in determining when circumstances call for collective action.

In particular, strenuous efforts have been made throughout the history of the League and the United Nations to work out a precise definition of aggression so that all might know exactly what the organization would consider unlawful and be prepared to resist. This, many have felt, would avoid confusion and delay in deciding when the common security was threatened, and largely remove the question from political influence and considerations of immediate national interest. The decision-making bodies would simply check to see if the facts in an alleged case of aggression fitted the definition.

But aggression has proved far more difficult to define than to outlaw, and the efforts to do so have not yet reached fruition.

Four main possibilities have been explored. These are to define aggression as: (1) concrete acts of hostility by one state against another; (2) refusal of a state to pursue peaceful methods of settling a dispute; (3) resistance to collective measures undertaken by the international organization; or (4) efforts to overthrow a government or otherwise undermine the independence of a state by indirect means—subversion, assisting a rebellion, and so on. The proposals have usually been open-ended, providing that the international organization might decide that actions other than those specifically defined would be aggressive in particular situations.

Aggression as Hostile Action. Definitions of the first type have a long tradition, and were anticipated by provisions of international law generally restricting states from forceful intervention in the affairs of others. The London Disarmament Conference in 1933 proposed a set of five tests of aggression: (*a*) a declaration of war; (*b*) invasion; (*c*) attack on the territory, vessels, or aircraft of another state; (*d*) naval blockade; (*e*) support to armed bands invading a state from the territory of another. These were incorporated in several regional nonaggression agreements in the middle thirties, but were not accepted as the official yardstick for League of Nations action.[9]

The Charter of the United Nations deliberately avoids an attempt to define aggression, but the United Nations has been repeatedly urged to approve a list of hostile acts that it would consider aggressive. The Soviet Union has taken a prominent lead in this movement, as it did during League days. The strongest other exponents have been smaller states, some, like Yugoslavia, ironically seeking by this means to secure additional safeguards against Soviet pressures. The proposed definitions were comprehensive and explicit. They covered most of the usual forms of military pressure, direct and

---

[9] See Martin, *op. cit.,* p. 115. Note the London Convention of 1933 between the USSR, Afghanistan, Estonia, Latvia, Persia, Poland, Romania, and Turkey; and the Balkan Entente of 1934.

indirect, putting the responsibility for aggression squarely on the state first to commit these actions, and specifically excluding as justification for an attack such well-tried pretexts as the backwardness or internal disorder of the victim state, its alleged violation of treaties, repudiation of debts, religious or antireligious measures, or economic boycott. These proposals have been debated both in the International Law Commission and the General Assembly. The Secretary-General and a Special Committee of the Assembly have made studies of the problem. As yet, no broad agreement has been reached on a particular definition or even on the desirability of having a definition, though a majority of members do favor continued efforts to arrive at one.[10]

Refusal of Peaceful Settlement. The second type of definition was attempted in the Geneva Protocol, put forward in 1924 as a means of supplementing the provisions of the League Covenant. The formula appeared simple and direct. States would undertake to submit to compulsory arbitration the disputes they could not settle otherwise. Whoever went to war without submitting to arbitration, or failed to comply with the decision rendered in arbitration or an alternative international proceeding, would be considered guilty as an aggressor. The same would be the case if the League Council were disobeyed when it called for a stop to hostilities already in progress. This bold and ingenious move was rejected, however, because some important states like Britain did not wish to be bound so strictly in regard to determining who was an aggressor and, consequently, against whom they would have to act.

The United Nations has not revived this approach, because the Charter effactually severs peaceful settlement obligations from the procedures of collective enforcement.

Resistance to International Authority. United Nations condemnation of Chinese Communist aggression in Korea reflected a widespread feeling that a government automatically brands itself as an aggressor if it forcefully opposes actions of the international organization. The People's Republic of China, declared a majority of the General Assembly in 1951, "by giving direct aid and assistance to those who were already committing aggression in Korea and by engaging in hostilities against United Nations forces there, has itself engaged in aggression in Korea."

The converse was also clearly implied—that the use of force under authorization of the United Nations could never be considered aggressive (this in the face of Communist charges that the U.N. label was being used merely to cover Western, and particularly U.S., aggression in the Far East).[11]

---

[10] See Martin, *op. cit.*, pp. 189–90; Goodrich & Simons, *op. cit.*, pp. 357–60.

[11] For effective discussion of this issue, see Goodrich and Simons, *ibid.*, p. 358; and Martin, *op. cit.*, pp. 119–22.

It is too early to tell whether armed action by a state against the community of states as represented in the United Nations will henceforth be regarded as an obvious and extreme case of aggression. The General Assembly persists in its stand on China. On the other hand, this remains a unique instance, and the Assembly was by no means unanimous in its decision. Many states demurred on the grounds that such an action would sharpen the struggle and make truce difficult to achieve. The Chinese People's Republic has, of course, given no indication that it is prepared to accept this definition of aggression, at least as applicable to itself.

Indirect Aggression.   Paradoxically, more progress has been made toward a definition of indirect aggression than of the direct varieties. The United Nations has been able to broadly resolve that actions by one government to incite and support rebellion against another amount to aggression. While the full range of such activities has not been precisely laid out, the ban clearly applies to the furnishing of arms and a base of operations to rebel forces. Conspiratorial organization, and especially terroristic activity, assassinations, and the like, are uniformly considered indirect aggression when supported by an outside government. Some have insisted that abusive propaganda conducted by subversive agents or by radio under the control of a foreign government also qualifies as aggression, but this is not firmly accepted as yet.

No United Nations organ has yet found the occasion to fit the definition to a concrete case. Charges of indirect aggression have been hurled in Security Council and General Assembly debate, notably against the United Arab Republic and the Soviet Union in regard to the 1958 revolts in Lebanon, Jordan, and Iraq. But these did not result in a successful vote of censure. So the United Nations definition of indirect aggression remains one of words alone.

It is surprising that the members of the United Nations have spelled out a definition of indirect aggression as precisely as they have. For one thing, quite a few of them have themselves acquired a reputation for practicing such activities. The Soviet Union is known as the past master of the technique on a worldwide front, but the United Arab Republic, various Latin American Countries, and even the United States (in the case of the overthrow of the leftist government in Guatemala) are under accusation on occasion. One might expect such countries to oppose an effort to limit their maneuvers. Yet, they have given the move ostentatious support. The action is all the more curious because it seemingly limits the discretion of the United Nations as a security organization at the very point where balanced judgment rather than rigid definitions would be more likely to uncover true aggression. In the circumstances of indirect aggression—real or presumed—responsibility and intentions are obscured by charges, denials, and countercharges. The clandestine character of much of the activity is likely to defy a finding of facts which would conclusively settle whether aggression in terms of the definition had actually occurred. So indirect aggression—as defined—might well be underway but the United Nations unable to prove it. Conversely, a limited or garbled set of facts might fit the definition, and aggression thereby be determined when in reality the accused government was not responsible. In either case, the United Nations would be under pressure to guide its action strictly by the formal definition rather than to reach a decision on the basis of its own assessment of what was really going on.

Determining Aggression without Definition. The position at the moment is that no definition of aggression provides an effective yardstick for the international organs charged with the responsibility of deciding when a state has transgressed. In effect, aggression is *any* action considered such by a vote of the Security Council or the General Assembly.

Many would rather have it this way. They contend that vesting such wide discretion in the competent international authorities avoids "on the one hand, the possibility that the aggressor might turn any detailed definition to his advantage, and on the other, the danger of premature action." [12] They fear that a would-be aggressor might devise actions not prohibited by the definitions and then claim the security organization had no business preventing them. The other argument in favor of wide discretion is that the organization might have a chance to head off a collision with a state not really intent on aggression if it avoided crowding the accused state into a corner by a premature condemnation. A fixed definition, it is argued, would give the organization no choice but to condemn such a state out of hand if it had committed one of the forbidden acts.

The United Nations Charter clearly confers the widest possible discretionary authority on the Security Council to determine when an act of aggression, a breach of the peace, or a threat to the peace has occurred. It prescribes no limiting definitions of these terms. The Uniting for Peace Resolution has given the General Assembly almost as much scope.

Nevertheless, there have been occasions when each of these organs was persuaded to act as thought it had no discretionary power. One was in reference to Palestine. The French delegate told the Security Council in 1948 that it "cannot, under Article 39, refuse to note the existence of a threat to the peace when such a threat exists." The United States fully supported the position.[13] Then there was the situation, previously mentioned, in which the General Assembly was told by the United States that it was duty-bound to judge Communist China an aggressor. In both cases, other states protested that such decisions were neither obligatory nor wise. Governments such as Britain, Canada, and Belgium urged that the United Nations was under no

---

[12] See Goodrich and Simons, *op. cit.,* p. 352, referring to U.S. Department of State, Charter of the United Nations, Report to the President of the Secretary of State, pp. 91–92.

[13] U.N. Security Council, 296th and 298th meetings, May 19 and 20, 1948.

obligation to reach decisions either on the basis of facts or of morality, but should act only if convinced it would thereby contribute to peace and security.[14] The more peremptory view prevailed in these instances, but the results were conspicuously satisfactory and strengthened the reservations of those who defended the exercise of fuller discretion.

Practically, in these and in all other cases, control of votes—not definitions of duties—has determined the decisions of the Security Council and the General Assembly. Under the United Nations system, politics—not law—settled the vital question of when circumstances call for collective enforcement of the peace.

THE MEANS OF ENFORCEMENT—
COLLECTIVE SANCTIONS

The system of collective security presumes that peace and security must, in the last analysis, be enforced by collective power. It envisages that the community of states responsible for the maintenance of peace will be able to pool so overwhelming a concentration of power of various kinds that no state would successfully challenge their mandate to keep the peace. Knowing beforehand the sanctions that could be mobilized to restrain them, few states, it is assumed, would then attempt aggression. If they did, application of the collective power should promptly and effectively prevent their realizing any gain from their actions and, at the same time, provide immediate protection to the victims.

The system of sanctions has generally encompassed three main features:

1. Provisions for application of a wide variety of pressures against a recalcitrant state by members of the security organization, including use of armed force on a major scale;
2. Coordination and direction of these efforts by international cooperative action (in contrast to a structure of command); and
3. Primary reliance on voluntary participation by member states in sanctions (rather than on measures directly under international control).

The Range of Sanctions

The collective measures designed to restrain states from threatening peace or security have been of three main types—moral (including diplomatic pressures), economic, and military. All three are specified in the arsenal of the League of Nations and United Nations.

Moral or diplomatic sanctions subject a state to censure for its conduct. They may go to the limit of breaking off diplomatic relations with the offending state, but more usually involve protest by resolution or commu-

---

[14] See Goodrich and Simons, op. cit., pp. 353–54.

niqué. The principal intent when such measures are applied collectively by a large body of states is to exert influential moral pressure through conveying to the people and government of the state concerned the sense of a strong and united world public opinion opposed to their behavior. Diplomatic sanctions also imply a warning that harsher actions may follow if the "decent opinion of mankind" is disregarded.

Economic sanctions deprive a state of normal access to the resources of the outside world. The intent may be specifically to strangle its capacity to wage war. Or they may aim to force a change of policy by making it difficult for the government to provide financial and economic stability and sustain the living conditions to which its people are accustomed. The range of available economic sanctions is very great. At the extreme, all trade to and from a country could be cut; its foreign assets frozen; all postal, telegraphic, and travel communications prohibited. Something of this sort was actually envisaged in the original conception of the League of Nations—a complete economic ostracism of the covenant-breaker by the rest of the community of states. But the view that came to prevail and has carried over into United Nations planning is that economic sanctions should be selective rather than comprehensive. Measures should be chosen so as to pinpoint peculiarly vulnerable spots in the economy of the recalcitrant state. For instance, an embargo on oil might be a far more significant deterrent than one on foodstuffs or even on arms, if the country had no oil resources of its own and the objective was to immobilize its armed forces. On the other hand, freezing its assets, cutting off purchases of its exports, or even suspending favorable trade agreements would put great pressure on a country heavily dependent for its livelihood on foreign trade and not in a position to better this situation by a swift military coup. At least, this has become the established rationale of collective economic sanctions.

The hub of the collective enforcement system, however, is professedly military. Diplomatic sanctions are judged weak and economic sanctions too slow when the threat to peace is serious and determined. The security organization must be able to engage on its own terms a state that resorts to war, and overwhelm it. To accomplish this end, the League and the United Nations provided in somewhat different ways for the mobilization and use of the armed forces of their members under international authority.

The Charter's Uncut Teeth. The arrangements intended by the Charter were much more explicit and elaborate than those of the Covenant, which had provided simply that it was the Council's duty to recommend to members in any concrete case what effective military, naval, or air force they should contribute "to the armed forces to be used to protect the covenants of the League."

The Charter outlines three distinct elements in the military apparatus for enforcement action:

a) specific national forces, assistance, and facilities, including rights of passage to be made available to the Security Council on its call—details of the arrangement to be worked out by the collective members in accordance with special agreements negotiated with the Council;

b) national air force contingents to be held immediately available for combined international action—strength and degree of readiness to be laid down in special agreements above;

c) entire air, sea, and land forces of members to be used in demonstrations, blockade, or any other operations considered necessary by the Security Council.

Neither the Covenant nor the Charter provided for forces of any kind to be organized as a distinct international army or police force. The national identity of the military units used in collective enforcement was to be preserved at all times. The Charter does provide, however, for earmarking special contingents within the national military establishments for "combined international enforcement action." (Art 45.)

Even this international tinge has gone by default. No special agreements to designate such contingents or other forms of military assistance have been concluded, because the five permanent members of the Security Council could not agree on the overall composition of the forces to be held available. The Russians insisted that each of the five states contribute exactly equal components of every type, while the United States and the others wanted a force that would be balanced on an overall basis but into which each country would put different quantities of various types of forces, depending on the nature of its own establishment. The full scope of the differences need not be described here, and it is not exactly clear why the countries were unable to resolve the impasse. But the effect was to nullify the Charter's elaborate structure of military deterrence. It meant that the United Nations, like its predecessor, would have to face a challenge to the collective security system with no prearranged facilities for collective compulsion.

"Collective Measures"—the Assembly's Untried Sanctions. In the face of this default of the great powers and against the background of the Korean crisis, the General Assembly made an abortive attempt to substitute an alternative arrangement with a broader base for military sanctions. It sought to universalize the responsibility for military enforcement, recommending in the Uniting for Peace Resolution, that each member "maintain with its national armed forces elements so trained, organized and equipped that they could promptly be made available, in accordance with its constitutional processes, for service as a United Nations unit or units." It specified that the use of such forces could be authorized by the General Assembly, as well as by the Security Council. A 14-nation Collective Measures Committee (from which the Soviet Union was conspicuously absent) was assigned the task of studying and proposing methods of making this and related recom-

mendations effective, including procedures for the advance preparation and coordination of the forces to be proffered for United Nations service.

But few firm bids appeared. Some lesser powers, such as Turkey, Greece, and Denmark, said they were ready to create the special United Nations units as requested. Most of the states that had so readily voted themselves an invitation to share in the collective military measures of the United Nations declined an advance acceptance of specific commitments. They pleaded other engagements—in Korea, in Malaya, in Indochina, in Europe, under the North Atlantic Treaty. Others, including the United States, would do no more than review, examine, and consider sympathetically how they might at some time in the future strengthen their capacity to assist the United Nations. Some states were openly hostile to the plan. The Soviet bloc, for example, branded it as a violation of the Charter which, they insisted, precluded any arrangements for military measures except those explicitly authorized in Chapter VII.

In these circumstances, the project could never materialize. Even before the Korean conflict terminated, the General Assembly was ready to concede rebuff to any plans dependent on securing precise military commitments from its members. It watered down the very mild recommendations proposed by its Collective Measures Committee so as to make absolutely clear that each state could act just as it chose in a particular situation.[15]

U.N. Police Power—the Korean Model. The United Nations has explored one other approach to the mobilization of military sanctions. On the initiative of the United States and under the mantle of its military might, the United Nations Command was organized to repel the attack on South Korea. This sudden improvisation, unlike anything envisaged in the Charter, vested the primary responsibility for United Nations sanctions in a single one of its major members.

The United States was authorized to designate the commander, to direct the conduct of operations in the field, to accept or reject assistance from other member and nonmember states, and within very broad limits to determine major policies to be followed in carrying out the United Nations police action. Sixteen members placed certain of their armed forces at the disposal of the United Nations Command. Others contributed in nonmilitary ways at various stages of the enterprise. The United Nations authorized the use of its auspices and its flag. But the essential feature of the action was not its international but its national character. In substance and control, the United Nations sanctions were indelibly marked, USA.

The implications of this experience for collective security are evaluated in the next chapter. It is clear, however, that so far the United Nations action in

---

[15] The sterility of the Collective Measures Committee is effectively analyzed by Stanley H. Hoffmann, "Sisyphus and the Avalanche: The United Nations, Egypt and Hungary," *International Organization,* Summer, 1957.

Korea remains a unique approach to the implementation of collective sanctions. Nothing attempted before or since has so closely identified the cause of the international security organization with the military power and policy of one member state.

The Voluntary Basis of Collective Sanctions

The provisions for enforcement, formidable as they appeared in the blueprint stage, were not self-operating. That is, they were not built into the organization of the League of Nations or the United Nations so that the international bodies could directly control the means necessary to put them into effect. The application of sanctions has remained voluntary with each member state. Each decides for itself whether to join in the enforcement operation, and if so, how and to what extent. Consequently, the bark of the collective security system has belied its bite.

Certain provisions of the Covenant and Charter did definitely obligate members to apply sanctions. But, in practice, these have been reinterpreted or neglected. Members of the League deliberately voided their explicit commitment in Article 16 to impose drastic economic sanctions immediately and automatically against a covenant-breaker. The United Nations has allowed Articles 25 and 48, which bound members to carry out decisions of the Security Council, to remain paper pledges. Not once has the Security Council hazarded a peremptory call for action by U.N. members—even when freed of the shackling Soviet veto in the peculiar circumstances of the Korean attack. States were obviously unwilling to surrender freedom to make unilateral decisions unless all five major powers were willing to support the concerted action and thus remove the risk.

Other provisions of the Covenant and Charter relating to sanctions are clearly permissive. For instance, in regard to military sanctions, the League Council could only *recommend* what forces the members should contribute. Under the Charter, the marshaling of military force hinged on the conclusion of special agreements with the affected states to be ratified "in accordance with their respective constitutional processes." (These agreements, as noted above, were never completed, so there is no mandatory commitment in effect.) A searching review of the problem of implementing sanctions by the Collective Measures Committee concluded that any and all measures undertaken in the absence of the special agreement authorized in Article 43 would have to rest on the immediate consent of each state. This conclusion accorded fully with the sentiments of virtually every U.N. member, as expressed through the concurrence of the General Assembly.

Compulsion by Cooperation

Proponents of collective enforcement have had to consider whether sanctions dependent on voluntary implementation could possibly be inclusive enough and firm enough to be effective. If each policeman reserves the right to decide for himself whether to heed a call for help and, if so, just how far he will go in responding, how strong will the police power be? Yet, this being the only basis upon which international policemen can be recruited, should one give up the system of law enforcement entirely? Sanctions of overwhelming power versus voluntary implementation—are not these two accepted principles of collective security mutually contradictory?

Hopefully, the designers of the system anticipate a linking third factor—the cooperative coordination of effort among a very large number of states genuinely impelled by mutual interest in putting a stop to a common threat to their security. The expectation is that the enforcement activities voluntarily undertaken by each state can be effectively integrated into a powerful deterrent by truly collective action—that is, through a process of concerted decision-making and probably through a joint, rather than a unified, structure of direction and command.

This concept of cooperative responsibility for the mobilization and fielding of the enforcing power—so alien to the habitual presumptions both of military command and public administration—underlies the entire operational philosophy of collective security as it has been attempted through the League and the United Nations. Except for the Korean episode, the planning and the practice of these organizations in regard to enforcement measures have aimed at securing united action by negotiating common agreement among the would-be enforcers. The belief that consultation and joint decision-making could produce agreement on measures adequate for the occasion explains why states have been, on the one hand, reluctant to abandon the idea of collective enforcement and, on the other, insistent on retaining independent control over the means of enforcement. It explains the phenomenon in both Covenant and Charter of making councils and committees (such as the Military Staff Committee in the U.N.) responsible not only for major policy decisions, but also for the actual operational direction of enforcement. When confronted with unforeseen problems, the tendency in both organizations was to create additional, ad hoc committees to prepare for and actually to implement sanctions, as for instance in the Committee of Eighteen which stage-managed most of the League's efforts to restrain Mussolini's attack on Ethiopia.

The expectation that sanctions could be made a thoroughly cooperative undertaking is further shown by the provisions in both the Covenant and the Charter for distributing the sacrifices entailed among the entire membership of the organizations. The members of the League agreed, for instance, that they would "mutually support one another in the financial and economic measures which are taken under this Article [16] in order to minimize the loss and inconvenience resulting from the above measures." The United Nations Charter, somewhat less specific. assured a state which "finds itself confronted with special economic problems arising from the carrying out of these measures shall have the right to consult the Security Council with regard to a solution of those problems." (Art. 50.) The Collective Measures Committee declared much more bluntly that agreements for an equitable sharing of burdens in the application of sanctions, whether undertaken by the Security Council or on recommendation of the General Assembly, had a direct bearing on the readiness of states to participate. It explicitly urged as a basic principle of equitable sharing that each contribute in accordance with its ability, and recommended setting up machinery through which consultation could be undertaken promptly on how to compensate those states which suffered an undue burden as a result of the collective action.

The spirit of cooperation has not persisted to the point where states could cash in these paper promises, however. The United Nations has not set up the machinery proposed by the Collective Measures Committee. The Korean action came and went with no serious proposal for an "equitable sharing of burdens," despite wide public grumbling in the United States over the disproportionate American share of the cost in blood and dollars. And, in the League's experience, the cooperating states deftly evaded a request by Poland for economic assistance to offset the losses it incurred by faithfully imposing a League-directed embargo on coal exports to Italy during the Ethiopian campaign. It therefore seems fair to conclude: (1) the actual (rather than the verbally expressed) assumption underlying the cooperative principle in collective security is that the degree of cooperation will be governed by the immediacy of the threat felt by each state; (2) states will *not* respond to the challenge of aggression or a breach of the peace with an equal sense of responsibility for the security of the community, but rather in the degree to which each considers its own security at stake; and (3) one must expect this varied response to result in uneven and inequitable cooperation in compulsive actions, undertaken by a limited group rather than the whole body of states in the collective organization. Cooperation under the present design of collective security is, therefore, partial rather than universal, and proportionate to national interest rather than to the national capacities of the participating states.

Whether cooperation on these terms is sufficient to sustain the weight of an effective collective security system is the problem which the League and the United Nations have had to confront. The tests to which they have been put do not yield a reassuring answer.[16]

---

[16] See the searching critique of collective security by Inis L. Claude, Jr., *Power and International Relations* (New York: Random House, 1962), chapter 5.

Chapter 4

Testing Collective Security

From one standpoint, the collective security system has never had a full and fair test. Neither the League nor the United Nations has actually employed the complete range of enforcement powers with which their creators endowed them, and in the manner in which they were intended to operate. Confronted with international violence, the member states have either refrained from invoking the sanctions provided for or plunged into the fray with split forces instead of the expected array of solidarity. The practice of collective security has not conformed to its design.

Consequently, advocates of collective security say that the epidemic of war and aggression in the second quarter of the twentieth century does not prove the failure of the system, but only the unwillingness of states to fulfill the obligations it entails. This seems to beg the issue, however. For if the success of collective security as a deterrent of force in international affairs rests on illusory expectations of national conduct, then it is premature if not totally misconceived. At the least, the system would need drastic overhauling before it could qualify as a useful approach to international order.

The experiences of the two global organizations charged with the enforcement of collective security indicate that the deficiencies of the intended system are, indeed, so basic as to render it inoperable. This conclusion applies alike to the three variants of the system as represented by (1) the League's security organization in the thirties, (2) the United Nations' original structure provided in the Charter, and (3) the reorientation of the United Nations' security establishment authorized in the Uniting for Peace Resolution.

As the League and the United Nations struggled to prevent the outbreak and spread of war and to restrain aggression by applying collective security, the following serious shortcomings emerged.

1. States were readier to fix responsibility for threatening peace and security than they were to shoulder the commitments of collective enforcement required to put down the threat. The competitive demands of other national interests, as well as the immediate risks of the collective action, whittled down the disposition to serve as world policeman and brought about a steady disintegration of communal solidarity as the rigors of the operation increased. Indeed, if the prospects of successful deterrence were too slim, nations simply did not start turning the wheels of enforcement, however much they engaged in moral condemnation, repeated pledges of loyalty to the world organization, and expressed sympathy for the victims.

2. The diverging and often conflicting interests of the major powers usually prevented the overwhelming consolidation of power that the collective security system presupposes will be brought to bear on the peacebreaker. In the absence of general disarmament or international control of national armaments, collective enforcement directed against a major power or its satellites therefore ran a grave danger of erupting into major war—the very occurrence the system was intended to prevent.

3. Collective measures short of war—the ones that hesitant partners in the policing enterprise were most easily led to adopt—were hardly adequate to deter serious, or even minor, disturbers of the peace.

4. Once embarked on military enforcement (as in the case of Korea), the collective operation became increasingly identified with the policy of the principal supplier of military power, and subject very largely to its direction. It became extremely difficult to maintain a truly collective responsibility for the undertaking.

5. This, in turn, extended the purposes of collective security beyond immediate deterrence, toward the end of punishment or a permanent liquidation of the source of aggression. Such confusion and distortion of the originally limited scope of the enforcement action invited even more stubborn resistance from the already firmly determined outlaws, and rallied behind the outlaw even greater support from states that identified the collective security operation as an extension of policy by powerful rivals. Thus, the action approached the dangerous point of no return—for both sides, but especially for the collective enforcers—and collective security dissolved into a harsh contest of the world's power titans.

6. In such circumstances, it became extremely difficult to end a collective enforcement operation in anything like a satisfactory manner. The peacebreaker, in the entire history of collective security, has never been overwhelmed and brought completely to heel. The defiant state by persisting in its defiance has confronted the enforcers with a most uncomfortable dilemma—either to undertake a vastly greater coercive effort with all the added sacrifices and risks of extended conflict that this could involve, or to give up the effort, ignominiously acquiescing in the culprit's misdemeanors. Under the ominous threat that the collective security operation would mush-

room into world war, ignominy has usually seemed the lesser evil. The exception was Korea. Even here, to hammer out a tolerable settlement required 18 months of intensive and frustrating negotiations during a military stalemate maintained by costly commitments of men and material and by an extraordinary exercise of diplomatic and military self-restraint on both sides to keep the war confined to the Korean peninsula. Whether the operation would end in a truce or blow up into a war of uncontrollable proportions was, indeed, nip and tuck.

In sum, collective security has assumed a greater "collective disposition" than the present generation of nation-states seems to possess—at least when it comes to pooling their powers for mutual defense across the globe. It has, therefore, overestimated the amount of collective power that can be effectively mobilized to confront a violator of the peace. And it may well be that it has underestimated the possibilities of noncoercive methods of preventing or ending war—indeed, it may have impaired the use of such methods.

THE TEST CASES

These conclusions derive from examination of the half-dozen situations in which the League of Nations or the United Nations were led to apply some or all of their enforcement powers. It is remarkable how few these occasions were, considering the epidemic proportions of international violence in the lifetime of the two organizations.

States were not only reluctant to apply sanctions. They were eager to avoid calling them such, and usually refrained from invoking the formal provisions of the Covenant and the Charter, authorizing coercive measures (Arts. 16 and 39, respectively). This meant that most actions amounting to enforcement were undertaken without specifically determining that a given state was guilty of an offense. As against the arguments of legal purists that such a finding was required before the organization could legitimately use its enforcement powers, the majority preferred to avoid the fixing of blame, hoping in this way to maintain flexibility in negotiations while building up pressures that would persuade the state to mend its ways without a major showdown.[1] Thus, the collective security system was modified in practice at

---

[1] See Leland M. Goodrich and Anne P. Simons, *The United Nations and the Maintenance of Peace and Security* (Washington, D.C.: The Brookings Institution, 1955), pp. 353, 360–61, and 369–72 for a detailed review of the question of determining whether to cite a state under Article 39 of the Charter for disturbing the peace or committing aggression. Article 39 was actually invoked by the Security Council for this purpose only when a temporary cease-fire was broken in Palestine in 1948, and then only to determine in general terms that a threat to the peace existed. Not even in regard to the attack on South Korea did the Council base its actions on an application of Article 39. In several cases, the Council did act without explicitly invoking Article 39. These included, in addition to Korea, the Spanish question, 1964 frontier incidents between Greece and its communist neighbors, the Indonesian-Dutch conflict and the Berlin issue (1948). See *Repertory of United Nations Practice* (New York: United Nations, 1955), pp. 331–56.

the very starting point of the enforcement process. The clear distinction that was supposed to be made between procedures of peaceful settlement and enforcement action against violators of the peace was blurred.

The discussion that follows refers to cases in which the League or United Nations actually did resort to some type of compulsive sanction, whether or not it was appropriately authorized. Beyond these, there were a few occasions, such as the situation in Palestine in 1948, when a threat of action was used to persuade.[2]

In addition, there is a roster of cases in which enforcement action was urged on the organization by some members but the majority would not go along. The significance of these is that they demonstrate how wide is the area of collective *inaction*. Understandably, most states did not wish to activate the League's or U.N.'s enforcement machinery if it meant taking sides in a confrontation between the great powers. Thus, they stood aside when one or the other cold war protagonist tried to push resolutions through the Security Council to fix responsibility on the other for endangering the peace (as, for instance, in the 1948 Berlin crisis).[3] In fact, the U.N. Charter's veto provisions were deliberately intended to exclude enforcement action in such cases. But the area of inaction seems to be getting even wider. Incidents such as the Indian takeover of Goa indicate that a whole range of other acts may now be politically immune from the restraints of the collective security system if they are labeled anticolonial. A United Nations majority simply could not be mobilized to condemn, much less to contest, India's resort to force, despite the moral strictures and legal pleadings of the United States and other purported champions of the organization's commitments to resist aggression.[4]

THE FUTILITY OF ENFORCEMENT BY THE LEAGUE OF NATIONS

The League's great test came with Italy's attack on Ethiopia in the fall of 1935, in flat defiance of patient and restrained efforts to arrange a pacific settlement—on terms weighted in Italy's favor.

In essence, the League's response was: first, an unequivocal condemnation of Italy for going to war in violation of the Covenant; second, the rupture of diplomatic relations; and, third, the organization and gradual imposition of a

---

[2] In this case, the threat by the Security Council to act under Chapter VII if the Arabs and Israelis did not stop hostilities seems to have been an important factor in getting them to agree to a preliminary cease-fire. See Goodrich and Simons, *op. cit.,* pp. 346 f.

[3] See Goodrich and Simons, *ibid.,* pp. 439–43, for review of considerations affecting initiation of collective measures to maintain or restore international peace and security.

[4] See Quincy Wright, "The Goa Incident," *American Journal of International Law,* July, 1962.

series of economic sanctions designed to deprive Italy of essential war supplies and to squeeze her financial and economic resources.

These actions won substantial support from the League members, despite awesome threats of retaliation from Mussolini and behind-the-scenes machinations of French and British political leaders to engineer a deal with Italy. Exposure of the so-called Hoare-Laval Pact so outraged opinion in England that Hoare was replaced as foreign secretary by Anthony Eden, identified as an all-out champion of collective security. From then on, the League pushed ahead strongly on its campaign of economic sanctions.

But members of the League turned away from the prospect of war with Italy. Not only did they refrain from direct military counteraction. They finally shied at the imposition of an embargo on oil when Mussolini swore he would treat this as an act of war. Meanwhile, his legions were racing to a rapid conquest of Ethiopia, while countries outside the League, notably Germany and the United States, actively supplied Italy with many of the items League members were striving to cut off. To compound matters, the League, as well as outsiders, rendered no direct aid to Ethiopia.

The affair ended in tragic ignominy, with the League Assembly listening in unresponsive silence as the exiled Ethiopian Emperor Haile Selassie pleaded for at least their continued moral support. Italy returned to full and good standing, complete with her new colonial acquisition. Total failure is the only appropriate score to register for this first head-on test of a collective security system. The League was left completely demoralized as a security instrument.

The reasons for failure have been the subject of intensive scrutiny and wide debate. On balance, the following factors seem to have been critical in causing the breakdown of the League's sanctions.

1. Not enough states cooperated to the wholehearted degree necessary in the application of sanctions to make them effective. Some, like the United States and Germany, that were not members of the League felt no sense of obligation and openly flouted the League's efforts. Other states, though members, were so eager to avoid war that they did not dare risk action which would seriously antagonize Mussolini. Still others felt their national interest was so remotely affected that they were unprepared to make any major sacrifice for the security of Ethiopia. This all resulted in an uneven burden on those states that did cooperate, so that their enthusiasm also waned.

2. The application of sanctions was too long delayed, and states did not act simultaneously when they did apply them. Thus, much of their punch was lost; Italy had time to stockpile essential items and also to push its military gains to a decision. Part of the trouble was that the League had made no prearrangements for the imposition of sanctions, an operation which turned out to involve intricate and different problems of implementation for each of the countries cooperating, as well as difficulties of overall coordination.

Fundamentally, the problem was that most states were unwilling to entrust the direction of sanctions to a central body with authority. Each wished to retain the power of decision for itself.

3. The sanctions applied were probably not extreme or forceful enough to deter so determined an aggression. At least in this case, they did not result in a vital impairment of Italy's capacity or will to wage war. The experience strongly suggests that at least the readiness to use military force, if not its actual use, would have been required to stop Mussolini.

"The question remains," concludes the definitive study of the League's attempt to enforce peace through sanctions on Italy, "whether if the world lacks the spirit of courageous and self-sacrificing cooperation on which sanctions depend, any alternative is available to avert war."[5]

The League did have a second and even more pathetic try at using its enforcement powers, when the U.S.S.R. attacked Finland in 1939. By this time, the League had had to default on its security functions in the face of each successive step of aggression by the Axis powers: their blatant intervention on Franco's side in the Spanish Civil War; the Nazi absorption of Austria; the full-scale Japanese attack on China starting in 1937–38; the German liquidation of Czechoslovakia, following the Munich Pact; and, finally, the Nazi attack on Poland, starting World War II. Ironically, considering what later happened over Finland, the strongest voice calling for collective action through the League on these occasions was that of the Soviet Union. But the fight had gone out of most of the League members, and they readily heeded the cautions of Britain's new prime minister, Neville Chamberlain, that the best the League could do was do nothing. When Poland was attacked, neither the victim nor its Western allies even appealed for help to the League. "The one passionate desire of the smaller countries was to keep out of war at all costs," writes the man who was deputy secretary-general of the League at the time, "and the governments in London and Paris, having themselves rejected the obligation to aid the victim of aggression [in the cases of Spain, China, and Czechoslovakia] did not think of asking aid from others."[6]

But the Russian assault on Finland, coming on top of the Soviets' deal with

---

[5] See Royal Institute of International Relations, *International Sanctions* (New York: Oxford University Press), 1938.

[6] F. P. Walters, *History of the League of Nations* (New York: Oxford University Press, 1952), Vol. 2, p. 801.

In the summer of 1937, the League Assembly did vote 32–2 to declare an end to the nonintervention policy toward Spain. This policy had been adopted outside the League under British initiative to try to confine the conflict to Spain. In practice, it worked to deprive the Republican government of support from those countries which honored the agreement, while Franco was supplied with matériel and even by armed forces from countries like Italy and Germany which flagrantly violated it. So the League's action was intended to give moral sanction to any countries that wished on their own responsibility to help the hard-pressed established government. In a sense, it very mildly asserted that the Spanish

Hitler and their role in the obliteration of Poland, provoked a worldwide burst of moral indignation. Resentment was all the more keen because of long-harbored fears of communism and, on the other hand, widespread respect for Finland's tradition of freedom and impeccable international conduct. Sympathy for the Finns grew even stronger as they put on a display of heroic and unexpectedly effective resistance. When the Finnish government appealed to the League, therefore, they received a more prompt and favorable response than had any previous victim of aggression.

On the moral front, the Assembly solemnly condemned the Russian aggression and resolved that Russia had placed herself "outside the Covenant"; the Council, on the same day, for the first and only time in the League's history, used its power under Article 16 to expel Russia from the organization for having violated the Covenant. On the more practical side, the Assembly called on the members to give Finland all the material help they could, and instructed the Secretary-General to organize their actions. This, too, was an innovation. The League had never before moved to concert assistance to an attacked state.

However, the action studiously avoided any implication of *military* involvement, and no sanctions, except moral, were pointed at Russia directly. Assistance was mainly limited to relief and medical supplies, though a few states sent war matériel. Furthermore, despite the Secretariat's vigorous initiative, the operation never became collective, but splintered into isolated efforts by the individual states that responded. It had, of course, no effect on the outcome of the war. Finland, overwhelmed, made peace on Soviet terms.

FRUSTRATIONS OF THE MORAL AUTHORITY OF THE UNITED NATIONS

Turning to the experience of the United Nations, the organization has often tried to enforce its will simply by the exercise of moral or diplomatic

situation was, indeed, the League's concern, however much the major powers had bypassed the organization up to this point in dealing with it.

This was a far cry, however, from the tough measures of collective restraint needed to stop illegal foreign intervention in the Spanish War, or the vigorous mutual assistance the Spanish government needed to withstand the massive assault—foreign-engineered—that had been thrown against it. The resolution merely tossed the ball to whomever in the League might want to carry it. Formally, even this action was without standing, because Portugal and Albania voted against the resolution, preventing the unanimity needed under League rules for authoritative action.

In regard to the Japanese attack on China, the League Council in September, 1938, took much the same sort of action. It declared that members of the League were entitled to carry out measures under Article 16—in other words, to apply sanctions against Japan, and to support China, if they individually chose to do so. But no one so chose.

As the definitive historian of the League of Nations puts it, the Council and the Assembly "went through the motions of international action as a man may go through the motions of a ritual which has lost all meaning for his mind and will." F. P. Walters, *ibid.*, p. 738.

pressure. The General Assembly, in particular, has practiced the art of appeal and condemnation to induce states to behave peaceably and respect the "decent opinion of mankind."

The first instance was in regard to Spain. In 1946, Poland and other Soviet-oriented states called for action against the Franco regime, declaring its existence and activities had led to international friction and endangered international peace. Other members of the Security Council could not agree that the regime posed any immediate threat to the peace, and therefore declined to authorize direct enforcement measures. But the question was then taken up in the General Assembly. It voted to recommend that all members recall their ambassadors and ministers from Spain, and that Franco Spain be barred from membership in international agencies and conferences related to the United Nations—a seemingly forthright diplomatic sanction, albeit a recommendation rather than a directive. The Assembly further recommended that if a satisfactory government were not established in Spain within a reasonable time, the Security Council should consider adequate measures "to remedy the situation."

Despite the near unanimity with which these actions were finally adopted, the first exercise of the new system of collective peace enforcement did not fit the basic pattern laid down in the Charter. It really presumed a far more radical function than had ever been intended. In the first place, the United Nations was attempting to use its enforcement power to give vent to ideological condemnation (and possibly a desire to punish a hated collaborator of the now-vanquished Axis enemies) rather than to put down an obvious act of aggression; it was, in effect, extending its role from policeman to political censor. Second, the object of the action was clearly to encourage the overthrow of a government, not merely to restrain it from international hostilities, thus implying authority on the part of the United Nations to brush aside the customary limits of national sovereignty and carry its policing function to the point of overseeing the internal political order of a country. The Soviet bloc actually urged far more drastic coercive action to accomplish this end.

Far from having any such results, however, the United Nations action fizzled out with no trace of an impact on the Spanish government. For a time, member-states largely went along with the agreed sanctions. (For many, this meant no change from previous policy.) But misgivings over the implications of the action steadily rose, as well as recognition of its ineffectiveness. More important, the cold war sharply altered the Western outlook toward Spain, and turned Franco from pariah into valued partner in the containment of Soviet influence. In 1950, the General Assembly finally revoked its actions (over vehement Soviet objections, of course). To complete the farce, Spain was later admitted to full membership in the United Nations with the concurrence even of the Soviet Union (as part of a package deal admitting Soviet satellites as well)—all without the slightest modification of Franco's government or policies, and with no act of penance or apology for his fascism or his wartime benevolence toward the Axis. The United Nations, in apply-ing its moral police power against Spain, had obviously been pushed into action as inappropriate as it was inopportune.

Ten years after Soviet initiative had directed the United Nations moral and diplomatic sanctions against fascist Spain, violent Soviet repression of the Hungarian revolt prompted the United Nations to try its hand once again at moral enforcement—this time against the Soviet Union and its puppet government in Budapest. The results were equally disheartening.

The uprising had, at first, succeeded in ousting the previous Communist regime and obliging the new government under the premiership of Inre Nagy (himself a Communist) to pledge greater freedom and appeal for the withdrawal of Soviet troops from the country. But the Soviet army, after a deceptive lull of a few days, seized the new Hungarian leaders and struck in force at all centers of resistance.

This hit the United Nations just at the moment when it was struggling to call off the equally unexpected British-French-Israeli attack on Egypt and the Suez Canal. The Security Council, blocked by a Soviet veto, could not act, except to call an emergency session of the General Assembly to make appropriate recommendations. This body, literally bleary-eyed from day-and-night sessions over the Middle East crisis but now profoundly alarmed over the epidemic of violence, mustered a 53–8 vote, with only the Soviet bloc in opposition (and seven abstentions), calling on the U.S.S.R. "to desist forth-with from any form of intervention, particularly armed intervention, in the internal affairs of Hungary . . . and to withdraw all of its forces without delay from Hungarian territory." The Secretary-General was instructed to arrange for immediate, on-the-spot observation of the situation and suggest methods for ending the foreign intervention. The General Assembly repeated its admonition to the Soviet Union within a few days, and urged free elections under United Nations auspices to determine the form of govern-ment desired by the Hungarian people.

All these appeals fell on deaf ears. The Soviet Union, with an amenable regime now firmly installed, rebuked the Assembly for interfering in Hun-gary's domestic jurisdiction. The Hungarian government refused any United Nations observation, including a visit by the Secretary-General.

The Assembly now turned to outright censure. At each successive session, it denounced the Soviet action in debate and by resolution as a violation of Hungarian independence and of the United Nations Charter. It also author-ized an intensive investigation of the revolt by a Five-Member Committee. The report of this Committee, based largely on interviews with escaped Hungarians (in default of permission to gather information in Hungary itself), presented a withering indictment of Soviet conduct during and since the uprising. It refuted the Soviet charge that the revolt was instigated by Western imperialists and Hungarian reactionaries. The General Assembly endorsed the report (60–10, with 10 abstentions), and again called on the Soviet Union to cease and desist from repressive measures against the Hungarian population, including mass deportations, and to respect Hungarian national independence.

The United Nations has gone as far as words can go in its actions on the Soviet intervention in Hungary. The awesome power of the accused neither modified the vehemence of the indictment nor prevented an impressive majority of the members of the United Nations, cutting across almost all their other controversies, from uniting to return the indictment. But Soviet policy has not yielded, and the inescapable conclusion is that enforcement of collective judgment by moral sanction has again been frustrated.

Similar results have attended United Nations censure in a whole group of cases in which countries have been accused of violating human rights, such as the charges against Hungary, Romania, and Bulgaria for persecuting political and religious leaders, and against the Union of South Africa for racial discrimination. (These are discussed in detail in chapter 18.) As in the Spanish case, the accusers have insisted that the international repercussions of these nominally internal practices justified moral intervention in the name of preserving peace. As in the Spanish case, neither the argument nor the censure has been persuasive. The accused categorically refuse even to discuss the matter, often carrying their rejection to the point of outright boycott of General Assembly debates.

To sum up, the experience of the United Nations in applying moral sanctions suggests the following conclusions. (1) It is relatively easy to secure a sweeping moral condemnation of states for conduct or policies which others consider reprehensible, even if the situation is largely internal to the country condemned. (2) However, the moral or diplomatic sanction has no influence on the affected states, except to provoke a sharp rejoinder and exacerbate their relations with the United Nations. The lack of effect is equally apparent, regardless of the power of the states accused. (3) To some extent, at least, the frustration of the United Nations' moral sanctions seems related to the kind of objectives for which they have been used—namely, securing a fundamental political change inside a country. (4) Support for this type of enforcement action noticeably slackens as its ineffectiveness becomes apparent.[7]

---

[7] Fernand Van Langenhove, longtime permanent delegate of Belgium to the United Nations, takes a somewhat more optimistic view of the results of the General Assembly's moral pressure, especially when backed up by actions throughout the world, such as parliamentary resolutions, press comment, and diplomatic initiatives of various governments. The effect is most pronounced, he feels, in democratic countries, but has even been evident on the U.S.S.R. He admits there was no effect at all in regard to the Hungarian uprising, and that it is not possible to measure the effect directly and precisely even in countries like France and Britain. See *La Crise du Système de Securité Collective des Nations Unies, 1946–1957* (La Haye: Nijhoff, 1958), pp. 182–90.

RESTRAINT BY EMBARGO

On three significant occasions, the United Nations has authorized material sanctions—but short of military force—to reinforce its efforts to maintain peace.

In the case of Palestine, the Security Council called on all governments to assist in implementing the cease-fire it had arranged between Israel and the Arab states by imposing a nondiscriminatory embargo on shipments of arms and fighting personnel to both sides.

Dealing with the situation in the Balkans in 1949, the General Assembly sought to pinch off the assistance Greek guerrillas were receiving from Albania and Bulgaria by calling on all states to refrain from sending arms or other materials of war to Albania and Bulgaria until a competent organ of the United Nations had determined that their unlawful assistance had ceased.[8]

The third instance was in regard to Communist China, following its condemnation by the General Assembly as an aggressor for its participation in the Korean war. Here, the Assembly, carefully sidestepping a course of general military action against China on the mainland, called for a broad embargo on shipments of strategic goods.[9] Each country was to decide for itself the specific articles to be embargoed as well as the procedures it would follow in applying the embargo.[10]

Although these material sanctions were not applied in pursuance of an outright United Nations directive and were not organized through any centralized machinery (as had the League against Italy), a considerable number of countries did respond to the appeal for action. The most inclusive response came in regard to Palestine, and until about 1955, complaints from both Israel and the Arab governments about the embargo testified to its reasonable effectiveness, except for surreptitious deals. This was, of course, the one situation in which for a period the Soviet Union and the Western powers were not at loggerheads. But in 1955, even this dam broke as Egypt made an arms trade agreement with the Soviet orbit and the Western states began to build up the Baghdad Pact countries and Israel, each side accusing the other of being the first to disturb the peace.

In the other cases, the apparent response to the United Nations authorized embargo was illusory. The embargoes were chiefly implemented by countries already committed to anti-Communist policies, and, of course, were openly flouted by the Communist world. The action was, in other words, no true demonstration of collective enforcement, but a side skirmish in the overall

---

[8] Resolution 288 (IV), November 18, 1949. See Goodrich and Simons, *op. cit.*, p. 430.

[9] Resolution 500 (V), May 18, 1951.

[10] See Goodrich and Simons, *op. cit.*. p. 439.

power struggle which now gripped the world. In the circumstances, it is not surprising that the contribution of these moves to collective security is hard to detect.

A new call for the imposition of economic sanctions is now pending and promises to pose a test of quite a different order. This is the sequel to the long history of unavailing moral sanctions against the Union of South Africa. The struggle between the overwhelming anticolonial U.N. majority and an absolutely recalcitrant South African government sidesteps the cold war and comes close to meeting the classic conditions assumed for the operation of collective security—a specific country branded by virtually the entire community of states for violations of the Charter (albeit *not* for acts directed internationally against other states). The Western powers, trying to avoid the appearance of condoning South Africa's apartheid, have had to reluctantly agree to Security Council action: first, embargo the sale and shipment of arms and materials for arms manufacture; and, second, study and prepare for the application of general economic sanctions. This portends a conclusive exercise of the United Nations' power to constrain without military force, for these actions have been undertaken without dissent and reflect an intense and widely shared conviction that the only alternative to an African blood bath is the united pressure of the United Nations directed at the base of South Africa's economy. Whether this will suffice to bring about a change of policy or change of government without violence is the crucial and so far unanswered issue.[11]

KOREA—THE ULTIMATE CHALLENGE TO THE UNITED NATIONS' POLICE POWER

There remains the one presumably supreme test of the collective security system—Korea. Here, for the first and only time, an act of aggression was met head-on with military might under the aegis of international authority. Even though the full conditions of the United Nations Charter were not met—notably, the provision for concerted action by all the five major powers—the defense of the Republic of Korea was undertaken by armed forces drawn from 16 nations, acting in the name of the United Nations and pursuant to resolutions approved by a majority of the members. Thus, responsibility for the enforcement action was at least nominally collective, and the enforcers went almost to the limit of compulsive power applicable within the immediate area of the aggression. Ill-prepared though the United Nations was at the beginning of the Korean experience for a testing of its enforcement role in such proportions, the length of the ordeal insured that the potentialities and limitations alike would be rigorously exposed.

---

[11] See U.N. Security Resolution of June 18, 1964; also, *Report by the Secretary-General to the Security Council,* April 20, 1964 (U.N. Doc. S/5658).

There were four distinct phases in the development of the Korean experience from the standpoint of its significance as an experiment in collective security: (1) determination of responsibility for the breach of peace; (2) organization of collective support for South Korea through a unified command under United States direction, and its deployment against North Korea; (3) extension of the operation beyond the thirty-eighth parallel, followed by China's massive intervention, and then achievement of a military stalemate; and (4) negotiation and final conclusion of an armistice.

The United Nations' Response to Aggression

The first phase was surmounted expeditiously, although in the process the United Nations had virtually to alter the Charter while overriding intense Soviet opposition.

The Attack on Korea. The Security Council—with the Soviet Union deliberately absent and insisting that any action in its absence was illegal—made successive decisions on June 25 and 27, 1950, which fixed responsibility on the North Korean authorities for armed attack on the Republic of Korea, determined that this constituted a breach of the peace, called for an immediate cessation of hostilities and withdrawal of North Korean forces to the thirty-eighth parallel, and within less than 48 hours found the North Korean authorities responsible for failing to comply with these directives. This laid the formal basis for authorizing United Nations police action to repel the attack and "restore international peace and security in the area."

The promptness and decisiveness of the Council was surprising in view of the difficulties that confronted it. The attack was so sudden and unexpected that few of the governments had been able to assess its significance and formulate even an immediate reaction when the Council was called into emergency session. Delegates had to consult their home governments constantly while debate was in progress. Some had to refrain from voting because instructions did not come in time. Voting on the fateful resolution of June 27 was actually held off until the Norwegian delegate heard that he should vote for it, thus providing the necessary margin for passage.[12]

The Soviet seat, though vacant, cast a long shadow over the Council table. There was first a tricky legal problem: Could the Council take any action when one of its permanent, veto-wielding members was absent? The Charter specified a vote of substance had to have the concurrence of the permanent

---

[12] The June 25 resolution was adopted by nine votes, Yugoslavia abstaining and the U.S.S.R. absent. The more decisive resolution of June 27 was passed with only seven affirmative votes, Yugoslavia opposing it, India and Egypt not voting, and the U.S.S.R. again absent. Later, India announced it had accepted the resolution; Egypt announced it would have voted "no" had instructions arrived in time. Only the bare minimum of seven votes was available to pass the July 7 resolution establishing the unified command—China, Cuba, Ecuador, France, Norway, United Kingdom, and United States.

members. The Soviet Union had plainly specified that its absence was deliberately intended to negate all Council action until its demand for the representation of Communist China was met. Furthermore, all Council members were aware that Soviet power lay behind the North Korean thrust, and knew that at issue in their decision might be a struggle with a world titan, not just the minor puppet. Nevertheless, a majority of the Council was persuaded to take up the awesome challenge; and a legal improvisation contrived by the United States was accepted as at least justifying Council *recommendations* to United Nations members in the circumstances.[13] The Council bypassed the question of using its mandatory powers, judging that recommendations alone would provide sufficient authority and impetus for those members who wanted to take action, and that nothing the Council could do would compel support from those countries which did not want to give it—above all, the Russians. Furthermore, Council members were only too well aware that the entire military machinery for collective enforcement authorized by the Charter was a dead letter. The United Nations had no teeth in being.

Several factors contributed to the United Nations' initial vigor of decision in the Korean crisis. Foremost was the policy leadership of the United States. The fact that the United States government clearly and unequivocally committed itself to withstand the Communist assault—even in advance of the United Nations' decision—encouraged the other countries to endorse a strong United Nations stand. Several were convinced that the United States commitment automatically insured the effectiveness of any action the United Nations chose to take, probably even without the engagement of major military forces. In any case, with United States' underwriting, the risks of enforcing peace by collective action appeared minimal. On the other hand, some countries supported the collectivizing of action under the United Nations out of fear that the United States if left to go it alone would almost certainly provoke Russian counteraction. Better a joint enterprise, limited and controlled by collective authority, than the direct confrontation of the two superpowers with their global war potentials. Whatever their reasons, the majority of the Council took their cue straight from the United States, which formulated the key resolutions, laid down the main lines of debate, provided much of the moment-to-moment information on developments in Korea, and simultaneously—with sharp, bold presidential declarations—turned the spotlight of public expectancy onto the United Nations, while mobilizing American forces. The United Nations decisions were engineered by the United States, even though, in form, the United States purported to join in a truly collective act. It is doubtful whether the decisions could ever have been made without the kind of support from the United States that was indistinguishable from pressure.

---

[13] See discussion of this legal issue in Chapter 3, pp. 61–62.

The North Koreans themselves helped to weld the forceful United Nations decision. The bluntness of their attack, its evidently premeditated character, and their refusal to make even a pretense of favorable response to the United Nations' call for cessation of hostilities left no doubt as to where immediate responsibility lay. And the overwhelming weight of the attack persuaded the Security Council majority that it had to choose at once between complete acquiescence or supporting the United States in major military resistance. The North Koreans seemed to have left no opening for a middle course of negotiation as at first advocated by Yugoslavia and others.

The presence on the scene in Korea of the United Nations Temporary Commission which was to have assisted in the country's unification was another circumstance that facilitated the Council's decision. This body was able to give an independent account of the attack, and to assess for the Council the location of responsibility through its on-the-spot consultation with the South Korean authorities and its frustrated attempts to communicate with the North Korean authorities. The Council thus felt it had reliable information on which to base its decisions, although it acted on June 27 before receiving the commission's definitive report which chronicled a background of unheralded South Korean capabilities as well as the overt aggressive actions of the North Koreans.

The Council was persuaded to act so decisively, too, because of the pervading sense that the United Nations was confronted with a truly momentous decision on which the security of the whole world really did hinge. To forego collective resistance at this point many felt would doom the organization to the futility of the League and expose everyone to ever more serious aggressions. For the United Nations to mobilize all possible resources and stop the aggression would revive its prestige and enable it to fulfill its expected function of guaranteeing the peace. Now or never was the mood inside and outside the Council chamber as the delegates struggled over the decision. At this moment, there did seem widespread that sense of collective responsibility for the peace which the system of collective security presumed.

The Chinese Intervention.   Six months later, the United Nations General Assembly found it far harder to reach a decision on holding the Chinese Communist government responsible for aggression, even though hundreds of thousands of Chinese "volunteers" had joined the fray and the Chinese regime had clearly become the principal antagonist. (The Security Council, with Russia now ever present, obviously could not duplicate its earlier action on Korea.) The United States position was as clear-cut as ever. It urged the unmistakable branding of the Chinese Communists as aggressors for their support of the North Koreans and attacks on the United Nations forces. In the end, this view prevailed, but only over substantial opposition and with very considerable misgiving by some of the states which finally yielded to United States insistence.

Reluctance to follow the Security Council's precedent certainly stemmed in part from a changed estimate of the risks involved. United States might did not seem so mighty after six months of testing in Korea, and especially in the gloom of the Chinese-forced retreat from the Yalu River. The Chinese loomed unexpectedly as a force of formidable proportions. Who could envisage a means by which the collective security operation could be brought to an effective conclusion against them? Then there were always the Russians, formally unengaged but available and helpful to the other side.

In these circumstances, there was a strong demand to explore every possible avenue of a negotiated settlement before formally committing the United Nations to enforce the peace against another opponent, even though it was already under attack by him. This disposition was strongly reinforced by dissatisfaction with United States strategy in the war, which some felt had provoked the Chinese intervention by pushing for the complete occupation of North Korea up to the Chinese border. This will be discussed in more detail later. Suffice it to say at the moment that United States leadership was no longer so unquestioned and respected as at the inception of the Korean crisis.

Another factor working against a precipitate decision was the ill-defined line of responsibility for the Chinese forces in Korea. The government persistently disclaimed official responsibility for the "volunteers," and—more adroit than the North Koreans—was modestly responsive to overtures for a negotiated truce. This made it more difficult than in the case of North Korea to fix the onus for aggression squarely on the Chinese government.

Nevertheless, in assessing the workability of collective security in the Korean situation, the conclusion is warranted that the United Nations, with respect both to North Korea and the Chinese People's Republic, successfully overcame great legal, political, and organizational obstacles to make the basic decisions on responsibility for breach of the peace and for aggression which were the necessary precursor to enforcement actions.

The Unified Command—Americanized Collective Security

The organization and fielding of an international force—with no advance preparation—in time to hold and then throw back the well-conceived North Korean attack was a remarkable military and political achievement. But ironically, the very condition that made possible this initial physical success for the United Nations effort jeopardized its effectiveness as a collective enforcement action in the longer run. For the United States, with the only substantial forces immediately available, asked for and was given the responsibility of supreme command over the entire operation.

This produced unity and vigor in the mobilization and direction of the military effort, but the United Nations gradually found that it had thereby surrendered effective policy as well as operational control to the United States, and that it could not make and execute judgments truly representative of the sentiments of the organization as a whole. This became an especially serious problem when the United Nations sought to terminate the operation but felt bound to funnel negotiations through the United States government.

The organization of the Unified Command was authorized by the Security Council, July 7, 1950, in the simplest of terms. It recommended that governments make available "to a unified command under the United States" all military forces and other assistance they would furnish to help repel the attack. It requested the United States to designate the commander of such forces and to report to the Security Council "as appropriate" on the course of action taken under the unified command. It authorized the use of the United Nations flag, at the discretion of the Command, concurrently with the flags of the various participating nations.

The Pivot of Control. General Douglas MacArthur, who was named Supreme Commander by President Truman, promptly fashioned an elaborate and highly centralized structure of control, with the pivot of responsibility located at his Tokyo headquarters. From the beginning, the U.N. Command was overwhelmingly American in character and composition, but more than that, was run as an extension of MacArthur's personal staff. MacArthur insisted that the power of decision was exclusively his, not only over military operations in the field but on every matter affecting Korea. He decided whether to accept or reject the assistance offered by the United Nations members, and precisely where and how it was to be used, regardless of their sensibilities. He included a token number of British and other non-American officers on the headquarters staff, but kept them in subordinate positions and rarely consulted with them even when their countries' forces were involved. He demanded, and acquired, from the Security Council control over all civilian relief assistance to Korea. The pattern of command was thus hierarchical in the extreme. Unity was achieved through the assumption of total personal control rather than by the close-knit coordination of the participants. While this was generally conceded to be appropriate to the conduct of the strictly military operations, its extension to areas of civilian life and especially to the determination of political decisions of broad import was sharply challenged within the United States, as well as by other governments, as incompatible with the international character of the enterprise.

The problem was complicated by the failure to establish a clear line of responsibility from the United Nations through the United States government to the United Nations Command, e.g., Douglas MacArthur. It is important to realize that the United Nations had no direct supervision over the United Nations Command, and virtually no channel of communication with it except through the United States government. Furthermore, there was no United Nations organ to which the United States was really accountable for its conduct of the United Nations police action in Korea. The Security Council virtually abdicated responsibility when it authorized the United States to establish a unified command, anticipating accurately that it would no longer be able to function responsibly in regard to Korea when the Soviet Union reoccupied its Council seat. It was months later before the General Assembly assumed a policy-making role concerning Korea, and then it was in an equivocal position regarding the Command because it had not established it. The United States had received, in effect, an irrevocable power of attorney from the United Nations, but there was no assurance that the attorney would always either understand or be ready to implement the wishes of his clients.

The United States government had its own problems in insuring that actions of the United Nations Command would reflect responsible policy. Aside from General MacArthur's strong-minded disposition to carve out policy on his own (a disposition which ultimately led to his dismissal), there was considerable confusion within the government over who had the authority to tell the United Nations Commander to do what. His appointment was from the President. As Commander of United States forces in the Far East, he reported to the Joint Chiefs of Staff, who prepared his instructions. But policy relating to the United Nations was the business of the State Department, and it was the channel of communication to and from the Security Council. Despite earnest efforts in Washington to coordinate the various aspects of Korean policy, enough loopholes were left so that MacArthur enjoyed quite a free hand, and frequently presented the presumed policy-makers with a fait accompli.[14]

The Narrow Base of Collective Support.   If the organization and direction of the United Nations Command belied its international origins and functions, the assistance furnished by the United Nations members other than the United States and the Republic of Korea was not sufficiently large and widespread to give it an unmistakable collective character. This was especially true of the military forces incorporated into the Command. These were provided by 15 nations, aside from the United States and the Republic of Korea.[15] British ground forces amounted to about a division. The other units were much smaller. Several nations contributed only minor naval or air support. As of December, 1951, the contributions of the 15 totaled only about 9 percent of the ground forces, 7 percent of the naval forces, and 1

[14] See Leland M. Goodrich, *Korea: A Study of United States Policy in the United Nations* (New York: Council on Foreign Relations, 1956), p. 121.

[15] Australia, Belgium, Canada, Colombia, Ethiopia, France, Greece, Luxembourg, the Netherlands, New Zealand, the Philippines, Thailand, Turkey, Union of South Africa, and the United Kingdom.

percent of the air forces.[16] In addition, a wide range of supplies and services were contributed by these and other members of the United Nations, some of it for military use and a larger amount for civilian relief and reconstruction.

Altogether, however, the United Nations Command—in substance as well as in leadership—was disproportionately American. That this should have been so was fully as much the result of default by the United Nations membership as it was the result of overzealous United States initiative. The paucity of collective participation in the enforcement operation can be explained in part by the pressure of other dangers on some of the members. The French were heavily engaged in fighting Indo-Chinese rebels, the British were involved in guerrilla warfare in Malaya, and Western Europe was generally nervous about Russian intentions. But many members of the United Nations, including most of those in Asia and the Middle East, were never genuinely committed to the Korean police action. In time, they came to suspect it as essentially an extension of American anti-Communist policy—especially after the Chinese became involved—rather than a United Nations action to put down aggression. Whereas a majority could always be rallied for a vote of lip-service to the avowed objectives (many out of deference to United States influence), only a small minority believed so strongly in the importance of the Korean war as a test of collective security that they were ready to make substantial sacrifices toward its waging.

This fact made little difference in the actual outcome of the hostilities, at least in the beginning. If anything, American predominance probably made the conduct of operations easier. Most of the forces were already integrated, uniformly equipped, with a common background of training, and accustomed to the same pattern of military organization. Non-American units were simply sandwiched into the American contingents, and quickly adapted to the American system, though retaining identity as combat units. MacArthur was able to impose the American logistical system on all forces except the Commonwealth units, thus simplifying the supply problem. Undoubtedly, operational unity, which the solid American core made possible in the United Nations Command, was a critical factor in enabling the skilled and tenacious defense of the Pusan perimeter, the bold counterstroke at Inchon, and the impressive rout of the invaders within three months of the North Korean attack.

Had the Korean war ended at this point, the uncollective nature of the United Nations enforcement action would surely have gone unnoticed in the wide rejoicing over the first great success of a collective security system. But in the moment of apparent victory, serious mistakes of policy were made,

---

[16] See *United States Participation in the United Nations* (Department of State publication, International Organization and Conference Series III, 80, 1952), p. 288. There were certain additional offers of assistance, notably from the Chinese Nationalists, which the command refused for various reasons.

which turned the event into an even yet unconcluded nightmare. The mistakes must be laid at the door of those who had the responsibility for the operation—the Americans, including General MacArthur and all those who should have held him accountable for major policy decisions. But more profoundly, the miscarriage of the operation resulted from abdication by the United Nations as a whole, and United Nations members individually, of responsibility for the active direction and control of the most portentous action the organization had ever authorized and to which most members had given their endorsement in one form or another. Collective security failed in Korea, therefore, not so much for lack of collective support—American power filled this deficiency—but for lack of sufficient collective responsibility at a critical juncture.[17]

The Fatal Mistake—Pursuit of Total Victory

The fundamental character of the United Nations action in Korea changed when the decision was made to seek the total destruction of the North Korean forces, the unconditional surrender of the North Korean government, and the occupation of North Korea with United Nations forces, pending a permanent settlement in accordance with United Nations directives. A police action limited to repelling armed attack and preventing the alteration by force of the status quo suddenly turned into an expedition "to enforce the decrees of the United Nations," in the terms of the flamboyant ultimatum delivered by General MacArthur as "United Nations Commander-in-Chief" to the North Korean commander on October 8, 1950. Though this rather overstretched the implications of the specific mandates the General had received—from Washington or the United Nations—it was not repudiated and could, therefore, properly be taken as staking out the extended scope of the mission.

This would have been a decision of major import for the United Nations in any circumstances, for it involved a drastic revision of the role and powers of the organization as conceived in its Charter. The United Nations was not authorized to issue or to execute decrees. Even in connection with the enforcement of peace and security, the Charter-prescribed function was to "restore peace," not to impose a settlement or even to punish the peace-breakers. Though the United Nations had from time to time shown a temptation to indulge in decision-making (witness the Palestine partition), there was clearly no precedent for the kind of sweeping compulsiveness now to be applied to the Korean situation. In regard to Palestine, the Security Council had explicitly refused to become the enforcing agent for the General Assembly's plan of settlement.

---

[17] On the question of responsibility for determining the objective of the operation and relationships between the U.N., the U.S., and the unified command, see the careful review by Goodrich and Simons, *op. cit.,* pp. 467–80.

The gravity of the decision was immeasurably increased, because it overrode the vehement objections—and outright warnings of counteraction—of both Chinese and Russians and entailed the direct confrontation of these hostile powers at their own borders. The risk of vastly extending the conflict was present, however much discounted by General MacArthur and others who minimized the Communist threats and Chinese capabilities.

Despite the serious implications of the situation, the United States and the United Nations as a whole evaded a deliberate facing of the issues and adopted a policy which, in effect, left the destiny of events in MacArthur's hands without benefit of a clean-cut collective decision by the governments concerned. It appears to have been the considered position of the United States that United Nations forces could cross the thirty-eighth parallel into North Korea with no other authorization than that which could be inferred from the original Security Council resolution of June 27, recommending "such assistance to the Republic of Korea as may be necessary to repel the armed attack and to restore international peace and security in the area."[18]

Nevertheless, the United States did turn to the General Assembly for a review of its mandate prior to the crossing (the Security Council being stymied by Soviet objection to any action on Korea).[19] It requested broad and flexible powers to deal with the changing situation, and temptingly suggested that a decisive military victory could lead to the creation of a unified and independent Korea in line with the previously declared aspirations of the Assembly. At the same time, it promised caution in exercising its powers. The Soviet bloc strongly urged, instead, the ending of hostilities forthwith, followed by the withdrawal of foreign troops, and all-Korean elections under United Nations observation to establish a national government.[20]

Others than the Soviets, however, expressed reservations about the carte blanche requested by the United States, and wanted to take every step possible to end the fighting quickly. The Indian government, in particular, took seriously the threat of Chinese intervention and also foresaw prolonged North Korean resistance if the United Nations entered North Korea. Yugoslavia objected that the use of armed force by the United Nations to change the status quo ante would set a precedent for intervention that would tend to embitter international relations.

But the majority—including those who had joined forces in Korea—were not prepared to bridle the United States, especially when under its leadership

---

[18] See Goodrich, *op. cit.,* p. 127.

[19] The thirty-eighth parallel was actually crossed by South Korean forces before the Assembly reached a decision. But MacArthur held up his ultimatum and the full engagement of United Nations forces in North Korea until the Assembly acted on October 7, 1950.

[20] This major reversal of the previous Soviet hands-off approach coincided neatly with the turn in the fortunes of the North Koreans.

the forces of the United Nations stood, in the words of the United States delegate, "on the threshold of military victory." Without explicitly authorizing the Unified Command to press the war into North Korea, the General Assembly backed a United States drafted resolution which sweepingly endorsed all appropriate steps "to insure conditions of stability throughout Korea," and all constituent acts necessary for "the establishment of a unified, independent and democratic Government in the sovereign State of Korea." A provision that United Nations forces would not remain in any part of Korea except as necessary to achieve these objectives clearly implied that they would go to—and stay in—North as well as South Korea *until* these objectives were secured. On the final vote, only five opposed the resolution (the Soviet bloc) and seven abstained.

Accustomed as it was to one-nation leadership, the United Nations was not prepared to exercise independent statesmanship in making the most critical policy decision of its venture into collective security. Its responsibility for what followed is none the less because it chose to acquiesce in United States initiative rather than to call for strict adherence to the well-defined limits of the United Nations enforcement function. In a sense, this was a failing more serious than the reluctance of many members to furnish substantial material support. For by rejecting the restraints the Charter prescribed for collective enforcement of the peace, the United Nations majority undercut the moral authority it claimed for its action. When policemen themselves cavalierly ignore the rules that supposedly govern their conduct, they impair the foundations of the social order, even though one easily understands their overwhelming desire to have done with the lawbreakers once and for all. The United Nations forsook the police role when it made itself party to the decision to conquer North Korea.

The military repercussions hardly need review here. Contrary to MacArthur's confident predictions, the Chinese Communists did intervene, and with such vigor and massiveness as to spell near disaster for the United Nations forces. MacArthur wanted to strike back at the Chinese in their homeland. But he was firmly blocked by his United States superiors all the way to the President, who in concert with the whole United Nations were now thoroughly alarmed over a possible global extension of the conflict and skeptical of following any further the United Nations Commander's insights. The Chinese and revitalized North Koreans pushed the United Nations forces back roughly to the old dividing line. There, a military stalemate developed a condition of deliberately limited war that lasted until prolonged negotiations finally produced an armistice two and one-half years later.

What the United Nations was not judicious enough to do of its own volition—set proper limits to its attempt at collective enforcement of security—was thus done by Chinese force of arms and the overhanging threat of having an international police action mushroom into the nuclear annihilation of the world.[21]

The Conclusion of Collective Security

The United Nations now confronted the extraordinarily difficult problem of having to negotiate for its objectives after failing to impose them by force. The problem was further complicated, because to the original aims of restoring peace and security were now added interests and responsibilities which the United Nations had acquired as a belligerent. What should happen to the thousands of prisoners captured by both sides had obviously to be settled before the action was concluded. The United Nations was also by now so closely intertwined with the political and economic life of the Republic of Korea that it felt many of the obligations of guardianship; while the Korean government of Synghman Rhee pressed its own direct political interests so aggressively that it nearly wrecked the United Nations' efforts to reach a settlement on several occasions.

These multiple and often contradictory objectives had to be pursued against wily and bitter antagonists with whom the United Nations refused any official relationship. Neither the Chinese nor North Korean government was permitted representation within the United Nations; and the Chinese at least acknowledged no governmental responsibility for their forces in Korea. Negotiations had to be conducted exclusively in the field, even though it was obvious that almost all decisions had to be made by political authorities. And at the governmental level, there could be no direct consultation. (The situation was eased by the Indian and certain other governments, which maintained diplomatic relations with China and played an informal but frequently vital intermediary role. The Soviet Union was actually the instrumental party in getting the negotiations started.)

Finally, the United Nations and the United States had not worked out the means of insuring that the policies pursued on behalf of the United Nations would consistently reflect a collective judgment, although in the end the restoration of peace would require the concurrence, at least, of all the direct participants in the conflict, and presumably of the United Nations as a whole. Although the conduct of military operations was largely entrusted to one-nation control, the conclusion of a truce involving broad political considerations was considered by many nations a matter for joint decision. Hence, it was a serious question whether the unified command which had been forged

---

[21] A contrary view of the proper limits of collective security action is taken by Leo Gross. He considers the broader objective of punishing the aggressor as both legitimate and necessary. See *American Journal of International Law,* January, 1958. But Goodrich and others share the conclusion expressed here that Korea illustrated the grave danger of trying to do more than stop an aggressor, as mandated by the Charter. It entails the risk of general world war.

to provide absolute concentration of direction in the hands of a single government's designated officer could conduct effective negotiations for a group of states that now wished to reclaim the power of final decision. The end of the collective security operation really required two different sets of negotiations—those with the enemy and those consultations necessary to work out a common stand among the United Nations. Both sets had to mesh. For this complex task, neither the United States nor the United Nations was adequately tutored.[22]

There is no point in reviewing the details of the tortuous negotiations which finally led to the signing of an armistice agreement in August, 1953. But it is important to determine some of the factors which contributed to this outcome and to assess the implications of such a conclusion of the United Nations enforcement effort.

Stalemate—The Condition of Truce.   Basically, the persistence of military stalemate appears to have been an essential condition for negotiation. The Communists rejected proposals for a cease-fire and a negotiated settlement when they were flushed with military success, just as did the United Nations when it felt on the threshold of victory. When it became clear to both sides that neither could decisively defeat the other—at least not without great danger of extending the area of the war—they became receptive to feelers for a truce. During the negotiations when deadlocks developed, one side or the other often sought to strengthen its military position, probe for signs of enemy weakness, and thereby gain a bargaining advantage, only to discover that the line was firm and that there was no alternative to working out mutual concessions.

Limiting the Collective Security Objective.   A second condition was the readiness of both sides to accept the military-political status quo as the basis for a stable settlement of indefinite duration, and to execute guarantees that neither would attempt to change it by force. For the United Nations, this meant a full retreat from the extended objectives it had adopted when crossing the thirty-eighth parallel, but it did not have to surrender the original limited objectives of its police action. The status quo did preserve virtually intact the political independence and territorial integrity of the Republic of Korea as it existed before the North Korean invasion. The

---

[22] An especially troublesome hurdle was confronted at the very beginning of the search for a way to conclude the conflict. General MacArthur was so vehemently opposed to any settlement by negotiation that he would not execute the policies decided on by the United States government in consultation with other United Nations members. On a number of delicate occasions, he acted in ways which actually threatened to intensify the war rather than to open the way to truce negotiations. His dramatic removal by President Truman in April, 1951, finally enabled the United States government to insure that policy decisions would be made by the governments concerned, not by the commander in the field, and that the unified command would faithfully carry out the instructions it received during the conduct of negotiations.

Communists, of course, had to explicitly renounce their intention of acquiring control of all Korea by force.

Aside from the problem of devising means of implementing the truce which would make certain that the Communists could not successfully renew their aggression in the future, the principal stumbling block here was the South Korean government. It did not want to give up the prospect of achieving the unification of Korea (on terms that would insure its exclusive control by the South Korean government) and was convinced that only force would do it. President Rhee stubbornly insisted that the United Nations should not give up its collective enforcement until it had secured the "unified, free and democratic Korea" which it had previously pledged. He refused to be bound not to fight for this end, even if it meant going it alone with his own troops. To the United Nations members, including the United States, this appeared complete folly; yet they were caught in such a situation that they could not avoid responsibility for South Korean actions, nor cease their involvement without giving the Communists a blanket assurance against any attempt to alter the existing situation by force. They confronted the ironic necessity of imposing restraints on the victim whom they had rescued from aggression so as to make possible the conclusion of their effort on the only practical basis of security available. Their dilemma was all the greater because during the hostilities a relationship of such close mutual dependence had developed between the United Nations forces and the Koreans that a break now seemed unthinkable, for moral as well as practical considerations of military security. President Rhee ruthlessly exploited every element of influence and pressure available to him as a result of this situation; but the clear contradiction between his demands and the minimal conditions for ending the war finally forced the United Nations to guarantee full compliance with the terms of the armistice, even if this should require its forcibly preventing the South Koreans from defying the arrangement.

The Recapture of Collective Responsibility. The third essential element in ending collective enforcement was the reassertion of the collective responsibility of the United Nations for policy direction and guidance. While the United States continued to take the lead in every aspect of the situation and to maintain its exclusive control over the channels of negotiation through the Unified Command, it came to accept consultation with the United Nations as a regular practice (in particular with the 15 members whose forces were fighting in Korea). Of greater importance was the insistent concern expressed within the General Assembly over the conclusion of peace.

This concern grew immediately after extension of the operation into North Korea. Many members quickly became alarmed as the behavior of General MacArthur belied the American assurances that great caution would be exercised not to provoke Chinese or Russian intervention. When the Chinese did intervene, members individually and in General Assembly discussion strongly pressed the United States government to resist the clamor, sparked by MacArthur, for drastic retaliatory measures. When the Secretary of State announced a decision to permit the hot pursuit of enemy aircraft across the Yalu River as a "military necessity," the governments with troops in Korea refused to concur and persuaded the United States to withdraw the policy. When President Truman off the cuff inferred that the atomic bomb might be used, Prime Minister Attlee flew to Washington to remonstrate. Instead of responding immediately to an American demand that the Chinese People's Republic be declared an aggressor and be subjected to a blockade and other sanctions, the General Assembly insisted on first trying to achieve a cease-fire. The military reverses and the evidence of an American disposition to recklessness crystallized a judgment throughout the United Nations that the time had come for strenuous effort to call a halt to the operation.

The General Assembly itself took on the task of exploring the means of bringing this about, feeling that by acting independently of the United States and the Unified Command it could have a better chance of securing agreement with the Chinese. Proposals were formulated for a cease-fire, a general political settlement in Korea, and consideration of other problems of concern to the Chinese, such as Formosa and representation in the United Nations. A group of nations not involved in the hostilities was asked to approach the Chinese and seek their agreement to negotiate on these proposals. Although the Chinese rebuffed this effort and the Assembly compounded its difficulties by yielding to the pressure to condemn China for aggression, the United Nations had, nevertheless, established the precedent of taking collective responsibility for the basic decisions that would determine the conclusion of the enforcement action.

The truce negotiations were finally initiated and conducted on the field by the opposing commanders, a procedure adroitly proposed by the Soviet delegate at the United Nations to save face all around. The Chinese government did not have to admit responsibility for hostilities it insisted were conducted by volunteers or to negotiate with governments that had branded it an aggressor. The United Nations did not have to negotiate directly and on terms of equality with a government which refused to purge itself of the verdict of aggression and continued to war on the United Nations.

On a day-to-day basis, the United Nations Command received its instructions from the United States government. But these were worked out in close consultation with the Committee of Sixteen (the governments with armed forces in Korea). And the General Assembly, though it took no direct part in the negotiations, made repeatedly clear that it favored the maximum possible concessions to achieve a cease-fire without sacrificing the minimum collective security objectives. Also, after prolonged deadlock over the exchange of war prisoners, the General Assembly on Indian initiative worked out proposals which were transmitted directly to the Chinese Communist and North Korean governments and opened the way to ultimate agreement.

The armistice was formally concluded by the respective commands on behalf of the two "sides" to the conflict. Its implementation was and is the responsibility of the "sides." But it seems certain that a most important influence toward the armistice was exerted by the United Nations when it assumed an active responsibility for terminating the operation it had authorized, and did so in a manner that distinguished its broad interest in restoring peace from the special interests of one side in the conflict as epitomized by the United Nations Command.

The Nonbelligerent Initiative within the United Nations. This leads to consideration of a final factor in the conclusion of United Nations enforcement of security in Korea. In a very vital way, it was the "neutral" element in the United Nations that made the armistice finally possible and prevented the deterioration of collective security into a limitless world war. From the beginning, some countries had genuine reservations about the wisdom of involving the United Nations in military action in Korea. These grew as the Korean hostilities became more and more identified as but one front of the struggle between the Western alliance and Communist power. Most Asian and African members of the United Nations, as well as others, wanted to avoid alignment in the broader conflict, and feared that Korea might easily light the fuse of a global war which would engulf them all. They spearheaded efforts to bring the fighting to a close and to disengage the United Nations from the semblance of an anti-Communist crusade.

Aside from using their influence within the United Nations to encourage self-restraint and negotiability, the neutrals, with India in a prominent lead, played a most important role in opening and maintaining lines of communication to the Chinese and, through them, to the North Koreans. At points, they were apparently able to go beyond messengering, and exercised considerable persuasion on the Communists to modify rigid stands and come to terms with the United Nations Command. In the final analysis, the Indian government's readiness to take on major responsibilities for the implementation of the armistice—accepting custody from the United Nations Command of Chinese and North Korean prisoners who refused to be repatriated and serving as a neutral member of the armistice supervisory commission—resolved the issues that had most seriously deadlocked the negotiations. In a sense, the neutrals enabled the United Nations to stand on middle ground—the proverbial spot of the effective peacemaker—at the same time that it continued as one side in the fight. This ability to operate simultaneously in a dual role—to wear two faces, as it were—was instrumental in bringing about the conclusion of an enforcement attempt insufficiently collective to give it the physical force and moral authority to overwhelm the aggressor. The United Nations, unable to make its will fully effective in the police role, was able to extricate a tolerable basis of security, at least in part, because it could switch over at the critical juncture to the peacemaker role. The inclusiveness of its membership, covering the gamut of political interest and loyalties, gave it protective coloration, so that in the moment of danger it could adopt the appearance appropriate to the surrounding circumstances.

The Lessons of Korea

There is still the sharpest disagreement over the implications of the Korean experience as a test of collective security. Those who look primarily at the surviving Republic of Korea, free of Communist domination and nominally at peace, acclaim the United Nations effort as a successful repulse of aggression which prevented the conquest of a sovereign state by force. Those who look at a Korea still divided, the governments responsible for aggression unpunished and in a powerful position to threaten security again, and the United Nations unable to implement its recommendations for a permanent settlement that would establish a free, independent, and democratic country, consider collective security to have failed totally, at a frightful cost in lives and misery on all sides. Others who recall the dominant leadership of the United States throughout the operation, and the correspondingly minor role of the rest of the United Nations, insist that Korea was not a test of collective security at all, but of the American policy of containment, carried out in this instance under the convenient but essentially false label of a United Nations police action.[23]

Each of these appraisals, within its own perspective, is pertinent. However, if Korea is viewed from the standpoint of the essential design of collective security—how international organization was *expected* to fulfill the functions of keeping the peace and preventing aggression—a conclusion along the following lines emerges.

The United Nations—or at least an effective part of it—did deliberately authorize the defense of South Korea as an action of collective peace enforcement. The action seriously miscarried, with tragic consequences for all concerned, though the final outcome did deny the attackers their objectives. The

---

[23] See Arnold Wolfers, "Collective Security and the War in Korea," *Yale Review*, June, 1954. Wolfers argued strongly against applying the label of collective security to the Korean action. "Intervention in Korea was an act of collective military defense against the recognized No. 1 enemy of the United States and of all the countries which associated themselves with its action." He foresaw disillusionment with collective security when it was discovered that U.S. forces would not be available against any aggressor anywhere, and danger of resentment against other U.N. members for failing to live up to their supposed commitments.

On the other hand, he concluded that the U.N. had gained stature by being useful to the free world in defense against Communist aggression without giving up its universal character and mediating possibilities.

miscarriage is attributable in part to the radical departure from the pattern of collective security laid out in the Charter and the substitution of an entirely new and previously untried design. On the other hand, the circumstances did not permit implementation of the original pattern. The uncomfortable conclusion is that the Korean experience demonstrated certain fundamental conditions of contemporary international life which make it impossible for the United Nations to fulfill the function of providing collective security worthy of the name, regardless of the particular form or method chosen for accomplishing it. Considering the present outlook of the United Nations members, as they view the Korean action in retrospect, it seems most unlikely that either the General Assembly or Security Council (leaving aside the procedural hurdle of the veto) could be marshaled to support any similar action in the foreseeable future.

These are some of the lessons learned in Korea which have led to such widespread skepticism of the appropriateness of collective security as a function of international organization today.

1. It was extremely difficult to maintain a distinction between the collective purposes of an international police action and the strictly national interests of those participating in it. This was particularly serious, because the occasion of action was precipitated by, and intertwined with, conflict among the major powers.

2. The operation could not maintain a truly collective character because many states, for various reasons, contributed little if any material support, even though they joined in authorizing it. The extraordinary disproportion of participation resulted in a quite understandable disproportion of responsibility for the enterprise, with the United States virtually monopolizing its direction.

3. Apart from their reluctance to sacrifice substantially in the common cause, many members of the United Nations shirked the responsibility of exercising independent judgment in making vital decisions on the basic objectives and strategies of the operation. This, too, undercut the collectiveness of the action.

4. The collective irresponsibility was most obvious when it came to making self-restraining decisions. Most United Nations members were no more scrupulous than the United States in holding the operation within the strict limits of the enforcement task when it seemed that force could secure much broader political objectives. Indeed, this suggests that collective judgment is in no sense a guarantee of respect for lawful and reasonable procedure in an international police action. A more likely conclusion is that the more overwhelming the power available to enforce collective security, the greater the danger of its improper exercise.

5. Another lesson of Korea was that the use of force, even under collective authorization, runs a grave risk of triggering a chain reaction of ever

widening violence. The hazard of a police action's unleashing a major war is very great, given a general international situation of tense controversy.

6. Finally, stopping an enforcement action proved an infinitely more complex problem than starting one, and the international organization found that it had compromised much of its peacemaking potential (as an essentially impartial spokesman for world opinion) by becoming identified as a "side" in the hostilities. It is strange that with all the attention given to defining the responsibilities of international organization for the initiation, organization, and conduct of collective measures against aggression, the procedures necessary to terminate them had been so little thought about. Korea demonstrated the seriousness of this omission in the design of a collective security system.

Chapter 5

Regional Organization for Security

Security-minded governments have never really put their faith in global systems of collective security. Despite professions of support for the League of Nations and the United Nations, they have continued to concoct defense alliances with states sharing common fears of specific enemies. Some of these alliances of expedience, however, are now considered to have introduced a new, more promising approach to security by establishing commitments and procedures for mutual defense on a regional basis.

Commonly, the term regional has a geographical connotation, and the so-called regional defense pacts presume that the basis of association is location of the member states in the same geographical area. This is held to produce a keen joint interest in preserving peace and security within that area and to provide a sound strategic base for the organization.

In fact, political, rather than geographical, ties have determined most groupings. The "regional" security organizations encompass states widely scattered over the globe. Some groups, paradoxically, do not include states that are geographically at the heart of the region. Consequently, these arrangements are more aptly described as instruments for selective, rather than regional, security. They may unite any combination of states in "collective self-defense," regardless of geographic location. The essence of the approach is that a *segment* of the world organizes its own security system outside the system for universal security that the United Nations was expected to become.[1]

Whether these defense pacts are corollary to the broad evolution of international regionalism in the mid-twentieth century is not yet clear, but in several instances, they appear to complement other, nonmilitary aspects of

---

[1] This distinction is made effectively by Inis L. Claude, Jr. See his *Swords Into Plowshares* (3rd ed.; New York: Random House, 1964), pp. 225–27.

association among groups of states that think of themselves as cohabitants of a region. Common cultural traditions, similar political ideologies, and interdependent economic interests have linked American republics, members of the Commonwealth of Nations, Western European countries, and some Arab and African nations. In the Soviet orbit, Communist political control has produced a kind of political community which undergirds their security system. On the other hand, some major security pacts, such as the Atlantic Alliance, have not been built upon a foundation of previously existing regional ties. This lack has so disturbed proponents that they have deliberately sought to stimulate consciousness of mutual interests in an Atlantic community in order to create regional foundations for the alliance where none existed before. Overall, the relationship between genuine regionalism—that is, some kind of persistent cultural, economic, or political affinity among peoples—and the purportedly regional security pacts seems to have been largely fortuitous. Defense partners may, or may not, have had much to do with each other in other respects.

The basis of the collective mutual defense pacts is really not regional at all—either geographically or otherwise. What matters is that certain governments accept the need of one another's assistance in their own struggles for security. This means they recognize a common menace—usually a specific enemy but sometimes (as in the American republics) a more general threat from sources outside the group, or even within the group. They recognize, too, their impotence in the short or long run to cope with the threat single-handedly. So they seek the assurance of united action. Each envisages essentially the same problem: an insufficiency of power to insure its defense against those it fears. Each aspires to the same solution: an alliance of the fearful sufficiently strong to ward off intruders from their respective premises.

This is the core of the so-called regional security pact, a simple alliance of expedience, promising (sometimes with reservations) military or other forms of support if any of the allies is attacked. Unlike most alliances in the past, however, these pacts have rapidly given rise to new international institutions—treaty organizations with highly developed procedures of international collaboration to implement the commitments, and in the case of NATO an integrated international military command structure. These innovations in the system of alliances have resulted especially from the anticipatory character of the pacts. They have stressed joint action before, rather than only in the event of, attack. They have, therefore, entailed ongoing consultation and planning, and in most cases a program of mutual aid in strengthening one another's defenses. In the name of mutual security, the allies have exchanged resources, mapped common defense strategy, and coordinated policy—at least toward the common enemy.

Yet, they have not, in any of these arrangements, made a fundamental surrender of sovereignty. Each state has retained the ultimate power of decision, and usually the organizations have operated on the basis of unanimous consent concerning day-to-day decisions as well. The organizations are definitely international, not supranational. Even the most highly integrated programs (such as NATO's joint military command) remain at all times subject to control by the national governments rather than by a common authority.[2]

A vital function of the regional security organizations is to keep peace within the family. Effectiveness in organizing joint defenses against an external enemy presumes unity among allies. Somehow, the organization must compose conflicts of interest, or keep them in check so that they will not block achievement of the central purpose. The members uniformly undertake commitments to settle controversies with one another by peaceful means, and they have generally agreed that the organization should take a hand in the process whenever the situation becomes serious. The Organization of American States has devised elaborate facilities to assist in the settlement of intraregional disputes. Others have left the matter to be handled informally.

In many ways, regional organization of security has aped the collective security system whose failings it was designed to overcome. Both approaches depend on the organization of collective power by mutual assistance among states to deter aggression and insure security. Both approaches presume this can be accomplished without sharp limitations of the prerogatives of sovereignty, and both expect voluntary commitments by national governments will produce the necessary amalgam of power to ward off threats to the peace. Both demand peace among their members as a prerequisite for effective functioning of the security system.

On the other hand, there are three clear and fundamental differences. The regional group concentrates on a particular target; it assumes it knows in advance where the principal threat to security will originate. In this regard, regional organization for security is grounded on a devil theory of war. By contrast, the collective security system anticipates that any state may break the peace and that action to enforce peace must, therefore, be able to veer freely to meet challenges to the international order from any quarter.

The second difference is the obvious one that the regional organization calls for much more limited commitments—more limited in number of states to whom assistance is pledged and in contingencies in which each is obligated to act. Collective security demands a blanket commitment to protect peace everywhere, for everyone, against anyone.

This reflects a third difference in diagnosis of the "epidemic" character of war and aggression. The regional pacts presume that breaches of peace can be effectively localized so that war erupting outside the regional area need not

---

[2] The Organization of American States has authority to impose nonmilitary sanctions by a two-thirds vote. See below, p. 132.

spread to involve those inside. They expect that the region, by its consolidation, can be largely sealed off from the impact of international controversy even though some members may individually have major interests in other parts of the globe. Collective security is based on the premise that the day of isolation is gone for regions as well as for separate nations. No area can be made safe, apart from assuring the security of every state in the world, for peace and war alike are indivisible in the contemporary international environment.

In the present mood of international diplomacy, dominated by uncompromising struggle between Communist and Western worlds, the regional approach has taken precedence. Ironically, the turn to regionalism in the security field occurred primarily in response to this global confrontation of rival political and ideological systems. Of the principal multipartite security pacts in effect since World War II, all except the Arab League and the recently established Organization of African Unity have been aligned on one side or the other. On the free world side, they have been interlocked by overlapping memberships, with the U.S. holding the guide reins. Even associations that antedated the onset of full-blown conflict, like the Organization of American States, have revamped their security provisions with a view to fitting into place in the composite jigsaw pattern of cold war relationships. The regional pacts grew in significance and substance as the world struggle became more intense. They have lost momentum when the conflict has eased off. Regional organization for security is thus basically a creature of world insecurity, and its evolution belies its premise that the problem of defending one group of states is separable from the problem of preserving peace throughout the international community.

The results of these efforts are inconclusive. On the surface, the security of those associated in regional pacts has so far remained unimpaired, and some comfortably assume that this has come about because their mutual security ties have frightened off aggressors. No member has been exposed to direct attack, and subversion organized from without has not overthrown an established government. On the other hand, these states had similar good fortune before they fashioned their organizations, though confronted with much the same potential challenges. Meanwhile, the many neutralist states that have remained outside all regional groupings have also survived. Furthermore, the intensified political warfare and stepped-up rearmament to which the rival blocs have goaded each other have done nothing to calm the general international atmosphere or to encourage an enduring security—for them or for anyone else. There is also some evidence that the lure of regional collective self-defense had diverted support from, and perhaps even blocked, United Nations efforts to keep the peace.

In terms of their capacity to maintain themselves and grow into firm, well-knit international bodies, the regional security organizations have had mixed experiences. All have had to contend with strong centrifugal pressures which continually threaten to pull them apart: conflicts of interest with one another, basic cultural and political divergences, strong introverted domestic forces in some nations, traditional habits of independent action of sovereign states, and the wear and tear—the costs and sacrifices—entailed by effective cooperative endeavor.

If one looks behind the window dressing put on for public appearance, most regional security ties seem very flimsy. The more specific and formal the commitments, the greater the amount of time spent in adjusting and compromising serious cleavages among partners and in trying to hold the team together. The capacity to make these adjustments has sometimes been acclaimed as a sign of vitality.[3]

But in most cases, adjustment has had the effect of loosening, rather than strengthening, the ties. The associates have agreed to do less with and for one another, rather than more. Only on terms of attenuated commitments have they been able to perpetuate the institutional form of the association. (The process of attrition has often started with demands by some members for much greater assistance from one or more of the others as the price for their continued participation—a kind of poor cousin's blackmail against the scions of the family. If the invitation is rejected, as it usually is, accommodation to a lower level of contributions ensues. This perpetual tug-of-war over each one's share of the burdens of association is probably the most insidious of the disruptive influences.)

NATO, after 15 years, looks as though it may prove an exception. It has survived some extraordinarily grave internal crises. Though it has not realized the full range of its objectives in collective self-defense, it has steadily extended the scope of joint operations—political and economic as well as military. The continuity of these common efforts and the growth of common institutional mechanisms to direct them have given NATO a bureaucratic foundation that the other associations have lacked. In addition to many officials who have regular ongoing NATO responsibilities, the individual governments are now infiltrated with NATO-conditioned personnel at all levels. Officialdom's orientation toward NATO is not yet matched by a deep or widespread loyalty or consciousness of unity among the populations, but, given persistent government support, NATO might acquire the broader base. In this connection, the closeness of political and cultural traditions among a core of the nations composing NATO should reinforce deliberate governmental policy.

NATO's comparative success does not indicate that its experience is generally duplicable. It started with the great advantage of a foundation of close mutual interest and support in many relations among most of its initial members. It had an exceptional undergirding quite outside the security field;

---

[3] See, for instance, the analysis by Ernst B. Haas in "Regional Integration and National Policy," *International Conciliation*, No. 513 (May, 1957).

its participants had already worked their way out of the postwar economic chaos by means of unprecedented economic collaboration through the European Recovery Program. A group of these states was already working toward closer economic integration in Western Europe. There was in being a nucleus of military collaboration in the arrangements made by Britain, France, and the Low Countries for their permanent joint defense, with an eye originally on Germany but equally applicable to other threats such as that from Russia. NATO's base of regional interest was therefore not completely artificial. Furthermore, it was uncontaminated by vestiges of local resentment against former colonial overlords, a bane of some of the other security combinations. Undoubtedly, the Soviet leadership must also be credited with a powerful indirect assist by its singularly inept diplomacy which continually reinforced the Western coalition's worst fears of Communist aggressive intentions. Finally, NATO was blessed with exceptionally brilliant leadership at the infancy of its organizational life: Eisenhower was its first joint military commander and Lord Ismay first Secretary-General of the Permanent Organization, backed by an able supporting staff that gave prestige to the enterprise and forged the pivotal centralized institutions and processes through which the various national governments were drawn together continuously in policy-making and joint operations.

The conclusion that seems most justified on the basis of experience is that regional organization directed at the protection of security matures only in exceptional circumstances and when it coincides with other movements toward regional integration. Even then, its deterrent effect must be discounted by the provocative impact such organizations frequently produce on those outside the region. Normally, the regional approach to security suffers from the disadvantage of the collective security system in that it does not bind states to reliable commitments of mutual assistance, and it does not have the comprehensive perspective of collective security (which at least attempts to get at all threats to the peace, in whatever part of the world they originate, in time to prevent their endangering the general security).

THE AREA OF DEFENSE

Ten multipartite pacts form the main patterns of regional security organization. At least 92 countries have joined one or more of the pacts, stretching the network to cover part or all of the five continents.

As can be seen from the following membership list, they vary greatly in comprehensiveness: the Organization of American States includes the 20 Latin-American republics and the United States; the Organization of African Unity has 32 members; but ANZUS has only three in the association (Australia, New Zealand, the United States). This naturally affects both the breadth and complexity of the commitments.

PRINCIPAL REGIONAL ORGANIZATIONS WITH MUTUAL SECURITY COMMITMENTS
(as of July 1, 1964)

ANZUS Pact

Australia
New Zealand
United States

Arab League

Algeria	Saudi Arabia
Iraq	Sudan
Jordan	Syria
Kuwait	Tunisia
Lebanon	United Arab Republic
Libya	Yemen
Morocco	

Central Treaty Organization (CENTO [formerly Baghdad Pact])

Iran	(Iraq)[3]
Pakistan	(U.S.)[1]
Turkey	
United Kingdom	

Commonwealth of Nations

Australia	Nigeria
Canada	Pakistan
Ceylon	Sierra Leone
Cyprus	Tanzania
Ghana	Trinidad and Tobago
India	Uganda
Jamaica	United Kingdom (including colonies
Kenya	and dependencies)
Malaysia	(Union of South Africa)[3]
New Zealand	

North Atlantic Treaty Organization (NATO)

Belgium	Netherlands
Canada	Norway
Denmark	Portugal
France	Turkey
Greece	United Kingdom
Iceland	United States
Italy	West Germany
Luxembourg	

---

[1] Associate member or observer.   [2] Nonmember covered by security guarantee.
[3] Former member (withdrawn or expelled).   [4] Member whose government has been expelled.

PRINCIPAL REGIONAL ORGANIZATIONS WITH MUTUAL SECURITY COMMITMENTS
(Continued)

Organization of African Unity (OAU)

Algeria	Madagascar	Upper Volta
Burundi	Mali	
Cameroun	Mauritania	
Central African Republic	Morocco	
Chad	Niger	
Congo (Brazzaville)	Nigeria	
Congo (Léopoldville)	Rwanda	
Dahomey	Senegal	
Ethiopia	Sierra Leone	
Gabon	Somalia	
Ghana	Sudan	
Guinea	Tanzania	
Ivory Coast	Togo	
Kenya	Tunisia	
Liberia	Uganda	
Libya	United Arab Republic	

Organization of American States (OAS)

Argentina	Mexico
Brazil	Nicaragua
Chile	Panama
Colombia	Paraguay
Costa Rica	Peru
Dominican Republic	Venezuela
Ecuador	United States
El Salvador	Uruguay
Guatemala	(Bolivia)[3]
Haiti	(Cuba)[4]
Honduras	

Southeast Asian Treaty Organization (SEATO)

Australia	Philippines
France	Thailand
New Zealand	United Kingdom
Pakistan	United States
	(Cambodia)[2]
	(Laos)[2]

Warsaw Treaty Organization (WTO)

Bulgaria	Poland
Czechoslovakia	Romania
East Germany	U.S.S.R.
Hungary	(Albania)[3]
	(China)[1]

---

[1] Associate member or observer.   [2] Nonmember covered by security guarantee.
[3] Former member (withdrawn or expelled).   [4] Member whose government has been expelled.

Western European Union (WEU)

Belgium	Italy
France	Luxembourg
Holland	United Kingdom
	West Germany

Typically, these regional associations define a precise area for mutual defense. The territory of member states is the heart of the zone. But because intercommunication among them is held vital to their successful defense (and in deference to the regional myth), the geographical limits of the commitments are usually set so as to enclose an entire contiguous zone, including marine and land space, stretching around and between frontiers of the allies. Within this area, an attack on anything belonging to the members is to be considered, according to the standard formula, "an attack on all." Conversely, the pacts do not obligate members to support one another in actions occurring outside the prescribed confines.

Charts of the regional defense areas convey a misleading impression of geographic unity and strategic defensibility. Within the far-flung perimeters, formidable physical obstacles deny close and 'tight communication among all members, even in the air age. Sometimes, the zones are cut up by states that have chosen to remain outside the pacts—as, for instance, India, Burma, Indonesia, and others in the Southeast Asian area; Sweden, Switzerland, and Yugoslavia in the North Atlantic area.

The truth is that the zones, for all their geographical specificity, have been laid out primarily to accord with political rather than strategic demands. Politics has affected both that excluded from the defense area and that included. From this standpoint, the pacts represent a compromise between an interest in having the widest possible participation of states that sense a common threat and a reluctance of states to become involved in the defense of others where it does not seem vital to their own security. In the formation and evolution of most of the pacts there have been strenuous continuing pulls in opposite directions: to *constrict* the defense area so as to increase its defensibility by strengthening the intimacy of accord among the allies, and to *expand* the area so as to increase the numbers of defenders and simultaneously widen the horizons of protection.

Expanding the NATO Club

This problem confronted NATO sharply at four stages of its development. When the defense area was first being defined in 1949, the question was what to do about the colonies and other overseas territories of France, Britain, and several other key members of the association. Were these to be mutually defended just as the home territories? The other proposed members, including the United States, indicated they had no enthusiasm for such globe-encircling commitments, including, at the time, the onerous assignment of helping France keep control of Indochina. The colonial powers did not press the point, but France insisted on placing Algeria within the North Atlantic area. They accepted the regionalist premise that action should and could be restricted to a relatively contiguous area whose defense everyone would feel vital to his own security, even though this meant they must provide on their own for the defense of those possessions orphaned by the regional association.

Spain's position posed an especially acute issue for NATO, pitting strategic against political considerations. Strategically, its inclusion would surely have strengthened the organization, and many American military and political leaders have pressed repeatedly for its membership. Politically, Franco's unregenerate totalitarian government was too indigestible for a group of nations that identified themselves as the core of the free world and professed a common dedication to "principles of democracy, individual liberty and the rule of law". (See the Preamble of the North Atlantic Treaty.) They stretched the point to include Portugal, with its mild personal dictatorship. Spain, they felt, would make too blatant a contradiction.

The situation was reversed in regard to Greece and Turkey. They were originally left out of the organization because their extreme eastern Mediterranean location placed them beyond a seemingly reasonable strategic definition of the North Atlantic; indeed, facing directly on the frontiers of the Soviet Union and its satellites, they were far more highly exposed from the standpoint of conventional defense strategy than were the Western countries. Including them meant adding considerably to the common gamble—more than could be gained by having Greek and Turkish troops at NATO's disposal. Nevertheless, key NATO members, such as the U.S. and Britain, were eager to keep Greece and Turkey thoroughly committed to a Western alignment. They pressed the other members to admit the two on essentially political grounds: give them the prestige of first-class citizenship in the main anti-Communist alliance, with a voice in its councils, instead of continuing them as only Anglo-American protégés. NATO membership, extended in 1952, was, in effect, a reward for firm political resistance to Communism and for military support the two countries gave to the defense of South Korea—on the other side of the globe from the Atlantic!

NATO's most acute crisis over extent of its defense area was precipitated by the U.S. demand for inclusion of Western Germany. Here, strategic considerations ran headlong into the most strenuous political objections and ultimately won out. The U.S., supported by the judgment of NATO's military staff, urged that only by rearming Germany and adding a substantial number of German divisions to the available NATO forces could the organization hope to set up an effective shield against a Soviet attack.

The U.S. contended, too, that German participation would permit a "forward strategy" to confront Soviet forces as far east in Europe as possible, with a view, hopefully, to absorbing the brunt of an attack in Germany before it reached the lands of the charter NATO members. To the U.S. government, the problem and the solution were obvious and urgent, especially against the ominous background of the Korean war in which almost all U.S. forces were committed.

But recreating the German army was a disturbing prospect to countries liberated from German occupation for only a half-dozen years. In their new fear of Russia, they could not dissolve their profound memories of Germany as a three-time aggressor, nor dispel a suspicion that the urge might return if the means were at hand.

Repercussions in Germany were almost as intense. Widespread opposition developed on many counts, but above all to auctioning a German conscript army for the privilege of serving as the main battlefield in a Soviet–NATO set-to. Chancellor Adenauer, however, agreed to go along in return for two formidable political payoffs—unequivocal recognition of German sovereignty (ending occupational status) and full equality in any defense arrangements involving German participation (implying membership with full standing in NATO).

After a frenetic search for a formula to reconcile these mutual fears and divergent aspirations (including the ill-fated European Defense Community that proposed a completely integrated European army under supranational control), an intricate arrangement was devised to bring Germany into NATO. But to control its rearmament through the Western European Union, the arrangements for joint defense *against* Germany made by Britain with France and the Low Countries in the 1948 Brussels Treaty were revised.

The character of these commitments will be analyzed in more detail later. What is significant here is that NATO could not be extended to include a potentially powerful and strong-willed country like Germany until internal safeguards were devised to satisfy the most fearful members. The minimum needed to satisfy France under the given conditions included: (1) verbal plus tangible guarantees by the other associates to guard against German attack, (2) arms control under mutual agreement but collectively supervised, (3) retention of independent national military establishments. The French rejected the European Defense Community because they did not want to lose their own military identity; they chose, rather, to live with a separate national German army, hopefully restricted by international agreement so that it would never threaten the NATO allies.

The Sacred Hemisphere

Defining the defense areas of other regional organizations has posed fewer issues than NATO, but has been just as political. The oldest association—the Organization of American States—developed around the idea of keeping the 21 independent American republics free from intervention not only by powers outside but also those within the two continents (at the insistence of the Latin-American states, with eyes focused on the U.S.).[4] The limits of the defense area have been set by what these republics consider their vital political concern. They have boldly encircled the Western hemisphere from the North to the South Pole, and far out into the Atlantic and the Pacific. In this inner zone, they decree, armed attack on any will be considered an attack on all, calling for immediate measures of mutual assistance. In addition, they agree that any fact or situation outside this area which might endanger the peace of America calls for joint consultation on measures of common defense.

Technically, territories within this vast region that do not belong to the 21 republics are not covered by the defense pact. Canada, though intimately linked with the U.S. in mutual defense arrangements, is not a member of the Organization of American States nor a signatory of the defense pact, nominally because of her closer extra-American associations with Britain in the Commonwealth of Nations. The present and formerly dependent territories of Britain, France, and Holland in the American hemisphere are also outside the formally guaranteed defense area. But the Inter-American association has made clear that any alteration in the status of such territories is a matter of concern to them and will be resisted, especially if brought about by force. (This stand antedated conclusion of the formal Inter-American defense pact—the 1947 Rio de Janeiro Treaty of Reciprocal Assistance—having been precipitated by the Nazi conquests of Holland and France in the second world war.) Obviously, these arrangements do not reflect a matured strategic concept of a defensible region but, rather, a reaffirmation with geographical precision of the traditional hands-off-the-western-hemisphere expressed in

---

[4] The inter-American system is based on a series of interlocking pacts concluded over a considerable period of time and involving far more than security and defense commitments. The principal relevant treaties are the Act of Chapultepec (signed at Mexico City, 1945), the Inter-American Treaty of Reciprocal Assistance (Rio de Janeiro, 1947), the Pact of Bogota, concluded in 1948, and the Charter of the Organization of American States, adopted at the same time. For a concise summary of the evolution of the system, see Covey Oliver, *The Inter-American System and the Cuban Crisis:* The Third Hammarskjöld Forum (Dobbs Ferry, N.Y.: Oceana Publications, Inc., 1964), pp. 4–14. For comprehensive treatment, see Charles G. Fenwick, *The Organization of American States* (Washington, D.C.: Pan American Union, 1963); also, John Lloyd Mecham, *The United States and Inter-American Security, 1889–1960* (Austin, Tex.: University of Texas Press, 1961); and Ann van Weynen Thomas and A. J. Thomas, Jr., *The Organization of American States* (Dallas, Tex.: Southern Methodist University Press, 1962).

the United States' Monroe Doctrine and successive noninterventionist declarations of the whole body of American republics.

Plugging the Gaps in the Free World Security System

The SEATO Hodgepodge. The Southeast Asia Treaty Organization's intricately contrived defense zone takes account of the many political reservations encountered. Within the treaty area's wide perimeter, from the western borders of Pakistan to the Philippines, armed attack on, or threats to territory or independence of, the parties would be considered a common danger. But the area is so drawn as to exclude the home territories of some of the principal members—the U.S., Britain, France—and also some of their possessions in spots particularly vulnerable to Chinese Communist attack, like Hongkong. The Asian members had no mind to take on even the most modest commitments to help the outside sponsors when the risk was not closely related to their own security. SEATO is the one regional security organization that does not cover the areas most vital to all participants. It is largely a vehicle for one-way guarantees *to* the region from the outside, rather than a truly mutual and reciprocal relationship among the members. This same reluctance to become embroiled in faraway and unduly provocative conflict accounts for carving the area south of Formosa. In this case, few members inside or outside the region wanted to defend the Chinese Nationalist government.

SEATO's problem was further complicated by a refusal to join from several key states lying squarely within the region. Some, like India and Indonesia, were in basic policy firmly opposed to an alignment in the cold war. Others, such as newly formed Laos and Cambodia, were so exposed that they dared not join. South Vietnam's future was in a state of suspension (the Geneva agreements ending hostilities in Indochina had provided for elections to determine its unification with the Communist-held North). SEATO could hardly force mutual defense commitments on unwilling countries. Yet, their noncooperation meant not only that the whole defense area was badly cut up, but also that territories most vulnerable to Communist pressure and crucial to the defense of key SEATO members, such as Thailand, could not be directly supported and readied for firm defense as part of the collective operation. Therefore, SEATO provided that the organization itself by unanimous agreement might designate states or territories outside SEATO as beneficiaries of its protection, without their joining the association. SEATO thus laid out a kind of no-man's-land and publicly declared it would be prepared to meet security threats therein, even though countries made no prior commitment in return. Deferring to widespread Asian suspicions of Western imperialism, SEATO pledged defense of these territories only at each government's invitation or with its consent. In practice, SEATO has adopted this position of standby guarantor toward the three non-Communist legacies of the French withdrawal from Indochina—Laos, Cambodia, and South Vietnam. (But Cambodia seems to have rebuffed the offer.)

These arrangements obviously were makeshift, pending, SEATO members hoped, the growing attraction of the organization to others and the rounding out of its defense area to include the whole of Southeast Asia. But SEATO's open invitation to all Southeast Asia "to share its benefits and responsibilities" has gone unanswered, and it has had to continue its role of unrequited protector. The SEATO Council rather plaintively observed in 1957:

It was hoped that as time passed and the value of SEATO became more widely appreciated that those who criticized it today would eventually be willing to welcome it. . . . Council members wish to stress that it was genuine concern for the security of the area which led to their voluntary association in SEATO; all nations of the area whether members of SEATO or not, are benefiting from the protection provided by SEATO's collective deterrent strength.[5]

ANZUS and CENTO.   The two remaining free world security pacts— ANZUS and Baghdad—rely, like SEATO, on commitments by outside powers to defend the countries inside the treaty area. In ANZUS, the U.S. took on the defense of Australia and New Zealand; in the Baghdad, Britain promised to protect Iraq, Turkey, Iran, and Pakistan—the so-called "southern tier" in the global circle around the Communist world. In each case, the relationship has raised delicate questions concerning the respective roles of the U.S. and Britain in areas where they have no substantial territorial stake and where each has had a strong political interest. The U.S., responding to the desire of Australia and New Zealand for closer and more formal defense ties, set up a threesome that elbowed Britain out of any say in the relationship, despite the traditional intimate association in the Commonwealth of Nations. The U.S., in effect, took over defense of a section of the Commonwealth—of which it is not member—neither asking consent from, nor even consulting, the principal member. The British were gentlemanly, but frankly miffed.

The Middle East situation was almost the reverse. The U.S. strongly pressed for organization of the southern tier, persuaded the British and the others to take on the necessary mutual commitments, but then stayed out itself. All Baghdad Pact members repeatedly urged the U.S. to come in, but domestic political reservations limited its role to benevolent observer. Understandably, the members felt left out on a limb, especially when the Soviet Union stepped up its political pressures.

The Baghdad arrangement was further complicated by a revolution in Iraq, taking that country out of the alignment and forcing a restructuring and rechristening of the association. Now known as the Central Treaty Organization, it includes only charter members Britain, Turkey, Iran, and Pakistan, with the U.S. as a paying sponsor.

---

[5] SEATO Council of Ministers Communique, Canberra, March 13, 1957.

The Communist Orbit

The Warsaw Pact's defense region neatly coincides with the Soviet span of political control. Yugoslavia lies outside—by its own determined volition. All other European Communist-controlled states are included—even Albania, geographically separated though it is. The multilateral treaty among nominally sovereign states is but an expression of the Soviet's political–military organization in what it views as its own "security zone."

Arab Affinities

The Arab League has not indulged in geographical acrobatics in defining its defense areas. It has simply accepted members' territories as objects of collective defense; membership is open to "every Independent Arab State."

This did not settle Palestine's status, however. An implicit League objective has been to secure independence for Palestine as an Arab state—a political and military objective well beyond the purported scope of the Pact and involving, in the Arab view, prevention and then elimination of Israel. Meanwhile, not being independently governed as an Arab state, Palestine did not belong to the Arab League—a sore point with Palestinian Arabs who felt their interests were not adequately represented through Jordan, Egypt, and the other states where they resided as refugees after Israel was established.

The League has also demonstrated its overriding political character by helping to secure independence for Arab groups in North Africa. It lent moral, propagandistic, and some financial support to the causes of Tunisian, Moroccan, and finally Algerian Nationalist self-determination. Following independence, these states became members of the League. In effect, the League has established a "defense area" as expansive as Arab political aspirations, even though its formal commitments are held to the immediate defense of the member states. This ulterior design completely disregards existing national jurisdictions in favor of an almost mystical concept of cultural and ethnic affinity. It bears, of course, no relationship at all to geostrategic considerations (nor to the actual degree of political cohesion among the Arab states).[6]

African Solidarity

Despite the divergence and often outright conflict of their particular political aspirations, leaders of most independent African states decided in 1963 to form a continent-wide association in the name of Africanism, anticolonialism, and a common interest in achieving a better life. The Organization of African Unity superseded a number of fractional African

---

[6] For a systematic review of the organization of the Arab League, see *Chronique de Politique Étrangère* (Bruxelles), Vol. XII, Nos. 3 and 4 (May–July, 1959).

groupings whose short lives indicated the shallowness or opportunism of the ties on which they were based.[7] But the OAU already has provided practical demonstrations of cooperative action, expressive of a determination by African governments to find African solutions to African problems.

In security, the African states have defined their problem of common defense in terms distinctive of their colonial heritage and present political instability. The Addis Ababa Charter puts forth three sets of commitments unique among regional organizations, in addition to the standard defense of sovereignty, territorial integrity, and independence of each state.

1. The states propose "to eradicate all forms of colonialism from Africa" (Art. II, sec. 1[d]) and dedicate themselves to "the total emancipation of African territories which are still dependent" (Art. III, sec. 6).
2. They express "unreserved condemnation, in all its forms, of political assassination as well as of subversive activities on the part of neighboring States or any other State" (Art. III, sec. 5).
3. They affirm "a policy of non-alignment with regard to all blocs" (Art. III, sec. 7).

Thus, the area they would defend is both geographical and ideological. But the ideological zone is drawn in terms of aspiration for self-determination—"liberation" from colonial domination in any form—rather than in terms of the cold war confrontation of political systems. Indeed, the OAU in committing itself to "non-alignment" seems to assert that these alternative ideological bases are incompatible, and rules that anticolonialism shall be the exclusive test of legitimacy.

The membership reflects these commitments, both in regard to those states included and those left out. According to the charter, "Each independent sovereign African State shall be entitled to become a Member," and all islands surrounding Africa as well as continental states may qualify. But only states that pledge themselves to observe the organization's principles are eligible, so the Union of South Africa and any other states that might practice racial discrimination are excluded.

What, then, is to be defended? The right to be "emancipated" from colonial rule, and the sovereignty and independence of states so emancipated. Conversely, governments that perpetuate the vestiges of colonialism in any form are not only ostracized but are to be eradicated by concerted action in an effort to purge the continent of all "illegitimate" influences.[8]

---

[7] For a review of early attempts at African international organization, see I. William Zartman, "The Sahara—Bridge or Barrier?" *International Conciliation*, No. 541 (January, 1963).

[8] The establishment and early development of the organization of African Unity is described in Boutros Boutros-Ghali, "The Addis Ababa Charter," *International Conciliation*, No. 546 (January, 1964). This publication also includes the text of the Charter. See, also, Norman J. Padelford, "The Organization of African Unity, *International Organization*, Summer, 1964.

The Mystique of British Heritage

In many ways, the firmest and most dependable association of states is the Commonwealth of Nations. Yet, it has no formal mutual security commitments. Nor does it possess any geographical regional unity. Spread over all five continents, members of the Commonwealth are knit only by a common heritage as present or former parts of the British Empire, by a purely nominal declaration of association within the Commonwealth, and by a set of understandings and informal agreements to consult together on matters of common concern. So tenuous are the organizational ties and so dispersed the members that the Commonwealth often is not considered a regional security organization.

Yet, in practice, it has functioned with a high degree of cohesion on many matters, including the rally of material and political support in defense of members' independence and territorial security.

Most remarkable is that this relationship of mutual support has continued between Britain and many of its former colonies and dependencies. Despite their long and arduous struggles for independence from Britain, most have chosen to enter the Commonwealth as full and equal associates with their old overlord.

It should be pointed out that the security understandings are not entirely mutual. Britain sees itself committed to the defense of all the Commonwealth, but some members have made no general commitment, even informally, to come to the defense of each of the others (even of Britain itself!).

Nevertheless, we feel that the Commonwealth's practical cohesion is so significant and its experience so revealing of the bases of an international association of states that it must be included in this analysis.

The Political Basis of Regional Security Commitments

This review of the defense areas of so-called regional organizations—areas in which groups of states declare they have an abiding common security interest—indicates that particular political interests, far more than geographic togetherness, strategic coherence, or even cultural and ideological affinity, determine the basis of a security association and therefore set the practical limits to collective action in defense. The area of defense seems to have little meaning unless it coincides with a bonafide area of political cohesion. Hence, the basis of regional security commitments is as firm or weak, as lasting or momentary, as the strength and continuity of the partners' common political aspirations.

Furthermore, the regionalization of security, as we shall see, must be reconciled with a large degree of national autonomy in control of defense means because the allies are not confident that their common security interests will always coincide with their national interests. In many instances, they feel they must actually guard against the possibility of mutual hostilities (note the continuing fears of Germany within the NATO alliance, and the fallings-out among various OAS members). This means the defense area can extend no farther than the available safeguards *against one another* are judged by the partners sufficient to meet the dangers of mutual hostilities. The defense area is, thus, the resultant of balancing internal suspicions against external fears, modified by whatever political ingenuity can devise to lessen the intensity of the associates' distrust of one another.

THE TIME FOR ACTION

Most regional security organizations are committed to act collectively not only in such strictly military contingenies as outright armed attack but also in numerous other, essentially political, threats, thus reflecting the ideological basis and subversive techniques of contemporary international conflict. Also, the organizations have been intensely preoccupied with preparation for eventualities, which has involved facing political, economic, and diplomatic problems as much as those of military scope.

The Contingency of Armed Attack

Typically, the regional pact's core commitment, anticipating the most formidable danger against which associates will seek protection by making common cause, declares that "armed attack" or "armed aggression" against any in the defense area will be considered an attack against all and will call forth the maximum assistance pledged.[9] This formulation of the contingency is more explicit than parallel provisions of the League and U.N. Most regional organizations have adopted—as the collective security organizations did not—a definite, preset yardstick to determine at least the decisive time for action—military assault.[10]

---

[9] See: Inter-American Treaty of Reciprocal Assistance (Rio de Janeiro, 1947) (cited as Rio Treaty), Art. 3, par. 1; North Atlantic Treaty (Paris, 1949), Art. 5; Southeast Asian Collective Defense Treaty (Manila, 1954) (hereafter cited as SEATO Treaty), Art. 4; Treaty of Friendship, Cooperation and Mutual Assistance (Warsaw, 1955) (cited as Warsaw Pact), Art. 4; Pact of the League of Arab States (Cairo, 1945), Art. 6.

The full texts of these treaties are reproduced in Ruth C. Lawson (ed.), *International Regional Organizations* (New York: Frederick A. Praeger, Inc., 1962).

[10] The contingency is defined in the Warsaw Pact as "armed aggression" and in the SEATO Treaty as "aggression by means of armed attack," but the use of the weasel word "aggression" probably does not greatly alter intent in the provision for joint action.

The Arab League Pact, however, refers more vaguely to "aggression or threat of aggression" as the occasion for action. This leaves the way open for varied interpretations—both narrower and broader than armed attack—presented to the Arab League and the U.N.

The Baghdad (CENTO) Pact is so vague as to leave the whole question of contingencies virtually unsettled. The parties simply agree they "will cooperate for their security and defence. Such measures as they agree to take to give effect to this cooperation may form the subject of special agreements with each other." (Art. 1.)

Except the Arab League, no regional organization has had to confront this extreme contingency. So it is not possible to tell whether such an exact prescription has the effect of increasing the certainty of collective action.

The Arab League so far has been an exercise in futility, at least in the fulfillment of its security commitments. Officially, the Arab states hold that they have been subject to actual and continuous aggression ever since the state of Israel was formed on what they consider Arab territory. Together they have publicly and repeatedly pledged to resist this aggression and to liquidate Israel as a separate state. A special convention adopted in 1950 provided for cooperative measures of common defense. Yet, no collective military action has occurred since the Israelis repelled Arab forces in 1949. For reasons not yet fully known, the League did not function even in the face of direct armed attack on Egypt by Israel, Britain, and France in 1956.

Possibly, the Arab response has been restrained by United Nations interpositions to restore and keep peace. But there is also reason to think that internal particularism and political rivalries within the Arab fraternity have been at work to keep the regional security commitments a dead letter, at least as long as efforts to dislodge Israel would entail an all-out and devastating war.

In a unique position, the Organization of African Unity undertakes to act immediately and continuously to expel those it considers present beneficiaries of former aggressors—namely, colonial or white supremacist governments in Africa. From their standpoint, they are readying themselves to roll back aggression *after* the fact. This puts them in the practical position, in the context of the present moment, of taking the initiative and precipitating attack instead of defining any specific enemy actions as the occasion for collective counteraction.

The Contingency of Apprehended Aggression

Regional security organizations may be distinguished from traditional alliances by their provision for joint defensive preparations in anticipation of aggression. They will not stand idle until an overt act of armed attack has occurred. Parties to most of the pacts agree, as in the North Atlantic Treaty, to undertake "continuous and effective self-help and mutual aid" to "maintain and develop their individual and collective capacity to resist armed attack." These commitments, calling forth by far the most vital collaborative action in the associations, have not depended on any specific occurrence to give them effect. Action has been prompted by a live fear of aggression rather than by an outright act of aggression. The contingency for the most basic regional security undertakings has, therefore, been the allied governments' subjective state of mind. If acutely afraid, they would intensify their collective defense efforts; if they felt reasonably secure and the threat of aggression seemed removed, they would tacitly assume the contingency was not at hand.

It should be emphasized that this is not the formal intent of the pacts. They assume the threat of aggression is constantly present and the commitments for mutual defensive aid must be continuously implemented.

But, in practice, it has not been possible to maintain a consistently intense fear of aggression, even with the most strenuous efforts to demonstrate that the Soviet Union and world Communism on the one side or capitalist imperialism on the other are intrinsically aggressive. Fear has had to feed on aggressive acts or evident threats rather than ideological resupposition. Consequently, the actual contingency for vigorous defensive preparations has tended to be some grave challenge to the existing balance of power: the attack on Korea; the Communist successes in Indochina; Soviet pressures in the Middle East; the recurring crises over Berlin and unification of Germany; Castro's Cuban beachhead for Communist revolution in the Americas; or, from the Soviet standpoint, the Hungarian revolt that threatened to collapse the entire satellite system. Each of these injected new fervor into the respective regional defense operations. Between crises, the efforts lagged.

The Contingency of Indirect Aggression

The pacts differ markedly in attention to defense against subversive activities and other essentially nonmilitary threats. The Inter-American system and SEATO are specifically designed to ring the alarm in such circumstances, and to concert joint measures of counteraction. Whenever the territorial inviolability or integrity, or the sovereignty or political independence, of any member is "affected by an aggression which is not an armed attack or by an extra-continental or intra-continental conflict, or by any other fact or situation that might endanger the peace of America," the Rio Treaty provides for immediate consultation on measures for common defense. SEATO's provision is almost identical. Both organizations by subsequent resolutions and actions[11] have made their concern over indirect aggression even more explicit.

The Organization of African Unity has expressed serious concern over subversion, though it has not laid down specific measures to counter it. It has noted not only actions inspired outside the continent by Communist and anti-Communist forces, but also the machinations of revolutionary groups operating out of one African state against another. The murder of President Olympio of Togo was fresh in the minds of African heads of state when they met in Addis Ababa in May, 1963, to draft and sign the OAU Charter. It affirmed the principle of "non-interference in the internal affairs of States" and unreservedly condemned "in all its forms, . . . political assassination as

---

[11] The vigorous responses of the Organization of American States to subversive activities initiated by the Dominican Republic and by Cuba are reviewed in Chapter 10, pp. 295–96.

In regard to SEATO's actions, see M. Margaret Ball, "SEATO and Subversion," *Political Science* (New Zealand), March, 1959.

well as . . . subversive activities on the part of neighboring States or any other State." (Art. III.)

The North Atlantic Treaty is more general. The parties simply declare they will consult together whenever, in the opinion of any, the territorial integrity, political independence, or security of any one is threatened.

The other regional pacts make virtually no provision for defense against political, in contrast to military, attack. One may suppose the Communist bloc associated in the Warsaw Pact feels rather immune to this kind of threat. Perhaps the same is true of the well-integrated and settled democracies of the West, each regarding itself quite competent to handle this type of challenge on its own. Indirect aggression is a problem peculiar to countries with weak political institutions and under severe economic and social pressures that can be easily channeled into political revolt. So it is natural that such strong emphasis should have been placed on the organization of political security in the Southeast Asia and Latin-American areas.

THE MEANS OF DEFENSE—MUTUAL ASSIST-ANCE BY TALK AND INFRASTRUCTURE

Considering that the regional security pacts were concluded to furnish stronger assurances of mutual defense than were found practicable through the United Nations, their formal commitments of collective support are unusually tenuous.

Against indirect aggression, they promise only mutual consultation concerning measures that might be undertaken. Against armed attack, action is limited by various escape clauses to whatever each state in its own discretion decides to undertake. Regarding preparative action to strengthen one another's capacity to resist attack, the most explicit commitments, in the North Atlantic and Southeast Asian Treaties, are to provide "continuous and effective self-help and mutual aid." In practice, this last provision has been supplemented by a series of corollary mutual security agreements between the U.S. and other members of the anti-Communist alliances, nailing down specific and substantial measures of assistance. These, however, require implementation by annual decisions of the respective legislative authorities, so they do not provide firm, long-term guarantees. The scope and character of assistance has changed drastically from year to year.

NATO has been the only organization able to build on this foundation a defense structure that has the marks of permanence, and even it suffers from frequent reminders that its basic commitments are only as durable as the immediate disposition of the governments to fulfill them.

The Commitment to Consult

Concerning defense against subversion and other forms of indirect aggression, the regional allies make no advance commitment to action, but agree only to consult whenever, in the opinion of any, the territorial integrity, political independence, or security of any is threatened.[12] These provisions are couched in terms (note the expression "in the opinion of any of them") that enable any member to initiate the consultation process, even if it is not the one immediately affected, thus guarding against the possibility that a government under pressure might refrain from publicly charging a neighbor is responsible for subversive activity against it for fear of further embroiling its relations. Another government can spotlight the situation and relieve the threatened country of onus.

These commitments have resulted in successive declarations of solidarity by segments of the anti-Communist coalition, especially SEATO and the OAS, against Communist aims and methods. The declarations have been buttressed on occasion by cooperation in training and equipping police and special forces to suppress subversive and terrorist activities.[13]

The regional organizations have not yet succeeded, however, in finding an approach that would clearly differentiate between defense against indirect aggression from outside a country and repression of bonafide internal political opposition. The problem is immensely complicated, especially in areas of political instability, because those attempting resistance against entrenched governments (of whatever character) seek sympathy and support wherever they can find it, and often turn outside their own borders to organize and develop their revolutionary movement. Thus, foreign governments can become implicated, especially if they tend to sympathize with the rebels, even though the main core of subversion is indigenous.

The problem of defense against Communist subversion, for instance, has become entwined with the question of intervention by associated members in the internal political struggles of their neighbors. This happened in Caracas in 1953, when a revolt against the Venezuelan dictatorship occurred and was bloodily suppressed while the Tenth Conference of American States was drafting a strongly worded resolution against subversive Communist activity. Even though the Caracas Declaration, at Mexican insistence, was drafted so as to relate to dangers originating outside the hemisphere,[14] many partisans of democracy in Latin America took the conference's action as an affront to efforts to unseat dictatorial regimes on the continent. They were particularly incensed over allegations that the outbursts against Latin-American

---

[12] See, for instance, Rio Treaty, Art. 6; North Atlantic Treaty, Art. 4; SEATO Treaty, Art. 4 (2); and the Arab Treaty of Joint Defence, 1950, Art 3. The SEATO Treaty also provides for consultation in the event of threats against designated territories outside the parties' own jurisdiction. See discussion above of the SEATO defense area.

[13] See Ball, *op. cit.*, and Oliver, *op. cit.*

[14] See C. G. Fenwick, "The Tenth Inter-American Conference: Some Issues of Inter-American Regional Law," *American Journal of International Law*, July, 1954.

dictatorships were evidences of Communist intervention, demonstrating the need for hemispheric defense.[15]

The Option to Fight

The regional pacts, except the Western European Union and the Organization of African Unity, do not commit their members to specific measures of mutual defense, even in the event of armed attack. Nor do they, except in the Inter-American system, bind members to accept the organization's decisions in this regard. The North Atlantic Treaty deftly limits the obligations of each party to "such action as it deems necessary." In SEATO, each party agrees that it will act "to meet the common danger in accordance with its constitutional processes."

The Arab League's assurances are more absolute and obligatory in tone. Members "undertake to hasten to the aid of the State or States against whom such an aggression is made, and to take immediately, individually and collectively, all means available including the use of armed force to repel the aggression and restore security and peace." (Article 2 of the Treaty of Joint Defence and Economic Cooperation, June 17, 1950.) But as the League acts only on the basis of unanimity; each state makes its own decision on when and how to implement its pledge. In the one major test case it has faced—the 1956 attack on Egypt—no one came to Egypt's support. This should be interpreted in the light of the Pact's terms, which make decisions binding on members only when they are adopted unanimously. Thus, no one is obliged to act unless he agrees, which is hardly a firm obligation.[16]

The Western European Union spells out specifically the size and characteristics of the common defense contribution expected from members, and also the strength and armament of their internal defense forces. These are the subject of special agreements among the members, supplementing their basic commitment in the Brussels Treaty to afford an attacked state "all military

---

[15] The meaning of the term "intervention" has been widely disputed. The U.S. has customarily held to a definition that connotes only coercive pressure on another *government*. Thus, any action agreeable to the government in power would not constitute intervention. But Latin-American jurisprudence and the prevailing view among less developed countries insists that *any* interference in the political affairs of a country by an outside government is intervention, whether it is pro or anti the regime in power. This explains why the OAS and SEATO antisubversion declarations have been so widely attacked as interventionist in their respective areas, when their sponsors have consistently looked on them as instruments of defense against intervention (having in mind Communist machinations directed from Moscow or Peiping against the governments in office). For a thorough discussion of this issue, see C. Neale Ronning, *Law and Politics in Inter-American Diplomacy* (New York: John Wiley & Sons, Inc., 1963); and Mecham, *op. cit.* Refer also to Chapter 10 below.

[16] The Secretary-General of the League, Mr. Hassouna, has urged that the pact be modified to make majority decisions binding, but his views have yet to be accepted. See *Chronique de Politique Étrangère, op. cit.,* p. 325.

and other aid and assistance in their power."[17] Altogether, the allies declare they have established a "system of mutual automatic assistance in case of attack." Though the system has not been put to a test, quite possibly it can insure an automatic response because of its concrete commitments and the close integration of defense plans and organization it establishes among the members. On the other hand, certain important questions, such as increasing the levels of defense contributions, can be decided only by unanimous consent, and each country retains ultimate control over its own forces. So a substantial margin of discretion is still left to each state. The Union does not contain the built-in guarantees the abortive European Defense Community would have provided through its scrambled international army and thoroughly integrated decision-making structure.

The inter-American system is the one regional organization that can institute defense measures without the consent of all members. The Rio Treaty provides that in the event of an armed attack the "Organ of Consultation" may by a two-thirds vote agree on measures of collective defense that shall be binding on all members, "with the sole exception that no State shall be required to use armed force without its consent." Therefore, organization may require states to break diplomatic or consular relations, and partially or completely cut economic relations and communications. It may also direct military action, though, as noted, subject to individual consent of the states involved. Whether these provisions for peremptory collective action could be effectively implemented—especially if a sizable minority of members were recalcitrant—is still an open question. They were invoked for the first time when the requisite majority of the Organization of American States (acting through the foreign ministers as the Organ of Consultation) resolved on July 26, 1964, to cut off diplomatic relations, sea transportation, and trade with Cuba (foodstuffs and medicines for humanitarian purposes excepted). In due course, the objecting minority fell in lines on the diplomatic sanction (with the notable exception of Mexico), but several have ignored the trade ban.[18]

---

[17] See Treaty of Economic, Social and Cultural Collaboration and Collective Self-Defense (Brussels Treaty, 1948), as amended by Protocols I–IV (the "Paris Accords"), October 23, 1954. Texts are reproduced in Lawson, *op. cit.*, pp. 149–72.

[18] This historic resolution declared that "the acts verified by the investigating committee constitute an aggression and an intervention on the part of the Government of Cuba in the internal affairs of Venezuela, which affects all of the member states," and warned that if Cuba persisted, the members might resort to armed force, individually or collectively.

The Organization of African Unity also acts on substantive questions by a two-thirds majority of its Assembly of Heads of State and Government (simple majority on procedural). But the charter is vague in regard to the obligatory nature of these decisions, and there is no mention of a specific obligation on states to fight or impose sanctions pursuant to decisions of the Assembly of Heads or any other OAU organ.

Strengthening Capabilities for Defense

The major emphasis in regional organizations for security has been placed on measures of mutual assistance designed to help each member strengthen its military capacities prior to attack. The central feature of these arrangements has been cooperation in preparing for the eventuality of attack.

Three assumptions have influenced this approach.

1. Effective defense under modern conditions of warfare requires a far greater state of readiness. Without substantial previous preparation of all the allies collectively, one might be overwhelmed before the others could come to its assistance.

2. Effective mobilization and organization of defensive capabilities may dissuade aggressors from starting an attack. This is the vacuum theory applied to international politics. A strong buildup of collective military force at the weakest points of the alliance would, it is held, "fill the vacuum" and deter those disposed to aggression by making it unprofitable for them. Effective preparation for war probably would thus prevent a test of arms altogether.

3. Intensive mutual assistance prior to actual attack will tend to insure fulfillment of the allies' commitments to help one another. If each is already deeply involved and has invested a considerable amount of its own resources in the defense of the others before an aggressive act occurs, the chances will be less, it is held, that the ally will pull back at the fateful moment. If each is committed not only by words but by "hostages" of men, hardware, or money, its participation in joint defense is just that more assured.

Article 3 of the North Atlantic Treaty is typical of the formal commitments for preparative assistance: "In order more effectively to achieve the objectives of this Treaty, the Parties, separately and jointly, by means of continuous and effective self-help and mutual aid will maintain and develop their individual and collective capacity to resist armed attack." The key concept is expressed in the words "continuous," "mutual aid," and "collective capacity to resist."

There are corresponding provisions in the SEATO Treaty (Art. 2), the Warsaw Pact (Art. 5), and the Baghdad Treaty (Art. 1), the third supplemented by Article 2 of the bilateral agreement of cooperation between the United States and members of the Central Treaty Organization (Turkey, Pakistan, and Iran). The Arab states have also agreed to a common policy of strengthening one another's capacity to wage war. (Art. 4 of the 1950 Arab Treaty of Joint Defence and Economic Cooperation.) While the Brussels Treaty, which forms the basis of the Western European Union, does not contain explicit provision for mutual preparatory assistance, this is implied in its recognition of a tie-in with NATO.

However, the elaborate provisions and mutual commitments of the Organization of American States do not cover arrangements for collective organization of mutual defense, reflecting the deep-seated Latin-American reservations about actions that might imply intervention in their internal affairs. An Inter-American Defense Board has been established by resolution of the foreign ministers, but its activities have been largely consultative. The United States, on a bilateral basis, has furnished military and economic assistance for "defense support" to several Latin-American countries. But the OAS as a whole has not been persuaded to accept responsibility for collective defense preparations. The Arab League also has shied away from any commitment to forge joint defense facilities or to undertake any program of mutual assistance in advance of an actual contingency.

On the other hand, the African states have made a show of organizing direct military as well as nonmilitary action to accomplish the eradication of colonialism. Following a resolution of the heads of state, an OAU Committee of Nine was set up, with headquarters in Dar es Salaam, Tanganyika, to coordinate anticolonial pressures, including aid to African "freedom fighters," an economic boycott, diplomatic sanctions, and creation of volunteer corps "to assist liberation." All 34 members have contributed to the "Freedom Fighters Fund," most of which has gone to support Angolans. Formation of a continental African army is pending.

This army might function beyond the anticolonial struggle to help maintain peace among and order within the African states. A plethora of border disputes, mutinies, and coups d'etat has plagued the new states, and led them to an embarrassing dependence for their security on their former colonial rulers. Some African leaders hope a common army, under OAU control, will obviate this necessity. But problems of composition, command, payment, and occasions for use have not yet been resolved.[19]

It seems clear that many states, especially those not caught up in the whirl of sophisticated military operations, have yet to be convinced of the need for collective *preparation* for defense, however much they may wish to have assurance of help in the event of actual attack. While the interlocking of defensive preparations has become the dominant feature of those regional organizations that wage the world power struggle, it has not caught the fancy of states that feel they may be able to stand on the sidelines. The preparative side of regional security is specifically a consequence of superpower conflict.

The extent of mutual assistance has varied widely, depending in part on how seriously members of the security organizations have felt threatened. The more severe and imminent they perceived the threat to be, the wider the scope and the larger the volume of mutual preparation they were prepared to

---

[19] See *New York Times,* March 3, 1964, p. 11.

undertake. But, characteristically, not all states have agreed in their estimates of the threat, nor have their estimates remained constant. Hence, the scope of mutual assistance, even in NATO, the most highly developed organization, has fluctuated.

The character of mutual assistance has also reflected the organization's particular strategic doctrines. This, too, has been an uncertain and changing element because of the tremendous rate of technological development in the means of warfare. NATO's initial program of assistance, geared to a situation in which the United States' monopoly of nuclear weapons was considered a complete and absolute deterrent, was quickly outdated by Soviet nuclear and missile achievements. The dual sword-and-shield strategy then devised —relying on the concept of *mutual* deterrence in recognition of each side's retaliatory capacity—was thrown into question when people began to wonder whether the nuclear powers would really pay the price of self-annihilation for an ally in limited aggressions by conventional means. Still another strategic dimension was opened up when the development of tactical atomic weapons made tenuous the distinction between the effects of limited conventional war and nuclear warfare, at least for the populations of crowded countries. The point is that development of a rational program of mutual assistance has been bedeviled by the extraordinarily rapid change in the circumstances of defense. With unclear and fleeting knowledge of what the regional security organization must be prepared to do, it has proved extremely difficult to devise a sufficiently stable strategy on which to base long-range defensive preparations.

Typically, assistance has taken the form of military modernization. The most advanced in the security organizations have furnished to their less sophisticated allies a package of weaponry and the training to go with it. The items have varied according to the strategic location of the country receiving them, its expected role in the general defense strategy, and its demonstrated capacity to use the modern tools of warfare effectively. In return, these countries would supply, by compulsory or voluntary recruitment, the contingents of manpower jointly agreed to be needed; bases and other facilities necessary for use of foreign contributions; and, usually, commitment of part of its productive capacity to military requirements. The pattern of mutual assistance has thus tended to reflect the great gap between the modern and traditional, the developed and undeveloped, the advanced and retarded military estate of the partners. The advanced have provided the tools and know-how of modern war; the undeveloped have offered their men and territory.

There have been two important amendments to this formula. The modern partner has never been willing to make available the finest part of his armature or know-how. Neither the United States, nor the Soviet Union, nor Great Britain has been willing to turn over to fellow members the most sophisticated of their military developments—particularly nuclear weapons and know-how, which have been held back for the senior partner's exclusive use. It is true that members have been gradually given access to increasingly sophisticated hardware and technique, but customarily, only after the weapons have, in effect, become conventional and, interestingly enough, after the opposing side—the enemy—has acquired a full arsenal of newer weapons. There seems to be a kind of unwritten agreement that first-class weapons shall be the exclusive property of first-class military powers. Only when all first-class powers have acquired more sophisticated devices will they pass on the fruits of their military technology to second-class powers. As will be seen below, this implicit class distinction within regional security organizations has been a major cause of strain and dissension.

In return, the major powers have had to reassure the lesser of the reliability of their commitments and, in particular, their readiness to fight by placing some of their own manpower either at the disposal of the organization or, at least, so deployed that they would become inescapably involved were any member attacked. For instance, when the United States and Britain were trying to fashion some kind of alternative for the European Defense Community after the French refused to ratify it, they agreed to specific long-term commitments to station their armed forces in Europe as part of the Western European Union Treaty revision. This was apparently a crucial requirement to secure French acceptance of a revived German army to be integrated into NATO. Similarly, the United States has used its commitment of forces to Europe as leverage to strengthen the unity and support of NATO—a demonstration that it was fully prepared to share the cost of blood with its allies. It is significant, however, that all these commitments are revocable. Furthermore, they are unilateral.[20] In other words, the holdback principle has been carefully reserved for use of security organization members whenever they see some overriding interest in doing so. France under de Gaulle, and even before de Gaulle, has on occasions pulled back from NATO some or all of the naval and air force divisions it had assigned to the organization. Perhaps it is not surprising that France has expressed the greatest skepticism about the durability of the U.S. and even British manpower commitment to NATO. But the British themselves stirred doubt when they insisted on withdrawing troops from WEU in 1957 and 1958, albeit with the reluctant assent of SACEUR and the WEU Council.

While placing military forces at the disposal of the common defense has usually been taken as the ultimate in assuring good faith, the action is not without its liabilities, even from the standpoint of the protected state. The presence of foreign troops on one's soil so easily connotes occupation rather

---

[20] See Paris Accords, *op. cit.*, Protocol No. 2 on Forces of Western European Union, Art. 1, par. 3: "The statement of these maxima does not commit any of the high contracting parties to build up or maintain forces at those levels but maintains their right to do so if required."

than protection, and dependence rather than interdependence, that it has often led to serious criticism and political opposition within the countries presumably benefiting from their presence. This has particularly been so where control over men and their bases has been the exclusive prerogative of the foreign power. Consequently, this form of mutual assistance usually suffers an ambivalent response. On the one hand, it is demanded both as a proof of sincerity and for immediate practical strengthening of the country's defenses. On the other, it is protested as an infringement of sovereignty and, in some instances, an actual threat to the security of the small power since it is thereby exposed more immediately to countermeasures from the other side—"The lightning rod attracts the lightning." These elements of local sensitivity have resulted, except in the European confrontation between Soviet and Western power, in limiting manpower assignments to a short-run and emergency basis, as in the American deployment in Thailand during the 1962–63 threat of a Communist takeover in Laos. The Thais, at first, virtually insisted on American involvement to prove that SEATO was worthwhile. When the crisis eased, they became almost equally insistent that the Americans get out promptly.

Actually, in terms of the likely conditions of interregional warfare today (in contrast to local actions between particular smaller states), the significance of forward strategy, involving direct engagement of large bodies of military forces at short range, seems to have greatly diminished. The contribution of manpower commitments rests far more on psychological impact than on military role, and it seems increasingly dubious that psychological reassurance, as in the NATO alliance, will long be sustained by a physical presence of foreign troops, which responsible leaders recognize is contingent from moment to moment on the independent decision of the home government.

The Pattern of Control

This leads immediately to the crucial question of the pattern of control. Regional security organizations have had to decide whether to pool their resources of mutual assistance into an integrated, jointly managed common defense establishment or to keep to the traditional pattern of each country's controlling its own defense resources and facilities. The complexity of modern military operation and the need for intimate human and technological coordination to mount an effective, comprehensive defense program has appeared to master strategists and planners to allow only a completely integrated international or collective approach, extending from the planning and command level to the organization of infrastructure and standardization of production. This was attempted in the European Defense Community, the Western European Union, the Warsaw Pact arrangement, and in NATO, each with a somewhat different pattern. But the tug of national independence has kept these organizations from achieving anything like full international integration defense means and management, while the other regional associations have been kept quite deliberately loose and voluntaristic, deferring completely to the principle of national sovereignty.[21]

EDC—Abortive Supranationalism.   What was proposed for the European Defense Community was a full supranational organization to direct and control an integrated European army, merging German military units with French, Italian, Dutch, Belgian, and Luxembourgian. The pattern of control was modeled on the European Coal and Steel Community, with a supranational commissariat responsible to an international parliamentary assembly. The single European army would operate within the framework of NATO as the principal European contribution to the defense of the North Atlantic area, but none of the six participating governments would have had a separate say in the organization and management of the European army per se. The intention was to so scramble the armed forces and arms production of the six countries that it would be virtually impossible for any one of them to act independently in defense of its home territory.[22] French initiative produced this radical plan, ingeniously contrived to permit German rearmament but insure that it would never again be used to threaten its Western neighbors. For German troops and German arms would be continuously and permanently and completely under joint control of all the partners. But in the end, reservations about entrusting control over their own capabilities for defense to supranational hands were held by enough Frenchmen to defeat ratification of the project in the French Assembly. Thus, the one attempt to fashion a truly integrated supranational security establishment never had a chance to be tested.

Western Union—Intergovernmental Check and Balance.   In its place, the strange and complex patchwork of the Western European Union was fashioned, largely by British initiative.[23] Western European Union emphasis has been on control of armed forces and arms production rather than on their direction and development. The approach has been to subject to international observation and decision the maintenance of maximum levels

---

[21] Typical of the extreme voluntarist pattern is the Arab League, whose council (the general policy organ), permanent military committee, council of defense (consisting of the various countries' defense and foreign ministers), and permanent secretariat have no powers of decision or action independent of the decisions of the individual national governments.

[22] There was some allowance for separate action, especially by France, in overseas territories and colonies.

[23] British reluctance to join the European Defense Community was widely criticized as one of the factors that led to French rejection. Some French leaders apparently felt that British participation was essential to offset the very great influence the Germans were expected to acquire because of the weight of their military contributions. For their part, the British were profoundly reserved about surrendering control over a major segment of their defense to an organization in which they would only have a partial say.

of forces and categories of armaments. While these measures were primarily to limit the independent discretion of Germany in rearmament, the agreement to allow international inspection and to subject to international decision changes in agreed levels of arms and forces has also been applied in many respects to other WEU members. The Council of the Western European Union, set up by the governments and representing them directly, is authorized to make the critical decisions. It is advised by an Agency for the Control of Armaments which scrutinizes national data and conducts inspections of production installations. Voting procedures have been designed to subject to the approval of all members any fundamental revision in the limits on levels of forces, but to allow the majority to decide the level of stocks each may maintain on the mainland of Europe (except for Germany, committed by the agreement not to manufacture any atomic, chemical, or biological weapons; long-range missiles; war ships; and strategic aircraft).

A unique feature of the Western European Union is its Assembly. Consisting of parliamentary representatives of the WEU states who act and vote as individuals rather than as representatives of their governments, the Assembly has come to play a role more significant than its constitutional powers of consultation and recommendation would have made likely. While the Council is the only organ with the power of decision, the Assembly has taken on itself the task of maintaining a Western European perspective toward defense, even challenging Council action when it seems to have reflected national, rather than international, concerns. With no real authority, the Assembly has exerted growing influence on a common defense policy, standardization of arms, joint production, and equitable distribution of costs. It has been a principal force in urging Western European states to harmonize their defense policies with NATO and to view their national and European interests within the broader framework of the "Atlantic community." Perhaps its most significant supranational influence has been the Assembly's review of Council reports and its practice of questioning the Council of Ministers on their action and inaction. In effect, the Assembly has been able to institute the interpolation common to continental parliamentary institutions and corresponding to the British parliamentary question period. Members of the Council have been induced to meet regularly with the assembly and to respond to written and oral questions posed by assembly members.[24]

One should recognize, however, that this is a pattern vastly different from the one envisaged in the European Defense Community. This is an intergovernmental arrangement, not a supranational one, no matter how much supranational perspective may be emphasized by the Assembly. Western

[24] See Ernst B. Haas and Peter H. Merkl, "Parliamentarians Against Ministers: The Case of Western European Union," *International Organization,* Vol. 14, No. 1 (Winter, 1960). Also see, Ruth B. Lawson, *International Regional Organizations* (New York: Frederick A. Praeger, Inc., 1962), pp. 150–54.

European Union responsibilities are fundamentally limited to control and limitation, rather than direction and management, of armament. Nevertheless, in the organization's evolution it is true that its important control functions have enabled it also to play at least an indirect part in management and direction, partly because all participating countries have become preoccupied with increasing rather than limiting their separate and joint defense capacities. They have been more concerned with getting one another to undertake larger defense responsibilities than with preventing anyone from exceeding the levels prescribed in the WEU protocol. They have been "inflation minded" in the defense field, so the WEU has performed the unexpected function of prodder and guide rather than brake or censor. Furthermore, WEU has always operated on the assumption that the major responsibilities for international direction and control of joint defense would be carried by NATO. There is, then, a kind of agreed division of labor that has made unnecessary a strictly European counterpart to NATO's command structure.

Warsaw Pact—Centralized Separation. The Warsaw Pact has achieved a major degree of integrated control over the entire spectrum of military organization, strategy, deployment, equipment, and production. But its approach has been pivoted around the single, centralized national authority of the Soviet Union, in contrast to the Western European attempt at truly mutual international organization. Although the pact provided for establishment of a "Unified Command to which certain elements of their armed forces shall be allocated by agreement between the Parties and which shall act in accordance with jointly established principles" (Art. 5), a Russian commander-in-chief and a Moscow command headquarters direct the disposition and training of Warsaw Pact forces.[25]

There is, to be sure, a political consultative committee, with a secretariat and standing committee for foreign policy coordination, but this group has met infrequently. Brzezinski suggests that inactivity of the formal organs of international association may be due not only to resistance of some satellites, such as Poland, to any more "coordination" under the Soviet Union than absolutely necessary, but also to unwillingness of the Soviet Union to push development of the Warsaw Treaty Organization too far, lest it become a medium for genuine international consultation, generating pressures for more extensive Soviet sharing of control and military information.

It is important to recognize that the Warsaw Pact as a military organization does not involve a merger of the participating countries' separate

---

[25] See Zbigniew Brzezinski, "Organization of the Communist Camp," *World Politics,* January, 1961. See, also, George Modelski, *The Communist International System* (Research Monograph No. 9, Center of International Studies, Princeton University, 1961); and Kazimierz Grzybowski, *The Socialist Commonwealth of Nations* (New Haven, Conn.: Yale University Press, 1964), esp. chap. 5, pp. 177–90.

national armed forces. Soviet troops are maintained as completely independent, self-contained units, whether stationed in the Soviet Union or on the allies' territory. The presence of Soviet troops in the satellite countries since 1956 has been regularized by bilateral agreements, using the Warsaw Pact as the juridical basis, without, however, involving any limitation on the Soviet Union's authority to direct their use and disposition. The reality of control was abundantly demonstrated in Hungary in the fall of 1956, when the new leadership tried to take the country out of the Warsaw Pact and establish its full independence of Soviet political and military control. Soviet troops in Hungary were completely responsible for its subjugation, with no pretense of consultation with other Warsaw Pact members or joint military decision-making.

Apparently, the armed forces of the other allies also remain separate and nationally self-contained. They are, of course, Russian equipped and Russian trained, but they are not merged with the Russian military forces and are officered by their own nationals. This circumstance was also demonstrated during the Hungarian crisis, particularly in Poland which was experiencing a somewhat similar internal upheaval within its leadership. It is reported that when Khrushchev and other Russian leaders came to Warsaw at the height of the crisis to assert their control over Gomulka and the new leadership, their threat to use Russian forces in Warsaw to enforce their will was countered by a declaration that Polish forces were positioned so that they could and would attack the Russians. Gomulka stated bluntly that he would not be responsible for Khrushchev's safety if the Russians decided to use force.

Thus, behind the apparently total, monolithic military integration directed by the dominant power, the Warsaw Pact seems, in reality, to represent only some essentially political consultation—a channel of communication among the command levels of the eight allies' separate national forces and a framework within which the Soviet Union may share with its allies any mutually acceptable facilities, hardware, and training. It does, to be sure, preclude any military cooperation or association by the members with others, and it has insured unanimity in all major issues of the bloc's external relationships. But it is indeed far from accomplishing a pooling of the members' defense capabilities in a common effort.

The NATO Model of Mutual Assistance. The most strenuous effort to forge an effective instrument of international military control has been made through the North Atlantic Treaty Organization. The NATO pattern is unique. It is also fluid, so that it is hardly a single pattern but rather an evolving one. Indeed, when NATO began, none of its members apparently anticipated development of a major organizational structure that would attempt to integrate the defenses of each into a common enterprise. As it has evolved over 15 years, predominant characteristics of the NATO model are: (1) a joint international command; (2) a set of "balanced collective forces" responsible to the command; (3) a coordinated infrastructure organized and operated by the joint international authority; and (4) an organ of consultation and coordination of policy decisions, set up, paradoxically, on the conventional basis of international association—namely, required unanimity among all members.

NATO, therefore, represents a curious attempt to combine substantial unified, international operative direction with the traditional decentralized pattern of decision-making on the policy level. Each country retains its full freedom of action regarding its commitments (financial, political, military, etc.), but where all partners have agreed to pool resources they have accepted unified direction.

The Joint Command. While joint direction has meant that all members would be involved some way in the common operation of NATO defenses (contrast the Warsaw Pact pattern, where full control is vested in a single nation), this has not meant the partnership would be equal. The Military Staff Committee, responsible for top-level strategic planning, represents only the U.S., British, and French chiefs of staff. In appointments to key posts in NATO's command structure there has been a clear recognition that responsibility would quite largely correspond to effective military power. The supreme commanders of the NATO forces in Europe and the Atlantic naval command have been Americans; under SACEUR, the officers principally responsible for theaters and operational forces have been predominantly British and French. Since the accession of Germany to NATO, German officers have played an increasingly prominent role, and a German was placed in the top command position over all ground forces in Europe. Distribution of these assignments has not been made without considerable grief and injury to national pride. The British found it peculiarly difficult to accept an American in the principal naval command post; the French were most put out over appointment of a Britisher to the Mediterranean naval command, which contributed to a decision, in due course, to withdraw French naval forces from the NATO direction.

A further limitation on the integration of NATO's command structure should be noted. SHAPE acquires the authority of full command only on the outbreak of war. Therefore, in practice, it must secure each government's consent to its decisions, even in the day-to-day operations of NATO defense forces. SHAPE cannot order the forces nominally under its command; it cannot take the place of the countries' own general staffs in directing the training or deployment of the forces, except in the event of actual hostilities. In effect, the NATO Command is not an instrument of command but an instrument of high-level coordination and persuasion.

This pattern of joint command has required a most delicate balancing of military needs and qualifications against considerations of national prestige.

Despite occasional discomfiture, the process has been accomplished with a deftness that enabled SHAPE (the Supreme Allied Headquarters) to become a viable, well-knit, and competent instrumentality. Indeed, SHAPE is probably NATO's most outstanding accomplishment. Once officers have been appointed, they have apparently been able to work together effectively, despite their nationalities, and to become an unusually compact and integrated team. At the strategic planning level, the preparation of defense needs estimates, and the overall organization of forces assigned to them, including joint training, SHAPE has operated as a single entity, viewing its tasks and responsibilities in terms of the overall problems of the alliance. This has not meant an absence of internal debate and severe disagreement over policy within the SHAPE group. But apparently, the organization has not broken down into national blocs, and the officers, regardless of nationality, have been willing to function within a decision-making structure based on the hierarchical principle customary in military organization and to accept as final the decisions reached at the top.

The "Balanced" Collective Force. The second NATO innovation in mutual defense has been the formation of a collective combination of forces contributed by members, its different elements "balanced" according to the requirements of NATO's strategic plan for defense. Significant of this approach is that the NATO force was recruited as a joint force, not simply a hit-or-miss pool of whatever a nation volunteered. Planning for the force was unified, and the joint command then specifically requested from each country the contribution it felt would best meet the overall need.

It was assumed throughout that these forces could be moved about as seen fit by the command and could be used together without regard to national origin. In practice, the contingents have been kept as national units; German divisions have not been mixed with French, or the Danish signal corps with British. But the various units have trained together in integrated military maneuvers, and there has been a considerable exchange of officers. It should be recalled that none of these forces is irrevocably committed to the NATO Command. The French, in particular, and the British, on occasion, have withdrawn units they had agreed to commit. This has, of course, seriously upset the "balance" the NATO Command is striving to maintain. Furthermore, the NATO Command has never been able to secure the full complement of forces they have insisted is necessary for adequate defense. They have felt continuously frustrated and shortchanged by the limitations and uncertainties imposed on them by decisions of their political superiors. They have never known from day to day what forces they could rely on to meet their targets. Therefore, the NATO Command ideal of a balanced collective defense force has been realized more in concept than in flesh, in a training process rather than a force-in-being.

The Infrastructure. The third, perhaps most impressive, NATO achievement of integration has been in the field of infrastructure, or organization of the logistical base for joint operation. It has developed a network of serviceable military airfields throughout the NATO area; it has laid fuel pipelines throughout continental Europe; it has established thousands of miles of signal communications systems.[26] The NATO Command has been directly responsible for expenditure of the funds allocated to the program by member governments, and has been able to design and develop facilities according to its own integrated plan. Each government has, of course, consented to the facilities on its territory, but the construction, use, and operation of these facilities has been a responsibility of the NATO Command. This is the most visible and continuing evidence of the regional security organization.

Those who have urged fuller integration have long hoped that NATO might accomplish in the defense production field what they have done in regard to infrastructure. Central to such an accomplishment would be agreement on standardization of military equipment. If single models of a given item could be accepted for use by all national contingents of the NATO alliance, then, it has been held, production could be distributed among the NATO countries wherever efficiency and security considerations made the location of a defense plant most reasonable. But the governments have largely balked at major proposals for standardization. Sometimes, progress has been possible on a bilateral basis; the United States, for instance, agreed with West Germany on a common model for a medium-size tank. And it may be that more agreements will come on a NATO-wide basis if certain strong reservations about sharing patents and secrets can be overcome and if Americans become less insistent that Europeans accept their models as the basis for standardization.[27] But at present, NATO seems to be far from solving the problems of fully integrated military production.[28]

Decisions by Engineered Consent. The fourth feature of NATO's pattern is its permissive and consensual approach to coordination of decision-making. In the beginning, it was assumed that basic policies would be determined at a council of foreign ministers of the NATO allies (the NATO Council), and economic decisions would be considered by the respective finance ministers. As provided in the treaty, all such decisions would require the consent of every ally. Recommendations were received from the military command of NATO, reflecting their judgment viewed in the perspective of the overall

---

[26] For a summary of achievements in the infrastructure program, see Alastair Buchan, *NATO in the 1960's* (Frederick A. Praeger, Inc., 1960) p. 111; also, Lord Ismay, *NATO, The First Five Years* (Paris: North Atlantic Treaty Organization, 1954); and reports of Supreme Allied Commander Europe (SACEUR) to the NATO Council.

[27] See Buchan, *op. cit.,* p. 121.

[28] See Gardner Patterson and Edgar F. Furniss, Jr., *NATO, A Critical Appraisal* (Princeton, N.J.: Princeton University Press, 1957), pp. 57–58.

NATO defense task. But they were balanced against the full range of competing diplomatic, political, and economic pressures on each country, internally as well as externally. It soon became evident that concerting policy among 14 foreign ministers, 14 defense ministers, and 14 finance ministers to achieve an effectively integrated defense program for the entire alliance was a highly complex undertaking in such a completely decentralized setting. Consequently, the governments accepted several devices of a more integrated character to help in engineering the process of agreement on major policy-making. At the same time, the power of decision was carefully reserved to top-level officials as they met in council.

One helpful device is a permanent Secretariat for NATO, with a secretary-general as a kind of diplomatic counterpart to NATO's military supreme commander. The task of the Secretariat, internationally composed as is SHAPE, is in part secretarial and in part diplomatic. Its initial task was to see that an adequate job of preparation was done for the Council meetings, to provide the ministers with a clear understanding of the issues and alternatives among which they must choose. As the ministers wrestled with their disagreements, the NATO Secretariat developed a diplomatic initiative all its own. It sought to insure, first, that problems *were* solved, and, second, that decisions would go beyond the least common denominator of agreement and reflect the general interests of the entire community of NATO countries. Decisions may still be blocked by the veto of no more than one recalcitrant member. But the Secretariat is committed to "engineering consensus" and, without any express authority to do so, represents the "collective interests" as against the individual separate interests of the different nations.

A second device to facilitate integrated decision-making has been to delegate to a small Council subgroup or to technical experts the task of formulating compromise solutions in serious disagreements. Here again, the power of final decision is not delegated, but the formulation of a viable program is turned over to a group small enough and sufficiently removed from immediate political control to look at the problem in the whole. In the end, pressures for agreement on proposed solutions have been great enough to secure acceptance, especially when the alternative might be breakdown of the whole collective defense system. This device was used at a crucial time in 1952 when the NATO allies could not agree on the budget necessary to carry out recommendations of the NATO Command, nor on the share of the budget each country should contribute. In the impasse, three "wise men" were designated to come up with a plan. While they did not satisfy the full requests of the military command, they did propose a much more substantial NATO budget than the governments separately had been willing to pledge, and in the end their proposal was accepted by the entire Council. This curious combination of separate national authority for accepting decisions and joint responsibility for formulating decisions is now generally referred to as "the NATO method."

It would be too much to claim that this decision-making system succeeds in resolving questions with a high regard for the general interests of NATO in contrast to the prevailing views of the separate nations. On the cost problem, for instance—a problem that continues to bedevil the organization despite the brilliant ingenuity of the three "wise men"—the way out of the standard impasse between demands at SHAPE and maximum commitments that individual governments have been willing to undertake has typically been to revise the "estimate of the situation." In other words, the budget demands have been scaled down on an arbitrary assumption that the Russian threat has decreased! The budgeteers have solved their problem by juggling the very foundation assumptions on which the entire existence of the organization is based.[29]

It seems fair to conclude that NATO decision-making may have set an ingenious pattern of integration as far as process is concerned, but that, in substance, decisions are still largely dictated by separate national calculations of interests. A NATO "decision" more nearly resembles the least common denominator of agreement (or no agreement) than it does a judgment hitched to a view of NATO's overall collective interest. As will be seen later, many of NATO's weaknesses can be traced to this determination to restrict the degree of international integration in the crucial act of policy decision-making.

The Limits of the Integrative Approach to Regional Defense

In appraising regional security organization experience, the following conclusions emerge in regard to integrating the means of common defense:

1. Nations have been unwilling to entrust basic decisions regarding their defense to a common authority unless they themselves retain an ultimate veto.
2. Even for purposes of organizing and strengthening the effectiveness of common defense capabilities, nations have been reluctant to join in common command arrangements. In the one major experiment with integration—NATO—joint responsibility has been sharply limited to implementation of policies set at the political level by intergovernmental agreement. There is no indication that even this limited form of joint operational control has been so appealing as to attract imitation by other regional security organizations. The NATO pattern of joint command in the development of defense capabilities has failed to catch hold, not because it has been ineffective but rather because many national governments fear it may become too effective; that is, they may lose much of their

---

[29] See *ibid.*, pp. 58–59.

independence of action in the face of the strong initiative and momentum of the joint command they have created.[30]

3. Nations have demonstrated their complete unwillingness to merge their means of defense in any permanent fashion, and they have not been willing to entrust more than a limited portion of their military and economic resources to the task of mutual defense. Mutuality, even on the most intimate of regional bases, stops far short of the point where countries will pool all they have in a common effort. The noble declarations of purpose committing each country to defend the others as though it were itself under attack are belied by the restraint they show in preparing to meet these commitments through concerted action.

The question, then, is whether in the absence of integrated policy-making, operational direction, and resources it is possible for the pattern of regional security organization to add significantly to the security of individual members. With the possible exception of NATO, the candid conclusion from experience to date is that the regional approach has added little, if anything, to the safety of states beyond what may have been accomplished by direct bilateral arrangements between major powers and their associated satellites. Regionalism has not succeeded in forging either a common sword or a common shield of substantial scope or durability. It has, at most, provided a façade for a set of activities in which the participating states have jointly exercised their muscles; but the exercise has been insufficient to develop reliable habits of response, and certainly not to develop unified and coordinated powers of decision and direction.

---

[30] One must not be misled by the tendency to couch reports of regional security organizations in terms of the NATO mythology. SEATO, CENTO, and ANZUS in reality have nothing comparable to the degree of integration and coordination achieved by NATO. Practical military cooperation is limited to training. Even in this respect, joint exercises and other programs are usually decided on, instance to instance, by each government (and not necessarily all members at any one time). The pattern of organization is essentially consultative, not integrative or directive.

Chapter 6

Testing the Regional Approach to Security

TESTS OF EFFECTIVENESS

In evaluating the contribution of regional organizations to maintenance of international security, at least three tests should be applied. First, deterrence: To what extent have acts of aggression and war been prevented? Second, cohesion: How well has the organization held together? Third, global compatibility: How acceptable to the world at large are the regional arrangements, and how consonant with general security requirements?

Enthusiasts claim, especially on behalf of NATO and the Western alliance network, that these arrangements have been principally responsible for (1) deterring aggression from outside the region, (2) maintaining peace within the region, and (3) strengthening the conditions of peace throughout the world.

Skeptics note that (1) tensions and pressures of the conflict between Communist and anti-Communist coalitions have not slackened, and aggression by subversion as well as outright armed attack remains imminent; (2) regional alliances have been continuously beset by internal crises, revealing their inability to resolve basic conflicts of purpose and interest among members; (3) war, by accident or design, is now a greater threat to world security, because the unarrested arms race has proliferated the spread of critical weapons, made them more devastating than ever, and increased the probability that any serious outbreak of violence would engulf the whole world.

Accurate appraisal is complicated by the "what if" problem. We cannot really tell whether results would have been different if other alternatives had been followed. History does not lend itself to controlled experiment, and mere coincidence of two sets of circumstances does not establish cause and effect between them. Neither claims of success nor charges of failure are verifiable when they attribute a particular outcome directly to the development of regional security organization. Such a statement as, "The unity achieved by NATO saved Western Europe, Greece and Turkey from the danger of being overrun by communism"[1] is simply incapable of proof, or disproof.

On the other hand, one can ascertain whether events that have happened or did not happen accord with the purposes, expectations, and underlying assumptions of the regional approach to security. One can also draw a negative conclusion: the actions of regional organizations, such as they were, did *not* forestall events that did occur and did *not* precipitate events that did not occur. Finally, one may explore the ways in which the evolving organizations specifically influenced governmental policy decisions inside and outside the organizations. Evidence concerning outside influences is not easily available nor completely reliable, but such as it is, it comes closest to indicating the direct impact on international politics.

Measured in these terms, the effectiveness of regional security organizations in meeting the tests of deterrence, cohesion, and global compatibility is far from confirmed. The record seems rather to sustain the skeptics' judgments.

THE MIRAGE OF DETERRENCE

To be sure, no major armed attack on a regional ally has occurred from a source outside its alliance.[2]

More tenuous is evidence that the area of Soviet pressure has shifted away from Europe as NATO and the Western alliance have matured their collective defenses, and that the Communists reoriented their tactics from military to political and economic means as they confronted the military buildup of anti-Communist coalitions.[3] The problem of evaluation is the unavailability of solid information either as to whether the Soviet leadership has, in fact, deliberately changed its policies or, if it has, whether it has done so specifically because of the West's security organization. One is dependent on "guesstimates," none of which the Soviet leaders have seen fit to corroborate.

By contrast, the evidence is conclusive that (1) each side's capabilities for armed attack have vastly increased; (2) tensions between the blocs have intensified, with most of the controversial issues unsettled and even less negotiable now; and (3) in some areas (such as the Americas), security has

---

[1] University of Pennsylvania Foreign Policy Research Institute, *United States Foreign Policy: Western Europe* (Study No. 3, for Committee on Foreign Relations, U.S. Senate, 86th Cong., 1st sess., October 15, 1959), p. 13.

[2] Some proponents of regional alliances as a basis of security take particular satisfaction from the fact that the only direct attack by a leading state since World War II was by China on India, principal protagonist of nonalignment.

[3] Such views were expressed—but also sharply disputed—at an international conference on NATO, held at Princeton University. See Gardner Patterson and Edgar S. Furniss, Jr., *NATO: A Critical Appraisal* (Princeton, N.J.: Princeton University Press, 1957), pp. 15–16.

been profoundly subverted in the face of all the military defenses regional organizations could devise. From the standpoint of the anti-Communist coalition, not even its military position has improved as a result of all the collective efforts, let alone the overall conditions of security.[4] Deterrence, in the sense of increasing assurances that nations will be secure against aggression or annihilation, has not been achieved.

Indeed, there is specific indication that the regional alliances have had a mutually provocative effect. Each side has intensified its military preparations to counter what it considers an increasingly threatening posture of the other. Each has adopted unyielding positions on even minor issues in fear that the other would interpret readiness to negotiate as a sign of weakness. Each has repeatedly declared the existence of the other's alliance constitues a major threat to its security (while, of course, professing its own completely pacific intentions). If the reactions of the protagonist countries to regional security organizations can be taken as at least a partial measure of their impact, then the organizations appear to have triggered a chain reaction of mutual irritants, suspicions, and fears, resulting in a sense of heightened insecurity that, at points, reaches traumatic proportions.[5]

A telling sign that regional security organizations have been unable to effect a condition of stable deterrence is the rapid turnover and obsolescence of their strategic doctrines. This is particularly obvious in NATO. As noted, it switched strategic plans at least four times in the first fourteen years of its existence. There is less consensus now on an adequate strategy of collective deterrence, because each previous plan continues to have advocates.[6] Some see in this record a commendable adaptability to changing strategic conditions and military technology. A more sober conclusion is that the organization has been unable to devise a strategy that will meet the test of stable deterrence, given the framework of regional alliances within which it has chosen to operate. Much of the critical disaffection that has permeated

---

[4] A wide range of such assessments is summarized in Harold and Margaret Sprout, *Foundations of International Politics* (Princeton, N.J.: D. Van Nostrand Co., Inc., 1962), pp. 617–18.

[5] George Kennan gave a trenchant critique of NATO's provocative effect and the fallacy of the concept that negotiation is more feasible from a "position of strength" in his sixth Reith Lecture, delivered over the B.B.C., on "Strengthening NATO."

[6] For thorough review of the strategic issues, see Alastair Buchan, *NATO in the 1960's* (New York: Frederick A. Praeger, Inc., 1960); and Klaus Knorr *et al., NATO and American Security* (Princeton, N.J.: Princeton University Press, 1959). For recent critique of alternative strategies, see Henry A. Kissinger, "Strains on the Alliance," *Foreign Affairs,* January, 1963. See, also, Dean Acheson, "The Practice of Partnership," *Foreign Affairs,* January, 1963. Acheson, one of NATO's original architects and its inveterate defender, now repudiates the sword-and-shield doctrine he formerly espoused, and pleads that NATO needs a "sound" strategic plan (p. 248). We cannot analyze here the various issues in this debate. Our point is that the whole strategic base of NATO has been volatile; the most authoritative exponents of strategic doctrine change their minds and contradict one another. A similar situation prevails in the other alliances, but is less obvious because the strategic problems are more primitive.

NATO recently reflects the frustration felt as the promised goal of security through deterrence has continually receded over the horizon.

The problem may be that the fundamental assumptions of regional security organization are invalidated by the present conditions of military conflict. Regionalized strategy generally counts on limited warfare to "contain" states that use arms to press their objectives, and on the "balance of terror"—that is, the threat of nuclear retaliation—to keep wars from becoming unlimited. The current strategy of regional deterrence, then, is simply to confront a potential aggressor with a formidable military hurdle so he finds the price of accomplishing his objective "unacceptable."[7] Regrettably, no sure line separates limited from unlimited war. The risks of "escalation" are great once war of any size is begun, and particularly great when states bind themselves to one another in collective defense. For then, trivial or irresponsible action by any state on either side will likely involve everyone, each persuaded that his refusal to back up an ally will cause the whole alliance to crumble. Thus, the essential premise of regional organization—all shall stand together in the face of a common threat—virtually insures that all shall constantly face the threat of total annihilation through accident or misadventure.

The basic problem with regional security strategy is one that has bedeviled all strategies that rest on the balance of power concept. There seems to be no way to assure that a balance can be made stable. The very process of balancing precludes a firm and lasting one. Each opposing side feels fundamentally insecure unless it is confident that the balance is tilted in its favor. Because the regional approach is predicated on division of the world into tightly aligned and perennially competitive blocs, its strategy cannot escape the balance-of-power dilemma—the dilemma of intrinsic instability. The regional approach plunges states into a dialectical process whereby the more effectively a group organizes, the more insecure it makes its opponents feel, impelling them to more extreme counterdefenses. It has no means of transcending the power struggle to create conditions of security in which all competitors have a high, mutual stake.

PROBLEMS OF COHESION

The elemental condition of effectiveness is that the regional security organization hold together. Members must maintain sufficient cohesion to carry out the basic collective functions essential to their common security, both when all members feel severely threatened and when pressure seems less. Continuity and permanence is demanded if collective self-defense is to provide assurance of security any greater than that states may achieve on

---

[7] See the major exposition of NATO strategic doctrine by General Lauris Norstad in April, 1959. This is effectively reviewed by Robert E. Osgood, "NATO: Problems of Security and Collaboration," *American Political Science Review,* March, 1960, pp. 122–23.

their own or through shifting attachments on the basis of immediate expediency.

Yet, the short history of these organizations is one of recurring internal crisis, testifying to the strong pull of many centrifugal forces. Sharp clashes of interest between members have gone unresolved, sometimes even reaching the point of violence. Agreement on strategic plans and priorities has proved difficult and subject to continual challenge and revision. Disputes over sharing the costs, both in money and manpower, have been especially bitter. Most members' contributions to the common defense have been grudging and "parsimonious," to use the delicate term of one authority.[8] No meeting of minds has usually been possible on issues of general foreign policy, political or economic. The question ever-present is whether the least common denominator of a common security threat will be enough to overbalance the forces of mutual dissension.

To be sure, most of the organizations have survived so far, in form and membership.[9] But strains within the alliances are generally acknowledged to have grown. Of deeper significance is that the range and amount of cooperative action have failed to grow appreciably; in some cases, they have actually declined. In the early stages, proponents confidently predicted the groups would quickly overcome growing pains and each year of collective life would add to their disposition and capacity for collective action. Such does not appear to be so, with the possible exception of NATO.

Friends of NATO insist that many of its current divisions are temporary and will pass with de Gaulle's "mystique." They are confident that the organization has become more firmly integrated as it has weathered successive crises. On the other hand, NATO has been unable to subordinate the profound policy cleavages among its members, to sustain its image as custodian of freedom in the face of the allies' contradictory ideological predilections and political systems, or even to persuade all partners to fulfill the minimum security commitments each had undertaken. These troubles seem chronic and not so different from those of the other organizations to conclude that NATO has successfully solved the cohesion problem.[10]

---

[8] Klaus Knorr, *op. cit.* For a more optimistic view of the cost-sharing problem based on NATO's early experiences, see Lord Ismay, *NATO, The First Five Years* (Paris: North Atlantic Treaty Organization, 1954), pp. 115–16.

[9] In terms of membership, the OAS lost 3 of its 21 members, all on the basis of unresolved conflicts with their neighbors—the Dominican Republic, Cuba, and Bolivia. The first two were excluded by action of the organization; the third withdrew in dudgeon over the organization's refusal to take its side in a dispute with Chile. The Dominican Republic was later reinstated, and the loss of the others may also be temporary.

[10] See Sprout and Sprout, *op. cit.,* chap. 21, for a summary of various views concerning persistent weaknesses in the anti-Communist coalition of security organizations. With reference particularly to NATO, see Klaus Knorr, *op. cit.* Buchan, *op. cit.,* takes a somewhat more optimistic view, but developments since his publication do not bear out several of his more sanguine hopes.

Zbigniew Brzezinski notes that the Communist coalition has not been spared similar

The difficulties in achieving regional cohesion have been serious and persistent enough to prompt searching diagnosis. Four main explanations have been advanced.

First, it is suggested that the regional partners have failed to develop and use effective processes of mutual accommodation. With attention riveted on external dangers, the need to confront serious internal dissension has not been sufficiently recognized. The problem is not so much lack of formal machinery for peaceful settlement but, rather, the degree of collective responsibility the organization as a whole shall assume—or be permitted by its members to assume—in resolving internal disputes.

Second, an interest in security against a specific threat may not be a base broad enough for building a firm and lasting international association. Perhaps the functional basis must also include common political, economic, and cultural interests. Some suggest an ideological affinity, with commitment to common values, is necessary.

Third, the pattern of responsibility for decision-making may be the critical problem. Much internal tension has revolved around the question of whether one or more of the partners shall exercise a dominant role in controlling the organization's policies and actions. A related issue is whether the decision-making process can insure that each ally will live up to its commitments.

Fourth, regarding institutional structure, the issue is whether cohesion can be assured short of the creation of supranational organs through which states agree their joint security efforts shall be fully and irrevocably integrated.

These four problems call for detailed examination.

Keeping Peace within the Family

The interdependence of security inside a region and security against threats from the outside is nominally recognized in virtually all regional security pacts. They commit members to refrain from acts of violence against one another and to settle disputes peacefully among themselves. Usually, special machinery and procedures are provided for settlement of intraregional controversies.[11]

---

strains. See his "The Organization of the Communist Camp," *World Politics,* January, 1961. See also George Modelski, *The Communist International System* (Research Monograph No. 9, Center of International Studies, Princeton University).

[11] The Arab League Council is supposed to "mediate" in all differences that threaten to lead to war, and its decision is declared to be "enforceable and obligatory" in all cases when the dispute does not concern the independence, sovereignty, or territorial integrity of a state. The newly formed Organization of African Unity has created a permanent Commission of Mediation, Conciliation and Arbitration to help settle disputes among member states. In the case of NATO, the Council (in the aftermath of the debacle over Suez in 1956) decided that members should submit disputes they could not settle among themselves to "good offices procedures within the NATO framework" and do so *before resorting to any other international agency* (except for disputes of a legal or economic character). The NATO Secretary-General was empowered to implement these procedures with the assistance of up to three of the permanent representatives on the council. The elaborate machinery established for the settlement of inter-American disputes is reviewed in Chapter 10.

However, with the notable exceptions of the Organization of American States regional organizations have tended to wash their hands of troubles within the family. This has not been because of a lack of intraregional quarrels. Indeed some of the conflicts have reached the stage of internescine violence. Yet on the whole states have avoided making these questions a matter of joint concern and action by the regional organization.

To mention a few examples: NATO took no direct action through its Council or other machinery to resolve the falling out of France and Britain on one side and the United States on the other over Suez in 1956; nor did it intervene when Greece, Turkey and Britain became embroiled over the Cypriote demands for "enossis" with Greece. When, after independence, Cyprus again erupted into violence, a proposal that NATO organize a peacekeeping force on the island was flatly rejected by Greek Cypriot leaders. NATO had to stand aside (in favor of U.N. initiative) even though two of its members (Turkey and Greece) were at the point of war, a third (Britain) was eager to have NATO help in the task it had assumed as a guarantor of the island's peace under the treaty of independence, and a fourth (U.S.) was prepared to provide substantial backing for a NATO-sponsored action.[12]

SEATO took no formal action in the sharp disagreement between the U.S. and Thailand over Laos during 1961–62, when the Communist Pathet Lao threatened to overrun the entire country. The Arab League did not act as a league in serious conflicts between Egypt and Iraq or Egypt and Jordan, or in the Yemen revolution in 1963.

In some of these situations, fellow organization members did attempt by direct diplomacy to mediate the conflicts and keep them from getting out of hand. But usually, proposals to bring the questions before the organizations as a whole for collective mediation or conciliation have not met with favor. States preferred to nurse their grudges without interference, even from their bosom allies.[13]

The OAS Formula—Collective Peacemaking. The Organization of American States, however, has an entirely different record. In this instance the contributions of the regional organization to peace *within* the region have in recent years become its most outstanding accomplishment. This is all the more remarkable because of the long and deep-rooted tradition of non-

---

[12] Later, the Cypriots did agree to let a NATO representative try to ease tensions on a personal basis—although the U.N. was entrusted with the major official responsibility for mediating the crisis.

[13] Some authorities are more sanguine about the record of intraregional accommodation. Ernst Haas, for instance, suggests that a capacity to make internal adjustments to meet sharp differences and changes in policies and situations of individual members has been major in the evolution of NATO, and even in such organizations as SEATO and the Baghdad Pact. See "Regional Integration and National Policy," *International Conciliation*, No. 513 (May, 1957), pp. 401 and 403 f.

intervention which has characterized the policies of Latin American states and their highly suspicious disposition toward any kind of outside involvement in disputes to which a Latin American state is a party.[14]

Broadly, what has happened has been the development of a doctrine of "collective responsibility" for the maintenance of peace and security within the hemisphere. The Organization of American States has been able to intervene in disputes between its members—through one of several instruments—and bring about a tolerable settlement with a degree of initiative which would have been resented and rejected by the disputants had the action been taken by any particular nation or group of nations acting on their own responsibility. This experience is reviewed in considerable detail in Chapter 9.

Generally, the strategy of the Organization's actions, and the basis of its successes, has been the maintenance of a territorial and political status quo among the member states. It has supported the integrity of each state, and its immunity from *external* pressures, regardless of the form, *internal* practices or ideological affinities of its government. (Exceptions to this approach have proved abortive, as noted in the discussion below.)

What is not clear is whether the Organization can function effectively to keep the peace within the association when it is torn by genuine, deep differences in social and political objectives. What happens when people within a country refuse to accept the status quo as tolerable and try to revolt? calling on sympathetic groups and states outside for support? Or, as in the case of Cuba, what happens when it exports its own revolution, allying itself in the process with powers outside the hemisphere which are perceived by its neighbors as a dire threat to their political, if not territorial security? To date, the OAS has teetered between action designed to maintain the traditional principle of non-intervention, and an emerging strategy of ostracism directed against states like Cuba which are held to have subverted the fundamental principles and conditions of regional solidarity. The two approaches are in effect contradictory, and this is the current dilemma of the OAS. However impressive its record of encouraging mutual accomodation among its members, in the acid test, namely, Cuba, accomodation has if anything been pushed farther off by the policy of political ostracism. Yet accommodation seems to many of the regional associates in this case to be tantamount to political suicide.

---

[14] The early experience of the Organization of African Unity indicates that it may be on the way to establishing a similar precedent of active initiative in the face of Inter-African conflicts. It succeeded for instance in negotiating a ceasefire and then arbitrating a border dispute between Algeria and Morocco in 1963. Its Council of Foreign Ministers heard each side present its case, then appointed a seven-nation ad hoc arbitration commission to examine the problem and submit concrete proposals to the opponents. Within months, agreement was secured to end the conflict. See B. Boutros-Gali, *op. cit.,* p. 42f.

The Commonwealth Formula—Quarrel in Private. The lesson seems to be that regional solidarity depends far more on willingness to live and let live than on machinery of peaceful settlement, even if used to its maximum effectiveness. Unless the regional group is prepared to use all its resources to enforce conformity to standards and practices acceptable to the majority, there would seem to be no practicable alternative to nonintervention or, in effect, laissez-faire. This is, indeed, the approach to intraregional conflicts deliberately and consistently followed by the most cohesive regional organization, the Commonwealth of Nations, as well as by most other regional security organizations, in practice, if not in word.

The Commonwealth practice has been to limit consultation and joint action to issues to which no member took exception. For instance, there is no evidence that the Kashmir dispute between India and Pakistan or the serious objections of India and other Commonwealth members to the racially discriminatory practices of the Union of South Africa have ever been the subject even of discussion among the Commonwealth Prime Ministers. They limit themselves to issues on which their interests coincide.[15]

Furthermore, Commonwealth conferences follow the practices of "elective discussion." Some topics will be considered only by members interested in that specific question. At defense discussions, for instance, neutralist members are absent, so those members concerned with common defense problems confer separately. Thus there is, in effect, functional subdivision within the association; individual members freely opt to join or not join in considering an area of concern.

A third related practice is to leave each member free to determine for itself whether its interests are compatible with the fundamental Commonwealth obligation—the obligation to inform other members and consult with them on questions of common concern. If a member considers that even this mild obligation conflicts with its particular national interest, then it seems free to move ahead on its own, in complete disregard of the concerns of its associated nations. The matter came to a head in the Suez crisis, when Prime Minister Anthony Eden took the position that Britain was not obligated to inform the other members of its intentions (on the grounds that India, in particular, might not be trustworthy because of its general sympathy for Egypt). Despite serious objections by some Commonwealth nations and even British leaders, Eden's position seems to have been in keeping with prevailing practice, and it is now widely held that the obligation to consult does not presume an obligation to supersede the interest of a member as seen by that member.[15]

The extraordinary conclusion of the Commonwealth experience is that its

---

[15] See J. D. B. Miller, *The Commonwealth in the World* (London: Gerald Duckworth, 1958), pp. 72 ff.

ultrapermissiveness for, and avoidance of, disputes among its members seems to have been important in holding the association together. "The bitter disputes between members are prevented from tearing the Commonwealth apart by the determination of nearly all concerned to treat them as domestic matters which are not susceptible to general Commonwealth adjudication."[16] This practice virtually reverses the position assumed in most regional security commitments; but it coincides with the general practice of other organizations, which, as we have seen, tends to ignore the unhappy quarrel within and concentrates collective attention on the threat from outside.

Nevertheless, one hesitates to generalize from the Commonwealth experience because it is so widely held to be a unique and nonduplicable international association held together by a special cement—British ties. Could one expect any other association without these special elements of cohesiveness to survive unless some effective action were taken to mitigate and resolve serious internal conflicts? The variety among states that belong to the Commonwealth, especially since admission of new members who have secured independence from British colonial rule, indicates that the Commonwealth experience may be generally applicable. The essential cohesive factor is apparently not so much British origin of membership as it is recognition of mutual advantages that outweigh the disadvantages of association. Under these conditions, the prerequisite of continuing association is self-restraint. Each member refrains from injecting into Commonwealth consideration issues that would cause others to break up the association or withdraw from it rather than face the need of thrashing out the question in public. It is understood that the pursuit of mutual disputes shall be conducted outside the forum. The condition of stability is to avoid organizational responsibility for intraregional conflicts rather than to accept responsibility for resolving them.

In summary, one of two conditions seems imperative if a regional security organization is to have a chance to effectively maintain its solidarity as against the outside world: Either it must be willing to pursue a "minimalist" approach to controversies and conflicts within the region, letting the disputants directly thrash them out and excluding them clearly from the purview of the organization's collective functions; or it must adopt a "maximalist" approach, taking all measures necessary to keep its members at peace with one another and in line with the commitments and principles to which all have nominally subscribed. So far, even the OAS in practice has not been willing to follow the second approach to its ultimate conclusion. Hence, sidestepping intraregional controversy, however profound, has emerged to date as the customary condition of the regional security association. The more

---

[16] Miller, *ibid.*, p. 255.

profound and serious the divisive issues, the more necessary it is for the regional group to close its eyes to them.[17]

A Functional Basis for Association

The stated objectives of regional security organizations include promotion of cooperation in many areas outside the security field. NATO members are pledged to promote "conditions of stability and well-being" and to "encourage economic collaboration between any or all of them." (Art. 2.) SEATO's commitments include "the further development of economic measure, including technical assistance, designed both to promote economic progress and social well-being." (Art. 3.) The Arab League has ambitious aims to bring about prosperity and raise the standard of living by encouraging cooperation in the "development of their economies and the exploitation of their natural resources," facilitating "the exchange of agricultural and industrial products." In addition, they make elaborate provisions for cooperation in communications, cultural and social affairs, and health problems. (Arts. 2 and 4 of the Pact and Arts. 7 and 8 of the Joint Defence and Economic Cooperation Treaty.) The Warsaw Pact and subsequent Charter of the Council for Mutual Economic Assistance dedicate most of the Communist countries to strengthening their economic and cultural ties, and to accelerating one another's economic and technical progress. (Art. 8 of the Pact and Art. 1 of the Charter.) The Organization of American States has been bequeathed the responsibility for implementing the vast Inter-American commitments for economic, social, and cultural cooperation undertaken over the last 75 years.[18]

This is not the place to review the development of regional cooperation in these spheres.[19] In general, organizations that owe their origins primarily to a

---

[17] This conclusion is at odds with the viewpoint of several careful students of regional security associations. See the reference above to Ernst Haas's study "Regional Integration and National Policy." Amitai Etzioni observes that groups of nations often work out consensus at a level lower than the United Nations and other organizations of universal scope, and by so doing facilitate a broader international consensus that might not otherwise be possible. See "The Dialectics of Supra-National Unification," *American Political Science Review*, Vol. 56, No. 4 (December, 1962), pp. 927–35. Etzioni, however, is considering particularly the experience of regional blocs caucusing in the United Nations, rather than the situations within regional security organizations. Our point is that regional groups have a peculiarly difficult time in reaching consensus on their own internal squabbles, especially when major ideological and political issues spill over from the world at large into the orientation and direction of governmental policies and systems within the states. It may be quite possible for adjustments and consensus to be worked out in questions involving relations outside the region, while impossible to do so in questions critical among the regional neighbors.

[18] See Ruth C. Lawson, *International Regional Organizations* (New York: Frederick A. Praeger, Inc., 1962) for the full texts of the agreements cited and also of major regional treaties devoted specifically to economic and social cooperation.

[19] See Chapter 15 for a consideration of regional economic development and integration, and Chapters 17 and 19 for the record of cooperation in social and cultural affairs and protection of human rights.

concern for security have been halfhearted in extending themselves to other fields. The major efforts in economic and social development have proceeded apart from security arrangements and frequently have no institutional link to them. Little coordination of policy and action between security and other spheres has occurred.[20]

Where an attempt has been made—as among the American states—to graft security functions onto a tradition of economic and cultural cooperation, a somewhat broader and better integrated functional base has been achieved. But addition of the security function seems to have made Inter-American solidarity more fragile. To hold the association together, it has been necessary to drastically step up cooperative effort and mutual assistance on the economic and social fronts through the Alliance for Progress and other means.

This experience demonstrates that the international cohesion necessary to sustain a common security effort must be forged outside the military and paramilitary fields, and that it comes at a high price in terms of the haves sharing their resources with the less privileged. Interest in security per se does not seem to generate other mutual interests and ties, nor is it self-sustaining. It is parasitic in that it must feed on whatever aspirations or values the cooperating states and peoples may already have in common. If people feel they haven't much to lose, fear of its loss does not drive them to great sacrifices for the region's, or even their own nation's, security.

This conclusion is confirmed by an intensive study of the bases of political community in eight historical cases of international association, undertaken by the Princeton University Center for Research on World Political Institutions. Among conditions found to be essential for development of firm "security-communities" are: (1) mutual compatibility of major values, and (2) capacity for political responsiveness to one another's needs—that is, a readiness in decision-making to give real weight to messages from other member governments. On the other hand, one outstanding condition that tended to destroy security-communities was excessive burdens as a result of excessive military commitments.[21]

The basic functional weakness of regional security organizations is that the common stake is not real enough, large enough, or evident enough to the peoples concerned. They are not convinced that what they want to live for

---

[20] The Western European Union may be an exception. See Ernst B. Haas and Peter H. Merkl, "Parliamentarians Against Ministers," *International Organization,* Winter, 1960, for an account of the substantial cultural and social activities initiated under WEU. It should be noted, however, that they are closely integrated with the parallel development of the European Common Market and other profound functional links among the Western European "Six."

[21] Karl W. Deutsch *et al., Political Community and the North Atlantic Area* (Princeton, N.J.: Princeton University Press, 1957), pp. 58–59 and 66.

depends on someone else's help, or that another can really be counted on to help. Mutual interests must be positive, tangible, and wide and deep before fear can become a reliable unifying force and drive people to be ready to die for one another.

Decision-Making and the Dominant Power

The problem of cohesion within regional security organizations may be traced to the pattern of decision-making, and especially to inequality in determining the most critical policies and controlling the use of the most vital weapons.

In form, most of the organizations reach decisions by unanimity of the participating governments. Each presumably has an equal vote and the right of veto.[22] In reality, the organizations have been subject, by one device or another, to the predominant influence of the major military power or powers. Sometimes, the influence is kept under wraps by tactful self-restraint, as in U.S. relations with the OAS.[23] Often, it is exercised indirectly through key officials of the organization whose appointments are contingent on their acceptability to the principal powers. But fundamentally, influence stems from these states' capacity to decide quite independently the measures they will take on behalf of the collective defense, and the conditions under which they will agree to make the critical contributions without which the alliance would be unable to function.

This capability for unilateral decision-making on matters fundamental to the organization's survival and its members' individual security has most persistently aggravated relations among the partners. There have been two main complaints, usually not from the weakest but from the next-to-strongest allies. First, they have feared their senior associate might exercise its power of vital decision either rashly or in pursuit of interests they do not consider of immediate importance to themselves. They would then be drawn into mortal danger against their will, or at least without a chance to decide for themselves whether the risks are warranted. Second, almost the reverse, the reliability of the great power's commitment to the common defense is

---

[22] The OAS may act by a two-thirds majority on most questions; the WEU has various voting requirements, depending on the nature of the issue, but unanimity is virtually required to change fundamental provisions of the original arms control limitations.

[23] But even in the OAS there is basic ambiguity in the self-restraint of the U.S. Its modesty and flexibility are constantly tried by the need for initiative, in the absence of which the Latin Americans are reluctant to push forward. Meanwhile, in response to the reality of U.S. dominance, an undercurrent of resentment and uncooperativeness flows. The U.S. is damned if it leads and damned if it doesn't. These are among the conclusions reached in a penetrating critique of U.S. relations with the OAS by a Northwestern University study group. See Northwestern University, "The Organization of American States" (Study No. 3 for the Subcommittee on American Republics Affairs, Committee on Foreign Relations, 86th Cong., 1st sess., December 24, 1959), pp. 40–41.

questioned: When it alone retains the right of final decision to go all out, how can anyone be sure it will risk vast self-destruction to salvage an exposed ally, especially if the aggressor nibbles?[24]

The issue has been joined most sharply in NATO, probably because some members feel that their own growing power gives them possible alternatives to so much dependence on United States discretion. De Gaulle, in particular, has demanded arrangements that would give France a more decisive voice in alliance affairs; in default, he would limit its NATO commitments drastically and press vigorously toward an ever more independent defense posture and policy. West Germany has shown a similar inclination, though it has not expressed it so bluntly as de Gaulle. Even the British have at times been restive under too much U.S. initiative, though they enjoy a relationship of special intimacy with the U.S. and, as a member of the "nuclear club," share much more closely in consideration of vital defense decisions.[25] Particular developments in military technology have brought the dispute to a boil. Countries like France are creating an "independent nuclear capability" over the opposition and without the assistance of the United States. With the Soviet Union able to deliver a devastating attack by intercontinental ballistic missiles directly on the United States, reliability of the American NATO commitment is increasingly questioned.

As a result, NATO is casting about for a different decisional process. The bolder rebels call for codetermination. They want major policies, major commitments, and ultimate decisions on the use of weapons to be agreed on by all allies. Each should have the same voice. Thus, the NATO "method"—applied through the Council and its related organs mainly to operational questions—would be extended to the full range of defense policy issues. The U.S. would give up its right to make independent decisions on the disposition of its nuclear weapons, at least insofar as they affected NATO. All such matters would be subject to decision by consensus of the full alliance. Codetermination would multilateralize big decision-making as well as small; NATO's practice would be made to conform to the letter of its Charter.

This approach runs afoul of a view that those with the major military investment should retain the effective power of decision over its use—a view

---

[24] For review of the arguments over these issues, see Patterson and Furniss, *op. cit.,* pp. 38–41.

[25] Note, for instance, the Skybolt controversy when in 1962 the U.S. peremptorily decided to discontinue production of a missile the British considered vital to their defense.

From de Gaulle's standpoint, that Britain did enjoy a special status of semi-independence made France's position even more intolerable. If Britain, why not France? See discussion in Patterson and Furniss, *op. cit.,* pp. 73–74. A clear understanding of the French position is provided by Edgar S. Furniss, Jr., "de Gaulle's France and NATO," *International Organization* Vol. XV, No. 3 (Summer, 1961).

especially widespread in the United States.[26] That greater authority should go with the greater practical responsibility of greater power is also conceded by some who do not have the sword or the shield, but they concede not so much from a sense of equity as of expediency, feeling that this is among the imperatives to be accepted in international political life.[27] From a strategic point of view, the demand for codetermination is rejected on the grounds that too many fingers on the trigger would prevent its being pulled in time to deal with an emergency. (Perhaps it is a question of having too many safety catches.)

However, advocates of extending the decision-making base have failed to resolve a deeper dilemma that results from a certain contradiction in the demands of the lesser partners. They want maximum assurance of commitment from the leading power; yet, they want full share in policy determination for themselves, without being willing or able to assume obligations corresponding in any way to those of the great power. In substance, they want more than equality. They ask for veto power and also, in effect, for power to commit the alliance to action on their behalf. By threat of noncooperation or a reckless move of its own, any state can plunge the entire alliance into war or steps leading to war just as surely as can the major ally. Under a system of codetermination, the power of effective decision tends to pass to the weakest and least responsible members.

As an alternative to full codetermination, the concept of "Atlantic partnership" has been strongly espoused. It was advanced with vigor by President Kennedy during his visit to Germany in June, 1963:

> We are partners for peace, not in a narrow bilateral context, but in a framework of Atlantic partnership. . . . It is not in our interest to try to dominate the European councils of decision. If that were our objective, we would prefer to see Europe divided and weak, enabling the United States to deal with each fragment individually. Instead we have and now look forward to a Europe united and strong—speaking with a common voice—acting with a common will—a world power capable of meeting world problems as a full and equal partner.[28]

---

[26] Note the "McNamara doctrine," enumerated by the Secretary of Defense in an address at the University of Michigan, June 16, 1962.

[27] American leaders, such as Dean Acheson, have great difficulty in understanding why this position is not congenial to many Europeans. They resent implication that the U.S. might not use its power responsibly in the common interest. They see little need for Europeans to share in control as long as the U.S. allows them to share in planning. Rejecting the contention that an independent European "deterrent" is necessary to give Europe more say in the alliance, Acheson protests that the "alliance would indeed, be in sorry shape if joint planning and control of defense had to be coerced by this sort of blackmail." *Foreign Affairs,* January, 1963, p. 258. A searching critique of what he calls the American "schoolmasterish approach," especially apropo of the McNamara speeches, is given by Henry A. Kissinger, *op. cit.* See especially pp. 272–73.

[28] Address of President Kennedy in Frankfurt, Germany, June 25, 1963, as quoted in *New York Times,* June 26, 1963, p. 16.

While the exact implications of partnership have not been spelled out or incorporated into a specific proposal, the Kennedy concept envisages

a more closely unified Atlantic deterrent, with genuine European participation. . . . The proposal before us now is for a new Atlantic force. Such a force would bring strength instead of weakness, cohesion instead of division. It would belong to all members, not one, with all participating on a basis of full equality. And as Europe moves towards unity, its role and responsibility, here as elsewhere, would and must increase accordingly.

Pillars of the partnership would be a "cohesive Europe" and the United States. Europe's internal regional unity is a prerequisite of its having a greater share in control of common Atlantic policies and resources. It must earn the right to decision-making equality by approaching equality in its overall contribution and by harmonizing the interests of its national parts so that it can speak with one voice. Equality, the American message seems to read, must be a fact before it can be a meaningful principle of decision-making. Meanwhile, partnership will involve much consultation but will reserve vital elements of control to the senior partner.[29]

But the partnership idea faces two formidable hurdles. First is strong opposition in the United States itself, including the Congress, to any moves that would take the power of important decisions from established U.S. procedures. Beloff notes that ever since announcement of the Marshall Plan, arguments about Atlantic unity have tended to be circular ones; the U.S. government officially prods the Europeans to greater unity, while facing at home both legal and popular restraints on any surrender to joint authority of its freedom of action.[30] Second is widespread European resistance to being Europeanized by American insistence. While Dean Acheson resents Europeans wielding independent deterrents as blackmail to secure more say in Atlantic alliance affairs (quote above), many Europeans resent Americans bribing them into unity by promises of more voice in their partnership. Hence, response to the vision of Atlantic partnership and the first steps proposed to activate it has been markedly cool. A multilateral NATO nuclear fleet, including Polaris-equipped ships with international crews, was proposed by the United States, welcomed by the West German government, flatly rejected by de Gaulle, and quietly "postponed" because Britain and Italy would not commit themselves in their "present political climates."

---

[29] American interest in European unity has a long history. It has been expressed in support of moves toward economic integration (through the OEEC and OECD) on the one hand and the European Community of the Six on the other, toward military integration (through the WEU), and toward at least moderate political integration (through the Council of Europe and other prototypes of parliamentary institutions). For an important review and critique of this aspect of American diplomacy, see Max Beloff, *The United States and the Unity of Europe* (Washington, D.C.: Brookings Institution, 1963).

[30] *Ibid.*, p. 118.

Failing establishment of true multilateralism in decision-making, notwithstanding all its potential hazards and frustrations, regional security organizations seem unlikely to harness their centrifugal forces and assure their capacity for unified action. NATO's experience would indicate that there is no stable halfway point between allies' full and equal participation in control of joint efforts and each one's going its separate way as soon as it feels able. The lethal risks of having, as Knorr puts it, "too many fingers on too many triggers"[31] are not sufficiently appreciated to outweigh the fancy for national independence in security decisions—a fancy that so far keeps each state, regardless of its power, from entering a partner relationship with others when it does not have, in the last analysis, the ultimate word on its own destiny.

Institutionalizing Political Integration

The roots of disunity within regional security organizations may have grown because the groups have failed to develop common institutions strong enough to offset the centrifugal forces by generating and expressing what Haas calls "maximal collective thinking."[32]

The typical regional security approach, as we have seen, stresses procedures of consultation rather than institutions for policy-making and administration. Initiative comes from the national governments. If common policy emerges, it does so from intergovernmental consensus. Joint action, when it occurs, results from ad hoc agreement, limited to a specific undertaking. The regional "community" is as weak or strong, as casual or intimate as the momentary convergence of national interests and fears. Paradoxically, it thrives when the danger is most acute; it withers as the threat of outside attack seems to recede. The association's growth and survival appear to depend far less on its intrinsic qualities and capacities than on the ebb and flow of the enemy's bellicosity.

The institutionalists argue that establishment of permanent regional organs, with a broad mandate to organize and direct common actions, would greatly increase regional solidarity. NATO appeared for a while to bear out their belief. Under the impetus of the Korean war and other signs of Communist aggressiveness, NATO rapidly fashioned central institutions for both military and political coordination.[33] Effectively led and staffed, these became a pivotal influence in promoting a sense of common purpose and creating a viable structure of common defense. They came to epitomize

---

[31] As quoted in Sprout and Sprout, *op. cit.,* p. 629. With particular reference to the issues confronted in establishing a multilateral nuclear capability, see Klaus Knorr's study, *A NATO Nuclear Force: The Problem of Management* (Policy Memorandum No. 26, Center of International Studies, Princeton University, N.J., 1963).

[32] Haas, *op. cit.,* pp. 418–19.

[33] These have been briefly described above.

NATO. They were "NATO-in-being"—a visible, tangible, physical presence. NATO became something more than a treaty and an occasional meeting of diplomats. It was a supreme headquarters, a permanent organization, a command, a network of air bases and pipelines. People worked for it for long periods of time; officers and men were assigned to "NATO."

Nevertheless, NATO has not overcome its problems of cohesion. Some suggest they may have become even more serious. Perhaps institutionalizing has not gone far enough. It has not reached the crucial point of common policy-making. Some leaders now propose creation of a "political framework" for the Atlantic Community, with new institutions to define common goals and make common decisions on fundamental political issues of common concern. Lord Avon (Anthony Eden) would have a political "general staff"—a group of experts—prepare guidelines for the heads of government. President de Gaulle wants a big power "directorate" of the chiefs of state. These do not go far or deep enough for most Atlantic Community protagonists, as evidenced in resolutions adopted by the NATO Citizens Convention in Paris, January, 1962. They call for a permanent "High Council"—at the highest political level—"to concert and plan, and in agreed cases to decide, policy on matters of concern to the Community as a whole." They also crave a consultative role for a more broadly representative organ such as the NATO Parliamentarians Conference or an Atlantic Assembly. Pending such institutional innovations, they will settle for strengthening the present NATO Council.[34]

There is, as yet, little responsible support for truly comprehensive supranational organization, paralleling on the political side the economic institutions of the European community's six members. Many West Europeans do not want moves toward Atlantic unity to sidetrack the possibility of uniting their countries politically. An implicit contradiction between the concepts of an Atlantic community and European community is especially evident when the issue of supranational organization is raised. The question of who shall be preeminent has yet to be resolved to the mutual satisfaction of "Europeans" and "Atlanticists."[35]

Of deeper import is whether the peoples and governments of the Atlantic

---

[34] See Christian A. Herter, "Atlantica," *Foreign Affairs,* January, 1963; Dean Acheson, "The Practice of Partnership," *op. cit.;* and Henry A. Kissinger, "Strains on the Alliance," *op. cit.* One of the most persuasive European spokesmen for development of stronger instrumentalities of political collaboration is Paul Henri Spaak, NATO's Second Secretary-General. See his "Atom Bomb and NATO," *Foreign Affairs,* April, 1955. The monograph by Kurt Birrenbach, *The Future of the Atlantic Community* (New York: Frederick A. Praeger, Inc., 1963), contains the text of the "Declaration of Paris," adopted by the Atlantic Citizens Convention in January, 1962. A more moderate approach to NATO reform is advocated by Buchan, *op. cit.,* pp. 105–6. Beloff, *op. cit.,* traces development of some of these ideas on both sides of the Atlantic. See especially pp. 104–15.

[35] On this issue, see the searching account by Beloff, *op. cit.,* especially chap. VI.

nations have developed a consciousness of common interests and ideals sufficient to support even the more limited moves toward political integration that have been proposed. One is assured that "the existence of a spiritual and cultural community of the North Atlantic nations" is a "fundamental and enduring reality." It is "indivisible," and "the United States is an integral part of it."[36] But the political behavior and attitudes of the United States and the other presumed members of this community hardly confirm this vision. They demonstrate, rather, the continuing, paramount force of direct national loyalties and distinctive national interests that resist absorption by a vague mystique of transoceanic spiritual communion. However much expediency may dictate an Atlantic framework for mutual defense, the imperative for such cooperation is primarily concern for the security of one's own nation, not an outpouring of supranational feelings of common Atlantic brotherhood.

This deeply rooted nationalism stifles the growth of political solidarity within regions just as it does globally. Hence, the organization of security institutions, on a regional or broader than regional basis, cannot presume a preexisting base of strong common loyalties that pulls together the people and leaders of different nations, for generally such a base does not exist.[37] The following conclusion, reached in a study of Inter-American relations, appears to apply almost everywhere, with the possible exception of Western Europe: " . . . Interdependence among the nations derives largely from the need to cooperate against others to maintain national autonomy. Thus, an underlying ambivalence in the Americas is induced by the states' desire to work collaboratively in the pursuit of non-collaborative goals."[38]

This is the fundamental contradiction built into regional security organization as it now stands, and an intrinsic source of its weakness and fragmentation. Its goals are "non-collaborative"; each nation is striving above all to protect its *own* security, which at rock bottom means its autonomy, its capacity to make decisions for itself. It is not truly interested in protecting another state's autonomy unless this contributes to its own. The more a state is asked to subordinate its autonomy to collective decision-making processes, the less convinced it is that collaboration is serving its ends. It begins to wonder whether the threat of outside aggression is so serious as to justify attrition of its independence within the regional group.

In these circumstances, establishment of regional political institutions of greater scope and powers may undermine, rather than strengthen, the associa-

---

[36] University of Pennsylvania, Foreign Policy Research Institute, *op. cit.,* p. 13.

[37] One study by competent scholars does conclude that in the North Atlantic area values may be sufficiently compatible to sustain political integration, though in some other respects (such as "mutual responsiveness") the conditions are not so favorable. They concede that Spain and Portugal cannot be included within the area where values are compatible. Deutsch *et al., op. cit.,* pp. 123–33.

[38] Northwestern University, *op. cit.,* p. 18.

tion's solidarity. To jump the gun and form communal political institutions with governmental authority before a community really exists may prevent its emergence altogether. Meanwhile, the institutions will lie impotent to provide any greater mutual security than nations individually decide they are willing to buy.

The experience of the Commonwealth of Nations seems to bear out this conclusion. It has fewer institutional trappings than any other regional organization; yet it has greater coherence. It survives and leads a vigorous collective life, despite sharp differences in the members' internal political systems and in many aspects of their foreign policies. It is, of course, an association with more than security interests—undoubtedly an important factor in its cohesion (as suggested above in considering the value of a broad functional base). But its institutional pattern is essential to its effectiveness.

Britain's position is crucial, for primarily the relationship to Britain makes the Commonwealth association appear profitable to the members. The key to British policy toward the Commonwealth is its ultrapermissiveness. Rather than "running the Commonwealth," it refrains from exacting obligations, strengthens common interests, plays a moderating influence on hostilities among the members, and actually pays a considerable price in economic and other arrangements to make the relationship attractive. In terms of decision-making, Britain claims no special privileges. But probably of greater significance—in view of the profound reluctance of states to lose control of their own decisions—the Commonwealth has chosen not to integrate the decision-making procedures and instrumentalities of the separate countries, or to superimpose institutions that would attempt to make decisions jointly for the Commonwealth. Its approach is to rely fully on voluntary consultation, at the level of prime ministers and below, as desired, to bring about whatever common policies and action the members feel will be beneficial. As has been noted, members are free to join in some areas and not in others (such as defense) entirely at their individual option. The relationship is aptly described as one in which "each member can treat each other as an independent state with confidence that the term 'independence' has some meaning."[39] Why doesn't the Commonwealth fall apart of its own looseness? Perhaps the very looseness of its institutions permits maximum growth of the cohesive power of mutual interests.

THE IMPACT ON GLOBAL SECURITY

Nominally, members of regional security groups have undertaken to act in ways consonant with their global security obligations, especially under the United Nations Charter. Whether they have, in fact, made their regional

---

[39] J. D. B. Miller, *op. cit.*, p. 251. See also pp. 273–76 for analysis of Britain's role.

behavior conform to either the letter or the spirit of United Nations commitments is open to serious question.

The regional pacts typically declare: (1) they do "not affect, and shall not be interpreted as affecting, in any way the rights and obligations of the Parties which are members of the United Nations" (NATO, Art. 7); (2) they do "not affect and shall not be interpreted as affecting in any way the . . . responsibility of the United Nations for the maintenance of international peace and security (SEATO, Art. 6) or "the primary responsibility of the Security Council for the maintenance of international peace and security" (NATO, Art. 7); (3) the parties undertake to "refrain in their international relations from the threat or use of force in any manner inconsistent with the purposes of the United Nations" (NATO, Art. 1); (4) measures taken to repel an armed attack "shall immediately be reported to the Security Council" and "shall be terminated when the Security Council has taken the measures necessary to restore and maintain international peace and security" (NATO, Art. 5), as required by Article 51 of the U.N. Charter.[40] Furthermore, they invariably assert that the regional defense treaties are appropriately authorized under the United Nations Charter, especially by Article 51 which explicitly recognizes the "inherent right of individual or collective self-defense if an armed attack occurs against a Member of the United Nations, until the Security Council has taken measures necessary to maintain international peace and security," and Article 52 which states that the U.N. Charter does not preclude "the existence of regional arrangements or agencies for dealing with such matters relating to the maintenance of international peace and security as are appropriate for regional action provided that such arrangements or agencies and their activities are consistent with the Purposes and Principles of the United Nations."

Neatly camouflaged within these professions of global commitment are at least three loopholes through which regional alliances have been able to evade, if not actually to flaunt, the carefully restrictive requirements of the U.N. Charter.

First, regional groups do not agree to report *all* their actions to the Security Council, only those they take in response to an actual armed attack. They remain unaccountable to the U.N. for everything they do in advance of an attack, which, of course, covers literally everything they have undertaken so far. They claim this keeps to the letter of Article 51, but it is more difficult to square with Article 54: "The Security Council shall at all times be kept fully informed of activities undertaken or in contemplation under regional ar-

---

[40] Corresponding provisions in the regional security treaties are to be found as follows: North Atlantic Treaty, Arts. 1, 5, 7; Charter of the Organization of American States, Art. 102; Inter-American Treaty of Reciprocal Assistance (Rio) 1, 5, 10; Arab League Joint Defence Treaty, Arts. 2, 11; Warsaw Pact, Arts. 1, 4; Western European Union Treaty, Arts. 5, 6; Southeast Asia Collective Defense Treaty, Arts. 1, 4, 6.

rangements or by regional agencies for the maintenance of international peace and security." To get around this awkward provision, the treaties (except the Inter-American Treaty of Reciprocal Assistance)[41] have carefully avoided labeling their arrangements or institutions "regional." But if they are not regional, they presumably have no right to undertake such preparative mutual security activities, for Article 51 concedes a general right of collective self-defense outside the framework of the U.N. only *in the event of an armed attack.* If they are regional, they should report. If they are not, they are obliged to function through the U.N. until an attack occurs. These bothersome restrictions have simply been brushed aside.[42]

Second, the prohibition in Article 53 of the Charter against any "enforcement action . . . under regional arrangements or by regional agencies without the authorization of the Security Council," is not even recognized in the regional pacts, let alone honored in practice. The regional groups have never asked for nor received Security Council approval for their actions. The customary rationalization is again that they are not legally "regional."

Third is an evasion of which NATO, in particular, is guilty in that it now includes Western Germany as a full ally, entitled to all the security privileges of the Alliance, even though it is not a member of the U.N. Yet, Article 51—mainstay of NATO's legitimacy—recognizes the right of "collective self-defense" outside the U.N.'s compass only "if an *armed* attack occurs against a *Member of the United Nations.*" (Our italics.)[43]

Beyond these technical considerations, the fundamental issue is which shall take precedence—the regional security arrangements or the U.N.'s security system. The Charter was drafted to insure the U.N.'s unqualified paramountcy in the event of contradiction or incompatibility, with the Security Council's exercising the ultimate power of decision on any issue of incompatibility. (The one allowable exception is the right of defense against armed attack as provided in Article 51, to be exercised only until the Council acts.) Regional security arrangements were accepted as potentially useful adjuncts of the U.N. system—primarily in deference to Inter-American sensibilities —but never should they supersede or displace the U.N.

Under the impetus of the East–West power struggle and disillusionment with the U.N. as an instrument of general security, the regional alliances

---

[41] The American States, entangled by a long history of pronouncements that they form the pristine "regional community," formally admit their comprehensive obligation to report to the Security Council (Art. 5), but generally ignore it in practice.

[42] The point is sometimes made that the right to undertake military preparations is generally implied, because Article 51 is part of Chapter VII, which concerns action with respect to "threat of peace" as well as actual "breaches of peace" and aggression. See Norman Bentwich and Andrew Martin, *A Commentary on the U.N. Charter* (New York: Macmillan Co., 1950). Such an interpretation seems, to this author, farfetched and unsupported by the record of the U.N. Charter negotiations at San Francisco.

[43] See Andrew Martin, *Collective Security* (Paris: UNESCO, 1952), p. 171.

have, however, successfully asserted a prerogative of independent action, and have insisted that theirs was the primary responsibility for security both within their spheres and against their outside enemies. Proponents of each regional group repeatedly deny that their group has any conflict of interest with the U.N.[44] But whether there is or is not a conflict is held to be a matter for each subgroup to decide for itself, rather than one for the encompassing world organization to determine. In these circumstances, there can be no effective means of ascertaining impartially whether regional security actions are, in fact, compatible with either the formal global obligations of each group or, more important, with the basic conditions of general world security.[45]

The regional alliances' precedence over the U.N. in security matters and their repudiation of any practical global accountability for their actions have come to be taken for granted. Rarely is an issue joined in which complete regional autonomy is challenged. When it has been—for instance, in Russia's 1956 suppression of Hungary or the 1954 overthrow of the Guatemalan government—the group has abruptly brushed aside the U.N. protests to the contrary notwithstanding. The Russian-installed Hungarian government firmly rejected every move for a U.N. inquiry, including a visit by the Secretary-General, claiming the privilege of "domestic jurisdiction"; while the Warsaw Pact members insisted the only international implications concerned them as Hungary's allies. The Guatemalan case was strikingly similar. Though the Arbenz government appealed to the United Nations, facing as it did a hostile majority in the Organization of American States, the OAS group asserted that it should have a chance to act first. With the threat of a U.S. veto in the Security Council, the OAS was able to enforce its demand; before it took decisive action, the government was overthrown and the whole matter dropped.[46]

Only when the great regional alliances have faced each other "eyeball to eyeball" and come to the verge of major hot war has the U.N. been permitted

---

[44] See, for instance, Christian A. Herter, *op. cit.,* p. 304: "The development of a strong Atlantic Community need not be in conflict with the United Nations. . . . The fact is that the development of the Atlantic Community into a closely knit group might well strengthen the existing machinery for the maintenance of peace."

[45] For a trenchant analysis of the issue of compatibility between regional security arrangements and the maintenance of security through the U.N., see Commission to Study the Organization of Peace, 16th Report, *The United Nations, Regional Arrangements and the Free World* (New York: American Association for the United Nations, 1963). The issue as it has arisen between the U.N. and the O.A.S., is searchingly examined by Inis L. Claude, Jr., "The OAS, the UN and the United States," *International Conciliation,* March, 1964.

[46] See Claude, *ibid.,* for detailed analysis of this case and others in which the question of the autonomy of the O.A.S. vis-a-vis the U.N. was confronted. OAS sanctions against the Dominican Republic in 1960 were reported to the Security Council, which "took note" but no further action, by a vote of 9–2 (U.S.S.R. and Poland). *U.N. Review,* October, 1960.

to take a hand. Even then, its role has been limited and short-lived. In the confrontation over Cuba in October, 1962, the U.S. and the U.S.S.R. agreed that the United Nations should be responsible for insuring that Russian missiles were removed and sites dismantled as a condition of the U.S.'s lifting its partial blockade and pledging not to attack Cuba. This was an important element in securing the detente; although in the end Cuba blocked the U.N. from carrying through the mission, and security had to hang on the self-restraint of the nuclear giants.[47]

The conclusion seems inescapable that the regional security arrangements have not only bypassed the United Nations, they have deliberately prevented the United Nations from discharging its functions of maintaining peace and security both within and between the groups. The regionalization of security, whatever its justification in terms of more adequate provision for the collective self-defense of some, has emasculated the global security commitments undertaken to provide for the defense of all.

CONCLUSION

Attempts to assure peace and security through the regional organization of collective self-defense have yet to prove themselves. They have had a short history—less than one human generation. Each has its own life history, reflecting differences in strategic situation, cultural background, and political leadership. None has faced really decisive tests. So overall generalizations are probably both premature and unreliable.

Nevertheless, signs indicate that these regional approaches have failed to come to grips with the essential elements of today's security problem. Despite their current vogue, they may be quickly forsaken as an anachronism in our time, given the present dimensions of warfare and the interdependence of human actions.

First, they are a response to a particular power conflict rather than to the general problem of international security. They are oriented to the interests of particular groups of nations, not all nations. Most regional defense organizations relate to the bipolar struggle between East and West, Soviet bloc and American orbit of influence, Communist camp and free world. Important as is this dimension of contemporary international relations, it encompasses only a limited area of the world's concern. Many nations are far more preoccupied with other conflicts close to home and, indeed, with issues quite apart from military security, such as the internal political and economic development of their countries.

The strictly security-oriented organizations (NATO, SEATO, CENTO,

---

[47] See previous chapters for a review of the Berlin crisis of 1948, when the U.N. performed an important, but again limited, function of moderating interbloc conflict.

ANZUS, Warsaw), and even some impelled by the midcentury power struggle to follow suit, are caught in a Western "culture bind." They emphasize interests and goals that appeal primarily to persons who take the Western state system for granted as the most suitable political framework in which to achieve their aspirations. The whole notion of the "Atlantic Community," for instance, attaches special value to the political institutions and cultural heritage presumably distinctive to this region. This cannot help but appear exclusive to those on the outside. To make matters worse, many of the Western regional groupings are affiliated to the recent system of European colonial rule. These organizations are then perceived in the non-Western world not only as limited to purposes of no concern to anyone else, but as imperialist tainted, if not imperialist motivated. (The Communist alliance has been less vulnerable because of its anticolonialist revolutionary ideology, but its critics have made some headway with the charge that it is aggressively pushing a system of neocolonialism on the rest of the world.) Consequently, the regional security approach has caught hold much more in Europe and the western Atlantic than in Asia or Africa, and there seems little prospect of its becoming more relevant in these other areas in the future.

A second limitation of the regional security approach is that its actions are predicated on the indefinite continuance of present international power-political alignments. It presumes that the regional groupings which form the base of the collective defense alliances will be more or less permanent. Yet, historical evidence indicates that such political attachments are temporary rather than timeless. Less than a generation has passed since the major international alignment pitted the Nazi–Fascist Axis against the "united nations," and the Western democracies stood allied with the Soviet Union in the immense war for mutual survival. Why should one expect the present alignment to be more enduring? Fissures in each bloc already indicate that the lines of association are fluid and herald the possibility of major realignments. Though ideological commitments supposedly harden the cement that binds each group and make the conflict between groups peculiarly bitter and unyielding, the mortar evidently is loosened by other sets of interests which cut across the commitments. The regional security organizations, hitched as they are to quite specific territorial, political, and ideological orbits, are not likely to survive events that seriously jostle the present order of international attachments.

Some advocates of the regional approach concede that it may meet conditions of security only for the moment. But they maintain this is prerequisite for any permanent solution—an essential step toward peace, even if further steps will be necessary to achieve a lasting, universal security. This presupposes that it is possible and acceptable to indefinitely freeze a given balance of power, or division of spheres of influence. In this period of the most dynamic development in history of the instruments of military and economic power, and in this time of political, social, and ideological revolution, such an assumption appears dubious at best.

Furthermore, regional security organizations have largely bypassed a crucial aspect of the security problem in the nuclear missile space age—control and limitation of the means of destruction. They have focused on the protection and containment of particular states rather than the containment of war. In emphasizing territorial security, they have tended to lose sight of the overriding risks of mutual annihilation posed by the worldwide proliferation of immensely destructive weapons. This accounts for the air of unrealism that pervades debates over regional defense strategy. The regional strategists fancy that by rational calculation they can "graduate deterrence," determining just how much power will make the price of aggression "unacceptable" or, if the calculation goes awry, at least creating a "pause" for recalculation by both sides. Security-minded though they are, they fail to see the overwhelming factor of insecurity: the totality of war and the danger that any military recourse, however limited its intended effects, may quickly get out of everyone's control and "escalate" into all-engulfing destruction so long as the development, deployment, and use of arms are not effectively restrained.

Regional approaches have also tended to isolate the military security problem from the problems of social, economic, and political development, failing to recognize the deeper threats to security posed by demands for social change and political recognition. They have seized a handle that runs only a limited aspect of national behavior, ignoring the things that matter most to most people. This means they do not really get to the taproot of the general security problem, and hence do not command broad and abiding support, even within their own constituencies let alone the rest of the world.

All this adds up to the final conclusion that the regional organization of security has made little if any contribution to developing a general system of international order. It simply has not confronted the essential elements of instability.

Chapter 7

The U.N.'s Peace-Keeping "Presence"

Three years after armistice in Korea, the United Nations was subjected to another sudden challenge to its security mission. Israel attacked Egypt, and Great Britain and France immediately launched their own curious version of a police action, in which they undertook to establish security by forcefully ousting the Egyptians from the Suez Canal area.

Amidst a stunned, really anguished, world reaction over so blatant a transgression of the rules of decent behavior in the international community by two of the leading expositors of virtue, the United Nations, to restore peace, engaged in the most creative and imaginative action in the history of international organizations. It invented an entirely new approach to the problem of maintaining security and preventing countries from using force in the pursuit of national policies. By forming the United Nations Emergency Force, it substituted for the concept of collective enforcement, which had dominated the security strategy of international organization, the idea of patrol, acting with the consent and in the interest of all parties to the conflict, as well as the world community as a whole.

Some precedent had been set for this kind of an operation by United Nations supervision of the truce in Palestine and the cease-fire line in Kashmir between India and Pakistan. But the problem in Egypt was much more formidable, because there was no disposition on the part of any of the fighting states to agree to a truce. The United Nations was in no position to force even the Israelis to accept a truce on terms that would respect Egyptian rights, let alone to compel Britain and France to back down. Quite apart from the ability of these two to block Security Council action by the veto (which they did), memories of Korea were too painful for any kind of an enforcement action to be favored, especially against these particular offenders. The question over which the delegates agonized at the emergency session of the General Assembly during the night of October 30, 1956, was whether the

United Nations could do anything at all that would alter the course of events. The situation was made all the more ominous by a barrage of Soviet threats of direct intervention in Egypt's behalf, with all the dangers of total war this implied.

UNITED NATIONS PEACE FORCE—BY COMMON CONSENT

The unique and bold suggestion that provided the miracle solution to the crisis was that the United Nations should assume direct and full responsibility for maintaining conditions of general security in the area, interposing a "peace force" between the belligerents. Obviously, such a plan could work only if all the hostile governments would agree to let the United Nations take over the job, and would voluntarily stop fighting and withdraw their forces as the United Nations moved in its force. The United Nations simply had no means of mobilizing sufficient compulsive power to make even the weakest of the belligerents yield to this arrangement against its will. The initial condition of success was, therefore, to persuade all four governments that they should give up their use of force, whatever their claims and interests, in return for what assurance the United Nations could give that the area would be immunized from acts of force from any side.

As a first step, the General Assembly by a vote of 64 to 5 (the only opposition being the three attacking countries plus Australia and New Zealand, acting because of their close ties with Britain) expressed "its grave concern over these developments" and urged:

1. An immediate cease-fire and a halt to the movement of military forces and arms into the area.
2. Withdrawal of Israeli forces behind the Egypt–Israel armistice lines previously negotiated by the United Nations in the Palestine conflict, and scrupulous observance of the armistice provisions by both sides, including the stopping of raids.
3. An embargo by all United Nations members on introducing military goods in the area of hostilities, and in general, avoidance of any acts that would delay or prevent implementation of this resolution.
4. Steps to reopen the Suez Canal and restore secure freedom of navigation as soon as the cease-fire became effective.
5. The Secretary-General to observe and promptly report on compliance with this resolution.

The Assembly decided to remain in emergency session pending compliance.[1]

Fortunately, the British government was now fully impressed by the gravity of world reaction to their move. More than the Soviet threats, both

---

[1] Resolution 997 (ES–I), Official Records of the General Assembly, First Emergency Special Session, November 2, 1956.

strenuous objections from United States government and public opinion caused misgiving. The outcry at home was also widespread and vehement. Prime Minister Eden was amenable to a way to get out of the precarious situation, and the French more reluctantly followed suit. The Egyptians were cooperative, as might be expected as long as there was assurance of respect for their "sovereign rights," but the Israelis yielded only to the utmost pressure applied within the United Nations and outside, especially by the United States.

While moral and diplomatic pressure succeeded in winning the consent of the combatants to the Assembly's call for cease-fire and the withdrawal of attacking forces, this was conditional on the capacity of the United Nations to organize and place between the combatants a force that would effectively shield each party from assault. This force could not itself use armed power to accomplish the task. The General Assembly called on Secretary-General Hammarskjöld to design such a delicate and novel instrument within 48 hours. In less time, he presented the Assembly with a preliminary outline of UNEF. He completed appropriate terms of reference and secured assurances of support necessary to put it into effect within another 48 hours. The Assembly immediately and without dissent approved the plan, though there was some grumbling by the Soviet Union and the United States because they were not invited to have a share.[2] (The plan, as discussed below, adroitly disqualified all the major powers from active participation so as to minimize the intrusion of ulterior political motives.[3])

THE PRINCIPLES OF UNEF

The basic principles laid down by the Assembly on the Secretary-General's recommendations were consistently applied and proved vital to the project's success.

---

[2] Resolutions 998, 1000, 1001, Official Records of the General Assembly, First Emergency Special Session, November 4, 5, 7, 1956.

[3] An excellent account of the dramatic negotiations leading to establishment of the UNEF is given by William R. Frye, *A United Nations Peace Force* (Dobbs Ferry, N.Y.: Oceana. Publications, Inc., 1957). Frye also effectively reviews and evaluates the operation of the force, and considers the possibilities and problems of establishing a permanent force on this general model. See also the substantial study by Gabriella E. Rosner, *The United Nations Emergency Force* (New York: Columbia University Press, 1963).

It is apparent that when Lester Pearson, the Canadian foreign minister, first broached the idea of a United Nations "police" he did not have in mind that it would be necessary to secure Egyptian or Israeli consent. He envisaged, rather, that the United Nations would take over control of, and thus internationalize, the purported "police role" of the British and French, hoping that this would provoke less international complication. But it soon became evident that the Egyptians would continue to resist any form of coercive intervention they felt violated their sovereignty, and the whole point of the United Nations' action would be lost. The Secretary-General was clear from the beginning that success depended on having full Egyptian consent, and at least sufficient acquiescence by the Israelis so that they would not put up a fight when the United Nations force moved in to occupy the areas they had conquered.

First, the principle of collective responsibility was unmistakably established. The force was so organized and directed as to be immediately responsible to United Nations organs—not, as was the unified command in Korea, to one member of the United Nations, nor to a group of countries. The United Nations wanted to carefully avoid any impression that it was "deputizing" the British and French as policemen with its moral and legal backing. The chief responsible officer was appointed by the United Nations, and his authority was so defined as to make him fully independent of the policies of any one nation. He reported directly to the Secretary-General (on the same basis as the chief of staff of the United Nations Truce Supervision Organization in Palestine, who, conveniently, was the person named to command the new force and was thus thoroughly accustomed to this line of responsibility). This made certain that only the General Assembly and/or the Security Council—by collective decision—could set the policies that would govern the conduct of the force. The General Assembly appointed a seven-nation Advisory Committee, *under the Secretary-General's chairmanship,* to do what planning was necessary beyond the immediate responsibility of the chief of command. Of most significance, the Assembly vested in the chief executive officer of the United Nations—the Secretary-General—full administrative control over such vital matters as recruitment of the force, its deployment, and all regulations essential to its effective functioning.[4] UNEF was thus a truly international agency.

Second, as suggested above, was the principle that the force should be unmistakably neutral and impartial, sealed off from the major crosscurrents of international political controversy. This was made explicit in the decision to recruit the force entirely from states other than the permanent members of the Security Council. It was further implied in the Secretary-General's firm insistence, backed by the Assembly, on a free hand in determining the composition of the force. The British and French had urged that the parties involved (including themselves, of course) should have to agree on who was to join the force—in other words, to have the right to veto participants. But the Secretary-General decared this could not be reconciled with the development of an international force. Even though he was fully agreed that the operation as a whole could not function without the consent of the interested parties, he wanted to make absolutely clear that the force itself was completely independent of control by any particular nation.

Third, the force was frankly set up on an emergency basis so as to emphasize that its tasks were strictly nonpolitical, e.g., to secure and supervise the cessation of hostilities in accordance with the terms of the General Assembly's original resolution. This shrewdly nipped at the very beginning any implication that the force might become an instrument for internationalization of the Suez Canal or accomplishment of other long-run political

---

[4] See General Assembly resolution of November 7, 1956, 1001 (ES–I).

objectives desired by the Western powers or Israel but anathema to Egypt. The Secretary-General was at pains to repeatedly stress the temporary and limited nature of the assignment and to note that it was reserved to the General Assembly itself to determine the tasks and legal basis of the force. "It follows from its terms of reference" he said in his definitive statement to the Assembly on November 6, "that there is no intent in the establishment of the force to influence the military balance in the present conflict and, thereby, the political balance affecting efforts to settle the conflict."[5]

Fourth, the terms of reference sharply excluded the force from exercising any enforcement role. Although lightly armed (for personal self-defense as were the observers of the truce supervision organization) it was not a force with military objectives. All operations of the force, including the question of where it would be stationed and how long it would stay, were subject to the consent of the government on whose territory it was present. The Secretary-General made the point most explicitly.

> While the General Assembly is enabled to establish the force with the consent of those parties which contribute units to the force, it could not request the force to be stationed or operate on the territory of a given country without the consent of the government of that country. . . . The setting-up of the force should not be guided by the needs which would have existed had the measure been considered as part of an enforcement action directed against a member country. There is an obvious difference between establishing the force in order to secure the cessation of hostilities, with a withdrawal of forces, and establishing such a force with a view to enforcing a withdrawal of forces.[6]

In other words, the relationship of the force to the host country was almost that of invited guests, rather than of policemen, thus recognizing both the sensitivity of newly independent states over their rights of sovereignty and the unwillingness of states who volunteered for patrol duty to become involved in actions that would require their shooting down Egyptians, Israelis, or anybody else. This rejection of any implication of enforcement in the function of the force was extremely hard for a collective security conditioned public to understand or accept, yet it was imperative for the success of this enterprise.

Fifth, the United Nations adopted the principle of assuming all those costs of the force which arose from its functions on behalf of the United Nations. Nations contributing units to the force continued to carry the salaries and equipment of their men, just as though they were on a national assignment. But the United Nations has financed their transportation, their maintenance on the scene, and all administrative costs out of a specially raised budget to

---

[5] U.N. Doc. No. 3 (A/3302 Official Records of General Assembly, First Emergency Special Session, Annexes).

[6] U.N. Doc. No. A/3302, *Ibid.*

which all the members were called to contribute proportionately to their share of the regular United Nations budget. This established more clearly than anything else that the force was acting for the international community as a whole and not for a particular part of it. Although the burden of the force fell more heavily on those who shared their own forces with it, payment of the operating costs by the general membership of the United Nations tangibly demonstrated that their support was not simply verbal.[7]

THE FORCE IN OPERATION

"One of the fastest diplomatic-military crash operations in history" was a well-informed analyst's estimate of the United Nations' emplacement of its Emergency Force on the line of cease-fire.[8] Eight days after the General Assembly passed its definitive enabling resolution, the first contingent—45 Danes—landed by air near the Suez Canal's northern entry. Within two months, the force built up to its peak of about 6,000 officers and men, and it strung out in the desert from Gaza to the Gulf of Aqaba, gradually moving up from the canal area as the Israeli army reluctantly retreated behind the original Egypt–Israel armistice line. Contingents from 10 countries, selected from the offers of 24 United Nations members, formed the UNEF.[9] These included all the necessary supply and supporting units to make UNEF a self-sufficient body.

UNEF continued operations far beyond initial expectations. During its oversight, no alteration by force of the political or territorial situation occurred. Acts of violence have been isolated. While no permanent settlement of the Egyptian–Israeli conflict is in sight, UNEF has apparently insured the stability and peace it was its purpose to secure.

The quiet that now prevails is a tribute to the successful resolution of extremely delicate problems which the United Nations, particularly the Secretary-General, confronted in the course of organizing the force and placing it in operation.

Entry by Permit—The Bargain for Egyptian Consent

First, the Egyptians were unexpectedly sensitive to terms that seemed essential to maintain the international initiative and accountability of the force, and without which it would hardly have been able to satisfy the minimal demands of the countries which were asked to withdraw their forces. Although UNEF was to be the instrument of Egypt's salvation from

---

[7] See p. 184, below, and also Chapter 2 for discussion of the problem posed by some members' refusing to pay the assessments for UNEF.

[8] Frye, *op. cit.,* p. 21.

[9] Brazil, Canada, Colombia, Denmark, Finland, India, Indonesia, Norway, Sweden, and Yugoslavia. In September, 1958, the Finns and Indonesians withdrew.

complete defeat, the Egyptian government balked at letting the force enter its territory—the place the immediate tasks obviously lay—unless assured of virtual control over every aspect of its operation, including who was to compose it. This appeared to many as an intolerable attempt by the beneficiary to dictate to the United Nations—almost as brazen as the previously rejected British–French demand for a final say on UNEF. Yet, the United Nations stood committed to acting only with the consent of the parties concerned, and especially consent of countries where the force would be stationed. Egyptian agreement was imperative for the force to be able to function at all.

The most acute part of the problem concerned composition of the force. Egypt, in effect, wanted to pick the countries that would participate and, therefore, have troops on its soil. It wished to exclude the Commonwealth countries, some of whom were among the project's strongest supporters, because they were identified with Britain. It would have been glad to have had Soviet bloc contingents. At issue were both the principles of international responsibility for the force and its essential neutrality. In addition, rebuffing generous offers of assistance was not calculated to sustain the broad base of moral support in the United Nations and the public enthusiasm that was beginning to form in back of the project.

The Secretary-General and his aides executed a series of rapid and adroit diplomatic maneuvers, thus resolving the impasse sufficiently to get at least a token force on its way to the scene. They reasoned correctly that this was the vital point—to get UNEF physically "on location" so that all could see it as a reality and count on its presence. Then, some of the other issues as they arose could be handled in the concrete, rather than on the basis of conjecture.

The key to satisfactory relations with Egypt was sidestepping explicit assurances of any kind in favor of a "good faith" understanding. The Secretary-General gave his personal interpretations of the relevant General Assembly resolutions, approved by the Advisory Committee, which accepted the general proposition that Egypt could determine where UNEF should be stationed, that it would stay no longer than Egypt was willing, and that it would never act to impose outside decisions on Egypt. On the matter of composition, organization, and operational direction of the force, he maintained the United Nations' inescapable responsibility but did "defer" action on accepting contingents to which the Egyptians were strenuously opposed. However, he successfully persuaded the Egyptians, at least partially, to retract their objection to Canadian participation—an important achievement from a symbolic as well as a practical standpoint, because Canada stood as UNEF's chief architect and one of the first to offer concrete support.[10]

---

[10] Canadian air and logistic support was accepted, but the Queen's Own Rifles, crack Canadian regiment, had to return to barracks after being all set to sail for Egypt. Apparently the Egyptians were concerned lest the Canadians be mistaken for Britishers and treated to a hostile reception. See Frye, *op. cit.*

On this general basis, the Egyptians accepted the presence of the force. A few days after the first UNEF contingents reached Egypt, Secretary-General Hammarskjöld flew to Cairo and settled with the Egyptian authorities the public form of their understanding. The government of Egypt declared that "when exercising its sovereign rights on any matter concerning the presence and functioning of UNEF, it will be guided, in good faith, by its acceptance of the General Assembly Resolution 1000" (the basic resolution which authorized the creation of UNEF and provided for its international character and direction). The Secretary-General declared, for the United Nations, that the activities of UNEF "will be guided, in good faith, by the task established for the Force in the aforementioned resolutions, in particular the United Nations, understanding this to correspond to the wishes of the Government of Egypt, reaffirms its willingness to maintain UNEF until its task is completed." Then the Egyptian government and the Secretary-General agreed that they would "explore jointly concrete aspects of the functioning of UNEF, including its stationing and the question of its lines of communication and supply."[11]

Hammarskjöld later worked out details and the General Assembly approved an agreement with Egypt on the status of the UNEF. The presence of the force was accepted on a blanket basis in the entire "area of operations," including lines of communication and supply. Its personnel were obligated to respect Egypt's laws and to refrain from actions incompatible with their international status. But they were granted immunity from Egypt's jurisdiction on the understanding that their respective national states would exercise jurisdiction over them for crimes or offenses committed in Egypt and that civil claims could be settled on the same basis as claims against the United Nations. Disciplinary authority on UNEF premises is exercised by UNEF military police, who have been given the power of arrest over members of the force by the commanding officers of each national contingent. Egyptian authorities usually take charge outside the premises, immediately turning over to UNEF any of its personnel they arrest.

The Egyptian government provided the premises of the force (free when government owned). It assured freedom of movement within the area of operations and unrestricted communications.[12]

Israel's Recalcitrance

The second critical operational problem was posed by Israel's refusal to agree to any terms for the UNEF to function on its side of the armistice line. This, for a time, jeopardized the entire arrangement, because the Egyptians

---

[11] This *aide-memoire,* U.N. Doc A/3375, was noted with approval by the General Assembly on November 24, 1956—Resolution 1121 (VI)—and constituted the basic understanding between the United Nations and Egypt concerning UNEF.

[12] See the Agreement on the Status of U.N.E.F. (U.N. Doc. A/3526 and Annexes, Official Records of the General Assembly, 11th sess., Annexes, agenda item 66).

felt that the Israelis, of all people, should be under UNEF watch, having launched the attack, and that a one-sided stationing of UNEF in Egypt would suggest an occupation rather than a patrol. Hammarskjöld persuaded the Egyptian government, however, that it was better to have what could be secured—namely, the peaceful replacement of an Israeli occupation by UNEF—than to risk further war. Then, there was always the possibility that Israel could be persuaded to let UNEF in at some later date, though this hope was never realized.

Recruiting and Organizing

A third difficulty was how to piece together a workable, balanced, and self-contained force, appropriate to the task at hand, from the heterogeneous offers of the contributing countries. In contrast to the Korean and other experiences, the United Nations was bombarded by governments that proffered their help. Often, it was a question of politely declining offers of certain types of assistance—troops, for example—when the offers exceeded what could be used effectively. Saying "No, thanks" required the highest order of diplomatic finesse—the customary protocol was to "defer" accept-ance, pending further evidence as to the precise scope and character of the needs after UNEF was functioning on the field.

But there were gaps to fill, and the Secretariat went on a hunt for donors of specific types of assistance. Quick transportation to the scene was essential. The United States supplied an airlift for the initial dispatch of UNEF contingents from their home bases to a staging area provided by Italy at Capodichino airport near Naples. Then they were flown to Egypt by Swiss Air Force and later by the Canadian Air Force.

There was an acute shortage of well-trained technical and administrative staff and of mobile units, particularly needed for a desert operation of this kind. An independent signals company was required. Headquarters engineer, transport, shop repair, and medical personnel were needed. A light air unit was essential for functions inside the UNEF operations area. The problem was accentuated, of course, because of the decision to exclude from active service nationals of the very countries which had the largest and best-equipped military establishments—the major powers. Also, other militarily well-developed countries like Czechoslovakia and Turkey were barred be-cause they might have a political interest too close in the situation.

The formidable recruitment problems were overcome swiftly, however, as the Secretariat boldly asked for what they needed. Yugoslavia delivered a reconnaissance battalion, complete with equipment, to Port Said by November 28. Canada (holding no grudge over Egypt's initial testiness) was a principal source of technical personnel and air support, as well as providing a fully equipped light armored squadron.

All of the disparate elements were effectively integrated in a joint working relationship under an organizational structure as international and cooperative as the Korean command had been national and authoritarian. Chief of Staff General Burns, the Canadian head of the United Nations Truce Supervision Organization in Palestine, headed a military staff composed of officers from each of the national contingents. The commanders of each contingent were responsible for the proper functioning of their personnel and were free to communicate with their home governments on all matters affecting their units. Despite this somewhat dual line of responsibility, and the large degree of autonomy left with each contingent, the arrangement worked with remarkable smoothness. The practice of agreeing to assignment of functions among contingents was followed, which enabled each to maintain its separate identity and internal cohesion, and avoided the difficulties of trying to weld together elements of different nationalities with different training and methods of work. Thus, the Indian contingent took responsibility for the supply depot, Norway and Canada covered medical needs, Canada and India provided transport and signals.

Procurement and delivery of supplies was a complex problem, because there was no established pipeline available for such an operation as UNEF. A mixed solution was worked out. The participating governments directly furnished much of their own troops' requirements. United Nations Headquarters procured supplies when it could do so economically, and UNEF itself set up a supply office in Italy to get what it could appropriately from European sources, especially the military forces in Germany. Also, local supplies were sometimes purchased.

Moving to Location

The actual deployment of the force in between the combatant forces was an operation of greatest delicacy. Though the cease-fire was formally in effect, tempers were high and trigger fingers nervous. No one was quite sure how firm the truce was going to be. Egyptian civilians and guerrillas were not under tight control.

Maintenance of both public order and respect for the truce, pending withdrawal of foreign forces and reestablishment of Egyptian authority in the evacuated areas, was UNEF's immediate responsibility. This was accomplished largely through negotiation by the UNEF Command with the respective commanders of the withdrawing forces and the Egyptian army and also with local Egyptian authorities. Precise agreements on the timing of withdrawals made possible their almost simultaneous replacement by UNEF. The Egyptian army was called on to exercise the greatest self-restraint against acts of violence or premature entry into the evacuated areas, and the Egyptian government appealed to the local populations likewise to cause no trouble.

UNEF troops, when attacked, had the right to fire in self-defense, but they were never to take the initiative in the use of arms. This made them virtual sitting ducks for infiltrators, guerrillas, or ordinary looters as well as any organized attack. Fortunately, such incidents were few.

Financing

Financing UNEF has proved to be its major continuing headache. The member states have not contributed voluntarily in sufficient amount to pay for such a large and costly operation.

According to the principles originally agreed on, the costs, over and above the normal salary and equipment of the troops, were to be covered out of a special budget. For several reasons, this seemed preferable to charging them up to the regular United Nations budget. Among them: the costs could not be precisely estimated when the scope and duration of the assignment were uncertain; it was unclear how much of the cost could be met from the various offers of assistance without charge to the United Nations; and, above all, it was necessary to avoid any delay that might result from haggling over who should pay the bill. The General Assembly consequently made blanket authorizations for the cost of the force, totaling close to $170 million through 1964, and appealed to member states for contributions to meet it.

As only about half the first year's authorization was pledged, the Assembly decided on a scale of assessments on everyone, similar to that for the regular budget. But a number of states have refused to pay the assessment. The Soviet Union, for instance, has maintained that all the cost ought to be charged up to the "aggressors." The net effect of such action has been to cause the United Nations administration great difficulty and, ultimately, to saddle an even greater burden on cooperative states. More support has eroded away as the operation has dragged on far beyond the expected duration, so that even though relatively stable conditions have enabled UNEF to reduce its costs, the problem of insuring its fiscal base remains serious.[13]

Morale

The morale of the force has not posed a major problem, although it had to work in circumstances which were most uncongenial. The force is deployed along a line of almost 200 miles in rugged terrain, mostly hot, uninhabited desert, and in 76 observation posts around the perimeter of the Gaza Strip. Their duties of day and night observation and patrol are undramatic and unchanging—there is no break in the boredom or the isolation.

UNEF has followed the practice of frequent rotation for the troops, paying the costs of transportation for home leave. It has also provided leave centers in Cairo, Beirut, and Alexandria, and developed a varied welfare and recreational program.

Nevertheless, the good spirits and exemplary conduct of the force are

---

[13] See Chapter 2 for review of the financial crisis that has beset the U.N. as a result of these refusals to support its peace-keeping operations.

mainly a tribute to its high sense of commitment to, and consciousness of, its unique international security role.

THE UNEF MODEL—CAN IT BE FOLLOWED ELSEWHERE?

The accomplishment of UNEF has been widely hailed as a miracle—wonderful but unrepeatable.

Others insist that it offers a precedent for the United Nations to follow in other crises, and they urge that it or something like it be made a permanent part of the United Nations organization—a "United Nations Peace Force" available for instant use. Granted that UNEF was formed under conditions which make it "an accident of history," could not adequate planning based on its experience significantly increase the United Nations' capacity to *prevent* future crises from erupting into war, instead of leaving it to improvise ad hoc arrangements to stop a war that has started? Is not the principal lesson of UNEF that the United Nations has stumbled onto an entirely different and much more effective way of keeping the peace in many circumstances than any of the formulas for collective security?

The case, on the face of it, seems so conclusive it is surprising to find that Secretary-General Hammarskjöld, who had more responsibility for the creation and functioning of UNEF than anyone else, demurred over most proposals for establishing such a Force on a permanent basis. He also voiced skepticism about following the UNEF model in such situations as the Lebanon–Jordan crisis of 1958 or the Berlin crisis of 1959.

His reservations stemmed from a conviction that the UNEF approach could be successful only if (1) the political conditions were such that the United Nations could command almost universal support for its actions on the part both of the countries immediately involved and the world outside, and (2) the principles of UNEF were scrupulously observed. He suspected that many members of the United Nations are not genuinely disposed to generalize the United Nations' action in the Middle East to all situations in which security is threatened, nor prepared to subscribe to the basic principles that guided the UNEF operation. In other words, UNEF was, he felt, really a precision instrument made to order for a particular set of circumstances, not a tool of general utility for security purposes. Its use should be reserved, therefore, for appropriate occasions, and appropriateness could hardly be known in advance. Hence, he concluded there was little point to having UNEF permanently in being, for the conditions were likely to vary greatly from situation to situation.[14]

---

[14] See Report of the Secretary-General, United National Emergency Force (Summary Study of the Experience Derived from the Establishment and Operation of the Force, U.N. Doc. A/3943, October 9, 1958), chap. 7.

Adaptation—The Crisis over Lebanon and Jordan

For instance, Mr. Hammarskjöld was convinced that it would not have been possible to interpose a United Nations force between conflicting parties in Lebanon or Jordan in 1958, when their governments felt threatened by the United Arab Republic. The United Nations Force would have had difficulty in distinguishing its presence and functions from those of the government's own troops in each country.

In Lebanon, particularly, the United Nations would have been hard put to it not to become involved in the internal conflicts that were part and parcel of the unstable situation. United Nations experience with these various Middle East situations persuaded the Secretary-General that

> . . . in each new conflict situation in which the United Nations might be called upon to intervene with military personnel, the nature of the actual organization required and its paramilitary aspects would be determined by the particular needs of the situation and could not therefore be anticipated in advance. Thus, for example, stand-by arrangements for a force designed for a UNEF-type operation would not have been of practical value in either of the situations in Lebanon or Jordan, where conditions required an approach in all relevant aspects quite different from that employed in UNEF.

The United Nations Observers Corps.   What the United Nations did in Lebanon was to send in a corps of observers—at one point, almost 200 of them—to determine whether substantial assistance was moving across the border from the United Arab Republic (Syria–Egypt) to support rebel forces against the government of President Chamoun. The situation was extremely confused by internal political rivalries as well as by powerful appeals for Arab unity, stimulated by supporters of Egypt's Nasser, and overtones of the Western–Communist struggle. It was much further complicated when the United States, on the request of the Lebanese President, landed forces to keep his government from being overthrown and, presumably, also to keep Lebanon independent from Nasser's control. Meanwhile, the Lebanese army did not seem to be fully engaged in suppressing the rebellion—evidently because its officers, including the chief of staff, were anxious to avoid major bloodshed that would further split the country. The United Arab Republic, for its part, denied that it was engaged in any aggression against Lebanon.

In such circumstances, Hammarskjöld considered the wisest course for the United Nations was to make certain of the facts concerning outside intervention. The process of international observation might serve simultaneously to check temptations to intervene in the future.

This is precisely what occurred. The observers quickly secured permission from both the government and rebel forces to move to the Syrian border—a denial of permission by either side would have been tantamount to admission that their respective claims were unfounded. The observers reported they could detect no evidence of sufficient outside support to affect the outcome of the conflict. The government vehemently objected that the observers were misled and, in any case, could not be aware of what had gone on before they arrived. Whatever the earlier situation may have been, as the observers patrolled the frontier with increasing thoroughness they were able to assure the United Nations as to the current state of affairs. This greatly eased the tension, for with the United Arab Republic out of the picture as an active protagonist, the United States was under pressure to withdraw promptly from its intervention. It should be emphasized that at no point did the United Nations representatives do more than observe. They refrained completely from any attempt to patch up an internal political settlement. This the United Nations made clear was the business of the Lebanese themselves. Nor did observers take on a military role—in contrast to UNEF in Egypt—because their task was merely to ascertain that foreign countries were not engaged in actions that violated Lebanon's independence and integrity as a sovereign state. This complete neutrality was a critical factor in the success of the mission.[15]

The United Nations "Presence." In stabilizing relations over the longer run between the United Arab Republic and those of its Arab neighbors which feared its expansionist aspirations (Lebanon and Jordan particularly), the United Nations offered still another variant of its security role. The problem now seemed more political and diplomatic than military. The danger of armed attack, direct or indirect, had been minimized by the operation of the Observers Corps. But relations were left embittered by Egyptian pressures, and the bloody overthrow of the Iraq government still had everyone in jitters. Some suggested that the functions and area of operations of UNEF should be extended to include patroling all the frontiers of Middle Eastern countries, not just the demarcation line between Israel and Egypt. But this raised objections on two grounds: it would identify UNEF with the particular governments in power, and it would imply a dependence of these governments on the United Nations, amounting to a derogation of sovereignty. Furthermore, it would require an immense expansion of the force and of its costs.

Hammarskjöld therefore proposed, and the General Assembly and concerned countries agreed, that the United Nations would establish a "presence" in the Middle East to assist the countries in communicating with one another on problems that disturbed their relations and to aid in preventing their aggravation by unilateral acts. This presence, as ultimately devised by

---

[15] For a careful study of this experience see Gerald L. Curtis, "The United Nations Observation Group in Lebanon," *International Organization,* Autumn, 1964.

Hammarskjöld, was a United Nations-appointed diplomatic officer, though not officially designated as an ambassador of the United Nations, whose job was to maintain regular contacts with the leading officials of each government on matters affecting stability in the Middle East.

These experiences reinforced the Secretary-General's conviction that the United Nations needed to maintain flexibility in its security role, ready to apply different measures as the varying circumstances of each situation dictated.

THE CONGO NIGHTMARE

A crucial opportunity to test the U.N.'s new style of peace-keeping came unexpectedly, under conditions completely different from those in the Middle East, underscoring Hammarskjöld's foresight about the need for flexibility. In the Congo, the United Nations was called on to maintain internal law and order, as well as to prevent external intervention, in the face of raw anarchy. All governmental authority collapsed when the former Belgian colony gained independence with no unity of political leadership, indigenous administrative experience, or national consciousness. Tribal and personal rivalries made a shambles of the central governmental structure which was supposed to be established, and sparked secessionist movements that were fanned by foreign mercenary or political interests (Belgians seeking to salvage some of their stake, Communists on the make, etc.). Violence broke out all over as mutinous soldiers and police themselves indulged a taste for power, and terrorized both population and their nominal commanders and government.

A detailed account of United Nations efforts to cope with this incredibly complex situation is not possible here.[16] An attempt must be made to identify the principal courses of action undertaken, explain why they were undertaken, assess their consequences, and try to determine why they were or were not effective.

An overall evaluation would recognize the United Nations' Congo operation as the most perplexing, the most involved, and the most costly of its history, with the end results still hidden in the jungle of Central African politics. Financially, the peace-keeping military force sent to the Congo in July, 1960, and maintained at varying strength until June 30, 1964, cost about $450 million; civil aid to support the area's economy, and to restore and develop its governmental and social services added about $50 million

---

[16] Two quite comprehensive accounts are: King Gordon, *UN in the Congo* (New York: Carnegie Endowment for International Peace, 1962); and Thomas M. Franck and John Carey, *The Role of the United Nations in the Congo* (working paper for the Second Hammarskjöld Forum, published for the Association of the Bar of the City of New York) (Dobbs Ferry, N.Y.: Oceana Publications, Inc., 1963).

more. While in the perspective of national defense budgets this may seem picayune, the refusal of many U.N. members to share in these expenses plunged the organization into a state of virtual bankruptcy (see Chapter 2). On the personal side, serious casualties were suffered, including the loss of Secretary-General Hammarskjöld.

U.N. Operations

The U.N. engaged in three quite distinct types of activity.

1. It formed and deployed an international military force the United Nations Operation in the Congo (ONUC) similar in organization to UNEF, but different in purpose and, ultimately, in conduct.
2. It provided massive technical assistance, and substantial economic aid as well, to help the government function effectively and to make the country viable economically and socially.
3. It undertook a highly delicate task of political negotiation, unique in its experience, to bring the country's rival leaders and factions together and get them to accept a workable form of government. In other words, the U.N. went into the business of constitution-making and nation-building in the vacuum created by the Congo's precipitous plunge into independence.

It was the first of these that became the focal point of controversy, though the other actions were just as vital and almost as frustrating. What happened was that the role of the U.N. force quickly became the decisive factor in at least three interrelated struggles for political power: the many-faceted international machinations of Congolese leaders; the attempt of Belgian colonials to hold on to property and influence by exploiting the conflicting ambitions of the Congolese; and the thrusts and parries of the cold war opponents on the battleground of a new country. In addition, other African countries were tempted to nurture their own special interests in the Congo backyard, while uniting in a common concern to send all "colonialists" packing and reserve Africa for Africans to run. Given this situation, the small, polyglot U.N. "army," never numbering more than 20,000, held the reins of destiny because it was the only disciplined, centrally accountable power in the country. How it was used would control the outcome of all the power struggles; hence, it became itself the target of all the protagonists. Everyone wanted the U.N. to throw its weight on his side, and was angry when it did not.

Three Mandates for ONUC

The force was ultimately given three distinct mandates: to maintain law and order; to prevent foreign intervention; to unify the country. These did not, in practice, turn out to be mutually consistent.

The first seemed simple and straightforward, though really unique in U.N.

experience—to help the new government's national security forces "to meet fully their tasks," namely, to insure civil order. This was military technical assistance, requested by a government unable on its own to preserve internal peace and security.

From the beginning, however, this was linked with the second objective—to prevent foreign intervention in the Congo. The immediate task was to secure withdrawal of Belgian troops who had come back during the wave of violence against Europeans which had swept the country after independence. This was the dominant motif of the Congo government's original appeal to the Security Council. Its President Kasavubu and Prime Minister Lumumba stressed that "the essential purpose of the requested military aid is to protect the national territory of the Congo against the present external aggression which is a threat to international peace." They accused the Belgians of instigating the secession of Katanga, the Congo's richest province, in order to perpetuate the "colonialist regime".

This cast the situation in the more familiar light of UNEF's role in the Suez crisis, with focus on the U.N.'s interposing its presence in a manner that would remove all occasion for foreign states to do any "policing." There were familiar overtones also in prospects that the great powers might take a hand, as Lumumba had broadcast appeals both to the U.S. and the Soviet Union, and the Soviets had given a ready and enthusiastic response.

Consequently, the Security Council urgently called on Belgium to withdraw its troops, and authorized the Secretary-General "to take all necessary action to this effect." It was not anticipated that this would require more than diplomatic pressure; but they did not figure on an exceptionally recalcitrant Belgian government and a die-hard core of officers, soldiers, and former colonists who would not budge from the Katanga haven provided them by Moise Tshombe in return for buttressing his control as president of the secessionist province. Strident demands for the U.N. force to use force to throw them out came variously from the central government, the Soviet phalanx, and several of the African states that had supplied troops to the U.N. This was ultimately authorized in an exceptionally stern resolution by the Council, following Belgian-led attacks on U.N. forces stationed in Katanga and Hammarskjöld's death enroute to attempt a peaceful settlement of the Katanga situation. Meanwhile, the Belgian government finally buckled and withdrew all support of the freebooters, even to canceling their passports. The U.N. force then expeditiously rounded up the foreigners (now including some French and South Africans) and deported them, only to find them filtering back to resume their gadfly tactics.

ONUC was more efficacious in preventing other foreign intervention. The principal problem was an influx of Soviet materiel and personnel, first to buttress Mr. Lumumba's campaign for complete personal power, and, after he was captured and murdered by his political enemies, to enable Lumumba followers to control and detach the big Oriente Province from the central government's authority. But the U.N. force took over the main airports and denied their use to all foreign aircraft, except those supporting its operation, thus cutting the critical routes of supply to this virtually landlocked country.

The third mandate—to keep the country from disintegration—was not stated with the directness and precision of the others. This may have been due to the constitutional confusion that prevailed for almost two years, during a large part of which no government in operation had a sound legal basis for governing anywhere in the Congo. Yet, all the U.N.'s actions were consistently conducted on the presumption that the Congo was a single political entity and should remain so.

The problem was that few of the Congo's leaders were interested in unity unless they could run the country. First one and then another would launch a separatist move, built around the core of his own tribe; his competitors would try by force or guile to make him heel to the command of the central government; when the pressure mounted, the separatist would come to the conference table and try to reverse roles by maneuvering into a winning coalition. The chips were held mostly by those who held the guns—as Mr. Lumumba, the only leader who could command a semblance of national following, found out when he was summarily ousted by Colonel Mobutu, heading the so-called national army, and was in the end murdered when he was turned over for "safekeeping" to Tshombe's Katangese army.

The U.N. had a bad time threading its way between the mandate for unity and one of the most fundamental of its guiding principles—a firm commitment not to "be a party to or in any way intervene in or be used to influence the outcome of any internal conflict, constitutional or otherwise." (Security Council Resolution of August 9, 1960.) It never did find a clear way out of this dilemma, for whatever it did to foster unity inevitably had a profound impact on the internal political struggle. In general, its strategy was: (1) to deploy the U.N. force throughout the country, on its own initiative, without consent of provincial authorities (like Tshombe), as a physical demonstration that it recognized only one country and one authoritative government at the center; but (2) to withhold the force from active military operations against secessionists, at least until a truly responsible central government with the widest possible support and some semblance of legitimacy could be formed.

Thus, unification was sought primarily through political diplomacy rather than military action, a course fraught with frustration as the U.N. representatives sought a consensus that would tie together the slippery eels of Congolese politics. These labors earned Hammarskjöld and his staff the bitter Soviet denunciation of being imperialist lackeys, and even some of the early staunch participants in the U.N. operation began to pull out, impatient for more forceful action to end the secessions and firmly entrench a strong national government.

Katanga was, of course, the sharpest thorn, led by the wily Tshombe with the principal wealth of the Congo at his disposal, the backing of the Belgian mining and financial interests, and a well-knit, professionally led fighting force built around a core of Belgian and other foreign military and paramilitary personnel.

Ultimately, politics gave way to force, and the U.N. force was turned from peace-keeping to winning a civil war on behalf of a reconstituted central government (the official rationale was "to prevent civil war"). It is still uncertain whether Hammarskjöld himself authorized this basic change from a policy he had considered fundamental to successful "preventive diplomacy"—that is, a policy whereby the U.N. peace-keeping force would steadfastly refrain from all use of force except in self-defense. It seems more likely that O'Brien, the U.N.'s mercurial chief in Katanga, infuriated by Katangese humiliations and provocations, took matters into his own hands, confident that he could clean up the whole mess by a few bold strokes unhampered by headquarters. In any case, the move badly miscarried, and Hammarskjöld was killed while flying to straighten it out.

But this made the Security Council and newly-elected Acting Secretary-General U Thant determined to suppress all Katangese interference with, and attacks on, the U.N. forces and officials, and, in the process, to end the secession once and for all. In the second round of force, the U.N. was more successful, and Tshombe finally gave way, "recognized the indissoluble unity of the Republic of the Congo," accepted the authority of the central government, and agreed to join in preparing a new constitution.

This was not the end, however. After a year of negotiations, Tshombe was still running his Katanga, having skillfully evaded all decisive steps toward unification, while agreeing in principle to a Plan for National Reconciliation sponsored by the Secretary-General when direct talks among the Congolese leaders broke down. After a careful buildup of ONUC, with the U.S. furnishing it additional equipment, a third round of fighting completely eliminated all resistance in Katanga. Tshombe left the country. U Thant could declare that the U.N. had now safeguarded the unity, territorial integrity, and political independence of the Congo. But the declaration was premature; as was the withdrawal of ONUC on June 30, 1964, under pressure of financial boycott by its antagonists and the attrition of concern on the part of its supporters.[17] For no sooner had the U.N.'s blue helmets left, than the country seethed, heaved and blew apart. A new orgy of factional violence erupted, inviting a rush of foreign intervention, collapse of the

---

[17] The financial boycott of the U.N.'s peacekeeping operations is reviewed in Chapter 2. See p. 43–47.

central authority, the destruction of all internal security, and, in the most ironic twist of all, the return of Tshombe, this time to take over as *national* Prime Minister, talking national reconciliation and unification: Thereupon, disorder escalated into full-scale civil war, waged with increasing ferocity and atrocity, and massively supported on both sides from the outside. Tshombe reconstituted an army of white mercenaries as the spearhead of his bid for control. The leftist groups drew supplies and leadership from North Africa, Russia and apparently even China. At a crucial point, the U.S. and Belgium took a forceful hand: a sudden, short, in-and-out paratroop operation to rescue several hundred white persons held as hostages by the leftists, which simultaneously opened the way for Tshombe's army to take control momentarily of some of his opponents' key strongholds.

The end of the Congo's agony is not in sight. For the outside world at the moment seems in no mood to reactivate the U.N.'s peacekeeping mission; and no substitute has been put forward, though there has been some talk in the Organization of African Unity of forming an all-African force to "police" the Congo.

Guiding Principles

In organizing its Congo mission, the U.N. tried to apply the basic principles which guided UNEF (see above).

1. It justified its presence on the grounds that the government concerned had asked for it: ONUC was in the Congo by invitation and consent. (But the UN. sharply distinguished between the original "legitimate" central government, which had extended the initial invitation, and all usurping or secessionist governments. From these it neither asked consent nor admitted any obligation to do so. During the chaotic months when no unified constitutional government was operating, Hammarskjöld simply proceeded on the basis that the consent, once given, had never been withdrawn by proper authority.)

2. The United Nations alone decided on the composition of its force, while taking into account the views of the host government. (As in the case of Egypt, the U.N. had uneasy moments effecting this delicate balance, but for different reasons. Some of the troops were recruited from governments such as Ghana which demonstrated partisanship in the infighting among Congolese factions, but the U.N. successfully resisted demands for their removal.)

3. Deliberately omitted from ONUC were military units from any of the permanent members of the Security Council.

   But an important exception was made to the related principle of excluding all other parties that might be considered as having a special interest in the situation. Alive to the widespread African sensibility that African problems were peculiarly the business of Africans, the Secretary-General explicitly called on African governments to supply a large part of the force, sought out Africans for many of the political and technical assistance assignments, and placed himself under the policy guidance of an African Advisory Committee.

4. The U.N. insisted that its forces and personnel should have full freedom of movement and all local facilities necessary for their tasks. As we have seen, some fighting was necessary to enforce this demand both in the secessionist areas and against the unruly national army.

5. The entire operation was accountable through the Secretary-General to the main organs of the United Nations, and acted in pursuance of Security Council or General Assembly resolutions. Personnel on U.N. duty were held exclusively loyal to the aims of the U.N., and demonstrated this loyalty with exceptional devotion and courage. It was, throughout, a truly international operation, in composition, direction, and collective responsibility.

Three of UNEF's guiding principles, however, proved inapplicable in the Congo.

1. Try as it could to honor the mandate to be no party to internal political conflict, the U.N. seemed drawn inexorably into a position where its every action did influence domestic politics. And, as we have seen, producing a viable government and stamping out secession came to be officially sanctioned by the organization as a principal mission of the operation.

2. The basic principle that force was not to be used except in self-defense was abandoned when the U.N. ultimately committed itself to compulsory unification as an integral part of its mission. It should be noted, though, that Hammarskjöld himself held doggedly to the no-force principal as a crucial requirement for this kind of international peace-keeping operation, at the cost of grave misunderstanding, the personal abuse of the Soviet Union, and, in the end, his life.

3. The principle that all member states are obligated to share the costs, according to their normal scale of contributions to the U.N., has been upheld by International Court of Justice opinion and General Assembly resolution, but denied in practice by the outright refusal of many states to pay and by the arrears of others.

Outcomes

Tallying the score for the U.N.'s four years of travail in the Congo, it is clear that the U.N. did do a major part of what it was commissioned to do, *while its commission lasted.* But it was pushed and drawn into some assignments incompatible with the fundamental nature of the organization; and it departed, at critical junctures, from certain of the basic principles which had governed its successful ventures into peacekeeping in other situations.

Its greatest success was in immunizing the Congo from foreign power politics and insuring that the Congolese would have at least the opportunity to manage a country of their own if they wanted to and could. The U.N. made independence a reality (during the life of its mandate) by removing the vestiges of Belgian colonial rulership, by keeping the cold war out, and by channeling all other extraneous influences (especially the various political crosscurrents of the country's African neighbors) through the collective instrumentalities of the U.N. presence.

Second, it had constructed a government and set it up in business, although presumably both U.N. Charter and Security Council directives prohibited all domestic interference. This unprecedented initiative by an international organization, reaching even to the point of drafting and imposing what amounted to a constitution for the country, was taken in response to the unprecedented conditions it faced. Some measure of internal stability and governmental responsibility was an absolute prerequisite for effective independence; and in the political jungle that was the Congo, someone from the outside had to do what should have been done before independence—create a workable frame of government. The exceptional features of the U.N.'s handiwork were: first, what is usually strictly a homemade product was, in this case, largely put together by outside hands; second, what is usually a politician's art became an exercise of technical craftsmanship. The reasons are plain: There was neither sufficient aptitude nor the minimum degree of personal disinterestedness necessary for local political initiative to put a government together.

Third, the U.N.'s civilian technical assistance mission had patiently laid the basis for social and economic rehabilitation and development, with emphasis on the organization of sound indigenous institutions and training of a Congolese administrative cadre capable of conducting essential public services, *given* conditions of peace and political stability.[18]

On the other hand the U.N. was least successful in what was to be its elemental task—keeping the peace within the Congo. It, indeed, dampened down a good many fires of violence, but it was unable to establish security for keeps throughout the country. Tribal, ideological, personal, and apparently racial hostilities kept major outbursts erupting first in one area, then another, and the U.N. force was often unable to do much more than conduct rescue operations. This highlighted once again the critical deficiency—lack of an effective government, able to command respect for its authority. The problem was not only that of secessions. The government never had a firm hold on its own security forces. For one wild year, the "army" itself ran things (within the area it could control), and this meant that soldiers would decide whether they would prevent violence or indulge in it, and when and whom

---

[18] It should be noted that the U.N. technical assistance mission continued its operations after ONUC was pulled out, heroically attempting to build foundations for the country's future, as well as distributing food and other vital supplies to the civilian population through all the turmoil.

they would beat and fight (including the U.N.'s own troops and officials). The basic problem was still unresolved when the ONUC mission terminated. But however unsatisfactory the U.N.'s peacekeeping record may have been, what followed the withdrawal of ONUC vividly demonstrated what can happen in default of such collective responsibility by the international community.

PATTERN FOR THE FUTURE

At this point, evaluation of the significance of the U.N.'s new approach to the preservation of peace—interposition of an international peace-keeping "presence" in turbulent areas of high tension, or what Secretary-General Hammarskjöld called "preventive diplomacy"—is necessarily tentative. The first tests are still running, with the results not all in. But already there is enough to warrant the conclusion by a careful scholar of international affairs that "this approach to the stabilization of the precarious international order appears to offer the organization its greatest opportunity to render significant political service in the cold war era."[19] And in demonstration of their confidence that this is so, a number of the smaller states which have contributed most heavily in men and resources to U.N. peacekeeping efforts in the past (notably the Scandinavian countries) have decided to recruit, train and maintain special volunteer forces of their own, to be available on call for United Nations duty. Furthermore, there seems no end to "opportunities" for the U.N. to become embroiled in peacekeeping initiatives—witness the call for it to keep a lid on the bitter violence between Greek and Turk on Cyprus, thereby forestalling an international war between Greece and Turkey which neither craved.

The case is made, however, that the effectiveness of preventive diplomacy depends above all else on consent on the major cold war antagonists to its conduct. Both powers must "attach such great value to the avoidance of general war that they be disposed to welcome the neutralization of potential breeding grounds of such war in the zones outside their blocs."[20] This was the essential difference between the Middle East and Congo experiences. In the Middle East, both sides clearly wanted to avoid a direct confrontation that held the potentiality of mushrooming into thermonuclear

---

[19] Inis L. Claude, Jr., *Swords Into Plowshares* (3rd ed.; New York: Random House, 1964), p. 302.

[20] *Ibid.*, pp. 298–99. For further systematic analysis and evaluation, see: Arthur L. Burns and Nina Heathcote, *Peace-keeping by UN Forces*, (New York: Praeger, 1962); and Lincoln P. Bloomfield *et al.*, *International Military Forces*, (Boston: Little, Brown, 1964). (See especially essays by Herbert Nicholas and Brian E. Urquhart on "UN Forces and Lessons of Suez and Congo").

war. In the Congo, the Soviet Union, while agreeable at the start to the U.N. role, turned vehemently against it and sought by every means to scuttle it. The reason it gave was that the U.N. had actually betrayed its trust. Instead of keeping the cold war out by neutralizing the Congo, it had taken sides with the imperialists and sold the country back into colonialism—a point of view which, curiously enough, received a kind of corroborating echo from the other side as Americans gloated over the "victory" that U.N. action in the Congo had given the West.

On the other hand, the record shows that great power consent may *not* be an absolute prerequisite for U.N. peacekeeping. Even in the Congo, after all, the U.N. did carry out extraordinary responsibilities, despite the lack of consensus among the powers, granted that the Soviet onslaught immensely complicated its life. The key issue is: What persuaded or restrained the cold war protagonists from more active intervention, especially with the Soviet Union feeling the way it did? One answer is the very fact of the U.N. mission. So long as it was on the scene, and effectively in control of the country's logistics, neither the Soviet Union nor the U.S. could step in without expecting immediate counteraction and a confrontation hardly worth the danger. Hence, the Soviet Union had to try to liquidate the operation from within the U.N. But here, Hammarskjöld's skillful diplomacy had made the U.N. mission a vehicle of African unity. Because the African states were invited to exercise a major influence in conducting the operation, they did not succumb to the temptation of playing on anyone else's interventionist team. It was they who principally gave the lie to the Soviet charge that the U.N. operation was an imperialist conspiracy. This was their show, and they would not give it up. In effect, Hammarskjöld transformed the special African interest into the disinterestedness or "international interest" on which the success of this kind of operation fundamentally depends.

Far more serious than the loss of Soviet consent was the result of being plunged into the Congo's internal political life. This virtually wrecked the operation, for the U.N. lost its appropriate role—a medium of collaboration among states—and became, instead, a political force within a state. By contrast, UNEF has consistently operated as a peace-keeping instrument *among* states, and has led a much calmer and more confident life. Perhaps the U.N. chose the only responsible course it could in venturing onto the shoals of domestic political management in the face of the chaos that was the Congo. But the crucial point in assessing the guidelines for future conduct is that the two roles of international peace-keeping and internal political tutelage do not seem to mix well. From the standpoint of the first, Hammarskjöld set forth at an early stage of the Congo ordeal what still appear to be the most cogent guiding principles in the light of the U.N.'s experience. The U.N. might have functioned better as peace-keeper if it had applied these principles with fuller consistency throughout its Congo venture:

The question before the General Assembly is no longer one of certain actions but one of the principles guiding them. Time and again the United Nations has had to face situations in which a wrong move might have tended to throw the weight of the organization over in favor of this or that specific party in a conflict of a primarily domestic character. To permit that to happen is indeed to intervene in domestic affairs contrary to the letter and spirit of the Charter. To avoid doing so is to be true to the letter and spirit of the Charter, whatever disappointment it might cause those who might have thought that they could add to their political weight by drawing the United Nations over to their side.

This is, of course, the basic reason for the principles spelled out at the very first stage of the Congo operation, and approved by the Security Council, to the effect that the United Nations force is not under the orders of a Government requesting its assistance and cannot be permitted to become a party to an internal conflict, be it one in which the Government is engaged or not. . . .

Further, as I have said, this is a question not of a man but of an institution. Use whatever word you like, independence, impartiality, objectivity—they all describe the essential aspects of what, without exception must be the attitude of the Secretary General . . . I would rather see that office break on strict adherence to the principle of independence, impartiality and objectivity than drift on the basis of compromise.[21]

This, then, is the basic pattern for United Nations action to maintain peace and security that, in the light of its experience to date, appears most likely to be effective. By definition, it cannot provide defense against armed attack pressed by a determined aggressor. Nor is it easily applicable to situations of deeply rooted and violent civil conflict. But the United Nations clearly can act to stabilize tense situations by interposing its presence in one form or another. The conflicting parties then know that their actions will, at least, come under international observation, as in Lebanon. In the event the United Nations has gone to the length of stationing a full-fledged peace force on the scene, no aggressive action could be undertaken without first sweeping aside the contingents of a dozen neutral countries, representing the entire community of nations—an action that would surely arouse the most extreme worldwide condemnation and resistance. The United Nations' police role banks for its effectiveness on the expectation that governments will not wish to incur the repercussions which would follow from an unmistakable and blatant act of violence observed by or directed against the international organization as a whole. The United Nations "police," be they observers or peace force, act as a trip wire. They cannot physically prevent aggression, but they restrain the

---

[21] Statement before the General Assembly, September 26, 1960, as quoted in *New York Times,* September 27, 1960, p. 16.

disposition to commit aggression, because their presence makes certain that the action will set off an alarm the world will be unable to ignore. At the same time, United Nations policing prevents the sending in of false alarms that could otherwise start actions against a state on the basis of unfounded suspicions.

Chapter 8

Security through Disarmament

Efforts to insure international peace and security have confronted, at every turn, the stark reality of a hundred armed nations, each in a position to start war on its own independent initiative. This is in marked contrast to the situation in a well-ordered society where a common governmental authority strictly controls use of weapons of destruction and often monopolizes their possession.

As we have seen in previous chapters, attempts to restrain nations from using the force at their command by organizing counterforce (through collective or regional security arrangements) have, at best, had limited success. The U.N.'s alternative approach—to interpose a peace-keeping "presence" in explosive situations—is admittedly completely dependent on the self-restraint of the nations involved. Any one of them can precipitate uncontrollable violence by either deliberate or unplanned use of the arms at its disposal.

The maintenance of peace is necessarily precarious as long as nations individually retain the capacity to wage war. Recognition of this fact has prompted the prolonged, complex, and as yet inconclusive search for security through disarmament.

The term "disarmament" is actually something of a misnomer, for, as customarily used, it refers not only to the giving up of arms but also to any limitations placed on their development or deployment. It covers proposals ranging all the way from complete elimination of national armament to a simple freeze on certain types of weapons or the "hot line" by which the U.S. and Soviet heads of government can immediately get in touch with each other if a nuclear missile has been misfired.

The essence of the approach is to restrict the means of military attack by one nation against another. The underlying assumption is that this will reduce the probability of attack and, in turn, of counterattack or "preventive" attack: first, because countries will hold back from war if they are not fully equipped and poised to wage it effectively; second, because countries will be less fearful of being attacked (and, hence, less prone to make an attack themselves) if their likely enemies are not mobilized for imminent war.

The strategy of disarmament, or arms control, is, in one sense, the exact reverse of the collective security system and the regional security alliances. Instead of trying to scare countries away from war by confronting them with a formidable "deterrent" force, disarmament seeks to establish conditions that will assure a country that others are neither intending to attack it nor capable of doing so, at least in the immediate future. The strategy is to unwind rather than to build up a confrontation of armed force.

This not only contradicts the basic premises of the collective and regional security approaches, but also flies in the face of the deeply held popular conviction that the measure of a nation's security is its own capacity for armed defense. It is not surprising, therefore, that the 50 years' history of the diplomacy of disarmament has produced mostly talk and little practice. Governments have been unwilling to risk a radical departure from traditional patterns of fending for security, no matter how insecure the old habits have left everyone.

Now the situation has changed, as the technology of destruction has overwhelmed all possibilities of physical defense and made national and human survival inescapably dependent on the nonuse, rather than the use, of arms. Recent negotiations demonstrate a new sense of urgency and the beginnings of genuine consensus on the design of international arrangements for arms limitation and control of far-reaching significance.

There is little point to reviewing here the tortuous chronology of the disarmament negotiations, and the shifts and turns of national positions on particular issues. For the past diplomacy of disarmament bears little relationship to the practical problems of organizing a workable system for dismantling the world's armaments. Because most governments did not consider disarmament a genuine objective of policy, the negotiations became a political sparring match. Expediency in the pursuit of strategic or political advantage dictated the stands taken, rather than serious concern to find a mutually acceptable basis for arms limitation.[1]

On the other hand, the intensive studies that proceeded alongside the diplomatic talk and double-talk have thoroughly explored major technical

---

[1] For detailed review of the record, see Philip Noel-Baker, *The Arms Race* (Dobbs Ferry, N.Y.: Oceana Publications, Inc., 1958); and Bernard G. Bechhoefer, *Post War Negotiations for Arms Control* (Washington, D.C.: Brookings Institution, 1961). The view that disarmament negotiations have amounted to little more than a form of political "gamesmanship" is argued by John W. Spanier and Joseph L. Nogee, *The Politics of Disarmament* (New York: Praeger, 1962).

and substantive issues, and have devised proposals of great versatility and ingenuity for meeting many of the critical requirements. The knowledge is largely at hand, if governments finally decide to meet the dangers of the uncontrolled arms race.[2]

The problem is that policy-making seriously lags behind technological change. Decisions which might have led to effective control a few years, or even a few months, ago, can no longer achieve such results. Opportunities for some of the most crucial decisions have been allowed to pass by and are irrecoverable. Failure to take bold steps at the right time limits what may now be accomplished toward security through disarmament. These limitations will quickly become greater if the major armed countries of the world stall on the steps they can still undertake.

Disarmament under international control is the very nub of the world security problem. Now, after more than half a century of study, negotiation, and advocacy, it brooks no further postponement. The solution it affords to the problem of international war is evanescent. It has to be seized today, or it will be gone for good, incalculably increasing the perils of the international society and the risk of destruction to all of mankind.

The following two chapters appraise the purposes underlying disarmament negotiations, examine the role of international organizations in the negotiating process, and analyze seven critical issues that have arisen persistently throughout the long struggle for disarmament:

1. Must disarmament be preceded or accompanied by other security arrangements?
2. Is the settlement of major political issues a precondition of disarmament?
3. The level of disarmament—how much should there be?
4. Who should disarm?
5. Methods of disarmament—what should be cut or limited, and how?
6. Timing—how quickly and in what sequence should nations disarm?
7. The problem of control—how can compliance with disarmament arrangements be insured?

---

[2] The general and technical literature on disarmament has now reached tremendous proportions, including massive official records of negotiations and important scientific contributions both inside and outside of governments. The negotiations are searchingly analyzed by Philip Noel-Baker, *op. cit.*, and Bernard G. Bechhoefer, *op cit.* The first covers the period before World War II as well as since. Three notable symposia on major contemporary issues are: American Academy of Arts and Sciences, "Arms Control," *Daedalus,* Special Issue, Fall, 1960; Donald G. Brennan (ed.), *Arms Control, Disarmament and National Security* (New York: George Braziller, Inc., 1961); and Seymour Melman (ed.), *Disarmament, Its Politics and Economics* (Boston: American Academy of Arts and Sciences, 1962).

Recent research in the United States is identified in a preliminary bibliographical report to the Ford Foundation by Eric Stevenson and John Teeple, *Research in Arms Control and Disarmament, 1960–1963.* A selective bibliography of official and unofficial sources is included in Lyman M. Tondel, Jr. (ed.), *Disarmament* (The Fourth Hammarskjöld Forum of the Association of the Bar of the City of New York, 1964).

WHY DISARM?

Progress toward security through international control of national armament has been complicated and impeded because of a confusion of perceived "purposes." Characteristically, governments and pressure groups have juggled a multitude of objectives having little to do, and sometimes quite inconsistent, with the central problem of how to keep nations from using armed force to disturb the peace. All too often, they have put their own national or special interests first, and freedom from war second.

Power

Many of the major states, for instance, and some of the lesser ones, too, schemed to preserve or strengthen their own power position while purportedly engaged in bonafide attempts to work out an overall limitation of arms in the interest of general security. Their real purpose has been to alter the balance of power in their favor or, conversely, to prevent another state from altering it adversely.

This aim was obvious in the victors' one-sided imposition of disarmament on the defeated states in two world wars, though couched after World War I in high-sounding terms as a first step toward general disarmament. It was just as obvious that the principal objective of Germany in the interwar disarmament negotiations was to change this situation. Demanding "equality," it really sought to justify rearming, for most of the other states clearly had no intention of disarming to the level they had set for the Germans.

Quite apart from the issue between victor and vanquished, the major armed states and many lesser ones have usually shaped their positions at disarmament conference tables with meticulous regard to their own specific power objectives, however much they may have rationalized their stand in the public eye as a disinterested contribution toward a satisfactory disarmament agreement.

For instance, the United States' dramatic offer in 1946 to internationalize control of atomic energy—an act of apparently unparalleled generosity and self-sacrifice in view of its presumed atomic monopoly—was, at first, so designed that the U.S. would not surrender its control over atomic weapons until after all nuclear development in other countries was removed from national control and placed under international management in which the U.S., because of its lead in the field, would have a predominant voice. There was some substance to the Russian charge that the plan would, in effect, have frozen an American atomic monopoly indefinitely.[3]

---

[3] See the penetrating analysis of this question in Inis L. Claude, Jr., *Swords Into Plowshares* (2d ed.; New York: Random House, 1959), p. 315–16.

But the Soviet call in rebuttal for an unconditional ban on the use, production, and stockpiling of atomic weapons was even more specious, especially at the time when it had only begun its drive for atomic power. Because these proposals were motivated, at least in part, by the power interests of their sponsors, they did not receive dispassionate consideration on their merits as systems of arms control to provide for general security. Instead of fruitful negotiations looking toward a basis of common agreement, an impasse developed as each side sought to avoid any action that might concede an advantage to its rival in the struggle for power. Such superimposing of national power-political objectives on the disarmament effort—unfortunately a consistent feature of the record—has resulted in what cynics have all too aptly described as the transformation of disarmament negotiations into armament conferences.

Propaganda

Disarmament negotiations have frequently been perverted for purposes of propaganda, pure and simple. Governments have participated with no real interest in limiting arms, but with an eye primarily on gaining prestige as a peace lover or making a rival appear as a warmonger. The cause of disarmament has been made the victim of its popularity. Publicly accepted as almost synonymous with peace itself, it has suffered manipulation for sheer domestic or international political advantages that have nothing to do with achieving greater security or preventing war.

These ulterior purposes have been so skillfully camouflaged that even sophisticated observers have had difficulty in disentangling what governments really have been after in disarmament negotiations from what they avowedly were trying to accomplish. This has muddied an understanding of the genuine problems of arms control. It has also soured opinion on the efficacy of the whole disarmament approach to peace and security.

Social Objectives

Even those who have genuinely advocated and sought disarmament are not all agreed on the nature of the problem they expect disarmament to solve.

Some have worked particularly for the moral and humanitarian purpose of limiting the horrors of war. To this end, they have concentrated on barring from use in war those weapons that cause mass and indiscriminate destruction of human life, or unusually cruel and painful injury—gas, fire, bacteria, and, supremely, nuclear weapons.

Others have struck at problems caused by the extraordinary economic cost of the preparation and waging of war. They have pressed for disarmament as a means of easing financial burdens, protecting the stability of the national economy, and releasing work and resources for productive use in raising living standards.

Still others have seen in disarmament a means of preserving democratic processes against the inroads of a highly militarized state, with its concomitants of a conscripted "nation in arms," restraints on civil rights, secrecy, and comprehensive government control of economic enterprise.

Another segment of the disarmament movement has aimed to eliminate profiteering from the business of war and to protect the common man from being exploited for the special interests of those engaged in the manufacture of arms.

Worthy as these objectives may be in and of themselves, they bear little on the problems of achieving a world order secure from war. Often the kind of approach that might be advocated as appropriate to a solution for one or another of these other problems would have little use as a deterrent of war. The horror of a weapon, its cost, the profits gained from its production, and the undemocratic results of girding a nation to use it or defend itself against it do not fundamentally affect its role in undermining international security. Banning the weapon might make little difference in an attempt to resolve the security problem, though it would eliminate that particular atrocity in combat. Nations might agree to spare themselves the cost of particularly expensive items of military hardware, and yet, with their remaining armament, pose just as great a threat to peace as before.

The Security Problem and Arms Control

Those who have seriously undertaken to promote general security through the control of arms have analyzed the nature of the problem along one or more of the following lines. First, the possibility of sudden, surprise attack is a vital factor in perpetuating a state of insecurity, particularly if it is likely that such an attack would result in giving the aggressor a sure hold on victory. To guard against such a possibility is a major incentive to a nation to arm, and this, in turn, opens the opportunity for it to initiate the surprise.

Second, among states at a high level of armament, mutual suspicion and fear grow and give rise to psychological insecurity quite as unsettling as the real danger of being victimized by overwhelming attack. Indeed, the intensity of the fear may be exaggerated far beyond the point justified either by the intentions or capabilities of the suspected enemy.

Third, there is under modern conditions of military technology such a contraction of the time allowed for vital decisions that the danger of war by accident is seriously increased. Faulty communication, misinterpretation of information, or panic by a staff officer could precipitate irrevocable decisions to fight, if states are mutually equipped with the full armature for total war.

Fourth, collective security arrangements to guard against aggressions are unworkable if the international community is unable to muster preponderant power against the violator of the peace. As long as individual states retain independent control over the potential for major war, enforcement of collective security will require a most formidable array of armed might and, probably, military operations on a scale tantamount to war. Assuming that many states would be reluctant to pool their forces in the face of such a prospect, the system could be made effective only against weakly armed states, leaving the major powers and perhaps many others subject to no restraint.

The purposes of arms control as seen by those making this kind of an analysis of the problem of security are, therefore: (1) to eliminate so far as possible the element of surprise in military operations; (2) to prevent the rise of unfounded suspicion; (3) to limit the repercussions of irresponsible or ill-informed decisions; and (4) ultimately, to bring the military capacity of all states within such bounds that they could not effectively resist the properly authorized restraining measures of the general community of states.

New Dimensions of the Security Problem

The new technical dimensions of warfare opened up by nuclear weapons and rocketry have heightened the importance attached to establishing these conditions as a basis for security, but have tremendously aggravated the insecurity of states and peoples in the absence of effective arms control.

First, from a strategic point of view, the power of offensive action has become so overwhelming that defense, in any real sense of the word, is no longer possible, nor does it appear likely in the foreseeable future. Arms have lost direct protective function. No state can any longer militarily shield its land and people from devastating attack, regardless of the scale and character of the defensive armament it creates. In these circumstances, the major powers have substituted a strategy of deterrence for a buildup of physical defenses, hoping that the threat of a massive retaliation would scare off a government from unleashing its lethal might. Resting as it does, in the last analysis, on human calculations, this "balance of terror" is highly unreliable. The technical triumph of the offense has put security at the mercy of whatever factors, rational or irrational, can influence the decisions of government leaders. Security has thus been transformed from an essentially military problem into a critical psychological problem, and it seems destined to remain so unless a system for the limitation of these new means of offense can be devised.

A second result of the new military technology is to annihilate space as a security factor. Given the present trend and tempo of development in missiles and atomic powered submarines, quite apart from the existing capabilities of manned aircraft for long-range delivery, no part of any country can expect immunity from planned attack, whatever its distance from the launching.

Third, the element of time has ceased to provide a potential measure of security. The swiftness of attack made possible by the new weapons—a matter of minutes between pressing the control buttons and the hitting of the targets—and their constant readiness for use without elaborate mobilization leave no opportunity either for last minute efforts to avoid the war or for measures to minimize the impact of the attack.

Fourth, the possibilities of effectively concealing a country's major armament have greatly increased, especially after the weapons have been produced and stockpiled. Foreknowledge of a state's intentions, gained from awareness of its military posture and dispositions, is so limited that it can no longer contribute to a sense of security. Given the immensely increased opportunities for surprise provided by the new weapons, the temptation is strong to assume the ever-present likelihood of surprise attack and to live in a state of perpetual high tension and mutual suspicion.

Finally, and most obviously, the new weapons (especially thermonuclear) have so extended the scale of destructiveness that the outright liquidation of the major centers of population and production in all countries drawn into a full war is now an accepted calculation in strategic planning.

Human Security

Until now, security has meant national security—the preservation of a country's independence and "national" interests—matters primarily political. But new weapons have made security a bare physiological and biological issue—a question of human survival. Always before, one could count on the major portion of the human race to survive even the most devastating of wars, capable of repairing its ravages over time, even in the most stricken of battlefields. Now, the unrestricted preparation of the implements of war, let alone their use, can contaminate the food supply throughout the globe, shorten the life span, and measurably affect the hereditary process.

This situation has come about particularly as the result of unleashing the power of nuclear *fusion*. Terrifying as were the consequences an atomic bomb could occasion by nuclear *fission,* it was the hydrogen bomb which really scared the experts. The almost limitless extent to which explosive power can be increased by the fusion of elements at high temperature, the compactness and stability and, hence, ease of delivery of thermonuclear weapons as well as their long-lasting legacy of radioactivity to the atmosphere are among the factors that make these instruments literally capable of annihilating most of mankind.

To protect the race from irreparable damage if not near-extinction—in other words, to provide elemental *human* security—has, therefore, emerged as the supreme objective of many of the more responsible arms control proponents.[4]

THE NEGOTIATING ROLE OF INTERNATIONAL ORGANIZATION

International organizations have made three principal contributions to disarmament negotiations.

1. They have taken the initiative in starting negotiations and have been primarily responsible for keeping them going.
2. They have established procedures of consultation through which the concerned states have been brought together to exchange and discuss proposals (both formally and informally).
3. They have made disarmament the business of all states, enabling the smaller and less powerful to become so well informed about the problems that they have been able to exert an increasing influence on the actual conduct of negotiations.

In addition, international organizations are expected to carry major responsibilities in implementing arms control agreements, a subject discussed in the next chapter.

Planning for disarmament was made one of the original tasks of both the League and the U.N., and has had priority attention throughout the life of each organization. Their mandates differed somewhat. The League was instructed to formulate plans for an outright *reduction* of national armaments; the U.N.'s assignment was less committal, and called only for their *regulation*. In practice, each has considered the full gamut of possibilities for international agreement—elimination, reduction, limitation, or control of weapons and armed forces. The U.N.'s responsibility quickly came to include also the special problem of how to limit the use of atomic energy to peaceful purposes.

The function of the international organizations was supposed to be strictly exploratory. They were to prepare proposals. It was up to individual governments to decide what to do about them. But the process of planning understandably merged with the process of actual negotiation, for the plans would

---

[4] The frightening risks resulting from the new arms technology are penetratingly analyzed in such studies as Sir Stephen King-Hall, *Defense in the Nuclear Age* (London: Gollancz, 1958); Jules S. Moch, *Human Folly* tr. by Edward Hyams (London: Victor Gollancz Ltd., 1955). Philip J. Noel-Baker, *op. cit.;* Albert Wohlstetter, "The Delicate Balance of Terror," *Foreign Affairs,* January, 1959; George Kennan, *Russia, the Atom and the West* (The Reith Lectures, British Broadcasting Corporation, November–December, 1957); and Klaus Knorr (ed.), *NATO and American Security* (Princeton: Princeton University Press, 1959) (especially chapters by George W. Rathjens, Jr., "NATO Strategy and Total War," Thomas C. Schelling, "Surprise Attack and Disarmament," and Klaus Knorr, "NATO Defense in an Uncertain Future").

be meaningless if they did not reflect what nations would accept. So, in reality, the international organizations became the focal point for most of the efforts to reconcile conflicting national defense policies and hammer out international agreement on the technical and political bases of disarmament arrangements.

The League Council and the U.N. Security Council were initially made responsible for this work. They created special bodies to study the problems involved and develop proposals: a Permanent Advisory Commission for the League Council, composed of high-ranking military officers; two commissions for the Security Council, one concerned with atomic energy and the other with "conventional" disarmament. But the issue soon spilled over into the assemblies of the two organizations, because the larger bodies became dissatisfied with the negative results and deadlocks that developed.

The League Council ultimately appointed another commission to produce a Draft Disarmament Convention. This ill-fated proposal was submitted to the full-dress Geneva Disarmament Conference in 1932, only to run afoul of the contradictory security policies and political objectives of major and lesser powers, and the militant stance of Hitler's Germany.

In the U.N.'s experience, the General Assembly has itself largely taken over from the Security Council responsibility for full debate of the issues by all sides, pressing the major powers to continue negotiating, and devising procedures of negotiation acceptable to them.

Negotiations have sometimes been conducted outside the framework of international organizations, either directly among some of the major armed powers or through special multilateral bodies they have set up for the purpose.[5] Among the reasons for bypassing the established international organizations have been a desire to avoid exposure to the limelight of other nations' concern, the need to involve countries that were not members of the organization (the U.S. in 1922, for instance), and a belief that agreement might be easier to reach if only the crucial states who had to agree took part. Actually, the third consideration has often been accommodated within the procedures of the League and the United Nations by turning over the detailed negotiations to small commissions composed just of the key military powers.

The critical factor in choice of forum is really nothing more than what is currently acceptable, for whatever reason, to the states whose participation is essential for the negotiations to be meaningful. International organizations have recognized that keeping the powers at *some* conference table is more important than having them sit around the *family* table. Usually, whenever

---

[5] Notably in the case of the Washington Arms Limitation Conference in 1922, and the nuclear test ban negotiations in 1962–63. The 10-nation and 18-nation disarmament committees that conducted the major negotiations since 1960 were endorsed by the U.N., but were really set up and operated independently by direct agreement between the U.S. and U.S.S.R.

negotiations bog down, the ball is bounced to some other body—a face-saving procedure to get them going again. For instance, the Soviet Union has been insisting in recent years on "parity" in the negotiating process. It strongly resented being outvoted in the commissions first set up under the U.N., especially when the Western powers claimed special virtue for their "majority" positions. When the U.S.S.R. refused to continue negotiating in such a context, a new committee was formed with equal representation from the Soviet bloc and NATO. This was later expanded to include some nonaligned countries, who carefully avoid, however, upsetting the parity balance and, instead, play a go-between role.

As time has gone on, the number of nations taking part in the active negotiations, as well as in the general discussion within the U.N., has increased. This was one result of a deadlock between the five "nuclear powers" who took the first crack at the problem after the U.N. was organized. Both the Soviet Union and the West sought to appeal their cases to the wider audience of the General Assembly. In the process of justifying their positions, they passed on information, and in due course found it necessary to respond to ever more penetrating questions first by adjusting their tactics and then, to some extent, modifying the substance of their policies. At first, the West could count confidently on a large majority of votes to support its stands without qualification. This changed as representatives of other nations gained more direct insight and concluded there might be more tolerable alternatives that would open ways out of the impasse. The emergence of this quizzical "neutral" point of view, which urged the importance of finding some basis for mutual agreement instead of holding to either side's fixed position, had much to do with loosening the bind of the negotiations. In the end, both sides felt impelled to invite other governments to join them in the negotiating club. In the 18-nation disarmament commission appointed by the U.N., and also in a corresponding body set up outside, unaligned nations came to wield an extraordinary power of initiative and innovation. Taking advantage of greater flexibility in the approaches of both the U.S.S.R. and the West, the middle nations succeeded in substantially widening the area of consensus on the terms of a general and comprehensive disarmament agreement, though important differences still remain to be reconciled.

THE DISARMAMENT—SECURITY CONUNDRUM: WHICH COMES FIRST?

For a long time, disarmament efforts bogged down in bootless controversy over whether disarmament or security should come first. Proponents of the "direct approach" urged that the reduction and limitation of arms would itself increase the security of nations by reducing the capacity and readiness of states to attack one another. Advocates of the "indirect approach" countered that states would not disarm unless, in place of the arms they gave up or agreed not to produce, they could rely on other states to give them equivalent or greater protection. Thus, firmly knit alliances or a functioning collective security system would have to be in operation *prior* to disarmament.

Generally, the major armed powers have given the indirect approach right of way. Except for the Washington Naval Limitation Conference in 1922, serious negotiations for the limitation of armaments after World War I stalled while ill-fated efforts were undertaken to supplement the League's system of collective security with firmer guarantees of mutual defense, and after the second world war, disarmament negotiations were mainly subordinated to the development of opposing security systems for the Western nations and the U.S.S.R. The direct approach has only once been given an actual trial—in the Naval Limitation Agreement of 1922. It worked fairly well in that particular and rather narrow context.[6]

But on various other occasions, three leading states have advocated the direct approach. First, the United States between the two world wars pressed for the limiting of arms without attendant security arrangements. This position changed with the onset of World War II, however, and since then, U.S. proposals for arms control have usually been skillfully designed so that they would take effect only as alternative political and military security devices were strengthened.

Some authorities maintain that even the U.S. prewar position assumed the existence of solid security systems in Europe and the Pacific, though the U.S. was not itself an active party to them. To this author, a more reasonable interpretation is that U.S. policy, strongly influenced by a vigorous nation-wide disarmament movement and perhaps by isolationist suspicion of entangling alliances, sought through direct disarmament an effective means of preventing war that would substitute for either a commitment to the League of Nations or other formal security pacts. Its advocacy of the direct approach was thus genuine and unequivocal, and its later recantation no less so because of the conviction that we had done wrong in not putting our strength wholeheartedly behind a collective security system.

The second case of a direct approach to disarmament was the British stand at the Geneva Disarmament Conference called by the League of Nations in 1932. Urging immediate abolition of various types of weapons which, from its standpoint, were "offensive."[7]

The third and most consistent supporter of the direct approach has been the Soviet Union. Why, is a question still much debated. Some contend that its motivation has been completely propagandistic—its disarmament policy

---

[6] See Noel-Baker, *op. cit.,* for a defense of the Washington agreement as a resounding disarmament success.

[7] See below, section on Qualitative Disarmament.

easily stamps it as a champion of peace. Others have reasoned that due to Russia's military weakness until recently (and its traditional reliance on distance for defense) any cut in arms by the major powers would have improved its relative military security. They predict a switchover in policy now that Russia has acquired a formidable armament. (There are some indications that it now does lay more stress than before on perfection of favorable arrangements for maintenance and expansion of its "security orbit" as a corollary to its disarmament proposals.)

Still another explanation plausibly links Soviet espousal of the direct approach with its ideological commitment to political revolution rather than to military warfare as the principal means of policy. In a largely disarmed world, according to this view, organization for a Communist seizure of power could go forward more expeditiously. Armies usually stand in the way of the proletarian revolution.

The Soviet protagonists themselves have been careful to shield the opportunistic character of their disarmament policy—if it is such—so that their stand in public represents a straight-out defense of the proposition that the way to disarm is to disarm, and that security will automatically increase as countries agree to cut back or, preferably, eliminate large parts of their armament. They repudiate the indirect approach as an attempt to evade disarmament and even to conceal preparations for war.

Although the direct approach has generally not been fashionable in the West, its validity is now being seriously reappraised. With a settled universal system of security beyond the horizon, governments are considering whether they might not cut their risks by accepting direct international regulation of arms, conditioned, of course, on reciprocal controls over the defense establishments of their rivals. There is even evidence of a broadening body of expert opinion convinced that disarmament, given present international realities, is both feasible and imperative—as a security measure—regardless of the weakness of other security arrangements.

POLITICAL CONDITIONS FOR DISARMAMENT

The major block to disarmament has been the insistence of key nations on settling controversial international political issues to their satisfaction before they would accept limitations on their arms. They have balked at restricting their capacity to defend or to alter the status quo by force until assured of a world political order tailored to their specifications. Complex as have been the technical problems of arms control, these political conditions have been more formidable—insuperable, so far.

To hitch disarmament to the perfection of a settled international political system presumes that states must reconcile their most fundamental differences of interest and ideological purpose before they can agree on limiting recourse to force. This is a tall order when the divergence of national objectives is as profound as it has been since World War II. Yet, this is the implication of the stand taken on disarmament first by one side, then by the other, and sometimes by both at the same time as they have driven the negotiations since World War II into one impasse after another.

This issue is related to, but much broader than, the question of a direct or indirect approach to disarmament, discussed above. The advocates of the indirect approach are preoccupied just with establishing a security system—that is, with arrangements for effective mutual defense in case the limitation of arms breaks down. While this is intertwined with important political questions (a solid security system implies acceptance of given national frontiers and nonintervention in the internal affairs of states), it does not call for a decisive substantive settlement of outstanding international controversies. The indirect, or "security first," approach shares with the direct approach a belief that the use of force can be restrained in international relations, even while major political conflicts continue. Those who hold out for full-scale political settlements as a prerequisite for disarmament doubt, at heart, whether states can remain at peace when they differ greatly on political aspirations. In reality, they expect war, because they do not consider the major political conflicts reconcilable. Hence, to them, disarmament appears utter folly—an invitation to national suicide.

The Abortive Prewar System

Disarmament efforts between the world wars assumed that most of the essential political conditions had been established by the peace treaties. Negotiations did not get embroiled in such questions as the future of Germany, or even the status and objectives of the Russian Communist state. These were taken as givens. Demands for revision of the international political system when they arose were confronted outside the disarmament conference room. An exception to this was the Washington Naval Limitation Conference, which went forward side by side with the Nine Power Conference to hammer out political agreements among the powers with major interests in China and the Far East, and, in particular, to define the legitimate limits of Japan's "special" interests in China. Marriage of the Nine Power Treaty and naval disarmament resulted. Some authorities are certain that states would not have accepted the disarmament without the treaty. This is open to speculation, but, at any rate, in this one instance it proved possible to conjoin arms limitation with what states, at the time, felt was a reasonably appropriate settlement of their principal political controversies in a particular region.

Advocates of the political approach argue tellingly that failure to follow this model in the thirties when the existing political order was challenged in all parts of the world (except possibly in the Americas) was the principal reason for frustration of the disarmament negotiations. You could not expect agreement on arms control among states deeply at odds over their rightful places under the sun. But a persuasive case in rebuttal maintains that the wisest course was, indeed, to keep the political and military questions separate in the hope that a limitation of arms implemented in time would have held the political conflicts within peaceful bounds.

The Postwar Deadlock

The situation after World War II has not permitted even the pretense of general agreement on the permanent character of the political order. There are many who insist that the inherent expansionist aims of world communism under the direction of the Soviet Union (and the Chinese Communist leaders) rule out any possibility of a modus vivendi. They naturally also rule out disarmament under *any* conditions, as a fatal weakening of anti-Communist defenses.

Others take the view that the Soviet government will accept and live with political situations that rest on "positions of strength," which it cannot hope to change by the various pressures at its command. Those accepting this perspective argue that it is vitally important to maintain and build up elements of "strength" on the periphery of Soviet power until Soviet leaders are persuaded to accept a political status quo which confines Soviet influence within its present expanse for the foreseeable future. Then, and then only, may disarmament agreements be effected; and they must be so designed as to insure that the Soviet Union, and China, acquire no absolute or relative military advantage which would enable them to challenge the political settlements they had been pressed to make. This is, broadly, the strategy which has dictated the Western approach to the political conditions of disarmament.

In the background of the negotiations, if not set forth explicitly in each formal proposal, the U.S. and its allies have demanded that in conjunction with an arms limitation agreement the question of European security be settled on the basis of German reunification, with Germany free to continue its association with the Western powers in NATO. In essence, the Soviet Union was asked to withdraw its control over East Germany, retract the limit of its European orbit to the Polish–German frontier, and acquiesce in the permanent consolidation of the Western alliance inclusive of the whole of Germany—all of this as a condition for the limitation of arms. From time to time, the matter of Soviet control over the Eastern European satellites was also raised, and it was invited to withdraw from there as a contribution to the atmosphere of trust and the conditions of political freedom and stability in which a disarmament agreement might happily flourish.[8]

No doubt all of this would have made for a world much more comfortable and secure for the democracies, producing a "condition of international confidence and security," to use the oft-repeated Western phrase. But the Soviet Union could scarcely be expected to consider it an even bargain.

---

[8] See, for instance, stands taken by U.S. and U.K. in the U.N. Commission for Conventional Armaments, 1947–48.

The traditional Soviet position has maintained that disarmament need not be linked to political settlements. Faced with the Western conditions, however, the Russians shifted tactics and laid down equally onerous political conditions of their own—a neutralized Germany under international oversight in which the U.S.S.R. would participate. The Soviet Union has, of course, persistently sought to demobilize NATO.

Had the negotiations reached the point where China's participation was needed to make the agreements comprehensively effective, the political issues would certainly have multiplied, with both the U.S. and China prescribing mutually irreconcilable conditions for the limitation of arms.

Positions became somewhat more flexible during the really serious negotiations of 1954–57. Not that the Soviet Union and the West came any closer to agreeing on the fundamentals of a political settlement. But the democracies appeared willing to consider adopting at least partial measures of disarmament without reaching political agreement, while the Soviet Union tried packaging together substantial disarmament along the lines advocated by the West, coupled with mutual disengagement in Germany or all of Central Europe. This Soviet package was submitted to the U.N. Disarmament Subcommittee, May 10, 1955, and was by all odds its most detailed and comprehensive proposal to date. There is every evidence that it was drafted with meticulous care, and it represented major departures on almost every issue from the stock Soviet positions. It accepted a very large portion of the Western program as put forth by the British and French in 1954. The political-military recipe it proposed for Germany rested on a quid pro quo rather than the winner-take-all approach of the West, though it was skillfully designed to accomplish a major Soviet objective—the blocking of Germany's intergration into the Western Alliance.

But the Western nations were determined that nothing was worth the price of barring West Germany from active partnership in the Western alliance. Far better that the consideration of political conditions be relegated to the *last* stage of a phased disarmament program—which is exactly where the matter was put in the West's "last offer" package as presented in 1957. The import of this was that limited measures of disarmament might be undertaken without political conditions (such as accepting ceilings for armed forces at a rather high level, beginning inspection, suspending nuclear tests, special safeguards against surprise attack). Then, after this first stage was successfully completed, the governments would be prepared to "negotiate a further limitation of their armed forces and armaments upon condition that . . . there has been progress toward the solution of political issues."

Unhitching the Political Conditions

In retrospect, the attempt to hitch disarmament to political conditions has resulted only in frustration and rising peril. Promising progress toward solving the difficult problems of effectively controlled and balanced limitation of arms has been stalled at crucial points by the injection of the political issue. The major political controversies have proved so intractable that there is no prospect of settlement. Meanwhile, the tensions and dangers of the arms race mount, while, in the words of Dr. Robert Oppenheimer, "the atomic clock ticks faster and faster."

There is impressive support for the view that disarmament definitely ought to be unhitched from political conditions. Conceding that political problems were an impediment to substantial disarmament, the Senate Subcommittee on Disarmament nevertheless concluded, after an exhaustive review of the question, that

. . . to await the solution of all political problems before proceeding to attempt the control of armaments is unrealistic and can be dangerous for the future security of this country and, indeed, the world. It is unrealistic, because many of the political problems confronting the world today are so basic that solutions, if they come about at all, can occur only gradually. It can be dangerous, because as time goes on the armaments race is continued at an accelerated pace, and the threat of nuclear catastrophe becomes more acute. . . . What we must try to do is to diminish or halt the arms race on the premise that limited and safe measures will in themselves help to reduce world tension.[9]

Similarly, Jules Moch, the French disarmament expert, urged on the U.N. Subcommittee that it "had no right to wait . . . for a settlement of the most serious political disputes. Indeed, they were practically insoluble in an atmosphere of distrust, whereas they would constitute no major problem once included in the general framework of agreement on disarmament." And Philip Noel-Baker, leading British authority on disarmament, appealed to the Western governments as their urgent duty "not to delay matters by posing hypothetical and undefined political conditions, but to put forward the proposals for large-scale reductions, and the detailed clauses for carrying them out, which are the first and indispensable step to a more peaceful world."

The course of the renewed and serious negotiations of the 1960's suggests that these warnings have been heard and, at least to some extent, heeded. Although neither side has backed away from its fundamental political commitments, and the ideological cleavage is as great as ever, proposals for both comprehensive and limited measures of arms control and reduction have been considered on the merits of their contribution to security—without political prefixes or prerequisites. It would be too much to say that calculations of political implications have not influenced acceptance or rejection of specific plans. The question of Germany's military posture and political alignment especially dominates the disarmament strategy of both East and

---

[9] U.S. Senate Report No. 1167 (85th Cong., 1st sess., September 6, 1957).

West. But such considerations no longer seem to stall the hunt for physical safeguards against the risk of war to be secured by international agreements for the reduction and regulation of arms. The political roadblock to negotiation has been removed, and it may be that the costs of war are so great that governments will be willing to buy the security of disarmament at the price of agreeing to pursue political objectives by political means.

TOTAL OR PARTIAL DISARMAMENT?

A vital issue in the strategy of disarmament is the comprehensiveness of measures necessary to make a significant contribution to security.

Those who make a strong case for nearly total disarmament—down to the level and kinds of weapons and armed forces required solely to maintain internal security—argue that this system would be the easiest to verify, and would provide maximum insurance against states' launching sudden or annihilative wars.

In practice, only the defeated states after the two world wars experienced anything approaching total disarmament, and even these one-sided tryouts were short-lived. It did not afford a test of what acceptance by all or most states of such a scale of disarmament might accomplish. It indicated, however, that large-scale disarmament could enjoy massive local support, even though the foreign occupation accompanying it was thoroughly detested. Also, it freed the disarmed countries for extraordinary economic progress.[10]

So acceptable was total disarmament in both Germany and Japan after World War II that rearmament was instituted only over intense domestic opposition and under strong pressure from the United States, their conqueror. Many preferred to take their chances unarmed, and uncommitted, in the burgeoning power struggle rather than to become partners-in-arms, however potent the allies.

As a policy for general consumption (not just for the conquered), total disarmament has had only one major governmental sponsor—the Soviet Union. The proposals presented by Maxim Litvinov to the League of Nations Preparatory Commission on Disarmament startled but did not persuade the delegates from other countries, even when convinced that the Russians were not acting facetiously. Traditional reliance on a balance of arms as a vital element of security would not yield to the logic and prescience with which Litvinov outlined the assurances states would enjoy were they all to implement complete disarmament under international control. As with so many facets of Soviet policy, the motivation and ultimate intentions of its disarmament policy have not been surely deciphered. Some of the interpretations previously discussed with reference to the objectives of disarmament

---

[10] See Noel-Baker, *op. cit.;* also Stephen King-Hall, *op cit.,* and Seymour Melman, *op. cit.*

and Soviet espousal of the "direct approach" are also relevant to its stand on total disarmament.[11]

The question of total disarmament did not become a live issue of negotiation until long after World War II, following round after round of virtually fruitless efforts to work out more restricted arms limitation agreements between the Soviet Union and the major Western powers. But in September, 1959, at the Fourteenth General Assembly of the United Nations, Premier Khrushchev in person proposed a program for "general and complete disarmament" to be carried out in three stages over a four-year period. It provided for such specific and drastic measures as:

disbandment of all armed forces;
destruction of all types of arms and ammunition;
complete prohibition of atomic and hydrogen weapons—discontinuance of their production, their removal from the armaments of states and the liquidation of their stockpiles;
complete termination of the production and the destruction of all types of rocket weapons;
prohibition of the production, possession and storing of the means of chemical and bacteriological warfare and the destruction of stockpiles;
liquidation of military bases of any kind in foreign territories;
liquidation of military production;
discontinuance of all military training;
abolition of war ministries, general staffs, military educational institutions and all kinds of military and paramilitary establishments and organizations;
discontinuance of appropriations for military purposes in any form;
prohibition by law of war propaganda and military education.

Only strictly limited contingents of police would be allowed each country to maintain internal order. An international control body would supervise the implementation of the whole program, its functions, and powers to correspond in nature and scope to the disarmament measures being carried out.[12]

In contrast to the interwar response, the call for total disarmament this time commanded serious and widespread attention, although the Western powers scarcely generated enthusiasm for the project. "Complete and general disarmament" became the avowed goal of further negotiations. The General Assembly sealed its approval in a resolution, unanimously sponsored and unanimously adopted November 20, 1959:

Considering that the question of general and complete disarmament is the most important one facing the world today, [the General Assembly] *calls upon*

---

[11] See the penetrating analysis by Marina Salvin, "Soviet Policy Toward Disarmament," *International Conciliation,* February, 1947.

[12] See address of Premier Khrushchev, September 18, 1959; also the U.S.S.R.'s official declaration of same date (U.N. Doc. A/4219).

Governments to make every effort to achieve a constructive solution of this problem . . . *Expresses* the hope that measures leading towards the goal of general and complete disarmament under effective international control will be worked out in detail and agreed upon in the shortest possible time.

Practically, however, agreement on the goal did not speed up the process of reaching it nor, indeed, of reaching any measure of arms limitation. Three main issues embroiled the subsequent negotiations. Two concerned the question of how to unravel the arms race: What should be the sequence of steps and their timing—in other words, the problem of *phasing* the move from here to then? How should the system of international control be set up to insure that everyone was living up to his agreement and carrying out the measures specified? These vital questions are examined in some detail later. Suffice it to say here that they have so far been unresolved, though the area of technical disagreement is not very great.

The third issue concerned what provision for international, as opposed to internal, security would be necessary, assuming the goal of complete disarmament was to be achieved. In the United States view, effectively expressed by Secretary of State Herter, in February, 1960, two types of peace-keeping machinery had to be developed prior to total disarmament: (1) an international enforcement body with adequate police power to guard small states against aggression by more populous ones (whose larger internal security forces would pose a threat even in the so-called fully disarmed world); (2) stronger international organization to insure just and peaceful settlement of disputed issues.[13]

Other Western states generally agreed, and so, in due course, did the Soviet Union—with an important gimmick. In its comprehensive plan submitted on June 2, 1960, to the 10-nation Disarmament Committee, it allowed that measures should be undertaken in the course of the final stage of disarmament to insure keeping the peace thereafter. But in its view, the proper model was to be found in the enforcement machinery originally spelled out in the United Nations Charter—detachments from the various states placed at the disposal of the Security Council, and subject, therefore, to a veto on their use and disposition by the five permanent members of the Council. By contrast, the United States and its associates called for a truly international "peace force," permanently established within the United Nations, "with agreed personnel strength and armaments sufficient to preserve world peace."[14]

How much opportunity there may be for bridging the gap on this issue is not yet clear. The question of accountability has been sharpened by vehement Soviet objections to the recent trial run of a United Nations "Peace Force" in

---

[13] Address of Secretary Herter before the National Press Club, February 18, 1960, Department of State *Bulletin*, March 7, 1960, p. 354.

[14] See U.S. proposal of June 27, 1960.

the Congo (see Chapter 7). But in one of its unpredictable reversals of policy, the U.S.S.R. agreed to support a permanent U.N. force staffed by countries *other* than the five big powers, *provided* it was set up under Security Council direction.[15]

Nevertheless, looked at in terms of overall strategy, the total disarmament approach can no longer be shelved, however baffling may be the questions of implementation. For the degree of disarmament and the effectiveness of its control have become inextricably intertwined. The longer controlled regulation of arms is postponed, the more comprehensive will be the dismantling of military establishments required to make possible adequate safeguards over the arsenals of states. The newest and most critical weapons are, on the whole, the most invulnerable to control. Hence, if states wish reasonable assurances against evasion of a disarmament agreement, they may have to bring down their level of armaments to a very low point, both quantitatively and in kinds of weapons and forces maintained, in order to make sure they will be within the capacity of a reasonable control system to check.[16]

On the other hand, setting the goal at total disarmament has not eliminated the necessity of considering partial measures of arms limitation in the interim, either as steps toward the goal or on their own merit. Actually, the meat of the disarmament negotiations has concerned the devising of such partial measures on a piecemeal basis or in packages relating several measures to one another. This method of attack, it was hoped, would enable a beginning on specific areas of disarmament where agreement was possible, without having to resolve all the problems involved in a more comprehensive arrangement. Initial steps, even if quite restricted, might open the way to broader agreements by stimulating confidence among the cooperating states and giving them experience in implementing arms control.

A great variety of formulas for partial disarmament have been proposed. Some of these will be discussed below in reviewing the problem of control. Broadly, they have taken one or another of the following points of departure.

1. They have tried to regulate certain types of weapons or forces without limiting others. Battleships were restricted by the Washington Naval Limitation Agreement, but agreement could not be reached on cruisers or submarines.

---

[15] USSR Memorandum to the Security Council July 10, 1964 (UN Doc. S/5811). See also, interview with Ambassador Platon D. Morozov, deputy permanent representative of the U.S.S.R. to the United Nations, reported in *WAR/PEACE REPORT,* October, 1964. The contrasting positions on this issue are examined by Marion H. McVitty, *A Comparison and Evaluation of Current Disarmament Proposals as of March 1, 1964* (New York: World Law Fund, 1964). For close analysis of the problems of establishing an international peace-keeping force as an element of general disarmament, see Lincoln P. Bloomfield *et al, International Military Forces* (Boston: Little, Brown, 1964).

[16] See Noel-Baker, *op. cit.*

For a long time after World War II, control or abolition of atomic weapons was sought, quite apart from action on conventional armaments. Discussions are now under way seeking a system for restricting the use of outer space to nonmilitary purposes (e.g., abolishing military missiles)—this without necessary reference to any other phase of disarmament.

2. Alternatively, formulas for partial disarmament or limitation have aimed to define maximum levels of permissible armament for various countries in one or more categories of arms; to fix a proportional cutback of armament; or, more modestly, to secure a "standstill" agreement whereby countries would stop further expansion or development of specified weapons. It is along these lines that the serious negotiations of the fifties proceeded, looking toward agreement on a "first stage" of disarmament which might include stopping nuclear tests, setting limits on the armed forces and corresponding weaponry of the major powers, and possibly a standstill on further production of nuclear weapons. In all these measures, the emphasis is on setting a partial limitation to the *scale* of the country's military establishment and development.

3. A third type of partial limitation has sought establishment of some kind of machinery for verification of a country's state of armament and its fulfillment of any other measures of limitation to which it has agreed. The various methods proposed for such control will be reviewed below. The point made by the partial-measures advocates is that implementing even very modest measures of inspection or census-taking may provide a valuable start on disarmament (and, incidentally, diminish the threat of surprise attack).

Critics of partial measures stress their insufficiency—the measures are too partial to do any good. They may also raise false hopes among the ill-informed that would result either in quick disillusionment or a naive sense of security where none existed. Either way, the effects would be injurious to the attainment of solid steps toward security.

On the other hand, such criticism leads directly to a do-nothing stance. For these opponents are rarely prepared to turn to the total disarmament alternative. They discount *any* attempt to limit arms, not just partial measures.

The vigorous search for agreement on partial measures has in recent years had the positive effect of greatly increasing the flexibility of negotiations and permitting intensive exploration of specific aspects of the disarmament problem. There is no reason to suppose that some of these measures, when finally worked out and implemented, may not form important pieces of a broader system of arms control that states may be led to adopt as they increasingly sense the precariousness of too limited and unintegrated regulation. However vital a total disarmament system may prove to be, its acceptance will surely not be impeded by the introduction of partial measures. If anything, awareness of their insufficiency—and their experimental accomplishment in breaking the ice of a totally uncontrolled situation—should dispose governments to undertake more comprehensive commitments.

WHO MUST DISARM?

The range of countries that must join in an arms control arrangement to make it effective and the terms of their participation are questions of vital import in planning for disarmament.

A small but respectable group has urged that it only takes one nation to put the wheel of arms limitation to turning. Unilateral action, they predict, will be contagious and, in any case, will bring no greater jeopardy to the nation than continuance in the arms race. This point of view has found particular support in Britain, where alarm over the implications of nuclear war has led to strong demands that the country on its own quit the triumvirate of atomically armed powers.[17]

Governments have so far shunned such a course of action and insisted that any regulation of arms in which they participated would have to be multilateral, and reciprocal, at least to the extent of involving states by whom they have felt seriously threatened. They have customarily thought that refusal of even one dangerous rival to join the disarmament club would make it impossible to limit arms without undercutting their security.

Some have gone farther. They have argued that disarmament can only be effective if virtually all states subscribe, regardless of their power or location. Every state would be a potential threat to others unless it were subject to equivalent regulation to insure that no one was left out. This position immensely complicates the disarmament process, of course, because it holds up any step until the last obdurate state can be persuaded to go along.

Since the second world war, disarmament has been widely considered the particular business of the heavily armed states, especially those with the resources for nuclear power. It has been taken for granted that any agreement they reached would be welcomed by others. But, in any case, they alone could insure the effective implementation of an arms control arrangement, so overwhelming is their mastery of the world's armaments. At the same time, the major powers, while concentrating on the problem of controls they themselves would agree to accept, have made clear that other states shall not be left exempt from the same regulations. They, too, evidently subscribe to the proposition that disarmament must be inclusive to be effective.

In this connection, failure to include Communist China in the negotiations at any point poses a very troublesome problem. If effective control of arms requires full acceptance by all states with substantial armament, China's

---

[17] See, for instance, King-Hall, *op. cit.*, who pursues to its ultimate conclusion a consideration of what could happen were Britain to do without atomic arms. He concludes that at the very worst—e.g., a Russian occupation of England—the country would have a better chance of defending its essential interests than through the amassing of nuclear armament in association with the U.S.

compliance will be essential for almost every control measure. But there can be no assurance that it will automatically accept the terms worked out by the other powers. As a matter of fact, it has categorically declared on several occasions that it would not. China's inclusion in the negotiations seems imperative if they are to produce a practical result.

The same holds true for France. But whereas China has never been invited in, the French have on their initiative opted out after a long and intensive participation, much to the dismay of its Western allies. The issue is de Gaulle's blanket rejection of any arrangement that might limit French development of independent nuclear power.

The procedure in each case has been to carry on negotiations in the expectation that once an agreement is reached among the others, its practical contribution to security and the pressure of world opinion will persuade both the pariah and the lone wolf to accept it.

Regional Disarmament

Arms limitation has sometimes been approached on a regional basis. The Rush–Bagot agreement between Canada and the United States produced the longest and most permanent demilitarized frontier in history. Pacification of several of the fierce feuds among Latin American states has entailed measures for reciprocal reduction and control of arms among them. An essential element of the agreements setting up the Western European Union in 1954 was the limitation of German armament under the control of the Union. Germany accepted the arrangement as a condition of its joining the Union. A regional circumference for arms control has the advantage of narrowing the number of separate interests to be reconciled to put a system into operation. On the other hand, such agreements touch but little on the world security problem unless they tie in with more inclusive arrangements.

The Condition of Reciprocity

Disarmament proposals have generally presumed a relationship of *reciprocity* among the participating states. That is, acceptance of limitations by one state depends on the others accepting equivalent restrictions. This principle was not followed in the terms of disarmament imposed on the losers of the two world wars. Their one-sidedness proved a constant source of friction and a factor in bringing about their early demise, as soon as the defeated states began to regain status in world affairs.

Few states are apparently willing to voluntarily give up the claim to equality, even though they realize that in terms of armed power this can have only a mythical significance. Reciprocity is the convenient formula by which vast differences in absolute power can be reconciled with the maintenance of titular equality among sovereign states. The object is to work out a give-and-take of concessions that will be roughly proportional to the existing situation of the various participants, or, speaking of controls, to have each state accept the same degree of restriction and oversight as the others. While reciprocity is clearly the only basis on which states are currently willing to negotiate for the limitation of arms, the problem is to find specific terms that every state will accept as truly reciprocal. This has proved a major stumbling block in the disarmament negotiations.[18]

METHODS OF LIMITATION

Assuming that, for the moment, any disarmament will have to be partial, reciprocal, and inclusive of most armed states, the problem remains of determining what kinds of limitation will have the desired effect of reducing threats to national and human security. Five main methods have been proposed.

1. *Quantitative* limits on size of armed forces or amount of specific weapons.
2. *Qualitative* disarmament in which regulation is applied particularly to major weapons of offense and mass destruction.
3. *Geographical* disarmament (currently described as "disengagement"), which involves withdrawal of forces and armament from certain areas.
4. *Financial or Budgetary* limitation, restricting national expenditures on arms.
5. *Disclosure of information* concerning national military establishments and planning.

All these approaches have been advanced in one form or another, and sometimes in combination packages during the sequence of disarmament negotiations. No nation has stuck consistently to one method, though at certain stages a particular country has often stood as champion of a given approach.

Quantitative

Quantitative limitation was tried between the wars and succeeded in preventing an imminent race for warships during the brief period that the agreements were in effect. The five major naval powers scrapped ships or stopped construction of new ones so as to keep to the agreed 5–5–3–1.75–1.75 ratio (as between U.S., U.K., Japan, France, Italy). They could not agree, however, on limits for other categories of ships. Nor did the prolonged negotiations for general disarmament in the interwar period succeed in fixing any limits for land armaments. Since World War II, however, the Soviet

---

[18] Unilateral disarmament would avoid the problems implicit in the reciprocal approach, but we have already noted that governments so far have ignored this alternative. For a positive critique of reciprocity as a basis for arms control arrangements, see Lawrence S. Finkelstein, "The Uses of Reciprocal Inspection," *Daedalus*, November, 1963; also, on this general subject, Fred C. Iklé, *Alternative Approaches to the International Organization of Disarmament* (Santa Monica, Calif.: The RAND Corporation, February, 1962.)

Union and the Western states have come very close to agreement on the size to which they would limit their respective armed forces in both a first and a second stage of a general disarmament arrangement, assuming they overcome differences on other parts of the package. (See Charts I and II at the end of this chapter.)

The principal difficulty with quantitative limitation has been the problem of the ratio. States tend to demand a higher limit for their own armaments than their competitors will admit is reasonable relative to the limits for others. The problem is complicated by the many variables that affect the comparative military strength of nations, and by the inability to calculate with any exactness the relative "security value" of different kinds of weapons or forces. How can one compare the worth of fighters and bombers, cruisers and submarines, men under arms and trained reserves, to mention only a few of the conundrums, without taking into account differences in the quality of equipment and training, or in the strategic location and commitments of various countries? Furthermore, the infinite complexity of a large military establishment and the need to mesh its many elements in a balanced, coordinated whole have made military experts shudder at the prospect of fixing and implementing quantitative limits on the separate components of the establishment. They have feared that, quite apart from the danger of finishing up on the short end of a ratio, they would find themselves left with a fighting force so straitjacketed by limitations that they could not properly integrate it and insure its maximum effectiveness. Another pitfall of quantitative disarmament is that it does not restrict military research and the development of new weapons and techniques of warfare likely to be far more dangerous than those that are limited.[19]

The advent of nuclear weapons has, in one sense, simplified the problem of quantitative limitation, but has also made such limitations far less important to the achievement of an overall system of arms control. The problem of the ratio ceases to have much significance when countries have pushed their armament to a point of saturation—where they have at hand all the power necessary to destroy their most formidable enemies. Stockpiling beyond that point, of men or of arms, hardly improves the ratio; conversely, expansion of other nations' establishments beyond saturation does not affect the ratio adversely. Quantitative limitation of conventional armaments, therefore, becomes practicable for atomically armed states, which can afford to disregard some of the troublesome detail of the ratio problem.

But the supreme menace of total war with "absolute weapons" would, of

---

[19] German armament was severely limited by the Versailles Treaty after World War I, but ingenious research and planning produced many of the formidable instruments of German military might in World War II before Hitler ever broke the limitations outright—the pocket battleship, the long-range submarine, the dive bomber, and the strategic pattern for use of panzer divisions.

course, remain untouched, for nuclear weapons, especially when coupled with missiles, are not susceptible to control by the quantitative approach. A limit higher than zero already exceeds the minimum requirement for safety. Moreover, it may be technically impossible to disperse the existing stockpiles even if the atomic powers were to agree to some limitation on their size.[20]

The renewed interest in quantitative limitation is partly the result of a fresh slant on the problem introduced in 1952 by the French and British during negotiations in the United Nations Disarmament Subcommittee. They suggested that a simple limit on the overall size of the armed forces might serve as a basic yardstick for limitation of all other aspects of the military establishment, without the need of spelling out figures for specific items of hardware or distinguishing between categories of forces. One would assume that each country would equip and dispose of its allowed force in whatever ways it considered gave it the strongest possible posture. The limit on numbers would tend to automatically limit equipment to what could be used most effectively by the force under arms. As the operation of advanced weapons requires increasingly specialized technical skill, and the progress of military technology rapidly outdates both weapons and previous training, size and preparation of the current professional force is a much more decisive factor in determining military strength than is possession of quantities of various types of weapons on the verge of obsolescence. This line of argument is obviously most applicable to states whose technology enables them to rely more on firepower than manpower. The French–British approach presumed, however, that if the major powers accepted quantitative limitations, they would be in a position to insist that other states follow suit, more or less proportionally, thus bringing down the entire world level.

The terms of an agreement along these lines have been largely worked out between the Soviet Union and the Western powers. It is not yet implemented, however, because the states have been unable to agree on other problems—notably, a system of control that would effectively verify compliance, and correlation of this move with measures for the limitation of atomic weapons.[21] But the major powers seem satisfied that this kind of quantitative limitation does provide a solution for this phase of the disarmament problem.

Qualitative

Qualitative limitation was put forward during the negotiations of the thirties as a way out of the apparently unresolvable dilemmas posed by the quantitative approach.

---

[20] If one assumes, with the exponents of contemporary doctrines of limited war, that nuclear armament cancels out in a stalemate of mutual terror, then conventional arms regain a decisive influence, and the problem of the ratio will have to be faced once more. The problem would persist in any case for countries outside the nuclear club.

[21] See Charts I and II below, pp. 238–42.

The British originally proposed a virtual prohibition of military aircraft, warships over 10,000 tons, submarines, heavy mobile guns, and tanks—the critical offensive weapons from their standpoint. This kind of limitation had already been imposed on Germany. Lord Cecil, at the Disarmament Conference in 1932, urged all nations to accept the same prohibitions. President Hoover placed the U.S. substantially in accord, and President Roosevelt endorsed a similar position. Many other governments came to accept the principle of qualitative disarmament.

The project foundered, however, over the issue of abolishing aircraft. A fierce struggle in the British Cabinet was won by air force enthusiasts who took the position that only large aircraft—bombers—were truly offensive and should be restricted. Negotiations then bogged down over defining the size and number of aircraft necessary to make them an aggressive rather than a defensive instrument. Similar haggling occurred over the size of tanks, ships, and guns that would give them an offensive quality.[22]

Since World War II, interest in qualitative disarmament has centered almost entirely on nuclear weapons, although the offensive power of aircraft, submarines, and many other weapons has also reached extreme proportions. The immensity of nuclear destruction and the fact that total elimination of nuclear weapons appeared technically feasible at the early stages of their development caused governments to give this problem priority. There has been little argument over the desirability—indeed, imperative need—for nuclear disarmament. The Soviet Union and the Western powers have constantly professed conviction that the use of nuclear energy for military purposes should be completely prevented. They have failed to agree on practicable means of control, and in the meantime the pace of nuclear development may have made control impossible.[23]

Aside from the question of control which must be considered in more detail, the great difficulty with qualitative disarmament now is the vast range of offensive armament at the disposal of nations. In order to effectively crimp offensive capabilities, the qualitative approach would require a sweeping, virtually total disarmament of modern arms. Whatever is done to control nuclear weapons, a system that left in being strategic air forces, ballistic missiles of even the shortest range, and tank divisions would allow the threat of massive attack to remain. The great opportunity for qualitative disarmament was missed in 1932–33. Had it been adopted at that time with vigor, World War II could hardly have been fought. Now the time has passed when it is practicable, unless it is part and parcel of a comprehensive system of control, covering all arms.

---

[22] An excellent review of the negotiations on this question is given by Noel-Baker, *op. cit.*

[23] There is some opinion that countries should retain atomic weapons for "tactical" use indefinitely, but official policies still advocate as an ultimate objective complete restriction of nuclear power to peaceful uses.

Geographical

Geographical disarmament has worked with fair success in limited areas, either when contiguous states have demilitarized their frontiers or other states have joined in neutralizing the area as a part of a general security settlement.

Reference has already been made to the long-standing demilitarization of the U.S.–Canadian frontier. Sweden and Norway installed a demilitarized frontier when the two countries separated in 1905, and it has been an important factor in their peaceful relations ever since. Similarly, disarmed frontier zones have minimized tension and dangerous incidents between hostile Latin American countries, between Russia and some of its neighbors in the twenties, between Greece and Turkey after bitter warfare in 1920–23, and elsewhere.

The second type of geographic disarmament—neutralization of buffer zones, secured by guarantees that other states will keep their forces out—has survived over long periods. Although the violations are recalled more vividly than the record of stability, the fact remains that the neutrality of Belgium (which actually owes its national origin to a nineteenth-century buffer zone experiment of the great powers) lasted almost a century, and Holland's stood for an additional generation, until swept aside by German aggression in the two world wars. What did not function well was demilitarization imposed one-sidedly on an unwilling state; even pacific Germans after World War I resented the demilitarization of the Rhineland as an injustice dictated by the Versailles Treaty. Changing this situation became a prime objective of German policy long before Hitler's rise.[24]

Complete disarmament of the Axis powers at the end of World War II might have instituted a new experiment in geographical disarmament had it been part of an overall peace settlement and affected the disposition of the victors' forces as well. But with the onset of the cold war, the Soviets and the West converted these disarmed areas into outposts of their own. Instead of sealing off the areas as buffers and guaranteeing their continued disarmament, the two sides encouraged their *rearmament* as part of the alignment in the power struggle.

The Austrian peace treaty was a great exception. It established Austria's independence on a basis of its own commitment to permanent neutrality and on agreement of the occupying powers to pull out all their forces. While Austria has maintained modest armament of its own, this arrangement effectively ended the direct military confrontation between the U.S.S.R. and the Western powers at a point of very great tension. Notable calm has since prevailed in this area.

---

[24] A definitive study of these experiences up to the thirties has been made by Major-General J. H. Marshall Cornwall, *Geographic Disarmament* (London: Oxford University Press, 1935). See also Noel-Baker, *op. cit.*, pp. 509–21.

Proposals to similarly "disengage" Soviet and Western forces in Germany and Central Europe have come to the fore as cold war tension has heightened. George Kennan, onetime chief of the State Department's Policy Planning Staff, provoked sharp debate by urging the mutual withdrawal or reduction of Soviet and Western forces in Germany, coupled with a restriction on Germany's military attachment to either side. Most especially he cautioned that arming either Germany or other European countries with atomic weapons would seriously increase military tension and the risk of war.[25]

Disengagement became a subject of active diplomatic negotiation when Poland proposed in the Rapacki Plan that the Soviet Union and the West clear their forces from a large zone in Central Europe, and that all concerned states agree to keep the area free of nuclear weapons and production. Under the plan, too, neither part of Germany would retain military forces. The Soviet Union declared it would accept some such arrangement for an area approximately 500 miles on each side of the dividing line in Germany and including as well states in a belt of similar width running from the Arctic Circle to the Mediterranean. The United States and other principal Western states have so far rejected the approach, because it would require them to reorganize NATO without German participation and limit the area for deploying NATO forces. They prefer to keep their existing collective "shield," though it brings them toe-to-toe with vastly superior Russian forces.

Nevertheless, the idea persists that a geographical separation of opposing forces and demilitarization, or at least denuclearization, of major areas of confrontation between the superpowers would greatly lessen occasions for tension and improve the prospects for general security. The approach obviously has great appeal to the peoples who are caught between the jaws of the East–West conflict, and the Poles have tried again to find a way of moving in this direction with the more modest suggestion of a freeze on existing forces and arms in Central Europe.[26]

A principal criticism of geographical disarmament is that it does nothing directly to reduce the capacity of states to wage war, nor does it provide in and of itself a means of deterrence to keep states from breaking the arrangement and seizing control of the disarmed areas. Such schemes create a power

---

[25] See George Kennan, *Russia, the Atom, and the West* (the Reith Lectures, British Broadcasting Corporation, November–December, 1957). The hazards of installing nuclear stockpiles and missile bases in Germany and making it, thus, a bastion of nuclear power are also sharply exposed by James M. Warburg, *The West in Crisis* (New York: Doubleday, 1959) and others.

[26] The Western powers were willing to consider establishment of zones for *inspection*, but not *demilitarization*, in their spheres of control. Proposals of this type are reviewed in the next chapter. The U.S. even objects to a freeze, for this would prevent the development of a multilateral nuclear force with German participation.

vacuum, it is asserted, which tempts powerful states to expand to fill it, gravely endangering the security of others and the maintenance of peace.

The point of this method of disarmament, however, is to reduce the danger of war by incident. Experience strongly indicates that it does just this, especially when linked to the neutralization of otherwise independent states which consider it much to their interest to prevent the use of their territories as battlefields. So far as enforcement goes, knowledge that violation of the demilitarized zone will probably unite all concerned states in reprisal has acted to prevent infractions, unless a state has determined to take on the consequences of full-scale war. Thus, geographic disarmament can avoid the buildup of friction from close physical proximity of opposing and nervous forces, forestall accidental acts of hostility, and remove a fertile source of pretexts for belligerence.[27]

Geographic disarmament also may have the important advantage of disentangling some questions of a military nature from the web of critical political controversy. Mr. Kennan has put the point pithily in reference to the defense of Europe. Geographically separating the forces of the great nuclear powers may result in

. . . excluding them as direct factors in the future development of political relationships on the continent . . . if there could be a general withdrawal of American, British and Russian armed power from the heart of the Continent, there would be at least a chance that Europe's fortunes might be worked out, and the competition between two political philosophies carried forward, in a manner disastrous neither to the respective peoples themselves nor to the cause of world peace.

He concludes that he "would not know where else this chance is to be looked for."[28]

Budgetary

The limitation of defense expenditures has not usually been regarded as in itself a primary technique of disarmament. For one thing, money spent does not furnish an accurate guage of military power. How it is used, and how

---

[27] Hitler's abrupt remilitarization of the Rhineland in 1936 is often cited to prove the futility of geographic disarmament. This is not a reasonable conclusion, considering that the arrangement was a one-sided instrument for the restraint of Germany by the Allies, and never accepted by Germany as contributing to its own security as well. Its implementation did not rest on reciprocal guarantees, but on the compulsive power and will of victors. It was thus not a geniune disarmament accord. Its repudiation by force suggests the ephemeral nature of peace systems relying primarily on a power-political basis rather than the ineffi-ciacy of agreed disarmament.

A far more damaging indictment is furnished by the German attack on Belgium in World War I and on both Belgium and Holland in World War II. These certainly show that geographic disarmament is not self-sustaining. It will not prevent a government committed to war from going to war and seizing the disarmed area for its advantage if it can.

[28] Kennan, op. cit., Lecture IV.

efficiently, varies so much from country to country that it becomes practically impossible to compare the results in terms of military value. Chances for evasion of a budgetary limitation are also considerable.

The idea has received thoroughgoing examination, however, as a yardstick to estimate the overall trend of national defense establishments and as one control method to see if countries are complying with a disarmament agreement. Governments have not yet put a plan for international fiscal arms limitation into operation, but its acceptance as one element in a comprehensive disarmament system now appears probable.

In the negotiations for general disarmament during 1955–56, both the Soviet Union and the Western powers included in their respective proposals provisions for inspection of budgetary appropriations for military needs, although they did not go the length of advocating outright fiscal limitations. At the Geneva Summit Conference in 1955, however, Premier Faure of France specifically urged the reduction of military expenses, with a new twist. Elaborating on an earlier suggestion of President Eisenhower, he proposed that savings resulting from the limitation of arms expenditures be devoted to an international fund for economic development and mutual assistance.

The technical aspects of budgetary limitations were well worked out by the League's Preparatory Commission and the Disarmament Conference of 1932. They went into the matter exhaustively and drew up a detailed plan for the use of budgetary control as a check on the trend of military expenditures. The plan was tested on actual financial data furnished by 29 states, representing the budgets and accounts for 90 per cent of the world's military expenses in 1931–32. The conference's Technical Committee concluded that the system was workable for the purposes of verifying any budgetary limitations that might be adopted.[29]

Disclosure

The remaining method of limitation—disclosure of military information—is subtle, for it does not appear on the surface to involve any direct restriction on how much or in what way a country arms, but only on keeping its doings secret. Nevertheless, the effect of thoroughgoing disclosure of military preparations and plans to the world at large, including all potential enemies, might make this method the most important restraint of all.

The League of Nations actually established a system of disclosure which functioned until feverish preparations began for World War II. The Covenant obligated members to "interchange full and frank information as to the scale of their armaments, their military, naval, and air programmes and the condition of such of their industries as are adaptable to warlike purposes." The League invited nonmembers also to cooperate in this arms census, and

---

[29] See Noel-Baker, *op. cit.,* pp. 498–508.

was able to compile and publish a comprehensive annual inventory of most of the world's visible armaments. The system relied on honest reporting by each government, so there was always the possibility of some evasion, especially in regard to research and development of new weapons. It worked sufficiently well, however, so that the League's yearbooks were generally accepted as authoritative on major military resources.

The United Nations has so far made no provision for a world arms census. At various points in the 15 years of disarmament negotiations since World War II, proposals for disclosure have been advanced, but they have been sidetracked in the search for much broader international controls over arms. Disclosure at the sole discretion of national governments and unaccompanied by international controls to ascertain its veracity has not found favor with the Western powers, though the Soviet Union has, on occasion, justified it as a step valuable in itself. To the West, another vital objection to accepting comprehensive obligations for disclosure was the need they felt for secrecy in the whole field of nuclear development until a "foolproof" system for its international control was in operation.

The Soviet Union unexpectedly precipitated the question into the first session of the General Assembly in 1946 with a proposal for a census of armed forces and bases maintained on *foreign* territory—a skillful political jab at the U.S. and other Western states whose power position depended far more than the Soviet's on a worldwide dispersal of military strength.

The West countered by proposing an internationally verified inventory of armed forces and installations at *home* as well as abroad. Molotov agreed, to everyone's amazement, and for a few hours overnight, on December 5, 1946, agreement seemed at hand on an extreme measure of informational control that would have subjected all the world's military establishments to outside observation, and would have ended the suspicion-breeding secrecy with which each side was enshrouding its military programs. The United States promptly hedged on exposure of its atomic developments (unless an entire package of international atomic management and ownership was accepted), and the deal was off.

During 1948–49, a French proposal for a census and international verification limited to conventional armaments and military forces was approved in various United Nations organs, but opposed by the Soviet Union and vetoed when brought before the Security Council. Russia contended that the census was meaningless unless it included information concerning atomic weapons; that it would not contribute directly to a reduction of arms; and, in the meantime, would serve only as a channel for military intelligence.

The Soviet Union proved no more responsive to the proposal of President Eisenhower at the Geneva Conference in 1955 for an exchange of military "blueprints" as a means of easing tension, building confidence, and reducing the threat of surprise attack. This idea was tied in with machinery for verification and, in particular, with provision for unrestricted aerial reconnaissance—the notable "open skies" proposal.[30]

In further negotiations, the question of disclosure has been consistently treated as one aspect of the larger problem of establishing systems of control to implement specific types of arms limitation agreements. Efforts to use disclosure as a method of limitation per se have apparently been abandoned.

There are currently two principal difficulties with disclosure of vital military information as a means of limiting the arms race. First is the possibility of evasion in precisely those areas where a country is building up its most potent means of attack. Methods of verification are technically most troublesome in ascertaining such matters as stockpiles of nuclear weapons and missiles, location of launching sites, results of research and testing, and strategic planning. Governments are understandably reluctant to divulge this kind of information and submit to procedures of verification unless they can be sure they will secure in return complete knowledge of what their potential enemies possess.

The second obstacle is the importance that secrecy itself has acquired as a weapon. Formerly, the nightmare of military planners was that their opponents might in the course of a war come up with a single, decisive secret weapon. Now the element of *initial* surprise figures as such a critical determinant of the final outcome that many strategists demand undercover treatment for every detail of defensive—and offensive—preparations. Overall secrecy covers up weaknesses the enemy might exploit if it knew about them, as well as the paraphernalia to deliver a series of unexpected knockout punches. From this point of view, any leak through the dike of concealment, whether through espionage, inept speechmaking, Congressional inquiry, or authorized disclosure in pursuance of an international agreement, is a blow to the nation's security.

Much of the force of this second argument is lost once knowledge escaping through the leaks has revealed the essential character of a country's defenses, and its rivals have clearly advanced to a similar level of preparedness. In such circumstances, secrecy does not help to preserve a vital edge of superiority, but merely exacerbates relations and contributes to self-deception.

Those who think they have a secret when it is already out make clumsy and often dangerous strategists. The tragedy of postwar negotiations for a system of disclosure is that in 1946–47, at a time when verification could have been effectively accomplished in all areas of the military establishment

---

[30] Discussed further, below, p. 250.

(including atomic development before large stockpiles had been amassed), the United States clung to its mantle of secrecy for atomic weapons in the false confidence that its know-how could be kept hidden for at least 5 to 10 years if its plans for international control were not accepted. By that time, it expected its lead would be beyond challenge. Ironically, at that very time, unbeknown to the United States, the U.S.S.R. was on the verge of crashing the atomic monopoly. Thus, maintaining the system of secrecy boomeranged on its proponents, even at a time when there seemed to be the most to hide. Now, the area of effectively hidden vital military information is probably much smaller and the reasons for holding back on disclosure even less cogent.[31]

However, the technical difficulties of verification are now so great in certain respects that it remains to be seen if they can be resolved. Substantial facilities for international inspection would be required, so the problem of disclosure has now become interwoven with the general problems of control.

If a system of verified disclosure can be worked out, it would probably go a long way toward reducing the fear of surprise attack and would provide a base line from which to calculate cutbacks in armaments. Information, reciprocally shared and validated, may also prove an antidote to the suspicions fostered when states try to conduct their military competition in secret.

TOWARD A BALANCED AND PHASED DISARMAMENT

The main thrust of negotiations after 1952 has been to bring together various types of arms limitation and control in an overall plan, to be implemented in a series of stages.

This was designed to meet the problem presented by the vastly different commitments and strategic situations of the major powers, which make any particular measure of arms limitation appear to bear unevenly on their respective power positions. The negotiators tried to devise an approach that by interlocking several measures would enable countries to balance their risks—that is, match the losses estimated from one measure of disarmament with gains from another.

The purpose as defined in the U.S.–U.S.S.R. Joint Statement of Agreed Principles (the McCloy–Zorin agreement) was to insure that disarmament would "be balanced so that at no stage of the implementation of the treaty

---

[31] President Eisenhower's exchange-of-blueprints proposal seems to bear this out. He proposed a *complete* exchange, evidently including atomic facilities.

could any state or group of states gain military advantage, and so that security would be ensured equally for all."[32]

This concept of "balanced" disarmament was coupled with the idea of "phasing" its implementation so that in the prevailing atmosphere of intense distrust states would not have to take big and irrevocable steps all at once. The hope was that agreement would be facilitated if initial commitments involved only limited risks. If these first steps were faithfully executed with no ill effects, more portentous steps would follow in the next stage.

The crucial question, of course, is what amount and what kind of disarmament to introduce at each stage of the program. To get agreement, each country must feel that it will be no less secure at the end of a stage than at its beginning. It will not accept paper assurances of future performance by others; therefore, the steps undertaken at each stage must in themselves form an acceptable self-contained package and be put into effect simultaneously by all concerned. In effect, each stage involves implementation of a group of partial measures of limitation or reduction of arms, leading to ever more extensive measures in succeeding stages. Taken altogether, they would accomplish the objective of "general and complete disarmament" to which, as previously noted, all the governments now stand committed.

Despite the intricacy of the venture, agreement has been reached on many aspects of a comprehensive disarmament program. The extent of consensus is indicated on Chart I (page 238), contrasting the positions of the U.S.S.R. with those of the U.S., Britain, and France as of 1957 when negotiations were broken off; and on Chart II (page 242), presenting the respective positions of the U.S. and U.S.S.R. in 1964.[33]

It should be pointed out that these positions do not in any sense represent firm commitments. They may be changed at will, at any time, until a treaty is finally accepted. Indeed, every provision of the carefully knit plan which had emerged by 1957 was officially scrapped when the negotiations abruptly ended; when they resumed in 1960, each government nominally started all over again with a slate clean of prior understandings. But there has actually been much continuity, as comparison of the two charts shows, and an overall trend toward greater consensus instead of less.

The matter of the breaks in negotiation needs explanation, because it casts light on some of the factors that have impeded agreement, quite apart from differences on the issues themselves. The nearness of agreement, rather than inability to bridge remaining gaps, may have had much to do with the 1957

---

[32] U.N. Doc. A/4879. This principle was incorporated in the U.S. draft treaty for general and complete disarmament proposed in 1962, and in a slightly modified version in the corresponding Soviet treaty proposal. See U.N. Doc DC/203, June 5, 1962 (ENDC/2, March 19, 1962).

[33] For a detailed analysis of the negotiations through 1960, see Bechhoefer, *op. cit.*

breakdown. Secretary of State Dulles came to Geneva at a point when major concessions on both sides seemed to have resolved most of the key issues; but instead of consummating the agreement, he set forth a position so much at variance with the previous American stands that the Russians felt the U.S. was not acting in good faith. They abruptly rejected a Western package proposal presented as a "last offer" on an all-or-none, take-it-or-leave-it basis, and adamantly refused for three years to reenter disarmament negotiations. Possibly accounting for Dulles' action was the buildup of pressure inside and outside the U.S. government against any disarmament agreement, when agreement seemed imminent.

Negotiations had hardly resumed in 1960 when the Russians again walked out. This time the occasion was unmistakable. They had brought down an American U–2 plane on a "spy" flight over Russia. President Eisenhower's refusal to disavow responsibility was the ultimate affront. They did not return to the disarmament conference table until long after the Kennedy administration took over in Washington, demonstrated a profound commitment to accommodation and disarmament, and strenuously sought to assure the Russians it would respect their sensibilities as well as territorial integrity.

In the light of the last round of negotiations (1962–64) it appears that the principal remaining stumbling blocks have to do with the question of controls to insure that the agreed terms of disarmament are carried out by everyone. This problem is analyzed in the next chapter.

Some disagreement also persists over the major substantive issue of the phasing of nuclear disarmament. For a long time, the two sides were uncompromisingly split over the sequence of restrictions to be placed on the development, production, possession, and use of nuclear weapons and nuclear delivery vehicles. Some of the former differences have become academic, and are recognized as such, because actions whose timing was previously a subject of debate are now technologically infeasible at *any* stage (for instance, total elimination of nuclear stockpiles). Other questions that tangled up the phasing problem, such as the nuclear test ban, have been separately settled and no longer have to be fitted into the sequence of general disarmament. The U.S. and U.S.S.R. still do not agree on the amount of cutback in nuclear delivery vehicles: in Stage I, the U.S. favors a 30 per cent cut, while the Soviets would make a wholesale cut (except for missiles to be held by the two titans as their ultimate *coup de frappe* until the last stage). The U.S. maintains that "the Soviet proposal is impractical because it would pose difficulties in control and implementation, and would result in a grave strategic imbalance in the world which the more gradual across-the-board reductions proposed in the United States plan would avoid."[34]

Such differences no longer seem irreconcilable, especially when viewed

---

[34] U.S. Arms Control and Disarmament Agency, *Second Annual Report to Congress, Jan. 1–Dec. 31, 1962* (Washington, D.C.: U.S. Government Printing Office, 1963), p. 166.

against the background of the great concessions already made to reach the present large area of consensus. For example, the U.S.S.R. has over the years changed its stand to accord with the West on such fundamental questions as:

1. Willingness to carry out disarmament by stages.
2. Beginning with a reduction in conventional armaments rather than with a total prohibition of nuclear weapons.
3. Agreeing to Western proposals for force levels in all stages of disarmament.
4. Accepting the West proposed time when prohibition of nuclear weapons would take place under a general disarmament program; and agreeing to begin by discontinuing the manufacture of nuclear weapons, then proceeding to their elimination from national armaments and the destruction of stocks.
5. Accepting control over rockets and satellites for peaceful purposes only.

These do not include other concessions with respect to the methods and timing of a system of inspection and control, which will be mentioned later.

Western concessions, reflected in the program for a balanced disarmament by stages, include:

1. Relinquishing the (Baruch) plan originally proposed for control of atomic energy by international ownership and management.
2. Abandoning the attempt to begin disarmament with a series of disclosures, starting with simple ones and proceeding to complicated ones, each followed by international verification, disarmament not beginning until this series of operations had been finished.
3. Agreeing to have nuclear weapons prohibited after 75 per cent of agreed reductions in conventional arms were completed, rather than waiting until the very end of the process.
4. Disarmament to begin with the Big Five (a Soviet idea) instead of having all countries start at the same time.
5. Agreeing that time limits should be set for certain of the stages to be completed.
6. Dropping political conditions for the entry into force of the first stage of the disarmament program.
7. Agreeing to place suspension of nuclear tests at the beginning of disarmament rather than at the end.[35]

The problem of control remains the critical unresolved issue. To this we now turn.

---

[35] From a memorandum prepared by Sydney D. Bailey for the American Friends Service Committee, Philadelphia, Pa., Dec. 30, 1957 (mimeo.), based on statements by Mr. Moch and Mr. Zorin before the U.N. Disarmament Subcommittee. See also Sydney B. Bailey, *The United Nations* (New York: Praeger, 1963), pp. 72–3.

CHART I

PROPOSALS FOR PARTIAL MEASURES OF DISARMAMENT
As of August, 1957

WEST	SOVIET

Preliminary
(on entry into force of a disarmament agreement)

Use of nuclear weapons

Renounce use except in self-defense vs. armed attack	Renounce all military use except for defense against aggression upon authorization of the Security Council (but see note *b*)

First Stage (see note *a*)

Armed forces and conventional armaments

Immediate freeze on armed forces, conventional arms and expenses (see note *c*)	Same

Reduce within one year all armed forces to:	Same (provided definite further reduction assured at later stage—see note *d*)

US	2.5 million
USSR	2.5 million
France	750,000
UK	750,000

Levels of other essential states to be determined later in negotiation	Same (proposed limit on China identical with US or USSR; others not to exceed 150,000–200,000)

Transfer to storage under international supervision of specified quantities of designated types of arms (see note *e*)	Agreed in principle

Bases

No provision	Agree to liquidate some foreign military bases during a period of one or two years (see note *f*)

Nuclear tests

Accepted Soviet position—assuming adequate control (see note *g*)	End nuclear tests as one of first measures, independently of other measures of disarmament—under international control (see note *g*)

Nuclear production

Study the technical feasibility of cutting off manufacture of nuclear weapons (see note *j*)	No specific provision

Missiles

Within three months after treaty enters into force, establish technical committee to study inspection system to assure exclusive use of outer space for peaceful and scientific purposes	Total abolition under international control of all missiles (of any range) suitable for use as nuclear weapons (see note *h*)

Second Stage

Conventional

Further reduction of forces on condition of "progress toward the solution of political issues," acceptance by other "essential states" of agreed force levels, and adequate inspection system

US	2.1 million
USSR	2.1 million
France	700,000
UK	700,000

Accepted, if reductions "were not made contingent upon the settlement of political and other issues" (see note *i*)

Nuclear production

Cut off manufacture of nuclear and other mass destruction weapons after above reductions have taken place, *e.g.*, after 50 percent of entire planned reduction of conventional forces has taken place (see note *j*)	Accepted

Third Stage

Conventional

Further reduction of forces, assuming conditions set for the 2d stage

US	1.7 million
USSR	1.7 million
France	650,000
UK	650,000

Accepted, as above (see note *i*)

Nuclear weapons ban

Complete prohibition of use of nuclear weapons after one-half of 3d stage reductions have taken place, *e.g.*, 75 percent of the total reduction for all stages; then begin transfers in successive increments of fissionable materials to non-weapons uses as means of reducing nuclear weapons stockpiles (see note *j*)	Accepted Western proposal on prohibition and elimination of nuclear weapons, to begin after 75 percent of agreed cutback in forces and conventional arms

Missiles

Ban on the use of outer space for military purposes (see note *k*)	Previously covered

Sources: This chart is based on a close analysis of the 1952–57 negotiations by Philip E. Jacob. See the Disarmament concensus, *International Organization*, Spring, 1960.

Except where otherwise noted, the Western proposals are those presented jointly to the UN Subcommittee on Disarmament, August 29, 1957 (UN Document DC/SC.1/66), by the US, UK, France, and Canada. Though put forward as inseparable parts of a single package, to be accepted together or not at all, the US and Britain have since "broken" the package and negotiated on some of the items independently of others. Also Mr. Selwyn Lloyd at the 14th General Assembly reintroduced the concept of a general program of disarmament steps to be undertaken in progressive stages along lines previously advanced by the British and French in 1954–1956.

The Soviet positions, except where otherwise noted, were defined in their proposals of May 10, 1955 (UN Document DC/SC.1/26/Rev.2), and April 30, 1957 (UN Document DC/SC.1/55). Despite the time lag between these sets of proposals and the differing contexts of the negotiations at their time of presentation, I have concluded that it is appropriate to integrate them as a composite statement of partial measures which the USSR is prepared to accept. Premier Khrushchev explicitly affirmed before the General Assembly in September 1959 that the Soviet government was convinced that the May 10 proposals "constitute a good basis for agreement on this vitally important problem" [*e.g.*, "partial steps in the field of disarmament"]. It therefore seems reasonable to assume that these represent the *latest* authoritative exposition of the Soviet stand with respect to these aspects of the problem. The 1957 proposals, insofar as they are basically compatible with the former, are assumed to be still in effect, as the USSR has not retracted them.

What is not completely clear is how inseparable the Soviet Union considers the various parts of these packages. Some it has explicitly declared independent of the rest, such as a ban on nuclear testing, the establishment of limited zones for the inspection and control of armament, and the withdrawal or reduction of forces in Europe. Others it has indicated rather definitely hinge on acceptance of related conditions. For instance, the amount of international control it will tolerate depends on how much actual disarmament the West will agree to implement. Considering the amount of flexibility demonstrated by the Soviet Union during the negotiations from 1954–1957, perhaps the exact tie-in of the different parts of its proposals is still open to discussion.

Notes: a) Soviet proposals were cast in a scheme of two stages, the Western proposals usually in a three-stage pattern as used in this chart. While there was considerable reshuffling of items from one stage to another as the plans matured, the basic sequence of steps remained the same as outlined in the chart with the exception of the ending of nuclear tests. The Western powers originally scheduled this step at the very end of the sequence; they finally moved it to the first stage as proposed by the USSR.

b) While the USSR has customarily propounded a total renunciation of the use of nuclear weapons, it has not shut the door to an exception in situations of self-defense. The formula indicated is the one set forth in the 1955 proposals.

In the 1957 negotiations the USSR suggested that the commitment might be couched in terms of an obligation not to be the *first* to use nuclear weapons. Later the Soviet delegate expressed interest in a Western counter-proposal to define the exceptions within the context of Article 51 of the UN Charter, permitting nuclear weapons to be used in individual or collective defense against an armed attack that could not otherwise feasibly be repelled. The USSR in the end rejected the Western formula as put in the August 29, 1957, proposals on the ground that it would "in fact legalize" the use of nuclear weapons. But this was incidental to the Soviet rejection of the Western package as a whole, and may not have represented a deliberate return to the demand for a total ban on use as a precondition for any disarmament.

See Informal Memorandum of May 31, 1957, from the Chairman of the US delegation to the UN Disarmament Subcommittee to the Chairman of the USSR Delegation; discussion on July 15, 1957, in the UN Disarmament Subcommittee; and statement of USSR representative, August 27, 1957 (UN Document DC/SC.1/65/Rev.1).

c) British-French proposal, March 19, 1956 (UN Document DC/SC.1/38).

d) This condition would no longer appear to hold, in view of the unilateral reduction authorized by the Supreme Soviet, January 15, 1960, to a level of 2,423,000 (*The New York Times,* January 15, 1960).

e) The Western proposals of August 29, 1957, represented a different approach to the problem of reducing armaments from that previously taken either by the West or by the USSR. They abandoned the earlier idea of a percentage cut in arms and military expenses (10 per cent cut proposed by the West vs. 15 per cent by USSR), because, without a reliable inventory of each state's complete armament at the time, it would be impossible to know what the cut really involved. It was assumed that the USSR would not agree to a full-scale report of its armament at such an early stage.

The Western powers therefore proposed as a more precise and verifiable arrangement, agreement on specific lists of items to be removed to disarmament depots under international supervision. (Cuts in expenditures would be put off until the International Control Organization was receiving information from the various powers about their military outlays.) See Informal Memorandum, US Chairman to USSR Chairman, cited in note (b) above; also, Four-Power Proposals of August 29, 1957.

The USSR agreed in principle with these suggestions. But it refused to discuss detailed procedures for dealing with armaments unless the other states abandoned their insistence on progress toward settlement of political problems as a condition of reducing forces to the levels envisioned for the next stages. See US Dept. of State publication no. 6676, *Disarmament: The Intensified Effort,* 1958, p. 47.

f) This formulation in the 1957 proposals was much less peremptory than in 1955 when the USSR called for a definite pledge in the first stage to liquidate all foreign bases, and fulfillment of the pledge in the second stage.

g) The US did not agree to consider a suspension of nuclear testing apart from other measures of arms limitation (in particular a cut-off of nuclear production for military use) until April 1958, in the face of a Soviet announcement that it would henceforth unilaterally cease testing provided others also refrained. (The USSR shrewdly timed its action right after completing a major series of tests, which reportedly produced an unusually large amount of fall-out.)

The USSR acceded to Western insistence on control as a condition of a test ban on June 14, 1957 (UN Document DC/SC.1/60).

All the parties now definitely accept suspension or elimination of nuclear tests as a first-stage step (see statement of Mr. Selwyn Lloyd, 14th General Assembly, September 17, 1959, UN Document 1/PV.798).

h) After the launching of the first Sputniks, the USSR demanded that control over missiles be specifically linked to the prohibition of nuclear weapons and the liquidation of US foreign military bases. See letter of Premier Bulganin to President Eisenhower, February 1, 1958 (US Dept. of State *Bulletin,* March 10, 1958 (Vol. 38, No. 976), p. 379), and statement of the Soviet Foreign Ministry, March 15, 1958 (*The New York Times,* March 16, 1958).

i) Statement of Soviet representative to the UN Disarmament Subcommittee, July 19, 1957. See Dept. of State publication no. 6676, *Disarmament,* p. 47.

j) This timetable was proposed in the British-French plan of March 19, 1956 (UN Document DC/SC.1/38). The Four-Power proposal of August 29, 1957, separated the cut-off of nuclear production and the transfer of stocks of fissionable materials to international control from any corresponding achievements in the limitation of conventional armament and made it dependent solely on the installation of an effective inspection system. The former position appears to coincide more closely with the Soviet position as set forth on May 10, 1955.

At the General Assembly on September 17, 1959, Mr. Selwyn Lloyd in effect reintroduced the Anglo-French timetable, proposing, however, that the reduction of stocks of nuclear weapons by transfers of fissionable material to non-weapons uses begin in the second, or intermediate, stage, and final reductions of conventional arms and manpower be effected concurrently with progress toward eliminating the remaining stocks of nuclear and other weapons of mass destruction.

k) Proposed for this stage by Mr. Selwyn Lloyd at the 14th General Assembly, September 17, 1959.

CHART II

DISARMAMENT PROPOSALS*
As of September, 1964

Stage I

USSR		UNITED STATES
18 months	Duration	3 years
Elimination of all bases in and withdrawal of all troops from foreign territories	Military Bases	
Cessation of all testing; and nontransfer of control of nuclear weapons to non-nuclear states	Nuclear Weapons	Cessation of all testing under international control; nontransfer of control of nuclear weapons to non-nuclear states; a halt in production of weapons-grade fissile materials and transfer of agreed quantities to non-weapons purposes
Elimination of all rockets (except a "limited contingent" of home-based intercontinental ballistic missiles to be retained until end of Stage III), aircraft surface vessels, submarines, and artillery systems capable of delivering nuclear weapons	Delivery Systems for Nuclear Weapons	30 percent reduction of specified delivery systems
Reduction of Soviet and United States armies to 1.9 million men each	Military Manpower	Reduction of Soviet and United States armies to 2.1 million men each
30 percent reduction from existing levels	Conventional Armaments	30 percent reduction from existing levels; an agreed limitation on the production of specified categories of major weapons
To be decreased "proportionately" to the reduction of armed forces	Military Budgets	Submission of reports on military expenditures and study of questions related to verifiable reductions
Agreement to refrain from orbiting nuclear or other weapons of mass destruction and to use outer space for peaceful purposes only	Outer Space	Agreement to refrain from orbiting nuclear weapons and to limit production, stockpiling, and testing of boosters for space vehicles
All states to place armed forces at disposal of the Security Council as provided by Article 43 of the United Nations Charter; the Peace Force to be composed of national contingents stationed in their own territory under national command.	Peace-keeping	Initial preparations for the establishment in Stage II of a United Nations Peace Force

Measures to Reduce the Risk of War by Accident, Miscalculation, or Surprise Attack	Prohibition of "large-scale" military movements or maneuvers effected jointly by two or more states; advance notification of movements or maneuvers by national armies within their own territories; exchange of military missions; and establishment of communications systems	Advance notification of major military movements; exchange of military missions; and establishment of observation posts and communication systems
Duration	24 months	3 years
Stage II		
Military Bases		"Agreed" bases to be dismantled
Nuclear Weapons	Elimination of all nuclear and other weapons of mass destruction; transfer of remaining weapons-grade fissile materials to peaceful uses	Reduction of nuclear weapons to minimum levels on the basis of agreed percentages; reduction of inventories of weapons-grade fissile materials
Delivery Systems for Nuclear Weapons		50 percent reduction from existing levels
Military Manpower	Reduction of Soviet and United States armed forces to 1 million men each	50 percent reduction from existing levels
Conventional Armaments	35 percent reduction from existing levels	50 percent reduction from existing levels
Military Budgets	To be further reduced in proportion to man-power reductions	
Stage III		
Duration	12 months	To be completed "as promptly as possible"
All armed forces, armaments, and arms-production plants would be eliminated, except as required for keeping internal order		
Peace-keeping	Contingents of national "militia" to be placed at the disposal of the Security Council; size and disposition to be specified in agreements with the Council; command of these units to be composed of representatives of "the three principal groups of States existing in the world on the basis of equal representation"	The United Nations Peace Force would be progressively strengthened "so that no state could challenge it"

* The proposals outlined include the most recent major amendments. Both the United States and the USSR proposals provide for IDO verification during each stage; however, while the United States insists that controls be extended to armaments retained as well as destroyed, the Soviet Union would extend them only to armaments destroyed.

Source: *International Conciliation*, November, 1964, pp. 26–27.

Chapter 9

The Organization of Arms Control

The success of disarmament efforts now hinges more than anything else on whether controls can be devised and established which will make sure that countries do what they have agreed to do and, if not, enable the facts to be published at once.

Disarmament must reckon with a situation in which nations presume each other's bad faith. Deception is an accepted instrument of policy for most governments in their international dealings, especially when power or security are at stake. For democracies as well as for totalitarian dictatorships, honesty defers to vital interest. Consequently, it is too much to expect that nations trust one another to faithfully implement agreements to "limit," "reduce," or "abandon" their arms when cheating might pay off with a bettered position in the military balance of power.

All sides concede that under present conditions of mutual distrust, disarmament arrangements will be unacceptable unless they provide for effective means of verifying their fulfillment *to the satisfaction of every party thereto.* This has been accepted as a basic premise of serious negotiation, at least since the second world war.

Before the war, the problem of control received scant attention. Almost everyone agreed that some form of supervision would be needed to make sure the terms of a disarmament treaty were carried out, but only the Russians produced a concrete and detailed plan of how it might be organized.[1] Why there was such indifference is not clear. Some governments, notably the

---

[1] The Russian proposal for control spelled out a comprehensive system of on-the-spot inspection, by foreign observers, of military installations, transportation hubs, arms factories, and records of defense expenditures. This was almost completely ignored in the negotiations. For an able review, see Marina Salvin, "Soviet Policy Toward Disarmament," *International Conciliation,* February, 1947.

influential British, apparently were just not ready to contemplate controls that would expose them to the oversight of foreigners and would rudely challenge the traditional prerogative of a sovereign power to handle its own defense affairs. This was also the position of the United States, though in 1933 the American delegate to the Disarmament Conference did call for "means of effective, automatic and continuous supervision" as part of any disarmament system. Most of the negotiators obviously thought the central and prior problem was to fix the substantive terms of limitation—to find a formula, in other words. If this had been accomplished, they might then have become more concerned over how to implement it.

By contrast, negotiations after the war have from the beginning been preoccupied with the issue of control. This was partly in reaction to the bomb and the immediate worldwide outcry for a system that would effectively prevent further development of atomic energy for military use. As the bomb's creator and original monopolist, the U.S. government felt under peculiar political and moral responsibility to explore the technical possibilities of such control and to propose measures that it would be prepared to accept.[2] The question of control thus came right to the forefront of nuclear negotiation, where it has remained through years of frustrating deadlock (as the Russians and Americans could not come to terms) and increasing complexity (as the nuclear arms race gained momentum and completely changed the conditions under which control would have to operate.)

Meanwhile, concern for control spread over into consideration of other types of disarmament: policing the limitation and reduction of "conventional" armaments, developing safeguards against surprise attack (especially in the light of spectacular advances in missile technology), and the attempt to keep outer space "disarmed."

What has made the negotiations unusually confusing to the nonspecialist is that the major powers have tended to deal with the question of control separately for each kind of disarmament, and what they have proposed for one kind, does not necessarily coincide with their approach to another. There is a sound rationale, as will be seen later, for flexibility in devising controls that are adapted to a particular arms limitation, rather than attempting to set up a single, comprehensive system for all possible types and degrees of disarmament. But it is difficult to fit each proposal and counterproposal into a coherent, overall profile of the issue, and it is doubtful if the governments themselves have until recently developed a unified and coherent approach

---

[2] The trail-blazing study of international control of atomic energy was the Acheson–Lilienthal Report, produced early in 1946 after the then Undersecretary of State and Chairman of the U.S. Atomic Energy Commission had organized a rigorous review of available knowledge. This formed the basis—but only in part—of the first official proposal for control, presented by Bernard Baruch as American delegate to the U.N. Atomic Energy Commission in June, 1946. (Mr. Baruch, largely on his own, added several elements.)

toward all aspects of the control problem. Improvisation under the pressures of political expediency and strategic opportunism seem to have dictated many of the positions on control, rather than far sighted consideration of consequences for national and world security as indicated by thorough technical study. This has often narrowed the vision of negotiators to the particular problem at hand—the nuclear test ban, the danger of an accidental nuclear attack, and others—simply because the amount of knowledge needed to grapple with the problem of control for more extensive and far-reaching disarmament is so great.

In recent years, expertise has developed to a point where this is no longer true. Negotiators are backstopped by continuous and exhaustive research. So there is evidence of an emerging area of common technical understanding of the various issues, which is reflected on the one hand in progress toward consensus and on the other in a much more exact identification of the real grounds for disagreement. Also, the same "teams" customarily direct and conduct all aspects of the disarmament negotiations. This introduces greater coherence, as does the present telescoping of most of the major questions into a single negotiating forum, the Eighteen-Nation Disarmament Committee.

Withal, sufficient agreement on control still has not been reached to complete the draft of a general disarmament treaty, or to put into effect any of a large number of possible partial measures. Three agreements have been made which do *not* involve control, at least from the outside on the territory of participating states—the nuclear test ban treaty, the commitment not to militarize outer space, and the hot line between the Soviet and U.S. heads of state. Some suggest that this all adds up to the infeasibility of control, and, hence, the improbability of any major breakthrough on disarmament unless there is a revolutionary change in the foreign policies of the powers, dictated by new political constellations or a radically altered strategic environment.[3] On the other hand, this is not the view of many of those who have had direct responsibility for the conduct of negotiations. Recognizing the tough ground still to be covered, they believe that many of the fundamental elements of acceptable control systems have now been worked out, and remaining questions are as negotiable as ones that have been settled.

This outlook was reflected in the decision of the U.S. and U.S.S.R. to resume negotiations on the basis of their Joint Statement of Agreed Principles for Disarmament Negotiations of September 20, 1961 (the McCloy–Zorin agreement), which was presented to and heartily welcomed

---

[3] See Lawrence S. Finkelstein, "Arms Inspection," *International Conciliation*, November, 1962, for a summary statement of such views. Such skepticism is characteristic of some American writers who view the problem from a preset view of the power-political impertives of national policies. See, for instance, Joseph Nogee, "The Diplomacy of Disarmament," *International Conciliation*, January, 1960.

by the United Nations General Assembly. On the subject of control, the statement declares:

All disarmament measures should be implemented from beginning to end under such strict and effective international control as would provide firm assurance that all parties are honoring their obligations. During and after the implementation of general and complete disarmament, the most thorough control should be exercised, the nature and extent of such control depending on the requirements for verification of the disarmament measures being carried out in each stage.

Thus, the Russians do not oppose control, as often alleged, but insist that the installation of control is inseparable from actual steps of disarmament—a position now conceded by the U.S., which formerly demanded that a control system should be established and prove its operational effectiveness *before* disarmament began.[4]

The seeming obstructionism or evasiveness of the Russians in the face of Western positions on control has reflected not so much their congenital hostility to international surveillance as a deeply held suspicion that inadequate or one-sided controls could be perverted into instruments of strategic intelligence. This position was expounded with his customary bluntness by Chairman Khrushchev in his disarmament proposals to the General Assembly, September 18, 1959.

We were and are for strict international control over the implementation of the disarmament agreement when it is reached. But we have always been against the system of control being separated from measures toward disarmament, against the organs of control becoming, in effect, organs for the collection of intelligence information in conditions where they would in effect be no actual disarmament. We are in favor of genuine disarmament under control, but we are against control without disarmament.

In the light of the McCloy–Zorin statement, there would now seem to be no argument with this general proposition.

However, the U.S.S.R. and the Western powers continue a running debate on what kinds of control are necessary, when specific measures should be put into effect, who should be responsible for carrying out the controls, and what should be done in case of violations. The rest of this chapter is devoted to an analysis of these issues and of the prospects for resolving them.

WHAT MUST BE CONTROLLED?

The kind of controls necessary to police a disarmament agreement obviously depends, first, on the kind and amount of arms limitation it is decided

---

[4] This point is examined in more detail below.

to put into effect, and, second, on the kind and degree of assurance demanded. For a long time, the major powers deadlocked on these issues.

The Western approach was originally based on the assumption that controls should be geared to implement very comprehensive programs of disarmament—such as complete prevention of the development and application of atomic energy to military purposes, and, simultaneously, a large cutback of conventional armed forces to offset the strategic loss of giving up nuclear weapons. Consequently, the Western proposals envisaged a very extensive net of control, encompassing virtually all objects and facilities related in any way to the production, storing, or deployment of arms and armed forces. For quite a while, also, the Western powers were convinced that the various aspects of disarmament were so interlocked that the control system had to be planned and put into effect as a single package, all at once, providing in advance for all the contingencies of controlling the complete program of disarmament, even though many of the steps of actually eliminating or reducing arms might not be taken for some time. The West insisted, too, on measuring the adequacy of controls by whether they were "foolproof," meaning that *any* evasion of any of the agreed on limitations could be reliably detected. This expanded even more the scope of objects and activities they felt should be subject to control.

This approach was entirely unacceptable to the Russians, for reasons along the lines indicated in the statement by Khrushchev quoted above. They have maintained that the amount of control demanded by the West far exceeded what was necessary to insure compliance with the amount of disarmament envisaged; hence, its purposes were clearly ulterior—expose Soviet defenses to Western espionage, and commit the Soviet Union to perpetual inferiority in areas where the West held momentary advantage (as in the earlier stages of nuclear weapons development).

This impasse was broken by an agreement on principle and a development of fact. When it was agreed to consider partial measures of arms limitation, either as stages of a program for general and complete disarmament or as valuable in and of themselves, it was also agreed that the different parts of the control package were separable and that controls should be tailor-made to meet just what was required for a specific type or degree of limitation. Thus, the amount of control would vary with the complexity of verifying compliance. A specific quantitative reduction of certain types or a certain amount of armaments could be checked by relatively simple observation of their destruction or transfer to an internationally supervised stockpile; but insuring that a country was observing a certain maximum level would be much more complicated, requiring widespread inspection to guard against hiding arms beyond the allowable maximum. Policing a nuclear test ban obviously does not require the widespread inspection of industrial facilities required to verify a cutoff of nuclear fuel production for military purposes. This diversified approach made negotiation for controls much more flexible, because it obviated the necessity of devising a single comprehensive system capable of detecting every conceivable kind of violation and enabled the design of control for one type of disarmament to be considered without waiting for agreement on others. Control was to be phased, in concert with the phasing of disarmament. Only that amount and kind of control would be implemented which was linked to the verification of a particular step or measure of arms limitation.

The development of fact is the end result of almost twenty years of feverish nuclear and military technology. The inventory of nuclear weapons is now so large and concealment so easy, the state of military technology so advanced and the dispersal of know-how so wide, that to establish anything approaching foolproof detection and control is admittedly beyond presently known technical and scientific capabilities.[5]

Realistic recognition of the limits to what was possible changed the test of what would be acceptable, and thereby greatly lessened the rigor of demands made on an arms control arrangement. The present disposition is to accept a plan, if it can provide assurance that violations of a scope capable of giving one nation a major advantage will be detected in time for threatened countries to take countermeasures, the present disposition is to accept the arrangement as a sufficient guarantor of fulfillment. The test of effectiveness is, thus, not whether *any* evasion can be detected, but whether a *serious* violation threatening immediate security or the basic strategic balance has been committed.[6] The U.S. has gone even farther from its original demand for "foolproofness" and suggests that statistical probability may be an adequate test of effectiveness for many types of control. Its proposals for "zonal inspection" are predicted on the idea that sampling procedures could establish a sufficiently strong probability that a country was not violating its agreements to satisfy others that their security was still secure.[7]

Applying these criteria, the negotiators have reached a large measure of common ground on the objects that will need to be controlled for several types and levels of arms limitation.

---

[5] See statement of U.S. representative to the U.N. Subcommittee on Disarmament, March 20, 1957 (U.N. Doc. DC/SC.1/PV. 89), p. 6. A Soviet admission to the same effect was contained in the proposals of May 10, 1955 (U.N. Doc. DC/SC.1/26/Rev. 2). The U.S. did hold out some hope that control of stockpiles might ultimately become sufficiently feasible to permit their gradual transfer to international control for peaceful use. If effective control of nuclear production were installed, it might be possible to establish within reasonable accuracy the amount of fissionable material previously produced. See statements of Ambassador Lodge, General Assembly (12th sess.), January 14, 1957 (U.N. Doc. A/C.1/783), and of U.S. representative at the U.N. Subcommittee on Disarmament, March 19, 1957 (U.N. Doc. DC/SC.1/PV.88).

[6] See L. Finkelstein, *op. cit.,* especially pp. 13–25, for a concise analysis of this point.

[7] See U.S. Arms Control and Disarmament Agency, *The Concept of Progressive Zonal Inspection,* January, 1963.

For instance, it is agreed that for a *general limitation and reduction of armed forces and conventional armaments,* control will be established at all military installations (including land, naval, and air bases and training centers), rail and road hubs, and factories manufacturing conventional weapons. (Should the concept of progressive zonal inspection be applied, only a sampling of the above would be necessary.) One still troublesome issue is how to secure an accurate military "census," determining, for example, the total existing stocks of each country and the size of its paramilitary forces at any given time. This is mainly a problem at the early stages of control, however, for a holdback of arms or forces would be increasingly hard to hide once control were fully operating at all the points indicated.

Agreement is substantial, but not complete, on the objects that would require control in an adequate system for the *cutoff of nuclear production for military purposes* and a *ban on the use of nuclear weapons.*

During negotiations in the U.N. Atomic Energy Commission over the Baruch plan (the original U.S. proposal for international control of atomic energy), the Western states asserted that control would have to begin at the original source of fissionable raw materials (the mining of uranium, thorium, etc.), continue through every facility involved in the process of creating nuclear fuel, apply to all storage facilities, and follow the distribution of nuclear products to their end use. The U.S.S.R. indicated that it would go along with most of this, but demurred on including related activities such as the production of graphite, heavy water, centrifuge pumps, and other materials largely used in nuclear production.[8] Since then, full agreement has been reached on the system of control used by the International Atomic Energy Agency to insure that its consignments of nuclear fuel, facilities, and products would not be diverted from peaceful purposes. As further experience is gained through operations of IAEA, even though the IAEA system applies only to countries that do not at the moment produce nuclear weapons, it seems likely that it will help to clarify the exact terms of an appropriate pattern for comprehensive control acceptable to all nuclear-producing nations.[9]

Agreement has proved stickier on the more limited question of immediate *controls to safeguard nations against surprise attack.* As against President Eisenhower's "open skies" proposal in 1955—to open the entire airspace of Russia and the U.S. to unrestricted reciprocal aerial reconnaissance—the U.S.S.R. at first held to methods of ground control. The Russians feared, they

---

[8] Compare Majority Plan with U.S.S.R. proposals of June 11, 1947. (Third Report of U.N. Atomic Energy Commission to the Security Council.)

[9] See the analysis of the IAEA system by John Stoessinger in *Organizing Peace in the Nuclear Age,* Commission to Study the Organization of Peace, 11th Report (New York: New York University Press, 1959). Also, Robert H. Cory, Jr., "International Inspection: From Proposals to Realization," *International Organization,* Autumn, 1959, pp. 495–504; and Alvin Z. Rubinstein, "The U.S., the Soviet Union and Atoms-for-Peace," *World Affairs,* Vol. 30, No. 1 (April, 1959).

said, that the aerial survey would be used for military intelligence unrelated to control over the reduction of armaments. During 1956–57, the two sides attempted to define specific geographical areas, outside as well as inside each country, that would be subjected to intensive inspection because of their strategic significance as bases for attack. (In this connection, the U.S.S.R. did consent to the use of aerial photography along with a system of ground control.) But they could not agree on the areas to be covered: "each side proposed aerial and ground inspection in the areas where it believed the other to have its strongest concentration of military bases."[10] A third approach was outlined by the Western powers at a special conference of experts called in 1958 to make a "technical" study of the problem: comprehensive surveillance of three types of weapons most likely to be used in surprise attack—long-range aircraft, ballistic missiles, and ground forces—and of the sites and areas from which such weapons might be launched.[11]

Concern for the control of delivery vehicles, especially those capable of carrying weapons of mass destruction, has mounted as advances in military technology, such as atomic-powered rocket-launching submarines and hardened or mobile launching sites for ICBMs, have rapidly increased the possible range, sources, and destructiveness of surprise attack. But the U.S.S.R. tends to see the problem of surprise attack much more in terms of enemy bases located near its territory, and most particularly in terms of the nuclear armament of Germany. Its essential formula is: dismantle all military bases on foreign territory, discontinue nuclear armed flights in Europe or elsewhere on the Soviet periphery, and completely prohibit nuclear weapons and missiles in Germany, or German access thereto. These demands the Western alliance rejects as political, involving as they would the practical abandonment of NATO as a security system.

The prevention of surprise attack has, therefore, been brought into the framework of negotiations for general disarmament, and relevant controls have been considered in relation to other measures of limitation that might be put into effect at various stages of the disarmament process.[12]

Much attention has been devoted to the problem of devising *controls for the specific purpose of detecting nuclear explosions,* in order to implement a

---

[10] *International Conciliation,* No. 519 (September, 1958), p. 10. Note that the issue in these negotiations was the definition of zones of inspection, in contrast to demilitarization or disengagement, as previously discussed in Chapter 8. The U.S.S.R. was prepared to combine inspection *with* demilitarization, but the Western powers would never go beyond inspection, at least for areas covered by NATO.

[11] See *International Conciliation,* No. 524 (September, 1959), pp. 9–12, for a succinct summary of the negotiations. The report of the conference is contained in U.N. Document A/4078, January 5, 1959. See also the statement of William C. Foster, Chairman and Senior U.S. Expert at the conference, Subcommittee on Disarmament, U.S. Senate Committee on Foreign Relations, 86th Cong., 1st sess., January 30, 1959.

[12] For a penetrating analysis of the problems and possibilities of preventing surprise attack, see Thomas C. Schelling, "Surprise Attack and Disarmament" in Klaus Knorr (ed.), *NATO and American Security* (Princeton: Princeton University Press, 1959).

comprehensive ban on nuclear testing. At first, it appeared that agreement would be forthcoming on a detailed plan, worked out by Soviet and Western scientific experts, for a network of control posts on land and sea (equipped with apparatus for recording seismic, acoustic, radio, and radiological data) combined with air sampling of radioactive debris and on-site inspection of events suspected of being nuclear explosions. As of August, 1958, these experts concluded that such a system would provide a good probability of detecting even very low yield explosions on the earth's surface, at low altitudes above it, in the ocean, or deep underground.[13] Later inquiry established the technical feasibility of detecting explosions at high altitudes and in outer space.

But on the basis of further American experimentation, the Western governments decided that a much more elaborate system of control posts and on-site inspection would be needed to reliably detect small underground nuclear tests and distinguish them from earthquakes. The Russians completely disagreed, and even though the Americans ultimately decided they could be satisfied with far less than they first claimed was necessary, the negotiations never entirely bridged the differences on the minimum amount of outside surveillance each state would have to accept on its own territory.

In the end, of course, the whole question of territorial control was bypassed. The present nuclear test ban treaty does not apply to underground tests, but only to those that can be detected by means of control located outside any given state—namely, to surface, marine, atmospheric, or outer space explosions.

METHODS OF CONTROL

Reliable inspection, it is generally agreed, is the cornerstone of an effective system of control to insure implementation of most measures of arms limitation and reduction. There are at least three reasons for this. Obviously, the threat of exposure tends to deter cheating by those so tempted. But of even greater importance in encouraging governments to live up to their disarmament commitments is the reassurance function of inspection—giving to each party confidence that it is not being cheated on. Finally, it provides the basis of a warning system, so that states can know if violations do occur and can take appropriate protective measures.[14]

There are those who have contended that inspection is altogether

[13] Report of the Conference of Experts to Study the Methods of Detecting Violations of a Possible Agreement on the Suspension of Nuclear Tests (Doc. EXP/NUC/28, August 20, 1958). The report is reprinted as an appendix to *Hearings on Disarmament and Foreign Policy* (Senate Committee on Foreign Relations, Subcommittee on Disarmament, 86th Cong., 1st sess.), Part 1.

[14] The functions of inspection are perceptively analyzed by Lawrence S. Finkelstein, *op. cit.*, pp. 16–17. Reservations as to the deterrent value of inspection are expressed by Fred C. Iklé, "After Detection—What?," *Foreign Affairs,* January, 1961.

insufficient to provide effective control for some kinds of disarmament. This was the position firmly staked out for the U.S. and the Western powers by Mr. Baruch in urging a system of international ownership and management to control the production and use of atomic energy. In due course, this approach was abandoned. The Russians wanted no part of it, and competent scientific and political opinion in the West came to challenge the assumption that this was the one and only way of insuring adequate supervision. Even the Acheson–Lilienthal report, pioneer American study of the problem, had suggested international ownership as but one possible line of attack on atomic control.

On the other hand, inspection has sometimes been rejected as unnecessary. The Russians frequently propose that simple declarations by national governments be accepted as adequate evidence of their levels of armament or fulfillment of pledges to disarm. It is hard to believe that they can be serious in expecting others—or themselves—to be satisfied with this, knowing as they do the wiles of international diplomacy. There are some types of agreements, however, which *can* be self-enforcing without inspection—or, at least, whose fulfillment can be ascertained without any formal arrangements for inspection. Such is the case, for instance, with agreements for joint research in the exploration of outer space, for the exchange of information, and for instantaneous intergovernmental communication, such as the Washington–Moscow hot line. The agreement is verified by the doing.

But for the most part, plans for arms control have been designed to rely on inspection. An immense amount of research has now gone into the technical side of inspection, and negotiations have come close to agreement on methods that could be effective in checking on many of the proposed types of arms limitation. The methods vary, of course, with the objects of control. Direct, on-the-spot observation by qualified inspectors is anticipated for many purposes, such as the control of arms production facilities, points of military concentration, and sites from which major attacks might be launched, in order to insure that no prohibited activity is going on. On-the-spot observation would also be required for control of nuclear mining and production facilities, and would include such functions as checking accounts: inventorying stocks; studying production operations; weighing, measuring, and analyzing fissionable materials; and prescribing rules for technological control of atomic facilities.[15]

---

[15] The last provision was interpreted by the Soviet delegate as including the possibility of requiring the "denaturing" of nuclear fuel during the production process to make it unfit for manufacturing nuclear weapons, were this to prove technologically feasible. On the other hand, the U.S.S.R. apparently did not concede the majority's desire to have the inspection agency conduct surveys and explorations (by air as well as on land) to discover and determine world supplies of source material as a further means of thwarting clandestine activities. See Majority Plan of Control, and U.S.S.R. proposal of June 11, 1947 (especially pars. 6 and 7), and related documents as presented in the first, second, and third reports of the U.N. Atomic Energy Commission to the Security Council.

An important additional function of the international control agency, all the states agreed, would be to conduct nuclear research so that it could keep in the forefront of developments in the field.

In the case of general disarmament, it is agreed that budgetary control would also be installed—e.g., examination of records relating to military appropriations and expenditures.

For some purposes, such as detection of nuclear explosions, inspection can be largely conducted, as has been mentioned, by scientific instrumentation without personal observation.

It is agreed that for some objects and activities there are *no* satisfactory methods of inspection at the present time. This is the case with stockpiles of nuclear weapons, as mentioned previously. The field of scientific research, vital to the furtherance of weapons technology, also defies effective inspection.

The role of aerial observation and photography has been in dispute. The Russians have objected to Western proposals for systematic aerial reconnaissance as a basic method of inspection at the beginning phases of disarmament, in customary fear of Western intentions to exploit knowledge of Soviet military dispositions before making a major cut in their offensive capabilities. However, the U.S.S.R. has declared explicitly that it would accept aerial inspection at later stages of a comprehensive disarmament program.[16]

The question of the *continuity of inspection* necessary to insure reliability was at issue for some time, especially in regard to regulation of atomic energy. In their original proposals, the Western powers contended that diversion of nuclear fuel to military purposes would be possible unless inspectors were always on the spot in the productive and mining facilities, keeping a running check on input and output as well as taking a constant inventory of nuclear fuel stocks. The Soviet Union objected that this would be tantamount to management, and it proposed, instead, periodic inspection with special investigations to be conducted on suspicion of violations.

If the Western majority suffered from myopia in regard to the issue of international ownership of atomic facilities, the Russians were unusually shortsighted in their initial proposals for inspection. Periodic inspections could never have sufficed to patrol the many subtle ways of possible diversion, given the rough techniques of input-output measurement and other methods of operations control then available. The special investigations contemplated in case of suspicion could hardly have plugged the gaps, especially with rights of normal access as tightly circumscribed as the Soviet government demanded. The majority leveled a telling criticism: With the

---

[16] See, for instance, U.S.S.R. declaration before the Fourteenth General Assembly, September 18, 1959 (U.N. Doc. A/4219). The U.S.S.R. has also agreed to aerial surveys of specific zones to guard against surprise attack.

scope of inspection so restricted, "there would in practice be no opportunity for the international control commission to become suspicious." Why this would not have been evident to the Soviet authorities, considering the stage to which their atomic development had advanced or what interest they felt could have been served by imperfect inspection, is one of the many mysteries of this stage of nuclear diplomacy. One could explain an outright rejection of international control in the interest of preserving intact their system of tight secrecy. But the halfway measures they proposed would have torn much of their curtain aside, without giving them the assurance of really effective control over the entire American apparatus of nuclear production.

In any case, the Soviet Union has now accepted the Western contention that inspection must be continuous. Its comprehensive proposals of May 19, 1955 (reconfirmed by Premier Khrushchev in 1959), provided that the international control organ would have "rights and powers to exercise control, *including inspection on a continuous basis* to the extent necessary to ensure implementation of the above-mentioned Convention by all States." (author's italics). This contemplated that continuing inspection would apply both in prohibiting production of atomic weapons and in regard to reducing conventional arms.[17]

THE TIMING OF INSPECTION AND CONTROL

For a long time, this issue deadlocked the negotiations. The Western states argued that a satisfactory system of inspection should be agreed to and in operation before any measures of disarmament were undertaken. The Soviet Union at first insisted on reversing the sequence: After definite commitments to disarm were made, then inspection could ascertain whether they were being carried out.

A way out of the impasse slowly evolved, as the concept of simultaneity was explored—inspection to begin at the same time the commitments to arms reduction took effect. This idea was first broached by the Russians as a major concession, then developed in detail by the British and French in a bold effort to achieve a synthesis of views on disarmament that would be acceptable to everyone. The formula, neatly phrased by Jules Moch, the French representative, was: "Neither control without disarmament, nor

---

[17] The U.S.S.R. departed from the concept of continuity, however, in the test ban negotiations. It insisted on severely limiting the number of on-site inspections that could be conducted to identify the origin of seismic disturbances, and it objected to the formation of permanent mobile control teams, favoring their constitution ad hoc in each instance an onsite inspection was called for. The reason for this different stand is apparently that the Russians firmly link the extent of inspection they are willing to accept to the extent of actual disarmament undertaken. A ban on nuclear tests, they maintain, involves no disarmament at all.

disarmament without control, but progressively, all the disarmament which can be controlled."[18]

As finally worked out, the plan called for the implementation of inspection and control to be divided into several stages, synchronized with stages of progressively more comprehensive measures of disarmament. Two treaties, one with the disarmament commitments and the other spelling out the control arrangement, would be adopted simultaneously. The machinery for control would be organized and sufficiently equipped to conduct the inspection of the limited measures of disarmament to be carried out in the first stage. The second stage would begin when the control organ had verified to everyone's satisfaction the accomplishment of the first, and when it reported that it was prepared to undertake the broader tasks of inspection which the second stage would require. Transition to the third stage would come after a similar certification.

The Soviet proposals of May 10, 1955, seemed to coincide closely with this concept of a progressive or phased implementation of increasingly stringent control. Each successive stage of integrated nuclear-conventional disarmament would be accompanied by extension of the functions, rights, and powers of the international control organ. Thus, by the second stage envisaged in these proposals, when the manufacture of nuclear weapons was to be discontinued, the international control organ would have installed "in all States signatory to the convention its own permanent staff of inspectors, having unimpeded access at all times, within the limits of the supervisory functions they exercise, to all objects of control." A cutoff of nuclear weapons production would come, therefore, only when satisfactory control machinery was established and ready to function in all countries concerned.[19]

This position was not reversed in Mr. Khrushchev's total disarmament proposal at the General Assembly in September, 1959, despite some interpretations to the contrary. He reaffirmed the May 10, 1955, proposals, and he explicitly stated that "there should be initiated a system of control over all disarmament measures, which *should be created and should function in conformity with the stages by which disarmament should be effected*" (author's italics).[20]

---

[18] U.N. Document DC/SC.1/PV.69, p. 10, quoted in U.S. Senate Committee on Foreign Relations Subcommittee on Disarmament, Staff Study No. 3, p. 179. Or, as expressed by Ambassador Lodge to the General Assembly's First Committee, "Progressive establishment of an effective inspection system concurrent with such reductions." U.N. Document A/C.1/783, January 14, 1957.

[19] See Philip Noel Baker, *The Arms Race* (Dobbs Ferry, N.Y.: Oceana Publications, Inc., 1958), Chap. 2. Acceptance of this approach represented a 180-degree reversal for the Russians, who had determinedly called for a complete prohibition of the use and possession of nuclear weapons as an unconditional *prerequisite* to control.

[20] The point was also made in the formal declaration submitted by the U.S.S.R. in conjunction with Mr. Khrushchev's address: "The scope of control and inspection shall correspond to the extent of the phased disarmament of states." U.N. Document A/4219.

The problem remains of securing agreement on a precise timetable for the implementation of controls, as this is necessarily linked to the kind of timetable finally adopted for the staging of limitations and reductions. Chart III shows how various control measures would mesh with a program of disarmament phased according to the near-consensus of 1957.

Substantial agreement has since been reached on a timetable of control to correlate with the stages of disarmament as worked out in the negotiations of 1962–64.

The principal discrepancies arise from the desire of the Western states to introduce in the first stage more extensive methods of inspection than the Soviet Union considers sufficient to supervise the actions to be taken at that time.

Recent negotiations have sought to define maximum time limits for the accomplishment of each stage, taking the indefiniteness out of the earlier proposals for phasing. The Soviets tend to be more optimistic than the U.S. on the time required to complete each stage and the overall program, but the differences are not formidable (as of 1963, five years envisaged by the U.S.S.R. for all three stages, as against a six-year period set by the U.S. for stages I and II).

The key to the entire arrangement is the understanding that each country would keep at least a portion of its nuclear weapons and missiles until the final stage of control, when the inspection and control system had reached its peak of development and its efficiency had been thoroughly tested. Thus, existing retaliatory power would remain, in case the system broke down along the line. But meanwhile, new production and the intensified competition that went with it would be diminished and finally stopped.[21]

WHO SHALL DO THE CONTROLLING?

The effectiveness of a system of control depends, it has been generally agreed, on its ability to inspire confidence on the part of each participating nation that the others are living up to their commitments. A crucial requirement, therefore, is the trustworthiness of those responsible for administering the various methods of control. States want to be sure, first, that they are competent and, second, that they are impartial (or at least not partial to the controlled state). They must be *capable* of detecting whether a particular type of limitation is or is not being carried out; they must be *willing* to report the facts accurately. Much of the effort to forge workable disarmament

---

[21] Acceptance by the U.S.S.R. of this critical proviso went a long way toward bridging the differences with the West over the phasing of control. See *Draft Treaty on General and Complete Disarmament Under Strict International Control,* presented by U.S.S.R., September 24, 1962 and amended February 4, 1964 (Chapter I, Article 5).

CHART III

PROPOSED TIMETABLE OF THE
IMPLEMENTATION OF CONTROL
as of August, 1957

WEST	SOVIET
First Stage	
Establish control organ and recruit its first elements	*Establish control organ* within two months after agreement is concluded; set up local branches, control posts, and position inspectors in good time to function when states begin executing agreed measures of limitation
Objects of control: armed forces, conventional arms, merchant ships and civil aircraft, financial records	*Objects of control:* armed forces, conventional arms, bases, factories manufacturing conventional arms, financial records
Methods of control:	*Methods of control:*
a) control posts at specific ports, railroad junctions, highways, and airports, to assure no dangerous concentration of forces	a) same, with reservation noted below (see note *a*)
b) access to all objects of control; control organ may send out mobile control teams and financial inspectors and conduct surprise visits	b) unimpeded access to all objects of control
c) secure information as considered necessary by control organ	c) states to furnish control organ information it requires on forces, conventional arms, and military expenses within one month after its establishment
d) unrestricted freedom of movement and communication for personnel of control organ in territory of participating states	d) commitment not specified
e) aerial surveys over any participating state	e) no provision at this stage
f) aerial surveys of a European zone in conjunction with either a Far Eastern or Arctic zone of inspection against surprise attack	f) aerial survey of a European zone (equidistant from NATO-Soviet dividing line) and/or Far Eastern zone including eastern USSR and western US
Nuclear tests: control system to be established prior to permanent cessation	*Nuclear tests:* same
Second Stage	
Objects of control: factories manufacturing conventional arms (including chemical and bacteriological), merchant ships and civil aircraft (under construction)	*Objects of control:* already covered in 1st stage

WEST	SOVIET
Inspection extended to new objects; resident inspection teams established at certain factories and installations	*Inspection placed on continuing basis;* permanent installation of inspectors and control posts
Development of control organ so that it can verify cut-off of nuclear production	*Development of control organ:* covered by blanket proviso of 1st stage

Third Stage

Objects of control: nuclear fuel production facilities, non-military nuclear stocks, facilities for manufacturing nuclear weapons	*Objects of control:* control organ shall have right to "exercise control to the extent necessary to ensure implementation" of agreement to discontinue nuclear weapons production, eliminate nuclear weapons stockpiles, and complete reduction of forces and conventional arms
Inspection extended to new objects of control	*Inspection:* aerial photography to be considered at a "specified" stage of execution of disarmament "when confidence among States has been strengthened"

Sources: This Chart is based on the analysis of 1952–57 negotiations by Philip E. Jacob. See "The Disarmament Concensus," International Organization, Spring, 1960.

The Soviet position is as outlined in U.N. Documents DC/SC.1/26/Rev. 2, May 10, 1955, and DC/SC.1/41, March 27, 1956. The latter proposals referred only to the control of partial measures of conventional disarmament. Modifications introduced in U.N. Documents A/3366, November 17, 1956, DC/SC.1/49, March 18, 1957, DC/SC.1/55, April 30, 1957, and DC/SC.1/60, June 14, 1957, are also take into account.

The Western position is based principally on the Anglo-French "synthesis" of March 19, 1956 (U.N. Document DC/SC.1/38), and May 3, 1956 (U.N. Document DC/SC.1/44). Some modifications introduced in the Four-Power proposals of August 29, 1957 (U.N. Document DC/SC.1/66), are also incorporated in the above chart.

Note a: The USSR later indicated that, if only partial measures of conventional disarmament were adopted, it would limit control posts to western USSR, eastern US, and the NATO and Warsaw Pact countries. Control posts at airfields would be postponed to the second stage. See U.N. Document DC/SC.1/55, April 30, 1957.

agreements has gone into the design of an international control agency or agencies that would meet these tests.

Other alternatives have been considered and sometimes adopted.

1. Each government can attempt to satisfy itself through its own intelligence facilities about what other countries are doing. This unilateral procedure of control is available in any case, whatever other machinery is established, and would serve as a double check on the reliability of international controllers. In the case of the nuclear test ban, this is the only procedure currently in effect. Each government depends on its own techniques of gathering information (or on its allies). The reliability is considered sufficiently great (except for underground tests) for countries to dispense with all other control machinery.[22]

2. Each government could police itself and report to the others on the fulfillment of its commitments. The Soviet Union has frequently maintained that

---

[22] See discussion of unilateral controls in Woods Hole Summer Study, *Verification and Response in Disarmament Agreements,* 1962, cited in Louis Henkin, *Disarmament* (New York: Association of the Bar of the City of New York, 1964).

such a system of national control would be adequate, and for certain stages and types of arms control has insisted that none other would be acceptable. Although this completely fails to meet the test of impartiality ("Who can trust the Russians?") it must be remembered that, in practice, the reality of national control would always be subject to check by available procedures of unilateral control, as indicated above. But the uncertainty of unilateral control, in the absence of open access to the territory (and security files) of other states, makes most governments quite unwilling to rely on either of these procedures if the possibilities of evasion are great.

3. Procedures of reciprocal control would go much farther toward meeting the tests of trustworthiness. This means that each country polices the others. It need trust only in the competence and impartiality of its own people, who are allowed access to the other countries to satisfy themselves that the agreed limitations are implemented. In effect, this substitutes partiality for impartiality: the controllers are accountable to their respective governments, hence, primed to be suspicious and demanding to be convinced. As a result, the practical effect of reciprocal control is that it switches the burden of developing confidence from the outside controller to the country undergoing control. It is up to the "policed" country to convince the controllers, instead of the controllers having to check out all possibilities of cheating. The condition of this arrangement is, of course, full reciprocity. Each must allow its competitor the same opportunities for inspection and control on its territory as it exercises on the other's.

This latter approach is receiving increasing attention, especially in reference to arms limitation arrangements where only two or three countries would be involved. President Eisenhower proposed reciprocal aerial inspection between the U.S. and U.S.S.R. (the "open skies" proposal previously mentioned); several of the other proposals concerned with reducing the danger of surprise attack have envisaged reciprocal inspection in regard to special zones or strategic points; and the control machinery worked out for the abortive comprehensive nuclear test ban (to apply to underground tests as well as others) provided for a form of reciprocity in that Soviet and Western nuclear powers were to appoint equal portions of the inspecting staff, along with a "neutral" segment selected from other countries.

There may be practical political obstacles to reciprocal control, however. Countries have to be willing to expose themselves to inspection by representatives of their most greatly feared and hated enemies. This means they have to secure both governmental and public acceptance of a totally different view of the role of secrecy in security. It is necessary to give the enemy access to places, things, and information that have been "classified" and jealously guarded, under severe penalties, from most of one's own population. This may involve more shock to the national nervous system than countries like the Soviet Union—and the United States—can absorb.[23]

---

[23] See L. Finkelstein, op. cit., for a persuasive statement of the case for reciprocity. For further references on this issue see Chapter 8, fn. 18.

The International Disarmament Organization

For these and other reasons, negotiations have generally focused on establishing multilateral international control machinery. This is what has been meant when the major governments (including the U.S.S.R.) have committed themselves to the principle of "international control" as an essential element of general disarmament agreements. There is now wide agreement on the character of an International Disarmament Organization so supervise implementation of the different phases of a general and complete disarmament program, including such functions as verifying a cutoff of further production of nuclear weapons, preventing unauthorized dispersals of fissionable materials, and checking on reductions of armed forces and weapons.

Composition and accountability

The operational responsibility must be vested in an international control authority, internationally staffed. Both the corps of inspectors and the central administration would be unmistakably international in composition. The staff would be recruited from different countries, and paid for by and accountable exclusively to the international organ.

The U.S.S.R. as well as the other negotiating powers have agreed that inspection could not be trusted unless it were conducted by an organ that was not beholden to the country being inspected. As early as 1947, referring to atomic energy control, Gromyko declared for the U.S.S.R. that "the International Control Commission must have at its disposal a staff of inspectors selected on an international basis. These inspectors will be accountable only to the Commission."[24] This position has been reiterated consistently—for instance, in the comprehensive Soviet proposals of May 10, 1955.

The control system would operate under the ultimate authority of the United Nations, though the International Disarmament Organization would be set up as an autonomous agency. On detecting violations, it would report to the Security Council and make recommendations for action. But the organ would not be its own enforcement agency. It would not be responsible for compelling a country to comply with the terms of the disarmament agreement. The job of enforcement is left to the Security Council, which, in effect (considering the veto), throws the matter into the laps of the major powers for whatever direct action each cares to take.[25]

---

[24] See letter of September 5, 1947, from the U.S.S.R. representative on the U.N. Atomic Energy Commission (Third Report of the Commission to the Security Council, Annex 3 [c]). See also U.N. Document DC/SC.1/26/Rev. 2.

[25] L. Finkelstein analyzes the contemplated relationship of the International Disarmament Organization to the United Nations, and concludes that it will have little significance either from the standpoint of making the control system functionally effective or strengthening the U.N. Only in reference to certain political functions, especially in the enforcement field,

Decision-making

The control authority must be free to operate by majority decision of its membership, no member having a veto. Contrary to widespread impression, the Soviet Union has not demanded a veto on the day-to-day operation of arms inspection and control.

It has accepted the proposition that decisions of the international control authority would be taken by a majority vote and that no nation would have the right to block the conduct of inspection on its territory. It has, however, cautioned that the control organ must function within the bounds of authority laid down in the disarmament agreement. It must not conduct "fishing expeditions" or inspections of objects other than those specified. Nor could it be permitted to slip over into a managerial role by issuing orders to national authorities—for instance, to cease and desist from certain actions. But its proper duties of inspection and reporting compliance or noncompliance would be immune from any interference, by veto or otherwise.[26]

Foreign Minister Molotov staked out the Soviet stand at the first session of the General Assembly, and it has not been repudiated in subsequent negotiations. In proposing that two commissions be established within the framework of the Security Council to control, respectively, execution of a conventional arms reduction and the prohibition of military uses of atomic energy, Molotov specifically denied that the Soviet Union intended to throttle their operations by subjecting them to veto in the Council. While the basic decision to reduce armaments would need the unanimous consent of the great powers, as reflected in a Security Council vote, he stated that:

It should be quite obvious that the question of the well-known principle of unanimity operating in the Security Council has no relation at all to the work of the commissions themselves. Consequently, it is entirely wrong to consider the matter in the light that any government possessing the "right of veto" will be in a position to hinder the fulfillment of the control and inspections. The control commissions are not the Security Council, and therefore, there are no grounds whatsoever for saying that any power making use of the "right to veto" will be in a position to obstruct the course of control.[27]

---

does he feel that the U.N. might perform better than a purely autonomous agency. See Lawrence S. Finkelstein "The United Nations and Organizations for the Control of Armaments," *International Organization,* Winter, 1962.

[26] The Russians have distinguished between the day-to-day operations of the control organ and enforcement action against violations. Over the first they have claimed no veto, at least in their control proposals relating to general disarmament (conventional or nuclear). However, in negotiations relating to the cessation of nuclear tests, the Soviet Union has held out for partial veto over operations.

[27] General Assembly (1st sess., 2d part), 1st Committee, 38th meeting, December 4, 1946 (Document A/C.1/114).

In an amendment to the first report of the U.N. Atomic Energy Commission to the Security Council, the U.S.S.R. similarly proposed that "the control organs and the organs of inspection should carry out their control and inspection functions, acting on the basis of their own rules, which should provide for the adoption of decisions, in appropriate cases, by a majority 'vote.' "[28] In 1950, Deputy Foreign Minister Vishinsky made the point even more categorically before the General Assembly's Political Committee: "Investigations would take place upon decision by the Atomic Energy Commission, and the Atomic Energy Commission's decision would be adopted not by the unanimous vote of any of its members, but by a simple majority . . . no state having the right to impose the generally hated veto."[29]

The point was firmly implanted in the joint U.S.–U.S.S.R. Statement of Agreed Principles for Disarmament Negotiations (the McCloy–Zorin agreement) of September 20, 1961, as follows: "This International Disarmament Organization and its inspectors should be assured unrestricted access without veto to all places as necessary for the purpose of effective verification."[30]

Right of Access

All the governments categorically assert that *the international inspectorate shall have "unimpeded access at all times to all objects of control,"* to use the language of the Russian plan put forward in March, 1956.[31]

The Soviet position still stops short of a complete carte blanche to the inspectors to roam a country at will. Their rights of access would be specifically related to facilities that, by terms of the international control agreement, they were authorized to inspect. (Access would also extend, however, to facilities the international authority suspected might be engaged clandestinely in prohibited activity.)

This proposal comes close to meeting the conditions of access defined by the Western powers as essential to insure effective inspection.

The Russians and the West alike provide for control posts to be located permanently on the territory of the participating states—in the capitals, at military centers throughout the country, and at nuclear facilities—the number and location of the posts to be specifically related to the amount and kind of control to be carried out at a given stage of disarmament.

In the case of nuclear control, inspectors would be guaranteed full rights to examine all the processes of nuclear production and check all financial and other records.

Unrestricted use of communication facilities is assured the control person-

---

[28] See Third Report of the Atomic Energy Commission to the Security Council, Annex 3(c), pp. 23 ff.

[29] General Assembly (5th sess.), 1st Committee, October 23, 1960.

[30] The veto would, however, apply to enforcement of sanctions against violators, as this would be a responsibility of the Security Council. The Western states have apparently come to concur in this position, at least since 1954.

[31] See the statement quoted above from the McCloy–Zorin agreement.

nel to keep in touch with the central authority to which they are accountable.

It should be understood that the above provisions represent consensus *only* in regard to machinery for the control of a program of limitations leading to general and complete disarmament. In the nuclear test ban negotiations, there was considerably less agreement on such vital issues as composition of the control commission, staffing of control posts, rights of access, and the extent to which control operations would be subject to veto. The Soviet Union took a more restrictive view in regard to the amount of external intervention it would accept from a control organization whose job was simply to police a suspension of tests rather than immediate cutback in the actual military power of its adversaries.

ENFORCEMENT

The issue of what should be done if someone violates a disarmament agreement and who should do it has been hard to resolve. This is partly because of fundamentally different appraisals of the role and importance of "enforcement." To Mr. Baruch, who originally represented the U.S. on the U.N. Atomic Energy Commissions, it was the keystone of the whole system of control, for it would provide states an assurance of safety in place of the arms they were called on to surrender. He felt, and the other Western governments at first agreed, that some such assurance was both politically and strategically necessary: politically, in order to persuade security-minded nations to accept any bold steps of disarmament; strategically, in order to guard the existing balance of power.

On the other hand, it was immediately apparent to the Russians, and, in due course, to others as well, that enforcement, especially if carried out by a supranational body, meant a drastic and probably irrevocable surrender of sovereignty. The power to enforce clearly presumed a power to decide when to enforce, and this involved a transfer of responsibility away from the national government for the most basic of decisions—determination of the country's "vital interests."

The struggle over enforcement, therefore, became much more than an item in the perennial diplomacy of the cold war. It pitted those whose loyalties were essentially national, and who stood committed to maintaining the system of independent national states, against a group who were ready to experiment toward a new world order out of conviction that the old was doom-bent on blowing itself up.

In terms of the specific debate on arms control, this confrontation took the form of argument over whether effective enforcement had to involve measures of restraint imposed by an authority external to a nation, or whether, in the last analysis, one had to depend on the self-restraint of each nation as it contemplated the consequences of a breakdown of the disarmament arrangements that would follow from its violations. Three main alternatives have been considered:

1. Enforcement to be exercised by an autonomous international agency, under powers granted by the governments setting it up as part of their disarmament commitments.
2. Enforcement to be entrusted to the United Nations, under its present constitution, meaning that the Security Council would be primarily responsible, and, hence, action would be subject to the veto of the five permanent members.
3. A permanent United Nations Peace Force to be created, which would take on the tasks of enforcement at a late stage of the disarmament program when the world was largely disarmed.

It will be seen that the first of these involves the maximum degree of external restraint; the second, the least (none, in effect, for the great powers). The third depends on whether the Peace Force operates exclusively under the Security Council (as proposed by the Russians) or under special provisions freeing it from Security Council control in veto-bound emergencies, along the lines authorized in the Uniting for Peace Resolution.

The first alternative seems to have been buried, as a result of obdurate Soviet objections to the plan advanced by Mr. Baruch in the original negotiations for atomic energy control. The plan provided for an elaborate system of penalties that the international control authority could direct against governments found to be violating the agreement. The U.S.S.R. insisted that enforcement should be left exclusively to the Security Council, the atomic control commission merely *recommending* measures it might undertake.

The great tragedy of these early negotiations was that each side became so obstinate in its views and so suspicious of the other that it would not seek and consider alternatives. The Western majority insisted on viewing the policing of atomic controls as a special problem distinct from other serious threats to security. They imagined that only a system of supranational sanctions at the disposal of a supranational authority could effectively deter states from committing violations of the agreements. Yet, in all other respects, these same governments assumed that the principal deterrent of aggressive activity was to be found in the readiness of states individually or collectively to take counteraction. In other words, the majority, faced with Russian rejection of what amounted to a world police authority, refused to consider that without any such special arrangement, states would still have available all the means of enforcement they normally used to protect their interests. Immediate restoration everywhere of nuclear production to military uses would be only one form of reprisal available against a government that persisted in violating the agreed restrictions. War itself would be the ultimate sanction in this as in other serious threats of aggression. Such considerations apparently did not receive serious attention, even when the alternative was a breakdown of negotiations and no atomic control at all.

Fortunately, both sides have come to take a fresh look at the issue. Recent negotiations have centered on the third alternative previously mentioned—a special permanent United Nations peace force to become fully operative at the third stage of the comprehensive disarmament program. While there is agreement that such peace-keeping machinery should be established, the U.S. and U.S.S.R. have not resolved the key question of whether the force would be completely under the direction of the Security Council and, hence, barred from acting by a great-power veto. On the other hand, the U.S.S.R. has yielded on its previous demand that the troika principle be applied in determining the composition and command of the force; in other words, that the force consist of equal national contingents from the Communist, capitalist, and neutralist "sides," and that it be commanded by a syndicate of the three sides, all having to act in concert. It now accepts the idea that the force should be recruited from countries other than the great powers, and have a single, unified command (more or less like the United Nations Emergency Force in the Middle East).[32]

CONCLUSION

This analysis demonstrates that a substantial consensus has emerged from the disarmament negotiations on many of the major technical provisions for a program of partial, but progressively more comprehensive, limitations on nations' capacities for mutual destruction.

To be sure, the provisions that now appear acceptable cannot guarantee the same degree of insurance against evasions as would have been possible had they been instituted before the U.S., the U.S.S.R., and Britain amassed stockpiles of nuclear weapons and begun the missiles race. Foolproof disarmament is impossible. Nevertheless, the present consensus does appear to project a base of control solid enough to sustain some bold moves to curtail the arms race.

It is no longer tenable to dismiss a disarmament program on the ground that the Soviet Union rejects effective inspection and control in its orbit and therefore cannot be trusted to carry it out. The control to which they have

---

[32] See above, Chapter 8, fn. 15. The positions of the U.S. and U.S.S.R. on the nature and functions of an international peace force are set forth in their draft treaties on general and complete disarmament presented originally on April 18, 1962 (US), and September 24, 1962 (USSR), and amended August 6, 8, and 14, 1963 (US), and February 4, 1964 (USSR). A major study of the problem was undertaken by the Massachusetts Institute of Technology, Center for International Studies. For its conclusions see Lincoln P. Bloomfield *et al, International Military Forces* (Boston: Little, Brown, 1964).

agreed would assure an extraordinary degree of penetration into the military posture behind the Iron Curtain under conditions that would not divest the West of its "shield" and certainly not of its "sword."

In connection with the limitation of conventional armament, it is hard to see how the accumulation and concentration of arms and forces could reach dangerous proportions without detection if international inspection of the kind the Russians specify were in effect. If Russia's mammoth military forces (over and above its nuclear and missiles development) pose, in fact, the serious threat to world security that the Western governments have assumed, then the sooner they come under the kind of inspection the U.N. negotiations have succeeded in blueprinting, the safer all will be.

Insofar as nuclear control is concerned, the risks of evasion and noncompliance are offset by each country's retaining possession of its stockpiles of nuclear weapons and a substantial contingent of conventionally armed forces until satisfied as to the adequacy of the control system. Even then, the states would not be obligated, under the proposed commitments, to give up their more modest arsenals until a change in the international atmosphere permitted the development of a full-blown world security system.

On these grounds, adoption of a program of control on the basis of present areas of agreement appears much preferable to having no control at all. The resumption of serious negotiations in the 1960's, looking toward comprehensive disarmament regulated by an International Disarmament Organization, indicates the acute discomfort felt at the top levels of government over continuing to gamble for security through the buildup of modern weapons systems. Responsible leaders of the major powers evidently share the concern voiced by President Eisenhower over "the enormous risks entailed if reasonable steps are not taken to curb the international competition in armaments and to move effectively in the direction of disarmament."

Chapter 10

Peaceful Settlement of International Disputes

In a world of independent states, each striving to advance its own national interests, disagreement and conflict among them is inescapable. The prevention of war in such circumstances has come increasingly to depend on the effectiveness of noncoercive methods of settling international controversies before one side or the other decides irrevocably to seek a decision by force.

Resort to force over a dispute, however justified the nation using it may feel, has usually provoked forceful countermeasures, and under modern conditions of interdependence even a minor and local fight involves the interest of others and may precipitate general war. Yet, neither fear of the disastrous consequences of war nor solemn obligations to refrain from it have restrained states from using force if they felt there was no other way to safeguard a "vital" interest or national "honor." The maintenance of peace and security has, therefore, demanded the development of international procedures and machinery that would enable disputes to be settled on terms sufficiently tolerable to all parties so that none would feel inclined to pay the price of war for something different. The peaceful settlement of international disputes has become a primary condition of forestalling international violence and establishing a foundation for world order.

THE METHODS OF PEACEMAKING

It is frequently maintained that peacemaking is preeminently the function of diplomacy, and that it should be the business of nations to settle their disputes peaceably by direct negotiation among themselves, without involving others. This has been the traditional practice, and undoubtedly most disputes still get settled this way. In fact, the League Covenant, the United Nations Charter, and a great many of the special treaties for peaceful settlement to which states have subscribed put the original and primary responsibility for resolving conflicts squarely on the disputing parties. And, typically, the first action of international institutions like the United Nations, when faced with a public controversy between states, is to call on them to work it out on their own, even though the organization has been given the duty and powers to "seize" such issues and take collective action to preserve peace.

This approach assumes quite a different concept of diplomacy than is implied in the familiar von Clausewitz dictum that war is diplomacy carried on by other means, or the snide description of a diplomat as a man sent abroad to lie for his country. It regards diplomacy as "a means of achieving peaceful compromise among the conflicting interests and purposes of states . . . a constructive and reconciling process whose objective is to find mutually satisfactory solutions of international conflicts."[1]

But diplomacy suffers from some intrinsic deficiencies as an instrument of peacemaking. For one thing, governments do use it, or misuse it, in pursuing *all* their objectives, acquisitive and defensive, as well as conciliatory. Hence, the same machinery and often the same personnel are devoted to waging conflict as to resolving it. It is difficult to switch roles and perform with equal effectiveness in each. It is also difficult to induce an attitude of reasonableness and trust on the part of one's protagonists if they are accustomed to a relationship of stratagem or belligerence. Basically, diplomacy cannot help but express one nation's point of view. It is the extension of that nation's policies and it will bring to the task of conflict resolution as myopic or out-ward-looking, as ignorant or informed, as self-righteous or mutually respect-ful a disposition as is held by the government in office at the moment.

This suggests that one can count on diplomacy neither for objectivity nor for continuity in tackling the solution of international controversies. Its success depends on the ability of the concerned governments to recognize, each for itself, a common interest in achieving an adjustment of their differences and the consequent necessity of "give" to meet the other side's interests as well as its own. This quality of statesmanship is by no means a perennial characteristic of national governments, and it is fortunate indeed if two governments can muster it simultaneously and unaided when they are at loggerheads over something serious.

The uncertainty of diplomacy has persuaded states that they have to

---

[1] Commission to Study the Organization of Peace, Thirteenth Report, *Developing the United Nations: A Response to the Challenge of a Revolutionary Era* (New York: American Association for the U.N., January, 1961), pp. 23–24. This report, in addition to its perceptive critique of the functions of diplomacy, also suggests methods for strengthening its conciliatory role.

provide alternative means of promoting peaceful settlement or face the probability that war will remain the final arbiter of major conflicts of national interest. Recognizing the growing danger that any war, however local and particular its origin, will become epidemic, the body of states have now generally agreed that any international dispute is a concern to the entire international community, over and beyond the countries immediately involved, and that a third party should be brought into the situation when diplomacy fails. One of the major functions of international organizations has been to institutionalize a variety of procedures for third parties to take a hand in promoting peaceful settlement. Sometimes, this has simply meant getting one or more other states to serve as go-between. But the main accomplishment has been the creation of what Claude aptly calls "synthetic third parties"—international organs acting on behalf of the general community of states.[2] Some of these are permanent, charged with ongoing responsibilities for the harnessing of disputes. Others have been created ad hoc to deal with particular cases as they arose. Their common and central feature is that they lift a dispute out of the context of a purely bilateral confrontation and expose it to outside examination and influence, although usually this may only be done if the disputants are willing. The procedures are permissive rather than mandatory.

There have been two fundamentally different approaches to the role of the third party in settling international controversies. In arbitration and international adjudication, the third party renders a positive and conclusive *decision,* determining the merits of the case according to objective standards of law or fact. The disputants agree in advance to accept this decision and end their dispute on the terms presented. In the other approach, the third party seeks to bring about a *mutual agreement* between the disputants, using techniques of conciliation, mediation, or good offices.

Although the first procedures would appear to assure greater certainty of settlement, as well as impartial objectivity, they have not been so widely applied as the second method, especially to serious controversies. The reasons are to be found in the continuing reluctance of states to entrust to anyone else a final power of decision over their conduct, no matter how limited or precisely prescribed that power might be. This disposition prevails even when, and especially when, states confront very grave dangers as a result of exacerbated tension over controversies left unresolved. Consequently, international peacemaking has had to emphasize persuasion far more than decision in the development of third-party functions.[3]

---

[2] Inis L. Claude, Jr., *Swords Into Plowshares,* 3d ed. (New York: Random House, 1964), p. 205.

[3] See J. L. Brierly, *The Law of Nations* (6th ed; New York: Oxford University Press, 1963), chap. VIII, for a classic review and appraisal of international procedures for peaceful settlement. Also, Lincoln P. Bloomfield, "Law, Politics and International Disputes," *International Conciliation,* January, 1958.

INTERNATIONAL ARBITRATION

The submission of disputes to arbitration is a time-honored practice among states. It was undertaken in medieval times and even by the Greek city-states. On many occasions during the last hundred years, this procedure has resulted in peaceful and satisfactory settlements. As a matter of fact, the record of successful arbitrations in regard to controversies over boundaries, fishing rights, private claims, and similar issues was so impressive that a large number of states obligated themselves in bilateral or multilateral treaties to arbitrate all their disputes with the other signatories, provided "vital interests" were not involved.

The Hague Convention of 1899 set up a special panel of arbitrators—the Permanent Court of Arbitration—with well-defined rules of procedure, so that states would have competent international arbitral machinery readily available whenever a case arose. States have usually preferred, however, to make their own arrangements for arbitration. Sometimes, the head of another state is asked to arbitrate; more often, each disputant names one or more members of an arbitration tribunal, and additional impartial members or an umpire are jointly agreed on. In each instance, the disputants set down in a special agreement, or compromise, the issues to be decided and the terms of reference (legal or other) by which the arbitrators are to be guided in making a decision. The parties pledge themselves to accept the decision as final and to carry it out in good faith.

The North Atlantic Fisheries dispute between the United States and Great Britain illustrates international arbitration at its best. The issue involved interpretation of a treaty by which the United States had secured for its inhabitants a perpetual right to fish on some of the coasts and bays of Newfoundland, while renouncing any right for them to fish elsewhere in British territorial waters in America. When Britain later sought to regulate the seasons, methods, and other matters connected with fishing operations in this area, the United States protested that its nationals had acquired complete freedom by the treaty and should not be bound by any such restrictions. The two countries agreed to submit this and other questions that had arisen over interpretation of the treaty and caused serious trouble between American fishermen and British authorities to a tribunal selected from the Permanent Court of Arbitration. The tribunal, which included an American and a Britisher as well as three outsiders, unanimously rejected the U.S. contention and upheld Britain's right to apply its regulations generally, so long as they were reasonable and did not discriminate between local and American fishermen. The United States accepted the decision, and Britain agreed to a further recommendation of the tribunal that a Permanent Mixed Fishery Commission be established to determine in the future the reasonableness of any regulations in dispute.

Arbitration has proved particularly effective in assessing the responsibility of governments for injury to the nationals or property of other countries. In the famous *Alabama* case, Great Britain was held liable for damages caused to United States shipping during the Civil War because she had permitted the building and outfitting of the Confederate commerce raider in violation of her obligations as a neutral.

Hundreds of "mixed" claims between the United States and Mexico were brought before a General Claims Commission set up in 1923 to settle cases that had arisen during a long period of friction and revolutionary develop-ment in Mexico. The commission served for all practical purposes as an international court, deciding claims "in accordance with the principles of international law, justice and equity." It examined each claim, heard evidence and argument presented by both governments, thoroughly explored the legal issues involved, and finally rendered a carefully reasoned opinion which determined whether the claim was valid and, if so, the amount of money that should be paid by one government to the other on behalf of the injured party. Some claims were dismissed. The commission decided that the Mexican government was not obliged to pay damages to the tune of $100,000 to the widow of a murdered American mine superintendent, because the Mexican authorities, though ineffective in apprehending the culprits, had not wilfully neglected their duties (the Neer claim). On the other hand, Mexico had to pay $12,000 on account of the murder of another American mine superin-tendent, because evidence showed extraordinary inefficiency and delay on the part of the authorities in undertaking to capture the criminal, even though his identity was well established and his whereabouts reported (the James claim). The decisions of the commission were accepted by both governments and carried out faithfully by them.

Sometimes, arbitrations have ended less satisfactorily, with one of the parties backing down from its commitment to accept whatever decision was made. The United States refused to abide by an award made to Mexico in a dispute over their Rio Grande boundary line, occasioned by a flood which shifted the river bed southward. The tribunal had decided (with the Ameri-can member dissenting) that the U.S. was not entitled to the extra territory resulting from this accident. On the whole, however, awards have been executed and an equitable settlement achieved when the issues in dispute have been essentially technical or factual, and the countries had once agreed to arbitrate. And even in the incident just cited, a happy ending occurred for the Mexicans after almost half a century of embittered protest. The United States agreed to return the Chamizal tract (with some alterations acceptable to Mexico), even though it meant buying up several hundred acres of now highly developed downtown El Paso, Texas, and also to pay 50 per cent of the cost of putting the Rio Grande channel back where it was before the flood. Total estimated cost to the U.S. government, including compensation to property owners to avoid injury: $39 million![4]

A more serious shortcoming of arbitration as a procedure of international settlement is that it has not been used in a great many disputes where the issues were political. An arbitrator can act only if the parties have been able to find a yardstick they will both accept as a valid basis for settlement. He is not empowered to seek a reconciliation, nor to work out a compromise of opposing demands, but only to apply the given yardstick objectively and determine that one side is right. If the arbitrator goes beyond this function, and takes other than the agreed on factors into consideration, a state may refuse to be bound by the decision. Where national "honor," political independence, strategic security, or territorial integrity are involved, however, states are extraordinarily reluctant to accept any other standard than their own judgment in determining what is equitable and right. For this reason, most states have carefully excluded "vital interests" as arbitrable issues, and have insisted on complete discretion in deciding whether a dispute concerned vital interests. This has virtually precluded arbitration in the most critical of international controversies.

Furthermore, international arbitration has been unable to build up, through precedent or dictum, a firm body of law or principles of equity that would govern the settlement of disputes. Though a particular decision undoubtedly has an indirect influence on similar cases later, especially when it has set forth a convincing statement of the legal issues involved, it has absolutely no binding effect beyond the case at hand. Each arbitration is considered an entirely new and separate matter, and the tribunal's sole and complete mandate is contained in the compromise by which it is created. This has meant that arbitration could not conclusively declare international law and thereby establish a more uniform and settled pattern of international conduct.[5]

THE INTERNATIONAL COURTS

To meet this deficiency—lack of an ongoing body that could authoritatively interpret and apply to settlement of controversies the rules of international conduct states had come to accept through treaties and other sources of international law—permanent international judicial machinery has been created.

Both the League of Nations and the United Nations parented a world

---

[4] Committee on Foreign Relations, U.S. Senate, 88th Cong., 1st sess. Hearings on Exec. N, Convention with Mexico for Solution of the Problem of the Chamizal, December 12, 13, 1963. This includes the text of the original arbitral decision of 1910.

[5] For a comprehensive study of this subject, see J. L. Simpson and Hazel Fox, *International Arbitration* (New York: Frederick A. Praeger, Inc., 1959).

court as an integral part of their organization to maintain international peace. The Statute for the Permanent Court of International Justice was prepared by the League Council in accordance with Article 14 of the Covenant, unanimously approved by the League Assembly in 1920, and ultimately ratified by 51 states, with the notable exceptions of the United States and the Soviet Union. Largely to satisfy the sensibilities of these powers, a new court—the International Court of Justice—was established as the "principal judicial organ of the United Nations" in 1945, and the older body discontinued. The two courts were almost identical in composition, functions, and procedure.

Composition

The present Court consists of 15 independent judges, each a national of a different state. They are elected by the General Assembly and the Security Council of the United Nations from a list of nominations made by members of the Permanent Court of Arbitration, acting in national groups, or by national groups appointed in a similar manner by governments not represented in that body. The judges serve for nine years and are not permitted to exercise any political or administrative function or engage in any other profession. Judges are expected to act as individuals without reference to the interests of their respective governments, but each party to a dispute is entitled to choose a judge of its own nationality to sit on the Court, in case one is not already present. The Court sits at The Hague, in Holland, and remains permanently in session (except for vacations and when there is no business).

Functions

The Court has two functions: to decide cases referred to it by states and to render advisory opinions to organs of the United Nations or other international organizations authorized by the Charter. The Court is *not* competent to hear cases brought by individuals. Nor does the Court have jurisdiction over international disputes unless the disputants voluntarily accept it, or are under some treaty obligation to do so.

The Court's competence has been extended somewhat by states' subscribing to the "Optional Clause" of the statute (Article 36[2]), thereby accepting the Court's jurisdiction as compulsory in all legal disputes, e.g., involving interpretation of treaties, questions of international law, questions of fact affecting an international obligation, or the reparation to be made for breach of international obligation. However, many states have not accepted this obligation, and the proportion has been shrinking (37 out of 60 parties to the statute in 1952–53; 39 out of 85 in 1959). Furthermore, states have made a habit of hedging their commitment with reservations, and the trend is toward more rather than less restrictive ones.[6] One of the most crippling was imposed by the United States Senate in adopting the Connally Amendment as a condition of ratification. This reserves to the U.S. government the right to decide by itself whether a case concerns matters within its "domestic jurisdiction" and, hence, is not subject to adjudication. This makes a farce of the entire commitment to accept the Court's compulsory jurisdiction, because the U.S. can prevent any case from going to the Court simply by declaring it involves matters *it* considers domestic, no matter how much another country may protest that its interests are at stake, or even if U.S. treaty obligations are clearly at issue. This happened in the Interhandel case, when the U.S. refused to let the Court decide whether it was entitled to expropriate former German assets, which Switzerland claimed belonged to a Swiss company under Swiss law, this despite a U.S. treaty with Switzerland to submit all such cases to adjudication.[7]

Assuming the Court does have jurisdiction, its responsibility is to decide cases strictly "in accordance with international law," applying relevant treaties, international custom, general principles of law "recognized by civilized nations" and, as a subsidiary source, judicial decisions, both national and international, that have dealt with international legal issues.[8] Its function is, therefore, not to conciliate but, in every sense, to adjudicate.

Procedures

The procedures of the Court are highly formal. Cases are brought by written application or notification of a special agreement to submit the dispute. The parties are represented by or assisted by counsel if they desire. Written memorials, countermemorials and replies supported by documents are sent to the court by specified dates. Then oral proceedings take place in public during which the Court hears witnesses, experts, agents, and counsel for both sides. After the hearings are closed, the Court deliberates and decides in private. A majority of the judges present decides. Reasons for the judgment are then published in an opinion, with dissenting judges entitled to

---

[6] See Julius Stone, "The International Court and World Crisis," *International Conciliation,* January, 1962, pp. 20 ff. Stone cites the following as among the types of cases frequently excluded: (1) past disputes, (2) disputes for which treaties in force provide other means of settlement, (3) disputes concerning questions that by international law fall solely or exclusively within a state's domestic jurisdiction, (4) disputes involving members of a special grouping such as the Commonwealth of Nations, (5) disputes as to territorial status, (6) disputes arising out of particular named treaties. In addition, time limits are often set to acceptance, particularly the right to terminate on simple notification. See *ibid.,* p. 22.

[7] For analysis of this complicated case, see Herbert W. Briggs, "Interhandel: The Court's Judgment of March 21, 1959," *American Journal of International Law,* April, 1959.

[8] If the parties agree, the court may also decide a case in the light of what it considers to be equitable and right, without being restricted to the limits of international law.

deliver separate opinions. The Court has complete control over its own proceedings, and there is no appeal from its judgment. A similar procedure is followed in regard to requests for advisory opinions, and every state or international organization entitled to appear is given full opportunity to present its views in writing or orally.

Judgments

Considering the elaborate organization and high professional quality of international judicial bodies, they have not been widely used and have not achieved a potent influence. During 25 years, the Permanent Court of International Justice rendered only 32 judgments and 27 advisory opinions. In the first 15 years of its life, the International Court of Justice received 34 cases and 11 requests for advisory opinions.[9] While some of these concerned important questions in the development of international law and organization, they rarely touched fundamental points of international conflict. In the Upper Silesian cases for instance, the Permanent Court of International Justice had to decide several claims made by Germany that Poland had violated the Minorities Treaty guaranteeing to respect the private-property and civil rights of German nationals who had chosen to remain in Silesia and acquire Polish citizenship after the territory was ceded to Poland following the first world war. The Polish government contended that the Versailles Treaty entitled it to expropriate any property in which the German state had had an interest and to expel former German nationals from holdings that had been leased from the German government. In several judgments and an advisory opinion to the Council of the League of Nations, the Court decided that Poland had no right to take such action and ordered the Polish government to restore the properties it had unlawfully taken or make full reparation for damages caused. Though these cases aroused great bitterness on both sides, and Poland acquiesced only grudgingly in the Court's rulings, the dispute did not really involve a major challenge to the security of either country, and a legal rather than a political settlement was therefore feasible.

A far graver controversy, the Corfu Channel case, was brought to the International Court of Justice in 1948 on recommendation of the United Nations Security Council. Two British destroyers had struck mines in Albanian waters, while passing through the Corfu Channel. There was serious damage and loss of 44 lives. The British government held Albania responsible and demanded full satisfaction for the injuries suffered. It charged that the mines must have been laid with the knowledge or even connivance of Albanian authorities, in an "international highway" through which ships of

---

[9] The record of the PCIJ is fully treated in Manley O. Hudson, *The Permanent Court of International Justice* (New York: Macmillan, 1943). For a preliminary critique of the ICJ, see Leo Gross "Some Observations on the International Court of Justice," *American Journal of International Law,* January, 1962.

all nations had the right of innocent passage. The Albanian government retorted that it knew nothing of the mines and that, furthermore, the British had violated Albanian sovereignty by proceeding through the channel (and later sweeping it) over its objections. Albania at first refused to submit the matter to the Court and challenged its competence to decide a case not brought to it by consent of both parties. On the other hand, the Court ruled that Albania had previously accepted the intervention of the Security Council, and thereby had really committed itself in advance to adjudication if the Council so recommended. Hence, no further consent was necessary. Albania acquiesced.

The Court then heard the arguments, examined witnesses and experts, and finally dispatched a fact-finding mission to determine on the spot the circumstances of the mine laying. On April 9, 1949, the judgment was rendered, holding by a vote of 11 to 5 that Albania was responsible for the explosions. The Court decided, 14 to 2, that the passage of the British destroyers had not violated Albanian sovereignty. But it unanimously held that the later mine-sweeping activities of the British navy did do so. Albania was ultimately ordered to pay £843,947 for the damages it had caused.

The settlement of this case on strictly legal grounds by an international tribunal is a notable—and exceptional—achievement, because profound political issues as well as considerations of national prestige were successfully sidestepped. The parties were, in reality, protagonists in an intensified struggle between Communist and Western democratic states for the control of Europe and the Mediterranean, and the incident involved a hostile act by a tiny state directly flaunting the sensibilities, renown, and traditional sphere of influence of Great Britain. "Vital interests" in every sense of the word were involved, and the offender was truculent and thoroughly unrepentant. Customarily, the dispute would have precipitated a serious diplomatic break or a resort to force to compel reparation and secure adequate assurance of future respect. Yet, both sides ultimately precluded any direct consideration of the extralegal implications of the controversy. If this action should become a precedent, the potentialities of judicial settlement of international disputes would greatly increase. But Albania's adamant refusal to honor the verdict and pay the damages assessed against it indicate that it, for one, does not propose to repeat the performance.

Advisory Opinions

The two world courts have exercised greater influence on the development of international procedures for peaceful settlement through their advisory opinions than by their judgments in particular disputes. On appeal from international organizations, they have ruled on crucial issues affecting the jurisdiction, rights, and powers of these institutions. The Courts' majorities have usually taken a broad view of the mandates given international agencies and have upheld the legality of the actions they wished to take to preserve peace. Among the important opinions that have undergirded the peace-keeping efforts of the League and the United Nations are:

1. The League Council was held competent to deal with a dispute between Britain and France over the application to British subjects of nationality decrees in Tunis and Morocco.

This opinion established the now determinative principle that a matter such as this ceases to be solely within the domestic jurisdiction of a state once it has been made the subject of an international treaty. Thus, the door is opened for international action in regard to a widening range of questions held at one time to be within the private domain of each state. Once "internationalized," such questions cannot be pulled back into the exclusive national preserve.

2. The General Assembly of the U.N. was upheld in its contention that annexation of Southwest Africa by the Union of South Africa would violate the international obligations it had assumed when it had acquired a mandate for the territory after World War I.

While the U.N. was not explicitly authorized to act as the inheritor of the League's powers and duties, the Court made plain that South Africa could not unilaterally duck out of its former commitments on the grounds that the League had ceased to exist. It implied that the U.N. was entitled to a watchdog role.

3. In 1949, the Court advised that the United Nations was empowered to bring claims against states for injury caused to the organization or to persons in its service. (This issue arose as a result of the assassination of Count Bernadotte and other casualties suffered as the U.N. undertook to restore peace in Palestine.)

The ability of the organization to act independently in its own right to protect its agents in the performance of their duties has, of course, been crucial to the effectiveness of its peace-keeping efforts.

4. Somewhat similar in effect was the Court's opinion that the General Assembly was obligated to pay damages awarded to members of the Secretariat who had been fired without just cause. (Several Americans had been dismissed by the Secretary-General on grounds of subversion when they refused to testify before Congressional committees, grand juries, and other American tribunals, during the "McCarthy era." But they were judged by the U.N.'s Administrative Tribunal to have discharged their *United Nations* duties properly.)

The point of this opinion was to protect the staff of the organization against direct or indirect pressure by a national government, and leave it unintimidated in the pursuit of its international tasks.

5. The advisory opinion with potentially the most far-reaching implications upholds the right of the General Assembly to *assess* each member for the costs of such peace-keeping operations as the Emergency Force in the Middle East and the U.N. force in the Congo. (This is reviewed in detail in Chapter 2.)

This seems to give the organization legal sanction to assure the financial life-blood for its undertakings, even to the point of obligating unwilling members to pay a reasonable share, and holding them in default if they refuse.

Limitations

There is no question, however, that the Courts have been limited to a comparatively narrow field of international controversies and issues, and ones that have not involved much danger of war. Use has actually diminished since World War II, as is also the case with arbitration.[10]

Many disputes are still not "justiciable." They must remain entirely outside court jurisdiction if they do not raise legal questions or are considered to involve matters within a state's "domestic jurisdiction." Yet, these are usually the most critical and dangerous disputes. In 1951, for instance, Iran categorically rejected the Court's jurisdiction in its conflict with Britain over the nationalizing of the Anglo-Iranian oil properties, though it had signed the Optional Clause. Iran rejected an "injunction" issued by the Court at Britain's request to restrain action that would prejudice the case, on the grounds that the question involved an elemental right of national sovereignty and was, therefore, not susceptible to judicial action. States that have not signed the Optional Clause are, of course, under no obligation whatsoever to submit even admitted legal disputes to adjudication. In the Albanian case, the Court was able to secure competence without Albania's express consent, but only because the Security Council had previously taken action and brought about agreement in principle on a third-party settlement.

Generally, the Court itself has taken a very cautious approach toward asserting jurisdiction unless both parties are fully agreed that it should.[11]

A further obstacle to effective adjudication is that implementation of the Court's decisions depends on willingness of the parties to carry them out, and this has sometimes proved insufficient. For instance, the Union of South Africa has not respected the Court's opinion that it had no right to unilaterally abrogate its mandate over Southwest Africa and to annex the territory.

The independence and impartiality of the judges has sometimes been questioned, and this also has impaired the Court's prestige and the influence of its decisions. In the advisory opinion that the project for an Austro-German Customs Union in 1931 was incompatible with Austria's peace treaty obligations, the Permanent Court split 8 to 7, with the majority composed mainly of judges who were nationals of countries strongly opposed politically to the

---

[10] See Julius Stone, *op. cit.*, pp. 31–32, for a cogent analysis of factors responsible for the growing unwillingness of states to accept third-party judgment. See also, Quincy Wright, "The Role of Law in the Organization of Peace," in Commission to Study the Organization of Peace, Eleventh Report, *Organizing Peace in the Nuclear Age* (New York: New York University Press, 1959), p. 40.

[11] See, for instance the decisions reached in disclaiming competence in the Anglo–Iranian Oil Company case (final action), and in the case of *Israel* v. *Bulgaria* over the shooting down of an Israeli civilian plane which had strayed over Bulgarian territory. The former decision is reviewed in *American Journal of International Law*, October, 1952, pp. 737–751; the latter decision is extensively reviewed by Leo Gross, "The Jurisprudence of the World Court," *American Journal of International Law*, October, 1963, pp.753 –766.

"Anschluss." In the Corfu Channel case in 1949, judges from the Communist states sided with Albania. In another case, they strongly dissented from a majority advisory opinion that held Bulgaria, Hungary, and Rumania were obligated to submit to arbitration, charging that they had violated the human rights provisions of their peace treaties with the United Nations. The Court's composition is sufficiently broad, however, so that it has been able to absorb the intrusions of politics and ideology remarkably well and establish a now rarely challenged reputation for integrity. This has been accented by some notable instances in which judges decided against the positions pleaded by their governments: in the Anglo-Iranian Oil Company case, the British President of the Court wrote the majority opinion rejecting the British contention that the Court could take jurisdiction over Iranian objections. In the Interhandel case, the American judge sided with the Swiss against the U.S. (while the Russian judge took the American side, which happened to coincide with the long-held Russian stand that the Court should respect a government's claim that a case lay within its domestic jurisdiction).

The basic reason for the Court's limited effectiveness lies outside the Court. It is simply that most nations balk at a judicial settlement of most international controversies. This is what lies behind the tortuous argumentation over the technical issues of jurisdiction. It comes out sharp and clear in the collective behavior of members of the United Nations. They have studiously sidetracked almost every proposition to refer actual cases to the Court (a procedure which the Charter fully empowers them to do when legal issues are involved and which turned out rather well when followed in the Corfu Channel case). While they have occasionally appealed for advisory opinions as we have seen, these have dealt mainly with the prerogatives of the international organization, not with the many legal issues that delegates debate in considering the disputes brought to the General Assembly or Security Council. The evidence is unmistakable that governments want to maintain a *political* grip on the processes of settlement, even when legal norms are relevant. They prefer not to have judicial rulings on the validity of any legal questions they raise, because this might limit their freedom to reverse positions on what is lawful or unlawful whenever they find it expedient to do so.[12] Consequently, one can only conclude, with Claude, that "the United Nations has clearly contributed little to establishing the sanctity of the principle of judicial decision.[13] Adjudication has, however, been more acceptable in regard to types of controversies which are essentially non-

---

[12] A systematic analysis of the positions of U.N. members on the "lawfulness" of actions undertaken by U.N. organs during a period of five years showed that very few were consistent in applying the same criteria of legality as they confronted different issues. Philip E. Jacob, "The Legality of United Nations Action," *University of Pittsburgh Law Review*, Fall, 1951.

[13] Claude, *op. cit.*, p. 215.

political, especially economic relationships. This has been particularly true within the framework of the Regional organizations of Western Europe, where special courts have been established with jurisdiction over issues arising under the Common Market treaties, and also in regard to implementation of the European Convention on Human Rights.[14]

SETTLEMENT BY MUTUAL AGREEMENT

Because of such limitations on the processes of international adjudication, nations have resorted to other, more flexible procedures for settlement of many of their controversies, especially those of a political nature. The aim of these methods has been to harmonize rather than to judge the opposing claims, and to achieve an agreement mutually acceptable to all the disputants. To provide adequately for reaching such agreements in cases where conflicts of national interest cannot be formulated in legal terms is by far the most vital problem in the development of effective means for the peaceful settlement of international disputes.

Three main methods have been tried to bring the disputing parties to a reconciliation in international controversies. (1) Where questions of fact have been chiefly at issue, an impartial *inquiry* by some third state or international body has often helped to settle the matter by establishing the real facts. In this procedure, the investigators study the situation and report their findings without, however, making any proposals for action. (2) If the disagreement is more fundamental and involves sharp conflicts of policy and interest, a third party may use its *good offices* to promote negotiation between the antagonists, either bringing them together face to face or serving as an intermediary. The intermediary, however, does not propose how they should settle their problems. (3) On the other hand, the third party may undertake *mediation,* or *conciliation,* in which it actively seeks a basis for agreement, exploring with the disputants the nature of their differences, pointing out where they are not far apart, and making positive proposals for settlement.

Formerly, action along these lines depended on the initiative of individual states and was, therefore, haphazard and unreliable. As a matter of fact, nations hesitated to take a hand in resolving disputes for fear they would be accused by one or both sides of ulterior motives.

The First and Second Hague Conferences in 1899 and 1907 attempted to regularize and encourage the use of inquiry, good offices, and mediation in the settlement of international disputes. A convention adopted provided that the offer of good offices or mediation should not be construed as an unfriendly act. It also recommended that parties to a dispute set up a commission of inquiry if they differed as to the facts (though not in case vital interests or

---

[14] See Chapter 18, pp. 594–600.

honor were involved). This procedure was followed successfully by England and Russia when the Russian fleet fired on English fishing vessels off the Dogger Bank during the Russo-Japanese War. A commission was appointed to determine whether Japanese ships had been among the English, as asserted by the Russian commander in justifying his action. The commission found none were present, and Russia paid reparation to England. Shortly thereafter, President Theodore Roosevelt brought the Russo-Japanese War to an end through an offer of good offices followed by personal mediation, demonstrating the important contribution which could be made by a bold and disinterested third party in resolving international conflict. On the other hand his action was exceptional and emphasized the lack of established machinery through which conciliation efforts could be put into motion promptly whenever a critical controversy arose.

The development of international organizations, with specific and continuing responsibilities for conciliation on either a regional or global scale, has been the most vital factor in promoting a peaceful settlement of disputes.

The "Bryan Treaties" were the first step in this direction. Negotiated by Secretary of State William Jennings Bryan in 1913–14, they provided that all disputes of any nature between the United States and other countries not solved by diplomacy or arbitrated should be submitted to permanent conciliation commissions, established in advance by the parties to each treaty. The commissions were to report their findings, within a year, including suggestions for settlement. During that time, the disputing nations were obliged to refrain from war or hostilities. As these treaties were bilateral, their provisions applied only to the relations between each two signatories.

But the fundamental principles—permanence of a peacemaking organ, its comprehensive right to investigate all disputes not otherwise settled, its capacity to propose terms of a settlement (which, however, were not binding on the nations), and requirement of a cooling-off period—foreshadowed procedures for peaceful settlement of the League of Nations and strongly influenced development of an Inter-American peace system.[15]

THE LEAGUE OF NATIONS AS CONCILIATOR

Great progress in the practice of international conciliation took place with creation of the League of Nations. For the first time, an organ representing most of the international community was made responsible for intervening in the disputes of its members to bring about a peaceful settlement.

Members agreed to place every acute dispute not submitted to arbitration

---

[15] This approach was also incorporated in the Locarno Pacts concluded between Germany and the Western Allies. Permanent conciliation commissions, as well as arbitration machinery, were provided to resolve disputes among them.

or judicial settlement before the League Council, which was empowered to launch an immediate investigation and to attempt to work out a solution acceptable to all parties. If unsuccessful, the Council published a report (within six months after the dispute was submitted), stating the facts and making its own recommendations for a just and proper settlement. If one of the parties preferred, the matter could be referred for similar action to the Assembly of the League instead of the Council. States were not obligated to accept any of the League's proposals, and were, in fact, free to go to war three months after the report was published. The League's task was to conciliate, not arbitrate. The League had discretion to use other and more flexible procedures when matters had not reached a critical state. Under Article 11, it could take any action that was "deemed wise and effectual to safeguard the peace of nations" when a member called attention to a circumstance it considered a threat to peace or "good understanding between nations." Many issues were simply discussed in the general debates of the Council or Assembly, or considered informally by a "rapporteur" selected by one of these bodies to consult with the states involved. Such action proved even more valuable on the whole than the formal inquiry.[16]

Though the practice of the League varied somewhat in accordance with the special characteristics and political circumstances of each dispute, its usual procedure included four main steps.

First, it asked the governments concerned to avoid action that would prejudice examination or settlement of the question by the Council, and particularly to refrain from hostile acts. When Greek troops crossed into Bulgaria in connection with a boundary dispute in 1925, Mr. Briand, acting president of the Council, wired both governments "to give immediate instructions that, pending the consideration of the dispute by the Council, not only no further military movements shall be undertaken but the troops shall retire behind their respective frontiers." Sometimes, the League actually fixed a provisional military frontier to avoid conflict, as between Turkey and Iraq in 1924, and Lithuania and Poland in 1920.

The League checked both sides' observance of its appeals for a cessation or avoidance of hostilities. In the Greco-Bulgarian incident, the Council asked the French, British, and Italian governments to immediately send officers to the scene and report within a time limit whether its request had been complied with. In the conflict between Colombia and Peru, the Council went so far as to appoint a commission of three neutral military officers that took over administration of the territory of Leticia (claimed by both sides) while negotiations for a settlement were carried on. In these instances, the measures

---

[16] The League's efforts to settle disputes are thoroughly analyzed in the definitive study by F. P. Walters, *History of the League of Nations* (New York: Oxford University Press, 1952). For the early cases, see also T. P. Conwell–Evans, *The League Council in Action* (London: Oxford University Press, 1929).

succeeded in reducing tension and creating an atmosphere conducive to a calm consideration of the substance of the dispute. Sometimes, however, a country refused to permit supervision within its territory. Then, the commission simply had to report the facts and confine its investigation to the other side. Of much graver consequence was outright rejection of appeal for a cessation of hostilities. Japan proceeded methodically to complete its conquest of Manchuria despite the League's efforts to conciliate, and the U.S.S.R. brusquely declined to cease its hostilities against Finland. These actions virtually destroyed the possibility of conciliation.

The second step in the process of conciliation was to appoint either a member of the Council as "rapporteur," or select a committee to examine the dispute. The rapporteur or committee studied the documents, engaged in private conversations with the disputants, and sometimes even entered into negotiations with them concerning a solution. For instance, a committee of three was asked to investigate a conflict between Colombia and Peru in 1933 and to seek grounds for agreement. In the course of a month, the committee communicated directly with the governments, held five meetings with their representatives, and submitted proposals to the parties. These were accepted by Colombia and approved by the Council, but Peru returned counterproposals which the committee considered unacceptable. A committee of five examined the Italo-Ethiopian dispute and made suggestions to the two governments for international assistance to be given Ethiopia in accomplishing administrative reform and economic development. These were acceptable to Ethiopia but not to Italy. In the end, the rapporteur or the committee reported to the Council, analyzed the allegations and responses of both sides, and suggested what further action it should take.

If these preliminary and informal efforts did not achieve a solution, the third step was usually for the Council to invoke Article 15 of the Covenant and appoint a formal commission of enquiry, or for the Assembly (if the matter was before it) to appoint a special committee for conciliation.[17] The commissions consisted of both civilians and military personnel, usually appointed in an individual capacity but with the approval both of their governments and of the parties to the dispute. Nationals of the disputing countries were barred from membership, but each country was invited to appoint liaison officers. The commissions' instructions varied. In two frontier disputes (Greece–Bulgaria and Yugoslavia–Albania), they were to assess responsibility for frontier incidents and consider measures to end the disturbances. On the question of Memel, a draft convention was to be drawn up, and in the Bolivian–Paraguayan dispute, an agreement for arbitration. In the Sino-Japanese conflict over Manchuria, the commission was specifically

---

[17] If legal issues were involved, the Council usually adopted the alternative of requesting an opinion from the Permanent Court, which, in effect, transformed the procedure into a judicial one.

limited to investigating and reporting to the Council on circumstances that threatened peace or "good understanding" between the countries. It had no authority to enter into negotiations or to interfere with the military arrangements of either country. In this case, the responsibility for active conciliation and the formulation of proposals for settlement was entrusted to a special committee of nineteen designated by the Assembly. The underlying purpose in each instance was to provide for a thorough exploration of possible bases for an agreement between the disputing countries by a competent body, devoting its full time to the task. This step was the crucial one in the process. The success or failure of the commission or special committee in winning the confidence of both sides and devising a mutually acceptable formula virtually determined whether the League could accomplish a peaceful settlement.

The fourth step in League conciliation efforts was presentation of a definite recommendation for settlement by the Council or the Assembly. Sometimes, as in the Greco-Bulgarian incident and the controversy between Finland and Sweden over sovereignty of the Aaland Islands, both sides agreed promptly to the League's proposition. On other occasions, one party rejected the recommendations categorically, as did Italy in regard to the Ethiopian crisis and Japan in regard to the Lytton Commission's report on Manchuria.

If all efforts to effect a settlement appeared futile, the League adopted and issued a report reviewing the controversy, explaining the reasons for failure, and publicizing its recommendations. While this usually ended the process of conciliation, negotiations were often continued, and in the dispute over Leticia they resulted in Peru's ultimate acceptance of recommendations it had previously rejected. Instrumental in accomplishing this result was the collaboration of the United States and Brazil, who were not members of the League but were concerned with the conflict as American states.

The League's record as conciliator was not reassuring, despite its earnest and painstaking attempts to resolve 44 disputes in 20 years. In some of these, the League undoubtedly made an important contribution to eventual settlement by providing a ready-made procedure for negotiation, an impartial investigation of the circumstances of the controversy without offense or prejudice to national pride, and the initiative of a disinterested body in recommending reasonable grounds for compromise. At times, the influence of the world organization's acting with unanimity was sufficient to prevent or stop hostilities, particularly in border conflicts between minor states.[18]

But the League was rarely able to discharge its task of conciliation effectively when a big power was involved. When a serious incident arose between Greece and Italy, and Italians bombarded and occupied Corfu, the League virtually abdicated, and the Conference of Allied Ambassadors ulti-

---

[18] Greece *vs.* Bulgaria, Turkey *vs.* Iraq, Colombia *vs.* Peru over Leticia.

mately resolved the issue (on Italian terms). In the Manchurian crisis, the result of the long and meticulous work by the Lytton Commission and efforts of both Assembly and Council was Japan's complete repudiation of the League to the point of actual withdrawal. Italy and Russia similarly rejected conciliation in their respective conflicts with Ethiopia and Finland, while the League was completely ignored in the succession of crises between the Axis and Allied powers which led up to the second world war.

Three factors chiefly account for the impotence of League conciliation in these situations. First, action was often so delayed or long-drawn-out, especially in regard to major crises such as Manchuria, that it failed to anticipate the consolidation of a fait accompli by force. In other words, conciliation was not swift, bold, or vigorous enough to come up with arrangements in time to be weighed and perhaps found preferable to undertaking the uncertain risks and costs of military action. There is evidence that Japan might have been persuaded to accept a settlement of the Manchurian crisis along the general lines of the Lytton Report had this been proposed within a month or two after the first outbreak. But the machinery for conciliation was cumbersome and rather inflexible. All major steps had to be thrashed out until unanimous consent was obtained from all states except those involved in the dispute. Furthermore, no experienced body of experts was readily available to work on the problems. Members of the League were caught unprepared to deal with issues of great complexity between countries with whose economic and political circumstances as well as foreign relations they were largely unfamiliar. Consequently, the League fell down badly on the preventive work necessary to bring conciliation into play before relations between disputants had deteriorated to a complete impasse.

The second factor responsible for the failures of League conciliation was the limited cooperation of the great powers, which crippled the moderating influence the organization could exert on the disputants and sometimes almost orphaned the commissions appointed to work for a solution. The United States was particularly wilful, even when the situation was of concern to it, as with the Inter-American controversies and the Manchurian conflict. Its insistence on acting independently of the League made concerted action impossible. The United States went only so far as to appoint observers to the bodies concerned with conciliation. It did not identify itself with and support the efforts made by them. It took an active hand in the Chaco and Leticia conflicts only when the League acknowledged defeat and, in effect, turned these situations over to the United States and other states to handle on their own. The great powers within the League were also extremely timid about active sponsorship of conciliation. They were eager to avoid decisions that might commit them to action, embroiling their relations with another major power, yet embarrassed to approve steps that might appear to appease. In such a dilemma, they stalled and vacillated, attempted to dodge responsibility, and in the process vitiated much of the League's prestige and power of initiative. Without the wholehearted support of the world's influential states, the League could not muster sufficient moral pressure to persuade a big power to temper its demands and adopt a conciliatory rather than an intransigent attitude.

A third fundamental shortcoming was lack of a basic and comprehensive commitment on the part of both members and nonmembers of the League to refrain from war in the pursuit of their national policies. The nations were obligated by the Covenant only to attempt a peaceful settlement before they resorted to war. They were not prepared, psychologically or politically, to admit that every dispute in which they might become involved must be settled by peaceful means. Hence, the contingency of war was ever present as an entirely legitimate alternative should conciliation fail to produce, within a very limited time, an agreement perfectly suitable to both sides. In the circumstances, the protagonists were inclined to put little faith in the conciliation process, but to concentrate instead on preparing for a resolution of the matter by the traditional methods of force. This skepticism increased as disarmament efforts failed, proposals by states defeated in World War I for revision of the peace treaties were rejected, and as countries like Japan, Italy, and Germany drove to expand their power. So long as war was generally accepted as a proper and probably necessary means of achieving national ends—at least when these involved substantial changes in the status quo—it was extraordinarily difficult to persuade the disputants to approach negotiations constructively with an attitude of determination to find agreement. The temptation was, rather, to maneuver so as to assure disagreement, with the onus, if possible, on the other side so as to lay the basis for a resort to force. Without a basic minimum of good faith and a willingness at least to seek a peaceful settlement, conciliation could not hope to succeed.

An attempt was made to supplement the League's conciliation machinery in the General Act for the Pacific Settlement of International Disputes proposed by the Assembly in 1928. This provided that states would submit every dispute that could not be settled by diplomacy (with certain possible exceptions) to permanent or special conciliation commissions set up directly by the parties to the dispute. They were bound to "abstain from any sort of action whatsoever which may aggravate or extend the dispute." This General Act, though ratified by over twenty states before the outbreak of World War II, had little effect. It was intended to facilitate conciliation by a simpler and more direct procedure than that provided by the League (which required action by the whole Council or Assembly). In effect, it extended the Bryan Treaties to a multilateral instead of a purely bilateral arrangement, and envisaged individual and specialized conciliation for each pair of countries. But the system was not put into operation in the critical international disputes that followed, and it became apparent that peaceful settlement was unlikely apart from action by some established international organ with a general responsibility for promoting peaceful settlement.

THE INTER-AMERICAN PEACE SYSTEM

The development of *regional* machinery for the conciliation of disputes met with greater success, especially among the American states, and to some extent afforded a practical alternative to the League.

Over the period from 1923 to 1948, an Inter-American "peace system" was forged, based on the assumption that quarrels between the American republics were of primary concern to them, and could, therefore, be most effectively settled by them. The long-standing policy of the United States against intervention on the American continent by non-American powers, and the growing disillusionment of Latin American states with the League of Nations as a peace instrument applicable to the Western hemisphere, as well as a growing desire to separate American disputes from European politics, were the drives that led to ever more elaborate arrangements for the maintenance of peace in the Americas.[19]

The first step was taken in 1923 with the conclusion of the Gondra Treaty, providing for the investigation of all controversies (aside from those submitted to arbitration) by a special Inter-American commission, which could be convoked by one of two permanent diplomatic commissions, stationed at Montevideo and Washington, on request of either party. Six years later, the functions of the Commission of Investigation were broadened to include conciliation, and the American states agreed to submit to it "all controversies of any kind which have arisen or may arise between them for any reason and which it may not have been possible to settle through diplomatic channels."[20] Later treaties reaffirmed the obligation to submit to conciliation, adding other procedures than the above, such as mediation by an eminent citizen of another American state. An important measure aimed at preventing controversies was adopted at the Buenos Aires Conference in 1936: the establishment of permanent bilateral mixed commissions, composed of governmental representatives to study "the causes of future difficulties or controversies" and to promote the regular application of the treaties in force between them.

Between 1943 and 1947, the Inter-American Juridical Committee (a semiofficial professional body of jurists and lawyers) worked on the preparation of a draft for an integrated and comprehensive "Inter-American Peace System," coordinating all the continental agreements for the prevention and

---

[19] For basic reference concerning the development of the inter-American peace system, see Charles G. Fenwick, *The Organization of American States: The Inter-American Regional System* (Washington, D.C.: Pan American Union, 1963), especially ch. VI; and, John C. Drier, *The Organization of American States and the Hemisphere Crisis* (New York: Harper & Row, 1962).

[20] General Convention of Inter-American Conciliation, 1929. Another treaty provided for arbitration of all disputes of a juridical nature.

peaceful solution of controversies. Its final product was placed before the Ninth International Conference of American States at Bogota in 1948, which revised and then approved it, formally establishing the system within the framework of the Organization of American States.

Prior to inauguration of the full-fledged system at Bogota, the Inter-American peace arrangements were anything but effective, either in preventing or in resolving conflicts. The Chaco War between Bolivia and Paraguay lasted eight years, although the states were among the smaller ones. Technically, both had not ratified the same treaties for peaceful settlement, and hence were not bound to follow the prescribed procedures. What was actually revealed was the startling inadequacy of any paper provisions for settlement, whether bilateral, regional, or worldwide, in the absence of effective international organization to help put them into effect, and the active concern and united support of the influential states in the area. The United States, Argentina, Brazil, and other American states were simply unprepared to get together and take on the onerous and thankless responsibilities of peacemakers in this confused and highly complex situation. Their own mutual suspicions and hostilities did not help matters. In the end, Bolivia tossed the job to the League, and after both sides were throughly exhausted, with neither completely victorious, a settlement was patched together from outside the American preserve. A better result was achieved in the Leticia controversy, when the United States and Brazil ultimately consented to work along with the League and persuaded Peru to become more amenable to the League's recommendations. But this dispute also pointed up a serious defect in the American peace arrangements. Both states had ratified virtually all the relevant treaties, but each insisted at one time or another that the question was one of "domestic jurisdiction" and the treaties did not apply. Fortunately, the breach was filled because the League was able to assert its jurisdiction and act. The Inter-American system as it then existed, however, was just not practical insofar as the usual type of international controversy that arose between American states was concerned. It had no application at all to the revolutions which are endemic in many Latin-American states. Nor did it operate in regard to the touchy controversies over "Yankee" intervention, which persisted until 1933 when the U.S. undertook to reverse its policy.

The present system has operated to much greater effect. In general, the Organization of American States has succeeded in mobilizing enough collective influence to exercise substantial restraint upon the practice of fomenting revolution against neighboring governments, the most persistent precipitant of Inter-American conflict in recent years.

The Pact of Bogota

The essential principles of the Inter-American peace system are: (1) an all-inclusive commitment to settle disputes peacefully, (2) a wide choice of methods of settlement, (3) acceptance of compulsory third-party decision in the event mutual agreement is not achieved by the disputants, (4) responsibility of a central organ representing the whole group of American states to assist in the efforts at settlement and assure proper functioning of the system.

Under the Pact of Bogota, every American state is obligated to settle *all* its disputes by peaceful means. Regional procedures are provided for every type of dispute, and they are so interlocked that if a settlement is not reached by one means, another must then be used. There are no loopholes if the states keep their obligations, and the system therefore presumes that no American dispute will have to be referred to the United Nations.

Four methods of settlement are recognized: (*a*) good offices or mediation either by a third state or an individual, (*b*) investigation and conciliation, (*c*) judicial procedure, and (*d*) arbitration. The disputants may begin with any of these procedures. But if mediation or conciliation is not successful, either party may push the case before the International Court of Justice and, if the Court decides it is without jurisdiction, compel the other to arbitrate. The compulsory jurisdiction of the International Court for all "justiciable" disputes is accepted. (It should be noted, however, that several of the most important states in the hemisphere, including the U.S. and Argentina, have refused to accept the obligations for compulsory arbitration or adjudication; others have entered different reservations; and some have yet to ratify the Pact at all.)

From a practical standpoint, three organs have been authorized to act on behalf of the Organization as a whole, in settling disputes.

The "Organ of Consultation," which consists of the foreign ministers of all the republics, may be called into session by a majority of the Council (an absolute majority) on the request of any member state "to consider problems of an urgent nature and of common interest to the American States." Under the Inter-American Treaty of Reciprocal Assistance (the Rio de Janeiro Treaty, 1947), the Organ of Consultation is given quite explicit powers in case of conflict between two or more American states, including the right to impose a variety of diplomatic and economic sanctions and the use of armed force, as well as to undertake actions of mediation and conciliation.

The second key institution of the OAS in dealing with disputes is the Council, composed of an ambassador from each member state. The Council, which meets frequently and regularly in Washington, is authorized to serve provisionally as the Organ of Consultation, and in this capacity has been the most active and effective instrument to implement collective peacemaking action among the American states.

A third useful organ has been the Inter-American Peace Committee, established by the foreign ministers in 1940 as a watchdog and to render good offices when asked by the disputants. Though it is not a formal part of the OAS machinery, it has been called upon in several situations to function, in effect, on behalf of the organization. In 1959, the foreign ministers gave the Committee temporary authority to study situations that threatened the overthrow of an American government or violations of human rights, even though the situation had not reached the stage of a major controversy. The Committee is composed of five members of the OAS Council selected from its membership.[21]

Strategy of Pacification

While the pattern of OAS action has been pragmatic and to a considerable extent adaptive to the different circumstances of the particular cases, it has tended to emphasize: first, a mutual accommodation among the protagonists themselves; second, a process of independent fact-finding by investigators accountable to the OAS directly (sometimes composed of members of the OAS Council itself); third, direct mediation or conciliation by an OAS body, if the parties did not settle the matter themselves or on their own agree to measures that had been suggested to them; fourth, a judgment of responsibility directed against one of the parties if the OAS suggestions for settlement were rejected; fifth, the imposition of sanctions in case the states continued to be recalcitrant. In one instance—the aftermath of the Trujillo regime in the Dominican Republic, the OAS went one step further and on the request of the new Dominican government actually undertook to advise and supervise implementation of new electoral provisions and selection of a new government.

A review of OAS actions indicates that they have tended, especially since 1959, to increase in vigor, rapidity of response, and readiness to use a considerable amount of pressure to reduce or eliminate what the OAS majority considered to be the principal threat to peace and stability in the situation. The OAS has, in effect, succeeded in making itself arbiter in the most serious fratricidal conflicts.

Dilemmas

There are two major limitations which affect the peacemaking mission of the OAS. First, the scope of its activity is necessarily regional. It is not in a position to cope effectively with conflicts that directly or indirectly involve a state outside the American hemisphere. Hence, its hands are largely tied in situations where an American state is either the opponent of a non-American

---

[21] In addition, a panel of "American Conciliators" is maintained by the Pan American Union (the secretariat of the Organization of American States), on whom the Council or disputing states may draw in setting up conciliation commissions.

state, or, as in the case of Cuba, its willing agent in an Inter-American dispute. The OAS cannot get at the other party.[22]

The second limitation is in regard to the handling of ideological revolution. The premise of the Inter-American peace system is nonintervention, which means, practically, the maintenance of the status quo. OAS action necessarily presumes that states shall be held to their commitments to respect the territorial integrity and political independence of their neighbors. The stumbling block here is that ideological revolution is by its nature transnational, and does *not* respect the political status quo in other countries—whether it is Communists, attempting to overthrow democracies; or dictatorships, democrats, and liberals, attempting to destroy dictatorships of right or left; or dictators, seeking to oust the democratic or Communist regimes by which they feel threatened. There is, thus, a fundamental contradiction between the noninterventionist commitments of the OAS on the one hand, and its nominally democratic professions on the other. This contradiction hamstrings OAS efforts whenever a dispute has ideological overtones. Yet, more and more, this is the nature of the situations it has to confront.

On the whole, the effect of OAS efforts has been to sustain the status quo.[23] In most instances, the organization was able to act with a substantial degree of consensus first in regard to the long-held principle of nonintervention, and second, with regard to avoiding of violence between states in pursuance of the fundamental commitments of the American Republics. In accordance with these two principles, the burden of responsibility for disturbing the peace would rest on any government that tolerated or supported efforts to impose its will on another state by force, whatever the state might feel was the justice of its cause. Acting within this frame of reference, the OAS could mobilize nearly unanimous pressure against a state which it determined was violating either the principle of nonintervention or the prohibition against violence. By reducing the issue to which it addresses its actions to these essentially technical considerations, the OAS has been able to keep the lid on most Inter-American conflicts.

The Costa Rican Case:—Preserving The Status Quo

Typical was a case which confronted the Organization within months after it was formally established.

---

[22] This problem has also precipitated serious and continuing controversy over the respective roles of the OAS and the United Nations in such cases, particularly over which should take precedence and how much autonomy the regional organization might properly claim in handling the dispute. See discussion in Chapter 6, pp. 167–71. Refer also to Inis L. Claude, Jr., "The OAS, the UN, and the United States," *International Conciliation;* March, 1964.

[23] See, Northwestern University, *The Organization of American States* (Study No. 3, prepared at the request of the Subcommittee on American Republics Affairs, U.S. Senate Committee on Foreign Relations, 86th Cong. 1st sess., December 24, 1959).

On December 11, 1948, Costa Rica notified the Council of the Organization of American States that its territory had been invaded by armed forces originating in Nicaragua and charged that Nicaragua had supported them. The Council was at once convened. It summoned a meeting of the foreign ministers to study the situation, and appointed a five-nation commission to investigate the alleged events on the scene. On December 17, the commission arrived in Costa Rica, examined weapons captured from the invaders, toured the frontier region for five days, and then reported: (1) the invading teams had been organized in Nicaraguan territory by a group of Costa Rican exiles; (2) the Nicaraguan government had failed to take adequate steps to restrain it, but after the expedition had started, did undertake measures to prevent aid going to it; (3) Nicaraguan armed forces had not participated, and there had been no actual contact between the forces of the two governments; (4) the Costa Rican government had failed to grant a previously agreed political amnesty to the exiles; (5) the Caribbean Legion had enjoyed official support and facilities in Costa Rica in preparing to overthrow certain Central American governments, including the Nicaraguan regime. In other words, there were definitely two sides to the question, and responsibility was mixed.

On December 24, two weeks after the initial complaint, the Council called on both countries to refrain from any further warlike activity, asked for categorical assurances from each that it would observe the principles of Inter-American nonintervention and solidarity, and appointed a five-man military commission to see that the Council's decisions were fulfilled, especially in regard to preventing the equipping and arming of persons in either country for the purpose of rebellion in the other. A full settlement was achieved with the signing of a "Pact of Amity" between the two governments on February 21, 1949, by which they agreed to observe fully and faithfully all recommendations of the Council of American States and affirmed their determination to prevent the repetition of similar incidents in the future.

But this kind of achievement has depended on the OAS closing its eyes to the underlying causes of major political and social conflicts within the hemisphere. From a long-run standpoint, the commendable record of peaceful settlement may have simply set up a temporary ban of restraint against the heaving forces of social change. As these forces gather intensity and are given ever more vigorous leadership, this policy of containing Inter-American disputes within the confines of the doctrine of nonintervention and nonviolence may prove increasingly difficult. The situation is effectively appraised by a Northwestern University study submitted to the U.S. Senate Foreign Relations Committee: "There has been almost no effort to change the underlying conditions which initially fomented the strife, since such basic causes reside within the nations themselves and since the OAS in its political activities tries scrupulously to avoid intervention in the domestic affairs of its member states, it does not attempt at present to deal with more than those surface manifestations of tensions that result in Inter-American disturbances."[24]

The Dominican Case—Intervention vs. Dictatorship

Nevertheless, there have been exceptions when the OAS deliberately raised its hand against dictatorships, of the right and of the left. In the case of the Dominican Republic, the OAS finally acted to impose restraints on the long-entrenched dictatorship of President Trujillo. Although the strong economic and diplomatic sanctions imposed on Trujillo were rationalized partly on the ground of his machinations against such governments as Venezuela's which were openly antagonistic to him, the major impetus came from the utter disgust among most of the American Republics at the ruthless supression of political and civil rights within the Dominican Republic itself. The OAS, in a remarkable break with its traditional practice, in effect declared that this kind of a political system was incompatible with the political ideals of the Organization; it demanded in the name of the collective ideology a fundamental internal change, if not on the part of the regime voluntarily, then under the compulsion of collective sanctions. It is generally held that the actions of the OAS were at least indirectly responsible for the internal crises which built up to the assassination of Trujillo and the decision of the caretaker government that followed to establish constitutional government with free elections. Having toppled the government, the OAS then helped to establish the foundations for the new system, even to the extent of appointing a commission to propose an appropriate electoral process and then to observe the first elections under the new system. Nominally, these latter actions were undertaken in response to a request for "technical assistance" from the Dominican government (one of the rare instances when technical assistance extended to the job of organizing a country's constitutional system). It was obvious, however, that the Dominican government made its request in view of the need to convince the OAS that conditions warranted lifting of its sanctions.[25]

But the OAS democratizing spark did not really strike fire. The Dominican accomplishment proved short-lived as Trujillo's son turned back the clock by a military coup.

And in neighboring Haiti, the OAS chose to avoid an outright challenge to "Papa Doc" Duvalier's authoritarian grip on his population.

Indeed, there has been a strong backwash among many Latin-American

---

[24] *Ibid.*, p. 29.

[25] See Henry Wells, "The OAS and the Dominican Elections," *Orbis,* Spring, 1963, pp. 150–63. For a detailed review of this case, see Jerome Slater, "The United States, the Organization of American States, and the Dominican Republic, 1961–1963," *International Organization,* Spring, 1964.

leaders against the tendency of the OAS to concern itself with the internal political pedigree of its member governments, of whatever breed. They oppose what they consider to be the OAS rejection of the principle of nonintervention as "a frank retrogression of Pan-Americanism." The case is vigorously put by a Mexican Foreign Office official, writing well before the more extreme recent instances of collective intervention by the OAS. He condemns the use of the enforcement measures of the Rio Treaty "not for their fundamental purpose which is to repel armed aggression or to serve as an instrument of collective security of the U.N. under the authority of the Security Council, but as a means of pressure to judge, condemn and eventually to overthrow the internal regime of the states, to the extent that they do not meet with the approval of the majority of the American Republics." Secondly, Mr. Castañeda concludes that the effect of such action by the OAS has been to transform a regional instrument of defense into an instrument of world policy to carry out extra-continental objectives of the United States.[26]

Revolution for Export—the Cuban Case

On the other hand, the full issue of intervention has been cast in a new perspective by the dynamism of the Cuban revolution. The question of Intra-American relationships, which have for so long been dominated by the role of the United States, now became intimately involved with the extra-continental issue of Communism. Perhaps it would be more appropriate to say that the Cuban revolution precipitated three sets of issues for the American Republics, all of them inextricably intertwined with one another: (1) internal social revolution and its counterpart of a political systemic revolution; (2) export of revolution from one American Republic to others which raised the traditional question of intervention; (3) support from outside the hemisphere for a state and an ideology in conflict with its neighbors.

In this melange, none of the precedents of Inter-American relationships seemed fully applicable. On the one hand, strict application of the principle of nonintervention would mean acceptance and association with a Communist-governed Cuba—a position which most American Republics seemed quite willing to accept. On the other hand, what should be done if Cuba itself were not inclined to keep its revolution to itself? Should the OAS undertake to act collectively to defend its members against Cuban-inspired political and social rebellion? Should it, in other words, undertake collective intervention to prevent national intervention directed toward a Communist takeover? Here, the American leaders were caught in a cruel dilemma. Having just espoused collective intervention to end the Dominican dictatorship, how could they justify action against a country that crusaded against

---

[26] Jorge Castaneda, "Pan-Americanism and Regionalism: A Mexican View." *International Organization*, August, 1956, pp. 382–86.

such conditions, or at least alleged that it was? Or, conversely, how could they undertake collectively to defend regimes similar to the one they had just helped to topple? The Cubans themselves helped to resolve this dilemma by focusing their aggressive actions, not on the remaining dictatorships, but on some of the constitutional democracies just in the process of establishing themselves after internal revolutions of their own. In these circumstances, the principle of nonintervention could be invoked against the Cubans, and collective action justified to counter Cuban aggression.

But it was the Cuban alignment with the Soviet Union which conclusively tilted the scales against it and led to the most remarkable of Intra-American collective actions. First, in 1960, the foreign ministers issued the Declaration of San Jose, which in general terms, without mentioning communism or the U.S.S.R. directly, condemned intervention by an extra-continental power in the affairs of the American Republics. In January, 1962, at Punta del Este, the foreign ministers unanimously (except for Cuba) condemned Cuba's Marxism–Leninism as incompatible with the principles and objectives of the Inter-American system, and agreed by a two-thirds majority to exclude the existing government of Cuba from participating in the system. This was the first time the sanction of exclusion had been used. In October, 1962, by a vote of 19–0, the foreign ministers approved the declaration of a limited blockade by the United States against Cuba and its demand for the removal of Russian missiles and military personnel from bases in Cuba. In 1964, the OAS investigated and confirmed charges that Cuba was instigating subversion and violence against the Venezuelan government, and by better than a two-thirds vote invoked its mandatory powers to order all members to break diplomatic relations and cut trade. (Mexico, Chile, and others objected, but as of 1965, only Mexico refused to go along with the decision on diplomatic sanctions.)[27]

This highwater mark of collective intervention by the OAS reflected the conviction of the American Republics that in regard to Cuba they no longer confronted just an ordinary Inter-American squabble but a general threat to the security of the hemisphere—a threat that called for the Organization of American States to exchange its hat of peacemaker for its sword of guardian of the hemisphere's collective security.[28]

Conclusion

In conclusion, the experience of the OAS seems to demonstrate that intraregional peacemaking is as difficult as achieving global international

[27] For text of the Resolution by the foreign ministers of the American Republic applying sanctions to Cuba, see *New York Times,* July 27, 1964, p. 2.

[28] See Chapters 5 and 6 for discussion of Inter-American security organization. For a succint analysis of the basis of OAS actions in regard to Cuba, with emphasis on legal aspects, see Covey Oliver, *The Inter-American System and the Cuban Crisis,* Working Paper for the Third Hammerskjöld Forum, Association of the Bar of the City of New York (Dobbs Ferry, N.Y.: Oceana, 1964).

harmony when the regional group is confronted by divisive issues of the same order as the world at large. The basic question is whether a regional security organization can function effectively to preserve peace among its members when divergences reach the point where states are unwilling to accept the status quo as tolerable and leave their neighbors alone. Or, what happens when one or more members of the regional group disagree so basically with the others that they turn outside the region for support and become partners of states perceived by their neighbors as vitally threatening their security? The response of the OAS to this issue has been, as we have seen, the policy of ostracism. But it is apparent that this policy has not yet provided a persuasive answer. Cuba is far from being brought back into the fold.

All this suggests the critical importance of the peacemaking potential of the general international community, over and beyond whatever may be the resources for peaceful settlement within particular regions.

Chapter 11

The Mediating Role of the United Nations

The most important development in the processes of conciliation in international controversies has taken place through the United Nations. Unexpectedly, the new postwar world organization was confronted with a succession of serious crises of a political nature that could not be resolved either through the customary methods of diplomacy or the processes of adjudication. Nor was the United Nations as yet equipped to impose a decision by force on the disputants, even had it considered such action desirable. Consequently, it was obliged to rely on its mediating potentialities. In its efforts to promote a peaceful settlement by mutual agreement among the protagonists, the United Nations has matured the machinery and skills of international conciliation to the point where they can be instrumental in avoiding war, even if not always successful in procuring a neat and final resolution of the controversy.[1]

THE U.N.'S PEACEMAKING MACHINERY

The Security Council was designed as the principal organ for achievement of a peaceful settlement of international controversies. Its mandate is sweeping. It is empowered to investigate and undertake action to resolve "any dispute, or any situation which might lead to international friction or give rise to a dispute." (U.N. Charter Articles 33, 34, 36, 37, 38.) The umbrella term "situation" is significant, because it gives the Council virtually unlimited discretion in considering any matter that is causing tension, even though

[1] For systematic analysis of United Nations' organization for the settlement of disputes and its first decade of experience see: Leland M. Goodrich and Anne P. Simons, *The United Nations and the Maintenance of International Peace and Security* (Washington, D.C.: The Brookings Institution, 1955).

it may not have reached the stage of a fully developed and clear-cut "dispute."

A dispute or a situation is easily brought to the Council's attention. One of the states concerned may notify the Council and ask its consideration. As a matter of fact, a member of the United Nations is obligated to refer to the Council every dispute "the continuance of which is likely to endanger the maintenance of international peace and security" should it fail to be settled directly between the parties by peaceful means of their own choice. Any other member of the United Nations may bring a dispute or situation before the Security Council (and before the General Assembly). The Secretary-General may refer "any matter which in his opinion may threaten the maintenance of international peace and security" to the Security Council. Finally, a *non*-member state may bring forward a dispute to which it is a party if it accepts in advance for the purposes of the particular dispute the obligations of pacific settlement under the Charter (Art. 35, par. 2).

The Security Council has a wide range of possible action open to it. After preliminary inquiry or investigation, it can simply call on the parties to attempt to settle their dispute by methods of their own choice, such as negotiation, mediation, arbitration, judicial settlement, or resort to regional agencies. (The disputants are expected to have made such an attempt in the first instance before coming to the Security Council, in case their dispute is likely to endanger international peace and security.) In the case of legal disputes, reference to the International Court of Justice is anticipated as a general rule. If the parties to a dispute so request, the Security Council may itself make recommendations for a pacific settlement. If a dispute or situation reaches the point where its continuance is considered likely to endanger peace and security, the Council may on its own initiative recommend both *procedures* of adjustment and *terms* of settlement it considers appropriate. In other words, the Council's freedom to act increases with the seriousness of the controversy, until it can assume the full prerogatives of a mediator. At the same time, it is limited to the function of a mediator—that is, it may only recommend steps to the disputants—so long as it is engaged in the effort of finding a peaceful solution in contrast to undertaking enforcement action to meet a breach of peace or threat of aggression. The role of the United Nations as peacemaker thus depends on securing the assent and cooperation of all parties to the controversy.

Peacemaking by the Security Council depends, furthermore, on assent of the Big Five, for to take any action in regard to resolution of a dispute or situation, the "substantive majority" of the Council must agree—that is, the vote of seven members, including the concurring votes of the permanent members. There is one major exception. As a result of the "Yalta Formula," proposed by President Roosevelt and accepted by Stalin and Churchill, a party to a dispute abstains from voting, even though it is a big power, in all action relating to the *pacific* settlement of that dispute.[2] In practice, another modification of the veto has been established in that the Council may place a controversy on its agenda and hear the case, even though a major power objects.[3]

Although the Security Council was clearly assigned primary responsibility for the peaceful settlement of disputes, the General Assembly has also taken a hand in this task and, as a matter of fact, has assumed an increasingly important role, because the Security Council has been unable to agree on action in several serious situations. The Assembly was specifically restrained by the Charter from making recommendations in regard to any dispute or situation while it was before the Security Council. But aside from this limitation, the Assembly's powers are very comprehensive. It "may discuss any questions relating to the maintenance of international peace and security . . . and except as provided in Article 12, may make recommendations with regard to any such questions to the state or states concerned or to the Security Council or both." Such questions can be brought to the General Assembly by the same four channels that lead to the Security Council: one of the immediately involved states, any other member of the U.N., a non-member willing to accept Charter obligations in regard to a dispute in which it is involved, and the Secretary-General. There is no limit to the action the Assembly may initiate, though according to the Charter, it is supposed to refer any question on which action is necessary to the Security Council "before or after discussion," thereby surrendering its right to deal further with it. In practice, however, the General Assembly has not restricted itself in this manner, but has proceeded to pass resolutions that recommend action, conduct investigations, set up commissions to carry out its recommendations, and generally take charge of the controversy whenever a question has come before it which the Security Council has not yet taken up, or has dropped from its agenda. This extended view of its powers it formally confirmed in the Uniting for Peace Resolution, adopted over vehement Soviet objections during the Korean crisis. (See Chapter 3.)

When the General Assembly assumed this increasing responsibility for action connected with international controversies, it set up at United States initiative an Interim Committee or "Little Assembly" to provide a greater continuity to its efforts. Consisting of one representative of each member-state, the organ was authorized to meet in between sessions of the Assembly, study the disputes the Assembly had taken up, and prepare recommendations for Assembly action. It was essentially a "committee of the whole," acting at

---

[2] This exception does not apply to *enforcement* action under Chapter 8.

[3] Since the Iranian dispute when the Council overrode Russian protests, this has been considered a "procedural" question not subject to veto.

the behest of the Assembly to follow up its efforts at international conciliation. The legality of this procedure was challenged by the Soviet bloc without
effect. In practice, however, the Little Assembly has hardly fulfilled either
the Soviet fears of displacing the Security Council or Western expectations of
an effective instrument of Assembly mediation. It has performed its most
useful function by making a thorough background study of the practicability
of various methods of peaceful adjustment available to the U.N. and by
recommending steps to strengthen the machinery for settlement.

THE CONTROVERSIES

The United Nations has attempted conciliatory action in four main types
of cases.

1. Violations of territorial integrity and political independence.
2. Issues arising out of the struggle for colonial independence.
3. Cold war confrontations.
4. Questions of human rights.[4]

First were charges that the independence and territorial integrity of a
country were being violated, either by direct forceful attack or by indirect
intervention in its internal affairs. As most of these represented skirmishes in
the cold war, the controversy involved high stakes not only for the countries
immediately concerned but for the major powers as well. Typical of these
disputes over the issue of political independence and territorial integrity
were:

1. The Iranian question, 1946. Iran appealed to the Security Council on
the grounds that the Soviet Union had failed to withdraw troops from the
country at the conclusion of World War II, as it had agreed to do together
with Britain and U.S. in 1942, when Iran consented to cooperate with the
Allies against the Axis. Iran contended that direct negotiations over the issue
had broken down; the Soviet Union insisted they were still in progress.

2. The Balkans question, 1946–51. This involved a succession of charges
of interference in the internal affairs of Greece and threats to its political
independence and territorial integrity. The Ukrainian Soviet Socialist Republic
first attacked Britain for maintaining troops in Greece and suppressing democratic opposition to the Greek regime. Within a year, the Greek government,
joined by the British and the United States, carried the attack to the Soviet
bloc, charging that Yugoslavia, Bulgaria, and Albania were actively supporting
guerrilla warfare in Greece and attempting to overthrow its government by
force. In turn, the Greek government was accused by the Soviet bloc of harboring

[4] A few others do not fit these categories—for instance, the Corfu Channel case previously
discussed. Although it clearly concerned a legal question—the right of passage through
territorial waters—the elements of national prestige and ideological alignment were so
strongly involved that the matter came before the United Nations Security Council as a
political question before it was passed on to the International Court for adjudication.

aggressive designs against her northern neighbors, as well as engaging in political persecutions, and their activities were alleged to have been instigated or abetted by Britain and the United States.

3. Czechoslovakia, 1948. Following the Communist seizure of political power in Czechoslovakia in February, 1948, the Chilean government requested that the Security Council investigate charges that the Soviet Union had actively intervened in connection with the coup, and had violated the political independence of Czechoslovakia by promising help to the Communists and, in reality, directing their efforts.

4. The political independence of China, 1949–50. The sweeping victory of the Chinese Communists over the Nationalist government led to grave charges by the Nationalists before the General Assembly against the Soviet Union for thwarting establishment of National authority in Manchuria, actively supporting the Communists in overthrowing the regular government of China, and itself seeking both economic and political domination of Manchuria. The Nationalist government asked that the United Nations call on its members to desist from all military and economic aid to the Chinese Communists and refuse diplomatic recognition to the Chinese Communist regime. The Soviet Union repudiated the right of the Chinese Nationalist representative to speak for the Chinese people, and refused to participate in any consideration of the problem.

5. Formosa, etc. 1950–present. As an outgrowth of war in Korea, the United States declared it would temporarily "neutralize" the island of Formosa under Chiang Kai Shek's Nationalist government, protecting it against Communist attack but leaving its ultimate disposition until the end of the Korean fighting. This action was challenged before the Security Council by the Peiping regime—even though it had no official status—with the support of the U.S.S.R., as a violation of Chinese territorial integrity. Likewise from the Korean War has followed a steady barrage of charges and countercharges by and on behalf of Communist China on the one hand, and the U.S. and the Nationalist regime on the other, arising out of their confrontation in the Formosa Strait and on the offshore islands of Quemoy and Matsu.

6. Soviet intervention in Hungary, 1956. Internal revolt overthrew the pro-Soviet Communist government in Hungary, and the new regime severed association with the Soviet bloc and called for Soviet forces stationed in Hungary under the Warsaw Pact to leave. But instead, the Soviet Union crushed the revolt and installed another regime amenable to its control. Before its demise, the government had time to appeal to the United Nations, and charge the U.S.S.R. with attacking the country and destroying its political independence. The question has been put on the General Assembly's agenda ever since, at the initiative of the U.S. and other Western states; while the going government in Hungary and the rest of the Soviet bloc have just as consistently rejected this and all other U.N. actions as illegal interference by the organization in its internal affairs.

A second major group of disputes has arisen in the process of imperial liquidation and the formation of new independent states out of former colonies or mandates in the Middle East, India, and Indonesia. Timing of the transfer of sovereignty, territorial limits of the new states, extent of rights still to be enjoyed by the "parent," and mutual obligations of the succession states to each other have exacerbated relations both between the imperial powers and their erstwhile colonies and, in the case of India and Palestine, between the various inheritors of the sovereign power. Some of these controversies as they have come before the United Nations are the following:

1. Syria and Lebanon, 1946.   These two countries, which had just acquired their independence after 25 years as mandates under British and French administration, demanded the immediate withdrawal of British and French troops from their territories. Britain and France objected to such action before they had negotiated an economic and political agreement with the two nations.

2. The United Kingdom–Egyptian dispute, 1947.   This controversy arose from the demand of Egypt for evacuation of troops from its territory and the Sudan, and termination of British administration in the Sudan. The United Kingdom contended that these arrangements were authorized by treaties which could not be changed without British consent, but Egypt contested the validity of these agreements.

3. The Indonesian question, 1947–49.   Establishment of the Indonesian Republic, demanding full independence from the Netherlands for all Indonesia, precipitated a succession of complex and increasingly bitter issues with the Netherlands, culminating in large-scale armed conflict, even though the Dutch were prepared to ultimately relinquish sovereignty in favor of some arrangement for self-government, provided their personal and property rights were safeguarded.

4. The question of West Irian (western New Guinea) 1961–63.   This was a further installment of the Indonesian question. Status of this territory was not settled when the Indonesian Republic was established. The Indonesians claimed it belonged to them; the Dutch maintained the inhabitants should have the choice of self-government and that it should remain under Dutch administration until the choice had been exercised. The Indonesians prepared to take it by force.

5. Palestine, 1947–present.   The United Nations became involved in this "second riddle of the Sphinx" when Great Britain placed before the General Assembly the problem of how to terminate its mandate and establish an independent state in Palestine. In the face of the irreconcilable views of Arabs and Jews as to creating an independent state of Israel within Palestine, the General Assembly nevertheless proceeded to recommend a plan of partition providing for such a state. When Great Britain terminated its mandate without assuming responsibility for implementing the General Assembly's recommendation, the Jews proclaimed the existence of the state of Israel, and warfare immediately broke out between it and the Arab states. Israel charged the Arab states with aggression, while the Arabs denounced the legality both of the United Nations' and Israel's actions and asserted they were being forcibly evicted from territory rightfully theirs. The United Nations was confronted with the immediate problem of stopping hostilities, and, later, with the much deeper issues of effecting a permanent political settlement for Palestine and the disposition

of a million Arab refugees who had been driven from their homes in the course of hostilities.

6. The Kashmir question, 1948–present.   Conflicting claims of India and Pakistan to sovereignty over the states of Kashmir and Jammu, following the ending of British control in 1945, led to hostilities, each charging the other with aggressive actions designed to seize control by force. The Indian government charged Pakistan with assisting raiders to attack the two states after their rulers had declared accession to India. Pakistan charged that Indian troops had marched in before the people (a majority of whom were Muslims), had had a chance to make their desires known, and had thereby prevented a just determination of the disposition of the territory.

7. Hyderabad, 1948.   Still another critical issue came before the United Nations as a result of Indian independence. The Nizam of Hyderabad complained that the existence of his princely state, which lay within the confines of India, was threatened by Indian intimidation and economic blockade; later, the Indian army entered the state and the Indian government took over its effective control. India claimed the question to be one within its domestic jurisdiction.

8. Morocco, Tunisia, and Algeria, 1951–62.   The demand for complete independence by these "protectorates" of France (Algeria was actually considered an integral part of France), and the actions of France in the face of these demands, were precipitated into the United Nations despite vehement French objections that these were strictly internal matters within its own domestic jurisdiction. There they continued to remain until independence was granted successively to each of them.

9. Angola, 1961–present.   In the same pattern, the revolt of Angolans for independence from Portugal is now a regular item on the General Assembly's agenda.

A third group of disputes—the most dangerous—involved at bottom the respective prerogatives and spheres of influence of the major powers in the postwar world. The United Nations was actually not intended to handle such issues. The Charter presumed a settled framework of peace settlements within which the organization would work after World War II. The great crises over Berlin and Korea were, however, the direct consequence of failure of the major powers to conclude the expected peace treaties, and thereby to define the role of the defeated states and the mutual relations of the victors.

1. The Berlin question, 1948–49.   The United Nations Security Council was requested by the United States, Great Britain, and France to act in regard to their claim that the Soviet Union was violating the Potsdam Agreement by imposing a "blockade" on traffic between the Western occupation zones of Germany and Berlin, and by attempting to drive them out of their rightful occupation of Berlin. Previously, the four states had failed to resolve their differences through direct negotiation. The Soviet Union insisted that the Western powers were responsible for the trouble. Should they drop their arrangements for a separate Western currency in Berlin and their plans for a West

German state, which it alleged were in flagrant violation of the Potsdam Agreement, the U.S.S.R. would agree to end the blockade. The West, in turn, insisted that the Soviets stop the blockade unconditionally prior to any reconsideration of the other issues. In the meantime, tension mounted as the Western Allies organized an airlift to supply Berlin with essential commodities and faced the prospect that the Soviet command might use force to expel them from Berlin altogether.

2. Korea, 1947–present. The problem of Korean independence first came before the United Nations in late 1947, after negotiations had broken down between the Soviet and American occupation authorities over the procedure of unifying the country and establishing a permanent and independent Korean government. The United States proposed that the United Nations take on the responsibility for establishment of a Korean National government, in consultation with Korean representatives and on the basis of free elections internationally supervised. The Soviet Union objected to this approach, refused to cooperate with the United Nations Commissions appointed for the purpose, and by the end of 1948 formally recognized creation of a Supreme National Assembly in North Korea, with full political authority. The United Nations faced the impasse of a Korea divided between two irreconcilable governments, each pledged to unification and independence, but neither ready to concede the conditions demanded by the other. To add to its embarrassment, the United Nations had recognized the Republic of Korea established under its oversight, but was unable as a consequence to make any contact with the North Korean regime, which held that it alone had proper authority.

When the situation erupted into violence with the North Korean attack on June 25, 1950, efforts to deal with the underlying controversy gave way immediately to mobilization of enforcement action to repel the attack. The U.N.'s machinery of conciliation was to all effects pushed aside until the devastating trial of arms had run its course and ground to a military stalemate. By July, 1951, the United Nations again confronted essentially the same issues in regard to the unification and independence of Korea, and faced once again the necessity of attempting settlement by conciliation.

The fourth group of cases concerned the international commitments of states to respect human rights. These are examined in detail in a later chapter, but in summary the principal issues were these:

1. The treatment of Indians in South Africa. In 1946, India called on the General Assembly to take action in regard to legislative discrimination by the Union of South Africa against the Indian minority, allegedly in violation of an agreement between the two countries to grant equal treatment to their respective nationals. The South African government maintained that this was entirely within its domestic jurisdiction and, hence, not a proper concern either of India or the United Nations.

2. South Africa's apartheid policies of racial discrimination. These have caused mounting concern as the United Nations has reflected the rise to political independence of colored people, and their sensitivity to any continuance of dis-

crimination, let alone the extreme measures of segregation adopted by the Union of South Africa.

3. Religious trials in Hungary, Bulgaria, and Romania. As a result of the trials of Cardinal Mindszenty and other religious leaders in Hungary, Bulgaria, and Romania, a wide group of Latin American and other Western nations accused these countries before the General Assembly of suppressing religious freedom and denying fundamental civil rights in direct contradiction of provisions of their peace treaties with the United Nations, guaranteeing full respect for such human rights. The accused states, not then members of the United Nations, rejected the charges as unfounded and refused to submit either to arbitration as specified in the treaties or to investigation by the General Assembly. The Soviet bloc, of course, took their part in the debates before the United Nations, and so the question inescapably became entangled with the cold war.

Hopefully, both the second and third groups of disputes mentioned above are "nonrepeatable." That is, once the basic lines of the mid-twentieth-century international political order are decided on, with reference, on the one hand, to disposition of the Axis territories and, on the other, to establishment of the colonial heirs to dissolving empires, then these basic issues ought to be laid to rest. For example, it appears unlikely that the Indonesian–Netherlands question will arise again in any serious fashion, because the fundamental issue—independence of the "colonials"—has evidently been disposed of by the parties directly concerned.

In the long run, therefore, the United Nations' conciliation capacities will be tested chiefly over the issue of maintaining the independence of existing "sovereign" states against the intervention of other states, large and small, in pursuit of their respective national interests. The problem of reconciling respect for national sovereignty with the exigencies of the "politics of power" is the really fundamental peacemaking task for the United Nations. It will stand or fall as a mediator by its effectiveness in persuading the superpowers to refrain from excessively rude and dictatorial domination over nations that do not willingly choose to cast their lot with one or the other.

THE STRATEGY OF U.N. CONCILIATION

The outstanding characteristic of United Nations conciliation has been its frankly pragmatic approach. Each situation has been handled with a view to discovering a basis upon which the particular protagonists would be willing at least to consult and, hopefully, negotiate in regard to the issues in dispute. No set formula or routine procedure of conciliation has crystallized. If initial recommendations were disregarded by one or more of the parties, United Nations organs willingly reconsidered the problem and sought to devise another and more acceptable approach. For the most part, the United

Nations has set aside considerations of its own prestige and of abstract justice and tried, instead, to find whatever approach would be most effective in dissuading the disputants from aggravating the situation, and in encouraging them to compromise their differences.

In the process of trial and error, the United Nations has developed four main types of conciliatory action.

A Hearing for All

From the beginning, the United Nations has adopted the practice of holding a general public hearing of the case, with all interested parties permitted to present their points of view directly before the Security Council or the General Assembly. On several occasions, the competence of the U.N. to hold such a hearing, or to permit representatives of some of the concerned parties to speak, has been challenged, but the U.N. has stood its ground. The Soviet Union objected in the Iranian case to Security Council consideration as long as direct negotiations were allegedly in progress between Iran and the U.S.S.R. But the Council insisted that it had an obligation to consider the case because the Iranian government had appealed to it. Thereupon, the Soviet delegate initiated the practice of boycotting the discussions as "illegal." Yet, the Council held the case on its agenda, pending an outcome it was convinced was satisfactory. In the early stages of the Palestinian crisis, the Arab states protested in vain the seating of a representative of the Jewish Agency during Security Council debate and in the General Assembly, on the grounds that only acknowledged national states were permitted to take part in U.N. deliberations. The Netherlands and India protested respectively the hearing of representatives of the Indonesian Republic and of Hyderabad, claiming in each case that they did not represent sovereign states. In each of these situations, the United Nations organ, sidestepping technical legal issues, agreed to listen to the representatives even before deciding whether to place the case officially on its agenda. The same decision was made in regard to a representative of the Republic of Korea, though a Soviet demand that representatives of the North Korean government be heard was turned down on the basis that no regime actually engaged in aggressive action was entitled to a hearing.

A most dramatic illustration of the United Nations' readiness to extend a hearing to any authority in a situation threatening the peace was the invitation to the Chinese People's Republic to present its charges regarding United States relations with Formosa directly before the Security Council. At a moment when Chinese Communist intervention was already under way against United Nations forces in Korea, General Wu was seated at the Council table in Lake Success, and he proceeded to denounce the United States, principal power behind the United Nations Korean action, for its Far Eastern policies.

It is clear that the United Nations has intended by this assurance of a full and fair hearing of all sides to reduce the excuses for arbitrary and precipitous action by one party or the other, and to confront the protagonists with the necessity for convincing others than their own peoples of the validity of their policies and claims. Such a hearing also lays the foundation for whatever further action the U.N. may wish to take, for it provides essential information and establishes direct, face-to-face contact between the U.N organ and the parties with whom it will have to deal.

Appeal for Another Try at Direct Negotiation

The United Nations has also inclined, especially in its earlier attempts at peaceful settlement, to the tactic of encouraging the parties to work out an agreement through direct negotiations and to report progress to the U.N. It has, in effect, tossed the problem back to the parties. But by assuming responsibility for the renewed initiative, the U.N. has sought to relieve both parties of the onus of backing down from the previous impasse. The U.N. has generally favored this procedure when hostilities were not too imminent, and when the parties were sufficiently responsive, reserving more active intervention until the situation reached a more critical state. For instance, the Security Council successfully prevailed on the U.S.S.R. and Iran to reopen negotiations, and to report results by a set date. Though the Soviet Union balked at the Council's assuming even this much responsibility, the negotiations proceeded to a mutually satisfactory conclusion. This was also the result of the U.N.'s encouraging the Dutch and Indonesians to negotiate directly over West Irian (though one may question whether the conclusion was genuinely "satisfactory" to anyone but the Indonesians).[5]

Fact-Finding and Good Offices

Where such negotiation has not appeared feasible or has failed to produce a settlement, the United Nations has itself undertaken either to ascertain and publicize the facts in the situation, or to promote reconciliation through the tender of its good offices. Frequently, these two functions have been combined, with the fact-finding mission's being authorized to facilitate the exchange of information and views between the disputants. Acting on the Greek question, the Security Council set up a commission to investigate on-the-spot the charges and countercharges regarding border violations and assistance to guerrillas. Each Balkan country involved in the controversy appointed liaison officers to the commission to assist it in securing access to the areas concerned. When the Soviet Union objected to the majority findings, and vetoed action by the Council on the basis of this report, the

---

[5] See Paul W. van der Veur, "The United Nations in West Irian: A Critique," *International Organization,* Winter. 1964.

question was dropped from the Council's agenda. The General Assembly thereupon created another commission, authorizing it not only to observe on the scene, but also to explore any means of establishing contact between the parties and fostering consultations between them to resolve their controversies.

The Indonesian question was at first approached very cautiously, with the Security Council merely requesting those of its members who had consuls stationed in Batavia to secure factual information from them regarding the conflict. In due course, the Council appointed a Committee of Good Offices, and this body established liaison between the Indonesian and Dutch leaders, paving the way for negotiation of the short-lived Renville Agreement, halting hostilities. Throughout the proceedings, the Committee scrupulously refrained from initiating proposals for a settlement, thus limiting its function strictly to serving as go-between in the traditional conception of "good offices."

Direct Mediation by the United Nations

In most of the major crises the U.N. has faced, the organization sooner or later assumed the role of active mediator, acting either directly or through a special commission or agent appointed for the purpose.

By an Individual Mediator. The outbreak of full-scale warfare in Palestine led the Security Council to empower Count Folke Bernadotte as United Nations Mediator to seek the bases of a truce, to supervise its execution, and to negotiate an armistice. With the assistance of a small staff from the U.N. Secretariat headed by Ralph Bunche, he went personally to the Arab and Israel leaders, asked for their respective terms for a temporary truce, himself proposed compromises of disputed points, secured acceptance by both sides (deliberately overlooking certain reservations), and set the date for ceasefire. Moving from truce to armistice proved a much more protracted and complicated matter, with charges and countercharges of breaking the truce, flareups of fighting, and, above all, an atmosphere so filled with mutual bitterness and animosity as to make effective negotiation of the vital issues impossible for a long time. Nevertheless, Mr. Bunche, who became acting mediator after Count Bernadotte was assassinated in Palestine, persisted in trying to bring the opposing sides together. With the backing of the Council, which insistently warned both sides against renewed fighting and demanded that they honor their commitments under the Charter to settle disputes peacefully, he finally persuaded the parties to meet on the island of Rhodes. He personally presided over the delicate proceedings which ultimately produced the armistice.

By the Secretary-General. In due course, the United Nations discovered its most potent resource for the diplomacy of mediation in the Office of Secretary-General, particularly when it could call on Dag Hammarskjöld's exceptional personal gift for this kind of statecraft. Directly or through a personal representative, he would explore the bases of controversy, propose procedures for negotiation, and sometimes suggest possible terms of a mutually acceptable agreement, always working carefully within the framework of Security Council or General Assembly resolutions (to whose drafting he lent a deft hand) and constantly reminding the disputants of their fundamental obligations under the Charter to keep the peace. This "preventive diplomacy," as Hammarksjöld called it, was skillfully applied in such divergent situations as the long complex of Middle Eastern crises and the always festering problem of Berlin, and even outside the U.N. family in arranging with the Chinese Communists for release of American fliers who had come down in Chinese territory.[6]

A noteworthy example of the Hammarskjöld technique was his mission to the Middle East in the spring of 1956, in an attempt to reestablish compliance with the armistice agreements and prevent a major blowup. His report to the Security Council, May 10, 1956, outlined a set of arrangements to which he had been able to win the assent of both Israel and the Arab states—a masterful achievement, demonstrating a clear understanding of the positions and circumstances of both sides, an astute sense of how to appeal to each, firmness in insisting on their fulfillment of obligations, and imagination in devising practical steps to reduce tensions. Unfortunately, the lid the Secretary-General's mediation had succeeded in fitting over the Middle Eastern kettle was blown off by a series of unilateral actions from outside the region by the U.S., Britain, and France vis-à-vis Egypt which ended up in the Suez Canal crisis and military attack on Egypt. What Hammarskjöld could not anticipate and forestall was the impact of precipitous and benighted great power diplomacy.

By the Security Council "Neutrals."   A different procedure of mediation was followed in the Berlin crisis. Representatives of the six nonpermanent members of the Security Council themselves assumed the task of mediation, under the leadership of Dr. Bramuglia, of Argentina, who was serving as Council president at the time. They sounded out the Western powers and the U.S.S.R.—in private consultations outside the limelight of the formal Council meetings—as to the technical issues in dispute, especially the controversy over currency reform in Berlin, and tried to persuade both sides to reduce the scope of their controversy to these specific questions. Specialists on the U.N. Secretariat, under the direction of Gunnar Myrdal, Director of the Economic Commission for Europe, drafted a plan designed to satisfy the essential economic conditions demanded by both sides. The "neutral powers" pressed for a settlement on the basis of such a technical agreement, urging

---

[6] Some of these incidents have been reported in previous chapters, see particularly Chapters 2 and 7.

both sides to lay aside the essentially unnegotiable questions of legal right and principle that each had by then advanced to the forefront of the controversy. In other words, they tried—unsuccessfully—to separate the political from the technical issues in dispute, and to put the powers in a position where they could achieve a mutually satisfactory settlement of the technical ones without loss of face, provided they would simply reserve their positions on the political ones.

By the General Assembly.   A fourth pattern of U.N. mediation was developed by the General Assembly in regard to the Greek question. In the fall of 1948, and again during its fourth session in 1949, the Assembly appointed a Conciliation Committee under the leadership of the President of the Assembly to meet with representatives of the four concerned Balkan states as well as the big powers, and to attempt to devise a formula for reestablishing normal relations. As in the Berlin question, the negotiations were kept private and personal. Similarly, promising progress toward agreement on the more technical issues ran into an impasse on broader political questions. The countries agreed in principle to the cessation of military hostilities on Greece's frontiers and to the guarantee of each other's territorial integrity. But Greece renewed her old claim to Northern Epirus (currently a part of Albania), and this was rejected by Albania with the backing of the U.S.S.R. The Communist states' demand for new Greek elections and the withdrawal of all foreign military assistance from Greece was unacceptable to Greece and her Anglo-American guardians.

By International Commission.   A fifth procedure of direct mediation has been the appointment of an international commission empowered to seek a settlement in negotiations with the states involved. In the Kashmir dispute, the Security Council, after its initial hearing of the case, asked three nations to designate representatives on a commission instructed to arrange a cease-fire, then effect a permanent truce, and finally work out the bases of a permanent solution of the issue. The commission conferred in India and Pakistan as well as in Kashmir proper with leaders of all concerned groups. There was such disagreement on both the basic issues involved and the prerequisites demanded by each side before they would begin negotiation that the commission finally made a series of proposals itself. One plan was rejected by India, another by Pakistan. The commission then made a last attempt to secure a formula that would enable hostilities to stop with assurance that the ultimate issue would be decided by a plebiscite. Receiving no encouragement from India, the commission left and reported back to the Council that it had not been able to fulfill its mission. Before the Council could seriously consider what to do next, however, India and Pakistan agreed to accept the commission's proposal, and announced the ending of hostilities on January 1, 1949.

The United Nations has used mediation or conciliation commissions on other occasions. After the armistice was arranged in Palestine by the acting mediator, a commission representing France, Turkey, and the United States attempted to effect a permanent peace settlement, which would fix the frontiers of the state of Israel, provide for the reestablishment or compensation of Arab refugees, and safeguard the status of Jerusalem. So deep were the differences between the Israeli and Arab governments that the commission decided not to initiate face-to-face negotiations, and, actually, it has done no more than to keep in regular contact with the various parties, watching for some sign of a change in their outlook that would justify more positive action.

In regard to Indonesia, the Security Council went the whole way from mere fact-finding, through the state of good offices, to appointment of a full-fledged mediating commission, as the situation progressively deteriorated. The commission consisted of representatives of the United States, India, and Australia, and came into being when the initial cease-fire agreement was broken by a Dutch "police action," which quickly resulted in seizure of the Indonesian Republican leaders and capital. The situation was further complicated because the Dutch denied the competence of the United Nations to intervene on the grounds that the whole question was within their domestic jurisdiction. Nevertheless, the Dutch finally yielded to the demands of the Security Council (apparently backed by strong direct pressure from the United States), and agreed to release the Indonesian leaders and negotiate with them directly, in the presence of the United Nations Commission. The role of the Commission was, therefore, transformed from outright mediation into friendly oversight, and the Dutch were able in the end to claim that they alone were responsible for effecting the agreement relinquishing sovereignty over Indonesia.[7]

Supervision of Agreements

In the course of its efforts at conciliation, the United Nations has undertaken certain special tasks of international supervision and administration to assure the proper fulfillment of agreements reached. This has been of particular importance in connection with implementation of cease-fire and truce arrangements. The United Nations has generally considered it essential to bring any fighting to a halt and to guard against its sudden renewal by one side or the other before undertaking settlement of fundamental issues. The reasons are obvious. Dispassionate deliberation and negotiation on the basis of the merits of the case are ruled out if each protagonist fears the other may at any moment seize its objectives by force. Furthermore, access to facts needed to work out a reasonable settlement is difficult if not impossible while fighting is in progress (for instance, determining the wishes of the people in

---

[7] The Indonesian case is discussed in detail in Chapter 20.

the territory). In addition, the continuance of hostilities can easily produce a raft of new problems and issues to resolve, such as the fate of refugees and the rehabilitation of devastated areas.

The United Nations has unhesitatingly assumed the position of neutral overseer in the execution of cease-fire agreements. In Palestine, the mediator not only effected the agreement in the first place, including the demarcation of the cease-fire line, but organized and directed on-the-spot patrol of the line by international truce teams, investigated charges of truce violation, demanded amends where justified, and reported to the United Nations whenever he felt one party had not properly lived up to its agreement. Similar, though not as extensively organized, action was taken in Kashmir and Indonesia.

In the Kashmir situation, the United Nations also proposed that it assume responsibility for conducting the plebiscite which India and Pakistan had agreed would determine the fate of the territory. An Administrator was appointed for this purpose, but could not secure Indian consent to the arrangements he considered essential to assure a fair and free vote, such as the prior withdrawal of both Indian and Pakistani forces. He thereupon resigned, and negotiations are still at an impasse in regard to the terms for the plebiscite. The Indians further objected to the United Nations' assuming temporary responsibility for civil administration during the time the plebiscite was in preparation, contending that the local authorities (sympathetic to India) should be undisturbed in their regular functions, while the United Nations Administrator should merely conduct the vote and check the results. To this, the Pakistani objected that only outside administration of the civil government as well as of the election itself could insure the population against intimidation or undue influence.

THE BALANCE SHEET OF UNITED NATIONS CONCILIATION

Clear calculation of the effects of United Nations conciliation is hardly possible as yet. Efforts to settle several of the disputes are still in progress. Other cases are deadlocked at the moment, yet they have not degenerated into war. Adequate information is not yet available regarding the various influences, apart from U.N. action, which affected the outcome of the controversies, as well as the actual impact of U.N. action itself on the policies and conduct of the principal protagonists. Nevertheless, on the record as now established, the initiative in conciliation undertaken by the United Nations appears to have been instrumental in bringing about the settlements that were achieved, or in freezing the currently unsettled situations short of a solution dictated by force.

In several cases, definite and apparently permanent settlements were reached. The Soviet Union withdrew its troops from Iran, and acknowledged Iranian authority over the border province of Azerbaijan, with the understanding that the Iranian government would grant 50-50 oil concessions to Russia in the northern parts of the country. Though the Iranian Parliament did not consent to the oil arrangement, the Soviet Union has not so far abrogated its part of the agreement. The Indonesian crisis was ultimately resolved when the Netherlands and Indonesian leaders agreed on terms for establishment of an independent state of Indonesia, and later for the transfer of sovereignty over West Irian. British and French troops and military authorities were withdrawn from Syria and Lebanon. The Corfu Channel dispute was brought before the International Court of Justice for a verdict. The 1948 Berlin case was finally resolved by direct negotiation outside the United Nations, but U.N. mediation paved the way for agreement. The same was true of the Balkan conflict between Greece and its Communist neighbors.

In such critical cases as Palestine and Kashmir, hostilities were brought to a stop and the basis laid for negotiations to settle the outstanding issues, but the process of peacemaking stalled short of final settlement.

Some situations have been completely deadlocked, and all United Nations action frustrated, though as yet there is no war. The Union of South Africa has turned down or ignored the various proposals of the General Assembly to negotiate with India in regard to its treatment of the Indian minority, and has completely rejected all moves to temper its apartheid policies. The same has happened with regard to U.N. action in regard to Hungary.

The United Nations has, in effect, defaulted on several cases. Though the matter of Hyderabad was placed on the Security Council agenda, no attention was given the matter after India took over administration of the state and compelled its ruler to withdraw his representations to the Council. On Chinese Nationalist charges against the U.S.S.R., the General Assembly expressed concern but indefinitely postponed action of either a conciliatory or enforcement character. The Assembly similarly refrained from taking any real steps to deal with the charges leveled against Russia in connection with the Czech Communist coup. Assembly condemnation of the religious trials in Eastern European countries and appeals for international adjudication of the issues raised were categorically repudiated by the concerned countries, and no further action appeared possible. The major failure to be chalked up is, of course, Korea. Whatever the outcome of the United Nations enforcement action, its efforts at conciliation, such as they were, were completely ineffectual even in regard to establishing a line of contact between the opposing sides, let alone in achieving bonafide negotiations looking toward a settlement. At a matter of fact, no real process of conciliation was undertaken in this situation. Instead, United Nations action resulted in its virtual identification with one of the parties to the dispute. Consequently, its offers at conciliation were repudiated by the other side as being insincere and spurious.[8]

The balance sheet thus presents a mixed picture of positive achievement, of deadlock, and of outright failure. What factors have tipped the scales in favor of, or against, the success of the United Nations in its conciliatory missions?

In the first place, the promptness with which the United Nations acted had a lot to do with its effectiveness. Even when there was considerable doubt as to the outcome of a particular course of action, a quick decision to intervene in a case usually forestalled precipitous action by one side or another which would have aggravated the situation. Conversely, delay by the United Nations and the consequent uncertainty as to what it might do (if anything) tempted nations to take unilateral action designed to strengthen or consolidate their positions. For instance, even though the Security Council did no more in the Iranian case than to hear Iran's complaint, urge further negotiations with the Soviet Union, and set a deadline for a report, the net effect was to ease tension that had arisen over the seeming impasse and to reduce the fear that Russia would force a decision. An atmosphere of watchful waiting developed, while the new negotiations progressed. By contrast, reluctance of the United Nations to act swiftly to guard against the outbreak of violence in Palestine and its long delay and hesitancy in pressing for a general settlement in Indonesia led to a serious worsening of relations between the states concerned and finally to direct hostilities. When even under such difficult conditions the United Nations reacted vigorously and quickly, its mediation commanded respect and even succeeded in inducing the surrender of momentary advantages gained by force when the protagonists realized the U.N. was on the job.

Second, the choice of personnel and the nature of its responsibility for mediation profoundly affected the results of U.N. action. On the whole, commissions composed of nationally designated representatives have been far less effective in the task of conciliation than have individuals chosen directly by the United Nations for the job at hand. The Kashmir, Korea, Palestine, and Balkans commissions and the Indonesia Good Offices Committee were slow, ponderous, indecisive, and sometimes inept. Even assuming good intentions and earnest effort on the part of the commission members—which was not by any means characteristic of all—they were hamstrung by the necessity of acting on their own government's instructions, as well as being accountable to the U.N. There was the constant possibility of serious division of opinion within the commission which would render it incapable of firm and clear action.[9]

---

[8] Leon Gordenker, *The United Nations and the Peaceful Unification of Korea* (The Hague: M. Nijhoff, 1959), provides a thorough study of this case.

[9] In regard to the Korean Commissions, see the trenchant critique of Gordenker, *op. cit.*

On the other hand, persons like Count Bernadotte, Ralph Bunche, and Frank Graham, chosen for their personal qualifications of unquestioned integrity, impartiality, and skill in negotiation and given wide discretion in the conduct of their relationships with the opposite governments, with a clear line of responsibility to an organ of the United Nations, were able to move quickly and directly to the heart of the problems.

The skill and experience of personnel assigned from the Secretariat to service the commissions and mediators was, likewise, of basic importance to their success. As the Secretariat learned from initial situations, it was able to contribute a greater sensitivity and know-how in the process of conciliation. Indeed, it is doubtful whether most of the commissions would have achieved any positive results without the constant guidance of the staff. This contribution has been cumulative as national governments developed respect for and confidence in the U.N personnel with whom they have had to deal. Perhaps the most significant result of the Palestine mediation was the worldwide reputation it gained for the peacemaking potentialities of the U.N. staff, which had become personified in Mr. Bunche. A most vital asset in the task of conciliation is the initial trust of the disputants in the mediator. If he can start with such trust, rather than having to win grudging acceptance, he can act with much greater speed and effect.

Third, the use of publicity by the United Nations seems to have had a generally wholesome effect, tempering national intransigence by the knowledge that a full accounting would take place sooner or later before the "bar of world opinion." On the other hand, shielding negotiations in their more delicate stages has been essential to promote give-and-take and a readiness to accept compromises. The United Nations has not been successful on many occasions in striking the proper balance between open and closed diplomacy in conciliation. Premature open debates hardened opposing positions to the point where compromise was virtually ruled out in the Greek and Korean situations, for instance, as well as in the Chinese Communist charges against the U.S. Yet, in the Palestine mediation was achieved a judicious mixture of open and vigorous Security Council discussion and of thoroughly private face-to-face talk between the mediator and the respective government leaders. This permitted publicity to function when the governments adopted so stubborn or unreasonable a stand as to endanger the whole course of negotiations, but shielded the negotiators from public criticism or pressures while they were seriously seeking grounds for agreement on specific issues in dispute. Effective conciliation has thus depended on the proper use and timing of open diplomacy, rather than on unlimited freedom of publicity.[10]

---

[10] The tendency among diplomatists and scholars alike is to favor privacy in negotiation, but U.N. experience demonstrates that public discussion can exert a constructive influence under some conditions. For a crisp discussion of the issue, see Lincoln Bloomfield, *The United Nations and U.S. Foreign Policy* (Boston: Little, Brown, 1960), pp. 141–42.

Fourth, of the various techniques that have been employed, no particular method of action appears to have been more successful than others, nor is there a clear indication that some methods have uniformly failed. Appeal for direct negotiations was sufficient in the Iranian and Syrian–Lebanese cases, but had no effect as between Egypt and the United Kingdom, or at one stage of the Kashmir dispute. U.N. fact-finding contributed to settlement of the Indonesian crisis, but had little appreciable effect in the Balkans, and was sharply rejected by Czechoslovakia and the satellite countries of Eastern Europe in the human rights cases. Airing the case before the United Nations helped in the Palestine mediation and Indonesia, but accomplished little or nothing in regard to Hyderabad, the South African cases, or Korea.

Fifth, insofar as the effectiveness of the different organs of the United Nations is concerned, the Security Council has for the most part made a more telling contribution than the General Assembly, thus confirming the original expectations of the Charter which assigned to the Council "primary responsibility" for the maintenance of peace. Most of the cases ultimately settled were handled by the Council, as were the Kashmir and Palestine mediations which, to date, have gone part way toward settlement. Many of the deadlocked or "defaulted" cases were handled exclusively by the General Assembly or by both Assembly and Council.

This suggests that the processes of conciliation have not suffered badly because of the veto in the Security Council. As a matter of fact, the veto has rarely kept the Council from *some* action under its peaceful settlement responsibilities (Chapter 7); its effect has been to block a *particular* course of action and force the Council to hunt for a more generally acceptable approach.

Actually, the Security Council has demonstrated rather exceptional capacities to deal with the complex problems laid before it. Its compactness has made for relatively expeditious action, while the diversity of the nations composing it has assured, in almost every instance, the fair presentation of conflicting points of view. Members of the Council have appeared acutely conscious of the weight of responsibility resting on each of them and have usually given painstaking attention to the issues before them. Because of its limited size, the Council has been able to conduct informal consultations "behind the scenes" to work over points of disagreement and find a mutually satisfactory plan of action. This has also resulted in considerable flexibility in the Council's approach to a controversy, and an ability to reconsider its steps when they have misfired. An excellent example of this adaptability to circumstances occurred in the Berlin situation, 1948–49. When faced with the unprecedented involvement in the dispute of four of its permanent members, the Council virtually transformed itself on the spot into an informal conciliation conference, with the "neutral" states striving to find grounds for agreement. While their efforts did not, at the moment, succeed, they narrowed the issues to a point where reconsideration by the disputants after the Council formally dropped the case led to a renewal of direct negotiations and an agreement. In this situation, the Council could not be persuaded to act according to any established procedure, or to invoke any of its presumed powers. What it improvised however, was sensitive to the delicacy of the situation. It recognized the limits of its capacities, and in the very act of confessing its inability to go further than it did made the great powers aware that in this instance they had to assume full responsibility for the consequences of their actions.[11]

The Assembly's behavior on similar questions has not shown any such sensitivity to the requirements of the situation, but rather a susceptibility to pressure for a vote that would define a stand or call for a sharp decision and a plan of action. The Palestine and Korean situations are cases in point. Rather than exploring patiently what means might ease the tensions between the opposing parties and enlist some measure of cooperation from all concerned in the dispute, the Assembly ground inexorably to a vote on fixed and rigid resolutions, identified with interests of one side or the other. Voting was primarily in accordance with "bloc" alignments, and was hardly ever modified by concern to meet the objections or counterproposals of those nations directly involved. In the end, the voted action aggravated rather than relieved the tension, and in both situations probably helped to precipitate violence.

These developments also indicate that the effectiveness of the United Nations as a conciliator depends very largely on a sixth factor—namely, its ability to maintain in its action as a world body a position of impartiality between the disputants. It cannot afford to espouse the cause of one side if it is attempting to bring about a settlement acceptable to both sides. Action such as approving partition of Palestine in opposition to the vehement feelings of the Arabs or establishment of the Republic of Korea on terms rejected by the North Koreans amounted to rendering a decisive judgment on the merits of the case. This is appropriate when both sides have agreed to adjudicate their controversy. But it disqualifies the "third party" as a conciliator if one side insists that the judgment is repugnant and unacceptable.

The ability of the U.N. to remain impartial has, of course, been deeply undermined by the hostility between the Western powers and the Soviet bloc. The cold war has engendered a vicious struggle for control and use of the United Nations as an instrument in the interests of the opposed groups. As the controversies brought before the U.N. came to mirror the clash of Soviet and Western aims, demands become more and more peremptory on

---

[11] The Council's reputation is undergoing considerable rehabilitation. See, for instance, the strong case made on its behalf by the Commission to Study the Organization of Peace. 13th Report, *Developing the United Nations* (New York: The American Association for the United Nations, 1961), pp. 25–30.

U.N. organs to take an unequivocal stand on one side or the other. When a majority of the Council or Assembly yielded and went on record as supporting the course of action proposed by the Western powers, the work of conciliation stopped dead.

By contrast, where the disputes have not stemmed from the cold war, and the great powers have not been in direct conflict over them, the U.N. has generally kept impartial and, as a result, has sooner or later been able to secure acceptance of its mediating role by both sides. This has happened even when one of the protagonists was itself a great power and a permanent member of the Security Council. However grudgingly, Britain, the U.S.S.R., France, and the U.S. have on one occasion or another acquiesced in the United Nations' intervention in their disputes with smaller states, even though they have not always accepted the U.N.'s proposals for settlement. This has, at least in part, been due to the realization that to flaunt the concern of a body of nations that was acting essentially without partisanship would have the likely effect of convincing many of those nations of the unworthiness of the great power's case. So long as the U.N. could maintain its nonpartisanship, both sides to a dispute had cause to temper their actions lest they incur a serious loss of prestige and respect. But as soon as the U.N. identified itself with one side, the other ceased to have any substantial incentive to cooperate.

The U.N. is now in grave danger of having its potentiality for conciliation compromised in disputes between "new" and "old" nations, and between the "underdeveloped" and the "developed." The U.N. majority is now overwhelmingly weighted in favor of the new and underdeveloped, and emotions run so deep that these countries find it impossible to allow the U.N. to adopt an impartial, or noncommitted, stance in regard to questions that strike to the moral and political roots of their vital interests.

A seventh factor is crucial. However circumspect the United Nations may be in maintaining impartiality and however skillful in organizing and conducting its mediation, it has been quite evident that in the last analysis its effectiveness in conciliation depends on a minimum measure of support from the great powers. It has not been, nor will it ever be, in a position to force an unacceptable solution on a great power. Indeed, it is unlikely that without the active support of several of these powers, disputes between the smaller states could have been resolved to the extent they were. Only when the United States put full weight behind the Council in the Indonesian conflict and backed vigorous intervention by the U.N. did the Dutch cooperate substantially with the Council. Mediation in Palestine was tremendously strengthened because both Russia and U.S. actively supported it. The responsibility of the great powers for U.N. conciliation is thus a difficult and delicate one. They must not interject their special interests and conflicts into the machinery to the point where they destroy the capacity of the organization to remain impartial; but if they do not concern themselves sufficiently with the controversies, the U.N. efforts will have an inadequate impact on the situations.

Finally, a basic limitation on U.N. conciliation must be admitted. There are some issues it probably cannot touch. First, fundamental questions of the balance of power between the major states lie outside its competence. This was recognized from the beginning in excluding from its responsibility the problems arising in connection with occupation of the Axis enemies and conclusion of peace settlements with them. Second, states are apparently unwilling to accept U.N. intervention even in the interests of conciliation of international tension when they consider the issues essentially within their domestic jurisdiction. Nor are they any more amenable if these issues are ruled by the United Nations itself to be "of international concern." Many of the cases in which no real progress toward a settlement has been achieved concerned such allegedly domestic matters: Communist seizure of power in Czechoslovakia; the similar occurrence in China (coupled with charges of Russian intervention); the Indians in South Africa; the apartheid policies; Soviet intervention in Hungary; the religious trials in Hungary, Bulgaria, and Romania; and the matter of Hyderabad. This same allegation of domestic jurisdiction was, furthermore, a major obstacle to effective conciliation in Indonesia, Kashmir, and Korea. One must expect further difficulty at this point, as long as the United Nations is unable to set up a generally acceptable procedure for determining what is, and what is not, within its sphere of responsibility, and as long as nations persist in claiming the right to decide for themselves when they will arbitrarily exclude all third-party consideration of their action on the ground that it lies within the sanctuary of domestic jurisdiction.

Summing up, the U.N.'s record of conciliation is promising but not perfect. Out of its experience, some of the elements of an effective strategy of international conciliation have emerged. The presence of an impartial third party is all-important. This has been the U.N.'s particular contribution. Its constant initiative in negotiating, exploring, and pressing for possible bases of agreement, and the high degree of its disinterestedness assured by the range of nations represented in it, have been vital in securing the concessions from both sides needed for settlement. While some of the United Nations' efforts have suffered because of inadequate personnel, the organization has been able to make available increasingly competent services from key members of its own Secretariat and from specially gifted individuals recruited from the outside for particular missions. The United Nations has also succeeded in focusing on the disputants the moral pressure of world opinion. By demanding and reiterating that a settlement must be reached by peaceful means, the organization has exercised a powerful influence on the negotiators, often causing them to avoid actions that would make them appear responsible for a breakdown of the conciliation effort and thus expose them to world censure. On the other hand, the threat of forceful coercion was not used by the United Nations to back up its mediation. Many of those who have carried on the work of settlement are convinced that, far from weakening their hands, the lack of enforcement power has actually been an important factor in their success. States were more cooperatively disposed when they knew that no solution would be imposed on them without their consent.[12]

The greatest challenge to the United Nations' peacemaking potential still remains. Can it promote a peaceful settlement between the principals in the world conflict of the cold war and forestall a full-fledged third world war? That this task may not be beyond the competence of the United Nations is evidenced by the important contribution made to the resolution of the Berlin crisis. But bold leadership from outside the Soviet and American coalitions is essential to provide the effective "third party" required for successful mediation in such controversies among the "titans."

In the end, the United Nations cannot compel the nations of the world to keep at peace. The ultimate decisions are up to national governments. But the United Nations can inform, it can appeal, it can persuade, it can maintain contact between hostile states, it can voice the world's will to peace. This is its true vocation in the struggle for world security. Its success will depend not so much on the strength of its "teeth" as on the responsiveness of its members to its reconciling mission.

---

[12] There appears to be a challenging parallel at several points between these findings concerning the experience of the United Nations and the record of conciliation and mediation in labor-management controversies, especially in the U.S. For a systematic comparison of peacemaking in these two areas, based on a study by a joint panel of experts in both fields, see Elmore Jackson, *Meeting of Minds* (New York: McGraw-Hill, 1952).

PART II

PROMOTING ECONOMIC WELFARE

Chapter 12

Arteries of Welfare:
The Channels of International
Communication

Increasingly, it has become the business of governments to promote the welfare of their peoples. And, increasingly, it has become apparent that under modern conditions of economic enterprise this cannot be accomplished without an elaborate exchange of resources among countries.

The problem of insuring the elemental requirements of livelihood, let alone a good and prosperous life, has therefore activated the development of international cooperative effort fully as much as the pursuit of peace and the struggle for national security. Indeed, the yen for economic security has stimulated by far the largest commitment to the regulation and organization of international relations, measured in terms of financial investment, range of action, and persons servicing international operations.

These efforts have moved in two main directions. One has involved the task of maintaining physical channels of mobility among nations—keeping open the arteries of commerce and communication by sea, land, and air. This has been accomplished by a wide variety of international regulatory arrangements and by a growing amount of coordinated technological services. This chapter reviews and appraises these developments.

In a second line of welfare action, certain nations have undertaken an extraordinary series of programs of mutual economic assistance, designed in the first instance to generate recovery from the immense devastation and dislocation left by world war. Growing recognition that economic interdependence is a permanent and globally pervasive fact of the twentieth century, whose consequences no country can hope to dodge, persuaded many governments to continue cooperative action, with a view, on the one hand, to effecting a fundamental and lasting international integration of their economic functions and, on the other, to resolving the riddle of persistent underdevelopment in large portions of the world. These unprecedented ventures in international relations are the subject of most of this section, Chapters 12 to 15.

In broad perspective, at issue here is whether a politically pluralistic world of 120 or 125 states, each insisting on a high degree of independence in making decisions that control the behavior of their people, can function with sufficient unity and regard for *mutual* interests to meet welfare conditions imposed by the demands of modern technology for ever more intricate collective human action. *Functional* international cooperation and organization is the principal device so far developed to meet this test. On its success or failure hinges to a large extent the viability of nations as well as the livelihood of peoples. For nations are not likely to survive unless they effectively feed, clothe, and house the human beings that compose them.

Commerce, as much as any other factor, has impressed on nations the advantages of cooperative, rather than antagonistic, relations. The material returns of trade to individuals and, through them, to their home states have depended on the maintenance of conditions of access from one nation to another. Especially when political and technological circumstances conspire to put self-sufficiency out of the reach of most states, their physical survival, let alone their general welfare, requires a steady flow of international commerce.

War—hot and cold—demonstrates the hazards of trying to keep this flow moving in the face of serious international conflicts. In the nineteenth century, even Britain found it difficult to insure by her own might the lines of communication necessary for her global commerce. Strategic theorists could glamorize Britannia's rule of the waves, but British diplomacy (consistently supported by the United States) patiently and steadily pressed for conditions that would avoid the necessity of using arms to keep open the sea-lanes and, in particular, sought to establish by international law the right of everyone to use the seas without interference. Conditions of the twentieth century make unilateral physical control of the media of communication—by air or land as well as by sea—even more precarious.

Gradually, states the world over have come to recognize that their common interest in using the main arteries of commerce could only be satisfied by agreeing on common rules and cooperative arrangements for their regulation. A body of international law, supplemented by specific international agreements, now determines the conditions of access to and use of international channels of transport and communication, while a series of international organizations administers a variety of regulations and services designed to protect and facilitate the flow of commerce among states.

The principles and patterns of regulation are far from uniform or constant, however. They reflect a consensus among concerned states with regard to a particular issue at a particular time. Governments have felt no compunction to be consistent in the rules they apply to the different media of communication, nor do they feel that a rule, once adopted, must remain unchanged if changing conditions make it unsuitable to their interests. Understandably, countries that stand to benefit by continuing an established rule object strenuously when others ask that it be altered. They take the position that change should occur only by common consent. But prevailing practice makes it clear that a rule is only as permanent as its fulfillment of a useful function for *all* those who are expected to abide by it. This is especially apparent now. The many new nations, and others that once had little influence (like the Latin-American states) are demanding and getting a say in adapting the "laws of commerce" to meet their interests more adequately.

Of utmost significance is the tendency for states, especially since the second world war, to treat new problems of international communication when they arise as matters for joint consultation and action, instead of each state's striking out on a separate approach. We can, therefore, expect the network of international regulation governing commercial contact within the community of states to become increasingly consistent and effective.

In the following sections, five major patterns of international regulation are examined; each has emerged as the particular set of arrangements on which concerned governments could agree at a given time for a given channel of communication. (1) In use of the seas, a complex body of international law, based essentially on the principle of national responsibility and jurisdictions, has evolved and is continuing to evolve. (2) A struggle has raged over whether international waterways should be regulated by an international authority or by the riparian states, with the odds now favoring the riparians. (3) Private regulation has largely governed the development of international railroad and road traffic. (4) Regarding use of the air, a rule of reciprocity is generally accepted. (5) Finally, in the area of international postal and telecommunications, true international administration has had a long history of reasonably successful operation.

At the moment, there is no strong indication that a unified approach will emerge. If anything, diversification seems to be increasing, along with a tendency toward asserting greater national, as against international, responsibility. This opens the way to a larger number of serious controversies, gaps in the structure of regulation, and impediments to the full and free flow of commerce and communication among nations. How soon critical impasse will be reached, forcing governments to consider a fundamental reorientation of their policies, is uncertain. In the area of maritime commerce, the point appears imminent on a number of issues, as will be apparent in the analysis which follows.

FREEDOM AND LAW ON THE SEAS—THE ASSERTION OF NATIONAL RESPONSIBILITY

The oldest body of rules commonly applied by states in their international relations concerns use of the seas. Some aspects of the "law of the sea" antedate by at least two centuries the beginning of formal international organization, and even now, maritime regulation is largely carried out by individual national governments through their administrative and judicial processes. Nevertheless, the conduct of maritime commerce is as effectively "organized" and controlled as any other aspect of international life. There are still gaps in the law where states have not fully agreed on an appropriate regulation, and several new issues have arisen for which no generally accepted rules have yet been devised. But states have gone a long way toward defining respective spheres of authority and mutual responsibilities in regulation of shipping and exploitation of the resources of the seas.

The legislative process by which these rules have been adopted has undergone major changes. At first, a rule simply grew out of common practices into a common law of the sea. Settled custom among the users of the seas was—and is—recognized by national courts as adequate evidence of the existence of universally applicable law, just as in England and several other countries the evolving common law has been accepted as an integral part of the domestic legal system.

During the nineteenth and twentieth centuries, a second source came prominently into play. With their eyes set on securing the most favorable possible conditions for maritime commerce, the principal maritime states issued a substantial body of their own national regulations. The British, in particular, laid down in their admiralty law what they considered desirable rules governing the movement and conduct of ships anywhere in the world. Though these regulations presumably were enforceable only in regard to British shipping and in territory and waters under British jurisdiction, the far-flung maritime influence of Britain resulted in many states' acquiescing in many of these regulations for themselves as well. Thus, tacitly or by specific agreement, such national regulations became sufficiently generalized to creep into the body of maritime common law.

Recently, however, states have turned to multilateral treaty-making as the principal procedure for formulating binding rules, and in the case of maritime matters, an ambitious attempt has been begun under United Nations auspices to adopt a set of treaties that would constitute a comprehensive, unified "law of the sea." The International Law Commission prepared proposals laid before two international conferences of concerned states (the Geneva Conferences on the Law of the Sea) which acted, for all practical purposes, as legislative bodies, their actions being subject, however, to ratification by the home governments. It was agreed that provisions acceptable to two-thirds of the participating states would be considered binding as international law (though not on objectors). This procedure was peculiarly significant, because it gave all nations an opportunity to review the existing state of maritime law and determine specifically for themselves what they were prepared to live with, at a time when the validity of many traditional principles was being challenged by states that felt they had had no effective part in shaping them. (86 states participated, making these the most inclusive ad hoc treaty-making conferences ever held.) Furthermore, issues on which there had been no previous general regulation were brought up for action.

The result was clarification and confirmation of a substantial body of rules governing use of the seas in peacetime, involving modification of some earlier positions to meet contemporary needs and the desires of new and smaller states, plus the design of acceptable provisions for handling new problems. There remain important unresolved issues, such as the width of territorial sea to be subject to exclusive jurisdiction of the coastal state. Also, a number of states are holding out for extreme positions at odds with the rules agreed on by the large majority. But a precedent seems to have been established in regard to the process to be followed in international legislating on such questions, and further similar action is anticipated to reach concurrence on the issues still in controversy or on new ones that may arise.[1]

The law of the sea embodies two basic but potentially contradictory principles: (1) freedom for the shipping of any nation to use the seas without interference by any other nation; (2) the independent responsibility of national governments to insure law and order on the seas.

To avoid conflict in the implementation of these principles of international freedom and national regulatory responsibility has required careful limitation of the maritime jurisdiction of each country, so that one nation's policing authority would infringe as little as possible on the shipping of others. This was largely accomplished by agreeing that nations would police their own ships, and also have the right to control ships within a belt of "territorial sea" next to their own shores. Where these jurisdictions overlapped, as in the case of one nation's ship in another's territorial waters, it was generally agreed that the territorial jurisdiction would have priority.

This pattern was developed and refined through practice and the settlement of countless disputes by negotiation and adjudication before national courts and, lately, international tribunals. Its main features have been

---

[1] The development of maritime law, with particular reference to the results of the first Conference on the Law of the Sea, held in Geneva in 1958, is reviewed by Max Sorensen in "The Law of the Sea," *International Conciliation,* November, 1958. Arthur H. Dean reports from the viewpoint of the principal American representative on "The Second Geneva Conference of the Law of the Sea," *American Journal of International Law,* October, 1960. For general critique, see J. L. Brierly, *The Law of Nations* (6th ed.; New York: Oxford University Press, 1963), pp. 194–218 and 222–40; and Percy L. Corbett, *Law and Society in the Relations of States* (New York: Harcourt Brace, 1951), chap. VI.

confirmed in conventions adopted by the 1958 Law of the Sea Conference on: (1) The Territorial Sea and the Contiguous Zone, and (2) The High Seas.[2]

Freedom of the Seas—the Law of Noninterference

After a long struggle against the closed seas policies of most maritime powers in the sixteenth and seventeenth centuries, the doctrine that the seas should be open to all, regardless of nationality, became firmly established. In its classic—and contemporary—form, this fundamental law includes the following provisions.

Freedom of the High Seas.   Every state has the right to sail ships under its flag on the high seas without interference by other states. This includes both freedom of navigation and freedom to fish.[3]

But the nuclear missile age has produced a serious challenge to the principle of freedom of the seas, because the nuclear club (U.S., U.S.S.R., and Britain) has proceeded to use the waters for nuclear testing or as a proving ground for long-range missiles, closing them temporarily to all shipping by unilateral pronouncement. Many states contend that these practices constitute an outright infringement of their rights under the international law of freedom of the seas. There is wide concern, too, over possible contamination of the seas and marine life by nuclear fallout and the results of underwater tests, and also by the disposal of radioactive wastes in the sea. These questions are under debate in the United Nations General Assembly, while the International Atomic Energy Agency has been asked to draw up internationally acceptable standards to prevent radioactive pollution of the sea.[4]

Innocent Passage through Territorial Waters.   Any vessel may traverse the sea immediately adjoining and under the jurisdiction of a coastal state, providing it does not commit acts prejudicial to the security of the state. This does not include the right to fish, however. A coastal state must try to keep the passage unobstructed, and publicize dangers to navigation of which it has knowledge. While it may suspend temporarily and in definite areas the right of passage to protect its security, it must publicize the suspension.

No charge may be levied on foreign vessels for passing through the territorial sea, and the coastal state shall not police the ship unless action on board has consequences that extend to the coastal state or "disturb the peace of the country or the good order of the territorial sea."[5]

---

[2] The text of these conventions is reprinted in the *American Journal of International Law,* October, 1958.

[3] *Ibid.,* Art. 2, Geneva Convention on the High Seas.

[4] See resolutions adopted by the Geneva Conference, April 27, 1958, concerning Nuclear Tests on the High Seas and Pollution of the High Seas by Radioactive Materials. Reprinted in *American Journal of International Law,* October, 1958, p. 864.

[5] Section III Geneva Convention on the Territorial Sea and the Contiguous Zone, *American Journal of International Law,* October, 1958.

There must be no suspension of innocent passage (even for warships) through straits normally used for international navigation between two parts of the high seas.[6] Regarding the Dardanelles, three centuries of struggle over its control has really concerned its military use and not the right of passage of merchant ships in peace, which has been conceded in all the varied conventions since the eighteenth century. The same principle applies to inter-oceanic canals, such as Panama and Suez, by virtue of the treaties negotiated in conjunction with their construction. Even warships have a right of innocent passage under some restrictions.

Access to Ports.   The idea of freedom has finally extended all the way to opening the use of ports, on a basis of equality, to ships of all nations. This principle has come hard, as states have long cherished the facilities of their harbors as something of their very own, to serve primarily their own nationals and to be extended to others only as a privilege and for special "consideration."

But in 1923, the Convention on the International Regime of Maritime Ports was signed, guaranteeing freedom of access to seaports and equality in charges and port facilities, regardless of the vessel's flag. This right was fully confirmed by the 1958 Geneva Convention. Under these principles, even a landlocked state may have an oceangoing fleet, for it need have no ports of its own at which to service its ships.

The Law of National Responsibility

The open seas do not mean lawless seas, however. National governments have individual responsibility under international law to police maritime commerce that comes within their respective jurisdictions, applying their own laws and also the rules of "admiralty" or "maritime" law commonly accepted by all nations. Sometimes jurisdictions overlap, in which case there may be disagreement over which nation shall take priority in regulating. But a long line of national and international judicial decisions and a growing number of conventions have standardized practices and narrowed the number of points of conflict between jurisdictions.

At present, nations exercise regulatory authority over shipping on three main bases: (1) the "law of the flag," (2) sovereignty over territorial waters, and (3) the repression of maritime outlaws.

The "Law of the Flag."   Ships possess the nationality of the state in which they are registered, and sail under its flag. On the high seas, they are under the exclusive jurisdiction of the state whose flag they fly. This means that everyone on the ship, and its owners, are subject to the laws of the flag state, regardless of their personal nationality. The state, in turn, is responsible for enforcing internationally accepted safety regulations concerning the proper use of signals, the load line, rendering assistance to vessels in distress,

---

[6] Decision of the International Court of Justice in the Corfu Channel Case. See discussion in Chapter 10.

and others. States are also responsible for drawing up regulations to prevent pollution of the seas by the discharge of oil from ships or pipelines under its jurisdiction.

In case of collision on the high seas, states other than the flag state may take jurisdiction under the following conditions: (*a*) claim for damages (a civil case) may be brought in the courts of any country where the ship charged with responsibility docks after the collision. (*b*) disciplinary proceedings against the master or other persons in the service of a ship (criminal case) may be instituted before the judicial or administrative authorities of the state of which they are nationals if different from the flag state.[7]

Sovereignty over Territorial Waters. All ships in the ports or territorial waters of a state are subject to its jurisdiction, regardless of the flags they fly, with the reservation noted above, concerning innocent passage. This means the owners of the ship, its operating personnel, and all other persons on board are bound to obey the laws of the territorial state, and it, rather than the flag state, will enforce all applicable maritime regulations. Responsibility for collisions in territorial waters, for instance, is determined in the state that has sovereignty over the area.

Rights of fishing and exploiting other natural resources in or under the territorial seas belong to the coastal state, and it is free to reserve them to its own nationals or extend them to others on whatever terms it chooses.

The coastal state polices its own waters, and can apprehend and punish anyone for violating its security, customs, fishing or other regulations, or international maritime law. There is also agreement that a coastal state may exercise control over a "contiguous zone," extending not more than 12 miles from the coast, to enforce its customs, fiscal, immigration, or sanitary regulations—meaning, in short, to prevent smuggling and catch escaping criminals. Furthermore, under the doctrine of hot pursuit, its patrols may follow a violator out into the high seas and capture it if the pursuit originates in the territorial sea or the contiguous zone and is continuous.[8]

But argument rages over the breadth of the territorial sea. A three-mile

---

[7] In the celebrated Lotus case, the Permanent Court of International Justice decided that criminal proceedings could also be taken by a state whose ship or nationals had received injury (objective jurisdiction). Turkey was upheld (by a closely divided vote) in punishing the French master of a French ship which had collided with a Turkish ship in the Mediterranean. But this decision has been hotly disputed, and in 1952 a Convention on Penal Jurisdiction in Matters of Collisions, signed by a number of major states, specifically dropped this basis of jurisdiction. "Its aim in so doing was to spare vessels and their crews the risk of criminal proceedings before foreign courts in the event of collision on the high seas, since such proceedings may constitute an intolerable interference with international navigation." International Law Commission, Comment on Article 10, Provisional Articles Concerning the Regime of the High Seas, *American Journal of International Law,* January, 1956, p. 200. The Geneva Convention confirms this last position, thus nullifying the Lotus decision.

[8] See, respectively, Article 24 of the Territorial Sea Convention and Article 23 of the High Seas Convention.

limit has been stoutly defended by Britain for over two centuries, and the United States has usually lined up on its side, though from time to time it has whittled away certain exceptions for its own purposes, such as the contiguous zone mentioned above and rights over the continental shelf, discussed below. But this distance has never been universally accepted either by treaty or in practice. Norway claims four miles as the breadth of its territorial waters; Yugoslavia, six; Mexico, nine; and the U.S.S.R., twelve, to mention a representative sampling. Peru, Chile, and Ecuador have gone as far as to claim sovereignty over a 200-mile-wide belt off their coasts, and for Peru, at least, this is not academic. It has made a practice of arresting and imposing huge fines on foreign (especially U.S.) tuna and whaling boats for fishing in this vast expanse. Other Latin-American states have supported this or similar positions.[9]

Reasons for espousing a given breadth also vary. The three-mile claim was originally justified on the grounds that this was the range of gunshot from the coast, hence within the practical capacity of the state to enforce its will; but this has long since ceased to be a valid criterion. The British case now is really twofold: (*a*) it is less complicated for mariners if the limit is uniform throughout the world; (*b*) no distance other than three miles has been set without arousing significant protest.[10] The U.S. feels that for security reasons the belt should be kept narrow; also, its fishermen would be barred from some of the best grounds off Canada, for instance, if the territorial sea was held to be much broader than three miles.[11] On the other hand, states like Norway cite a long historical tradition behind their particular limits. Other states urge that the speed of modern shipping makes effective law and security enforcement impossible unless the belt is broader. And some would say that geographical factors such as the continental shelf should determine the width of the territorial sea.

This disagreement seriously complicates the regulation of maritime commerce because of the fundamental difference in the rights and obligations of shipping and in the primary policing authority on one side of the territorial limit from the other. In the absence of an international consensus, ships are unlikely to have any recourse but to accept the decision of each coastal state as to the area of its sovereignty and to abide by its regulations within this area. This leaves the way open to extreme unilateral extensions, such as that declared by Peru, and invites a growing encroachment on the essential freedom of the seas.

---

[9] See Sorensen, *op. cit.,* p. 244, for tabulation of national claims at opening of the Geneva Conference.

[10] See Note Verbale, February 1, 1955, from the permanent delegation of Britain to the U.N. in the International Law Commission. Quoted in report of the Commission reprinted in *American Journal of International Law,* January, 1956, p. 274.

[11] See Arthur Dean, *op. cit.*

Neither the International Law Commission nor the Geneva Conferences (the second one convened particularly to deal with this issue) were able to bring about sufficiently wide agreement on a specific compromise to resolve the impasse. But the gap between the extremes was significantly narrowed. Britain and the U.S. said they would give up their historic commitments to the three-mile limit and settle for a six-mile limit; the U.S. also conceded a twelve-mile limit for fisheries jurisdiction by the coastal state (but preserved "historic rights" of fishermen who had fished in the area for at least the last five years). When the fisheries exception was abandoned, the U.S. and Canada were able to come together and jointly propose the "6 and 6" formula to the Second Geneva Conference, but it fell just short of commanding the needed two-thirds majority. On the other extreme, the Latin American 200-milers found no support, though they did not formally abandon their claims. The overwhelming majority clearly held that no state was entitled to extend its territorial sea beyond 12 miles.

But in the absence of a commonly accepted rule, anything goes, and states are continuing to determine the question unilaterally and act thereon, to the serious discomfiture of others (and often of themselves, too, as their actions boomerang and precipitate counteraction). Iceland is an example of what can happen in the present state of "lawlessness." It asserted an unqualified 12-mile limit and undertook to keep all foreign fishermen out. The British Navy then took a hand, protecting British trawlers up to the previous four-mile limit, and there were nasty moments of armed confrontation between these two historically friendly nations and current NATO allies. (In due course, Britain backed down and settled for a three-year concession, permitting its trawlers to fish at certain seasons in the 6–12 mile zone.)[12]

An attempt to partially fill the vacuum has been made by West European nations for their coastal waters. A modification of the "6–6" formula was agreed on: six miles in which the coastal state has the exclusive right to fish,

---

[12] Sorensen, *op. cit.*, pp. 242–52, concisely reviews the controversy over the breadth of the territorial sea. See, also, Dean, *op. cit.;* George A. Codding and Alvin Z. Rubinstein, "Problems Left by Discord," *U.S. Naval Institute Proceedings,* February, 1961; and R. D. Powers, Jr., and L. R. Hardy, "The Background and the Vote," *U.S. Naval Institute Proceedings,* February, 1961.

From a strictly legal standpoint, the International Court has held that states are *not* free to determine as they please the limits of territorial waters; "the validity of the delimitation depends upon international law." Decision in the Anglo-Norwegian Fisheries case, *I.C.J. Reports,* 1951, p. 132. But this does not help much on the question of breadth, because there is no agreement on what the law is. However, there is now a sufficient body of historical practice, judicial precedent, and treaty commitments to provide a basis for settling most *technical* questions of demarcation, such as the proper way of charting the "base line" along the coast from which the width of territorial waters is measured. The case cited specifically concerned this matter, and the Geneva Convention has laid down quite explicit provisions in this regard, much in line with the court's (and Norway's) position. See Sorensen, *op. cit.*, pp. 236–40.

while in a second six-mile belt, fishing is opened, but just to the other contracting parties and only if their vessels had habitually fished in the area during the decade 1953–62. Thirteen countries, including Britain and the Common Market group, have accepted this solution, but Norway and Iceland are holding out for an unconditional 12-mile limit.

The Repression of Maritime Outlaws. The regulation of maritime commerce is largely accomplished, as we have seen, by national states' enforcing their own laws, or internationally agreed rules, on ships flying their flag or on shipping inside their territorial waters. But some actions have been branded by the community of states as so reprehensible that the public authorities of any state are entitled to seize their perpetrators on the high seas and punish them. Against piracy and the slave trade, every state is deputized as an enforcing agent for the entire community of states. Any warship is free to stop and board a vessel when there is reasonable ground for suspecting it is engaged in these outlawed practices. But if the suspicion proves unfounded, the state making the seizure is liable for any damage it causes.

There has been considerable disagreement as to whether piracy is limited to acts by private persons for their own ends or whether it also extends to depredations committed by public vessels, including warships. The Nyon Treaty of 1937 branded as piratical acts the sinking of merchant vessels by submarines against the dictates of humanity. Warships engaged by rival governments in a civil war are also often accused of piracy. For instance, the Nationalist government of China was accused of piracy when its gunboats confiscated merchant vessels trading with the Communist mainland (since neither Nationalists nor Communists claimed to be belligerents). The International Law Commission concluded, however, that "to assimilate unlawful acts committed by warships to acts of piracy would be prejudicial to the interests of the international community" and would entail grave consequences if every state were duty-bound to seize such vessels. By omission, the Geneva Convention seems to confirm this view that a government and its agents can never be guilty of piracy, whatever they do. (However, if a government ship has been taken over by a mutinous crew, then any predatory acts of violence they commit are held to be piracy, just as though the ship were private.)

Protecting the "Living Resources of the Sea"

The traditional pattern of maritime regulation has featured freedom to use the seas and exploit its resources with a minimum of restraint. On three fronts, however, governments have been moving, separately and sometimes jointly, to limit freedom in their own interest or the general welfare. The objects of this increasing regulation have been: (1) to keep major grounds from being fished out of existence; (2) to control exploitation of oil and other resources beneath the seabed; (3) to promote the safety of shipping at sea.[13]

The problem of conserving fish has become acute, because the development of new techniques and equipment makes possible massive hauls, and a rising demand for fish and fish products stimulates competition among the world's fishing fleets. Yet, so firmly grounded is the tradition of freedom on the high seas that attempts by nations individually or in concert with a few others to restrict the catch and in other ways to protect the fisheries from exhaustion have been resisted as violations of international law.

A series of arbitral decisions at the beginning of the century, including the notable Bering Seal case, undercut several conservation arrangements. The pivotal issue was the lack of evidence of sufficient worldwide agreement to, and participation in, the schemes to warrant a conclusion that states had decided to change international law in this respect, so that nationals of countries which had not agreed to the conservation agreement would be bound thereby.

In recent years, two approaches have been taken on behalf of the fish, one to circumvent, the other to modify, the freedom of the seas. Some nations have unilaterally extended their jurisdiction over fisheries near their coasts, and claimed the right to police these areas and enforce conservation regulations. The alternative approach has sought to secure agreement of all major states concerned in a given fishing ground on a conservation arrangement they would jointly enforce.

Claims to Exclusive National Control. Examples of the first approach are proclamations by several Latin-American states that their national sovereignty extends over the seas adjacent to their coasts to the extent necessary to conserve and protect and make use of the resources of national wealth in such areas, as well as to prevent such resources from being exploited to the disadvantage of their own inhabitants. As noted above, Chile and Peru, among others, have asserted their right to protect and control all the sea to a distance of 200 miles from their continental or insular coasts. Argentina and Mexico asserted sovereignty over the continental shelf. The effect of these claims is to make the coastal state sole custodian of the fish in the designated areas, and to restrict fishing by nationals of other countries to whatever extent the coastal state decides is in the interests of conservation—or in its own interest. Despite the unilateral character of these actions, lifting vast stretches of ocean out of the hallowed area of the high seas, they have won wide support among other Latin-American states, and the sovereign right of

---

[13] The development of contemporary international law on the first two of these subjects is thoroughly examined and appraised by the distinguished Latin-American jurist, F. V. Garcia Amador, in *The Exploitation and Conservation of the Resources of the Seas* (Leyden: A. W. Sythoff, 1959).

conservation seems well on the way to becoming a principle of Latin-American jurisprudence.

The United States and other governments have vigorously protested, declaring that this extension of sovereignty outside the generally accepted limit of territorial waters violates international law and deprives others of their rights and interests in the high seas. But the United States itself proclaimed in 1945 that it regarded establishment of conservation zones in areas of the high seas contiguous to its coasts as proper, and would undertake to regulate fishing activities in them. Simultaneously, it conceded the right of other states to do likewise. In retrospect, it appears that this action emboldened the Latin-American "conservationists," although the U.S. has remonstrated that its decree was different. It claimed only jurisdiction, not sovereignty, over the zones. More important, it promised that if nationals of other states were engaged in "legitimate" fishing in these zones, it would undertake to work out agreements with their states concerning regulation and control. The American proclamation explicitly disavowed any intention to impede navigation on the high seas.[14]

International Fisheries Agreements. Nevertheless, the far-reaching repercussions of unilateral action on this problem and the dangers of encouraging exclusive national preserves under the guise of conservation zones have dramatized the importance of making regulation of fisheries the subject of international agreements. A growing number of bilateral and multilateral arrangements have been negotiated in recent years. Though they bind only states that are parties to them, enough of those with large fishing fleets have subscribed to put some regulation into effect over many of the major fishing grounds. Important bilateral treaties between the U.S. and Canada regulate salmon and halibut in the Pacific; U.S. treaties with Costa Rica and Mexico deal with tuna. A typical multilateral convention is the one applying to the rich area of the Northwest Atlantic off the coasts of New England, Newfoundland, Labrador, and Greenland. Ten nations adopted the Convention in 1949, including those whose nationals do most of the fishing in the area as well as those whose coasts are nearby. They established a Joint Commission responsible for (1) scientific investigation concerning methods for maintaining and increasing stocks of fish in the area; and (2) recommending conservation measures to be taken jointly by the contracting governments, such as establishing open and closed seasons, closing spawning areas, setting size limits for any species, prescribing an overall catch limit, and prohibiting certain types of fishing gear and appliances. These measures are put into effect only if approved by all governments concerned with the particular

---

[14] See Charles B. Selak, Jr., "Recent Developments in High Seas Fisheries Jurisdiction," *American Journal of International Law*, October, 1950.

subarea to which the measures are to apply (the convention distinguishes five such subareas). Each country then applies the measures to its own nationals. What is involved, therefore, is *self-regulation* by the 10 states adhering to the convention, guided by a technical agency representing all of them.

An agreement between the U.S., Canada, and Japan, covering the North Pacific, introduces a novel element in regulation. Each country agrees to abstain from fishing for certain species in given areas, leaving to one country alone the right to enforce conservation in each area. This is intended to avoid controversies over countries' policing one another's vessels, yet provide strong restraint. The problem of defining the areas of abstention is difficult, being based on the presumed source of the fish (salmon having U.S. "nationality," for instance). Scientists are not in full agreement on the spawning habitat of all species.[15]

Still another pattern of international regulation applies to "pelagic" sealing—that is, fishing seals out of the ocean rather than killing them "selectively" (young males only) in their breeding grounds. The U.S., Russia, Japan, and Canada agreed in 1911 to halt pelagic sealing because it threatened to extinguish the animals. In return, Russia and the U.S. agreed to turn over to Canada and Japan a percentage of the seals killed on their island breeding grounds, most of which were in their territories. The Soviet Union did not carry out the Russian part of the bargain, and Japan denounced the convention in 1940. Now it is in force again, though the countries find it difficult to agree on the size of the catch to which each is entitled. The problem is that Asian and American seals freely intermingle, disregarding territorial waters and defying experts to apply some of the criteria the countries have agreed should determine how many seals each should get; for instance, the proportion of Soviet, Canadian, Japanese, or U.S. fish that goes into the seals' diet!

These various forms of self-regulation by mutual agreement among concerned states leave much to be desired, however. First, they go only as far as the least concerned state is willing to go. Second, states that have not adhered to the conventions are completely exempt from their regulations and can fish whenever and however they please, thus undermining the effect of the others' conservation measures. Third, states that depend greatly on fishing off their coasts (by small, modestly equipped boats putting out from shore) feel present arrangements do not adequately protect their vital sources of supply against the heavy high seas fishing fleets with their techniques of massive exploitation. This is one of the reasons many of these smaller coastal states have been insisting on sovereignty over a wide belt of territorial sea, so that

---

[15] International Convention for High Seas Fisheries of the North Pacific Ocean, Tokyo, 1952. Reprinted in *American Journal of International Law*, Documents, July, 1954.

they can take unilateral action to restrain foreign fishing and thereby conserve their livelihood.

In an attempt to meet these problems and to establish a reasonable compromise between the historic right for anyone to fish freely on the high seas and the imperative need to protect the marine food supply of the world, the International Law Commission devised a global Convention on Fishing and Conservation of the Living Resources of the High Seas, adopted with minor changes by the Geneva Conference in 1958. This was a triumph for the little fishermen over the big, and for conservation over unlimited exploitation. It gives a coastal state the right to initiate unilateral measures of conservation in any area of the high seas adjacent to the territorial sea, and to demand that any state whose nationals fish in the area enter into negotiations with it for a conservation agreement. On the other hand, no state may have its nationals barred from fishing or otherwise subjected to discrimination; and any state, whether engaged in fishing or not, may call for conservation measures if it shows it has a special interest in an area and cites scientific reasons which make them necessary.

The crux of the Convention is its provision for what amounts to compulsory arbitration for any and all disputes arising over the measures to be put into effect. Any party can require binding settlement by a five-member commission, and call for appointment of the commission by the Secretary-General of the United Nations in consultation with the President of the International Court and the Director-General of the Food and Agriculture Organization, assuming no other procedure is agreeable to it. This means that a coastal state, or any other state, that is dissatisfied with existing arrangements (or lack of arrangements) can force the issue to a determination by a group of technically qualified persons, if the process of negotiation fails to produce a mutually acceptable solution. In contrast to the previous self-regulatory approaches which hinged on the *least* concerned state, this approach gives the power of initiative to the *most* concerned.

The International Law Commission, at one point, wanted to go farther and establish a central international regulatory authority empowered to lay down and implement universally applicable measures. But this was too much for the governments. Even the convention may be a departure too radical to secure effective cooperation. Latin American states and the Soviet bloc vehemently opposed the compulsory settlement provisions, and they were really put across by a procedural maneuver which required only a simple majority for adoption. As a result, ratifications are lagging, and, like all treaties, the convention binds only those that ratify.[16]

---

[16] Sorensen, *op. cit.*, pp. 211–25, from which much of this critique is derived; also, Arthur H. Dean, "Freedom of the Seas," *Foreign Affairs*, October, 1959, pp. 92–3. The text of the Convention is reprinted in *American Journal of International Law*, October, 1958, p. 851.

Exploiting the Continental Shelf

This trend toward internationalizing the regime of the high seas for purposes of conservation is not apparent in regard to the exploitation of oil and other natural resources which lie beneath the sea. Because technological advances now make rich reserves of such products accessible up to a depth of several hundred feet, nations are claiming full and exclusive sovereign rights over the bed of the sea many miles beyond their territorial waters, on the basis of the new doctrine of the "continental shelf."

Credence to the claims is derived from the geographical phenomenon of a sharp drop in the seabed surrounding the North and South American coasts, at distances from shore that vary from a few miles to over a hundred. The United States and other American countries argue that this shelf is geologically a part of their territory, and even if they allow free navigation and fishing in the waters above (which some of the Latin American states deny, as we have seen), the resources of the shelf are indisputably theirs and theirs alone.

But states that do not enjoy the presence of a shelf off their coasts have taken a different line, claiming that the real basis of sovereignty is the accessibility of the seabed, regardless of accidents of submarine geography. Wherever waters are shallow enough to permit drilling, there the coastal state rules—so this argument of practical expediency runs. In the Arabian Sea, this leads to extraordinary results, for oil technology has reached the point where exploitation can proceed well over a hundred miles out from shore. The Sheik of Abu Dhabi, for instance, claimed the right to dispose of oil concessions as he saw fit over an area that stretched almost half way across the sea.

This policy of each one's grabbing all he can of the seabed for himself, has given an indirect boost to those states that have unilaterally asserted their sovereignty over wide stretches of contiguous waters. They argue rather logically that to distinguish between the bed and the sea above is arbitrary and artificial. If some states are free to stretch their territory seaward, others are similarly entitled. Distance out, rather than down, they say, should be the criterion to determine the limits of sovereign jurisdiction.

So the continental shelf doctrine, sired by the United States, produced some very unwelcome offspring for countries that cherish the maximum of maritime freedom. The United States government itself tried to pull in the reins, having started the runaway. It began to protest all claims to exclusive national exploitation beyond the three-mile limit, including those advanced by its own states.[17] But these pleas had no effect at home, and the tendency abroad was to hoist the United States on its own petard.

---

[17] The State Department urged Congress, and the Department of Justice argued in the U.S. courts, that any action which had the effect of asserting exclusive rights by states or

The Geneva Conference, however, secured agreement on a Convention which now restrains the more extreme claims, while conceding the coastal states' sovereign rights to explore and exploit the resources of the seabed and subsoil of the continental shelf. Sovereignty is *not* recognized over the high seas above, which means the coastal states must not prevent, or unreasonably interfere with, use of the seas by others for navigation, fishing, scientific research, etc. They may set up oil drilling rigs and other installations, for instance, but must establish safety zones around them and be careful not to get too close to international sea lanes. The definition of the "shelf" is rather ambiguous, as it applies two criteria in an attempt to compromise the views noted above: it includes areas to a depth of 200 meters, but also recognizes any area deeper than that if it is exploitable. This means that the "shelf" expands as technology advances and makes possible operations at increasing depth—a pragmatic, functional test, but one which leaves room for controversy when the shelves of two or more states, so defined, meet and overlap. The most serious gap in the Convention is precisely the lack of provision for compulsory judicial settlement of disputes arising over the shelf. The International Law Commission had proposed such, but the Conference would not accept it.[18]

Safety at Sea

One of the earliest purposes of international cooperation was to provide facilities that would reduce the perils of "those that go down to the sea in ships."

Custom, hardened into international maritime law, has laid down "rules of the road" which govern the conduct of shipping the world over, and, indeed, has spelled out a universal language for navigation.

Nations individually have done what they could to warn vessels of hazards on their coasts and assist them when in distress. At some points of great danger, such as Cape Spartel in Morocco, where the local authorities were not able to provide adequate safeguards, several governments have jointly assumed responsibility for administering and paying for a lighthouse and other warning signals.[19]

The major international effort has been directed at the danger of icebergs. Following the Titanic disaster in 1912, the International Ice Patrol, supported by 14 nations was organized to locate and chart the course of floes,

---

federal government over submerged lands beyond the presently recognized limit of territorial waters would have serious international repercussions in encouraging extravagant claims by others.

[18] See Sorensen, *op. cit.,* pp. 226–31. The Convention is reprinted in *American Journal of International Law,* October, 1958, p. 858.

[19] See G. H. Stuart, *The International City of Tangier* (Stanford, Calif.: Stanford University Press, 1931).

destroy some, and warn ships of the presence of others. The Patrol now includes both cutters and aircraft, equipped with radar. It also conducts intensive oceanographic and meteorological studies to determine the factors affecting the limits and movements of icebergs and field ice.

Nations have also agreed on certain common regulations to reduce hazards resulting from human negligence or irresponsibility. To insure the seaworthiness of ships, the International Load-Line Convention, prescribing the maximum safe cargo load, was adopted. Then there are internationally adopted rules dealing with ship construction, minimum amount and character of lifesaving equipment, necessary fire alarm and fire-fighting appliances, and radio and other signaling devices.

So far, most of this action has been carried out by each country, separately applying the agreed rules to its own ships. But in 1958, the Intergovernmental Maritime Consultative Organization was established as a specialized agency of the United Nations to facilitate cooperation in improving and implementing such technical regulations and also to help remove discriminations against shipping in international trade. A variety of objections blocked its formation for a decade, and continue to limit its membership and effectiveness. A number of countries with small merchant marines felt it was weighted in favor of the big shipowning powers, and were fearful that actions might be taken that would adversely affect their interests. Though the organization's functions are labeled "consultative and advisory," it does have broad mandate to make recommendations concerning safety and other technical regulations, and also to consider questions of shipping policy, including charges of "unfair" restrictive practices. This last-mentioned function causes the principal rub, as countries demur over the possible intervention of the Organization in matters affecting their capacity and techniques for maritime competition, e.g., for waging commercial warfare.

A second bone of contention is the structure of the Council, which is the pivot of responsibility in IMCO. It alone may make recommendations concerning restrictive practices and discrimination, and the Assembly cannot reverse its decisions. It consists of 16 members, and as all major maritime states have seats, they can dominate the proceedings, both in getting action they want and in preventing action they find objectionable. (The Council as well as the other organs of IMCO—the Assembly and the Maritime Safety Committee—vote by simple majority which, in this case, gives the decision to the big shipping states if they stand together.) There is substance, therefore, to the charge that the structure is undemocratic, and only broad-gauged and disinterested policies by the "bigs" will build the mutual reassurance necessary for the organization to fulfill its functions effectively.

Present prospects are favorable in regard to the technical tasks, relating directly to the improvement of conditions for shipping. But serious difficulties have already been encountered in regard to resolving the economic and commercial policy issues stemming from the intense international maritime competition.[20]

CONTROL OF INTERNATIONAL WATERWAYS— THE REPUDIATION OF INTERNATIONAL RESPONSIBILITY

Historically, the great rivers of the world have met three vital human needs. First, they have served as major arteries of commerce. Second, they have supplied power—initially, turning the wheels of industry directly, now, the turbines of the age of electricity. And third, in many areas, life itself depends on the irrigation of otherwise parched lands.

But man-made frontiers have cut up many of the river systems and, especially in Europe, made their usefulness to mankind contingent on the consent and cooperation of nations through which they flow, e.g., the "riparian states." It lies within the power of any of these states to seriously injure the welfare of the others—by closing its stretch to traffic or levying heavy charges for the privilege of transit, or by damming up the river and diverting a large portion of the water to its own use. Of course, it will suffer in turn as the others retaliate. There are few areas of international relations in which the sword so clearly cuts both ways. European countries have had frequent cause to learn this lesson, as war and "curtains" close down international river commerce, if not the flow of the water itself.

So, over the last hundred years, nations have tried by various means to insure that "international waterways" would be regulated so as to permit their continuous and equitable use by all concerned. Three main approaches have been attempted: (1) a general international "law of rivers" similar to that of the high seas; (2) special international administrations for certain rivers, representing both riparian and other interested states; and (3) regulation by joint agreement among riparian states alone.

It is the third approach that has come to predominate in recent years. Riparian states assert that as the sovereign states through which the rivers pass they should be the primary regulatory authority, though they have been willing to concede to others the right to navigate the waterways without discrimination.

The Rights of Navigation

For some time, it appeared that international rivers, their tributaries, and even the man-made canals connecting them might be opened to the commerce of all nations as a general international right. Although no such right

---

[20] See David J. Padwa, "The Curriculum of IMCO," *International Organization*, Autumn, 1960; also, Alvin Z. Rubinstein, "The USSR and IMCO," *U.S. Naval Institute Proceedings*, October, 1959.

could be claimed by customary international law (as in the case of the high seas), important treaties, starting with the Congress of Vienna in 1815 and extending to the peace settlements after World War II, have consistently recognized the principle of free navigation on the major rivers of Europe. In 1921, on League of Nations initiative, the Barcelona Convention was negotiated, affirming and defining this principle as applicable to all "navigable waterways of international concern." The Convention has not been ratified by every concerned state, but does represent so general a consensus that its provisions are widely held to have the effect of international law.[21]

In brief, passage through international waterways is held to be open and nondiscriminatory for nationals of all countries. All are to enjoy equal treatment in regard to tolls and port facilities. Even the riparian states retain no special privileges for their shipping, except to reserve to their own nationals commerce among their own river ports ("petit cabotage"). Charges for use of the river are to be reasonable, usually limited to enough to pay the cost of upkeep of the navigation facilities. Navigation rights do *not* excuse vessels from respecting the customs, sanitary, and police regulations a state may adopt.

The right of open navigation for all without discrimination has also been confirmed for the major interoceanic canals, in treaties concluded between the states involved in building them, the countries through which they pass, and some of the principal users.[22]

In practice, riparian states have not honored these rights when at war or when they have felt their security threatened. Nor have they always fully accepted the doctrine of nondiscrimination as between riparian and nonriparian commerce. The Danube after World War II is a case in point.

The United States and Britain proposed that the river be reopened to commerce on terms of equality for all, with these rights guaranteed in the peace treaties between the defeated Danubian states and the Allies. Russia and the other Eastern European states objected that the question should be settled among the Danubian states alone, and apart from the peace treaties. They yielded on the principle, but left its implementation to be decided by a special International Conference held at Belgrade in 1948. Here, the Russians and the Danubian states, in a disciplined majority, overrode all Western

---

[21] See Clyde Eagleton, *International Government* (rev. ed.; New York: Ronald Press Co., 1948), p. 164; see, also, editor's note in Herbert W. Briggs, *The Law of Nations* (2d ed.; New York: Appleton-Century-Crofts, 1952), pp. 274 and 277, and relevant cases and documents reprinted therein.

[22] See the Constantinople Convention of 1888 re the Suez Canal; and re the Panama Canal, the Hay-Pauncefote Treaty of 1901 between the U.S. and Britain, and the Hay-Varilla Treaty of 1903 between U.S. and Panama. Similar rights were conceded by Germany for the Kiel Canal, in the Treaty of Versailles. Though this was denounced by Hitler, it is generally held that the provisions still apply to the canal. See J. L. Brierly, *The Law of Nations* (6th ed.; New York: Oxford University Press, 1963), pp. 233–36.

proposals and objections, and established exclusive riparian control and administration. The United States, Britain and France were convinced that this would lead to discrimination against the commerce of outsiders. Nevertheless, the new Danubian Convention, on the surface at least, fully recognizes the open navigation principle, providing in Article 1 that "Navigation on the Danube shall be free and open for the nationals, vessels of commerce and goods of all States, on a footing of equality in regard to port and navigation charges and conditions for merchant shipping. The foregoing shall not apply to traffic between ports of the same State."[23] Other sections explicitly guarantee nondiscrimination in the administration of sanitary and police regulations (Art. 26), port dues (Art. 40), and charges for port facilities (Art. 41).

Almost immediately, however, it became evident that application of these provisions would be subject to the political directives of the U.S.S.R. which dominated the new Danube Commission and controlled the conduct of the major Danubian states, except Yugoslavia. When the Cominform outlawed Tito, its principal sanction was an economic blockade against Yugoslavia, and this almost ended international commerce on the river. Paradoxically, it was a Danubian state itself that suffered most acutely from discrimination under the riparian regime it had helped establish.

This object lesson in the damages of undercutting the right of open navigation on international waterways may serve to dissuade such action in the future.

The principle of open navigation has been better respected by the custodians of the canals, though here, too, there have been some exceptions. It was probably too much to expect that enemy ships, especially warships, would be allowed passage in wartime, as supposedly guaranteed by the Suez and Panama Canal treaties. In any case, neither Britain nor the U.S. have allowed it during their periods of control respectively over Suez and Panama; and since Egypt took over Suez, it has excluded all Israeli shipping (and often other ships servicing Israel) on the grounds that it is at war with Israel.[24]

On the other hand, when it nationalized the canal in 1956, Egypt specifically reaffirmed "its determination to continue to guarantee the freedom of passage through the canal in conformity with the 1888 Convention."[25]

In the case of the Panama Canal, the principle of nondiscrimination

---

[23] Convention Regarding the Regime of Navigation on the Danube, August 18, 1948 (38 U.N. Treaty Series 181).

[24] The Egyptian actions have been widely condemned as illegal, but are little different from their predecessors except that a U.N.-negotiated armistice is nominally in effect between the two countries.

[25] Letter to the U.N. Security Council, September 17, 1956, from the permanent representative of Egypt to the U.N.

survived an early threat when President Wilson barely managed to persuade the Congress to hold off on legislation granting lower tolls to American ships, in violation of a treaty with Britain. This issue is now history.

Administration of International Waterways—An Issue of Riparian Privilege

The main issue between riparian and other states has concerned who should be responsible for keeping the rivers navigable and for regulating their use. Because some riparian states could not or would not undertake adequate dredging, construction and maintenance of locks, and other expensive operations necessary to make the river fully serviceable, the important using nations devised various international administrative arrangements to take over these responsibilities and, in a sense, to "govern" a river throughout its entire length. The record of these experiments in real international operational administration was excellent on the whole. Navigation facilities improved greatly. The rules agreed on by the participating nations were fairly enforced. But friction between the international authority and the governments of riparian states in whose territory it had to be exerted was incipient. As nationalist self-consciousness grew, these states came to demand, ever more insistently, full control over "their" river. They regarded a supranational regime as an infringement of sovereignty—which it really was—and an inference that they were incapable of doing an effective job of administration. Joint riparian administration has therefore become the general pattern of regulation.

The Danube again illustrates what has happened. By the Treaty of Paris in 1856, two Commissions were formed. One, composed of just the riparian states, was to conduct the general regulation and improvement of the river. The second, a "European" Commission representing other major powers, was to build important improvement works at the mouths and in the lower stretches of the river and to collect tolls to pay the cost of the works. The European Commission was intended to be temporary, but instead was extended and its powers strengthened because the Riparian Commission proved untrustworthy in upholding conditions of navigation that were fair and free for all. The European Commission, in due course, gained operational, financial, and even police and quasi-judicial powers. It deepened the river, built lighthouses, erected floating elevators, and licensed vessels and pilots. In addition to levying tolls, it borrowed funds for major improvements. The Commission supervised the police of the lower river and penalized offenses against its regulations, by fines or by revoking licenses of pilots (although local courts had jurisdiction over all criminal and civil cases). It also had charge of sanitary regulations, and after 1881 it appointed and discharged inspectors and supervisors of navigation at the major ports on the lower river. The Danube was declared a neutral river, and the Commission's own neutrality was guaranteed vis-à-vis the riparian states.

Following the first World War, the upper Danube also was placed under a general international, rather than exclusively riparian, administration—the International Danube Commission. The European Commission continued its separate responsibility, however, for the lower river, the dividing point now being fixed at Braila, which gave the Commission rather than the riparian states charge of the Iron Gates, the most vital of points requiring special facilities. Responsibility for some power and irrigation projects was added. Under these two Commissions, the entire length of the Danube (though not its tributaries), therefore, was administered and controlled on a broadly international basis, inclusive of, but not limited to, riparian representation.

Now the pendulum has swung all the way to riparian control. By the 1948 Convention, each state undertakes primary responsibility to maintain its section of the Danube in a navigable condition and to carry out most of the navigation works on its territory. On most stretches, regulations are pre-scribed by each state individually, or by bilateral agreement when the river forms a boundary. They also administer the sanitary, customs, and police regulations on the river. A single Danube Commission, consisting of one representative of each Danubian state, executes works individual states are not able to undertake, and establishes a uniform system of traffic regulations. It can levy charges to defray the costs of the special works constructed. The rest of its budget is met by equal contributions from the Danubian states. While the Commission acts by majority vote, it is explicitly restrained from outvoting the state on whose territory its actions are to be carried out. In turn, a state has no effective say on Danubian regulation beyond its own functions, as discovered by Yugoslavia during the period of its break with the Comin-form, when it was excluded from any part in the Danube Commission's functions, although its share of the Danube is longer than all the others. Thus, for all practical purposes, the Danube has returned to individual control by the riparian states, subject to the international rights of navigation they recognize.

The U.S. and Canada have completed a more harmonious half-century of international cooperation in the regulation of their long fluvial frontier. But their problem is far simpler than the Danube—only two riparian states are involved, and at no point have they had to recognize an international interest broader than a bilateral one in working out their pattern of administration. The two nations have formed the International Joint Commission, empow-ered to execute specific treaty agreements on navigation, and principally on diversion of water for irrigation and hydroelectric power. For instance, in 1950, the two countries agreed to divide the water of the Niagara River equally between them, after insuring a minimum flow to preserve the beauty of the falls. They also agreed that remedial works to keep the falls from being eroded away would be undertaken by the Commission.

Agreement has not always come easy, even between two such intimate associates as the U.S. and Canada. Internal sectional interests have generated domestic political pressures which, in turn, precipitated sharp international policy conflicts, leading almost to the point of arbitrary unilateral action. The St. Lawrence Seaway, major showpiece of the bilateral approach to development of an international waterway, came about only after decades of arduous and intricate "engineering of consent," especially on the U.S. side of the border and after Canada had decided to go it alone.[26]

Even more embittered were the 17 years of dispute within and outside the International Joint Commission over the development of the Columbia River before a treaty for this purpose was signed in 1961. The technical problems themselves were extremely complex. But the heart of the controversy was a struggle over the amount of water and power that would be allocated to promote the growth and welfare of the American as against the Canadian Northwest. The U.S., badgered by its western leaders, demanded the lion's share, so much so that Canada felt it would never be able to stimulate the development of its western provinces. Historical, legal, and other bases of the respective claims were argued to no avail. The Americans were insistent and uncompromising, until the Canadians decided on a fantastic scheme to completely change the course of the Fraser River so that it would empty into the Pacific without going through the Columbia, leaving the U.S. with virtually a dry river. This lesson in the functional imperative for give-and-take on an equitable basis in the management of international waterways finally got through. The treaty now provides for an ambitious and comprehensive program of flood control, power development, and stabilization of the river's flow, with each country's building dams and other facilities on its territory, Canada sharing *equally* in the downstream power benefits, and agreeing not to divert water from the Columbia Basin without U.S. consent, except as specified in the treaty.[27]

The assertion of direct national responsibility for control and administration of international waterways was dramatically demonstrated by Egypt's nationalization of the Suez Canal. From an administrative point of view, this meant an Egyptian governmental authority took over full charge of operating the canal, displacing the private international stock company that had been empowered to do so for 99 years by the Constantinople Convention of 1888. From a financial point of view, it meant that Egypt assumed ownership of the properties and collected the tolls, while compensating the expropriated company with Egyptian bonds. We are not here concerned with the strictly

---

[26] See William R. Willoughby, *The St. Lawrence Waterway: A Study in Politics and Diplomacy* (Madison, Wis.: University of Wisconsin Press, 1961) for this extraordinary story.

[27] See *Report on Executive C, Columbia River Treaty* (U.S. Senate Committee on Foreign Relations, 87th Cong., 1st sess., March 15, 1961). Also, William E. Kenworthy "Joint Development of International Waters," *American Journal of International Law*, July, 1960.

legal issues involved, nor with the background of events which precipitated the action as a particular retort to U.S. pressure in the diplomacy of the cold war. What is significant is that having taken the move, Egypt stood by it, against the demands of the principal Canal users for some form of international operating authority. (Secretary of State Dulles, trying to recoup from the catastrophic effects of his previous attempt to pressurize Egypt, proposed a "Canal Users Association" to run the Canal, and persuaded Britain and other deeply concerned states to go along; but Egypt would not budge, even before this powerful, united diplomatic front.) What is more, Egypt made a go of it, despite predictions that it was incapable of mobilizing the technical and administrative know-how. Years after the debacle of the British-French effort to turn back the clock by force, even these determined stakeholders in international administration gave up and came to terms with the Egyptians' implanted authority.

Thus, the primacy of riparian, or national, interest in the administration of international waterways seems established, regardless of the degree of "international concern" in which they are held, or the efficiency and equity of the various experiments with multinational or really nonnational regulation. Nations are loath to concede to the community of nations at large any larger share than they must of their territorial jurisdiction.

INTERNATIONAL TRANSPORT BY RAIL AND ROAD—A PATTERN OF PRIVATE INTERNATIONAL COOPERATION

What governments will not do, business sometimes can, if there is money in it. The ease with which the tremendous volume of overland rail commerce now moves across European borders in peacetime is largely the result of agreements worked out directly among the various railway administrations, or promoted by them when governmental action was necessarily involved.

International cooperation in four main matters is required to send the Simplon–Orient Express from Paris to Istanbul, or to ship a trainload of coal from the Ruhr to Italy.

Exchange of Rolling Stock

Each company needs assurance that it will receive proper compensation for use of its cars when they go outside the country and, of course, that its cars will come back. In turn, it must be prepared to pay other companies for the privilege of having its rolling stock go over their lines.

The European railway administrations (including both private and nationally owned companies) have formed the International Railway Union, one of whose purposes is to regulate the international exchange of rolling stock. Under its provisions, a loaded freight car or through passenger car is allowed to cross frontiers in proceeding to their destination. After unloading, it may pick up a return load for either an internal or international journey. The receiving administrations pay rent on a uniform rate per day in the case of freight, or mileage in the case of passenger cars, and a central payments bureau keeps and clears the accounts. Any disputes are settled by arbitration. Voting rights in the Assembly, which decides policy for the Union, is proportioned to the mileage of track each administration owns, and decisions are binding by a majority vote on these questions.

Uniformity of Physical Standards

Railroads, as public utilities, are under government regulation, even if they are not owned and operated by the government, and their equipment must measure up to set standards. If different governments prescribe markedly different rules, cars from one country may not be able to move into others. An extreme example is the difference in width of tracks that has necessitated a complete transshipment for all traffic crossing the Russian frontier from Europe. But clearances for bridges and tunnels, maximum weights tolerated on given roadbeds, brake requirements, and many other items must be similar if international rail traffic is to flow freely. So, on Swiss initiative, an intergovernmental agreement was negotiated in 1882 among countries in Europe—the Code d'Unité Technique—which standardized the gauge and prescribed common technical requirements for the essentials. No formal administrative machinery exists to carry these out, each country's doing so on its own.

Uniformity in Legal Responsibilities

Again, differing national legislation concerning carriers' responsibilities impedes international rail traffic, because railroads are reluctant to be saddled with greater liabilities if their cars happen to be moving in one country rather than in another. The Berne Union helped to overcome this problem. Not in reality an organization at all, but a set of complementary treaties that became part of the law of each ratifying country, it defined uniform responsibilities for carriers in regard to liability for damages, getting goods to their destination, and so on. It guaranteed that countries would not discriminate in the responsibilities they enforced on one railroad as against another, regardless of its nationality.

Rights of Transit

Fundamental to international rail communication, of course, is permission by governments to let foreign traffic move across their territory. Narrow nationalistic considerations of security or commercial interest have sometimes caused nations to embargo or severely discriminate against the transit of commerce from a neighboring state, and this danger made control of vital rail lines a sharp issue in negotiation of the peace treaties after the world wars. Countries wanted frontiers drawn so that they could directly control the whole length of a line to the sea or to an important communications center. But nationalism in rail communication boomerangs in a tightly knit continent like Europe, where frontiers, however drawn, are bound to cut across key transport arteries.

Most European states have therefore agreed to a kind of "law of the rails," by which freedom of transit is assured across their territories for goods moving from one country to another or to the sea. Inland states are permitted the use of "free ports" where they can transship their goods without discriminatory charges. In some instances, specific "railroad corridors" are guaranteed to a state to facilitate communication between different parts of its territory when a line runs through another country. These arrangements cannot operate, of course, when countries are at war or have broken relations.[28]

Despite the complete breakdown of all international rail traffic during the second world war, most of the arrangements have since been reconstituted, thanks in large measure to the work of the United Nations Transport and Communications Commission, the European Central Inland Transport Organization, and the U.N. Economic Commission for Europe, which assumed its duties. In 1948, the clearing arrangement for the exchange of cars was reintroduced after an intensive effort had "recaptured" for their rightful owners more than half a million freight cars lost during the war and had inventoried several million more.

Under the impetus of this experience, the European countries have begun to extend the principle of freedom of transit to their roads. Simplification of customs formalities now enable buses and trucks to roll across Western European frontiers with little difficulty. As a result, a whole new form of tourist travel has blossomed, and trucking has for the first time become a practical means of long-distance shipment in Europe. Consideration is now being given by some European countries to joint regulation of commercial truck traffic—similar to that of the railroads—which would standardize safety requirements, weight loads, publication of tariffs, and others.

THE LAW OF THE AIR—
REGULATION BY RECIPROCITY

Mastery of the air has all but wiped out the time barrier in contacts among nations, and because of this the practical development of civil aviation as a

---

[28] See Sir Osborn Mance, *Frontiers, Peace Treaties and International Organization* (New York: Oxford University Press, 1946); also Sir Ralph Wedgwood, *International Rail Transport* (New York: Oxford University Press, 1946), which gives a comprehensive summary of arrangements before World War II. International rail traffic outside Europe is so restricted that no general system of regulation has developed, except for bilateral agreements covering such international transit as occurs in the Americas and in Asia.

major channel for international commerce has posed regulation problems of peculiar difficulty. For understandable reasons, states have insisted on complete and exclusive sovereignty over the air above their territory ever since man-made gadgets became capable of international flight.

Some talk at the turn of the century of declaring airspace as "open" as the high seas evaporated when balloons, Zeppelins, and then airplanes were turned to military use. The Paris Convention on the Regulation of Aerial Navigation, signed in conjunction with the Peace Conference in 1919, set forth the principle of sovereignty that has prevailed in all subsequent agreements.[29]

Other obstacles to the development of international civil aviation have been the desire of states to protect and strengthen the position of their own commercial airlines as against foreign competition, and the great variations in national regulations relating to aviation. As planes must meet the standards and laws of the land over which they fly, the lack of uniform technical requirements among countries is a substantial impediment to international air traffic.

By the end of World War II, vast expansion of international civil aviation, including transoceanic flight, was technologically feasible, provided nations could agree on a mutually satisfactory pattern of regulation. For this purpose, the United States invited 50 countries to an International Civil Aviation Conference in Chicago in 1944. Immediately, alternative concepts emerged of how the problems should be handled.

The American Appeal for the "Five Freedoms"

The United States proposed that every country allow civil aircraft of all countries full freedom of *transit* and commercial *traffic* over and in its territories, provided they obeyed the nation's laws and respected such security zones as it might establish. In concrete terms, this meant that nations would obligate themselves to respect five freedoms of the air—two for transit and three for traffic:

1. Freedom for a properly registered aircraft to fly over another country.
2. Freedom to land for service and refueling.
3. Freedom to transport passengers and cargo from its own country to the country where it lands.

---

[29] Secretary of State John Foster Dulles hinted at possible modification of this position in commenting on a Soviet protest against U.S. weather balloons flouting Russian territory. He said that airspace above a certain height, possibly 30,000 feet, might be considered "open" for meteorological observation and similar purposes. There is no foundation for this view, however, in any international agreement, though this is one of the issues in negotiation over the control of "outer space"—e.g., is there a point at which "airspace" can be said to stop and outer space begin? See Lincoln P. Bloomfield's reasoned discussion of the "Prospects for Law and Order," in Bloomfield (ed.), *Outer Space* (New York: The American Assembly, 1962), chap. 7.

4. Freedom to transport passengers and cargo back again.
5. Freedom to transport passengers and cargo between the country of its destination and a third country.

On the transit Freedoms, there was prompt agreement among the countries represented in Chicago. These merely reiterated the right of "innocent passage" which the nations that signed the Paris Convention had accepted while declaring their sovereignty over the air. Unfortunately, several states did not attend the Chicago conference, including Russia, so even the transit Freedoms are not universally recognized. Several critical incidents arose during the tense period of the cold war, when planes straying off their course into Communist countries were shot down for "intrusion." While trigger-happiness is more under control now, these and other states still do not concede foreign aircraft the right to cross their territories without permission, and the custom is to invite intruders peremptorily to land and explain themselves.[30]

It was with regard to the traffic Freedoms that disagreement was sharpest. The British, strongly supported by most countries not yet in a position to compete effectively in international civil aviation, feared that given the full Five Freedoms American airlines with their big head start would so dominate the field that others would have no real chance to develop. The Fifth Freedom, in particular, was fine for the U.S., because its large, well-equipped air fleets could hop, skip, and jump all over Europe, Latin America, and Asia, picking up all the traffic they wanted from place to place, in direct competition with local lines whose costs had to be higher because they handled smaller volume. What would have made the game all the more uneven was the reservation of "cabotage"—traffic from point to point in the same country—to each nation's own airlines. This closed the lucrative domestic American trade to all foreign lines, but because the other continents were cut up into so many separate nations, all the important air traffic was international and, hence, open to the U.S. under the Fifth Freedom.

American eloquence could not convince the others that freedom to be run out of business was to their interest. What they asked was some form of regulation that would guarantee a share of international commercial aviation to any nation that wanted it.

International Civil Aviation Authority—British Model

The British counterplan envisaged a world authority with powers similar to the Civil Aeronautics Authority in the United States. It would establish

---

[30] See Oliver J. Lissitzyn, "The Treatment of Aerial Intruders in Recent Practice and International Law," *American Journal of International Law,* October, 1953. By virtue of the Geneva Convention on the High Seas, freedom of air transit over the high seas is recognized. On the other hand, the principle of national sovereignty is explicitly applied to airspace above the territorial sea, by the Convention on the Territorial Sea and the Contiguous Zone.

uniform regulations for international flight. It would operate air safety services. Pilots would secure from it their licenses for international aviation. And, above all, it would allocate routes to the different airlines, prescribe the maximum amount of traffic each could carry, and approve their rates. The authority would thus be fully responsible for all international civil aviation, under principles laid down by the governments that set it up.

The United States rejected the plan out of hand because of its restrictive features and the supranational character of the control envisaged. It did not want American airlines bound by outside authority.

The Chicago Conference was not able to resolve this impasse. Although the nations agreed to set up the International Civil Aviation Organization (ICAO), its functions were primarily technical, and it was given no authority to regulate commerce. Eighteen states did sign a convention accepting the traffic Freedoms, but a number of these demurred on the critical Fifth Freedom, and most of the key European states refused altogether.

The Compromise on Reciprocity

A partial solution was worked out through bilateral agreements, the pacemaker being the Bermuda Agreement between the United States and the United Kingdom, signed in 1946. The two countries agreed on a mutual exchange of traffic privileges, including the right to operate routes between each other, and to use each other's facilities. The British even yielded on the Fifth Freedom, but in return set limits on the number of flights and the routes American airlines could operate, using British territory as a stopping point. Rates were subject to governmental review. Disputes would be referred for advisory opinions to the ICAO.

With this all-important precedent established, the United States proceeded to sign up over forty other countries on similar terms, though sometimes it could not persuade them to grant the Fifth Freedom. The other nations interested in international aviation followed suit and negotiated their own network of bilateral agreements with the states with whom they wanted to conduct commerce. A "most-favored-nation" clause in many of these agreements meant that considerable uniformity was gradually achieved in regard to traffic rights, as countries extended their most liberal terms to everyone who had agreed to do the same with them. For all practical purposes, a world-wide system of regulation has now emerged (outside the Soviet-controlled areas), permitting a large degree of freedom for commercial airlines to engage in international business, but insuring a sufficiently large slice of the market to each nation so that its airlines can grow. By "reciprocity," even small nations have been able to bargain the privilege of using their facilities for concessions that would benefit their own lines.

This was pointedly illustrated when the United States had to renegotiate its agreement with Canada in 1949. Britain had relinquished its sovereignty over Newfoundland to Canada, so use of the Gander base as the major refueling stop on trans-Atlantic flights was no longer covered by the Bermuda Agreement. The Canadians insisted that the U.S. permit Canadian Air Lines to fly four new international routes, including the lucrative Montreal-New York-Bermuda route, in competition with Colonial Air Lines, in return for extending the use of the Newfoundland facilities to American lines. Colonial's protests, echoed by 49 U.S. Senators, could not prevail against Canada's "ace in the hole," and the agreement was concluded. Ironically, if the American way had won at Chicago, Canadian and other lines would now have unlimited right to compete with the U.S. As the foreign companies have become capable of effective competition, the Americans are less sure about the benefits of full freedom of the air.

Technical Regulation

With each nation sovereign in its own air, international flight must respect as many separate sets of safety and technical regulations as the countries it covers, and must be subject to as many different provisions concerning its legal responsibilities. Substantial progress has been made toward extricating international civil aviation from this maze by getting nations to agree on uniform regulations to govern international flights and by providing a central organization to coordinate their implementation.

Functions of the ICAO. The International Civil Aviation Organization has six main jobs.

1. It develops uniform technical standards to facilitate international air transport, securing agreement among its member states on such subjects as air traffic control, communications and navigational aids, and rules of the air. Experts keep these standards under constant review, bringing them up to date with technological progress.

2. ICAO arranges for financial and technical aid to maintain navigation and transport facilities at key points where a state feels it cannot adequately do so by itself, or where no state is fully responsible, as over the oceans. For instance, ICAO organized a system of 13 weather observation and air-rescue stations in the North Atlantic, and worked out an agreement among the principal North Atlantic nations for sharing the expense of a LORAN (long-range aid to navigation) station in Iceland. It is important to note that ICAO's service in this regard is dependent on persuading its members, or some of them, to undertake a project. It has little independent capacity to act. It could do nothing, for instance, to prevent the U.S. from pulling its 14 ships out of the Atlantic weather and rescue system when the Eisenhower administration decided that "the benefits derived by the United States are no longer commensurate with the cost."[31] The U.S. government contended that other

---

[31] Letter of Harold A. Jones, U.S. delegate to ICAO, quoted in *New York Times,* October 27, 1953, p. 47.

countries should pay a greater portion of the cost and, unable to carry its point, just boycotted the arrangement.

3. ICAO tackles particular regional aviation problems and helps the governments in an area to determine jointly what new navigation facilities and procedures are needed.

4. It encourages states to minimize the red tape of customs, immigration, health, and other formalities at international airports so as to cut down the delay in crossing boundaries. For instance, visa requirements have been eased to several Latin-American states for air passengers.

5. ICAO has become the principal forum in which international disputes over technical regulations are discussed and settled.

6. An ICAO commission is charged with promoting more adequate and comprehensive traffic agreements, with the long-run prospect of a new multilateral convention on air rights. Meanwhile, it encourages such action as Pakistan's allowing Indian aircraft to fly direct routes to Afghanistan over its territory, despite the political tension between these countries.

The Warsaw Convention.   One of the earliest agreements to facilitate international civil aviation (1929) defined common limits of liability that countries would enforce on carriers when engaged in international air commerce. These limits were set very low (a maximum of $8,292, unless the injury were due to "willful misconduct" of the carrier or its agents) so that airlines would not be deterred from international traffic by heavy risks.

Many cases have come before American and other courts to test the applicability of the Warsaw Convention, because injured persons stand to collect much more if they can show that this treaty does not cover their situation. But its language is explicit and comprehensive, and is held to cover damage to goods at a warehouse at the point of destination if they were internationally transported, injury to a person on a ramp while alighting from an international trip, and also accidents to international passengers, even though they were on a plane also carrying persons between cities in the same country. It was the Warsaw Convention that prevented singer Jane Froman from securing more than $23,000 out of a $1 million suit over the serious injuries she suffered when a plane crashed in Portugal.

The limits of liability were doubled in a revision of the Convention in 1955 (the Hague Protocol), but there is still widespread feeling that the airlines are now in a position to assume liability more in line with that expected of established common carriers in most countries. This is, of course, resisted by the companies engaged in international aviation, especially the smaller ones, because of the cost and danger to their competitive position.[32]

---

[32] This and related issues were the subject of a symposium at the 1962 meetings of the American Society of International Law. See its *Proceedings,* April, 1962, especially the statements by Oliver J. Lissitzyn and Stanley D. Metzger.

THE OPERATION OF INTERNATIONAL COM-
MUNICATIONS—THE ACHIEVEMENT OF
INTERNATIONAL ADMINISTRATION

A letter will be delivered anywhere in the world (in peacetime) for eight cents. A cable or radiogram costs more, but will get there in hours. An international telephone connection can be made in minutes. One's privacy in all these means of communication is essentially inviolate. These astounding feats of international communication, now largely taken for granted, are made possible by two of the earliest and most effective systems of international administration—the Universal Postal Union (UPU) and the International Telecommunication Union (ITU). These organizations also have the most comprehensive membership, including most countries of the world, regardless of ideology or political system.[33]

The two Unions demonstrate a pattern of real international regulatory authority.

1. The Congress of the Postal Union and Conference of the Telecommunications Union, at which all the members are represented, legislate basic policies. Conventions adopted by two-thirds of the members are binding on all (unless a dissatisfied state chooses to leave the organization entirely and thereby lose all rights and privileges). The act of ratification has become a mere formality. The UPU procedure for revising its acts between congresses is unusual. A request for a change is circulated by the organization to its members. Within a specified time limit, states can vote on the amendment. The article will be considered changed if the majority of nations replying do so in the affirmative. Those not replying are considered to have abstained. All nations automatically agree to the mail regulations when they become members.[34]

2. The two Unions provide machinery for the settlement of all disputes that may arise within their fields of operation. There is no appeal outside the organization.

3. Sanctions behind the Unions' decisions are automatic. If a state rejects a decision, it loses its right to the privileges of the association. For instance, if a state will not comply with the allocation of radio frequencies for international broadcasting made by the ITU Conference, it may be subjected to retaliatory action, other states being freed to use the frequencies previously assigned to it. Or the Postal Union could suspend regular postal communi-

---

[33] The Chinese Communist government has been excluded, however, as in all other U.N. and specialized agencies. A majority in the organizations holds that this is a "political problem" to be settled elsewhere.

[34] However, other services, such as parcel post, C.O.D., and subscriptions, can be subscribed to separately.

cations with a recalcitrant state. The importance of the privileges has so far outweighed the disadvantages experienced by some members; at least, none have gone the length of withdrawing. Even the French, who have at times threatened to leave the Postal Union in protest against the rule to "gratuity of transit" (by which a state receives only a nominal amount for carrying mail in transit to another country), have in the end backed down and continued to move their disproportionate burden of other people's letters.[35]

On the other hand, the lesser developed countries are consumers of mail (as they receive more second and third class mail than they send, or sell stamps for). Their distribution costs are great, and they have requested reimbursement. But they have never been able to rally enough votes to get this special consideration; they, too, choose to live with their defeat and pay up rather than get out.

The ITU has been less successful than the UPU in securing enforcement of unpopular decisions, especially where important political issues were at stake. The United States was thwarted in its request for a large number of new frequencies for the zone of Germany which it occupied. It went ahead anyway with the large-scale broadcasting programs of the Voice of America and Radio Free Europe, beamed to Eastern Europe. The U.S.S.R. has systematically jammed broadcasts originating outside its orbit, even when they were transmitted on authorized channels—a violation of the ITU's fundamental rules. There was little recourse against such action, however. Retaliation would only interfere further with satisfactory broadcasting, so the other states let the titans alone to wrestle over the airwaves. Meanwhile, the ITU kept working on the technical and scientific problems involved in perfecting an equitable code, against the day when reason could replace politics in the regulation of telecommunications.

4. The Secretariats of the two bodies have substantial administrative responsibilities. The Postal Union Bureau fixes the specific rates to be charged, following principles laid down by the congress, and handles the international accounts for mail services among members. It determines, by sampling the volume of mail at ports of entry at different times during the year, the amount each country should receive from the others.

The ITU Administrative Council and its technical committees are empowered to carry out the decisions of the Conference, rather than having the decisions referred back to the individual governments for action.

5. On the other hand, it should be emphasized that regulation does not mean *operation*. These organizations do *not* provide or conduct mail services or telecommunication facilities. These functions are left to governments to handle.

---

[35] As a matter of fact, France has a hard struggle to keep the Union from eliminating even the modest payment now made for mail transit; yet it continues to hang on.

6. Furthermore, the problems with which UPU and ITU are equipped to deal are technical, not political. It is plain that the success of these organizations in smoothing and speeding the flow of communication depends to a large degree on keeping politics out of their technical tasks. If left alone, they can devise rational solutions for complex questions. But their implementation inescapably requires cooperative action among the various governments, regardless of their political controversies. They have a choice: to use communications for communicating or to use them for waging political battle. This is a decision which UPU and ITU cannot make.

Typical of the problems with which the UPU can cope is the need for standardization and mechanization in order to lower costs. The Consultative Committee for Postal Studies was set up in 1957 to work out uniform envelopes, set up faster and more efficient mail-sorting systems, recommend better and more diversified means of transport and delivery, and in general to study the means of applying automation to the whole process of handling mail.

The major problem of the ITU is the allocation of a limited number of frequencies among many demands. Frequencies are a scarce international resource, with an absolute ceiling fixed by nature. But demands constantly increase with advances in technology and possible uses. For instance, at the ITU Conference in Atlantic City in 1947, nations were invited to submit requests for frequencies they felt would be necessary. They filed 3,236 to fill 235 availabilities requiring 16,100 kc's. The International Frequency Registration Board was set up to assign allocations, and the problem has been temporarily but efficiently solved through the Seasonal High Frequency Broadcasting Schedules which are regularly revised four times a year. But, obviously, a spirit of compromise must prevail to enable the ITU to fulfill this task satisfactorily. As noted above, this is by no means assured, especially when some countries are determined to carry on a war for men's minds via telecommunications.[36]

In retrospect, international administrative regulation in the field of communications has, despite competing economic interests and the intrusion of political considerations, generally maintained the conditions necessary for a free flow of messages among the peoples of the world. It has not been able, however, to transcend barriers of censorship, or to restrict other abuses of the channels of communications when governments have become obsessed with security and locked in a power struggle.

---

[36] For a thorough analysis of these issues see George A. Codding, Jr., *Broadcasting Without Barriers* (Paris: UNESCO, 1959); also, by the same author, *The International Telecommunications Union* (Leiden: E. J. Brill, 1952).

The organization and operations of the UPU are reviewed in M. A. K. Menon, "Universal Postal Union," *International Conciliation,* March, 1965.

Chapter 13

Postwar Reconstruction: A Triumph of International Cooperation

Peace after World War II meant for most of the belligerents, victor or vanquished, a desperate struggle for sheer existence. So immense had been the destruction of human and material resources that many nations stood on the verge of economic and social collapse, and some faced actual starvation.

An unprecedented global recovery effort was launched to meet the emergency. The United States, least damaged by the war, was necessarily the chief reservoir of funds and supplies, and its cooperation was vital. But mutual assistance among the devastated and the support of many other countries set a pattern of truly collective international action. Though the methods and terms of cooperation changed, the battle to recover from the greatest of wars accomplished a striking advance in the organization of world economic collaboration. Under the pressure of dire misery and hunger, many nations relinquished their jealous insistence on independent control of their resources and instead worked out and joined in cooperative action to advance their common welfare.

RELIEF: THE TRADITION OF PRIVATE CONCERN

Before the century of total wars, each nation had usually fended for itself after a war. Reconstruction took place as people trudged back to their homes and land, and started over again to plow and build. Occasionally, their governments might assist—lending materials, issuing temporary rations, or improving needed supplies if not available in the country. Debts incurred by the government during the war (mainly to its own citizens) would gradually be paid off out of new taxes—or, more conveniently, defaulted. Dislocations caused by the war were essentially internal, rather than international, and reconstruction consequently could be accomplished with relatively little assistance from other countries.

Gradually, however, humanitarian concern for victims of war prompted the voluntary organization of international assistance by private groups. National Red Cross Societies were established, primarily to aid the wounded soldiers of their own countries during the course of hostilities, but also to provide emergency relief to civilians in war and other disasters. The International Red Cross was a separate effort largely directed and supported by Swiss, aimed to improve the treatment of prisoners and to aid civilian victims of war. Churches and religious groups also contributed across national boundaries to ease the human suffering caused by war.

World War I generated emotional and political pressures that resulted in a demand for international reconstruction of a far different sort. The Allies as victors imposed on the defeated Germans the obligation of paying for all the damages of the war. Reparations were, in effect, a symbol of moral retribution and contributed little to actual reconstruction. Payment was demanded in money, not goods; and, as a matter of fact, Allied economic policies aimed to prevent the receipt of German goods in order to "protect" home production against competition. In the end, reparations did not provide the French with new homes nor the British with new investments to replace their war expenditures. Instead, an immense hypothetical credit was created. Unwilling to realize this credit through purchases directly or indirectly from Germany, the Allies largely forfeited German assistance in their own reconstruction.

Actually, the immediate physical impact of World War I was not serious except in Germany and German-controlled areas where normal imports of foodstuffs were shut off by the Allied blockade. The plight of the Belgian population in this situation prompted a unique private international relief effort even in the midst of the war. Under the leadership of Herbert Hoover, the Commission for Relief in Belgium was organized and arrangements made for shipment of food and clothing through the blockade to be distributed to the Belgians under neutral, nongovernmental observation. The German government permitted the distribution without seizing supplies for its war effort, and also contributed agreed amounts of its stocks for the purpose. The British government permitted passage of the supplies on assurance of the commission that no diversion to Germany was taking place. Funds were at first raised by voluntary contributions in many countries, but the Belgian and other governments increasingly subsidized the program.

By the end of the war, conditions of near starvation prevailed in Germany and Eastern Europe. Continuance of the blockade for nearly nine months after the armistice made it impossible for the German government to meet the emergency. Mr. Hoover promptly organized the American Relief Administration—also a nongovernmental effort, enlisting the cooperation of many religions and humanitarian organizations in the United States—which succeeded in mobilizing, transporting, and distributing food and medical supplies to the most needy among the former enemy population, and in addition reached into Russia, Poland, Austria, and most of the East European countries.

Such relief provided the critical margin between life and death for some several million persons during a period when economic relations between the defeated countries and the rest of the world were at an enforced standstill. The emergency, however, was primarily the result of Allied war and postwar policy, not of raw physical destruction. Once the policy changed, it was possible for these countries (except Russia) to get back on their feet rather quickly. The problem of relief, grave though it was, could be met by temporary action, largely on private initiative and with private resources.[1]

THE LEGACY OF TOTAL WAR

A situation of entirely different magnitude and character was confronted in the aftermath of World War II. The accumulated legacy of the two wars precipitated a total economic and social breakdown in the most devastated countries, which, in turn, deeply threatened the security and stability of those less directly hit by the conduct of hostilities. Recovery was a hydra-headed problem. It involved not just alleviation of momentary hunger but reestablishment of basic social institutions, regeneration of every facet of national and international economic life, resettlement of displaced persons, restoration of health and morale, and a rebirth of moral values.

The overwhelming material obstacle to recovery was the world scarcity of resources, resulting from the attrition of raw materials, industrial plant, and communications in both world wars. Aggravating this problem, the economic balance between countries had been so destroyed that those most in need could not pay for supplies from countries able to furnish them, such as

---

[1] Emergency wartime and postwar relief was rendered by religious and non-sectarian organizations directly as well as through the A.R.A. The efforts of Quakers were notable for their particular emphasis on relief as an expression of goodwill toward the populations of the defeated enemy states and on the restoration of bonds of common humanity.

As successive waves of suffering humans were presented by further wars, more limited in scope, but just as ferocious, and as devastating in their impact on people, the tradition of international private relief continued. Near East Relief, another largely American effort, was instrumental in assisting 2,000,000 Greeks to establish themselves in Greece after being forced to leave their homes in Asia Minor in an exchange of populations at the end of the Greek–Turkish hostilities in 1922. More or less partisan organizations helped each side in the Spanish Civil War (1937–38); while the Quakers again demonstrated their non-partisanship by gaining entree to both sides for distribution of various types of civilian assistance.

the United States. Inadequate production, inflation, exhaustion of former assets dragged Europe and Asia alike into a state of international bankruptcy, depriving them of any independent means of access to the resources necessary to rehabilitate their economic life. Furthermore, a human problem acutely hampered efforts at recovery. Much of the productive manpower of the world had been shattered. Aside from outright war casualties, disease, malnutrition, war tension, and the toll of concentration camp and persecution had worn down stamina and sapped incentive. People were tired, hopeless, resentful of enemy and ally alike. Between the have-not and the have, the barrier of distrust grew, the have-nots jealous to guard their independence, the haves indignant that proferred aid should be received with suspicion and even ingratitude. In addition, many millions of refugees, driven from their homes by the sweep of hostilities or by forced labor, were unable to find security or the means of providing for their own livelihood.

The problem of reconstruction was clearly one of fullest international dimensions. The devastated could not repair the material and human damage they had suffered without vast outside help. The Axis peoples in defeat were themselves full companions in the misery of the war's aftermath, unable even to feed themselves, much less to undertake the reparation of their victors' injuries. Hence, reconstruction depended, in the last analysis, on the cooperation of the undamaged. The United States and the other American republics fortunately recognized that in the postwar world their prosperity, trade, and security would depend on the revival of Europe and Asia. They could not, if they would, isolate themselves from the impact of impoverishment, starvation, disease, and social chaos on other continents. Reconstruction, like the war, compelled a total and a collective effort.

THE STRATEGY OF REHABILITATION: THE UNRRA PATTERN

In the midst of the war, the countries of the United Nations agreed on the necessity for a broad, joint program to rehabilitate "liberated" areas, and on November 9, 1943, established the United Nations Relief and Rehabilitation Administration to carry out this purpose.[2] UNRRA was the first operating agency created by the United Nations and the most ambitious experiment in international administration ever undertaken.

Underlying its organization were three basic assumptions: (1) the revival of the devastated nations would require not just *relief* to individuals (as after World War I) but also *rehabilitation* of the entire national economy and social life; (2) this would require such large resources that governments, not

---

[2] Germany and Japan were not included among the objects of UNRRA action, but were dependent exclusively for relief upon the occupying powers. Their entire reconstruction was dictated by the military governments.

private organizations, would have to assume the primary responsibility for action;[3] (3) this international effort, though of large scale, would be short-lived, dealing only with immediate emergency problems and not providing assistance in longer-run tasks of reconstruction, such as attainment of prewar levels of production and standards of living. In other words, postwar recovery was conceived as a two-stage process—the emergency stage of relief and rehabilitation administered internationally through the novel instrument of UNRRA, the second stage, reconstruction, left to independent national action or to other permanent international agencies.

The overriding principle in UNRRA administration was to "help people to help themselves." This purpose was dictated both by the necessity of enlisting maximum effort to assure effective rehabilitation and by considerations of national honor. The basis of the UNRRA approach was delicately expressed by the first Director-General, Herbert H. Lehman.

> Nations no less than individuals desire to live in dignity and self-respect. They wish to become self-reliant members of the world community. To this end they seek the opportunity to work, to produce, to trade. They turn to us with no idea of long-continuing relief, but like individuals overwhelmed by some catastrophic misfortune they merely ask for our help in order that they may surmount a dire national emergency.

To implement this principle of national self-help, UNRRA followed three basic policies. It conducted its operations through national governments; it required all member nations to contribute to the program, even countries receiving aid; and it stipulated that within each country most of the supplies furnished by UNRRA be sold rather than given to individuals, and that the funds so secured be utilized for other worthy internal reconstruction projects approved by UNRRA.

National Initiative

UNRRA acted only on the express invitation of a national government which requested assistance. The type of program, the quantity of supplies, and the methods of distribution were, in the first instance, proposed by each government; and, in the end, all arrangements were subject to its approval. In very few instances did UNRRA undertake direct distribution. For the most part, it merely procured the needed supplies and transported them to a country's border, then turned them over to the government for distribution through its own agencies according to an agreed plan. The intention was to

---

[3] Private organizations did make a supreme effort to meet urgent relief needs. In the United States, the Jewish Joint Distribution Committee, the National Catholic Welfare Council, the major Protestant Denominations, the American Friends Service Committee (Quakers), and separate committees for the different liberated countries raised unprecedented sums of voluntary contributions for relief. This was spent mainly for supplies of food, clothing and medicine, distributed either by relief teams on the spot or through churches and other institutions in the devastated countries.

avoid superimposing an expensive outside organization for handling the relief program, and to strengthen in every way the competence and responsibility of the country's own public institutions. UNRRA advisers frequently assisted national governments in setting up effective administrative machinery and guided them in the development of their reconstruction programs. But the power of decision, within the framework of a "basic agreement" negotiated between the government and UNRRA, rested with the national officials.

National governments, furthermore, participated in determination of overall UNRRA policies. The final authority was the UNRRA Council, in which every member government was represented and had equal voice, whether or not it received aid. A powerful Central Committee, however, was empowered to make decisions when the Council was not in session, and it actually exercised a more potent influence over the day-to-day operations. It consisted of four permanent members—United States, United Kingdom, Soviet Union, and China—and five others elected by the Council. Specially interested nations could be represented at the meetings, and all decisions were open for review when the Council convened.

"From Each According to His Ability"

Ability to pay was the chief criterion for financing UNRRA, but every country was obligated to contribute something. Those countries whose territory had not been occupied by the enemy bore the burden for supplies. Each was asked at first for contributions estimated as equivalent to 1 percent of its national income for the year ending June 30, 1943. Later, another 1 percent assessment was requested. Under this plan, the United States provided approximately 72 per cent of the UNRRA budget, though proportionately its contribution was no larger than the other unoccupied countries.

All member governments, whether or not their home territories had been occupied, shared in the administrative expense of UNRRA. In addition, each country receiving aid was asked to cover all costs of administration, transportation, warehousing, and local services within its borders, and often to contribute local products to the program.

These arrangements confirmed the character of UNRRA as a partnership of nations engaged in promoting their common interest, rather than an instrument of charity by the fortunate to the underprivileged. This stimulated an increased spirit of self-reliance on the part of those being assisted.

Double-Duty Relief

The most ingenious—and most controversial—technique of encouraging self-help was the UNRRA requirement that the bulk of its supplies be sold through commercial channels rather than given free to needy individuals.[4] A

---

[4] Some UNRRA supplies were distributed free especially through schools, orphanages, and public institutions for the aged and other needy.

national government, receiving foodstuffs, soap, horses and livestock, fertilizer or machinery, without cost to itself, was authorized to place them on sale either through government or private stores at fixed prices in the national currency. Any person who had the money could buy. If he wished, he could resell. All funds realized from the government's sale, however, were earmarked for reconstruction or relief purposes and could be used only with UNRRA's approval.

Strange and misunderstood results often occurred. The purchasers were unconscious of having received any benefit for which they should acknowledge gratitude, for they had paid from their own pockets for what they received. Hence, the contribution of UNRRA was not visible to them, and it did not arouse enthusiastic local support. UNRRA commodities turned up on the black or grey markets, as they were resold for higher prices or in exchange for other products wanted by the purchaser. Stories of administrative graft and corruption spread. In the end, this method of distribution brought on intense public and legislative criticism in some of the chief contributing countries.

Yet, three essential purposes were fulfilled. National governments were able to undertake such swifter and broader steps of reconstruction because additional funds were thus made available to supplement their heavily burdened budgets. Furthermore, this approach strongly counteracted inflation by making people use up their personal income for necessities, instead of having it free to spend after receiving food or clothing as a gift. Above all, the incentive to work was stimulated because people knew they had to earn their means of livelihood.

International Control

While UNRRA stressed self-help and national initiative, it insisted on international control and supervision to assure that certain fundamental conditions of the program were carried out. In the first place, the UNRRA administration itself screened each country's estimates of its needs and determined the final allocations in the light of available supplies and the relative needs of others. UNRRA controlled disbursement of all funds and directly undertook procurement of supplies. This strictly limited each recipient to the items approved for it. An UNRRA mission was stationed in every receiving country to check on distribution and ascertain whether the supplies were being used as specified in the agreed program. UNRRA demanded for its field staff freedom of movement, observation, and communication, and insisted on an accounting of the disposition of its supplies. An essential requirement was that distribution take place without distinction as to national, racial, religious, or political considerations.

The pivot of UNRRA control was the Director-General. Though he was responsible to the Central Committee and ultimately to the Council, he was given substantial discretion in execution of the program. In carrying out the far-flung operations, he depended on a staff which at one time reached almost 13,000, recruited from 55 nationalities. Particularly heavy responsibilities rested on the chiefs of missions in the various receiving countries. For the most part, these officials preserved a careful impartiality in regard to the nations in which they worked, and sought constantly to maintain the principles and policies of the organization as a whole. The director-generals steadfastly insisted that no nation could act contrary to the UNRRA Constitution or to the decisions of the Council and still receive assistance. On the other hand, an earnest attempt was made to work harmoniously with the various national governments, and to resolve differences by agreement rather than ultimatum.

The Accomplishment

In three years, despite formidable obstacles and serious shortcomings, UNRRA saved two continents from collapse. After a long period of planning, negotiation, and organization for tasks whose nature and scope would only be guessed at while hostilities were in progress, the agency's operations suddenly assumed formidable proportions. Beginning with Greece in April, 1945, the shipment of relief and rehabilitation supplies was extended to eleven European countries, three countries in Asia, and one in Africa.

At first, the primary emphasis had to be placed on relief. An immediate aim was to quickly rebuild the transportation network so that commodities could reach the neediest parts of each country. Trucks, locomotives, rolling stock, shipping, horses, and mules were poured in. Simultaneously, urgent action was taken to meet acute food shortages. During the winter of 1945–46 before the first postwar harvest was in, cereals and fats supplied by UNRRA literally provided the margin between life and death in Eastern Europe, Italy, and the Balkans. At that, rations in these countries declined until the normal consumer received little more than 1,500 calories a day, and large sections of the population much less. Outright starvation was averted only by the narrowest margin—but it *was* averted. Basic clothing, much of it contributed voluntarily in a mammoth worldwide collection, filled a critical need of millions, especially for the winter months. UNRRA health services and medical supplies were instrumental in preventing, for the first time after a major war, the wiping out of populations by epidemics.

As soon as the immediate emergency eased, UNRRA shifted to an increasing emphasis on basic economic rehabilitation projects. Seed, fertilizer, and farm machinery were distributed to help revive agricultural production. Dairy cattle and breeding livestock were brought in to rebuild the herds slaughtered during the war. Raw materials and tools were secured to start up local industries and crafts. UNRRA even procured equipment for mining and heavy industry. Meanwhile, technical experts assisted the economic and social welfare agencies of the recipient governments in planning and organizing their reconstruction efforts and in training local personnel.

The great diversity of the UNRRA operation is evident in a partial inventory of its program in China, which received the largest amount of assistance. Direct food relief was provided to over 10 million destitute persons through soup kitchens, work projects, or take-home allotments. Hospitals, medical schools, and clinics were rebuilt and reequipped. A large quantity of vaccine was shipped in to check cholera, typhus, and other epidemics, and emergency training in nursing was given to many Chinese. A flood-control, irrigation, and reclamation project organized in the Yellow River Basin restored four million acres to agricultural production. Three thousand blacksmith shops were equipped and technical assistance provided to set going a farm tool manufacturing industry. In a particular rehabilitation project, UNRRA furnished tractors, plows, combines, and cultivators to speed agricultural production. On the industrial side, UNRRA provided power plant equipment, waterworks equipment, construction and shelter supplies, coal mining supplies, and 660,000 bales of raw cotton for local textile production. UNRRA effectively restored inland water transportation in China by supplying 300 river vessels, cranes, dredges, and repair shops which made possible a monthly movement of half a million tons. It also equipped an air transport line and put some rail transport in operation by providing some 268 locomotives, 86,000 tons of rails, and a corresponding amount of other types of equipment.

In sheer volume, the UNRRA supply operation exceeded in two years the U.S. Army's total wartime shipments across the Atlantic. Over 20 million tons of commodities were procured and transported during 1945–46. Their value was about $3.7 billion, almost 93 per cent of UNRRA's total expenditures.

The net effect of UNRRA was to start each of the aided countries well along the road to recovery, while preventing an incalculable loss of life from starvation and disease. Summarizing the rehabilitation of European countries assisted by UNRRA, Fiorello LaGuardia, the second Director-General, reported to the United Nations in 1947: "Starvation has been averted. A substantial recovery has been achieved in agricultural production, transportation has been greatly improved and industry has begun to recover in most countries. No serious epidemics have occurred." Mr. LaGuardia also noted that UNRRA supplies had helped materially in the battle against inflation. At the same time, he warned that only the smallest beginning had been made in the replacement of capital losses such as livestock, industrial equipment, and housing, and only the first steps had been taken to rebuild the network of trade among European countries. A similar but somewhat more pessimistic evaluation would have held for the Far East. In brief, UNRRA had succeeded in starting recovery, but the process was far from completed.

UNRRA's Problems

In its complex and herculean task, UNRRA encountered grave problems of procurement, administration, inadequate cooperation from national governments, and public misunderstanding that hampered it and prevented fully effective action.

Most of the commodities needed for relief and rehabilitation were in acutely short supply both during and after the end of hostilities, and were under strict control of either United States or inter-Allied war agencies. UNRRA had to compete for allocations against both military and domestic requirements of the chief supplying countries. It could not freely purchase in the market the items needed. An equally stringent restriction applied to shipping, and this was a critical bottleneck throughout UNRRA operations. Again and again, delivery schedules were upset, threatening serious crises in the receiving countries, because shipping space was unavailable. The control boards were not unsympathetic to the requests on behalf of relief and rehabilitation, but generally gave them lower priority than other demands. Later, when controls in the United States were relaxed, the prices rose for scarce commodities, such as wheat and dairy products, and UNRRA's costs skyrocketed. The extraordinarily high American consumption of food immediately after the war (averaging over 3,500 calories daily) intensified the problem both of cost and procurement; and the government was unwilling to authorize and designate the sources of supply quotas for UNRRA as it had done for wartime purposes. Instead, it stimulated voluntary effort in two directions—to increase production of foodstuffs and to limit consumption. The first succeeded over a period of time, but the second had only a limited effect. In the most acute period of crisis, the winter of 1946–47, Mr. LaGuardia barnstormed the breadbasket of America, directly appealed to farmers to sell their products for relief, and stimulated the sending of several trainloads of food. None of these actions adequately met the problem of securing the supplies UNRRA really needed. The agency continually skirted the thin edge of disaster, and had to scale down its assistance to each country far below the level required for effective rehabilitation.

Shortcomings in UNRRA's administration resulted in inefficiency and waste. Personnel both at headquarters and in the field was often inexperienced and incompetent. Just as with supplies, the organization had to compete for its manpower against military and other national government demands. On the field, the temptations to venality strongly challenged the moral fibre of the staff. A few did exploit their positions of virtual life-or-death responsibility for their personal gain. This gave a bad reputation to the staff, even though most were above reproach. The administrative organization was unwieldy and poorly coordinated, at least during the initial stages. The functions of different sections overlapped, and some top officials resisted reorganization that would deprive them of any part of their bailiwick. Lines of responsibility, therefore, became confused, and control over personnel slack. In due course, appointment of a dynamic and highly capable Australian deputy-director, Commander R. G. A. Jackson, led to a drastic realignment of the organization, cutting out of incompetent personnel, clarification of functions, and sharpening of lines of responsibility. Loose financial and budgetary control also plagued UNRRA at the start. Effective auditing was not instituted for almost two years, and in the meantime disbursements had been made without a strict, centralized system of authorization and accounting. This made careful budgeting impossible and soon tarred the organization with a reputation for financial mismanagement which clung until its liquidation, though the problem was largely corrected and a final audit cleared the record.

UNRRA's work was jeopardized in several instances by the action, or lack of action, of participating governments. Some governments were so inefficient or irresponsible that they did not properly conduct the distribution of aid. In China, the UNRRA mission was especially critical, because the government failed to move supplies quickly to needy areas, and they consequently piled up on the docks in Shanghai and other ports. Friction between UNRRA and the Chinese government became acute when UNRRA began to carry out distribution directly, ignoring the terms of the basic agreement. Finally, when UNRRA temporarily suspended shipments because of the congestion of supplies, the government agreed to strengthen its Reconstruction Administration with borrowed UNRRA personnel, acting under its formal authority.

Several governments balked at permitting the degree of outside supervision UNRRA considered necessary to make sure the conditions of aid were being fulfilled. They objected that this reflected on their national competence or integrity, were sometimes recalcitrant about putting UNRRA recommendations into effect, and even asked that their own reports and assurances be accepted without further check as adequate confirmation of the satisfactory discharge of their responsibilities. Delicate negotiations were often required to maintain UNRRA's policies—observing distribution first-hand in the field and accounting meticulously for all supplies—without giving offense to a government that was not only "sovereign" but an actual member of the UNRRA organization. The implicit threat of losing the aid usually brought compliance, but sometimes only after a long period of strained and disagreeable relations.

The most serious difficulty with national governments arose when they let politics intrude into the UNRRA program. The distribution of relief offered a tempting tool to a government in power to strengthen its prestige and influence, and even to gain adherents outright. At one time, for instance, the Yugoslav government took public credit for handing out supplies provided by UNRRA. The Ukrainian government also inadequately publicized the international source of UNRRA assistance. The clearest example of political discrimination was the virtual embargo imposed by the Nationalist government of China on distribution of UNRRA supplies to Communist areas of the country. More subtle forms of partisan influence were reported at the local level in several countries. The UNRRA staff hit hard to prevent or correct such abuses. Supplies were boldly stamped with the UNRRA label. The missions closely watched all national publicity affecting the program and called firmly for accurate, continued, and full public explanation by the government of the source and principles of UNRRA aid. The field staff checked carefully to detect any local misadministration. As a whole, the intrusion of politics was kept at a minimum, but in the case of China, the UNRRA mission bluntly stated that it had been unable to effect equitable distribution according to need in the Communist areas. Not only did the government block by direct and indirect means the overland shipment of supplies, but Nationalist planes on one occasion bombed UNRRA ships enroute to the Communist-held port of Tsing-tao.

As a result of these and other problems, UNRRA labored under the handicap of public misunderstanding and criticism, which grew steadily more serious. Its reputation was especially poor in the United States, a most critical situation since American financial support and supplies were indispensable. Attacks in the press and in Congress charged inefficient administration, misuse of UNRRA aid for political purposes by the pro-Communist governments of Eastern Europe, excessive or unwise allocations of supplies, inadequate supervision, and a lack of thankful recognition by the recipients of the aid given. Many criticisms were without foundation. Others were exaggerated. Some were pure recrimination by persons fired from the UNRRA staff for incompetence. Some were based on a misunderstanding of the principles and methods of UNRRA—for example, its selling of consumer commodities to ward off inflation and secure local revenue for further reconstruction efforts. (This important policy and its justification was—and still is—almost completely unknown, even to the relatively well-informed.) Some of the charges were undoubtedly justified, particularly as related to UNRRA's first years. But however much the organization strove to correct its mistakes and overcome the staggering problems with which it was faced as the pioneer large-scale international administration, if failed to improve its public and legislative relations. In the end, this proved fatal.

An Untimely Death

UNRRA's operations were officially terminated in Europe at the end of 1946 and in Asia on March 31, 1947, largely at the initiative of the United States. At the fifth session of the UNRRA Council in Geneva in August, 1946, William L. Clayton, Deputy Undersecretary of State for Economic

Affairs, startled the other delegates by announcing that "the gravy train has gone around for the last time." Though UNRRA had originally been designed to last for only two or three years, few had anticipated that it would cease operations until recovery was more firmly assured. The United States government confidently asserted, however, that the postwar emergency was over and that the liberated countries should now be able to fend for themselves with whatever loans they could get from private commercial and financial sources, from the International Bank for Reconstruction and Development, or by bilateral arrangements. Furthermore, American officials indicated, the Congress and the American public would oppose any further contribution to UNRRA.

This ultimatum left no alternative. Arrangements were hurriedly made to transfer some of UNRRA's technical and social services to other bodies. Health activities went to the World Health Organization actually before it was in operation. An International Refugee Organization was specially created to provide for the million or more displaced persons still on UNRRA's hands. The United Nations was asked to take on such of UNRRA's social welfare functions as it could or would. A last-minute plea at the United Nations General Assembly in December, 1946, resulted in creation of an International Children's Emergency Fund under the United Nations. It would use whatever residual assets of UNRRA might be available and other funds that might be contributed for continuing the rehabilitation of children and adolescents. But no further provision was made for a planned international supply program for relief and rehabilitation. A warning by Director-General LaGuardia that the war-devastated countries were completely unprepared to meet their own needs and that major international help was still essential was disregarded. The first General Assembly of the U.N., meeting that fall, finally agreed to a compromise, requesting its members to provide further assistance, but directly to the countries concerned and on conditions determined in each case by bilateral negotiation.

Events quickly and catastrophically confounded the American premises on which UNRRA's precipitate dissolution was based. During the winter and spring of 1946–47, one of Europe's worst, food stocks sunk to their most dangerous postwar level. Fuel in many countries was virtually exhausted. Transportation stalled. Production slackened. European countries' financial resources, especially dollars, drained off at an alarming rate. International relief and rehabilitation, substantial though it had been, had not been extensive or prolonged enough to assure permanent recovery.

FOREIGN AID—AMERICAN STYLE

UNRRA machinery was still in operation, but the United States government did not turn to the organization it had disinherited. It decided, instead, to meet the renewed emergency by offering aid directly to such countries as would accept American conditions regarding its use and administration.

In contrast to UNRRA, the American foreign aid program had a conscious political objective. It was undertaken not only to relieve distress but as a means of combating the further extension of Communist influence and control in Europe. Acting unilaterally, the United States confined most of its economic assistance to four countries whose governments were under severe internal or external Communist pressure—Austria, Greece, Italy, and France. In the course of one year, 1947–48, a billion dollars worth of food, fuel, fertilizer, and medical supplies was given to these governments to help maintain minimum rations, increase production, and prevent epidemics. This was actually as large an expenditure on behalf of four countries as the U.S. had contributed for a corresponding period to UNRRA—which had assisted 14 countries, in addition to 10 to 12 million displaced persons. In return, however, the United States was able to choose the recipients, to control the distribution, and to reap the credit.

The terms of aid were fixed by American law, and each receiving country committed itself in a bilateral agreement to meet them. Direct supervision and control of supplies throughout the process of distribution had to be exercised by a mission composed solely of American citizens, cleared by the FBI as to loyalty and security. The American Field Administrator was empowered to retain possession of supplies up to the local community where they were used. Not only U.S. officials but also the American press and radio were assured the opportunity to observe freely and report on the aid program. The governments had to insure full and continuous publicity within their countries in regard to the "purpose, source, character, scope, amounts and programs" of the progress. All supplies had to be "marked, stamped, branded or labeled in a conspicuous place as legibly, indelibly and permanently (as possible) . . . in such manner as to indicate to the ultimate consumer . . . that such supplies or articles have been furnished by the United States for relief assistance." Supplies similar to those being furnished by the United States could not be exported. Any information requested by the United States government affecting the operation was to be provided, and the governments undertook to stimulate maximum efforts to produce and distribute local commodities. The United States retained complete discretion as to the supplies it would furnish, and where they would be purchased. In the interest of conserving American resources for home use, the Foreign Aid Act set definite limits to the amount of wheat that could be exported, and also discouraged export of American petroleum. On the other hand, not more than 10 per cent of the supplies could be procured "offshore" if the delivered price was higher than the U.S. price.[5]

---

[5] See provisions of Public Laws 84 and 389, 80th Congress.

In other respects, the program followed precedents set by UNRRA. Supplies were required to be distributed without discrimination "as to race, creed or political belief," and equitably on the basis of need. The method of distribution was to sell goods through government agencies at fixed and reasonable prices. Like UNRRA, the proceeds in local currency were placed by the government on deposit in a fund used (subject to American approval) for special projects contributing to relief or reconstruction. France, for instance, devoted a part of its "local currency fund" to modernizing some of its power and mining facilities and to reducing the national debt so as to combat inflation. The Greek fund went almost entirely to provide bread, clothing, bedding, and other relief to refugees. The Italian lira fund was spent in part on measures to relieve unemployment, such as financing public works, distributing food packages, and providing vocational training.

American administrators, reporting every three months to the President and to Congress, claimed important accomplishments as a result of the relief program. In Austria, 50–60 per cent of the 1,700 calorie target for the daily ration was supplied by U.S. aid. In Italy, a most critical food situation was transformed by the spring of 1948 into the best condition since the war—just in time for the vital elections on April 18, when the Communist bid for political victory fizzled. The French basic ration was also maintained to a large extent by U.S. supplies, following the terrible harvest of 1947 which produced less than half the prewar yield. In addition, large imports of cotton forestalled a shutdown of the textile industry when France, for lack of dollars, virtually stopped buying from abroad.

In the case of Greece, American economic assistance was associated with military aid in the first installment of the Truman Doctrine, designed to prevent Communist expansion in the Balkans. With guerrilla warfare threatening to overthrow the Greek government, disrupting transportation and devastating much of the countryside, top priority was given to strengthening the armed forces.[6] Nevertheless, the desperate economic conditions made imperative extensive relief and rehabilitation efforts, chiefly along lines already started by UNRRA.

The American mission in Greece was particularly concerned with reform of the government's economic policies in order to check the drastic inflation. American experts, "counseling" with the respective government departments, in effect drew up the national budget, imposing stringent economies that included the dismissal of thousands of government employees. They revised the tax system so as to bring in additional revenue from Greek businesses. An American was employed to head up a new Foreign Trade

---

[6] Of the $300 million initial appropriation for Greek aid, only 41 per cent was ultimately allocated for relief and economic reconstruction. Originally, economic and military aid were expected to be about equal, but the deteriorating military situation caused a transfer of $23 million to purchase additional military supplies.

Administration which regulated Greece's exports and imports and controlled foreign exchange. As a matter of fact, the American Mission became a "brain trust" for the Greek government—with the powerful suasion of funds and supplies to back up their recommendations.

The United States government liked this system of direct American control over international relief operations. It could insist on its own methods and standards of efficiency. It could secure swift correction of what it considered shortcomings or misbehavior on the part of another government. It could expect the dividends of political support as well as personal appreciation from dutifully informed recipients of American bounty. With this in mind, the missions paid particular attention to publicity, and were gratified by the thousands of inches of local press notices, the radio commentaries, window displays and public ceremonies, the letters of children, and the vivid posters that glorified United States' generosity and acknowledged the American share of the daily ration. Congress was told for instance, that "all Greeks knew that they were dependent upon American assistance, realized that they were getting it and expressed their gratitude for it."[7] An Austrian poster, distributed throughout the country, showed four-fifths of a loaf of bread as the gift of America. In Italy, a major battle for publicity was waged with the Communists—and was won, to judge by the 1948 election returns. For such reasons, the principle of donor control became firmly established as a prerequisite for further American efforts to promote world recovery.

VINDICATION OF INTERNATIONAL RELIEF ADMINISTRATION: UNICEF

The UNRRA tradition was not completely displaced by American initiative. The United Nations International Children's Emergency Fund (UNICEF) carried out, under the mandate of the United Nations General Assembly, a program of aid to children and adolescents in countries that had been receiving help from UNRRA and "for child health purposes generally." In its administration of these functions, the organization became an "international cooperative," drawing on nations able to help with money, goods, and services, and distributing that aid to countries not able to meet their children's needs out of their own resources.

Program

UNICEF is the only United Nations section that is essentially a supply program. The Fund operates no projects of its own but uses its money to purchase essential supplies and equipment not available locally. Initially, these supplies were emergency aid (mainly food, but also some clothing and

---

[7] Department of State, Third Report to Congress on U.S. Foreign Relief Program, March 31, 1948.

medical supplies). With recovery in Europe, governments of the economically underdeveloped countries began to insist that UNICEF shift its emphasis to programs of long-term benefit to children, particularly applicable to areas of chronic need.[8]

In 1950, the General Assembly extended UNICEF's life for three years with the intention of continuing it indefinitely if the Fund found it could work effectively in countries of massive need. In line with its general opposition to internationally administered supply programs, the United States was the only country to vigorously oppose this move and, in the end, to vote against the resolution endorsing it. UNICEF's unique experience with the provision of strategic supplies to stimulate government activity on behalf of children and its insistence on training national staff to carry out these provisions proved peculiarly appropriate for the developing countries. Consequently, the General Assembly, with the United States abstaining, voted enthusiastically to establish the Children's Fund as a semiautonomous body of the United Nations, on a permanent basis.

To insure technical competence and avoid overlapping programs, UNICEF has developed a network of cooperative relationships with those divisions of the United Nations and the specialized agencies in whose functional domain the fund operates. Thus, in the field of health, the World Health Organization not only approves the types of medical programs UNICEF may assist (through the UNICEF–WHO Joint Committee on Health Policy), but also sets the medical and technical standards and criteria to be followed in provision of supplies and equipment as well as operation of the program. WHO provides special consultants to advise governments on implementation of the projects and international personnel to support national medical leaders and provide on-the-spot training. Similar joint relationships for the conduct of programs in their respective fields have been worked out with the Food and Agriculture Organization, UNESCO, ILO, and the UN Department of Social Affairs.

Financing

The Fund has depended on *voluntary* contributions from governments, persons, and organizations, in contrast to UNRRA which could, in effect, *assess* its member governments. Based on the priorities of child needs in relation to UNICEF resources, the key to its workability has been the assurance of recipient governments that they would provide material contributions as well as guarantees to continue the services for children once the program was established.

By 1964, more than 118 countries and territories were making annual government contributions to this program, and the aided governments were

---

[8] For this aspect of the program, see Chapter 14, pp. 421–23.

spending about $2.50 of their own money on projects for every $1.00 given by UNICEF. This international "grant-in-aid" formula not only greatly increased the amount of resources available for the immediate program, but stimulated the recipient governments to bolder action in developing their permanent services for child welfare.

The voluntary feature of financing also encouraged direct participation in the United Nations by individuals and organizations who wanted to demonstrate their support for international assistance as well as their humanitarian concern for children. In the first two years of its existence, 45 countries and more than 30 territories conducted campaigns to contribute the equivalent of "one day's pay" to children. Since then, other forms of solicitation have increasingly gained public support, so that by 1964, 20 percent of the Fund's annual resources (approximately $35 million) were nongovernmental contributions.

International Responsibility

UNICEF principles of distribution have stressed the responsibility of the international agency as trustee between donor and beneficiary. It has scrupulously insisted that aid must be given without discrimination because of race, creed, nationality, or political consideration, and that it be used in such a way as to make a permanent contribution to child welfare. Though actual administration has been the responsibility of national government agencies, UNICEF missions have conscientiously checked on every step of distribution until the individual child was reached. The Fund went beyond UNRRA in retaining title to all its supplies until consumed by the ultimate recipient. All contributed supplies were clearly stamped "UNICEF," down to each separate diaper or school book. Posters, the local press, and official announcements have publicized the United Nations' source and responsibility for the program.

That UNICEF has been an integral part of the United Nations is to a large degree responsible for its ability to work effectively in all parts of the world, regardless of political and ideological conflicts. The Fund's 30-nation executive board includes all five major powers in the United Nations, and a number of smaller countries from every region, including some that are not even members of the United Nations. The board reports to the Economic and Social Council and, through it, to the General Assembly. The Executive Director and the UNICEF staff are appointed by the Secretary-General of the United Nations and are directly responsible to him.

The solid achievements of UNICEF won universal acclaim. The United Nations, the participating countries on both the giving and receiving ends of its program, the press and many private groups repeatedly praised the work as an outstanding demonstration of effective international cooperation. By its careful planning, scrupulous nonpartisan administration, high operating efficiency and economy, and, above all, the overriding sense of international responsibility for a humanitarian purpose that permeated the organization, UNICEF vindicated the role of international organization as agent for the relief of human need and misery.

THE BID FOR ECONOMIC STABILIZATION

Alongside the efforts to repair the immediate physical devastation of the war and restore the capacity of people to produce a livelihood, governments undertook an extraordinary set of international actions to insure economic stability in the longer run. Mindful of the disastrous consequences of the victors' policies after the first world war, which failed to recognize the mutual dependence of victors and vanquished, of creditors and debtors, the principal United Nations allies began to plan, long before the second world war ended, how to prevent another excursion into throat-cutting jungle economics.

The economic debacle between the world wars reflected, in part, contradictory and conflicting policies in regard to exacting reparations from Germany and its allies, paying allied war debts to the U.S., and achieving national economic security in the face of runaway inflation on the one hand and depression on the other. The central problem was that each government fended for itself, operating on the basis of what immediate advantage it might gain through the manipulation of international trade, exchange rates, payments and loans, and other instruments of economic intercourse. This led or forced others to do the same. As a result, virtually everyone became engulfed in full-scale international economic warfare and pushed the world, themselves included, over the brink of economic collapse.

A few sporadic attempts were made to stall the spiral and establish a measure of stability through international action. The most notable of these were the League of Nations' efforts to secure the financial reconstruction of Austria and five other European countries that were at the point of national bankruptcy in the twenties; and, also at the League's initiative, a move to stabilize currency exchange rates by setting up a world pool of funds that could be drawn on when countries were temporarily unable to meet international payments.[9]

The financial reconstruction programs at first scored considerable success but could not survive the avalanche of the depression. The currency stabilization scheme never got off the ground because the United States would not play ball. In the first flush of the New Deal, President Roosevelt was not

---

[9] See Martin Hill, *The Economic and Financial Organization of the League of Nations* (Washington, D.C.: Carnegie Endowment, 1946). A definitive study of the financial reconstruction programs is Royall Tyler, *The League of Nations Reconstruction Schemes in the Inter-War Period* (Geneva: League of Nations, 1945).

prepared to give up a nationally managed currency as an important device of American recovery from the depression. It took only one recalcitrant at this point to scuttle the plan and send economic nationalism on an unchecked course to the conclusion of the second world war. Hitler, of course, delivered the coup de grâce to all international economic stabilization efforts by his ruthless pursuit of autarky, carrying economic nationalism to the ultimate.

The approach to economic stabilization after World War II, while thoroughly repudiating the nationalist precedents, reflected two influences that did not fully converge. A contrite and liberally oriented United States was now strongly committed to the reconstruction of a world economic order largely free from government controls. On the other hand was the strong hold of Keynesian economics on leaders of other governments, especially Britain. Even U.S. policy-makers were not immune from the influence of the British economist who had so surely predicted the course to catastrophe after the first world war (in his epic monograph *Economic Consequences of the War*) and then gone on to point out how nations could extricate themselves from the toils of depression. The hand and mind of Lord Keynes himself were at work throughout the critical negotiations on the stabilization program, emphasizing the necessity of responsible intergovernmental management and control of fiscal and economic policies in the pursuit of conditions of stability, rather than depending on the vagaries of free enterprise in open markets.

A bargain was reached on four main steps to lay the foundations for a stable world economy:

1. The U.S. virtually wiped clean the slate of debts incurred by its allies during the war, completely reversing its policy after the first world war.

2. Reparations from Germany were put on a pay-in-kind basis, quite separated from the network of regular international economic and financial relationships. However unrealistic this was from the point of view of encouraging general reconstruction and recovery, it did sidestep the thorny problems of international payments which arose after World War I.

3. Loans were made to countries that needed help in financing economic reconstruction.

4. Currency stabilization was internationally guaranteed.

These four lines of attack, though launched separately, were inter-related. As a matter of fact, the third and fourth measures were specifically tied together.

The Bretton Woods Agreements

The 44 United Nations, while still at war, negotiated the Bretton Woods Agreements, and established two new international agencies—the International Monetary Fund and the International Bank for Reconstruction and Development. Countries joining the Bank (thereby putting themselves in line for loans) had to be members of the Fund, thereby accepting strict obligations to maintain the stability of their currencies and ultimately to allow their currencies to be freely "convertible," that is, exchangeable at a given rate with those of the other organization members.

The rationale behind the arrangement was this: if the creditor helps the debtor over his immediate difficulties, the debtor must refrain from sharp competitive practices against his benefactor. The United States, in particular, looked forward to a time when its international business could be conducted without the obstacles of exchange controls and unpredictable currency fluctuations. Granted that in the immediate situation most countries could not hope to achieve anything like a balance of trade with the United States, and hence could not keep their currency from depreciating in terms of dollars unless they strictly limited their imports from the U.S. by one means or another (or were extended credit in dollars from some source), the American hope was that this was a temporary condition which could be overcome. Then, the relative values of currencies would be determined, not by direct government policy, but by the flow of international commerce. In the meantime, rates should be set approximating the "market value" of the various currencies and not changed without some special cause. This would give reasonable assurance of stable conditions of trade and encourage its expansion.

The International Monetary Fund

The Fund, financially speaking, is a pool of money contributed according to agreed quotas by each member. 25 percent of the quota is paid in gold, the remainder in the country's own currency.

The Fund, as a code of financial conduct, binds its members, in the first place, not to alter their exchange rates more than 10 percent from the initial par value without the Fund's permission. Permission requires a majority of votes, and as these are weighted according to the size of a member's contribution, it actually means the consent of countries that have the major financial stake in the Fund. (The United States has 33 percent of the voting power and the United Kingdom 14 percent.) A second obligation of members is to furnish full information concerning their domestic and international financial position and factors affecting it. A third commitment was to restore free convertibility and transfer of currency after a transition period originally expected to last five years.

The principal function of the Fund in maintaining currency stability, is to sell to a member a limited amount of another currency to help it meet a relatively short-run need to balance its payments. In any one year a member can buy up to 25 percent of its contribution to the Fund, and over a period of years this could rise to a maximum of 125 percent of its quota. The purchase can be made, however, only for purposes approved by the Fund. In due course, the members are expected to buy back the amount of their own currency they have sold to the Fund, thus making it perpetually revolving. This repurchase occurs when the country improves its trade or otherwise manages to gain more gold and foreign exchange than it is spending. Once in this favorable situation, it is obliged to use half of each year's gain to buy back its currency from the Fund.

The International Bank. The International Bank had an authorized capital of $10 billion, with actually subscribed capital of $8.4 billion as of December, 1951. This, too, is composed of fixed quotas from each member: 2 percent paid in gold or dollars, 18 percent payable in the country's own currency on call by the bank, and 80 percent to underwrite loans secured by the bank from private sources. As a matter of practice, the Bank has borrowed most of its funds from private sources, successfully floating its own bonds (chiefly in the U.S., where they have been snatched up as a gilt-edged investment).[10]

The principal function of the Bank is to lend funds at a moderate rate of interest, or to guarantee loans made by others to governments or private enterprises of member countries for specific projects of reconstruction or development. Usually, it does not provide such assistance if it can be secured from other sources under reasonable conditions, or if it considers that the borrower will have difficulty in repaying the loan. This has resulted in the Bank's undertaking a searching examination of the proposed uses of the funds requested, and of the financial position and policies of the borrower, whether or not the applicant is a national government or a private business. It has frequently made approval of a loan conditional on changes in proposed projects and even in national fiscal and economic policies. It then follows its loans through to their "end use," checking to make sure that the borrower fulfills the terms of the agreement. The Bank thus functions not only as lender and guarantor but also as an international brain trust for the evaluation and guidance of reconstruction and development strategy.

Despite the mammoth size of its capital from the standpoint of a banking institution, the International Bank made only a modest contribution to the processes of economic reconstruction. It has consciously pursued a policy of cautious restraint, demanding assurances of repayment as ironclad as most private banks, and insisting in the words of its second president, Eugene R. Black, that the Bank is "not an agency for relief or emergency aid."

The Bank's largest loan for reconstruction purposes was $250 million made to the Credit National, a semipublic French corporation, in May, 1947. A loan of $195 million was granted to the Netherlands to aid in the reconstruction of Dutch productive facilities, $40 million to Denmark to

---

[10] The resources of the Bank and the fund were greatly expanded later. See Chapters 14 and 15.

finance imports of essential capital goods and raw materials, and $12 million to Luxembourg to purchase equipment for the steel industry and rolling stock for railways. All this was during the critical months before the beginning of the Marshall Plan. Small additional grants were made during 1948 and 1949 to Holland and Belgium. Finland and Yugoslavia also finally qualified for limited reconstruction loans. All told, the Bank put less than $600 million dollars to work on reconstruction in the first three years of its operation, as against more than $2,500 million applied for within the first few months after it opened shop. Every dollar went to Europe, on the grounds that here was the nerve center for world recovery.

The Bank's unwillingness to move more boldly and swiftly to bolster national efforts to revive production and trade was a distressing surprise to those who had counted on it as the major outside source of help to countries unable to finance their own recovery. As a matter of fact, the Bank quickly ruled itself out of any major role in meeting the requirements of reconstruction, as soon as the magnitude of the need became apparent. It discreetly limited its function to the financing of "projects which involve permanent additions to production capacity" and where interest payments and early liquidation of the loan could be foreseen.

Why didn't the Bank rally its full resources to meet the demands of the hour, and, if necessary, even call for expanded contributions from its members? The immediate answer is found in U.S. policy, which necessarily determined the Bank's decisions both because of the preponderant American voting power and because it was dollars for which the borrowers were clamoring. Put in a nutshell, the American government made a mistake in 1946—it bid too low for world recovery. Its decision that the Bank should be chary in lending dollars for reconstruction matched its other fateful decision of the same year to liquidate UNRRA and declare Europe and Asia rehabilitated. At the crucial moment when the maximum impetus was needed, the chief engineer throttled down the main generators created to power the postwar recovery. By the time the mistake was discovered, so much momentum had been lost that the resources of the Bank were indeed inadequate to the task, and the credit status of its customers was seriously undermined. Even though it finally loosened its purse strings in 1947, billions, not hundreds of millions, were now needed, and a gambler would not have bet on repayment of more than a fraction of it. Having held the Bank back from its intended reconstruction functions, the United States now faced on its own the mushroomed burdens of financing world recovery.

THE FRUSTRATION OF RECOVERY

Notable as were the accomplishments of international and American efforts in postwar rehabilitation, the fact remains that they did not produce the expected firm recovery of the devastated countries. By the end of 1946, when the projected timetable called for the march to recovery to have reached full velocity, the world was headed for economic collapse.

A disastrous food deficit stared Europe in the face, threatening widespread starvation. Coal production was bottlenecked so that the continent whose mines had usually supplied one of the world's main fuel lines had to turn to the United States to help meet its own bare essentials. Not only had industrial production failed to regain prewar levels, but it was actually on the decline in many places from the period of immediate postwar rehabilitation. Transportation was still disorganized. Trade was stagnant. With such severe shortages of goods, the black markets thrived, and inflation was no less real because it was illegal.

The international focus of the crisis was the "dollar famine." Countries simply could not find the wherewithal to finance what they needed to buy from America. Credits and reserves alike evaporated at an astonishing rate. A U.S. loan to Britain of over $3 billion which had been expected to last at least five years was almost used up in little more than a year. France used up in about the same period most of $3.2 billion of foreign loans and credits and faced the imminent exhaustion of its gold reserve.

These were the symptoms—and a few of the hard facts—of the crisis. How had this come about so suddenly and so devastatingly?

In retrospect, at least four factors appear to have contributed to the frustration of recovery at this stage. First, the gravity of the impact of the war on the world was seriously underestimated. The long-term effects of the attrition of resources, human exhaustion and malnutrition, and, in particular, the drastic unbalancing of trade and credit relations between the United States and the rest of the world were not fully realized. Something more fundamental than "emergency" aid was required to tide countries over to a good harvest and to repair their roads and factories.

The second factor impeding recovery was the legacy of hate for Germany and Japan left by the war. This resulted in an attempt to segregate the problem of rehabilitating the "liberated" countries from the objectives of occupation for the defeated. UNRRA aid was restricted, for instance, to those liberated (among which Austria and Italy were included by special dispensation), while under the policies of the Potsdam Declaration, German rehabilitation was sharply restricted by reparations, industrial dismantling, zonal divisions, and some of the more extreme phases of denazification. By such action, Europe was deprived of its industrial nerve center at the moment reconstruction depended on a maximum increase in all kinds of production, and essential channels of trade involving Germany were blocked, preventing integration on a continent-wide basis of the effort to restore European economic life.

A third obstacle was the emergence of serious political conflict between the

Soviet Union and the Western powers, which made impossible the conclusion of a complete peace settlement and left Europe in a state of uncertainty regarding the future. Increasingly strained relations prevented wholehearted cooperation in the tasks of rehabilitation, and led to recrimination and mutual suspicion that even produced official attitudes toward UNRRA. The situation of Germany was further aggravated, and economic barriers arose between Eastern and Western Europe. Rehabilitation became more and more subordinated to the dictates of political warfare.

Finally, as we have seen the United States government undermined the rehabilitation effort by repudiating international administration in favor of action it could more directly control. This nationalist approach to relief and rehabilitation was unable to retain the values of an international program which were essential for sound recovery. In contrast to the initial American foreign aid program, UNRRA and UNICEF greatly minimized the political influence of individual nations in rehabilitation; removed all implication of philanthropy, patronage, or domination on the part of the donors; and enlisted very extensive international support and cooperation, which strengthened both the resources and influence of the organizations. The United States' return to nationalism in the area of relief was particularly unfortunate in its timing. The liquidation of UNRRA came at the critical moment when continuation and expansion of its program was really needed to deal with the new elements of crisis which had emerged.

THE EUROPEAN RECOVERY PROGRAM: A REVOLUTIONARY PRESCRIPTION

In any case, by the spring of 1947, the architects of foreign policy on both sides of the Atlantic recognized they had not put the world back on its economic feet, despite the unprecedented relief efforts undertaken, and the new international institutions that had been forged. The problem of recovery was much deeper and more complex than even the soberheads had envisaged. "No one had a picture of the completeness of the disruption that had occurred," said Dean Acheson, as he thought back on the situation six years later. "We had operated on a theory of dealing with hunger, disease and unrest until one or two crops could come in. But the problems were more far-reaching and it grew upon us toward the end of 1946 that we were heading for very bad trouble."[11]

Meeting these problems called forth the boldest and most imaginative program of international economic cooperation ever devised—a partnership of Europe and America in reconstruction that tore down some of the tradi-

---

[11] Dean Acheson, Undersecretary of State, 1946–47, in an interview with Harry Bayard Price. Quoted in Price, *The Marshall Plan and Its Meaning* (Ithaca, N.Y.: Cornell University Press, 1955) p. 9.

tional moats around national economies and led countries to pull together in the battle for recovery rather than trying futilely to save their own skins. In terms of the immediate task—reversing the plunge of Europe toward economic chaos and organizing the basic conditions to enable people to make a living—the strategy of reconstruction developed in the European Recovery Program came close to success. Progress toward a fully stable and durable world economy was cut short, however, by the tragic return to military defense priorities after the outbreak of war in Korea, by the hard-yielding restraints of particular national economic interests, and by the inability to grapple effectively in so short a time with the fundamental problems of the economically underdeveloped areas of the world. Nevertheless, in the four years of the Marshall Plan experiment, two continents did go far toward learning and applying some of the basic principles of an orderly world economy, and they left a legacy of institutions and settled habits of international economic management which operate as vital factors in keeping disruptive forces in check.

The Dual Partnership

When Secretary of State George Marshall announced on June 5, 1947, at Harvard University, that the United States was prepared to take a new look at Europe's economic plight, he astutely turned the initiative back to the European nations, inviting them to get together and frame up an analysis of their needs, and proposals for meeting them. During the months of planning and negotiation which followed, a new pattern of international organization emerged—a twofold partnership.

First, 16 European states pledged themselves to work jointly for recovery. They agreed to set common targets for development of their production, mobilize full use of their productive capacity and manpower to meet these targets, modernize equipment and transportation, maintain financial stability, reduce trade barriers, remove obstacles to free movement of persons across their boundaries, and work together in developing common resources —almost a reverse Magna Charta of international economic *obligations,* rather than rights. Thus, they dramatically broke with the 30-year tradition of economic nationalism, at least among themselves.

The second aspect of the partnership was the American commitment to make up the deficits of the operation over a four-year period—a bill originally estimated at $17–19 billion—on condition that the European countries would put forth their maximum effort to help themselves, and that they would do it *jointly.* The United States was insistent on the partnership within the partnership. It wanted partnership with the whole of Europe, not with its separate parts, and it shunned the bilateral relationships to which it had turned in lieu of UNRRA (even though, in form, the U.S. assistance agreements were to be made bilateral). In effect, America served an economic ultimatum on Europe: "Unite or Perish." In addition to this general condition, the United States set up an intricate system of controls which insured that both basic policies and day-to-day operation would conform to standards considered sound by the moneyed partner. The Marshall Plan, despite the gibes of its critics, was neither a "giveaway" nor a cunning form of imperialism, but a hard-headed business arrangement based on a broad "calculated risk" and with firm management to satisfy both sides of the partnership that their mutual interests were being effectively served.

The Soviet Boycott

The European Recovery Program precipitated a final break in the economic relations of Eastern Europe with the rest of the continent, even while it heralded the beginning of a new experiment in Western European cooperation. The Soviet Union had at first seriously considered the American invitation, which had been delivered open-ended to all European states. A large delegation, headed by Mr. Molotov, met in Paris with French and British officials, but shortly withdrew when the others indicated they were prepared to engage in a closely knit joint enterprise in line with American desires. The Soviet leader insisted that each nation should work out its program and needs separately, and that the United States should make known its intended aid and offer it country by country.

The real basis of the Soviet refusal to go along still remains one of the mysteries of postwar diplomacy, for at the time they apparently stood to lose nothing and gain much. They professed, however, to foresee dangers of U.S. intervention in the vital economic affairs of recipient countries if a joint economic program were devised and made subject to American approval. As the European Recovery Program developed, American controls did emerge which undoubtedly would have been offensive to the Soviet Union and would have impaired its independence of action. Another possible explanation is that the Soviet Union feared its own economic controls over Eastern Europe would be weakened in any common program of recovery. Perhaps the underlying reason was that the Soviet Union was so habituated to nationalist economic planning that it could not contemplate the drastic reorientation involved by international economic planning. To have the center of gravity of economic policy making shifted from Moscow to a common European point would have required both an ideological and political about-face for Soviet leadership. For this would have meant that the Soviet Five-Year Plan and Fifteen-Year Plan would undergo scrutiny and possible revamping to fit into a European Four-Year Plan.

Whatever the reasons, the Soviet decision was firm. A mandate to its satellites to follow its example made even Czechoslovakia reluctantly shun the temptations of the Marshall Plan, and it thus brusquely prescribed the limits of European cooperation. Half of Europe, not the whole, agreed to pull together.

The Framework of Cooperation: OEEC

The European partners then decided on an organizational pattern for their cooperation which would be international rather than supranational. This reflected British reluctance to surrender national reins over economic policy. (The French were ready to have a central organization that would enjoy some autonomy and decision-making powers.) The essential features of the Organization for European Economic Cooperation (OEEC) were:

1. All important decisions required the unanimous consent of the cooperating governments, and were made by the *council,* consisting of a minister or his deputy from each country.

2. The small nations, as well as Britain and France, were active participants in the decisions and work of the organization. The *executive committee* of seven members had no authority of its own, but acted only according to instructions of the council.

3. The detailed negotiation of agreements was conducted in *technical committees,* some set up on a vertical basis to consider programs for specific commodities (food, coal, oil, electricity, iron and steel, etc.), others operating horizontally to consider the main areas of European economic relationship (production, trade, manpower, intra-European payments, overseas territories). These committees were working committees. The representatives of the various governments did not merely state official positions but studied problems and hammered out recommendations for action to be laid before their governments.

4. A small, but highly competent, secretariat of economic experts serves the organization.

The organization undertook three major tasks: (1) programming the total recovery effort of the cooperating nations, (2) allocating American aid among them, and (3) promoting intra-European trade.

Programming Recovery. A "programme" as developed by the OEEC is an entirely new activity in international relations. It involved the preparation and acceptance of a comprehensive, integrated master plan of economic activity for all 16 nations for a given year. Each government revealed its economic policies and plans, its estimates of productivity and trade, a complete inventory of its own resources, its anticipated needs of European and other foreign goods, and what deficits it foresaw. Never before had so many countries publicized such detailed information concerning their current economic operations and policies.

These national programmes were then put together and examined by the central organization in terms of the fundamental principles the nations jointly agreed should govern their recovery efforts. Adjustments were negotiated when it appeared that a country's plan was out of line. In order to achieve a realistic overall programme, a great many concessions were usually necessary, and individual nations had to cut back on their original proposals—voluntarily, of course, as final decisions required the consent of all. In the end, the OEEC produced for each year since 1948 a specific set of production targets for each of its members, a detailed breakdown of the nature and amount of exports and imports for which each nation should aim, and the main changes it should attempt in its fiscal position.

These were the main principles which have governed this programming: (a) to maintain financial and monetary stability, (b) to increase exports and earnings, (c) to reduce imports payable in dollars, (d) to facilitate payments for trade among themselves, (e) to coordinate the investment and modernization plans of the various countries, and (f) to find means of handling the surplus population problem.[12]

Allocating American Aid.   The stiffest task of the OEEC, testing its capacity to hold together on a basis of mutual consent, was cutting the pie of American assistance. This assignment, proposed by Paul Hoffmann almost immediately on assuming direction of the U.S. Economic Cooperation Administration, was unexpected by the Europeans, and at first unwelcome. They could not see how governments could reach agreement on parceling out an amount considerably less than the estimated absolute minimum needed. Officials would have to step out of their customary role of presenting and justifying their own nation's requirements, and consider, instead, whether another country should have priority in the interest of the total recovery effort. In one breath, they had to switch from representing the special interest of their own people to considering the general interest of Europeans, and this at a time when their countrymen labored under the pressures of a rock-bottom standard of living.

But shock treatment worked. By worrying through this painful process of decision, the OEEC established itself as an effective and responsible instrument of collaboration, capable not only of planning but also of disciplined self-management. "We feared it would wreck the Organization," recalled Baron Charles J. Snoy, of Belgium, Second Chairman of the OEEC Council. "Yet it was possible. We had to learn cooperation. No one could take responsibility for jeopardizing the whole plan, even if dissatisfied with any particular decision."[13]

Four experts (dubbed the "Four Wise Men") were given the task of trying to reconcile the estimates of need with the aid actually available. They examined and trimmed each country's program, generally keeping consumption of food and other consumer goods at the low 1947 level, trying

---

[12] See *Two Years of Economic Cooperation* (Paris: Organization for European Economic Cooperation, 1950).

[13] Quoted in Price, *op. cit.,* p. 82.

to find ways of cutting back planned dollar imports, and substituting supplies that could be secured without dollars.

Promoting Trade: The Liberalization Program.   The third and longer-range task of the OEEC was to loosen up the flow of trade among European countries so that they would not turn to the United States for goods available among themselves.

This was attempted partly through encouraging reduction of import quotas, which most of these countries had imposed to protect themselves from going bankrupt by purchases of foreign goods for which they could not pay. The OEEC adopted a Code of Liberalization which bound members to remove quotas at first from 50 percent of their imports. This was shortly raised to 60 percent and made applicable to each of four main categories of imports in order to counteract the tendency of some countries to concentrate most of their liberalization on areas where there was little competition with domestic production. (For instance, heavily agricultural countries at first lifted quotas on manufactures but kept them on farm imports.) A target of 75 percent was set in 1951. Then, the OEEC started work on a "common list" of products on which all 16 countries would lift quotas entirely, thereby providing full freedom of movement in Europe for at least these commodities. A five-man Central Group was appointed by the OEEC to set standards of compliance with the code and to rate each country's performance.

With establishment of the European Payments Union (see p. 390), the OEEC agreed on a rule to promote greater equality of treatment in intra-European trade. Each country was to apply its liberalization measures equally to imports from all member countries and to end all discrimination on grounds of balancing payments. In other words, a country might not keep a quota on a product imported from one country if it lifted the quota on the same product from other countries. Exceptions to this nondiscrimination rule were permitted if the OEEC found that serious damage was being done to the economy of one country because its products had not been sufficiently freed from import restrictions by another country.[14]

But it quickly became clear that these measures would be ineffective unless they were linked to an arrangement whereby each country could clear its accounts with the OEEC countries as a whole rather than with each separately. Otherwise, a country felt that in the interest of its economic stability it would have to limit imports from a neighbor to the amount it could pay for directly by its exports to that country. The knottiest part of this problem was the chronic deficit position of certain of the 16 countries, such as Greece and

---

[14] Steps were also taken to end restrictions on "invisible" transactions—services, shipping, tourist expenses, etc. For a comprehensive analysis of the OEEC program of trade liberalization, see William Diebold, Jr., *Trade and Payments in Western Europe* (New York: Harper & Bros., 1952), chap. 10.

Western Germany, in trade relations with some of the others, like Britain and Belgium, which were chronic creditors. The creditors were not enthusiastic about increasing the volume of a one-way trade that would bring them no immediate return, especially when they were husbanding their exportable resources to pay for imports from the U.S. and other non-European countries.[15]

The European Payments Union.   To meet this problem, the OEEC, prodded by the U.S., created one of the most ingenious postwar international economic institutions—the European Payments Union. The EPU was a clearinghouse through which each of the European countries paid its bills to the others *collectively.* The system worked as follows. Each member of the Union extended to the others a credit, in its own currency, which could be used to purchase its goods up to the limit it felt it could meet within the targets of its national economic programme. This, in turn, was transformed into "drawing rights" which each country could use to finance the purchase of goods from the others. In the beginning, chronic creditors were allocated extra slices of American aid on condition that they furnish correspondingly larger drawing rights to the chronic debtors in the Union. With the supplementary American aid, the total drawing rights used by members of the Union were expected to balance the total credits (or "contributions") made by them to the Union, and, in each case, a country's contribution (including the special allocation of dollar aid if it received one) was expected to match the drawing rights it was granted on other members. Transactions were handled through the Bank for International Settlements. This multilateral credit arrangement made it possible for countries to trade with each other, within the limits of their drawing rights, without worrying about direct repayment. The handling of West Germany's critical and persistent deficit in these years illustrates the EPU's effective technique of international financial management.

The EPU's German Crisis—A Test of Cooperative Integration.   In its first year of operation, the EPU found that Germany was buying far more from the other European countries than it was able to pay for by its own exports. It quickly used up its quota of credit in EPU, which meant that it would have to make up in gold for any further trade deficits. Having inadequate reserves, the only alternative was to drastically cut its imports. This would have injured not only Germany but also the countries exporting to it, thereby defeating the whole effort to liberalize European trade.

So the OEEC Council (which determined the EPU's policies) first approved an increase in the credit that EPU could grant Germany. But the deficit continued to pile up. This alarmed several countries because they

---

[15] The positions of Germany and Britain became completely reversed after a time, but the basic problem remained.

thought Germany might shrewdly be getting all it could on credit at the expense of the others, and would then demand further trading concessions from its creditors (for instance, special purchases of German products under threat of suspending further business with them). Memories of this policy of debtor's blackmail as conducted by Hjalmar Schacht under the Nazi regime were still painful.

So the OEEC, *with German consent,* worked out an arrangement for a selective restriction of German imports, so as to bring about an immediate trade balance, under the supervision and direction of a Mediation Group of three independent experts, appointed by the OEEC Council, who applied principles laid down by the Council. Germany was instructed as to the amount of imports it could license and the countries from which it might buy. (Countries that were themselves heavily in debt to the EPU and those that would suffer most from a cut in their exports to Germany were favored.) Germany reported to the Mediation Group every 10 days on the licenses it had authorized. Countries dissatisfied with decisions of the group could present their cases and even appeal to the Council—but *not* to Germany.

In a few months, the deficit was cleared. Germany soon became a creditor, and the whole crisis was resolved with a minimum of dislocation to the trade of the other countries. The significance of this achievement can hardly be overestimated, and the technique of mediation devised to cope with the problem is a model of effective international economic cooperation. The role of the Mediation Group was not that of

. . . three wise men dispensing justice according to their respective inner lights or disposing of full power over the structure and course of Germany's trade. They *mediated,* at the intersection of some 20 national interests and pressures. They could not dictate; they advised, but so long as they had mediated well, governments did well to take their advice.[16]

Some Germans complained that this was "intervention." To a large extent, they were right. Germany lost its power to bargain separately with its neighbors and to manage its trade controls independently. But throughout the operation, the OEEC could act only with the consent of Germany. Its decisions were really recommendations to the German government, and were frequently based on suggestions made by the Germans themselves. The Germans cooperated in this rigorous exercise in discipline because of the privileges they would lose if they did not. By accepting the Mediation Group's recommendations, they were protected against retaliatory measures by the other countries and were assured of the advantages of the EPU once they got back to a better balanced trade position.

EPU Contributions. In sum, the European Payments Union was the keystone of the program to knit together Europe's separate national econo-

---

[16] Diebold, *op. cit.,* p. 128.

mies. It gave countries greater freedom in trade relations, because each nation had only to balance its trade with the whole group in the Union, rather than having to achieve a bilateral balance of payments with each neighbor separately. The Union also provided a cushion against temporary shifts in a country's trade position so that it did not have to suddenly and drastically cut back its imports from others when it found it was running low on means of payment. A third contribution of the European Payments Union was to encourage coordinated action by all the partners to help a country overcome basic trade difficulties which seemed likely to persist for some time.[17]

The American Role

In the grand design of European recovery, the United States planned to furnish "friendly aid in the drafting of a European program and the later support of such a program," in the words coined for Secretary Marshall by the State Department Policy Planning Staff in May of 1947.[18] This broad view took concrete form in the various U.S. foreign assistance acts from 1948 to 1951 and in the actions of the Economic Cooperation Administration (ECA) set up to administer American participation.

Dollars. About 12 billion dollars of American assistance was given outright, and about 1 billion dollars loaned. In physical terms, this became food, feed, and fertilizer (29 percent); fuel (16 percent); machinery and vehicles (17 percent); raw material and semifinished products (33 percent); and other commodities. While most of this was American produced, about 20 percent was purchased outside the United States in the Americas, and 10 percent in other countries.

Almost half the aid went to the United Kingdom and France. Italy, Western Germany, and the Netherlands each received over a billion; Greece, Austria, and Belgium–Luxembourg over half a billion each. The remaining billion and a quarter went to the other eight countries.

Yardsticks. The U.S. advised the European countries in the preparation of their recovery programs, and ultimately approved them. The OEEC framed the proposals, in line with the basic Marshall Plan concept of

---

[17] The significance of the EPU for economic integration is evaluated more fully in Chapter 15, pp. 468–70. Unfortunately, for reasons reviewed there, this organization was liquidated after formation of the European Common Market by the six countries of Western Europe.

[18] The original Policy Planning Staff Memorandum outlining the "Marshall Plan" had been prepared at Marshall's request, following his return from the fruitless Conference of Foreign Ministers in Moscow during March of 1947. It was presented to the Secretary on May 23, 1947, and formed the basis of the Marshall address of June 5, which publicly announced America's readiness to be of help. See Price, *op. cit.,* p. 22. The background and development of U.S. policy toward European recovery is thoroughly examined by May Beloff, *The United States and the Unity of Europe* (Washington, D.C.: The Brookings Institution, 1963).

European initiative, but they had to pass ECA examination and conform to American legislated policy before qualifying for American support.

On most major objectives, the OEEC and the ECA saw eye to eye. But the United States exercised a whiphand in pressing for speedier and more complete intra-European economic integration than the European countries were generally prepared to initiate on their own. The creation of the European Payments Union and other moves to relax trade barriers were largely the result of insistent "advice" from the ECA, as was the application of a direct economic sanction, some grants of aid being made conditional on the acceptance of greater European commitments to integration.

The ECA also applied to the European recovery programs certain yardsticks of strictly American interest. For instance, ECA determined whether specific proposals for American assistance would have an adverse effect on the American economy, and if so, what alternatives could be substituted. Requests for steel and some foodstuffs in the early period exceeded what was felt to be the amount that could be supplied out of American production without risking serious domestic shortages and inflationary prices. Non-American sources of supply were explored, and where these, too, were insufficient, the demands trimmed.

Some of the criteria were mandated by Congress in the authorization of funds and reflected ends at cross-purposes with the broad policies of recovery. 50 per cent of the supplies had to be transported in American ships, though this added to the dollar expenditures of an operation whose immediate objective was to eliminate Europe's "dollar gap." American surpluses, of tobacco for instance, had to find an outlet in the recovery program, though they might not be the most vital commodities needed to generate the expansion of European production and might even be available from European sources. At one point, the House of Representatives actually voted to halt funds to Britain as long as Ireland was partitioned. The Senate, however, did not consider it necessary to halt European Recovery pending settlement of the Irish question. As the cold war intensified, and especially after the hot war broke out in Korea, the U.S. forbade re-export from the Marshall Plan countries to the Soviet bloc of supplies similar to those provided by American assistance, as well as a long list of materials considered "strategic." Whatever the political or military justification for these restraints, they hindered the expansion of East-West trade which was an important factor in achievement of economic recovery and stability for Europe.

For the most part, however, the ECA's role in programming was positive. The spirit of the American administration was to get on with a vital and urgent job, and to find agreement with the European governments as quickly as possible on the scope and character of the recovery efforts and the American assistance to be provided.

Counterpart. The terms of U.S. aid included a provision for counterpart funds, which gave the ECA an additional potent instrument with which to guide and stimulate the process of reconstruction in each of the European countries. As with UNRRA, a country agreed to put aside in local currency the equivalent of the dollars it received in aid from the U.S. Five percent of the fund was turned over to the U.S. government and used principally to pay the costs of American administration in that country. The remainder could be spent for purposes jointly approved by the ECA and the receiving government. Paul Hoffmann, ECA Administrator, considered counterpart the "essential catalyst" of the whole recovery program. "It made the difference," he said flatly, "between success and failure for the Marshall Plan in every nation that had a shaky government, and it helped mightily with those that had strong ones."[19]

The ECA used its power to release counterpart funds as a lever for persuading governments to adopt the stringent measures necessary to achieve and maintain internal financial stability. For instance, France was in the midst of financial crisis in 1948, and its political instability blocked strong anti-inflation remedies. The national budget was running at a big deficit, the government was printing larger supplies of money, and was allowing a vast extension of bank credit. Yet, it was faced with serious strikes and other signs of popular discontent, and was therefore reluctant to put on the brakes which would mean higher taxes, cutting down government welfare expenditures, and curtailing private credit. The ECA agreed to release counterpart funds to finance the Monnet Plan (a broad program of investment to expand production, and thereby also increase jobs and wages) *provided* the French government went ahead with firm measures of fiscal control. This put the heat on the government, but it also gave those leaders who wanted to take strong action anyway a means of sugarcoating the bitter pills they were prescribing for the French economy.

In other countries, the ECA approved the use of counterpart funds for retirement of national indebtedness, and investment in projects designed to increase agricultural and industrial production. The Netherlands was permitted to use much of its counterpart funds for reclaiming land from the Zuider Zee, which had been flooded during the war. Austria used some of its money to tame the Enis River. Germany built a power station in West Berlin, improved its coal mines, and built railroads. Italy put counterpart to work on drainage, irrigation, and flood control to reclaim agricultural land.

Generally, release was conditioned on strict American supervision and control to make sure that the funds were used as authorized. This feature of the program led a German statesman to remark that "the economy had been like a regiment drilling under its colonel." But he felt that the control,

---

[19] Paul G. Hoffman, *Peace Can Be Won* (New York: Doubleday & Co., Inc., 1951), p. 48.

though "not always morally pleasant," had contributed greatly to the recovery effort.[20]

Supervision. The American supervisory role extended throughout the whole of the program. An "end use" check was made by ECA missions on what actually happened to the funds put at the disposal of each country, even though it did not itself handle the procurement of the agreed-on inventory of supplies. A country's representative in Washington would submit an application to ECA to authorize the purchase of specific commodities. ECA ascertained whether the request fell within the allotment that had been approved in the overall program, and whether it conformed to other criteria, such as having no adverse effect on the American economy. A letter of commitment then issued to a cooperating bank guaranteed that ECA would reimburse it for financing the purchase. No funds were actually issued, therefore, except when the approved commodities were bought. Then the ECA country mission asked for an accounting of where the commodities were distributed, and it examined, on the spot, the ways in which they were used.

In addition to this detailed administrative follow-through, the ECA asked each government for a public accounting of American aid, both to its own people and to the American and world press. Projects supported by ECA funds were so labeled. Commodities were identified wherever possible as part of the American aid. The press could roam and inquire at will, a nonofficial, but nonetheless effective, supervisory instrument. The ECA itself organized a vast and imaginative public information program which worked with the various governments to interpret and dramatize the Recovery Program both to Europeans and Americans. Finally, the supervisory process included a large stream of congressional visitors engaged either in formal legislative investigation or personal junketing. Europe and its affairs were indeed exposed in a goldfish bowl for all to see.

Some friction developed under all this supervision which accompanied the "friendly aid" from across the sea, and it was not just Communist inspired. The American rode hard, driven by conviction of the critical importance to European recovery of efficient and responsible economic management, and dismay at the many examples in Europe of waste, maldistribution, and venality. Many ECA staff were more pro-European than the officials and business leaders with whom they had to work, and the temptation was strong to use the stick to back up "advice" when sufficient "cooperation" was not forthcoming on action the ECA considered vital. Furthermore, there was the constant pressure of having to show tangible results quickly in order to smooth the road for next year's appropriations.

Fortunately, top leadership in the program's administration on both continents were sensitive to the dangers in the situation and were able to achieve sufficiently close understanding of each other's problems to prevent a falling-

---

[20] Vice-Chancellor Franz Blucher, in an interview with H. Price, quoted in Price, *op. cit.,* p. 106.

out. European statesmen were aware that however rigorous ECA control might appear in Europe, the ECA staunchly supported European interests before the American Congress and people, and that their plight would be desperate if for any reason the pipeline of American aid should be shut off.

Technical Assistance. The American role was also to some degree a technical one. After the initial large-scale effort to meet the urgent need for basic commodities, the ECA turned increasing attention to the exchange of production and managerial skills and know-how.

The significance of securing this technical assistance was most promptly appreciated by the British Chancellor of the Exchequer, Sir Stafford Cripps, who responded immediately to a suggestion of Paul Hoffmann in 1948 that British and American management and labor leaders tour factories in each other's countries and study their methods of operation. The Anglo-American Council of Productivity was formed to plan and schedule the visits. The teams that came were skeptical at first as to what they could learn which would be applicable at home. But the net result was the quick adoption of new industrial processes, and equally important modification in the approach to human relations by management and labor. Other countries did not respond so enthusiastically as the British to this longer-run and more subtle means of increasing productivity by laying the technological and human bases for a greater output per man-hour. But in three years, the idea spread, and some 3,000 Europeans of different nationalities came to the United States to study not only its industrial techniques, but also the raising of hybrid corn, coal mining, civil aviation, road-building, and other enterprises related to their own country's economy. Americans, in turn, on a more limited scale learned from European experience.

The most important impression made on Europeans by the "American way," in the judgment of Paul Hoffmann, was the "primacy of the person in a setting of teamwork." American top management, reflecting back on some of their tough contract negotiations, perhaps would be surprised to know that to a British rayon-weaving unit "there appeared to be a most friendly and genuine attitude of co-operation between management and labor . . . a sense of camaraderie based on mutual respect." And some American labor leaders might be as surprised as the French unionist who reported that "the American employer seems to be a psychologist aware that his prosperity is tied directly with that of the workers."[21]

The Accomplishment

The Marshall Plan accomplished the immediate economic recovery of Europe. In human terms, as Paul Hoffmann put it, Europeans by 1952 were eating, they had jobs, they were working and working hard.

---

[21] Quoted in Hoffman, *op. cit.*, p. 54.

The longer-run impact is less clear, especially as sweeping demands for military defense against Communist expansion sidetracked the process of economic reconstruction before it had run its intended course. NATO requirements, the deteriorating French position in Indochina, intermittent economic warfare over a divided Germany, and, above all, the imperious commitments to Korea intruded on the second half of the European Recovery Program, and curtailed both the American and European resources available to it. The character and targets of the effort were, therefore, drastically altered.

Nevertheless, by 1953 Europe was a different place than it had been in 1947. What had happened?

1. Western European production had soared. Industrial output which in 1947 had been 15 to 20 per cent less than in 1938 (with 17 million more people than before the war) had reached 134 per cent of the prewar level. Europe was again self-sufficient in coal. Agricultural production had climbed from 86 per cent of the prewar average to 114 per cent, keeping pace with the population increase. The gross national product had gained $30 billion in three years, reaching a new plateau.

2. The economic dependence of Western Europe on the U.S. had been tremendously reduced. Between 1947–50, the dollar gap had been narrowed by $7 billion. Though various factors, especially the new defense burdens, caused it to rise by a billion in 1951, an intensified "dollar drive" recouped some of the loss the next year, chiefly by expanding European exports to the United States and Canada and further reducing dollar expenditures for imports. Europe still ran a trade deficit with North America, but its overall world balance of payments during 1952 and again in 1953 resulted in a small current surplus. In the first half of 1953, Western Europe was approximately in balance with the whole dollar area, including however, the heavy U.S. military expenditures in Europe, though not economic aid.[22]

Yet, Europe was not fully on its own. It had not reached the stage of self-support where it could be independent of outside assistance. There were still drags on its economic vitality. Its exports still fell well short of the amount adequate to support the steady expansion of imports needed to maintain an upsurge of production. By 1951–52, production had leveled off, although private consumption was only a little above the prewar standard. And incentives to make further basic changes in the patterns of domestic or intra-European economic activity were weak.

3. Financial stability had been achieved in most countries. This accomplishment required the most skillful balancing of inflationary and deflationary tendencies in all the cooperating countries, for the objectives pursued in

---

[22] *Progress and Problems of the European Economy* (Paris: Organization for European Economic Cooperation, 1954), pp. 24 ff.

the recovery program tended to counteract one another. The first main target, increasing production, required an emphasis on an expansion of investments. But financial stability at a time when inflationary influences were strong necessitated a limitation of investment. Furthermore, a severe financial crisis in 1949 led the British and then others to devalue their currency in terms of dollars. Inflationary pressures were then gravely boosted in 1950–51 as a result of the unexpected demands for military expenditures connected with the Korean war.

Nevertheless, by mid–1952, prices leveled off in most countries, confidence in the national currencies returned, and black markets in both commodities and currency began to go out of business. By January, 1954, the OEEC was able to report that "inflationary pressure has, on the whole, been eliminated in Western Europe."[23]

This was not only an economic but also a political feat of unusual difficulty, because it meant that the shaky coalition governments of countries like France, Germany, and Italy had to raise taxes, reduce government expenses for nonmilitary purposes such as social security, and persuade their people in the face of the drumfire of Communist criticism that all this was for their welfare.[24]

4. Some progress toward European economic interdependence had occurred. The volume of trade among OEEC countries increased 70 per cent over the four-year period of the Marshall Plan. The European Payments Union, closely linked to this development, survived although subjected to severe strain. But the most important evidence of greater interdependence was the continuation of the OEEC as a joint planning and programming organization for European economy after American economic assistance came virtually to an end. The value of cooperative economic direction and the coordination of national economic policies was a lesson that Europe had learned deeply during the four years of collaboration in the recovery program. Cooperation took "forms which would have been considered completely impossible before the war" in the judgment of Robert Marjolin, Secretary-General of the OEEC.[25]

On the other hand, real economic integration had by no means been realized. Despite a key decision, reached in 1949 by the OEEC, of the "need to form a single large market in Europe in which goods and services could move freely," intra-European trade barriers were still formidable. Quantitative controls over a considerable volume of imports and exports from and to other European countries persisted. Severe competition among European industries for both domestic and overseas markets appeared as recovery

---

[23] *Ibid.*, p. 10.

[24] Price, *op. cit.*, pp. 152, 154, 399.

[25] *Ibid.*, p. 223.

progressed. Obstacles restricted the movement of labor among European countries, although the OEEC had tried hard to find means of easing them.[26] And, of course, East-West trade had actually declined to an all-time low as cold war strategy tightened its hold over the export of European products to the Soviet orbit.

Perhaps the basic point of divergence among the European countries was over their respective policies of domestic distribution and welfare, which, in turn, blocked the fundamental integration of their foreign economic policies. Countries such as Britain, Holland, and the Scandinavian countries, which were committed to a broad sharing of economic benefits, could not throw in their lot completely with Italy, France, Greece, and, to some extent, Germany where economic enterprise was so controlled as to let special interests take a large cut out of the economy before its return "trickled down" to the mass of the population. It was difficult to build enthusiasm for greater European integration, unless there could be assurance that it would result in an improvement in the general living condition, not just the enrichment of the already privileged. (Later developments toward European integration are discussed in a subsequent chapter.)

A well-balanced, overall evaluation of the accomplishment of the European Recovery Program is presented by Harry B. Price at the conclusion of his thorough study of "The Marshall Plan and Its Meaning."

The Organization for European Economic Cooperation stood out as the first organization through which the disintegration of western Europe into autarchic islands had been checked and a reverse trend established. During the transition both immediate economic necessity and temporary American aid were important contributing factors. With advancing recovery these factors receded in importance. That the trend did not then collapse seems to have been due chiefly to the successful demonstration given by the O.E.E.C. and other emergent Europe institutions that positive benefits of distinct value to all members could be achieved by closer economic cooperation. . . . Integration as a goal synonymous with unification—economic or political—was still far from realization. But integration as a continuing dynamic process of joint effort to deal with common problems through reason and consent had become a new reality on the European scene.

---

[26] OEEC, *op. cit.,* p. 10.

Chapter 14

The Lure of Development

Relief, rehabilitation, reconstruction—all these phases of the attack on the economic aftermath of war called forth unparalleled ingenuity and cooperation in the manipulation of world resources for general recovery. Yet the horizon of world economic stability constantly receded, and most of the world has still been unable to set foot on the escalator of dynamic economic expansion. The attention of international institutions has been increasingly directed toward finding an answer to this quandary.

THE RATIONALE OF PERSISTENT INSTABILITY

It is customary to blame the persistence of economic instability on the international political conflicts and the stepped-up arm's race that have cut across the postwar world. Western and Soviet apologists condemn each other's "expansionist" or "imperialist" policies for diverting vital resources to military ends, blocking the benefits of trade, and blighting economic growth. In a more limited sphere such as the Middle East, razor-edge tension between Israel and its Arab neighbors has certainly strangled any major effort to better economic conditions. Such a diagnosis implies that economic stability—in an area, or worldwide—must await the achievement of political stability and that until a durable peace is won on someone's terms, any program of economic improvement will be short-lived.

Without denying the destructive impact of political struggles on international economic cooperation, perceptive analysts maintain that the evaporation of economic progress in the postwar period can be traced to the operation of basic economic factors. For reconstruction failed to take adequate account of all the economic realities of the present epoch, particularly the problem of underdevelopment in some of the densely populated areas of the world. Underdevelopment is no new phenomenon, but not until now has international contact reached the point where disparity between the have and the have-not seriously impinges on the well-being of the have.

Quite apart from the political challenge of discontented nationalism in areas of depressed economy, it is increasingly apparent that poverty and economic stagnation in any major population center in the world drags on the progress of areas that have already attained a high degree of development. Plans geared to specific targets of economic reconstruction, say in Europe, would succeed up to a point, and then stall when they ran into the economic development gap between nations within their own region or in different regions.

In addition to the problem of underdevelopment—or perhaps it would be more accurate to say disparity in development—the lack of adequate international economic integration is held responsible for the frustration of more substantial progress toward stability. Natural and human resources have not been used efficiently, and artificial barriers have impeded the growth of the market. This factor in part explains the paradox of large, unmarketable surpluses in some areas, while others struggle against scarcities of the same products; pools of unemployed in one country, while production is handicapped by a labor shortage in another; the serious depletion of natural resources in one section, while rich reserves go untapped in another; or the protection of excessively high-cost goods in one nation, forcing others that could produce them less expensively to turn, likewise, to less efficient enterprise.

The implications of this economic rationale are, first, that long-run economic stability demands a strategy even more far-reaching than the partnership of economically advanced countries achieved under the Marshall Plan. This strategy must somehow succeed in reproducing in the less-developed three-quarters of the world conditions which will foster economic growth and enable these people also to move toward a better life. Second, the grip of economic nationalism must be loosened even further and much more unified economic management be achieved among nations. Third, failure to press forward toward worldwide economic development and integration will exacerbate existing political controversies and breed new ones. Fourth, international action along these fronts may actually reduce areas of political tension by showing that vital interests can be secured—in fact, can only be secured—if nations bury their hatchets and concentrate on the problems of getting the most out of a day's work.

The validity of this rationale is being tested by a great range of experiments in international cooperative action to promote economic development and integration. This chapter considers the efforts to help development; the following one examines the approaches to economic integration.

THE PROBLEM OF UNDERDEVELOPMENT

Though experts differ on the technical definition of underdevelopment and the best yardsticks by which to measure it, they generally agree that the heart of the problem is *low human productivity* linked to *low human consumption*. In other words, a man has relatively little to show for his work in an underdeveloped area. The strategy of economic development is directed toward unleashing a larger productivity per man-hour and, within the democratic perspective, at translating this productivity into higher living standards for the general population.

The key marks of an underdeveloped country, succinctly put by one authority, are: (1) "mass poverty which is chronic and not the result of some temporary misfortune"; (2) "obsolete methods of production and social organization, which means that the poverty is not entirely due to poor natural resources and hence could presumably be lessened by methods already proved in other countries."[1]

A complex of economic and social conditions is usually tied in with this situation. The per capita use of energy is low, as is the industrial investment per worker. Food consumption is barely over the minimum necessary to sustain life, and frequently drops below. This, in turn, saps human energy. Health is generally poor, life expectancy short. Illiteracy is high, skilled labor limited.

The area of such underdevelopment is large, including most of three continents—Asia, Africa, and South America—and some of Europe. About two-thirds of the world's population lives in these areas.[2]

The degree of disparity between the developed and underdeveloped countries is striking. "In 1961, the developed countries, with about 20 per cent of the world population, accounted for nearly 60 per cent of the world real gross national product (GNP), while the developing and the communist trade bloc countries together, with 80 per cent of the world population, accounted for only about 40 per cent of the world GNP." (see Table 1).[3]

The disparities are, of course, even greater when one compares the U.S. situation, at the top of the income ladder, with the underdeveloped areas. Whereas 180 million Americans recently had an annual per capita income of

---

[1] Eugene Staley, *The Future of Underdeveloped Countries* (New York: Harper & Bros., 1954), p. 13.

[2] *Ibid.*, p. 14.

[3] Robert M. Stern, "Policies for Trade and Development," *International Conciliation,* May, 1964, p. 6. The table, reproduced from this monograph, was originally derived from P. N. Rosenstein-Rodan, "International Aid for Underdeveloped Countries," *Review of Economics and Statistics,* May, 1961, p. 118.

$2,300, two billion persons (65 per cent of the world's population) lived in countries where per capita income was below $200.[4]

Translated into terms of basic health and life conditions, these differences in income mean, for instance, that in the underdeveloped areas people live only 30 years on the average; in the developed countries, the life span is double that. 106 doctors serve 100,000 people in developed countries; only 17 are available in the underdeveloped regions.[5]

Furthermore, the relative situation is worsening for the underdeveloped areas; the gap between have and have-not is getting wider. During the 1950's, while per capita income was rising by over $200 in the U.S. and Western Europe, it rose by less than $10 in most countries of Africa, Asia, and Latin America.[6]

TABLE 1

WORLD GROSS NATIONAL PRODUCT AND POPULATION, 1961

	% of World Population[a]	% of World Real GNP[a]	Real GNP Per Head[b] (U.S. dollars)
Developed countries[c]	19.7	58.8	2,098
Developing countries	45.7	17.5	281
Communist trade bloc	34.6	23.7	716
World total	100.0	100.0	

[a] World population in 1961 was estimated at 2,993 million and total real GNP at $1,750 billion U.S. dollars.

[b] Calculations are averages weighted by the percentage distribution of total real GNP in the major regions in each group in 1961.

[c] Including Western Europe, Oceania, United States, Canada, Japan, and South Africa.

PRESCRIPTIONS FOR DEVELOPMENT

The central question in planning a strategy for economic development, both for leaders of underdeveloped countries and for those outside concerned with furnishing international assistance, has been where to break the circle of conditions making for chronic poverty so that the economy could be most effectively and permanently stimulated. The following are among the principal lines of attack advocated.

---

[4] Rajendra Coomaraswamy, "United Nations Technical Assistance in the Development Decade," in Richard N. Swift (ed.), *Annual Review of United Nations Affairs, 1962–63* (New York: New York University Press, 1964), p. 35.

[5] The second estimates were made in 1950. See *Supplemental Report on Act for International Development* (H.R. 7797) (House Committee on Foreign Affairs, 81st Cong. 2d sess., March 23, 1950), pp. 6–7.

[6] Coomaraswamy, *op. cit.*

1. *Industrialization.*   Governments of underdeveloped countries usually stress industrialization because they consider it to have been the key to rapid economic growth and prosperity in most developed countries. To many have-nots, development and industrialization appear virtually synonymous. On the other hand, industrialization requires a combination of resources—physical, financial, and human—which are not immediately available in these countries and are costly to secure from the outside. So some experts warn against overambitious and indiscriminate plans for industrialization, and urge that efforts be concentrated on strengthening primary resources.

2. *Expanding the output of agriculture and other raw materials.*   This would not only provide immediate improvement in living standards by giving people more food to eat, but also would contribute to the accumulation of capital by increasing the country's exports to developed areas. Furthermore, it would involve a minimum dislocation of people from their usual occupations.

3. *Expanding the power resources of the country.*   Those pressing for industrialization usually come up against a severe power shortage in an underdeveloped country and are forced to hunt for means of increasing the reservoirs of energy. They call for more intensive exploitation of local fuel—oil, coal, or hydroelectric power, depending on the country's condition—and the simultaneous development of better transportation to bring power, raw materials, and labor together. This is generally expensive development, and its advocates must solve the problem of an acute shortage of capital.

4. *Increasing the availability of capital for investment.*   Almost any major advance in economic growth requires a substantial push, in the form of new facilities, equipment, supplies, or training. Somehow, these must be bought. Yet, one of the characteristics of an underdeveloped economy is a very small margin of savings. Hence, very little domestic capital accumulates. What little there is may be concentrated in the hands of a small privileged group, which restrict its investment to purposes that may not contribute to the country's general economic development. As for capital from outside the country, private investment also looks for conditions of assured and reasonably prompt return. Such return may not be realized at the points of greatest need for sustained national economic growth and may run counter to nationalistic demands for independence from "foreign exploitation." The availability and limitations of foreign *public* funds to meet some of the capital needs for economic development are reviewed in detail later.

One other course is open—savings out of current production. In an underdeveloped country, this means taking a slice out of the little that people are able to produce—cutting back their already low standard of living—and using it, directly or indirectly, to start new enterprises. Strong government control is usually necessary to accomplish this, but the Soviet Union demonstrated that it could be done. The main source of capital for its economic development was the labor of its people, a generation of whom had to work until they dropped with no return except minimum subsistence—if that. What they produced over and above consumption—in wheat or roads or dams or machinery—was what the government took, physically or in taxes, to redeploy in its five-year plans of development. Some went in the form of exports to buy foreign equipment needed for industrialization. A great deal went directly into building Russian industry and power.

Implacable and unconcerned about the human cost as this policy was, it stands as a model of how an underdeveloped country can "pull itself up by its own bootstraps," turning inward for its capital. The method therefore appeals to countries as an ultimate way out if they cannot qualify for enough foreign capital on terms that enable them to guide and control their own economic destiny.[7]

5. *Opening markets.* Imports are required for significant development in an economically interdependent world. But to get them, a country must be able to sell what it produces itself (aside from what may be given it free). A problem facing underdeveloped countries is their inability to export at a good price even the limited resources they do produce, thus strangling their capacity to help themselves. Much attention is now focused on trying to provide more favorable opportunities for these countries to market their goods and services.[8]

6. *Providing technical know-how.* In the absence of know-how at various levels of the economy, the underdeveloped country is helpless to start a program of expansion. One strategy of development has therefore aimed to secure "technical assistance" from developed countries to train and educate people in skills that will increase their personal productivity and provide the country with the technical, managerial, and governmental expertise necessary for effective economic development.[9]

7. *Educating the people.* The capacity of a people to function effectively in a modern society seems to demand not only technical skills but also the

---

[7] England also used the up-by-the-bootstraps approach in initiating the Industrial Revolution in the early nineteenth century. In its experience, the rigors of the Malthusian struggle for existence, rather than the government, provided the control necessary for enforced savings. See Benjamin Higgins and Wilfred Malenbaum, "Financing Economic Development," *International Conciliation,* March, 1955, p. 282.

For a concise analysis of development strategies that emphasize the need to increase savings, see Gustav Papanek, "Framing a Development Program," *International Conciliation,* March, 1960, pp. 321–22. For a major exposition of the role of savings in development, see Arthur Lewis, *The Theory of Economic Growth* (Homewood, Ill., Richard D. Irwin, Inc., 1955).

[8] This approach is discussed in detail in the next chapter. See also, Robert M. Stern, *op. cit.*

[9] See U.N. Secretariat, *Technical Assistance for Economic Development* (New York: United Nations, May, 1949); also Papanek, *op. cit.,* pp. 316–21.

ability to communicate with one another in writing. "Fundamental" education, or literacy, therefore is urged as an elemental condition of development, followed by progressively more advanced general as well as vocational and technical education.[10]

8. *Strengthening the competence of governmental administration.* The achievement of development inescapably demands decisive and well-informed governmental action at all levels, even if the chosen procedures emphasize private as well as public enterprise. The Achilles' heel of development is often the inability or unwillingness of those with public responsibility to make and carry out the decisions essential to effectively direct and coordinate the collective efforts of people. A strong case is thus made for "political" development—recruitment and training of experts in various phases of public administration—as a prerequisite for economic development.

9. *Improving health conditions.* A sick people cannot produce. Therefore, some have urged that a frontal attack on disease be made a fundamental element in the strategy of development. An offsetting consequence of this approach, however, is the increase in population that occurs as better health practices cut the death rate, especially among children. A race is then on to see whether the adults can produce enough to keep pace with the additional children until they too can become productive.

10. *Relieving population pressure.* Because the pressure of population on resources is usually intense in an underdeveloped country, and the population is growing at a rapid rate, the benefits of economic advances tend to dissipate quickly. Especially in the early stages of economic development, the rate of economic growth may not match the increase in population, so the country faces the discouraging prospect of falling backward after trying to push forward. To cope with this dilemma, development planners have urged migration to sparsely settled areas as well as systematic efforts to encourage the mass adoption of birth control practices.[11]

Birth control has made little headway against deeply entrenched customs and prejudices. Migration efforts have foundered because of cost and the difficulty of finding hospitable areas for resettlement.[12]

11. *Social revolution.* Economic development is often hindered by archaic systems of land tenure or the unwillingness of propertied groups to widely distribute the return from production, such as it is. When the changes

---

[10] Note the emphasis on education not only of such specialized agencies as UNESCO, but also of such "hard-headed" disbursers of capital as the International Bank. See statement by Geoffrey M. Wilson, Vice President of the Bank, in *The Fund and Bank Review,* June, 1964, p. 24.

[11] See the Indian five-year plans.

[12] The interrelationship of population growth and economic development has come before the U.N. as a matter of urgent importance. It is undertaking major studies of the problem and is beginning to furnish technical assistance to governments engaged in efforts to control population growth.

required to speed up productive processes and raise living standards will not be made by those who hold economic power, some exponents of development insist that their first task must be to tear down the existing social and property system. Communists are by no means the only dispensers of this prescription. It is the familiar formula of nationalists in underdeveloped countries who demand not only that their governments "throw the foreigner out" but also, with equal vehemence, call for it to nationalize major natural resources, redistribute land, and take other steps to dispossess the economically privileged in the interests of "the people." This strategy assumes that direct government control of the key points in the national economy will make possible the initiation of major reforms in methods of production and organization of distribution, as well as the coordinated planning needed to secure a substantial advance in economic development.

12. *An integrated attack.* A further line of strategy attempts to combine some or all these approaches in a coordinated, multiphased plan of development, designed to improve particular conditions of a country or area so that roadblocks won't emerge to halt or divert the process of development. Recent international action to promote development has strongly stressed such an integrated attack, both because it promises a more even and lasting impact on a country's condition, assuring "balanced growth," and because it makes maximum use of available resources for international assistance. A report prepared by the United Nations Secretary-General in consultation with the heads of the specialized agencies urged that:

The problem must be attacked on several fronts at once. A great increase in output of food and other agricultural products is urgently necessary, but there must also be a concurrent development of industry and transport. The mechanisms of trade and finance must be expanded and improved. None of this is possible without simultaneously taking steps to raise the levels of health and education, to improve conditions of work and to provide basic social security.[13]

13. *Community development.* Much stress has recently been laid on the need to bring all these efforts to bear on the local community. Here, at the grass roots of a traditional and undeveloped society, lie the springs of action. Unless they can be released, the most nobly conceived development plan will wither. Hence, a strategy of coordinated economic and social assistance is urged to stimulate communities to become self-reliant and take a hand themselves in improving the conditions of their lives and livelihood.

---

[13] U.N. Secretariat, *op. cit.*, p. 6. Papanek, *op. cit.*, provides a competent overall review and assessment of the strategies advocated for development. Note, particularly, his critique of the concept of "balanced growth" as a criterion of development programming, pp. 333–34. He argues that it is difficult to define meaningfully, and often leads in practice to allocating resources to sectors and agencies that, in someone's opinion, are not getting their "due," rather than establishing priorities for projects on the basis of their relationship and contribution to a whole development program.

THE ORGANIZATION OF INTERNATIONAL ACTION

The bulk of development planning and action has been undertaken by the governments of the underdeveloped countries or by the remaining colonial governments for areas not yet independent. But the converging interests of nations on both ends of the range of development have led to a surge of international policy-making in this field and to the adoption of significant programs of international assistance. These efforts have been organized and conducted variously on a (1) global, (2) regional, or (3) bilateral, country-to-country basis.

On the global front, economic and social development has been a main preoccupation of the United Nations and the specialized agencies related to it. It is estimated that about 85 per cent of the funds contributed to these bodies, and 17,000 of the 20,000 persons working for them, are engaged in this type of work.[14] To emphasize this concern, the United Nations General Assembly dedicated the 1960's as the United Nations Development Decade, during which would be stimulated exceptional efforts to expand the flow of resources to underdeveloped countries and help them get on the road to sustained growth.

Regional development programs and institutions have been organized for the Americas under the Organization of American States; for the Commonwealth and associated countries in the Colombo Plan; by the European Economic Community specifically for the assistance of their overseas territories and associates; and by the Soviet bloc for one another through the Council for Mutual Economic Assistance. On a more general basis, 20 non-Communist countries have attempted to broaden and coordinate their assistance to underdeveloped areas through the Organization for Economic Cooperation and Development, formed as a successor to the Organization for European Economic Cooperation set up under the Marshall Plan.

The varied programs of development assistance undertaken by these *multilateral* international organizations are summarized in the accompanying table (Table 2).

It is evident that the programs are highly diversified in type and scope of assistance rendered, in beneficiaries of the aid, and in the control of the resources. Indeed, a major problem of coordination has arisen because of the diffused responsibility for development programming. In the absence of adequate procedures for joint planning and clearance (and, some would say, of central directing authority), different programs tend to overlap, or fail to mesh, or leave important gaps.

---

[14] See Coomaraswamy, *op. cit.*, p. 36.

Within the United Nations, progress has been made, as will be seen, toward integrating the programs, especially at the country level. A resident representative stationed in each country receiving assistance helps to coordinate the plans of U.N.-related agencies and guides the country's governmental authorities in shaping requests for aid in a manner that will gear in to the nation's general development program and to assistance received from other sources.

But the problem is immensely complicated because by far the greatest amount of foreign economic assistance is handled bilaterally, reflecting the preference of the United States, the Soviet Union, and other countries that control the major capital resources needed for development. These countries want to make their own decisions as to whom to aid, how, and under what conditions. As a result, it has proved practically impossible to work out arrangements for the coordination and integration of bilateral and multilateral programs (though the OECD, as previously mentioned, is making some attempt along these lines).

The bilateral approach has had other complicating effects. It has often run afoul of national pride in underdeveloped countries which resent any intimation of domination or exploitation by the haves. They tend to demand assistance as a right and to claim a fully equal voice in setting the terms for assistance from the developed countries. The donors have not always taken kindly to this self-assertive attitude, and real unity on development strategy has yet to be achieved between the needy and the "benefactors." The principal differences arise over (1) the intensity of industrialization at which development should aim, (2) the quantity of capital that developed countries should make available, and (3) the strings that should be attached to it. The U.S. and Britain have generally resisted plans for vast industrial expansion (especially in heavy industry) and demands for large, long-term loans to finance major development projects. The Soviet Union, on the other hand, has espoused extreme industrialization and made bold promises of capital assistance, which gives the appearance of aligning it with the characteristic point of view in the underdeveloped, rather than the developed, country. But, in practice, the U.S.S.R. has been even more tight and specific in control and direction of its development assistance projects than have the U.S. and other developed countries.[15]

Argument over the merits and demerits of bilateral as against multilateral responsibility has had little practical effect, however, on the organization of

---

[15] Quite apart from its propaganda significance, the Soviet Union's "line" can be explained by the recency of its graduation from the ranks of the underdeveloped and its deep-rooted ideological commitment to industrialization as the heart of the current stage of economic and social evolution. For a major study of U.S.S.R. policies toward underdeveloped countries, with particular reference to its relationship with United Nations economic and social agencies, see Alvin Z. Rubinstein, *The Soviets and International Organizations* (Princeton, N.J.: Princeton University Press, 1964), chaps. 2 and 3.

TABLE 2

MULTILATERAL AGENCIES PROVIDING INTERNATIONAL ASSISTANCE
FOR ECONOMIC DEVELOPMENT
Partial Inventory as of 1963–64

Agencies	Type of Assistance	Source of Funds and Supplies
I. UNITED NATIONS AND RELATED AGENCIES		
UNEPTA (Expanded Program of Technical Assistance).............	technical assistance	102 U.N. member governments (voluntary contributions)
Special Fund............	technical assistance (especially "preinvestment" projects—resource surveys and feasibility studies manpower training, research)	same as UNEPTA
Regular programs (U.N. and specialized agencies)	technical assistance	regular budgets of the organizations
UNICEF (U.N. International Children's Emergency Fund)..........	supplies for child and maternal health and welfare programs	U.N. member and other governments (voluntary contributions); private donations
World Food Program.....	food (including shipping services) to meet emergencies, feed special groups (i.e., children), and support experimental development projects	approx. 40 U.N. and FAO member governments (voluntary)
OPEX (Operational and Executive Services)....	senior executive and managerial personnel, especially for public administration	U.N. regular budget
International Bank for Reconstruction and Development............	"hard" loans for public and private "self-liquidating" projects; development planning surveys and technical assistance	capital subscriptions by 108 member governments (Soviet bloc *not* included); sale of securities to private investors; earnings rec'd from loans; repayment of loans; sale of IBRD loans to financial institutions
International Finance Corporation..........	equity investments in private enterprise	subscriptions by IBRD members

Amount	Beneficiaries	Control
$51 million (1963)	U.N. members	U.N. Technical Assistance Board (representing U.N. Secretary-General and specialized agencies); accountable to ECOSOC
$70 million (1963)	U.N. members (70 countries and territories)	Governing Council (representatives of 18 governments elected by ECOSOC); accountable to ECOSOC
$40 million (approx. for 1963)	U.N. members; members of each agency	each agency's governing body
$40 million (approx. annual)	115 countries, regardless of membership	UNICEF Executive Board (representatives of 25 governments, nominated by ECOSOC); accountable to ECOSOC
$90 million (approx. for 3 years)	U.N. members	U.N.—FAO intergovernmental committee (20 members)
$850,000 (annual)	U.N. members	U.N. Secretariat
$20 billion authorized capital ($2.1 paid in, balance callable only to meet Bank's obligations); $2.5 billion borrowed to 1964; $800 million earnings to 1964; and approx. $1.4 billion to 1964. Total actually loaned to 1964, about $6 billion	IBRD members (mostly underdeveloped countries)	Board of Governors (representing all member governments); voting weighted according to capital subscribed; operational direction by Board of Executive Directors (19, including 5 representing largest shareholders)
capital subscription of $100 million (total loaned 1956–62, about $70 million)	IRBD members (20 recipients through 1962)	Board of Governors (affiliated to IBRD)

TABLE 2—*Continued*

MULTILATERAL AGENCIES PROVIDING INTERNATIONAL ASSISTANCE
FOR ECONOMIC DEVELOPMENT

Partial Inventory as of 1963–1964

Agencies	Type of Assistance	Source of Funds and Supplies
International Development Association.......	"soft" loans (long-term, minimum interest, but repayable in convertible currencies); to assist agriculture, industry, education in countries with balance-of-payment difficulties	subscriptions by IBRD members (including local currency from undeveloped countries) *no* borrowing in the market
International Monetary Fund.................	short-term financial assistance to help overcome temporary balance-of-payments problems; establish conditions for currency convertibility; consultations and technical help on fiscal policies and currency stabilization	subscriptions (quotas) by 103 member governments
II. REGIONAL AGENCIES European Economic Community Development Fund............	grants to finance social institutions (hospitals, teaching and research, etc.) and economic investments of general interest	6 EEC member governments
Organization for Economic Cooperation and Development..........	review and coordinate members' development aid efforts and policies; continuation of OEEC technical assistance programs; research and training	20 Western governments and 3 in special status (Japan, Yugoslavia, Finland)
Organization of American States Inter-American Development Bank..........	ordinary loans for public and private productive projects forming part of a national or regional development program; ordinary loans to development-financing institutions loans repayable in local currency for special projects or operations	capital subscriptions by 21 OAS governments; contributions to Special Fund by member governments; sale of securities on private capital markets

Amount	Beneficiaries	Control
initial capital subscription of $780 million lendable funds; additional subscription of $750 million committed for 1965–67; rate of loans committed, about $300 million annually.	IBRD members (14 recipients through 1962)	Board of Governors (affiliated to IBRD)
capital subscription of $9.2 billion to 1958; 50% additional subscribed, plus new members' quotas yield total capital of $15 billion by 1964. Total assistance provided to 1964, over $11 billion (including unused standby arrangements)	IMF members, identical with IBRD (54 recipients by 1964)	Board of Governors and Board of Executive Directors (similarly constituted as, but separate from, IRBD)
$580 million for 5 years	present or former overseas territories of EEC members (especially of France in Africa)	EEC Council of Ministers, acting by weighted voting on proposals of European Commission; administrative operation by the commission
no funds directly disbursed	countries receiving aid from OECD members, bilaterally or multilaterally	OECD Council of Ministers, representing all members; Development Assistance Committee, representing major capital-exporting countries of the Western world and Japan
$850 million ($400 paid in); $150 million to the Special Fund	Latin-American countries	Board of Governors, representing each member government, voting based largely on capital subscribed; administration by board of 7 executive directors, including U.S.; U.S. veto on Special Fund

TABLE 2—*Continued*

Multilateral Agencies Providing International Assistance
for Economic Development

Partial Inventory as of 1963–1964

Agencies	Type of Assistance	Source of Funds and Supplies
Alliance for Progress....	grants and loans for top-priority projects in comprehensive country development programs (especially agriculture, industry, education, transport, communications, etc.)	grants by U.S. and Latin-American governments (except Cuba); private foreign investment
Colombo Plan...........	technical assistance; loans and grants for development projects (especially agricultural production)	contributions by Commonwealth countries, U.S., Japan; internal commitments of Asian countries
Council of Mutual Economic Assistance......	coordination of central economic policies, including direction of investment; trading credits; intergovernmental investment in industrial and extractive enterprises; technical assistance	Soviet bloc governments
African Development Bank...............	loans to countries; guarantees of regional projects	subscriptions by 32 independent African government members of Organization for African Unity

Sources:
The Fund and Bank Review, June, 1964 (Washington, D.C.: International Monetary Fund and International Bank for Reconstruction and Development).
Richard N. Swift (ed.), *Annual Review of United Nations Affairs, 1962–1963* (New York: New York University Press, 1964), pp. 36–38.
European Economic Community, Treaty of Rome, March 25, 1957. Implementing Convention Relating to the Association with the Community of the Overseas Countries and Territories, Articles 1 and 3, Annexes A and B. See, also, Serge Hurtig, "The European Common Market," *International Conciliation*,

development assistance. The growing political leverage of the underdeveloped countries has resulted in a modest increase in the flow of resources through multilateral institutions. This tendency has been encouraged by the proven effectiveness of such institutions as the United Nations and the International Bank in handling development programming and assistance to the satisfaction of both givers and recipients. But the haves continue to insist that the bulk of their assistance shall be made available only on terms of their choosing.

Amount	*Beneficiaries*	*Control*
$20 billion for 10 years in foreign aid and investment, in addition to direct internal commitments of Latin-American governments	Latin-American countries (except Cuba)	OAS panel determines priorities; U.S. and international lending agencies determine financial commitments
$14.9 billion total loans and grants 1960–1964	Asian members of the Commonwealth and other participating countries members of the Soviet bloc	Colombo Plan Conference of member governments and U.S.; Council for Technical Cooperation to arrange T.A. council, representing governments, under general Soviet direction
	members of the Soviet bloc	Council representing governments under general Soviet direction
capital subscriptions of $250 million	Members of Organization for African Unity	Council of Governors, representing member governments

March, 1958.
    U.S. Senate Committee on Foreign Relations, *Hearing on Inter-American Development Bank*, 86th Cong., 1st sess., June 23, 1959.
    Zbigniew Brzezinski, "The Organization of the Communist Camp," *World Politics*, January, 1961.
    Senator Hubert Humphrey, "A Report on the Alliance for Progress" (U.S. Senate Committees on Appropriations and Foreign Relations. 88th Cong., 1st sess., April 11, 1963).
    Colombo Plan Consultative Committee thirteenth annual report.

In this situation, there is a tendency for some initiative to pass to regional groupings that include both developed countries and certain underdeveloped ones in which the developed have a special political or economic interest. (An example is the Alliance for Progress, undertaken by the U.S. and the Latin-American republics, excluding Cuba.) This format gives the have-nots a sense of partnership in decisions affecting their welfare, while the haves can restrict their commitments to those they specially favor. The danger, of course, is continued fragmentation of the total world development effort, with a consequent waste of resources, as well as intrusion of political influences in shaping direction of the effort.[16]

In any case, the forecast is that all three types of organization—bilateral, regional, and global—will continue to coexist and compete in funneling international assistance to economically underdeveloped countries.

TECHNICAL ASSISTANCE AS AN INSTRUMENT OF DEVELOPMENT

International consensus has been reached regarding the importance of technical assistance in the strategy of development, and international cooperation has made possible an unprecedented worldwide sharing of technological, medical, educational, and administrative skills during the last decade. In one sense, "technical assistance began when the man who invented the wheel told somebody about it." And for at least the last century, private agencies—missionary, philanthropic, and business—have been giving or selling skills of all kinds to the peoples of underdeveloped areas. They have built and staffed schools and hospitals, and have trained workers in new methods of agricultural and industrial enterprise. Such assistance has probably far exceeded anything that governments have done.

Systematic government use of technical assistance as an instrument of international action to encourage economic development began during the second world war under United States auspices. After the war, the United States, the United Nations, the specialized agencies, and regional groups such as the Organization of American States and the Commonwealth of Nations felt the need to widen such services, and in due course organized separate programs of intergovernmental technical assistance.

The United States Bilateral Programs

Genesis in Latin America. The United States government first entered the technical assistance field in cooperation with Latin-American countries as an outgrowth of the wartime need for increasing production of raw materials. Two federal agencies, the Institute of Inter-American Affairs (IIAA) and the Interdepartmental Committee on Scientific and Cultural Cooperation (SCC), organized an extensive program of cultural and technical exchange. Latin Americans trained in the U.S. as public health doctors, nurses, engineers, agricultural technicians, and educators while American experts in agriculture, civil aviation, child health and welfare, and many other fields went to Latin America to provide in-service training. They established rural

---

[16] For a concise summary of issues involved in the organization of international economic assistance, see Robert E. Asher, "Multilateral versus Bilateral Aid: An Old Controversy Revisted," *International Organization,* Autumn, 1962.

health centers, constructed water and sewage systems, conducted campaigns against disease, improved vocational training techniques, and organized community action to overcome illiteracy.[17]

A fundamental principle of these inter-American programs was reciprocity, which meant, in practice, that the Latin-American governments contributed local personnel, facilities, and funds, and also shared in administration. By 1949, the recipient governments were carrying three-quarters of the total cost of the SCC program; the United States, one-quarter.

Another example of reciprocity was a unique arrangement of the Institute of Inter-American Affairs for administering field projects, called the *servicio*. This unit was staffed jointly by personnel appointed by the U.S. and the host government, was jointly financed by the two governments, and actually functioned as an autonomous bureau in one of the ministries of the Latin-American country. This pattern of partnership anticipated that the U.S. would eventually withdraw and that the receiving government would smoothly assume full responsibility for carrying the service forward on a permanent basis.[18]

"Point Four." In 1949, the United States government gave technical assistance a big push on a worldwide scale. In the famous "Point Four" of his Inaugural Address, President Truman urged "a bold new program for making the benefits of our scientific advances and industrial progress available for the improvement and growth of under-developed areas" and to this end pledged a twin American contribution in a cooperative effort with other nations: first, "the benefits of our store of technical knowledge," and second, the fostering of capital investment. When this was elaborated in legislation, technical assistance emerged as the principal undertaking.

Under the provisions of the Act for International Development, the United States really launched two programs: (1) an expanded program of technical assistance through the United Nations; (2) a strictly American program channeled to those countries with whom satisfactory bilateral agreements for "technical cooperation" could be reached. The second program received the mammoth share of the resources ultimately made available, transcended American partisan controversy, and, in due course, succeeded in establishing technical cooperation as "one of the great American missions of our times."[19]

The following guidelines governed the pattern of cooperation with the receiving governments:

---

[17] Department of State, *Technical and Scientific Cooperation*, February 1949, pp. 4 ff. See, also, Walter R. Sharp, *International Technical Assistance* (Chicago: Public Administration Service, 1952), pp. 4–6.

[18] *Ibid.*, p. 5.

[19] International Development Advisory Board, *Report to the Director of Foreign Operations*, December, 1953.

1. American assistance must be supplementary to local effort; the recipient government agrees to pay "a fair share of the cost of the program" and takes steps to make effective use of the assistance—for instance, by encouraging the "flow of productive local and foreign investment capital where needed for development."
2. American assistance should contribute to "the balanced and integrated development of the country."
3. Projects undertaken should clearly be needed and economically sound, with sufficient private capital available to finance them.
4. Receiving governments should give the program full publicity.
5. The receiving governments should cooperate in "the mutual exchange of technical knowledge and skills" with other countries participating in the program.
6. Fair labor standards of wages and working conditions and management-labor relations should be encouraged in the participating countries.[20]

Administration and Control.   Project planning is an intricate process of negotiation among agencies of the receiving government and concerned branches of the U.S. government, coordinated on the field by the American embassies and in the U.S. by the division currently responsible for general administration of technical assistance.

Usually, the receiving government first proposes a project. The U.S. technical assistance "mission," working out of the embassy in that country, evaluates the project and forwards a recommendation to the program administrator in Washington. It is then screened by the appropriate regional bureau of the State Department and the U.S. agencies that will be responsible for providing the kind of technical assistance requested (Department of Agriculture, U.S. Public Health Service, Department of Commerce, etc.). Presumably, the project's relationship to United Nations and other international programs is also reviewed. If approved, a three-way contract is made between the receiving government, the Technical Assistance Administration, and the U.S. agency that will operate the project, specifying the tasks and contributions each will undertake.

In this process, patterned on the European Cooperation Administration, initiative must come from the countries desiring aid, but approval is the prerogative in the United States government. Only sensitive self-restraint by those who hold the ultimate power of veto can in these circumstances insure

---

[20] Act for International Development, 1950, secs. 403 and 407. Some of these conditions were later loosened. For instance, in regard to the third point above, the U.S. government itself financed projects if private funds were unavailable. European countries were not at first included in the category of "underdeveloped countries" eligible for technical assistance under this program, but they did receive similar help through ECA (see Chapter 11). Later, all U.S.-administered technical assistance activities were consolidated under the Foreign Operations Administration, regardless of the area involved. In 1955, the Department of State assumed full jurisdiction. In still another administrative rearrangement, the programs were consolidated in the U.S. Agency for International Development.

a really free choice to the beneficiary country. To seek to propose whatever the donor will accept, is a great temptation, even for governments firmly resolved to maintain independent direction of their countries' economic development. One outstanding achievement of the U.S. Technical Assistance Administration has been its ability to draw a line between professional "evaluation" of a project's soundness and interference in general policy determination, a task often complicated by domestic American pressures to politicize technical assistance or to insist that recipient countries live up to a code of economic behavior that would safeguard the interests of "free enterprise."

The operation of technical assistance projects has been conducted not only by U.S. government agencies but also by an increasing number of universities and other private institutions. They have formally contracted to establish new educational institutions and training centers as well as to conduct a wide variety of demonstration programs and advisory services in the underdeveloped countries. Under this arrangement, American faculty members go abroad to organize and temporarily direct these projects without having to resign their jobs at home.[21]

The United Nations Programs

EPTA. Under the impetus of the Point Four proposals, the United Nations General Assembly, in November, 1949, approved an "expanded program of technical assistance for economic development of under-developed countries" to be conducted through the specialized agencies and the United Nations organization itself. The vote was unanimous, indicating the potent worldwide appeal of a multilateral effort to stimulate economic progress. General Romulo of the Philippines, President of the General Assembly at the time, expressed the prevailing response when he acclaimed the action as "one of the most constructive acts of international statesmanship ever undertaken under the auspices of the United Nations."

Not even the Soviet Union could afford to withhold its support from this American-sponsored move, though it had at first condemned Point Four as "just another colonial plan" and had voted against an Economic and Social Council resolution that recommended the expanded U.N. program, following the American initiative. But faced with an overwhelming General Assembly majority favoring the proposal, the Soviet Union withdrew its objections; its representative declared that the U.S.S.R. was concerned only "to elaborate principles which would insure the sovereign rights of the economically under-developed countries from political interference."[22]

---

[21] *Development of Technical Assistance Programs,* Senate Committee on Foreign Relations, 83rd Cong. 2d sess., November 22, 1954, p. 11.

[22] U.N. Official Records, General Assembly, Committee II, October 11, 1949.

In due course, it even contributed modestly in funds and technical assistance personnel.[23]

The Special Fund. Ten years later, the United Nations launched a second program designed to complement the Expanded Program of Technical Assistance. The particular commission of the Special Fund, as defined by its American Managing Director, Paul Hoffman (formerly head of the U.S. Marshall Plan Administration), was to conduct "pre-investment" surveys of resources and some pilot projects that would point the way to removing bottlenecks that hampered the progress of a country or region and thus lay the groundwork for further capital investment in its development.[24]

Creation of the Fund was actually the result of a compromise between the less-developed countries on one side and the United States and Britain on the other. The less developed had for years been urging establishment of SUNFED (Special United Nations Fund for Economic Development), which would have made outright grants to support development projects that could not be financed otherwise. But the two great holders of capital objected to any such United Nations organ having power to disburse funds and becoming, in effect, an "operating agency" of economic development programs. The line taken in public was that they had no more money to spend for economic development; creation of SUNFED would merely divert the already too limited resources of other programs, such as technical assistance. Off the U.N. rostrum, and especially in Congress, the blunt objection was that "the borrowers would run the bank." The real trouble was that in an agency like SUNFED, *international,* rather than *American,* decisions would govern the direction and terms of additional assistance to the underdeveloped countries, and such decisions could not be trusted to safeguard the economic, let alone the political, interests of the chief capital providers. So critical were the repercussions from this stand, however, that the United States finally came forward with its own version of the Special Fund, much more restricted in resources and limited to the purposes indicated.[25]

Despite the shackles imposed on its operations, the scope and significance of the Special Fund's activities have grown steadily. It has become, in fact, an important catalyst in the process of development programming and assistance—a sort of middleman between the governments of the underdeveloped countries and the reservoirs of capital (private, national, and inter-

---

[23] See Rubinstein, *op. cit.,* chap. 2.

[24] "The United Nations Special Fund," An Explanatory Paper by the Managing Director (New York: United Nations, 1959).

[25] A penetrating report on this set of decisions, now a classic illustration of the processes and determinants of action in the United Nations, is given in John G. Hadwen and Johan Kaufmann, *How United Nations Decisions Are Made* (Dobbs Ferry, N.Y.: Oceana Publications, Inc., 1962). See especially chap. 5.

national). It helps the underdeveloped to put together viable programs, and then peddles them to likely underwriters.

OPEX. A third United Nations program of an entirely different character is OPEX, the Operational and Executive Services, which recruits top-level administrators to temporarily fill critical gaps in the governmental services of countries that have not yet developed strong and experienced public administration. Customarily, the government appoints counterpart personnel to understudy the OPEX expert, whose job is thus twofold: to buttress the government's day-to-day operations in his own field of competence, and to train and guide potential successors.

UNICEF. Increased concern for the development of human resources and more general recognition that nutritional, psychological, and health damage sustained in a child's earliest vulnerable years disastrously affect him as a youth and as an adult have led governments to seek UNICEF aid for comprehensive plans that cover the whole intervening range of children's needs. This emphasis on preparing children for life has also resulted in a shift of UNICEF emphasis from assistance supplies to provisions for training in the form of equipment for training centers, teaching materials, and stipends for trainees. By 1964, one-third of all UNICEF aid was given for this purpose.[26]

Basis of Support. Three principles govern support for the U.N. programs. (1) Contributions are voluntary. This means that special funds must be raised apart from the regular U.N. budget (raised by assessments levied against all members). This is mainly accomplished now at an annual pledging conference, when the members are urged (and sometimes urge one another) to meet the estimated needs submitted by the governing bodies of the various programs. Actually, the total contributions to U.N. programs appear microscopic when compared with U.S. commitments to its own mutual assistance programs.[27] (2) Contributions may be made in any currency or in services. (3) But they must be unrestricted, that is, "made without limitation as to use by a specific project."[28]

Program Approval. The principal instrument for administering UNEPTA is the Technical Assistance Board, composed of a representative of the executive head of each specialized agency cooperating in the program and

---

[26] See "Help for the World's Children," *Landmarks in International Cooperation* (New York: United Nations, 1965).

[27] The UNEPTA budget rose from $20 million to $50 million for 1964–65; the Special Fund has averaged about $70 million annually; UNICEF received $33 million for 1964.

[28] U.N. Economic and Social Council Resolution 222 (IX), August 15, 1949, U.N. Doc. A/983. The U.S.S.R. attempted to earmark its contributions for use solely by the U.N. Technical Assistance Administration, excluding 10 specialized agencies. This limitation was refused, however, because it violated the principles laid down by the Economic and Social Council.

of the United Nations Secretary-General. The board is thus a group of top-level international civil servants, responsible individually to their respective international organizations and as a body to the Technical Assistance Committee of the Economic and Social Council, composed of 18 governments and exercising overall supervision on behalf of the whole United Nations.

The Special Fund is directed entirely from within the United Nations proper; its Governing Council of 18 states is elected by the Economic and Social Council and accountable to it. The Managing Director administers the Fund with sole authority to recommend projects to the Governing Council. Governments submit projects through him.

In UNEPTA, governments that want technical assistance lay their proposals either before an appropriate specialized agency or the Technical Assistance Board directly. All requests clear through the board, however, before approval is finally given by the agency that will actually carry out the project. This rather complicated arrangement was devised to provide: (a) maximum discretion to the requesting government to define its needs and choose the agency; (b) autonomy to the specialized agencies in determining and operating projects in their respective fields; (c) coordination of the whole program so that it would make an effective contribution to the total economic development of a country and not degenerate into a hodgepodge of unrelated projects.

For the first several years, effective coordination was hard to achieve, as the specialized agencies pushed their own separate interests strenuously and jealously guarded their independence both in policy-making and field operations. In fact, they competed so fiercely for shares in the technical assistance undertaking that the participating governments decided to allocate to each of the main agencies a fixed percentage of the funds available.[29]

Of course, this procedure seriously limited the flexibility of the program, because it prescribed, before actual requests from governments could be received and evaluated, the extent of the major categories of assistance. Furthermore, the procedure insured that programming would be completely decentralized, each agency enjoying sole authority over the disposition of its own allocation, even though it nominally discussed its proposed programs with the Technical Assistance Board. In these circumstances, only firm control by the receiving government over its own economic development planning could achieve an integration of the various efforts and prevent wasteful overlapping.

Dissatisfaction with this arbitrary approach to programming reached the point where, in 1954, the Economic and Social Council switched over to a system of authorizing allocations country-by-country, on the basis of compre-

---

[29] A succinct analysis of the U.N. program's operational system and its problems is presented by J. von Goeckingk, *United Nations Technical Assistance Board* (New York: Woodrow Wilson Foundation, 1955), p. 9–12.

hensive proposals for all forms of technical assistance submitted by governments to the Technical Assistance Board. The chairman of the Board (designated by the United Nations Secretary-General and with no particular axe of specialization to grind) was given wider authority to resolve conflicting claims of the agencies in terms of what would contribute most to a country's progress at its current stage of development.[30]

So the United Nations process of technical assistance programming now insures a true meeting of minds among recipients and donors, technical specialists and "generalists." Program approval is an *international* decision, in which the requesting government participates. It also is an *integrated* decision, in which the specific project has been fitted into an overall development program for the country.

The Conditions of Assistance.   United Nations technical assistance is rendered only to or through governments. Private agencies may not be used to channel assistance, as in the United States program. The receiving governments must fulfill economic obligations stricter in some ways than those demanded by the United States. They are normally expected to pay a "substantial" part of the cost, at least that part which can be paid in their own currencies. In practice, this has meant that the receiving country has supplied almost all the capital needed for any U.N. projects, because the U.N.'s meager resources have been devoted largely to personnel—technical assistance in the narrow sense without general economic aid to back it up. The U.S. program, on the other hand, has been able to furnish outright a considerable body of capital to finance its projects, either from appropriations labeled "technical assistance" or from those made more broadly for "economic assistance."[31]

On the other hand, no political strings are attached, implicitly or explicitly, to U.N. technical assistance. Neither the ideology nor political alignment of a government figures in the evaluation of its requests, and political logrolling has had little if any part in U.N. allocations. As a result, 96 countries and territories have drawn on the U.N. "global reservoir of know-how." By contrast, the American program has been specifically limited to helping "the free peoples of the world . . . to produce the things they need for a decent life," and its roster of beneficiaries is therefore more exclusive than the U.N's.

Problems of Implementation

Putting a program of this scope and complexity into operation and assuring its continuity and maximum effectiveness have been difficult. Many of the problems encountered arise from the very nature of the undertaking—a

---

[30] *Ibid.,* p. 12.

[31] Walter R. Sharp, "The Institutional Framework of Technical Assistance," *International Organization,* August, 1953, p. 344.

shortage of competent personnel willing to spend time on a project in an underdeveloped country, the uncertain impact of planned projects on a country's ultimate development, and resistance to change of long-established social and economic habits. Other problems—inadequate financial support, cumbersome, and overlapping administration, and motivational suspicions, for instance—reflect the controversial climate of world politics and the dictates of current U.S. policy within which the technical assistance programs have had to develop.

Securing Competent Personnel. The heart of technical assistance is persons with know-how adapted to a particular need and able to communicate it in a particular situation. Experience has shown that "effective technical assistance can come only from a meeting of minds and the resultant fusing of ideas for joint action."[32] The TA expert must therefore combine with professional competence an ability to achieve rapport with the local leadership and to involve them in what he is trying to innovate. He must somehow delicately bridge the gap between his knowledge and the experience of the local technicians with whom he works, and must also find ways of getting the general local community to understand and cooperate with the project. This calls for patience, tact, deep human sympathy, and a real sense of humility.[33] Such people are hard to find, and harder to persuade to leave home and job, often at the risk of professional advancement. As a result, there have been serious shortcomings, especially at the point of adaptability to the culture and conditions of the underdeveloped country. Personal attributes have too often been sacrificed in the mad scramble for expertise.

Efforts to "orient" staff before sending them out to the field have been too hurried to be adequate. Pressure is strong to get on with the job, and brushing up on language has often taken priority over thoughtful study of the culture. The problem has been complicated by the necessity of short-run programming and the inability of either the U.S. or the U.N. to offer the prospect of continuing possible career service to the proven specialist in intercultural technical assistance.

The U.N. has been more successful than the U.S. in finding persons who can adapt easily to the culture and conditions of an underdeveloped country. It enjoys the distinct advantage of being able to scout the world for its staff. Its teams are almost always multinational. They include specialists whose own cultures are similar to those where they are sent, and who are personally familiar with the practical problems and conditions of an underdeveloped country. Not only are they able to easily apply their technical competence to the situation at hand, but they usually experience little difficulty in establishing rapport with the people.

---

[32] Peter G. Franck, "Implementation of Technical Assistance," *International Conciliation,* February, 1951, p. 69.

[33] Sharp, *op. cit.,* p. 361. See also Sharp's definitive study, *Field Administration in the United Nations System* (New York: Frederick A. Praeger, Inc., 1961), esp. chap. 5.

The U.S. program, on the other hand, has had to rely almost entirely on American personnel, properly "cleared" in loyalty and security by procedures currently in force. This has restricted the range of choice at the principal bottleneck of the operation, and has resulted in a formidable problem of adjustment on the field for some personnel sent out. They have sometimes been at a particular disadvantage as Americans, being suspected of "imperialistic" motivations.[34]

Planning an Effective Program. How to choose projects that will have a lasting and significant effect on the country's overall economic and social development and not just peter out after a brief experiment is one of the most critical policy decisions in technical assistance administration.

The problem has been complicated by several factors: (*a*) The governments of underdeveloped areas are expected to take the initiative in proposing projects when they frequently lack the fundamental expertise to determine what would contribute most to their development. (*b*) Responsibility for approving projects is scattered, as we have seen, among international organizations and the United States and other governments, which often compete for separate programs rather than strive to discover what is most reasonable for the given situation and then integrating their different services in a common plan. (*c*) Experts often disagree on the appropriate strategy for economic development, and consequently arrive at different conclusions regarding types of assistance that should have priority. (*d*) Statistical data on many areas is unreliable and inadequate. (*e*) Noneconomic factors have shaped program decisions. Especially in the U.S., the imprint of political and strategic motivations on technical assistance has aroused the suspicions of countries like Burma, India, Indonesia, Syria, and even certain Latin-American countries, some of whom went so far as to reject American aid for fear it would compromise their position of neutrality.

In technical assistance administration over the years, a strong trend has developed toward balance and integration in designing and approving programs, and toward coordination between agencies in carrying them out. Closer teamwork between the receiving governments and the U.N. or U.S. missions has led to the tying-in of specific projects with general country development programs. In this process, the United Nations Resident Representative in each country has performed a pivotal coordinating function. As time went on, "country programming" became the instrument for achieving greater coordination among the assistance agencies. This was facilitated by the outcomes of technical assistance surveys which gave governments the basic frame of reference needed for intelligent evaluation of further projects. From a personnel standpoint, a United Nations Resident Representative appointed to each country has performed a pivotal function in this coordinating process.

---

[34] See Sharp, "The Institutional Framework of Technical Assistance," *op. cit.*, pp. 361–64.

Now the pattern of interagency cooperation seems well set. An increasing number of projects being planned involve closely knit action and integration of technical assistance resources by several organizations in the same country. Such coordinated programs are also being organized on a region-wide basis, with several countries integrating their plans and efforts under international guidance.[35]

Securing Adequate Financial Support. Despite its worldwide appeal and impressive accomplishments, technical assistance has been hamstrung by the uncertainty and insufficiency of its funds. The U.N. program, in particular, has suffered acutely for lack of support. Furthermore, continuity in programming cannot be achieved because of the general unwillingness of governments to pledge contributions for more than their current fiscal year. In some cases, also, the mere pledge by the country's U.N. Representative carries no assurance that appropriations of like amount will actually be forthcoming. So the technical assistance operations for a given year have to be planned and sometimes even undertaken without knowing the extent of resources available; yet its intrinsic nature requires long-run planning and personnel commitments for technical assistance to be really effective.

The U.S. is the major source of the U.N. program's financial headaches. Its contribution is the largest and, perforce, the most crucial. Yet it is limited to an American-fixed percentage of the total amount of contributions. So, the U.N. has no assurance that it will receive the whole U.S. appropriation, and the money is parceled out to it bit by bit, proportionately as other countries pay up. This may be a good way of prodding the sharing spirit, but it makes the total scope of the operation contingent on the weakest and least responsible governments. The U.N. Program Administrator has to refrain from committing both the uncollected pledges and the corresponding amount pledged by the U.S.

It is obvious that the present scale and method of financing severely restrict the effective implementation and continuity of both the U.N. and U.S. programs of technical assistance, though the U.N. has been the most crippled. The program faces a "crisis of success," for as work has proceeded and its quality improved, the flow of well-designed proposals for new projects has far outstripped the funds made available. Without sustained and substantial financial support, technical assistance cannot have the sustained and substantial impact on world economic development that is its mission.

Developing Local Responsibility and Carryover. Ultimate success in a program of this kind is to have the people of an underdeveloped country, with their newly acquired skills, take over and continue improvement of their economy on their own. One of the major problems of technical assist-

---

[35] Sharp, *Field Administration, op. cit.,* thoroughly analyzes the U.N. programming process and its problems. See, especially, chaps. 8–11.

ance has been to overcome such formidable barriers to self-help as weakness of governmental machinery, suspicions of "foreigners' ulterior motivations," and strong resistance to technological and, particularly, social changes by both the "power groups" and the masses in many countries. Incompetence, venality, ignorance, apathy, vested interest, superstition, prejudice, distrust of "colonialism," and pervading fear of the new and different confront the technical assistance administrator as he strives to insure a permanent follow-through on his projects.

Yet these resistances can be hurdled in several ways. The "self-help principle" of indigenous responsibility—the receiving governments initiating proposals, sharing the cost, and cooperating in planning and administration—is fundamental. Expertise in national governmental administration has been strengthened through such projects as OPEX and through the advisory services and consultation which form a regular part of the technical assistance operation. The joint staffing of projects with nationals and foreign experts, as in the "servicios" of the Institute of Inter-American Affairs, builds the core of a continuing local administration. The U.S. program and, to a lesser extent, the U.N. have insisted that "opposite numbers" be appointed by the receiving government at the national level—and sometimes the local—to work with the outside technical assistance administrators. The broad objective is to increase "the sense of shared participation."

The stigma of foreign authority directing local personnel and operations or controlling national policies must be avoided at all costs, even while inducing governments and people to accept needed reforms—social, economic, or possibly even political. In this respect, U.N. agencies have been able to go farther than the U.S., because they can appeal to a "proprietary as well as a consumer interest" in the recipient country. The government does not lose face by accepting a U.N.-directed condition for assistance, because it conceives of itself as one of the U.N.'s bosses; it is, in a sense, telling itself what to do.

Because of this and other reasons, the U.N. appears better equipped to engineer the delicate long-run process to strengthen sinews of responsibility with the underdeveloped country and assure a sustained impact of the technical assistance program.[36]

The Future of Technical Assistance

The overall case for technical assistance seems unassailable, whatever its limitations in specific instances of operation. "It is politically, economically and morally the right thing to do," reported the International Development Advisory Board, composed of American business, labor, and farm leaders—the "practical" men of economic enterprise. They declared that,

---

[36] See Sharp, "The Institutional Framework of Technical Assistance" *op. cit.,* p. 369.

economically, expenses for technical cooperation should be considered "ordinary and necessary business expenses, not giveaways"; that it was *"practical morality"* to share knowledge and help one's neighbor to improve his lot; and that, politically, technical cooperation stood as a symbol of partnership between the free world and the United States. The Board specifically commended the U.N. program and urged its expansion as the "best answer to the charge of American "imperialism."[37] A leading American authority on international economic relations agrees that an enlarged U.N.-sponsored technical assistance program, with sustained financial support over several years, would probably contribute more toward building a stronger and more unified "free world community" than any other action the world organization could take. But he warns that such action depends on "vigorous American initiative and the assurance of increased American funds."[38]

FINANCING ECONOMIC DEVELOPMENT

Economic development cannot occur unless capital is joined with know-how. Strictly "technical" assistance to underdeveloped countries cannot expand production without appropriate equipment—tools, machinery, seeds, fertilizer, fuel, and the mass of other resources a modern economy utilizes. These are the things a poor country lacks for the most part, and it also lacks the means to buy them. How to secure capital to launch the process of economic development and carry it through to the point where a country can begin to sustain its own further development is a most baffling problem.

Stated in economic terms, the problem is: (1) to stimulate a flow of capital large enough to increase production fast enough to outrun the growth of population and launch a process of cumulative expansion, and (2) to acquire sufficient foreign exchange to permit the country to import the raw materials and equipment it needs for development.[39]

How much capital is required to accomplish these ends varies greatly according to the particular conditions of a country, and reliable estimates are hard to arrive at because of the many uncertain factors that determine the rate of economic growth. Nevertheless, all estimates exceed amounts these countries are currently able to provide themselves, either through taxes or voluntary savings.

Totaling capital needs on a world basis, one careful analysis set $9 to $12 billion as the additional amount needed annually to achieve a bare minimum target of an annual 2 per cent increase in per capita income. About 50 per cent of this amount might be met domestically, it was estimated, by careful national budgeting, some increase in taxes, and an all-out effort to encourage

---

[37] International Development Advisory Board, *op. cit.*

[38] *Ibid.*, p. 375.

[39] See Higgins and Malenbaum, *op. cit.*, p. 278.

people to save, however limited their income might be. The difference of $5 to $7 billion could come only from outside the underdeveloped areas.[40] Other studies set higher figures. An early United Nations expert's report, *Measures for the Economic Development of Underdeveloped Countries,* estimated $19 billion per year—1949 prices—with a deficit after domestic savings "well in excess of $10 billion."

Using the United Nations Development Decade target of a 5 per cent annual rate of growth to be achieved by 1970 (considered modest compared with the actual rate of the 1950's and the required momentum to sustain progressive development), a later study carried out by the United Nations Secretariat projected a foreign exchange gap on current account of *$20 billion* in 1970. Only $9 billion of this would be met by the presently foreseen inflow of foreign long-term capital from private or governmental sources.[41]

Sources of Foreign Capital

The problem is: Where can the underdeveloped countries beg or borrow $5 to $11 billion a year, beyond what they are currently securing?[42] The main options are:

1. Private investors.
2. The U.S. government through its Export-Import Bank, or the Development Loan Fund (for loans), or foreign economic assistance appropriations (for grants).
3. The International Bank for Reconstruction and Development and its affiliates, the International Finance Corporation and the International Development Association.
4. Some of the British Commonwealth governments, associated in the Colombo Plan.
5. Some of the European governments, especially those in the European Economic Community who are now enjoying unparalleled economic expansion.
6. The Soviet Union, which apparently is now in a position where it can mobilize surplus capital for export.

The amount of capital available from these sources fluctuates greatly, influenced by many factors, but above all by the estimates of risk and return

---

[40] *Ibid.,* pp. 290–91.

[41] *World Economic Survey 1962:* Part I (New York: United Nations, 1963), pp. 6–7, quoted in Robert M. Stern, *op. cit.,* pp. 25–26.

[42] While there are precedents in which countries have achieved development without depending on a large influx of foreign capital, either through inflation or the up-by-the-bootstraps approach of enforced employment and controlled consumption (as applied by the Soviet Union), these experiences demonstrate that extreme social and political repercussions are likely to accompany such crash methods. See the trenchant critique by Higgins and Malenbaum, *op. cit.*

made by the holders of capital. In the case of governments, political as well as economic risks and returns may enter the calculations.

In practice, the flow of capital to underdeveloped countries in recent years has run as follows (in millions of dollars):

	1958	1959	1960
Bilateral:			
Grants	2107.7	2146.2	2400.3
Loans	1177.6	1127.3	1190.2
Total bilateral	3285.3	3273.5	3590.5
Multilateral:			
Grants	86.8	90.0	96.0
Loans	350.6	318.1	353.7
Total multilateral	437.4	409.0	449.7
Grand total	3722.7	3862.5	4040.2

SOURCE: *United Nations Statistical Yearbook*, 1961, p. 467.

The total obviously falls far short of minimum needs.

The search is on for ways to expand the flow from present sources or to discover new sources. On the other hand, a world shortage of capital may force contraction of the flow at some points and, in any case, step up competition for available resources. Allocating and guiding the use of capital in international assistance for economic development is one of the most fateful decisions of the time. Paramount responsibility rests with the United States, which controls the world's largest capital pool. Following is a review of the main choices.

Encourage Private Investment in Underdeveloped Areas. Advocates of this course stress that, first, sufficient public funds will not be made available to give important impetus to economic development everywhere; second, private investment has the inherent advantage of combining capital with applied technical knowledge; third, it consists almost entirely of equity investment involving no fixed return and no amortization—that is, the investor puts his capital into the country to stay and generally reinvests its earnings in the enterprise started.

On the other hand, the flow of private capital is held back because the hostile and discriminatory treatment accorded foreign business in many underdeveloped countries makes investment too risky for the return. Fearful of being "exploited" by foreign capital, these countries are often disposed to levy high taxes, restrict the export of profits, and in other ways limit the freedom of the investor to develop his enterprise. Then there is always the threat that a successful undertaking may be nationalized. Assurances of a fair deal for the private investor, it is alleged, would induce vast private capital resources to go abroad.

Efforts to increase the attractiveness of private foreign investment have been directed at securing some form of government guarantee that would reduce or eliminate risk and thus provide security for foreign investment. Point Four originally envisaged that the U.S. government would underwrite private investment abroad, but this was not really carried out. Governments of the underdeveloped countries have themselves made firm commitments to protect foreign business, and have even extended tax concessions and other privileges. To guard against a change of policy by some future government, the conditions of fair treatment have sometimes been guaranteed in treaties or agreements with other governments. The United States has insisted on such commitments as a condition for countries to secure any economic or technical assistance out of its public funds.

There is a constant running battle, however, between entrepreneur and nationalist. The businessman wants to decide where and how to use his money. He may not aim to get rich quick, leaving as soon as he takes out his profits. But he wants sooner or later to get back more than the safe 4 to 6 per cent he could earn if he were to buy A.T.&T. or Ford Motor Company securities. The nationalist in an underdeveloped country wants to control the development of his economy and to insure that private business contributes to his country's overall welfare and progress. He wants its returns plowed back into improved conditions of work and further productivity. Bridging this gap calls for long-term cooperative planning and better understanding of the mutual interests of investor and country.

International Finance Corporation.   A new approach to this problem has been undertaken with the creation of the International Finance Corporation, affiliated with the International Bank but with a separate capital fund of $100 million to be contributed by the member governments. It helps to finance private productive enterprises through equity investments and loans without government guarantee. It *supplements* what private investors themselves are able and willing to put in. It does not attempt to manage the enterprises in which it invests, but it tries to make sure the management is experienced. The contribution of the corporation is threefold: it enables private investors to undertake promising projects they cannot finance entirely by themselves; it publicizes the opportunities for profitable investment abroad; and, most important, it encourages great confidence among investors to embark on foreign projects, because its participation in the financing as an international body gives assurance that the legitimate interests of the investors will be respected in the recipient country. Operations of the corporation are frankly speculative. It expects losses. But it looks for profits on successful ventures to more than offset losses.[43]

---

[43] *Report on the Proposal for an International Finance Corporation,* Washington, D.C.: International Bank for Reconstruction and Development, April, 1952.

The genius of this undertaking is that governments, through the international agency, *share the risks* (and thereby reduce them) with private investors in development projects. But they do not guarantee the investor *against* risk. This approach has foundered because receiving governments are reluctant to make ironclad guarantees that undermine their independence and expose them to domestic political charges of selling the nation out to foreign interests, and the Congress has not been enthusiastic about letting the United States government "buy part of the chips but allow private investors to cash in on the winnings."[44]

With every effort, however, there appears to be no prospect of stimulating an adequate flow of private funds to underdeveloped areas in view of the current world shortage of capital. The contribution of private capital to investment in the underdeveloped countries has actually been declining in recent years; the net flow from capital exporting countries to the rest of the world dropped from $3.6 billion in 1958 to $2.9 billion in 1961. A major gap, therefore, remains between need and private supply. This forces consideration of larger public financing.[45]

Extend Direct American Governmental Loans and Grants for Development.   The bulk of development financing has actually been carried during the postwar period by the United States government. The Export-Import Bank has been authorized to extend loans or guarantees up to $7 billion to promote U.S. trade by encouraging economic enterprises in foreign countries that will use U.S. products. About 65 percent of its loans have been made to underdeveloped areas. A Development Loan Fund was established in 1958 to help finance projects that would increase productivity but could not be financed by private capital or from other public sources. Appropriations for such "soft" loans totaled about $1.5 billion through 1961. On top of this, the U.S. has added outright grants of "economic" or "development" assistance to selected Asian and Latin-American countries through its Agency for International Development and certain special programs. Appropriations for these purposes have been declining steadily, however, as Congressional and public sentiments in the U.S. have soured on "foreign aid." The figure was held at $3.2 billion in 1964–65.

The case for a substantial expansion of American government loans and grants for development purposes is, in brief: (1) No other source or combination of sources can furnish the amount of capital required. The limits on private investment and on public funds of other governments, especially since the war, make it out of the question for them to close the gap. (2) The U.S. government *can* mobilize the necessary funds without seriously overbur-

---

[44] Seymour E. Harris, *Foreign Policy Bulletin,* October 15, 1951.
[45] See Higgins and Malenbaum, *op. cit.,* p. 312; and Harris, *op. cit.*

dening its national budget or economy. About 3 per cent of the federal budget (about .5 percent of the national income) would do the job. In fact, the Export-Import Bank already has authority to lend more than it has. Only a policy decision is necessary to have it devote a larger proportion of its resources to the poorer countries of the world, instead of favoring those that can expand production of strategic raw materials and otherwise contribute to American military power. The total expense would be less than the U.S. carried during the postwar recovery period, and only a fraction of its wartime foreign outlays. (3) A large portion of the funds would return to the U.S. Loan repayments to the Export-Import Bank have been very high, and interest, though nominal, mounts up. Within 10 years, well-conceived programs of economic development will probably become self-sustaining, according to expert opinion, and countries should be able to carry a sizable amount of foreign indebtedness. This would be "good business" for the U.S., not giveaway.[46]

But there are reservations about this approach. (1) Direct American lending has in the past been hitched to specific American interests, which do not always gibe with the best strategy for economic development. Export-Import Bank loans usually must be used to buy American supplies, whereas buying supplies elsewhere, perhaps even within the country itself, might contribute more to the country's growth (and be more economical. Political and military objectives admittedly influence loan policy. U.S. security demands caused the Export-Import Bank to shift emphasis away from development objectives as such, jeopardizing the continuity of some countries' programs. (2) Underdeveloped countries are unusually sensitive about becoming subservient to foreign domination, and hesitate to tie themselves too closely to American policies, even at the sacrifice of financial aid. (3) Loans are conditioned on repayment, yet many basic and costly development projects, such as roads and power facilities, are the least likely to produce a tangible return in a reasonable time. Thus, countries may have to drain resources to pay back the U.S. precisely at the time they should be free to put everything into keeping up the momentum of their economic advance. This objection obviously does not apply to *grants* given by the U.S. (4) Export-Import Bank loans are limited by the customary requirement that their repayment be guaranteed by the receiving country's government. The practical effect is that few private enterprises can secure financing; governments prefer to guarantee only when they have some measure of control over the project. (5) As for U.S. grants, important segments of Congress and Ameri-

---

[46] Higgins and Malenbaum, *op. cit.*, pp. 308–09. See, also, the conclusions of the provocative study conducted by the Massachusetts Institute of Technology Center for International Studies: Max F. Millikan and W. W. Rostow, *A Proposal: Key to an Effective Foreign Policy* (New York: Harper, 1957).

can business in recent years have displayed an allergic reaction to foreign assistance not strictly military that may actually close down the pipeline, rather than increase its flow.

Expand International Facilities for Financing Economic Development. Two courses are currently open: (1) increase the resources of the International Bank and its affiliates and adopt policies that will enable them to lend funds more liberally for development projects; (2) strengthen the resources of regional development programs such as the Colombo Plan by inducing more countries to participate and to up their contributions as they become prosperous.

The International Bank. The Bank, after a slow start, has taken the business of promoting economic development very seriously. In 18 years, it made loans totaling almost $8 billion to finance the capital plant of specific development projects. Correlated with its funds has been its advice and expert help to governments in planning their overall development programs. Dramatic results are beginning to show.

The loans were made principally for transportation and communications, electric power, agriculture and forestry, and industry. Thus, the emphasis was put overwhelmingly on the basic requirements for development rather than on projects that could yield quick returns but would not stimulate long-run economic expansion.

Of major significance, the Bank has attracted private capital in its wake. The value of the projects assisted by the Bank is almost three times the Bank's own investment (which means other investors have put up $3.00 for every $1.00 committed by the Bank). Furthermore, a substantial amount of the Bank's own resources is supplied by private investors, who have bought its bonds to the tune of about $2,500 billion.[47]

But the Bank, too, has its limitations. (1) Its loans must be repaid with interest at a rate higher than Export-Import Bank loans and not much less than commercial banks. (2) Poorer countries may not be sufficiently good "risks" to qualify for substantial credits from the Bank. For a number of years, the Bank was leary of lending money except for "self-liquidating projects" which would be able to generate returns quick enough to pay back the loan out of its own proceeds. This stringent policy ruled out many of the most necessary basic projects. Now, however, the Bank appraises the total capacity of repayment from the economy as a whole. Even so, the neediest countries frequently cannot meet the test. (3) It lends only for the direct costs of *foreign* supplies required for a project. The local costs must be met completely by the country itself—often a burden heavier than should be borne in the early and most demanding stage of development in a poorer country. (4) The Bank requires a government guarantee (like the Export-

---

[47] Geoffrey M. Wilson, "World Bank Operators," *The Fund and Bank Review,* June, 1964, pp. 15–20.

Import Bank), which cuts out most private undertakings. (5) The total resources of the Bank as presently constituted could not support much more than $500 million new credit annually, especially when most of the loans need to be made for terms of 20 to 25 years.

A number of important steps have been taken to increase the scope and flexibility of the Bank's operations. Its resources were substantially expanded. Its capital subscriptions were doubled to $20 billion. (But of this amount, only about $1,700 billion is available to be loaned, as governments pay in just 20 per cent, most of it in their own currencies to be used only with their permission. The rest of the subscription remains in the hands of the governments on call to guarantee the Bank's own borrowings.) The Bank has been unusually successful in broadening the base of its borrowings in the capital markets of the world. More than half its bonds have been sold to investors outside the U.S. (especially in Germany and other countries of western Europe. As a result of these and other actions, the Bank has been able to step up the amount of its loans (to over $800 million in 1963–64, almost doubling the amount lent in the previous year).

The legitimate need for capital assistance over and beyond what could be provided under the Bank's strict conditions led to establishment, in 1960, of the International Development Association, operating as an affiliate of the Bank and completely integrated with it. It makes "soft" loans, at a lower rate of interest and for longer terms, when the Bank considers a project economically justified, the government's fiscal and economic policies sensible, but the country's overall balance of payments situation is unfavorable and it cannot soon repay large foreign debts.

Projects financed were at first similar to those backed by the Bank—railways and roads, power stations, and irrigation schemes. Its activities were then extended to provide assistance for basic agricultural services (farm-to-market roads, facilities for crop storage, and local agricultural credit institutions), to industry (helping establish new industries to reduce a country's dependence on exports of a few primary products, financing "maintenance" imports—replacement parts, etc.—and supporting privately owned industrial financing companies), and to education (supporting vocational and technical schools, etc.).

The value of the IDA was quickly recognized by both developed and developing countries. Its initial resources of about $765 million were quickly committed and a second round insured by a subscription of about the same amount. (It is significant that both developed and underdeveloped countries contribute, the underdeveloped putting up most of their funds in their own currencies.)[48] In addition, the Bank has decided to turn over to IDA part of the regular earnings it receives on its "hard" loans.

---

[48] *Ibid.,* pp. 21–25.

Clearly, the Bank is the proper instrument through which to channel the bulk of regular public lending for development purposes. It is now able to provide high quality technical advice and guidance in the whole field of economic development. It can help governments to devise and staff their projects so as to be efficient and make the maximum contribution to the country's progress. It has established a nonpolitical reputation, though it is sometimes criticized for reflecting the economic outlook of the developed countries (which it really does, since its decisions are made by those who hold a majority of its shares).

But the Bank still cannot, within its present terms of reference, (a) undertake to meet all the capital needs for economic development of the poorest countries, and (b) take major risks in the others and directly support private productive undertakings, however worthy.

The Colombo Plan. In 1950, seven members of the Commonwealth of Nations agreed on a program for the economic development of South and Southeast Asia. It included a six-year regional development plan, coordinating the separate plans of individual countries and taking account of their respective needs and resources. The Plan estimated the assistance they would require to produce some real improvement in a period short enough so that the peoples of the area could see real benefits. The combined programs called for an expenditure of about $5 billion over the six-year period—about two-thirds for India, one-seventh for Pakistan, and the rest for Ceylon, Malaya, and Borneo. The main focus of development was on agriculture, communications, and electric power, with more than 70 per cent of the program devoted to increasing production of food and agricultural raw materials to meet the overriding need of the half-billion people of the area. This joint planning process proved most effective and was continued at the expiration of the first period. While the initial core of collaboration was the group of Commonwealth countries, others in the region were welcomed into full association in the enterprise, so that now most non-Communist Asian countries participate (including Japan as a contributor).

An intergovernmental technical assistance scheme was organized to supplement aid from the United Nations and the United States. Under a Council for Technical Cooperation, a small bureau of technical staff arranges for training personnel, sending missions to study practices in other countries, and providing experts for advisory services in public administration, health, agriculture, industry, scientific research, and other phases of development. Equipment for training and demonstration is also part of the assistance rendered.

A coordinated plan of financing was devised. Initially, somewhat over $2 billion was to be raised internally by the Asian countries themselves. Toward the remaining $3 billion needed, the United Kingdom agreed to release about

$750 million of "sterling balances" owned by the Asian countries. (Though these really belonged to India and the others, Great Britain had been unable to let these balances be used because of her own precarious financial position. This action meant a real tightening of England's own financial belt in order to make so large an amount of capital available in so short a time.) Roughly, the Commonwealth countries outside Asia put up a total of $1 billion, leaving $2 billion to go. Part of this was borrowed from the International Bank by the participating governments. But the largest contribution was made by the United States, including loans from the Export-Import Bank and grants from the Foreign Operations Administration. This approach was continued and expanded after the initial period. By 1965, total aid provided under the Colombo Plan to countries of South and Southeast Asia had reached $14.9 billion; $13.5 billion of this came from the U.S.[49]

The Colombo Plan devised a new pattern of relationship between the underdeveloped countries and the countries that held the major resources of outside capital—a pattern that avoided some of the problems of direct bilateral assistance (such as resentment of foreign control), yet assured the donors a substantial voice in determining the use of their funds. This was a regional association, in which donors and recipients jointly agreed on the targets of development and the resources each could make available.

The organization of the Colombo Plan is distinctive in two respects (compared, for instance, with the way the Organization for European Economic Cooperation was set up). First, it operates without a centralized organization. This acknowledged British preference for a "conference approach" to decision-making, which preserves complete independence for each government to make its own policy, rather than an "institutional approach," which would encourage unified procedures of policy-making and press countries to identify their national interests completely with the common interests of the group. Second, the United States is included as a full and equal participant in the group rather than remaining more or less outside, exercising solitary parental authority over the petitions for assistance presented to it. This enables the U.S. to join in the planning process and to express its judgments at every point during execution of the program without appearing to dictate to any particular country the scope and form of its development program.

Since organization of the Colombo Plan, the U.S. has integrated its bilateral assistance to the member countries with the overall plan. In the absence of a central organization, its loans and grants are made directly to individual governments (as are the grants of the other countries). But the contribution is conceived as a regional one. There is a strong disposition on the part of the

---

[49] As reported in the Colombo Plan Consultative Committee Thirteenth Annual Report.

U.S. to favor this method of channeling funds for economic development, as it encourages a maximum coordination of effort among countries whose problems are interrelated.[50]

CONCLUSION

Where does all this leave the prospect for the underdeveloped two-thirds or three-quarters of the world?

A few countries appear close to joining the ranks of the developing, if not yet the fully developed. Mexico, for instance, seems to have acquired the momentum for sustained general economic growth. Yugoslavia may be on the way. In others, some sectors of the economy have been stimulated, but this has not spilled over sufficiently to assure a balanced development of the entire country.

Great areas remain stagnant, however, or seem actually to be retrogressing. Economic plans flounder under the weight of exploding populations, unyielding habits of life, ineffective public and private administration, and just sheer deficiencies of basic resources. The efforts of the international community to assist, substantial as they have been, have not yet succeeded in enabling these countries to shake the various shackles that restrain them from becoming what has been called "achieving societies."

The various programs of international development assistance have gone a long way toward establishing effective procedures for transferring physical resources and technical know-how from the economically advanced to the underdeveloped countries. Undoubtedly much more could be contributed than has been, probably to the good. But it is now clear that the mere input of resources, in whatever quantity, whether of capital or skills, will not automatically turn the wheels of economic development.

---

[50] The Alliance for Progress established a somewhat similar approach to expanding resources for the development of Latin-American countries. At the initiative of President Kennedy, but also in line with growing concern throughout the American continents over the stagnation of the Latin-American economies and the need for social reform to accompany programs of economic development, 19 republics (Cuba excepted) joined the U.S. in a 10-year, comprehensive program for social and economic development expected to involve at least $20 billion in foreign financing and equivalent commitments of domestic resources by the Latin-American countries.

The Declaration of Punta del Este, adopted in August, 1961, sets forth the basic objectives and commitments of the Alliance for Progress and is, in effect, its charter. After a shaky start, marked by policy disagreements and unimpressive indigenous response in some of the Latin-American countries, the Alliance appeared by 1964–65 to have gathered momentum and a sense of direction.

For early reports from differing perspectives, see the study prepared by Raymond F. Mikesell, "United States–Latin American Relations" (Subcommittee on American Republics Affairs, U.S. Senate Committee on Foreign Relations, 87th Cong., 2d sess., August 3, 1962); and the report by Senator Hubert H. Humphrey to the U.S. Senate Committees on Appropriations and Foreign Relations (88th Cong., 1st sess., Senate Doc. No. 13, April 11, 1963).

For one thing, the problem of how to infuse such resources into the lifestream of these countries so that they become self-propelling remains largely unresolved. Put another way, many of these countries are not able to absorb new resources because their economies are not successfully *integrated,* either internally or in relationship to other countries.

The prospect for development is seen increasingly to turn on the question of how to accomplish economic integration. The international aspects of this problem are the subject of the following chapter.

Chapter 15

Experiments in Economic Integration

The paradox of nations pursuing separate and often conflicting economic policies in a world whose technological advancement makes international economic relations inescapable has been the despair of those who long for conditions of stability and progress. They see in disunity, as well as in underdevelopment, a prime cause of stagnation and recurring crisis.

So inventive minds have designed schemes to "integrate" major facets of economic life across national boundaries, either on a world or a regional scale. Many of these plans have been stillborn. But others have had their trial runs. If these efforts have not yet ushered in the "brave, new world," they have certainly pioneered with brilliance and boldness previously unexplored paths toward a stable and productive international economy.

THE CHARACTER OF INTEGRATION

Like many sacred words, integration now means different things. Even when applied to the area of international economic relationships, it covers a variety of approaches, some of which are probably contradictory.

Table 1 illustrates the diversity of approaches to integration undertaken by major international economic organizations currently in operation. There are sharp differences of expectation even within the experience of a single organization. A penetrating study of the European Economic Community, for instance, identifies four conceptions, each of which has been reflected in the community's development: (1) integration as political unification, (2) integration as economic unification, (3) integration as economic and political cooperation, and (4) integration as free trade.[1]

---

[1] Leon N. Lindberg, "Perceptions of Integration," *The Political Dynamics of European Economic Integration* (Stanford, Calif.: Stanford University Press, 1963), chap. 6.

In reviewing the main definitions that have emerged in the immense literature on

TABLE 1

INTERNATIONAL ORGANIZATIONS CONCERNED WITH ECONOMIC INTEGRATION

Organization	Area Included	Object of Integration	Degree of Integration
Benelux............	Belgium, Netherlands, Luxembourg	trade controls, the whole economy	tariff union, economic union
Colombo Plan........	7 Commonwealth countries, U.S., British and Asian countries	development plans, investment, and technical assistance	consultation and unified aid
Council for Economic Mutual Assistance (CEMA or COMECON).......	Soviet bloc	whole economy, including trade, investment, production goals, development assistance	central direction and bilateral mutual aid treaties
European Coal and Steel Community (Shuman Plan) (ECSC)..........	France, Italy, Germany, Benelux countries	coal, iron, and steel industries	common market with supranational regulatory authorities
European Economic Community ("Common Market," EEC)........	same as ECSC	internal and external trade, industrial and agricultural development	common market with central institutions for policy formation and implementation
Euratom............	same as ECSC	nuclear energy production, distribution, and research	central institutions to organize research, finance common development, own raw materials, enforce controls
European Free Trade Association (EFTA).	Britain, Scandinavia, Portugal, Switzerland, Austria	trade	reciprocal, nondiscriminatory concessions
General Agreement on Tariffs and Trade (GATT); Organization for Trade Cooperation (OTC)............	89 nations	government trade controls	reciprocal concessions, nondiscrimination, collective decisions on grievances and exceptions

TABLE 1—*Continued*

INTERNATIONAL ORGANIZATIONS CONCERNED WITH ECONOMIC INTEGRATION

Organization	Area Included	Object of Integration	Degree of Integration
Intergovernmental commodity agreements for: wheat, sugar, tin, coffee........	46 nations	international trade in wheat; trade in sugar, tin, coffee	international contract, no organization
International Monetary Fund........	103 members (*not* including Soviet bloc)	currency stability and liquidity, national and international fiscal policies, balance of payments	international stabilization fund, regulation of exchange rates and balance of payments practices, consultation and recommendations
Latin-American Free Trade Association...	9 Latin-American countries	trade, transport, international payments, industrial complementarity	mutual tariff concessions, consultation and joint planning, international complementarity agreements
Organization of American States (OAS).............	21 American republics	trade, development	consultation and agreement, mutual aid
Organization for European Economic Cooperation (OEEC); including European Payments Union (EPU) (now inoperative)............	16 nations in Europe (including Britain)	production, international trade and payments, economic and fiscal policies, labor	consultation and planning, mutually agreed rules and goals, central fund and credits
Organization for Economic Cooperation and Development (OECD)....	18 nations in Europe, plus U.S. and Canada	trade, capital movements, development assistance	consultation and coordination of policies, monetary fund
Sterling bloc........	Commonwealth, also most Middle Eastern countries	financial reserves, fiscal and trade policies	consultation, agreement, pooled reserves
Uniscan............	Britain and Scandinavia	fiscal relations	consultation and agreement

TABLE 1—*Continued*

INTERNATIONAL ORGANIZATIONS CONCERNED WITH ECONOMIC INTEGRATION

Organization	Area Included	Object of Integration	Degree of Integration
United Nations Economic Commissions for:			
Europe (ECE)....all Europe, including U.S.S.R. and Britain; also the U.S.		trade, production, labor	consultation and recommendations
Asia and the Far East (ECAFE)...Asian members of U.N., also equal number of non-Asian U.N. members		trade, development	consultation and recommendations
Latin America (ECLA)........Latin-American countries, plus U.S.		trade, development	consultation and recommendations
Africa (ECA).....African members of U.N.		trade, development	consultation and recommendations

We shall be primarily concerned in this study with the development of two principal patterns of international economic association, each designed to finally accomplish the meshing of production and distribution of goods and services among nations to their mutual advantage, but each reflecting radically different assumptions regarding the means necessary to accomplish this end.

First is the effort to create conditions of economic freedom, "liberalizing" international economic relationships by removing trade barriers and discriminations. While the main thrust of this approach has been directed at restraints imposed by governments, it has also sought to prevent private restrictive

---

integration, Lindberg notes a major distinction between those who consider integration as a "condition," and those who identify it as a "process" of shifting loyalties, expectations, and political activities to a new center, with joint institutions demanding jurisdiction over preexisting national states. A principal exponent of the second concept is Ernst Haas. See, for instance, his *The Uniting of Europe: Political, Social, and Economic Forces, 1950–57* (Stanford, Calif.: Stanford University Press, 1958).

Lindberg himself modifies the process concept, putting primary emphasis on the development of joint or delegated decision-making, but without necessarily moving toward political community as defined by Haas. See Lindberg, "Definitions and Hypotheses," *op. cit.,* chap. i.

For an attempt at a systematic formulation of the integration concept for purposes of empirical research, see Philip E. Jacob and Henry Teune, "The Integrative Process: Guidelines for Analysis of the Bases of Political Community," in Philip E. Jacob and James V. Toscano (eds.), *The Integration of Political Communities* (Philadelphia: J. B. Lippincott Co., 1964).

practices, like cartels. The assumption has been, in agreement with a main line of classical economic theory, that the greatest advantage to all would accrue, largely automatically, if people were allowed to produce, sell, and buy—across national boundaries, as well as within them—in response to the incentives operating in an "open" market where no one arbitrarily controls the price or sets a limit on what can be made or purchased.

In the postwar world, this approach has been attempted on two different levels—on a worldwide basis and within particular regions. However, it is not at all clear that liberalization at the regional level is conducive to or compatible with the attempt to achieve global economic freedom, and vice versa, though this was at first the widely held expectation. The experience of the European Economic Community, reviewed later in this chapter, is a sobering case in point.

Furthermore, as will be seen, the liberalization approach has never reached the point of complete economic freedom. The unfreezing of some controls has itself depended on a complex network of international economic agreements. A growing amount of intergovernmental action, control, and organization has proved necessary to implement these agreements and to meet new needs arising as the former controls were relinquished.

The needs of developing countries have posed a particular challenge to the strategy of economic freedom. As these pushed to the fore, they raised a demand for a system of deliberate, managed, and long-term preferential treatment in favor of the underdeveloped. How to reconcile this with the basic liberal principles of economic equality, nondiscrimination, and minimal governmental control has been the conundrum of policy-makers on both sides of the have–have-not confrontation.

Second is the bold experiment of "economic community," brought nearest fruition by the six Western European countries that first forged a Coal-and-Steel Community, then created a similar setup for atomic energy (Euratom), and capped their handiwork with the comprehensive "Common Market," covering virtually all sectors of their economies. Captivated by this experience, or alarmed by its competitive implications, others are now trying either to join the Europeans or to apply the model to their own regions. (The Soviet bloc has fashioned its own model of economic integration, COMECON, achieving an extreme degree of centralized control within a rather loose formal framework of international economic cooperation.)

The community idea (as developed by the European six) is really a complex amalgam of three elements : (1) economic liberalization within the community, almost to the point of a single "free" market in many sectors; (2) highly coordinated economic planning by the concerned governments, operating through joint institutions and procedures of decision-making; and (3) specific control over certain segments of the national economies by central authorities exercising, in some instances, supranational powers over both private parties and the national governments.

To what extent integration, approached either through freedom or by community, holds the promise of economic stability and growth is the point of further analysis of these various experiments. At least four critical questions arise:

1. Is integration likely to be more successful on a regional than on a worldwide basis? And does regional integration tend to block the organization of measures for global stability?

2. Can integration in one economic sector—a particular commodity or industry, or international trade and payments—contribute to stability unless there occurs a much broader coordination of national economic policies and activities? And does integration of a sector tend to block or forward the widening of collaboration to include a broader sweep of the economy?

3. Can integration succeed without economic union, or at least some degree of supranational authority to control the economic activities integrated?

4. Can integration in economic matters succeed without substantial political unity, involving even some modification of national political authority?

An overview of the various attempts at international economic integration suggests the following broad conclusions.

1. The push toward integration has gone farther in certain regions than on the global scale, notably in Western Europe, the British Commonwealth, and probably the Soviet bloc. But there is little evidence that the experience of these areas is reproducible in other regions. A combination of fortuitous circumstances in a *particular* region has made possible the success of the *particular* measures undertaken in that region. Meanwhile, in almost every case, regional integration has generated toward the world outside the region attitudes and policies that have been disruptive and disintegrative of general international economic cooperation. The more integrated the region becomes, the less likely it is to contribute effectively and generously to the welfare of those outside. Regionalism seems to nurture a form of economic self-interest as ruthlessly competitive and myopic as the virulent economic nationalism that tore apart the world economy between the two world wars.

2. Experience seems to indicate that successful integration in one economic sector has a tendency to "spill over" into others and, conversely, that confinement of integrative measures to a relatively narrow range of international relationships will limit effectiveness even within the narrow area. This is not to conclude, however, that ambitious attempts to integrate everything at once are likely to succeed. Quite the reverse. "Gradualism" is the formula; but gradualism must be expansive and progressive if the process of integration is not to stall.

3. With respect to supranationalism, the implications even of the West European experiments are that advances toward integration depend far more on consensus formation procedures than on establishment of central decision-

making authorities with powers to mandate actions against the will of the constituent governments. Supranational institutions appear to be a result of integration rather than a condition of it. In the few instances when they function, they do so within a framework of agreed policies and purposes so well constructed and firmly based that their actions, in effect, conform to and implement a preexisting consensus. In such circumstances, supranational organs may be a convenience; they are not a prerequisite. Generally, the degree of integration has stopped well short of supranational authority. In practice, it has meant simply close functional cooperation among independent governments with common problems, rather than outright union—either economic or political.

4. Coming directly to the question of the political basis for international economic integration, experience so far indicates that considerable progress toward integration has been achieved with very little inroad on the political structure of the nation-state system. One must admit that divergent political policies have often severely limited the extent to which national governments have been able to develop cooperative economic relationships and adopt major integrative measures. But if the price of economic integration is understood to involve a substantial and permanent abandonment of the national pivot of political authority, no government or people has yet been prepared to meet it, even though some vigorous appeals have been made to persuade them to do so. In these circumstances, there has been no choice but to try to reconcile economic integration with political pluralism. The results are moderately encouraging to those who crave economic salvation but foresee no imminent millennium of world government or even of region-states.

INTEGRATION THROUGH FREEDOM

Much of the planning for long-run economic stability has been directed toward restoring a relatively free flow of goods, money, and people across national boundaries. The underlying assumption has been that adequate economic integration would come automatically among countries that agreed to let their people buy and sell their products and services unhampered by tariffs, quotas, exchange controls, and the other restrictive and discriminatory barriers which governments—and sometimes private business—have erected to protect the national economy or special interests from the stress of international competition. This "liberal" approach insists that over the long run the free play of basic economic forces, such as the relative efficiency of the division of labor, functional specialization, and supply and demand, will stimulate productive activity and still afford reasonable stability, provided one closes down a valve here or there in the channels of economic intercourse.

The major problem confronting the strategists of liberalism has been to find ways of opening the many valves already closed, at a rate and in an order that would not expose some nations to ruinous pressures on their economy while they were making the transition to freedom. They have also sought in the experiments with integration ways to cushion countries and groups against sudden and unexpected dislocations in trade that might occur when controls are lifted.

On a world-wide basis, the most ambitious attempt to organize economic life on foundations of relative freedom was the International Trade Organization, a charter for which was signed in 1948. But it was not ratified by enough countries (including its chief sponsor, the United States) to put the institution into operation.

In the meantime, the General Agreement on Tariffs and Trade (GATT) has been negotiated at three-year intervals. This eases tariffs multilaterally, and has made the principle of nondiscrimination in trade binding among the parties to it.

On a regional basis, considerable progress toward trade liberalization within Europe resulted from the efforts of the Organization for European Economic Cooperation. This accomplishment was closely bound to the success of the European Payments Union in enabling countries to settle their international payments on a regional, rather than a bilateral, basis. When it was decided to disband the OEEC and EPU, the Organization for Economic Cooperation and Development was formed, in part to continue the efforts to liberalize trade within Europe. The OECD was also expected to work out arrangements for extending the area of liberalization to include trade between Europe and North America.

Meanwhile, a complete removal of trade barriers was attempted among first three, then six, countries of Western Europe, through the Benelux customs union and the European Common Market, respectively. But, as will be seen later, while the Common Market countries have liberalized trade among themselves, they have devised a common *external* tariff that restricts others from sharing in the Market. This policy has precipitated serious interregional economic conflict and retaliatory action, including formation of the European Free Trade Association under Britain's leadership.

But Britain herself has had a long record of "preferential" trading and international financial arrangements with the Commonwealth and certain other countries associated in what has been known as the "sterling bloc." From the standpoint of facilitating trade among those in the sterling area, these arrangements have been highly successful. But the same privileges and principles have not been extended to the countries outside, and the policies and commitments of the sterling area have been a major stumbling block to both European and global integration efforts.

Several other regions have attempted to follow in the path of integration charted by the Europeans. Embryonic common markets have been formed or planned in Latin America, Central America, Africa, and among the Arab countries. It is still premature to predict their permanence or outcomes.

The Global Approach

The International Trade Organization—A Rejected Blueprint. The Havana Charter, signed but never implemented, culminated three years of intensive negotiation for a comprehensive reorganization of world trade. Boiled down to the bare essentials, this complex, technical, 106-article convention provided:

1. Nations, in principle, would not discriminate against trade with any member of the organization.

2. Quantitative restrictions on trade, such as import and export quotas or limitations, would be abandoned.

3. Nations would negotiate a substantial reduction of tariffs, would not impose more severe internal taxes and regulations on imports from other members than on domestic products, and would consult together whenever subsidies adversely affected international trade. In principle, therefore, nations would refrain even from discrimination in favor of their own nationals' trade.

4. Governments would prevent private business practices that would restrict trade; for instance, such common activities of cartels and monopolies as fixing prices, excluding markets, allocating customers, and fixing production quotas.

5. Intergovernmental commodity agreements would be worked out to regulate production and sale of products subject to damaging price and output fluctuations.

6. Certain exceptions to these rules would be tolerated when countries faced unusual economic needs (for instance, for postwar reconstruction, developing new industries or overcoming serious balance of payments difficulties). But, generally, countries would have to secure the permission of a majority of the members before they could take such action, and the exception would be considered temporary, to be revoked as soon as the particular condition that warranted it was corrected.

7. Nations would submit their trade disputes to international settlement if they could not work out solutions among themselves. Disputes could be arbitrated or submitted to the International Trade Organization itself.

The cardinal innovation of the ITO was its insistence that a nation justify before its peers any departure from the liberal code of open and nondiscriminatory world trade. From an economic perspective, the ITO thus aimed at freedom. But from a political perspective, it envisaged a far greater surrender of governmental freedom in trade and economic policy than had ever before been attempted. In reality, the ITO proposed that in an area where nations had exercised almost unlimited individual power of decision—to restrict and disciminate, or not, as each felt was to its own interest—all vital policies that conflicted with the interests of others would now be subject to international decision. To *gain* of economic freedom, nations would *give up* their freedom to control international economic relations as they separately saw fit.

This was strong medicine for many countries to swallow, especially when they had come to depend on tight controls as a principal instrument of survival in war and of recovery from war. It was also hard for many underdeveloped countries to face the rigors of competition with highly industrialized countries in an open world trading system. The British, for their part, were reluctant to surrender the system of preferences that formed an important tie with their empire and the Commonwealth. But the prospect of important trade concessions from the world's most lush market, the United States (and provisions for a substantial number of exceptions, especially during a transitional period), gradually prevailed over the reservations and objections. Then came the coup de grace. Soundings showed that the American Executive had outdistanced the Senate in rushing toward a free world economy and could not secure approval for ratification of the Havana Charter.

The demise of ITO was indicative of difficulties more basic and chronic than American protectionism. Nor could the troubles of the "transition period"—from war to recovery—or the exigencies of the new cold war and the rearmament that accompanied it be held primarily responsible for the frustration of ITO.

There was an inherent contradiction between a policy that sought stability primarily through a return to freedom from government controls in trade and the wide acceptance of government planning and regulation as necessary to keep a nation's economy on an even keel. At least since the depression days, people have come to expect governments to take positive action to insure their economic security and have been unwilling to place their welfare at the mercy of the vagaries of the free market. Can governments effectively discharge this fundamental welfare obligation to their people if they give up their powers to manage their international economic relations? The repercussions of integration by freedom of trade might mean instability and insecurity for some countries some of the time. Whatever long-run benefits might accrue, most people are inescapably preoccupied with the problems of their day-to-day livelihood, and governments will not last long if they merely hold out the liberal economist's assurance that everything will work out all right in the end if the "economic forces" are left well enough alone.

ITO foundered, therefore, on two rocks—the welfare state and national sovereignty. Primary welfare obligations bind governments to at least some degree of economic management. And insistence on national independence in policy-making as a political prerogative of sovereignty bars the kind of international control that ITO would have exerted.

The Attack on Trade Barriers—GATT. The General Agreement on Tariffs and Trade, however, has accomplished a considerable reduction of barriers to international trade by means of specific undertakings for a limited period of time in contrast to the blanket commitments of ITO. The first agreement was negotiated during the final stages of drafting the ITO Charter, and was intended to give the process of tariff reduction a head start while the ITO was getting organized. Twenty countries agreed to extend one another tariff concessions on some 40,000 items for a two-year period. The Agreement was renewed when it was apparent that the ITO would not be formed. Some additional concessions were negotiated, and other countries joined. Despite some serious conflicts of interest, which at times threatened to wreck the entire arrangement, GATT has been continued and now encompasses 89 nations.[2]

GATT has now acquired permanent institutional form. Functions carried on at first by the "contracting parties" at their occasional conferences without facilities for continuing responsibility are now the business of the Organization for Trade Cooperation, with its own Secretariat. It arranges for the tariff negotiations, conducts studies, settles disputes, and passes on applications for waivers from GATT provisions. It is able to initiate new trade proposals to the governments.

The GATT contains three main undertakings: (1) the specific tariff concessions each member is willing to apply to imports from all the others; (2) a set of principles of fair trade that each agrees to respect in its dealings with all the others; (3) a procedure for settlement of trade disputes that arise among the members. There is no provision for enforcing the agreement other than withdrawal of privileges by the other members from one who has refused to live up to its obligations.

The Rule of Nondiscrimination. The tariff concessions are extended on the basis of the most favored nation principle which insures nondiscrimination among the members. The rate imposed on a product imported from one member must be no higher than on the same product imported from any other country.

The members also promise to outlaw quantitative restrictions and quotas on trade among themselves. They guarantee freedom for goods to move in transit through their territories to third countries. Internal taxation of imported goods shall not exceed that on domestic products. Customs procedures are to be eased. Export subsidies shall undergo international scrutiny.

Escape by Consent. In some circumstances, these rules can be modified. The principal exceptions permitted are maintenance of agricultural price-support programs, protection of new industries in underdeveloped countries, prevention of a severe drain on a country's foreign exchange, or provision for military security. Generally, nations merely consult with the other members before invoking one of the "escape" provisions, explaining

---

[2] The early development of GATT is ably described in Raymond Vernon, "Organizing for World Trade," *International Conciliation*, November, 1955. Much of the following discussion is based on this account.

why they believe they must do so. But if the action they contemplate is discriminatory, they must secure a waiver from the group (by a two-thirds vote, including at least one-half of all the members). For instance, the countries that organized the European Payments Union had to ask for a waiver, because they had to be free to put quantitative limits on imports from a particular country if it was running up an excessively heavy trade deficit within the EPU. The European Coal and Steel Community had to negotiate for a waiver of the rule governing tariffs, because to form a common market which was the essence of the community, its six members had to abolish all trade restrictions, including tariffs, among themselves. Yet they were not prepared to do the same with the other GATT members (at least without their accepting the same obligations in return). Thus, these six countries would give one another a preferred position as against the other countries in GATT, violating the "MFN" principle. The negotiations were difficult, because some of the other countries, such as Britain and the Scandinavians, feared they would be shut out of trade in coal and steel products in the community area when they had to pay a tariff that German industry, for instance, did not. In the end, the waiver was granted (the community being recognized as a single nation for this purpose), but only on condition that the community limit the tariffs on coal–steel imports to the lowest rates previously imposed by any of the six members.

Even more difficult negotiations followed the formation of the European Economic Community, for now all products were involved, not just coal and steel. The formula of reconciliation reached here was that the tariff set by the six European countries for a particular product could be no higher than the arithmetical average of the six separate tariffs in effect when the EEC was established.

The GATT countries also acquiesced in United States discrimination against Czechoslovakia, waiving all the reciprocal rights and obligations of the two countries under GATT after Congress in 1951 directed the President to withhold from the Soviet bloc countries the benefit of all concessions negotiated under the Trade Agreements Act. Without judging the merits of the case, the other countries, in effect, granted a divorce on grounds of incompatibility, but continued the relations of each country with all the others.

The discussion of these exceptional cases should not detract from, but rather emphasize, the main point of the GATT experience, viz., the rule of nondiscrimination has been consistently recognized as a fundamental principle in trade relations, applicable on a basis of reciprocity even across the Iron Curtain and to be modified only in unique or extreme circumstances, and then by consent of the "contracting parties" rather than unilaterally.

Settlement of Disputes.   When trade disputes arise among the GATT nations or countries are charged with violating the agreement, the issues are usually aired before the whole group if the parties have been unable to settle the matter between themselves. The member countries as a whole decide who is to blame and recommend action they think will resolve the dispute, such as a change of administrative practice or perhaps even of legislation in order to bring the offending country into line with its obligations. In the rare cases when a country does not comply, the other members can rule that it has broken its contracts and can authorize retaliatory action by any nations so inclined.

The procedure customarily used to effect a settlement has been to appoint a working party, including the disputants and disinterested neutrals. This group seeks the facts, agrees on the GATT principles involved, and prepares a set of recommendations that is then considered and adopted by the entire group of GATT members. The process depends on mutual education and conciliation. The countries have now achieved sufficient confidence in one another so that they refer disputes to a "panel on complaints" which does *not* include the disputants and thus reaches decisions in a semijudicial manner. It hears disputants and confers with them to find common ground. But it prepares the final report to the GATT members on its own responsibility.

GATT's record of settlement is impressive. The following cases are typical. Chile complained that Australia was subsidizing the use of ammonium sulphate, an artificial fertilizer, which competed with Chilean natural ammonium nitrate. GATT ruled that Australia could properly subsidize one product and not the other but the subsidy did, in fact, deprive Chile of the advantage of a tariff concession on its product. Australia complied with GATT's recommendation that the subsidy be removed. Denmark and Norway complained that Belgium's internal taxation discriminated against certain of their imports. GATT members sustained the complaint and the discrimination was eliminated. On GATT recommendation, Germany removed the competitive inequality involved in import requirements stricter on Portuguese than on Norwegian sardines (sidestepping a technical issue over whether the two varieties were "like products"). GATT decided that Greece had violated its agreement by calculating tariff levies in artificially valued drachmas, with the practical effect of drastically increasing its tariffs. Greece withdrew the action.

The great majority of disputes never reach the GATT members, being settled directly in bilateral consultations based upon reference to the relevant GATT provisions. Britain repealed a ban on the manufacture of pure Virginia tobacco cigarettes on protest by the U.S. Appeal to GATT provisions has likewise ended many discriminatory buying and pricing practices.

The hardest cases to resolve are those requiring legislative action in countries where the legislative and executive powers are separated. The United States has been particularly at fault; Congress balks at the elimination of import restrictions on such items as dairy products, even though they violate GATT.

The Fight against Protectionism.   GATT's major problem has been to overcome the strong pressures for protectionism on all sides. Almost every country has bargained for some kind of special treatment, while trying to secure from the others substantial concessions for its trade. The tariff negotiating sessions have been long-drawn-out and complex. In the initial stage, pairs of countries bargain with respect to products for which each is a principal supplier to the other. But, in the end, all agreements must be made multilateral, by virtue of the most favored nation principle.

A number of key countries have resorted to various devices to avoid making substantial concessions. Some have tried to bargain on the basis of promising not to raise tariffs, rather than agreeing to reduce them. Countries have been quick to offer great reductions on items for which they had little demand anyway. France and then Italy attempted to get away with jacking up their tariffs just before their first negotiations began, then making "concessions" on the basis of the new schedule. The British have been reluctant to give up the imperial preference system under which trade was largely freed of duties among the Commonwealth countries, and it has been even more reluctant to give such privileges to all GATT members unless they, and the United States in particular, would abolish virtually all restrictions on British trade. The United States, for its part, became more niggardly in its concessions with each passing year, and even proceeded to raise its tariffs on such vital items in GATT members' trade as Swiss watches and English bicycles. In 1950, the United States was unable to reach any kind of agreement with the United Kingdom and other principal Commonwealth countries, and only very limited terms with other major trading nations such as France.

The main reasons for the increasing difficulties experienced by GATT were, first, the receding tide of economic liberalism in the United States and, second, rather paradoxically, the progress of trade liberalization among some of the other countries. Many of these had given up a fair part of their armor of economic controls—dropping quotas, easing exchange restrictions, etc.—so that the tariff was left as the principal remaining instrument by which to limit imports and protect the competitive position of their own products.

Nevertheless, prospects now look brighter for consistent progress toward less restrictive trade relations through GATT. In 1963, thanks to special legislative authorization, the U.S. government was able to initiate the "Kennedy Round" of negotiations, aimed at a 50 percent reduction in *all* tariff rates—across the board in contrast to the previous practice of negotiating product by product. While the object was not fully attained (partly because of the European Common Market's unwillingness to accept this approach in full), the movement toward liberalization received a strong boost. The members agreed on basic negotiating principles that took the 50 percent across-the-board cut as a common point of departure; then prepared "exceptions lists" which became the subject of bargaining under a general proviso that such exceptions had to be justified to the satisfaction of the other GATT members in terms of overriding national necessity.

The process of reaching agreement was arduous and seemed interminable, as fundamental disparities in the tariff schedules of different countries had to be overcome. The problem of reconciling policies with regard to the protection and support of agriculture was especially sticky, since tariffs are a principal instrument of such policies, and farmers have great political influence in most of the countries affected. The GATT multilateral negotiating process, however, provided the necessary vehicle for reaching consensus, as governments had to confront these questions in the presence of virtually the entire world trading community, thus subjecting them to countervailing pressures of international interest that somewhat offset the tug of domestic special interests.[3]

As the GATT agreement has been successively renewed, over a period of almost twenty years, it has brought a large measure of stability to the world's tariff structure and trade policies, even when substantial reductions were not accomplished. Its basic provisions have been accepted by national officials as an established part of international life, to be taken into account as a matter of course when trade policies are decided. A former American representative to GATT testifies that

> These officials and ministers have fallen into the practice of testing each prospective trade restriction against GATT's provisions. And there have commonly been efforts in major governments either to tailor such restrictions to GATT's limits of tolerance or to mitigate any violation of GATT if it could not be prevented altogether.[4]

International Fiscal Management. We have already seen how, in the postwar reconstruction effort, the promotion of trade was intertwined with the problem of making international payments and this, in turn, with the stabilization of currencies. Obviously, individuals and corporations are not likely to sell abroad if they do not get paid; but governments are not likely to tolerate payment (or the purchases that lead to the obligations for payment) if it jeopardizes national solvency or domestic economic stability.

A direct, nation-by-nation approach to this problem seems to leave no alternative but adoption of stringent controls over both foreign exchange and the flow of trade, so that each country may keep its obligations to others within its capacity to pay by exportable resources. Indeed, governments are prone, in these circumstances, to do their balancing on a bilateral basis, restricting the amount of purchases from any country to the amount that country in particular will be willing to receive from it in return.

---

[3] See Richard N. Gardner, "GATT and the United Nations Conference on Trade and Development," *International Organization,* Autumn, 1964, pp. 689–91.

[4] Vernon, *op. cit.,* p. 204.

It has been a major objective of the strategists of integration through economic freedom to establish international fiscal arrangements that would permit the growth of trade on a multilateral basis, subject to few or no restrictions. On a global basis, this has been attempted through the International Monetary Fund. Its efforts to establish international "liquidity" and to maintain a cushion of funds on which countries could draw when temporarily confronting an imbalance in their international payments have been the indispensable corollary of GATT's program of trade liberalization.

The setup of the Fund has already been described (see Chapter 13). It represented, as will be recalled, a compromise between two quite different approaches to stabilization—the American-favored emphasis on maximum freedom and the British commitment to fiscal management. Since the days of reconstruction, the Fund has developed policies that, in effect, blend these two approaches.

In the direction of freedom, it has seen to it that most of its key members live up to their original commitment to make their currencies "convertible," that is, exchangeable with any other currency in the world without special permission from the government. Par rates established for each currency have been kept remarkably constant; changes take place only by permission of the Fund on the ground of demonstrated need to correct a basic, long-term imbalance in a country's international economic position. Thus, one could reasonably count on a $1.00 being exchangeable for the same amount of francs, marks, yen, or sterling at one time as at another.

The condition of these achievements was the ability of the Fund to lend countries enough money on short term to pay their debts to others when they could not meet them out of current exports or financial reserves without endangering the stability and growth of their domestic economies. To do this has required a large expansion of the Fund's resources, especially as the volume of international trade and commitments has grown. Quotas were more than doubled; this, together with the contributions of new members, brought the Fund's own resources to more than $15 billion by 1964. Two-thirds was available in the form of gold and the currencies of the major industrial countries. In actual practice, $11 billion worth of loans had been made (up to April 30, 1963), most of it in the last five years.[5] In addition, the Fund negotiated, with 10 industrial countries, the "General Arrangements to Borrow," by which it can secure up to a further $6 billion in

---

[5] Statement by Pierre-Paul Schweitzer, Managing Director of the International Monetary Fund, before the United Nations Conference on Trade and Development, March 26, 1964. *International Financial News Survey,* Supplement, March 27, 1964. See, also, Frank A. Southard, Jr., "International Monetary Arrangements," *International Financial News Survey,* Supplement, April 3, 1964.

The amount derived from the new members is a small proportion of the total, as most of them are underdeveloped countries with extremely limited national income, which is the yardstick of fund quotas.

emergencies. This plan was put to a successful test in November, 1964, when the Fund called for help to tide Britain over an extraordinary financial crisis that threatened to destroy the value of sterling and jeopardize the position of countries relying on it as a principal medium of payment.[6]

In its regulatory or management function, the Fund has stringently maintained the Bretton Woods code governing multilateral payments relationships between its members. The code prohibits restrictive practices, unauthorized manipulation of exchange rates, and discrimination between countries in making payments. But the Fund has gone much farther. It has presumed to "advise" governments in serious and persistent balance of payments difficulties how to correct the situation. Linked to the power to grant or withhold loans, such advice is tantamount to command. And it extends deeply into the vitals of a country's budgetary and fiscal policies, including consideration of the wisdom of its government expenditures and the adequacy of its tax structure. Any aspect of national economic and fiscal programming is fair game for Fund review if it affects a government's capacity to meet international payments in a manner consonant with the rules of the multilateral system—that is, *if* the government has failed in the art of self-management and has needed to turn to the Fund for help.

The Fund has not been a universally popular taskmaster. Especially among the underdeveloped countries, proud of political independence and sensitive because of their economic dependence, the Fund is viewed as a hardfisted custodian of economic practices prescribed as "sound" or "orthodox" by the financial and industrial giants of the world.[7] Nevertheless, they join and remain as members (bringing the total to 103—virtually the entire world outside the Communist periphery). They feel they have no choice, given the Fund's imperative role in keeping open channels for trade and, it should be added, the fact that the Fund is, in effect, doorkeeper to the treasury of the International Bank. Membership in *both* these agencies is a condition for access to either.

Reorientation to the Developing Countries: The Have-Nots' Bid for Economic Preference. The needs of the developing countries have, however, exerted a compelling influence on the fundamental strategies of international economic cooperation, especially those directed toward achieving integration and stability by increasing the freedom of economic relationships.

---

[6] See *International Financial News Survey,* November 13, 1964, p. 401. See also, in regard to the problem of international liquidity, Pierre-Paul Schweitzer, Report of the Fund at ECOSOC, March 25, 1965, reprinted in *International Financial News Survey,* Supplement. March 26, 1965, pp. 118 and 120.

[7] See Miguel S. Wionczek, "Latin American Free Trade Association," *International Conciliation,* January, 1965, pp. 27–28. For the Fund's rebuttal see Report of Pierre-Paul Schweitzer to ECOSOC, *op. cit.,* p. 119.

From the standpoint of the impoverished, largely nonindustrial two-thirds or three-quarters of the world, easing trade restrictions has contributed but little to providing a world economic context favorable to economic growth. They require much more than mere access, on a basis of reciprocal nondiscrimination, to the markets of the industrialized countries. They need assurance of favorable trade terms for their products, that is, a good price. The return on their exports, after all, is their principal means of financing imports of the goods necessary to promote development (apart from depending on foreign gifts, loans, or investment.) This is the basis of their becoming able to "help themselves," assuming, of course, that they can produce goods that others want to buy.

Furthermore, the growth of new industries within these countries often demands the same kind of special encouragement that industrialized countries afforded their entrepreneurs in getting a start, namely, a protected internal market where they do not have to stand the full blast of competition from well-established, efficient industries in other countries.[8]

Recognition of these needs has had a profound effect on GATT, especially as its expanding membership (from an original 20 to 89 by 1964) gave underdeveloped countries an ever more powerful voice in the deliberations. GATT has modified its commitment to pure trade liberalization and has adopted policies which deliberately concede preferential treatment to the underdeveloped. This position was confirmed at a special Ministerial Conference in 1963, which pledged unanimously that "in the trade negotiations every effort shall be made to reduce barriers to exports of the less-developed countries, but that the developed countries *cannot expect to receive reciprocity from the less-developed countries.*" (Italics inserted.) In other words, the developed countries will grant greater tariff reductions to the less developed than they get in return. They agree to discrimination against themselves

---

[8] This thesis has been advanced notably by Paul Prebisch, prominent Argentine economist, and in studies produced by the Economic Commission for Latin America and other United Nations groups with which Prebisch was associated. He was for several years executive secretary of ECLA, then selected as Secretary-General of the special U.N. Conference on Trade and Development, convened in 1964. See, especially, the ECLA reports, *Economic Development Planning and International Cooperation* (U.N. Sales No. 61.II.G.6) and *Towards a Dynamic Development Policy for Latin America* (U.N. Sales No. 64.II.G.4), and the basic working paper prepared for the aforementioned U.N. Conference, *Towards a New Trade Policy for Development* (U.N. Doc. E/CONF.46/P/3, February 12, 1964).

This thesis has been strongly challenged by a number of distinguished Western economists. See, for instance, Gottfried Haberler, "Terms of Trade and Economic Development," in Howard S. Ellis (ed.), *Economic Development for Latin America* (New York: St. Martin's Press, Inc., 1961). Also, Charles P. Kindleberger, "The Terms of Trade and Economic Development," *Review of Economics and Statistics,* February, 1958, Supplement.

For a general analysis of these issues, see Robert M. Stern, "Policies for Trade and Development," *International Conciliation,* May, 1964, especially pp. 3–28; also, Isaiah Frank, "Aid, Trade and Economic Development: Issues Before the U.N. Conference," *Foreign Affairs,* January, 1964.

in the interest of promoting the economic growth of the have-nots. In this respect, GATT has been transformed into an institution for the global regulation and manipulation of trade preferences, instead of remaining a straight "free trade society." But it remains true to its basic objectives of promoting conditions that over the long pull will make possible the maximum of mutual benefit from the international exchange of goods and services. What has changed is the tactic, not the purpose.[9]

But far more drastic measures were demanded—nothing less than a complete overhauling of the system of international economic relationships to which the strategy of freedom had been pointing. This was the impetus behind calling the United Nations Conference on Trade and Development at Geneva in the spring of 1964. It turned out to be the biggest international conference in history, with over 2,000 delegates. In the eyes of the developing countries, it was viewed as the most important single event since the founding of the United Nations.[10]

Strenuous efforts to the contrary notwithstanding, the Conference could not avoid a direct confrontation of haves and have-nots so intense that it was questionable whether any significant common action might emerge. Perhaps this confrontation itself should be considered one of the important accomplishments, for the developing countries were able to work together as a cohesive bloc. The "Group of 75" (later expanded to 77) forged through a process of compromise among themselves, a joint stand on almost every issue, eventuating in a declaration made a part of the Conference's Final Act. As might be supposed, this led them to be uncompromising vis-à-vis the advanced and wealthy countries, and this invited stubbornness on the other side.[11]

On the other hand, both sides recognized that solutions could be achieved only by cooperative action, and some of the rich countries were disposed to consider substantial changes in their policies if they could be assured that the poor, in turn, would put forth the kinds of self-help effort and responsibilities crucial for economic development.

---

[9] See Stern, op. cit., pp. 43–45; also Gardner, op. cit., p. 695.

The full "Programme of Action" adopted by GATT to strengthen and reorient its approach is recorded in GATT Doc. MIN (63) 7, May 22, 1963. The text of the resolution adopted by the GATT Ministerial Conference, May 21, 1963, is reproduced in European Community, No. 63 (June, 1963).

[10] For a succinct appraisal of its results and significance, see Sidney Weintraub, "After the U.N. Trade Conference: Lessons and Portents," Foreign Affairs, October, 1964; also Ricard N. Gardner, op. cit., pp. 696–704. The background of the conference is effectively reviewed by Frank, op. cit., and Janez Stanovnik, "The Changing Political Context," Foreign Affairs, January, 1964.

[11] The curious position of the Soviet Union at the Conference was described as that of being "rich in the eyes of the poor, but not rich enough to have been interesting." Consequently the confrontation was not really North vs. South but West vs. South, with the Soviet Union left on the sidelines. See Gardner, op. cit., pp. 698–99; also Weintraub, op. cit. p. 40.

Substantively, the developing countries stressed the need for action to improve and stabilize the terms of trade for their products, especially primary commodities in comparison with the prices of manufactured goods. One suggestion was for a kind of insurance arrangement, whereby countries would be compensated if prices for their exports fell below a certain point, compensation to come from an international pool of funds contributed principally by the advanced and wealthier countries. Another possibility was to regulate prices and sales by international commodity agreements such as those currently in force for wheat, tin, sugar, and coffee. The merits and demerits of these and other recommendations were vehemently debated along lines familiar among economists long before the Conference. No specific decision was reached. The industrial countries rejected the concept of automatic compensation, and argued convincingly that commodity agreements were applicable only under certain limited conditions and might actually have an adverse effect by stimulating overproduction, checking the incentive to diversify, and in some cases causing potential purchasers to shift to cheaper substitute products.[12]

There was major controversy over the issue of preferences, involving as this did the fundamental question of markets for the developing countries. The Conference continued the debate started in GATT, with the poor bluntly demanding one-way discrimination: complete freedom of access for their raw material exports into the markets of the industrial countries but, on the other hand, substantial tariff preferences to encourage their own manufactures by discriminating against competition from the industrial countries. Here, the industrial countries split. The Common Market was willing to go at least part way, as was Britain; but the U.S. was adamantly opposed to such an all-out surrender of the principles of economic freedom.[13]

The most critical issue, from a practical standpoint, was the kind of international organization to carry on continuing responsibility for action on these problems. The developing countries wanted a new and powerful international trade organization in which each country would have one vote, thus giving them dominant influence and control. This reflected their distrust of other international economic institutions weighted in favor of wealth, including some of the U.N. organs and specialized agencies. (For reasons noted before, their feelings had softened toward GATT, and hence they were inclined rather to complement GATT or absorb it in the new organization than to set up a counterweight.) For equally cogent reasons, the other

---

[12] See Gardner, *op. cit.,* pp. 700–701; also Stern, *op. cit.,* pp. 44–53; and Frank, *op. cit.* The issues of commodity policy are analyzed forthrightly by John A. Pincus, "What Policy for Commodities?," *Foreign Affairs,* January, 1964. An early, comprehensive treatment of the subject is given in a report by the U.N. Secretariat, *Measures for International Economic Stability* (New York: United Nations, 1951). See, also, the symposium, A. S. Miller (ed.), "International Commodity Agreements," *Law and Contemporary Problems,* Spring, 1963.

[13] See Gardner, *op. cit.,* pp. 699–700.

countries would have no part of such a proposal. The result was a momentary draw. The "continuing machinery" is placed within the United Nations structure, to be activated by the General Assembly. The Conference on Trade and Development will be convened at least every three years. A 55-nation Trade and Development Board will meet between sessions of the Conference. A special Secretariat within the U.N. Secretariat will service the new institutions, and is headed by none other than Mr. Prebisch, the indomitable crusader for a new economic order centered on the needs of developing countries. The voting question was sidestepped by asking the U.N. Secretary-General to appoint a special committee to work out procedures for conciliation before voting and to design safeguards to protect "the economic or financial interests of particular countries" against injury by majority action—in straight language, to protect the resources of the rich against the votes of the poor.[14] This is a far cry from the glowing expectations of the have-nots when they entered the Conference. But it may well be that a ball has been set rolling which will gather momentum, and that the Conference did, in fact, initiate a chain of events ushering in a radically different world economic order than the one originally designed by the architects of the haves, however enlightened they may have felt they were at the time.

These experiences indicate that the problem left unresolved when the original blueprint for an international trade organization was rejected has returned to haunt us. Is pure economic freedom on a worldwide basis really an effective way to insure economic stability for less privileged countries or, indeed, for the world generally? Or is much closer and more rigorously controlled economic integration and more deliberate international economic management required?

If control and management are needed, can this be worked out satsifactorily on a global basis? Or must one look to regional ties as the cohesive force for the kind of integration of national economies that will both provide stability and stimulate a growing welfare?

Implications of Regionalism

In a parallel or alternative development to economic cooperation on a global basis, many governments have centered their pursuit of international economic integration around a regional hub. They have been convinced that within the context of a region were ties of mutual economic interest, or political and ideological affinity, that would make possible a much more intimate and beneficial association than could be achieved with countries outside.

The patterns of attempted regional cooperation have been diverse. Four will be examined here. First is a focus on planning, which has sought to

---

[14] See Final Act of the U.N. Conference on Trade and Development (U.N. Doc. E/CONF. 46/L.28), Part II, sec. V. See, also, Gardner, *op. cit.*, pp. 701–3; and Weintraub, *op. cit.*, pp. 42–44.

loosen trade relations within the region, coordinate national programs of economic development, and, in some instances, promote joint regional projects. Much of this has proceeded within the framework of the United Nations, which has organized commissions specially concerned with the economic problems of Europe, Latin America, Asia and the Far East, and Africa, respectively. Quite apart from the U.N., such established regional organizations as the Organization of American States, the Arab League, and the Organization for African Unity have made economic planning a major part of their activities. In addition, special regional organizations have sometimes been established to foster economic cooperation, a major function being joint planning.[15]

Second is the interlocking of financial and monetary systems in a manner which facilitates the settling of international accounts. The outstanding illustration of this approach is the sterling bloc. A move in this direction was also taken by the 16 European countries in the OEEC through establishment of the European Payments Union, but the attempt was short-lived for reasons discussed later in the chapter.

Third, in the case of the Soviet bloc, regional organization has provided a framework through which to attempt to reconcile centralized control over the economic life and relations of the bloc with the professed autonomy of each "sovereign" member.

Finally, regionalism has involved varying degrees of economic union, in which countries agree to treat one another as one for purposes of regulating production and marketing certain or most of their commodities, moving goods and persons across their respective borders, and others. In one sense, this could be considered an ultimate extension of moves toward the liberalization of trade and other economic relations among the countries within the region. But, as will be seen in examining the experience of Western Europe, union may also involve implications of supranational direction and policy-making on the one hand and exclusiveness vis-à-vis the outside world on the other, which run counter to fundamental premises of the strategy of integrating through economic freedom.

In evaluating these experiments in regional economic association, there are two critical considerations. First, how much have they contributed to the welfare of the countries in the region? Second, have they been compatible with advancement of the welfare of others through economic cooperation on a worldwide basis?

On the first question, evidence is insufficient as yet to justify a conclusion that any pattern of organization is directly responsible for the economic record of the region. It is even less clear that one region's experience is

---

[15] For instance, the Latin American Free Trade Association, which grew directly out of the experience and initiative of the U.N.'s Economic Commission for Latin America. See Miguel S. Wionczek, "Latin American Free Trade Association," *International Conciliation*, January, 1965.

transferable to another. On the other hand, if one judges by the self-satisfaction of the regional group's members and their readiness to continue the association and go on to even closer measures of integration, the regional experiments we are considering have done well, with two possible exceptions. Rumblings in the Communist camp suggest a bid for greater national independence in making economic policy than has been customary in COMECON. And in Europe, the dynamic integration of the six Western countries has been bought at the price of disintegration of the broader net of cooperative relationships that had knit together the countries associated in the European Recovery Program.

This experience anticipates the answer to the second question. On the whole, regionalism tends to thwart the development of strong and mutually supportive global measures of economic cooperation. The implications of regionalism are particularly serious for efforts in the direction of liberalization on a world scale. Except for planning, the main patterns of regional integration (as illustrated by the sterling bloc, COMECON, and the Western European economic communities) have generated a kind of parochial inwardness leading to actions of a protectionist character, untempered by regard for their impact on others. Whether regional integration along any of these lines can be oriented so as to avoid splitting the world into throat-cutting rival blocs is the grave issue of the moment. If this cannot be done, regionalism may well prove to be the road to economic disaster for everyone.

From this standpoint, the regional economic planning undertaken within the United Nations framework acquires special significance. For here, regional interests are kept in the perspective of world interdependence, and the impact of actions is weighed not only in terms of the immediate consequences for the region but of the general effects on economic growth and stability. This is partly the result of the commissions' accountability to the world community as represented in the principal United Nations organs; partly because the composition of the commissions customarily bridges across regions; and partly because a unified, "integrated," *international* secretariat provides initiative and orientation. The work of the Economic Commission for Europe illustrates at its best this pattern of fashioning regional integration within the context of global cooperation.[16]

---

[16] For the work of other United Nations regional economic commissions, see the definitive study of ECAFE by David Wightman, *Toward Economic Cooperation in Asia* (New Haven, Conn.: Yale University Press, 1963; in regard to ECLA, Miguel S. Wionczek (ed.), *Integracion de America Latina, Experiencias y Perspectivas* (Mexico City: Fondo de Cultura Economica, 1964). For a summary account of ECAFE, see C. Hart Schaaf, "The United Nations Commission for Asia and the Far East," *International Organization*, November, 1963. A penetrating study of Soviet involvement in ECAFE is Alvin Z. Rubinstein, *The Soviets in International Organizations* (Princeton, N.J.: Princeton University Press, 1964), chap. 4.

A Focus for Planning: The U.N.'s Economic Commission for Europe. The Economic Commission for Europe was set up initially to aid in the coordination of reconstruction efforts, but it has come to serve as a key center for long-term economic planning by all the European members of the United Nations, together with the U.S.S.R. and the U.S. As is customary with U.N. organs, its powers are limited to research, consultation, and recommendations to the member governments, and its operations require the unanimous consent of the members. It does not control or manage economic enterprise. Yet it has had a vital role in bringing about integration at focal points of the European economy, both during the reconstruction period and since. Much of the credit for its accomplishments is due the able and dynamic Secretariat, first headed by the Swedish economist, Gunnar Myrdal.

The Commission took responsibility for allocating European coal and for working out means to increase its production in 1947–49, when there was a virtual coal famine and Europe was importing huge supplies of expensive American coal. It inventoried the needs for mine machinery and brought producers and users together to arrange for meeting the needs as quickly as possible. It persuaded the European countries to accept limits on their coal requirements so that all could share fairly in the precious commodity. Later, when the situation was reversed and surpluses of coal were glutting the market, the ECE arranged for an orderly cutback in production and explored new outlets.

A similar program of continental planning to guide production and distribution was undertaken for other essential commodities. At the end of the war, timber, traditionally one of Europe's major exports, was extremely scarce. The ECE arranged a substantial loan to buy lumbering equipment needed to expand production. A few years later, surplus was the problem, and again the ECE analyzed the market possibilities and advised the governments to temporarily taper off this aspect of their economic activity.

ECE made a critical contribution to the rehabilitation of inland transport. It tracked down and arranged for the restitution of rolling stock and river craft that had crossed frontiers and, in the chaos of the war and its aftermath, never been returned to their country of origin. This reassured countries that they would not lose their transport equipment by letting it out of their territory, and it was possible once again for freight to move over the continent in continuous hauls without being transferred to new cars or barges at every boundary.

Another bit of informed planning put a large number of trucks back on the road. Lack of spare parts had stranded trucks in Eastern Europe. The ECE found that Italian parts would work, but the Italians demanded dollars for them, and the Eastern countries could not pay. The ECE Secretariat arranged an exchange of the truck parts for raw materials needed by Italian industry.

An intricate global negotiation enabled northern Italy's steel industry to expand. Refractories were needed to reline the furnaces. They could be made in Germany, but sufficient manpower was not available in the French zone to mine the quartzite from which the refractories are made. The Italians agreed to send manpower and take their pay in the materials produced. The British agreed to help get digging and transportation equipment. From Alaska, the United States secured technical expertise on how to mine in deep cold. The French gave official approval and extra cigarettes to the miners. One of the major postwar production bottlenecks, therefore, was broken.

The ECE's masterstroke of economic diplomacy has been the patient unfreezing of trade between Western and Eastern Europe. For a number of years, the cold war almost completely stopped the exchange of Eastern foodstuffs and raw materials for Western manufactures, which had for 100 years formed one of the principal elements in Europe's trade pattern. What trade did occur was largely worked out in bilateral agreements between a few Western countries and Russia. Meanwhile, the trade of Eastern European countries was wrenched from its westward orientation and tied increasingly to the Soviet Union. Mutual recrimination filled the air, even in the technical atmosphere of the ECE, until the Executive Secretary personally and privately asked each of the concerned governments, including Russia, to outline "shopping lists" of products it might be willing to buy or sell across the Iron Curtain. After comparing the lists, the Secretariat encouraged countries whose proposals matched to get together and agree on terms of trade. A trickle at first, the trade resulting from these negotiations steadily increased as countries became convinced that strategic imperatives need not rule out all the mutual advantages of commerce between East and West.[17]

The ECE's contributions to short-run and especially to long-term economic integration have been based on a solid foundation of highly competent research, conducted independently by its secretariat. The annual Economic Surveys of Europe have become recognized as the most significant diagnoses of the continent's state of economic health, noting with unusual prescience the critical problems calling for joint planning and coordinated action. These have been supplemented by detailed studies of special economic problems in the development of industry and agriculture. Under Myrdal's leadership, the Secretariat established an institutional tradition of "independent truth-seeking" in its research work. While it secured information from and consulted governments, it reached its own conclusions and published them without previously submitting its reports for review by any government. They were, of course, subject to criticism and rebuttal in the commission

---

[17] See United Nations, *The ECE in Action* (New York: United Nations, n.d.); also, *ECE: The First Ten Years* (Geneva: United Nations Economic Commission for Europe, 1957).

itself, but there was never prior censorship, no matter how controversial the positions taken.[18]

The Cement of Sterling. Reference has already been made to the sterling bloc as a working model of integration on a regional basis. Of course, the "region" comprised is not geographical, because the territories involved stretch over four continents. The members are: first, the United Kingdom itself and its colonial dependencies; second, the other members of the Commonwealth, with the exception of Canada; third, certain other countries that have developed financial ties to Britain, such as Burma, Iceland, Republic of Ireland, Iran, Jordan, and Libya.

The strange feature of this association is that it has no formal rules of membership, constitution, or organization. However, the group normally follows common practices. First, the central monetary authorities of the countries keep their reserves of foreign exchange in the form of balances of sterling on deposit with London banks (or in short-term sterling investments on the London capital market). This means they have a common dollar and gold pool that covers all their payments and receives all their income in transactions with countries outside the sterling area. Second, the countries usually keep the exchange value of their own currencies fixed in terms of the pound sterling. Third, and most important, there is almost complete freedom of payments by private persons and institutions within the sterling area, although payments outside the area are strictly controlled. In addition, the sterling area has enjoyed the benefits of the imperial preference system, whereby tariff rates levied on goods exchanged among the members are lower than those on imports from other countries.[19]

The sterling bloc has hung together through trying economic and political circumstances, including the tremendous pressures of the war. The United Kingdom has played the dominant role, virtually controlling the use of the common reserves. For instance, it kept countries like India and Ceylon from freely using their large sterling balances to purchase from the United States and other non-sterling areas during the postwar period when Britain's financial position was precarious.[20] But these restrictions have not caused the bloc to disintegrate, because the members have secured privileges in return. Britain has imposed few import restrictions against the other members, even

[18] See Gunnar Myrdal, "The Research Work of the Secretariat of the Economic Commission for Europe," *25 Economic Essays in Honour of Erik Lindahl* (Stockholm: Svenska Tryckeriaktie Bolaget, 1956), pp. 267–93. See, also, his general evaluation of the role of the secretariats in *Realities and Illusions in Regard to Inter-governmental Organisations* (London: Oxford University Press, 1955).

[19] See J. E. Meade, *The Atlantic Community and the Dollar Gap* (London: Friends of the Atlantic Union), pp. 6–9. The preferential tariff system was created at the 1932 Ottawa Conference as a means of offsetting some of the effects of the depression. The sterling area arrangement was consolidated in 1939 as Britain girded herself for the second world war.

[20] Under the Colombo Plan, a substantial portion of these balances has now been released.

though some of them have seen fit to protect their own industries against British competition. Britain has deprived herself of capital in order not to interfere with the flow of capital to the rest of the area.

Together, the sterling countries have agreed in the face of economic crisis to hold back on purchases outside the area and to check internal inflationary pressures so as to preserve the stability and solvency of the arrangement. This reflects, says an informed observer, "an intimacy of association among the concurring nations not to be found in many other inter-governmental organizations; [and] the long tradition of cooperation among the monetary and fiscal authorities of these countries, activated by the cohesive influence of the United Kingdom."[21] On the other hand, we have seen that this very intimacy within the sterling group has posed great difficulties in working out programs of economic integration in association with nations outside the sterling area.

The Ties of Comradeship.   The Soviet model of integration has been the most extreme in that it covered *all* sectors of the economy and concentrated both political and economic authority at a single center. It rejected outright, on both political and ideological grounds, the concept of freedom as a principle governing either the bloc's economic relations with the outside world or intrabloc relationships.

Formally, the Soviet approach has the appearance of a loose, multilateral association in which each country that belongs to the Council for Economic Mutual Assistance (variously abbreviated as CEMA or COMECON) consults with the others on common economic problems and decides independently to join in certain common policies of trade, investment, "mutual aid," and production.

Actually, the organization has "become the single most important organ for actively shaping policies designed to promote the Communist Camp's unity." A powerful bureaucracy, responsive to Soviet direction, manages a "world socialist market," implementing a network of bilateral mutual-aid treaties that, given overall state control of the economy in each country, "govern the totality of trade among its members, and since most of the foreign trade of the Communist states takes place within the Camp . . . these agreements have an important bearing on the future livelihood and development of the signators."[22]

There are signs, however, that the nature of COMECON may be changing

---

[21] Vernon, *op. cit.,* p. 172.

[22] Zbigniew K. Brzezinski, "The Organization of the Communist Camp," *World Politics,* January, 1961, as quoted in Harold and Margaret Sprout, *Foundations of International Politics* (Princeton, N.J.: D. Van Nostrand Co., Inc., 1962), p. 591. See also Andrzej Korbonski, "Comecon," *International Conciliation, S*eptember, 1964; and Brzezinski's *The Soviet Bloc* (Rev. ed. New York: Praeger, 1961.) for further description of the Soviet system of international economic integration. The most comprehensive study is Kazimierz Grzybowski, *The Socialist Commonwealth of Nations* (New Haven, Conn.: Yale University Press, 1964), particularly "The Council on Mutual Economic Aid," chap. 3.

in response to strong rumblings of opposition to monolithic Soviet direction and to demands by countries like Romania and Hungary for greater regard for specific national interests (let alone Yugoslavia, whose independent stance has left her variously ostracized by the bloc or holding the status of observer in COMECON). To avoid an epidemic of boycotts or secessions, practice is apparently being brought more in line with the formal image of an association of sovereign states, seeking through cooperative planning, agreed division and specialization of economic functions, and joint productive enterprises to promote one another's welfare. Whether the ties of ideological comradeship are sufficiently strong to prevail against the centrifugal pull of sharply divergent and often competitive national economic interests is the organization's major preoccupation now that it is no longer undergirded by a fully effective hierarchical system of political control. Will concessions to national autonomy and freer international economic relationships lead to the dissolution of Communist economic integration, or will they pave the way to a firmer and sounder association, based on a genuine recognition and support of mutual interests?[23]

Europe's Renunciation of Freedom. Europe, or rather that part of Europe drawn together by the Marshall Plan, has been the hub of the most intensive efforts to forge integration by knocking down international economic barriers. The distinctive—and, in some ways, the enigmatic—feature of these efforts is their exclusive intra-European character. The European nations considered that liberalizing relations with the rest of the world was secondary to establishing balanced and freer relations among themselves. Indeed, moves toward European integration appeared at times to contradict a global approach to economic freedom. Greater freedom inside Europe was often bought by measures that fenced off the continent from the outside world. And when the six Western European countries decided to form a "community" and move toward a completely free common market among themselves, they did so in a manner that largely broke up the structure of continent-wide economic cooperation so laboriously constructed under the impetus of the Marshall Plan.

The high command of the campaign for European integration was originally assumed, as we have seen (Chapter 13), by the Organization for European Economic Cooperation. The United States, principally through the Marshall Plan, provided initiative, strategic plans, and some financial ammunition in the earlier stages.[24] The major moves undertaken were (*a*) a liberalization of trade restrictions and (*b*) the multilateral balancing of pay-

---

[23] Korbonski, *op. cit.*, reviews changing attitudes toward COMECON and some of the modifications of policies and structure that appear to have been made in response to the assertion of independence from Soviet direction by some of the members.

[24] For a penetrating review of the background and development of American policy toward European integration, see Max Beloff, *The United States and the Unity of Europe* (Washington, D.C.: Brookings Institution, 1963).

ments (through establishment of the European Payments Union), together with a coordination of foreign trade and finance policies to correct or prevent serious unbalancing of intra-European fiscal relations.[25]

The results of these efforts are difficult to appraise accurately. The Europe of the OEEC (that is, all 16 Marshall Plan countries) did not achieve the single free market that full integration in a trade and tariff union would appear to call for. Tariffs and a motley array of other restrictions, including some quotas, continued to inhibit the flow of commodities from one European country to another. On the other hand, intra-European trade expanded enormously under the liberalization program, and the long trend toward national self-sufficiency appeared to have been definitely reversed. An accomplishment of major importance was that each of the 16 countries admitted accountability to the others for the effects its trade policies might have on them. When a country's performance in living up to a common code of trade rules is the subject of critical review by its associates, a fundamental step has been taken toward integration, even if governments still retain the power of final decision over these economic policies.

From the standpoint of financial policy and relationships, the European Payments Union succeeded in virtually removing the payments problem as an obstacle to trade. There are several measures of the EPU'S overall effectiveness.

First, almost three-fourths of the debts incurred by the members to one another were canceled out by virtue of the payments they received for their exports to the others. Sometimes, a country would run quite a deficit for a period, only to have its position change in a few months so that surpluses wiped out the deficit.

Second, the remaining debts were not permitted to interfere with continued trade. At the end of the accounting year, the EPU worked out arrangements between the principal creditors and debtors for handling the accumulated indebtedness. The usual formula was the debtor paid 50 percent of the debt immediately, and the creditor extended time for repayment of the remainder. Then the regular annual quota of credit was reestablished in the EPU for each member. Thus, trading without currency restrictions could continue, and no one had to make a drastic cutback in imports.

A third measure of success was the ability of the EPU to function with no special support from the U.S. after the first year's capital contribution of $300 million. The reserves were undoubtedly too low to cope with a major and long-continued imbalance of trade among the members. But whenever a debt had to be paid off in gold, the EPU was able to get either the debtor itself or, in extreme cases, the entire group to make sufficient resources available.

The EPU did confront three persistent problems: the extreme debtor and

---

[25] These actions have been described above, Chapter 13, pp. 389–92.

creditor position of some of its members; the intricate financial relations that arose because Britain was a pivotal member of EPU and was also kingpin of the sterling bloc; and the trade and payments relations of the EPU members with the rest of the world.

Over a period of several years, Britain, Italy, and some others ran continuing large trade deficits with the EPU countries. Belgium, Switzerland, and then Germany (in a remarkable turn of events) were the big creditors, constantly exporting more to the EPU area than they bought. The problem was eased in part, but only in part, because the debtors were in a relatively better position with non-European countries, and some of their earnings from the outside could be used to pay off their European creditors—but only if they earned dollars or some other currency that would buy things the creditors desired. There was steady pressure for the debtors to right their balance by discriminatory restrictions against the trade of the principal creditors. Though this never reached the acute crisis of the German situation in 1950–51, it posed a threat to the long-run stability of intra-European trade liberalization.

The problem of the sterling area almost prevented formation of the EPU in the first place. The British could not afford to let their trade relations with Europe drain their resources (either to pay trade debts or to extend trade credits, as in the first two years of the EPU when Britain's problem was that of the extreme creditor) to the point where they could not meet obligations to the sterling area countries of which Britain was financial custodian. The solution finally reached allowed Britain, in effect, to represent all the sterling countries in the EPU; the EPU countries agreed to settle all their accounts with the sterling group through Britain. For instance, French exports to Australia would be charged to Britain's account in the EPU, while Britain would be credited with the value of Australian products imported by France. If the sterling countries ran up a deficit by buying more from Europe than they sold, Britain had to pay the bill. If the sterling area as a whole sold more to Europe than it bought, European countries paid Britain. In one sense, this arrangement tremendously broadened the range of the EPU system, linking it with the far-flung sterling financial and trading area. But it also posed complications, because the sterling countries were not bound to integrate their policies with those of the OEEC nor to accept any of the EPU trade rules that aimed to reduce discrimination and restriction while insuring a balanced intra-European economy.

The third problem was whether the EPU could facilitate participation of European countries in a more general worldwide system of freer trade and easier international payments. Some authorities thought the EPU should be considered only a makeshift until conditions were ripe for countries everywhere to agree to the complete convertibility of their currencies. They felt that it was not sufficient for European countries to settle accounts among themselves by means of what amounted to a common currency for trading purposes. Western Europe does not normally balance its trade within itself, and to the extent that EPU tended to press each country to try to achieve an intra-European trade balance it was uneconomic from the long-run point of view. "Western European economic integration," it was asserted, "cannot reasonably be the primary goal of economic policy either for countries of the area or for the United States."[26]

On the other hand, the EPU Managing Board confidently asserted in 1954 that the institution had provided

. . . an international financial mechanism on which members can rely in case of need, and which can therefore help to give them the confidence necessary for the adoption of more liberal trading policies . . . it helps OEEC to continue to provide a central point in which members can meet to discuss their problems and to consider joint action for dealing with them.[27]

The whole situation took a radically different turn, however, when six of the sixteen decided to form a full economic community among themselves.[28]

Then arose the question: Would the OEEC accomplishments go by the board, with Europe splitting into rival economic blocs, each discriminating against the other. An ominous move in this direction occurred when the Common Market decided not to extend to other OEEC countries the tariff and quota reductions they accepted among themselves, unless these countries agreed to join the Common Market and accept all its other obligations.

Britain and some of the other outsiders (the "seven") first tried to counter this threat by forming the European Free Trade Association. But shortly they decided to try to join rather than fight, applying for admission on terms which would take at least some account of the special worldwide economic relationships and responsibilities in which Britain, in particular, was involved. The negotiations broke down largely because of obdurate French objections to any concessions. The stage seemed set for a complete dissolution of the ties the OEEC had striven to develop on a continent-wide basis and for revival of economic nationalism in the modified, but possibly more dangerous, form of economic regionalism or subregionalism.

To prevent this from happening, and for other reasons, the Organization for Economic Cooperation and Development was established in 1961 as a successor to OEEC. Its 20 members included all the OEEC group, plus the U.S. and Canada as full members (they had only been associates of the OEEC). But it is a pale image of its ancestor. Its functions are largely limited

---

[26] Diebold, *op. cit.*, p. 417.

[27] European Payments Union, *Fourth Annual Report of the Managing Board* (Paris: OEEC, 1954), p. 111.

[28] The formation and operation of the European Economic Communities is discussed in detail below, pp. 473–90.

to encouraging consultation and joint studies in an effort to secure economic policy coordination. It has taken over from OEEC the two "codes" for the liberalization of capital movements and current "invisible" operations that aim to ensure maximum freedom for financial transfers and transactions between the member countries. But the major trade liberalization codes have lapsed.[29]

A major casualty of Little Europe's venture into separate unity has been the European Payments Union. Perhaps it is not fair to charge this up entirely to the West Europeans; others refused to accept on a permanent basis the degree of external control of their economies that was involved in the strict mutual balancing of payments under EPU. As their individual economic positions strengthened, countries abandoned the instrumentality of collective self-regulation that had enabled them to avoid strangulation.

A feeble testimonial to the EPU was left in the form of a European Monetary Agreement, administered by the OECD, which makes possible short-term credits to countries in temporary balance-of-payments difficulties as well as multilateral settlement of payment balances between countries at guaranteed exchange rates. Paradoxically, the European Common Market, despite its vaunted boldness in integration, has yet to establish a system as satisfactory for handling its own mutual financial and payments relationships as the OEEC provided for its much more inclusive family through the EPU.

So the tug of national or subregional autonomy pulled back to independently determined economic policy-making enough countries to wreck an effectively functioning system of regional economic integration, at the same time blocking progress toward a worldwide liberalization of economic relationships.

The lesson seems to be that desperation and destitution generate cooperation and mutual assistance; the onset of affluence tempts nations to feather their nests separately and "let the devil take the hindmost."

INTEGRATION BY COMMUNITY

Benelux—Pilot Experiment in Economic Union

Three small countries pioneered in the most extreme form of integration—a complete economic union—and unexpectedly paved the way for the development of the most dynamic of integration experiments, the

---

[29] The terms of reference and operations of OECD are fully set forth in *The Organization for Economic Cooperation and Development* (Paris: OECD Publications, n.d.). In practice, OECD has been able to contribute much more to another mission—that of coordinating and increasing the flow of assistance to underdeveloped countries from capital-exporting members—than it has to maintaining and promoting the liberal trade arrangements among its own members which the OEEC had bequeathed.

European communities. Belgium, Netherlands, and Luxembourg tried at the end of the war to unite their economies—that is, to abolish all economic barriers among them, to adopt common economic policies toward the outside world, and to apply identical policies regarding all internal economic matters, including taxation, wages, and prices. What they achieved fell well short of this goal. They did form a "tariff union," with a common tariff on imports from the rest of the world and no duties on trade among themselves. And they tried hard, but for the most part unsuccessfully, to devise common policies on a number of key problems preparatory to launching the full union. Nevertheless, their difficulties and frustrations proved to be a valuable trial run, for the experience gained contributed immeasurably to the design of the more inclusive European Coal and Steel Community, Economic Community, and Euratom.

The principal stumbling blocks they encountered were: (1) a big gap in the economic conditions of the countries, and (2) important differences in their economic policies.

After the war, Belgium recovered quickly and was a relatively rich country. It was one of the few countries that did not have to worry about holding enough dollars to buy what it wanted from the United States. Holland, especially hard hit by the last months of the war, the loss of its prize colonial possessions in Southeast Asia, and the slow recovery of Germany on whom its economy was dependent, had great trouble in balancing its payments not only with the dollar area but with Europe as well. Then, the Dutch farmers produced more cheaply than the Belgians, and the Dutch worker received lower wages. In many respects, the economies of the countries were competitive. Hence, in a full economic union differences in costs, prices, and wages would cause serious trouble for those who were the less efficient or the more highly paid in corresponding occupations.

Partly because of these differences in condition, but also because of different political traditions, the Dutch maintained a high degree of government control over their economy, while the Belgians had a much more liberal, noninterventionist policy. Thus, the Dutch government had a broad social security program, kept prices of many essential commodities down, regulated wages, subsidized industry, and in general *managed* its economy. Naturally, its taxes were high. An economic union would require the Dutch to change these fundamental policies, or the Belgians to accept them, in whole or in part. However well disposed the governments were to unite their policies, many people in the three countries saw the immediate impact on their lives much more clearly than the long-run benefits that might accrue.

A small example of the dilemmas confronted in negotiating for union was the beer tax. The governments compromised on a figure that would have raised the tax on Belgian beer. The Belgian brewers promptly organized countrywide opposition around the theme, "Benelux perhaps—but pay more a pint for our beer, never!"[30]

The Benelux experience posed a vital question in regard to the feasibility of through-going integration. These countries attempted to align their divergent economies step by step, as a prelude to final union. They encountered such difficulties along the way that they never reached their goal, at least by themselves. Does this mean that full integration can occur only among countries whose economies already mesh naturally—in other words, where integration in effect exists at the beginning? If so, integration efforts could hardly extend far beyond the cooperative action on limited problems undertaken through the OEEC or GATT, because few countries have completely complementary economies with no important conflicts of interest.

Or does the Benelux experience argue for boldness in action to integrate, plunging ahead with major unifying steps and letting the adjustments and changes follow after? The issue is forcefully put by Diebold. Either of two alternative conditions must be met if economic union is to have major consequences: "Either the continued divergence between the two countries shall not be so important as to nullify the main purposes of forming the union; or the participating governments shall permit the divergent circumstances to change. . . . Change is an essential of economic union and policies that permit change are its pre-condition."[31]

The European Coal and Steel Community

An answer to the questions raised by Benelux is found in the successful formation of the European Coal and Steel Community, the European Economic Community, and Euratom. These events suggest the feasibility of a bold and decisive approach to integration, even when national economies are highly divergent and even competitive.

In the first of these revolutionary moves, six countries—France, Germany, Italy, and the Benelux group—have gone the limit in integrating the most vital sector of their industrial economy by merging their sovereign powers in a supranational community. For all its boldness and novelty, and the drastic adjustments in national policies it has embodied, the Schuman Plan was proposed, negotiated, adopted, and put into effective operation in less than three years. After three more years, it has become firmly established and has

---

[30] John Goormaghtigh, "European Integration," *International Conciliation,* February, 1953, p. 77. Goormaghtigh gives a clear summary of the major obstacles to the consumation of Benelux. See, also, Diebold, *op. cit.,* chap. 18.

[31] Diebold, *op. cit.,* pp. 348–49. Considerable study of the possibility of forming a five-nation customs union to include Italy and France ("Finebel" or "Fritalux") did not result in any definitive commitments. Similarly, an OEEC study of proposals for a Europe-wide customs union of some form did not convince governments that they should push toward this degree of integration. See Diebold, chaps. 7, 17, 19, and 20.

proved the practicability and usefulness of all-out functional integration among a limited number of countries with a common vital economic stake.

The fact that this Community was formed among countries that had barely stopped fighting one another, with memories of the German occupation bitter in France and the Low Countries, shows how even the most intense political conflicts can be sidestepped in a skillfully managed program of economic collaboration. In fact, ingenious diplomacy engineered the Coal-Steel Community project in part as a means of resolving some of the long-run security problems of the countries bordering on Germany, using economic integration as a means of harnessing German industry to serve the joint needs of the Community, thereby preventing its serving again as the base of German national military might.[32] The principal features of this functional Community of nations, the world's first really supranational organization, are as follows.

The "Common Market."   The six nations agreed that they would form a single market among themselves for their iron, coal, and steel industries, with a view to expanding production and employment and raising the living standard of their peoples. What this means, in essence, is that they accept common policies and common institutions for regulation of this sector of their economy. For all practical purposes, they unite as a single country insofar as production and trade in these industries are concerned. While maintaining full political independence, the six nations simultaneously give up their independent power of decision in regard to these economic matters by joining in the Community.

This dualism of government is the real innovation of the institution, as untried an experiment as was the political federalism fashioned by the American Constitution. Whereas American federalism permits two governments to operate simultaneously over the same people and territory, both are political authorities, and exercise their respective powers over all activities of public concern. But the Schuman Plan distinguishes between *political* authority, still completely reserved to national governments, and *economic* authority, which in the specified area is exercised by the Community government. This functional division of powers flatly contradicts the traditional concept of sovereignty, which holds that a true "state" cannot separate out the supreme authority of government. It also refutes the current widely held view that

---

[32] The diplomatic history of the Schuman Plan and its first years of implementation are concisely reviewed by John Goormaghtigh in "European Community for Coal and Steel," *International Conciliation,* May, 1955. For a detailed study of the negotiations, and analysis of the basic treaty, see Paul Reuter, *La Communauté Européenne du Charbon et de l'Acier* (Paris: P. Pichon et R. Durand Auzias, 1953). Full-scale studies of the actual workings of the community are William Diebold, Jr., *The Schuman Plan* (New York: Praeger, 1959); and Louis Lister, *Europe's Coal and Steel Community: An Experiment in Economic Union* (New York: Twentieth Century Fund, 1960).

national interest dictates the complete subordination of a nation's economic life to its own political authority.

The general tasks of the Community are:

1. To see that the Common Market is regularly supplied.
2. To assure consumers within the market equal access to the products (without discrimination in price).
3. To seek the lowest possible prices, allowing for reasonable costs and return on capital.
4. To expand and modernize production and improve its quality.
5. To improve and equalize "upward" the living and working conditions of labor in the industries.
6. To develop international trade and set equitable prices to be charged on the external market.

The Community governing powers are delegated to it by treaty for 50 years. Powers are limited to actions necessary to insure the successful operation of the common market, and do not include the powers of ownership or direct management of the industries. The Community is thus a "welfare superstate" with substantial regulatory powers, but is *not* a socialist state. Under its jurisdiction are both private mines and industries and nationally owned and managed enterprises. Its authority is exercised over individuals, corporations, and the national governments themselves.

The principal powers of the Community include:

1. Applying rules of fair competition and nondiscrimination in trade laid down by the treaty. The Community prohibits pricing practices that aim to acquire a monopoly position. It prevents the granting of preferential treatment to buyers of a particular nationality. All prices must be made public. In some instances, the High Authority of the Community may fix maximum prices to be charged within the Common Market as well as maximum and minimum export prices. Agreements among enterprises under the Community's jurisdiction are banned if they tend to restrict competition, such as agreements to maintain high prices or divide the market.
2. Helping to finance investment programs of the enterprises and improvement of their plants so as to increase production and lower production costs.
3. Assisting states in the reemployment and temporary support of workers displaced by actions of the Community in establishing the Common Market.
4. Eliminating discrimination in transport rates among the member states and otherwise reducing freight costs.
5. Programming modernization and expansion of production, and promotion of technical research in industrial processes.
6. Studying and forecasting markets and price tendencies.
7. Regulating production in times of crisis, the Community may temporarily set quotas allocating scarce resources and otherwise try to overcome emergency conditions of surplus or shortage. But normally, it does not intervene directly in the fields of production.

8. Recommending steps to improve wages if they are abnormally low. The Community is also impowered to see that no discrimination in remuneration or working conditions is permitted against immigrants from another member country working in the affected industries.

9. Fixing minimum and maximum rates for customs duties on coal and steel imported from outside the Community, and supervising the import and export licensing systems of the member states.

To give the Community free rein to develop and safeguard its Common Market, the member states are bound to eliminate among themselves all import and export duties and quantitative restrictions on trade in iron, coal, or steel products. The national governments must also refrain from subsidizing or assisting their own industries in a way that discriminates against enterprises in the other countries.

The High Authority. The administrative and operating arm of the Community is a supranational body, nonpolitical in character. That is, its nine members are chosen on the basis of their personal competence, and are accountable to the Community as a whole, not to their own national governments. The member states explicitly accept the supranational character of the High Authority and guarantee its members complete independence in the exercise of their functions. "In the accomplishment of our duty," declared M. Jean Monnet, first President of the High Authority, "we will accept instructions from no government or organization and we will refrain from any act incompatible with the supra-national characters of our functions."[33] Members of the High Authority are chosen for a six-year term. Eight members are elected by the governments acting together (a five-sixths majority can elect); the ninth is elected by the other eight, not by the governments. Nominations are made by the individual governments, each of which also has the right to veto two appointments and possibly others if the Community's Court considers its reasons justified. No more than two members of the High Authority may be of the same nationality.

The High Authority, by a majority of its members, may take three kinds of action: decisions, which are binding in every detail; recommendations, which determine objectives but leave the means for attaining them up to the parties concerned; and opinions, which are not binding. The Authority has the power to punish violators of its mandates, usually, in the case of an industrial enterprise, by a fine based on the turnover of coal or steel. Actual enforcement of the penalties is carried out by a national government on enterprises in its territory. If the violation is committed by a state, the penalty may also be financial; sums due the state by the Community may be suspended, or other states may be authorized to take retaliatory measures.[34]

---

[33] Quoted in Goormaghtigh, "European Coal and Steel Community," *op. cit.,* p. 392.

[34] Sanctions against a state require the concurrence of a two-thirds majority of the Council of Ministers. See below.

In practice, the Authority has followed a rather cautious policy and has relied more on consultation, study, and persuasion than on power. "Its policy has been to prescribe little, to observe what happens, and to test in its own Court the legality of procedures of which it disapproves," concludes a competent analysis.[35] But it has not shrunk from sanctions when milder measures were unavailing. In January, 1955, it fined two Belgian firms and an Italian one for violating its decisions on sales prices.

One of the vital tools of the High Authority, and an important source of its power and influence, is the money it can disburse for various purposes. Unlike other international institutions, it does not depend for its funds on allocations made at the discretion of the separate national governments. It levies a direct tax on the production of coal and steel at an annual rate not to exceed 1 percent of the value of the production, unless a higher rate is authorized by the Council of Ministers. The rate imposed has varied from 0.3 to 0.9 percent. With this, it finances the administrative expenses of the Community, provides compensation to workers who have lost their jobs as a result of actions taken by the Community, and encourages technical and economic research. The Authority also borrows money, which it loans out at moderate interest for modernization and improvement of plants to encourage industrial expansion. A loan from the U.S. government of $100 million was negotiated and allocated to 54 collieries and iron ore mines for these purposes.

Many of the Authority's actions during its early years of operation have concerned the complicated arrangements for bringing the Community fully into being. It decided when each facet of the coal-steel complex was to be "communalized," and supervised the legislative, administrative, and private steps involved in this process within each country. It published prices for which the various enterprises would sell their products throughout the community. It had to hear and decide on the many special problems of producers as they were forced to adjust to the new situation. It worked out terms of the Community's relationships to other international arrangements, such as GATT, and found a satisfactory basis for the association of Britain with the Community.

The British had refused to join the Community, and at first vigorously opposed its formation, fearing it would seriously undermine their efforts to rehabilitate and expand their own coal and steel industries. The British did not want to entrust the direction of a vital segment of their national economy to a supranational body. But their opposition gradually eased, and the British government indicated its willingness to cooperate with the Community and to harmonize policies with it as much as possible without actually becoming a member.

---

[35] Goormaghtigh, "European Community for Coal and Steel," *op. cit.*, p. 392.

One of the Authority's principal functions is to enforce the Community's fair-trading code, designed to prevent discriminatory practices and encourage competition among enterprises, thus stimulating their maximum efficiency and lowering costs. On one occasion, for instance, the Authority ordered the Italian government to stop preferential treatment of domestic iron and steel products bought by the Italian shipbuilding industry and to abolish a tax on coal and steel imported from other Community countries. It condemned and ended a Belgian system of tax exemption for domestic coal and steel delivered to public bodies because it was discriminatory. It told French steelmakers either to drop a discriminatory rebate to their French clients or to grant the rebate equally to all buyers in the community. The French chose to end the rebate.

To aid in the coordinated development of Community investments, the High Authority now reviews all investment projects over $500,000 for new plant and over $1 million for replacements or modernization. The firms are left responsible to carry out their own programs, but the Authority expresses its opinion on their plans.

Lines of Communal Responsibility and Control. Three different types of interest converge in the Coal-Steel Community, and its institutions recognize the right of each to be represented in some way in making community policy and in overseeing its administration. The Assembly, composed of delegates from the six national parliaments, presumably speaks for the general public states. Representation roughly takes account of the varying sizes of the states (18 seats each to Germany, Italy, and France; 10 each to Belgium and Netherlands; and 4 to Luxembourg). The Council of Ministers gives the separate national governments a say at those points where acts of the Community impinge on their other economic affairs. The Consultative Committee represents the functional interests of producers, workers, consumers, and dealers—those who have the most immediate stake in operation of the Community.

The Assembly is the body to which the High Authority is chiefly responsible. The Authority must report to it annually, and the Assembly may censure it. If two-thirds of the Assembly votes lack of confidence in the administration, the High Authority must resign as a body. But the Assembly does not itself legislate. It thus represents a compromise between a parliament and an advisory body. It provides democratic control of the administration, but it does not undermine the singleness of authority of the "executive." In practice, it has demonstrated a capacity to reflect the total political complexion of the Community rather than particular national interests. The liberal and Socialist delegates from various countries tend to pull together as against the conservatives.

The Council of Ministers has more real power to curb the High Authority, in the interest of protecting the sovereignty of the national governments. On most important policy decisions, the authority must secure the Council's assent. The Council can itself propose measures to the Authority. An intricate voting procedure insures that the Community will take no significant action against the desires of either France or Germany unless all the other states side with one or the other. In practice, the Council seems to have rarely interfered with the High Authority, and its members have tended to emphasize their responsibilities as an organ of the Community rather than as agents of their own governments.

The Consultative Committee advises the High Authority on its general objectives and program, and reviews its action in regard to investments, financial assistance, and cartels. It has no power to make policy or to overturn the Authority, but it has been an active organ, taking up problems on its own initiative and keeping close tabs on the authority's policies and actions. The Committee has fulfilled the expectation of providing a gauge of functional interests, because the lineup of positions tends to cross national lines.

The Court. The Court established for the Community is one of the rare examples of an international judicial organ with authority to decide controversies and to apply the rule of law without the consent of national states. Its decisions are as final as those of the United States Supreme Court when it deals with conflict between member states, or between governments and the High Authority of the Community. It also functions as an administrative tribunal with equally plenary authority in actions brought by industrial enterprises or associations against the institutions of the Community. In addition, it settles conflicts between one organ of the Community and another, and it can remove a member of the High Authority from office.

The Court's seven judges are appointed by common agreement among the governments, and they hold office for six years. Their complete independence is guaranteed by the basic treaty and by a system of immunities. The Court's judgments are enforced, as are the penalties imposed by the High Authority, through the legal machinery of the countries concerned.

The Court has assumed a very important role in the actual functioning of the Community, partly because its powers give it the final say on some critical issues of policy. In its first cases, the Court was faced immediately with the same fundamental question of constitutional interpretation that confronted the U.S. Supreme Court in the early days of the American republic. Is the Constitution (in this case, the Treaty) to be interpreted strictly or broadly insofar as its grant of powers to the federal authorities is concerned? The Community's Court so far seems to be following the course opposite from the broad construction of what is "necessary and proper" made famous by Chief Justice John Marshall. It has annulled decisions of the High Authority based on even a slight deviation from the literal provisions of the Treaty. For instance, the authority allowed steel plants a modest leeway of 2.5 per cent between their published sales prices and what they might actually charge. But the French and Italian governments argued that this violated the text of the treaty, and the Court upheld their position that the exact prices charged must be published.

The Court's independence and the finality of its decisions have so far gone unchallenged by the High Authority, governments, or private enterprises. It is a remarkable development in international relations to see two Frenchmen pleading before a tribunal; one on behalf of his own government, the other on behalf of an international body against whose order the French government is protesting. This, as much as any feature of the system, bears out the reality of the supranational character of the Community.

Achievements. The European Coal and Steel Community is a going concern. Its six member states have succeeded in welding together their respective industrial resources in a pioneer international institution to form the world's second largest integrated complex of iron, coal, and steel production. The concrete results attributable to the merger are not easily assessed at this stage of the undertaking. But, economically, there is no reason for the countries to feel dissatisfied with the course they have chosen. Steel output surpasses the joint production of the six countries at any previous time. Its expansion has corresponded to a very large increase in orders from inside the Community. Total output of coal and output per man-hour have increased somewhat in all the member countries, although it is not sufficient to meet the demands of the booming steel industry.

Trade within the Community has leaped. Prices have remained steady. Even when external demands dropped after the Korean war, new buyers were found in the Common Market, so prices did not fall sharply. The cost of freight has gone down as discriminatory practices have been abolished, differential rates reduced, and for goods crossing frontiers special "through-rates" introduced in place of the 15 to 20 per cent additional formerly charged.

Substantial loans have helped governments and industries to adapt themselves to the new competitive situation. In some cases, high-cost, "marginal" enterprises have had to close down or find ways of increasing their efficiency. Some French and Belgian coal mines have been particularly hard hit as the cheaper Ruhr coal and coke can now flow without tariffs to steel producers throughout the area. But the High Authority is subsidizing and resettling displaced workers and helping to develop new industries to employ them. It is also helping to finance the modernization of plants and, in the social field, the improvement of workers' housing.

Fears have been expressed that the Community may not be able to hold together in the face of strong national or industrial pressures. For instance, some have predicted that once Germany has consolidated a position of great strength politically and economically it will either insist on running the

Community to its own benefit or withdraw. And others have questioned whether the High Authority will be able to enforce the spirit and letter of the Treaty against the more powerful producers.

One thorough study concludes that the central goal of economic federation has not, in fact, been reached. The Community has become much more an intergovernmental agency than the supranational body the founders had in mind. "The difficulties encountered by a partial economic union devoid of political power . . . can be resolved only within a union encompassing more activities and more central power," concludes this observer.[36]

On the other hand, the Community has been accused of having within itself the seeds of a super-cartel, able to manipulate the gigantic resources of the industries in its jurisdiction in such a way as to overwhelm the competition of other countries' industries. Britain, the Scandinavian countries, and even American business have viewed with alarm the "crisis provisions" of the Community, which in times of shortage or surplus authorize centralized price fixing, production quotas, consumption priorities, and allocations as a means of stabilizing prices and securing the uninterrupted flow of supplies within the Community.[37]

Experience has not yet provided an adequate test of these fears. Up to now, the evidence points rather toward a growing sense of mutuality among the divergent groups brought together under the umbrella of the Community and a feeling of satisfaction at the progress they have made by fusing their interests. It is clear, furthermore, that the Community has enjoyed an unusual quality of leadership in its High Authority, both technically competent and politically sagacious. Its self-restraint, coupled with firmness in pressing forward on the central tasks of the Community, has won confidence from all sides, in and out of the area.

Fruition of the European Economic Community

The test run of economic integration in the European Coal and Steel Community proved so satisfying to the six partners that they decided to expand the scope of their association to other sectors. In so doing, they found themselves caught up in a dynamic process that swept them toward full economic union. The result, the European Economic Community, is a form of organization unique in international relationships. The national governments retain political autonomy, that is, the right and power to make their own decisions. But they have committed themselves to a series of joint steps by which they are transforming themselves into one country for virtually all

[36] Lister, *op. cit.,* as quoted in Twentieth Century Fund *Newsletter,* No. 38 (Spring, 1960).

[37] William A. Brown and Redvers Opie, *American Foreign Assistance* (Washington, D.C.: The Brookings Institution, 1953), p. 300.

economic purposes. And they have set up central institutions, not so much to govern as to engineer consensus among the six, and to carry out their common policies.

The association is *functional* in that it singles out for joint action only certain aspects of national life where common interest runs strong. Granted that the range of functions in this case is enormous, the EEC stops short of encompassing the whole range of national interests that full political union would involve. On the other hand, operation of the EEC is clearly *political* in that decisions on the vital economic issues with which it is concerned stem from the same sources as decisions on all other national policies (the policy-making organs and procedures of the six national governments) and are subject to the same internal and external political influences that play on policy-making within each of the countries.[38]

Within the area of its functional competence, the European Economic Community acts unitedly, but *not* supranationally in the ordinary sense of that term. In this, it differs somewhat from the Coal-Steel Community. Its institutions have few powers to direct governments or impose policy on persons and organizations over the heads of national authorities. The term "community" aptly describes its nature—*common-unity*. It embodies commitments to adopt common, and only common, policies in the progressive development of unity in their mutual economic relationships, and as between themselves and the outside world.

Some of these policies are specified in the voluminous Treaty of Rome that brought the Community into existence on January 1, 1958. (It contains 248 Articles, 4 Annexes, 13 Protocols, and 4 Conventions!) For the most part, however, left to the common institutions the Treaty created was the task of finding or forging agreement among the six on the immense number of concrete decisions and general policies necessary to implement the guiding principles adopted. The Treaty mainly established procedures for *joint* or *shared* decision-making—highly detailed and specific in some instances, quite general in others—and set up a timetable for common action on the many

---

[38] The distinction often made between functional and political integration is really rather fuzzy. Basically, it adds up to a difference in the scope and comprehensiveness of the functions entrusted to political institutions acting for a community. The functionalist usually envisages these institutions being preoccupied with *some,* rather than *all,* functions usually performed by a government, and their powers, whatever they may be, are limited to action on these particular functions. Thus, functional integration is partial; political is total. But both involve political institutions and processes of decision-making.

The distinction has nothing to do with the amount of power or authority exercised by the central or common institutions as against that retained by the constituent national governments. This is the "federalist," not the "functionalist" issue. Functional integration may be attempted by giving supranational powers to central institutions; or the power of decision may be left almost entirely in the hands of the separate governments; or it may be divided between national and supranational organs. Political integration has the same choice of alternatives.

different issues that had to be resolved before economic union could become fully operative. With few exceptions, the member states did not endow the Community's institutions with the power to make decisions, but only to try to bring them about. In practice, this has proved sufficient to accomplish a drastic overhauling of national policies and to effect the compromises among deeply divergent group and national interests necessary to secure unity and make the Community the vibrant economic "co-nation" it has become.[39]

The Links of Union.   Economic integration, as envisaged by the European Economic Community, comprises four major sets of actions.

Establishment of a "Common Market."   This means a customs union, and more. Barriers to trade and competition among the countries that form the market are to be terminated, including both governmentally imposed restrictions, such as tariffs and import quotas, and private restrictions on competition, such as price-fixing and monopolistic practices. It also applies to various actions that "distort" competition, like government subsidies to particular producers and price support policies that favor one country's farmers over another's.

An important corollary to the removal of barriers and discriminatory practices affecting the flow of goods is the assurance of mobility for labor to cross frontiers freely and to seek jobs without discrimination in any of the Common Market countries. Similarly, the Common Market calls for the free circulation of services and capital.

Setting a Common External Tariff.   This distinguishes the Community's approach from a genuine free-trade policy. The Market is free and unrestricted only to its members. It discriminates against outsiders (or, to put the point more gently, it accords a "preference" to insiders) by imposing on imports from outside countries duties that producers within the Market need not pay.

The crux of the arrangement is that the same duties shall apply to goods imported into *any* of the six countries. Thus, all of them had to agree to an identical tariff schedule—the same list of goods to be taxed at the same rates—no mean undertaking for countries with such diversified economies and commercial policies. Three were traditionally high tariff countries, committed to protecting home industries and agriculture. The others held to low tariffs, being primarily exporters and anxious to keep markets everywhere as open for their products as possible. This also means that all six must act as a unit in tariff negotiations with other countries, staking out a common stand on every question and agreeing to be bound by it.

---

[39] See Lindberg, *op. cit.,* for a searching review and analysis of the evolution of the Community's decision-making processes. He examines, in the light of EEC practices, hypotheses originally set forth by Ernst Haas in his pioneer work *op. cit.* Haas is concerned with identifying the factors responsible for integration, which culminated in the historic decisions to form the EEC.

Adopting Common Policies for Economic Development.   This has involved the extraordinarily difficult task of reconciling sharply differing philosophies and traditional practices of government intervention in the economy. Yet, fulfillment of the Community's objective of promoting economic growth through an expanding market demanded, in the judgment of its pilots, more than the negative action of knocking down trade barriers and letting competition run its course. It required positive steps to encourage both industrial and agricultural development that would open alternative opportunities to those who could not survive the stiffer competition to which they would be exposed in the Common Market. Indeed, the promise of a common development policy, especially in regard to agriculture, was for several of the countries a quid pro quo, without which they would hardly have agreed to the complete liberalization of trade expected in the Common Market.

Joint Support for the Promotion of Economic and Social Development throughout the Community.   The six countries agreed to devote substantial resources (with proportionately heavier contributions from the wealthier) to meet special needs in three areas.

A European Investment Bank (with capital of $1 billion) facilitates the financing of projects to aid less developed regions of the Community, to help modernize or convert enterprises, and to start up new economic activities.

The European Social Fund promotes employment and the mobility of labor, sharing the expense of occupational retraining, resettlement, and temporary assistance to displaced workers.

The Development Fund siphons $580 million over five years into the overseas dependencies of the member states (chiefly French) to stimulate their economic growth.[40]

Steps toward Integration.   It was completely agreed that these actions could not be put into effect at once. Indeed, a transition period of 12–15 years was set, during which the six countries would systematically prepare for the changes and adjustments the new relationships would inevitably bring about in their internal as well as international economic life.

But this was to be a managed gradualism, harnessed to an explicit timetable of sequential steps the countries pledged themselves to undertake, with some allowances for delay or speedup as circumstances unfolded. For in-

---

[40] The provisions of the Treaty of Rome are immensely detailed on each of the above subjects and cannot be treated in this brief summary, which seeks merely to identify the essential nature of the Community undertakings. For a major study of the substantive economic provisions and the initial actions of the Community in implementing them, see Isaiah Frank, *The European Common Market: An Analysis of Commercial Policy* (New York: Frederick A. Praeger, Inc., 1961). Lindberg, *op. cit.,* gives a concise synopsis of the Treaty, and follows with a comprehensive account of the handling of four major implementing decisions during the first stage of transition: relations with the European Free Trade Area, the decision to accelerate the timetable for transition to liberalization within the Market, adoption of the external tariff, and adoption of a common agricultural policy.

stance, in regard to cuts in tariffs within the Market, the Six agreed to cut 10 percent the first year, another 10 percent by July 1, 1960, and achieve a total cut of 30 percent by the end of the "first stage," which was to be three to four years after the Treaty came into force. In regard to the common external tariff, a "first approximation" was expected to be put into effect by December 31, 1961.

Some events actually moved faster than the original timetable. Exceptional prosperity, the unexpectedly buoyant response of business circles to the launching of the Community, and the ability of the Community to surmount its first crucial decisions with a minimum of internal friction and dislocation generated a momentum that led the Six to decide to accelerate and move some actions up to earlier dates (the external tariff was introduced a full year ahead). The critical overall decision—to declare the first stage completed and move to the second—was made on schedule, January, 1962, though only after the most strenuous of negotiations finally broke a logjam over adoption of a common agricultural policy.[41]

In addition to its specificity, the timetable had the imperative of irreversibility. The big decisions, once made, could not be undone, at least not without wrecking the entire project. This was particularly true for the decision just mentioned—to move to the second stage—because at this point each country had to determine whether the total package of measures so far agreed on enabled it to balance what it had had to give up against the advantages it could expect to secure and come out ahead. Each part of the package worked out in the first stage was contingent on the others. It was, in effect, an all-or-none proposition. Once accepted by every state as the condition of its going on with the more drastic steps of unification provided for in the second stage, no one could back away from *any* provision previously adopted.[42]

The Operational Process.   The EEC functions through institutions similar to those of the European Coal and Steel Community. Two, in fact, are identical: the European Parliament (formerly known as the European Parliamentary Assembly), composed of delegates appointed from the national parliaments of each state; and the Court of Justice.[43] These bodies operate, respectively, to express the crosscurrents of political opinion on issues before

---

[41] See Lindberg, *op. cit.,* chaps. 9 and 12.

[42] For a strong statement of the case that the European Communities are irrevocably committed to a process of supranational economic unification (despite de Gaulle's contradictory posture), see Ernst B. Haas, "Technocracy, Pluralism and the New Europe," Stephen R. Graubard, ed., *A New Europe?* (Boston: Houghton Mifflin, 1964).

[43] These organs are also shared with Euratom, third of the European "communities." Action has now been taken to merge the *executive organs* of the three Communities as well, beginning in 1966. They will be fused into a permanent, unified Commission of nine members. See *European Community,* March, 1965, for a report on this decision by the Council of Ministers.

the Community and to adjudicate disputes arising from implementation of the Treaty.

The active direction of community affairs, however, centers in the Council of Ministers (which, like the ECSC Council, represents the governments) and the ECC Commission, consisting of nine persons chosen by common agreement among the governments and charged with representing the general interest of the Community. The Council is given the major powers of decision. The Commission has vital powers of initiative, administration, and oversight. The situation would appear made to order to produce friction, divisiveness, and paralysis. But, in practice, an effective working relationship has grown up, in which the Commission functions delicately yet forcefully to overcome disagreements that prevent the Council from acting, and in which it fashions proposals that the governments, acting through the Council, are ultimately persuaded to accept as Community policy. The Commission's role is aptly described as that of negotiator and broker—the catalyst in the decision-making process.[44]

The Commission acquired its pivotal position in the formulation of policy in part, but only in part, as an outgrowth of its formal powers to originate the proposals on which all major decisions of the Community are based. Although it is the Council that finally decides, that body is usually limited to acting on a proposition of the Commission, *which it may not amend* except by a unanimous vote. (Art. 149 of the treaty.) The Commission, on the other hand, may modify its proposals at any time before the Council finally acts. This enables the Commission to become "the driving force behind the actions of the Council, which filters, controls and channels this force."[45]

The Commission has other powers that also contribute to its influence, notably, the right to represent the Community in all external negotiations (with countries outside the Community and with other international organizations), the right to represent the Community at the European Parliament before which it is responsible, and the right to participate in all deliberations of the Council and Parliament and in the preparation of their actions. The effect of these powers is to make the Commission, and it alone, spokesman and agent for the whole Community—the embodiment of its general interest. This gives the Commission impressive moral as well as political leverage as it confronts the other institutions of the Community and the constituent governments. Its recommendations always carry the presumption of being directed toward the welfare of the Community rather than reflecting a special national or group interest; conversely, objectors are cast in the unenviable role of defending special interests over the well-being of the whole Community. This puts the European Parliament, for instance, in the paradoxical, and to it

---

[44] See Lindberg, *op. cit.*, especially pp. 65–73, 202–5 and 243–52.

[45] Gerhard Bebr, "The Balance of Power in the European Communities," *Annuaire Européen*, V (The Hague: Nijhoff, 1959), p. 69 as quoted in Lindberg, *op. cit.*, pp. 32.

embarrassing, situation of debating and criticizing the Commission's actions (as it is supposed to do, representing the various national legislatures), yet wanting above all to uphold the Commission as symbol and custodian of the Community. What happens usually is that the Parliament upbraids the Commission for not being bold or forward enough in pushing the Council toward greater and more rapid integration.

The most important secret of the Commission's success is its skill in manipulating the peculiar decision-making pattern that has evolved in the Community, quite apart from the formal structures and complex procedures laid down in the Treaty. This pattern, as summarized by a close observer, "brings together the representatives of the Community interest (the Commission) and those of the Member states (experts, Ministers, Council) in a continuous problem-solving operation."[46]

The Commission's tactic is to involve the principal national civil servants concerned with an issue at every stage of the policy preparation process. The result is an extraordinary "interpenetration" of those responsible for decisions in the separate governments and those functioning in the central Community institutions. The regular staff of the community institutions, numbering over 3,000 by 1962, is itself largely drawn from the civil services of the six governments. Then, an immense number of committees and special groups of experts are called on by the Commission to study the many problems for which it is responsible, collect and analyze relevant information, identify the major points at issue between the governments, and draw together preliminary recommendations for the action the Commission should propose. Most of these groups are composed of high-level national officials, even though they do not participate as representatives of their governments in most of the work. Finally, there are the national delegations, each with its own sets of experts; and there is a network of intergovernmental committees that do function to represent the governments, heading up into the Committee of Permanent Representatives, set up to service the Council of Ministers and to provide continuous liaison between the governments and the Community. One estimate added up a total of 17,500 direct participants in the EEC decision-making process during one year, in addition to the regular staff of the Community. Obviously, this experience feeds back into the national bureaucracies a community-wide perspective that affects their own internal decision-making and paves the way for a receptive attitude toward the Commission's proposals. The national officials, in a word, become "engaged." The point has been well put by Haas.

The concept of 'engagement' postulates that if parties to a conference enjoy a specific and well-articulated sense of participation, if they identify themselves completely with the procedures and codes within which their decisions are made,

---

[46] Lindberg, *op. cit.*, p. 217.

they consider themselves completely 'engaged' by the results even if they do not fully concur in them.[47]

Thus, instead of jealously guarding its prerogatives as custodian of the Community interest and carrying on a running cat-and-dog fight with the Council and the various governmental representatives, the Commission has emerged as the mediator, the harmonizer, and, at times, the actual arbiter of intergovernmental controversies. Eschewing an attitude of supranational dirigisme for one of infinite solicitude for the views and policies of the separate governments, it has emerged a masterful pilot of unity, whose integrative influence is rapidly growing far beyond the limits formally prescribed in the Treaty, or ever intended.

In the last analysis, of course, the determination of Community policies rests with the national governments. The glow of successful unification tends to obscure the deep divisions that have had to be overcome; and the fact that a common stand has finally emerged on most issues does not indicate that the six countries started with consensus but rather that they agreed, after hard bargaining, to compromise. The Treaty of Rome did not, it should be emphasized again, itself confirm specific agreements on the major issues, nor even commit the parties to agree. It only bound them to try to agree.

It is true that on many matters the governments waived an individual right to veto. The highly detailed and complex voting provisions of the Treaty specify some actions that may be decided by a simple majority of the Council; others require a "qualified majority" designed to insure that none of the large states, nor the group of small states, can be overridden unless all the others stand together. The provisions are geared to a system of weighted voting, similar to that of the Coal-Steel Community.[48]

But unanimity is required on the questions considered most vital, such as expanding the membership of the Community. That this is no academic matter was demonstrated when France alone blocked Britain's application to join the Common Market, to the deep distress of the others. Normally, the veto is exercised implicitly, however, and less peremptorily. A country states the nature and basis of its objections to a proposal; the others, nudged by the Commission, go part way toward meeting them; and the objecting government is pressed to do some conceding of its own.

The Community's experience raises an intriguing question: Why have the six governments come to agree when they don't have to and when their

---

[47] Haas, *op. cit.*, p. 522, as quoted by Lindberg, *op. cit.*, p. 84. The process as it has functioned in the EEC is thoroughly examined by Lindberg, chap. 4.

[48] In the Council, France, Germany, and Italy have four votes each; Belgium and Netherlands, two each; and Luxembourg, one—a total of seventeen. Voting is also weighted in the other organs of the Community, though not in exactly the same proportions. In the financial organs—the social and development funds—Italy's weight is reduced to accord with its relatively smaller contribution, while that of Belgium and Netherlands is greater.

interests and policies conflict as profoundly as they do on many basic issues? The procedures of consensus formation previously discussed undoubtedly contribute to this result. But more important than the strictly procedural techniques has been the strategy adopted by the architects of Community decisions to resolve the substantive disagreements. They have "upgraded common interests" rather than attempting to "split the difference" between opposing governmental positions.[49] The planners have succeeded in demonstrating to the governments that they stand to gain on an overall basis from an action that will strengthen the Community's economy as a whole, even if on certain particulars and in the short run the interests of some of their nationals might suffer.

This leads directly to the matter of rewards. What actual or anticipated "payoffs" have persuaded the governments to pay the price of agreement on common policies for the Community? The most obvious has been unparalleled economic expansion—a booming internal market, a strongly competitive position abroad, and the resulting high levels of employment, rising standard of living, and general "good times." Whether this was coincidence or cause-and-effect related to the formation of the Community is in dispute among the economists. But from a political standpoint, the Community was held to have won a smashing success, measured in hard, material returns to the businesses, industries, and even the farms of the member countries.

On a narrower front, the Community's protectionist features vis-à-vis other countries seemed to some (notably the French and agricultural interest groups generally) to yield important benefits that they were eager to reserve to Community members exclusively. This was conceived as direct compensation for giving up discriminatory restrictions on trade with the other Common Market participants. This issue, however, more than any other, embroiled the Community's relations with Britain and countries closely tied to it economically, as well as relations with many underdeveloped countries and even with the United States, which had backed the Community almost as a godfather.[50]

The question was, and still is, whether community cohesion must be bought by policies that create special privileges denied to others; in other words, whether a prerequisite for integration among the Six (and whoever else is allowed to join) is that the Community provide some tangible rewards

---

[49] This perceptive analysis was made by Ernst Haas on the basis of his studies of European integration. See particularly, his "International Integration: The European and the Universal Process," *International Organization,* Spring, 1961. Lindberg, *op. cit.,* substantiates this conclusion in reference to the major Common Market decisions he examined. Note, for instance, his conclusions in regard to the acceleration decision, pp. 203–4.

[50] The background of the problem is sketched by U. W. Kitzinger, "Europe: The Six and the Seven," *International Organization,* Winter, 1960. Relations between the EEC and EFTA, the European Free Trade Association organized by Britain, are treated at length by Lindberg, *op. cit.,* chap. 7.

"for members only." The problem is that this approach may precipitate outright economic warfare with other countries, which may retaliate by counterprotectionism and undermine the whole movement toward economic expansion and development, which is the truly significant payoff for integration. This prospect obviously deeply disturbed most of the Community's adherents, who tried unsuccessfully to budge the French from their intransigent insistence on making Britain conform to the full protectionist regulations as the condition of joining the Market (thus obliging her to discriminate economically against her intimate associates in the Commonwealth).

The Community is, therefore, facing a critical choice, which is proving highly divisive within as well as alarmingly provocative to those outside. Is the Community prepared to integrate regionally at the cost of impairing economic relationships globally? Does its union demand rewards that are exclusive and incompatible with the welfare of others? Does membership in the European Community preclude membership in the world economic community? If so, will the bonds of regional union hold against the tug of global interdependence?

PART III

STRENGTHENING THE HUMAN POTENTIAL

The actors in the international arena are states. They fight wars; they make peace. They define and sustain international order. They arrange for international economic stability and development. Yet all these efforts—and at times they may not have been very vigorous —were never totally divorced from the fundamental objective of the well-being of man. At a minimum, states claimed to be motivated by the desire to provide the most proper environment for their people. Since the rise of the Great Democracies the individual became a focus of international cooperation.

In recent centuries, the idea of human dignity was prominently incorporated into Western ideologies. The health and welfare of people became a collective responsibility. The individual was recognized to possess rights not only in regard to his fellow man but also in his relationship to government. These rights, moreover, were not anchored in citizenship. They were not merely privileges to be enjoyed through membership in a national community. Instead they were derived from universal human nature. They were inalienable.

Concern for the protection of human rights and the advancement of human welfare invites international cooperation. In the fullest sense of the word an Englishman's liberty and right to equality is assured only through respect for the liberty and equality of all human beings. The health of a German is dependent to some extent upon the absence of epidemics in Africa. The standards of labor in America are not unaffected by the working conditions in Japan. Surely no less important is the realization that Congolese and Angolan national aspirations are contingent upon the popular commitment to the right of self-determination in Europe and the United States.

The advance toward internationalization of political rights and minimum standards of economic and social well-being confronts the cardinal principle of national sovereignty. Thus it has been a slow almost imperceptible advance. States continue to retain control over the populations within their territories. They define the scope and regulate the exercise of rights of citizens. Above all each state determines the extent to which the international effort to advance human rights and welfare are internally implemented.

Chapter 16

Safeguarding the World's Health

International cooperation in the field of health is a relatively recent development. For many centuries, perhaps millennia, man comprehended little of the causes of diseases and the way in which they spread. He accepted with resignation the outbreak and swift spread as part of the natural order of life or perhaps as a sign of divine disfavor. As long as man thought there was no way to control diseases there was little incentive for international cooperation.

Once medical science brought some understanding of the causes of disease it also offered a focus for effort. It was obvious that epidemics crossed borders without much difficulty; sometimes skipping over certain areas to break out in countries separated by many miles of land and water from the areas of original epidemic. As a minimum, a program to prevent contagion was clearly indicated.

At first it was a national effort. A system of quarantine and disinfection of ships arriving at ports was introduced. It was promptly and vigorously opposed by merchants and traders as interference with the flow of profitable trade. Worse still, it gradually became apparent that such a system proved inadequate in the absence of detailed knowledge of incubation periods and carriers. Clearly effective protection required control of epidemics at their sources, even though these were within the territories of other states.

France was the first to take action. Unilaterally it set up medical posts in the Middle East. The improvement was less than decisive. Most of the earth's surface, or what is more important, most of the world's population remained unaffected. Success, indeed, depended on a far more massive program, one which could not be sustained by a few colonial powers but required the voluntary cooperation of all states.

International cooperation in health once begun, did not stop at the control of contagion. It expanded to the prevention of epidemics, and the cure of a wide range of diseases. Dental care and mental health were included in the natural course of events. Good health today no longer means a mere absence of discernible ailment, but is a positive concept of well-being—physical and psychological. Good health is no longer an individual concern, but a focus of international cooperation.

TYPES OF INTERNATIONAL HEALTH ACTION

International health work has taken several forms. Over the years, these have become more complex and have involved different types of cooperation. In the following section, growth of the various types will be outlined to show how international health cooperation has evolved and developed.[1]

Regulation by Imposition

As mentioned above, France's failure to set up a workable system in the Middle East to prevent export of epidemics encouraged the search for more effective means. In 1838, some of the European states were willing to cooperate in an attempt to work out a solution. Although Europeans cooperated internationally, the system worked out was one involving imposition: Turkey was forced to set up a health council made up of Turkish and European representatives. This type of international action—European powers cooperating to force weaker areas into a system involving Europeans—was used in a number of Middle Eastern, North African, and Southeast European regions. It was possible only when weaker areas were unable to resist the pressure of more powerful states. Britain, with possessions in the area, was unwilling to have the system extended to cover her possessions and was strong enough to prevent "imposition."

The health councils established were often able to improve sanitary conditions in their areas. In Tangier, for instance, the European powers were able to force the sultanate to pave streets, to improve means of sewage disposal, and to make provisions for a pure water supply.

Regulation by Convention

The health councils were set up in an attempt to improve health conditions in ports from which epidemics might spread. These councils could often improve conditions, but their efforts never resulted in complete eradication of the danger, and it was necessary to supplement this approach with other safeguards. In 1881, a conference was called in Washington to investigate the possibilities. It was agreed that states had the right to prevent the spread

---

[1] For a general history of world health efforts in the pre-League period, see Linden A. Mander, *Foundations of Modern World Society* (Stanford, Calif.: Stanford University Press, 1948), pp. 203–10.

of disease into their territories and, therefore, were not obligated to permit "infected" ships to enter their ports. But how could a state know whether a ship was infected? It was agreed that ships should be inspected before leaving ports and be prohibited from sailing until they had received a clean bill of health.

The principle was a sound one, but there were two problems. First, the United States put forth the position that officials of states with high health standards should be permitted to examine ships destined for their ports from areas with low standards. The principle was rejected by most representatives on the grounds that it was a violation of a state's sovereignty. A further difficulty explored at the conference was lack of adequate scientific data on diseases and the methods of spread. It was recognized that no system of quarantine and inspection would be satisfactory until such information was available.

Although the conference had been useful for its exploratory work, it produced little of importance. States were willing to cooperate to enforce a regime on weaker areas, but few assumed responsibility for action in their own areas. England continued to refuse permission for an international health system in her Middle Eastern possessions. Cholera epidemics spread from that area to Europe almost every year between 1880 and 1892, causing the loss of thousands of lives.

The continued spread of epidemics finally convinced many that action had to be taken, and, consequently, several conferences were called in the 1890's. These resulted in the drafting of the first international sanitary conventions.[2] Measures for precaution and quarantine to be taken in ports, as well as heavy penalties to be laid on captains and steamship companies for violations, were now international obligations. Sanitary stations were set up in many of the dangerous ports.

These conventions marked an important step forward in international health cooperation. Obligations were now being taken equally by all states; imposition had proved inadequate to cope with the problem when dangerous areas could thereby be excluded.

Cooperation by Conference

The conference technique underlay both of the first two means of regulation; conferences were called to draw up conventions. But conferences came to be looked at as important techniques in their own right.

Until the beginning of the present century, health conferences were held on an ad hoc basis, i.e., when a special problem or a state was particularly concerned, a conference was called. As noted, the Washington Conference of 1881 had brought out the problem of inadequate knowledge about diseases.

---

[2] *The First Ten Years of the World Health Organization* (Geneva: World Health Organization, 1958), pp. 6–8.

To promote scientific investigation and to encourage cooperation, the United States sponsored the idea of holding periodic conferences among the American states—conferences that only medical and sanitary officers would attend. This cooperation was to be directed especially at a major American problem—yellow fever.

Men attacking health problems have found it is usually possible to search together for common solutions; those from different political, social, and economic systems—even citizens from "enemy" states—have found that their dedication to the search for good health can surmount most differences and bind them together in pursuit of common—health—"enemies." The ad hoc conferences at the end of the nineteenth and beginning of the twentieth centuries provided an opportunity for this kind of sharing.

Organization for Continuing Cooperation

The interchange at the ad hoc conferences often proved valuable, and there was pressure to establish some sort of regular machinery for exchanging information. In response, the International Office of Public Health (OIHP) was established in 1907, with headquarters in Paris.[3] The Office was to act as a clearinghouse for public health information and recent developments, and was to gather information and make regular reports on the status of infectious diseases within contracting states.

Although the Office was conceived of as a passive agency for collecting and passing on information, it became more active as time passed. It studied the sanitary conventions and made recommendations for revision and expansion, indicating how conventions could be kept in line with new scientific discoveries. It studied public health systems and drew up recommendations concerning particularly important types of control to have in the hands of governments—for example, drinking water. When established, states agreed to submit information to the office, but on a completely voluntary basis; 39 states had accepted compulsory communicable disease reporting by 1926. In 1938, states agreed to recognize the Permanent Commission of the International Office of Public Health as the technical advisory board on all sanitary conventions and agreed to consult the Commission when difficulties arose over interpretation of the convention.

Thus, the Office expanded in functions and authority over the years. It never, however, took direct action but remained, rather, a coordinating and advisory organization. One of its primary contributions was its permanence: a secretariat that worked year round, a regular forum for discussion of common problems.

During the Paris Peace Conference, the International Red Cross pressed for some type of health organization within the framework of the League of

---

[3] For a brief description of the work of the OIHP, see *ibid.,* pp. 15–21.

Nations. No separate organization comparable to the International Labor Organization was established at the time. In 1920, a conference drew up a plan for the League of Nations Health Organization, and it was adopted by the League Assembly in 1923. The organization was not to be autonomous as the ILO but was, rather, to be included within the League framework.

As the International Office of Public Health before it,[4] the League organization was conceived of primarily as an agency for coordinating the efforts of states and as a clearinghouse for information.

Organization for Service and Action

The functions of the League Health Organization began to change soon after it was established. It was not to be confined primarily to sharing information but was now to take on more and more the character of a service agency.

One reason for this new development was the national change in the concept of good health from a negative one—lack of disease—to a positive one—a state of well-being. At the same time, public health services were expanding and assuming more responsibilities and functions. With this development on the national level went pressure on the international level to expand—a pressure often met by the counterpressure of "national sovereignty" and by resistance to money-giving for international health work. In spite of opposition to expansion and interference, the League organization became a more active agency than its forerunners.

Another impetus to this change in function came from dissatisfaction with current means and techniques for cooperation. Just sharing knowledge and relying on national action proved insufficient to accomplish certain aims of the League Health Organization. For example, international efforts in epidemic control had been confined to containment by quarantine. Now the League was urged to do more. Even before the League Health Organization was actually established, a League Epidemic Commission began to function. An epidemic of typhus and relapsing fever struck Eastern Europe in 1920. The League body spent about one million dollars in coordinating efforts, and succeeded in stopping further spread of the epidemic. In Europe, the Commission acted successfully. Thus, from the beginning of the League period, the principle of the international organization's actual participation programs was established.

The principle of international action was continued after the League of Nations ended. Before the second world war was over, the Allies realized that, at liberation, health conditions in war-stricken areas would be grave and, further, national governments would be totally unable to cope with the problems. If epidemics were to be avoided and a beginning made to restora-

---

[4] The Office continued to function during the League period.

tion of good health in these areas, some sort of international action was imperative.

Thus, the more fortunate nations began to feel a sense of responsibility for those with crucial health problems. At first, this took the form of health aid to war devastated countries, i.e., as part of the Allied relief and reconstruction program. An important part of UNRRA's action was concerned with restoring health facilities and providing health aid to states.[5]

This concern for the health of peoples has expanded beyond care for war-afflicted areas. There has been a growing sense of international responsibility to raise the health standards of all peoples everywhere. With the increase in number of independent states, most of which are poor and have health standards woefully far behind those of older states, a new approach in health cooperation has developed—assistance to developing nations.

The concept that the have states should assist the have-nots has been evident in the field of health. Less affluent members have been pressing for assistance, while within the "richer states" there has been insistence—from many sources and for numbers of reasons—to respond. Various programs have been undertaken by international organizations to help the poorer states to achieve good health for their peoples. Today, the bulk of international health activity has been placed under the World Health Organization (WHO), a specialized agency of the United Nations.

The World Health Organization. From the beginning, it was accepted that WHO should engage in operational work[6] and that its concerns should embrace a wider variety of fields than had the League organization. WHO's program includes—with the exception of regulation by imposition—all the types of international cooperation outlined above.

While WHO is the most important international agency in the health field, in some areas it shares responsibility with other international organizations. Children's and mothers' health has been improved in many parts of the world as a result of the cooperative efforts of WHO and UNICEF.[7] WHO has cooperated with ILO on workers' health problems and with the U.N. on various aspects of narcotics control.

Organizationally, WHO was to be established on the same general pattern as most specialized agencies. There is a World Health Assembly, composed of representatives of all member states, which meets annually to decide on general policies of the organization, pass on the budget, and adopt conventions. Meeting more frequently is an Executive Board made up of 18 members chosen by the World Health Assembly "from among persons most

---

[5] See above, pp. 363–72, for a description of UNRRA's activities.

[6] Although provision was made in the organization's constitution, it did not—due to obstruction from certain states, including the United States—actually engage in any extensive programs until the United Nations Expanded Program of Technical Assistance was set up.

[7] See pp. 375–78, 421–22, 555–56, for a description of UNICEF's activities.

qualified by their technical competence in the field of health, preferably representing the national administration." Finally, the Secretariat is under a Director-General. There is also provision for setting up regional offices. The Pan American Sanitary Bureau, to promote health cooperation among the American states, had been functioning well, and some American states wanted to continue it as an independent agency, while other states urged a centralized organization. Use of regional offices, a compromise solution, was finally accepted. Regional offices, while providing for cooperation on problems peculiar to a region, have given rise to problems of organization and coordination which have been difficult to work out.

PROGRAMS AND PROJECTS

The previous sections have been concerned primarily with the impetus to international cooperative action and the means that have been adopted. We turn now to the types of programs and projects that have been tried out.

As mentioned, *preventing the spread of disease* has been an important part of international health activity. A second area of activity has been *curing disease.* It is not enough to stop diseases from spreading among areas; sympathy for those afflicted has resulted in a search for better ways to effect cures, and this concern has been reflected in international programs. Extending the idea of a positive state of health aroused interest in preventing disease—a goal that over the years has continuously expanded.

Preventing the Spread of Disease

Here the problem, as an international one, is definable. When a disease—especially one known to assume epidemic proportions—breaks out, the problem is to confine the disease within the borders of the state in which it started.

The means adopted, as mentioned above, include conventions that permit states to inspect ships leaving their ports and to issue bills of health. The conventions lay down standards and procedures to be followed in examining ships, and have been amended as more scientific information on the spread of diseases becomes available. The League Health Organization encouraged research into better ways of fumigating ships. During this period, the danger of disease spreading by rats came to be appreciated and more effective ways employed to combat them.

The conventions aim at preventing the spread of disease while at the same time interfering as little as possible with the flow of trade. By setting international standards for inspection of ships, states may permit ships to enter their ports without subjecting them to long periods of quarantine. An important contribution of WHO was the 1951 drafting of a single comprehensive sanitary convention[8] to replace the many in force, thus clarifying the obligations of states that had been complicated by multiple conventions with overlapping commitments and involving different states.

Another means employed was the councils.[9] The purpose of the health councils was to assure satisfactory sanitary conditions in ports from which ships were departing for European states. The system was used in ports where diseases were particularly prevalent and health conditions—as judged by European standards—especially deplorable.

The number of ports from which ships left was limited, and few travelers from these dangerous areas used means of transportation other than ships, so ships were the natural object of control. After the first World War, however, Europe was threatened with epidemics carried by land—from Russia. Here was a more difficult problem. Refugees from Russia, many bringing diseases with them, were crossing at many points along the borders with Eastern European states. The system adopted to prevent the further spread of disease was one of inspection and examination at centers for fleeing Russians, located at points along the borders. This project undertaken by the Eastern European states in cooperation with the League Epidemic Commission probably prevented the outbreak of a major epidemic in Europe.

The regime established under the sanitary conventions proved to be not so effective as had been hoped. As long as the duration of a ship's voyage exceeded the period of incubation for a disease, the system was fairly adequate. If a disease broke out during a voyage, a ship could be quarantined after it entered a port. However, it was possible for a ship to leave a port before an epidemic had broken out, so infected persons might be on board without anyone's knowledge. If the ship then landed in another port before the incubation period was over, it was possible for such persons to land without anyone's suspecting they were carriers.

The problem was again one of reconciling the need for protection with the demand for no unnecessary interference with trade. One way to reduce the danger was through a system of reporting. If a state in which an epidemic threatened would inform others immediately, appropriate action could be taken on boats arriving from the infected area. The aid of warning is shown in the effectiveness of precautions taken when epidemic threatened from Russia in 1922.

The first system of epidemological intelligence was set up for Eastern Europe.[10] Reports on certain diseases were collected and disseminated by

---

[8] This convention came into force October 1, 1952. The convention allows the organization to ammend provisions, these becoming binding on states unless rejected by a member within 18 months.

[9] See above for a discussion of establishment of the health councils.

[10] *The First Ten Years of the World Health Organization, op. cit.,* p. 29.

the League. In 1922, a bureau was set up in Singapore to report on the Far East—an area particularly plagued by frequent and severe epidemics.

Today, states agree to send information on outbreaks of the diseases covered to one of the four bureaus (Geneva, Singapore, Washington, Alexandria). Any situation considered urgent is reported immediately to the whole world by a series of radio bulletins. Each week, this information is summarized and confirmed in weekly publications which are airmailed out.

When there is danger of an epidemic and word has been received via the intelligence network, states have an opportunity to put into effect emergency measures, such as quarantining ships from infected areas or other precautions, depending on the disease. Today, however, although the system continues to function and is useful, it cannot offer much protection. Fast ships and jet airplanes can arrive days before there is any indication of an epidemic in ports of departure. By requiring vaccinations and by keeping passenger lists, states are able to take some measures once they have learned of the outbreak of disease.

Another type of program undertaken to prevent the spread of epidemics has been cooperative emergency aid at the source. Since it has been very difficult to contain epidemics, especially in states without adequate medical facilities and personnel for control, other states have sometimes been willing to offer assistance and to entrust the international organization with responsibility for coordinating and directing the operations.

A program of this type occurred in 1947, when a cholera epidemic broke out in Egypt, threatening all her neighbors. WHO acted as procurer of supplies and coordinator. Two U.S. drug firms agreed to expand vaccine production, and within 20 days a shipment was grown, tested, packed, and delivered to Cairo. Nine governments cooperated with the world organization in donating needed supplies. WHO organized much of the transportation, including air transport of 22 tons. The peak of the epidemic was on October 20, when 1,022 new cases and 581 deaths were reported. Within three months after the outbreak, Egypt reported to WHO that all port cities and upper provinces were free of cholera. The efforts of the World Health Organization and response of governments prevented the epidemic from spreading beyond Egypt. In the nineteenth century, five major epidemics, having gotten a good start in Egypt, had spread over Europe.[11]

This type of cooperation can be traced to the self-interest of states in preventing epidemics from spreading. However, once states are willing to contribute to fighting an emergency within a country, it would seem that they are being motivated by other considerations also. The plight of an area helpless against the ravages of a disease is often able to arouse sympathy—sympathy which is translated into positive action.

[11] C. E. A. Winslow, "World Health Organization—Its Program and Accomplishments," *International Conciliation,* No. 439 (March, 1948).

Curing Disease

Halting the spread of disease was the first objective of governmental health action. Once international cooperation proved itself in this area, there was pressure for broadening international action. Prevention was important—especially to those who were thereby spared—but what about those already afflicted? How could international cooperation contribute to curing diseases?

One of the first prerequisites for a cure is scientific knowledge—knowledge of what the disease is effecting and of ways to combat it. It was natural, once international health organizations were established, that this problem would be discussed among representatives at conferences, and also that there be urging for regular exchange of information and results of experiments undertaken nationally. These demands increased as studies of diseases multiplied and keeping up with research developments in all countries became difficult.

Use of the international organization as a clearinghouse for such information followed as a natural response to this need.[12] The international organization did not regard its role in this area as a completely passive one. International health organizations have continuously searched for better ways to disseminate information and for ways to encourage research into illnesses not being given sufficient attention.

The organizations have published especially important monographs, encouraged and helped support collective study tours, and have been influential in establishing institutes for the study of particular diseases. Recently, there has been special attention to diseases prevalent in the newer nations, from which older ones are spared. Since the newer nations are the poorer ones without the means—financial and personnel—to engage in comprehensive research, WHO has encouraged the richer states to do research on some of these diseases.

In the fight against disease, there has been an increasing use of serums and medicaments. Within states, there is usually a standard system for measuring units; that is, one unit of a product will contain the same strength whether produced in New York or California, and a doctor administering the substance will know what his patient is receiving. However, these units are national ones, and states adopted different measurements. As long as the medicaments were used mostly by nationals within the producing states and relatively few persons lived and traveled outside their own countries, this situation caused little difficulty or hardship.

However, increase in travel and in shipments of medicaments across borders has produced difficulties. During the first World War, the situation

---

[12] *The First Ten Years of the World Health Organization, op. cit.,* pp. 429–55.

became particularly acute. For instance, the use of antitetnus serum in France presented doctors with real problems. American and British doctors often had to use the French products, which were very different from their own: if the German unit is taken as one, 67 such units of the American serum or 2,500 units of the French would equal it.[13] It is impossible to estimate the number of deaths that might have been prevented had this confusion not existed.

Here, then, was a problem that demanded an international solution. National standardization would be adequate for the majority of cases, but the use of serums by foreign doctors was increasing. Tourists and other aliens with special illnesses needed to be assured that the units they were receiving were comparable to those at home, and in emergencies, such as the one in Egypt mentioned above, doctors needed to know what they were using. Starting in 1921, the League Health Organization concerned itself with the problem. Many conferences were held and studies made. Outstanding authorities undertook special investigations and studies. The results of these efforts were rewarding, and a system of international standardization is now well established.

During the League period, the principle of voluntarism applied to standards; under League auspices, standards were worked out and samples sent to any states requesting them, but adoption was left up to each state. WHO's contribution in this area has been to make new international standards binding unless specifically rejected by the state within a set period of time.[14]

The system used by both the League and the United Nations has involved working through, and in cooperation with, national health facilities. The Danish State Serum Institute in Copenhagen and the National Institute for Medical Research in London did most of the preliminary investigation for standardization and enlisted the cooperation of other national centers. The existence of such national centers and organizations has appreciably facilitated cooperation, not only in this field but in many others. A national institution that unites and helps coordinate research or other activities on a state level makes easier the difficult task of the international organization in promoting international cooperation. For financial reasons, the system is also an effective one; the international agency rarely has funds to undertake such projects itself, whereas state agencies often have funds, plus equipment and personnel, or can get them.

Recently, international organizations have taken a more active part in curing diseases and have actually been involved in campaigns. While older countries have diseases under control and are able to cope with most of the health needs of their citizens, many of the newer nations, where most people

---

[13] L. A. Mander, *Foundations of Modern World Society* (Stanford, Calif.: Stanford University Press, 1948), p. 217.

[14] *The First Ten Years of the World Health Organization, op. cit.,* pp. 403–8.

suffer from some disease, face mammoth health problems. And it is these countries that lack the means to handle the problems. In some cases, no cure has been discovered, but even where there is a cure, money or trained personnel are lacking.

International cooperation in fighting disease has been growing as the more advanced states have gradually begun to assume some responsibility for aiding in the development of less fortunate areas. Economic development cannot succeed where workers are debilitated from disease, so curing disease has become recognized as an important aspect of economic development. At the same time that the advanced nations have assumed some responsibility themselves, they have been exposed to pressures within international organizations to increase their assistance. The great expansion in memberships has increased attention to the problems in the less fortunate regions, and this has resulted in the allocation of larger portions of the budget to less developed countries and in attempts—not always successful—to increase the contributions of the wealthier nations.

WHO has tried to respond to the need for curing diseases in the less developed countries. As mentioned, it has been able to help by encouraging research into particularly prevalent diseases in these areas. Research has been done in some diseases for which a cure is known but involves costly medicines or requires numerous applications, thus limiting its usefulness. WHO has encouraged and helped to support research for means that are cheap and quick. Such a cure has, for example, been found for yaws.

Although most of the actual curing must, of necessity, be left to national governments, WHO—often in cooperation with UNICEF—has undertaken some programs. It has set up pilot projects to show how a campaign should be run; has provided for the training of the necessary personnel; has made preliminary surveys, required in any large-scale campaign; and has sponsored seminars and conferences at which techniques and experiences have been exchanged. In some countries, it has managed a campaign itself, usually with a high degree of success.

WHO and UNICEF can act as catalysts and can supply technical knowledge in the effort to cure disease; but the resources of these agencies are limited, and it is therefore not possible for them to engage in extensive programs. Some within WHO have objected to the organization's engaging in *any* such campaigns. One opinion is that the organization should concentrate more on projects that will benefit *all* states *equally*. Those for continuing to undertake campaigns, even on a limited scale, point to the publicity these give to the organization as well as to the need. Most campaigns have been so successful that they have aroused an appreciative interest in WHO, and some members hope this kind of interest will lead to increased contributions.

Curing disease has now become an accepted function of international health organizations. In carrying out programs in this field, health organizations have moved from the concept of an organization in which states share, giving and receiving on a more or less equal basis, to one which views health needs as worldwide and calls on the richer states to help with the problems of the poorer.

Preventing the Outbreak of Disease

Just as has been necessary in control and cure, effective programs in preventing the outbreak of diseases—third strategy in the fight against disease—have had to wait until research has yielded data on causes. Only when the cause is known is it possible to think in terms of what can be done to stop the disease from taking hold.

International cooperation in this area has proved particularly effective. WHO has helped to facilitate the exchange of findings and has itself promoted research into widespread diseases about which little has been discovered through national efforts. WHO has given assistance to research centers such as the Tubercular Research Office in Denmark, and has arranged for researchers to study there when their country lacks the necessary laboratory facilities. Like methods for curing disease, methods for preventing disease which are costly or require innumerable sessions cannot be used by the poorer countries, so WHO has encouraged research into preventatives that are cheap and require only one or a few applications.

WHO, often in cooperation with UNICEF, has undertaken pilot projects and campaigns employing some of these preventatives—especially BCG for tuberculosis and DDT for malaria. In some cases, a method or formula that has proved effective against a disease in one area has no effect at all when employed in another. Thus, experimentation often needs to be an ongoing process.

The campaign against malaria has been one of WHO's biggest all-out programs in recent years.[15] At the 1955 meeting of the World Health Assembly, it was decided that the organization should put its efforts behind eradicating this disease in all parts of the world.

The first task was to get states interested in undertaking campaigns nationally, for the world organization does not have the means to do this itself; it can only assist and support national efforts. By 1964, almost all countries had begun comprehensive programs.[16]

In order to carry out a satisfactory program, experience has shown that it is

---

[15] For accounts of the malaria eradication program being undertaken by WHO see "Seventeenth World Health Association," *World Health Chronicle,* April, 1964, pp. 119–23; "The World of W.H.O. in 1963," *World Health Chronicle,* April, 1964, pp. 134–35; "Malaria Eradication in 1963," *World Health Chronicle,* June, 1964, pp. 199–216.

[16] Some states that had not yet undertaken these are Cuba, Haiti, Maldive Islands, and Algeria.

absolutely necessary to have trained personnel. WHO has helped establish malaria eradication training centers and has provided personnel for them. Today there are regional centers in Belgrade, Cairo, Jamaica, Maracay, São Paulo, Tala, Lagos, and Lomé. Besides these regional centers, WHO has provided experts for national training institutions—for example, in Turkey. In some cases—Morocco is an example—special advisory staffs have been attached to projects to train personnel on the spot.

The first step in a campaign is an extensive survey. Before any program gets underway, it is necessary to know what areas of the country are affected, how many people are sick with the disease, what vectors are carrying the disease. The world organization has helped countries make surveys by training nationals in the various centers, by sending experts to work with national units, and by providing materials—the result of research sponsored or supported by the organization and of experience gained in other areas.

The planning stage is crucial for a successful campaign. Again, the organization has been able to make this stage more effective. It now provides comprehensive instructions on the preparation of plans.

The actual campaign gets underway with a mass and thorough spraying of the area. In some countries, it was thought that this could be done without professional personnel. However, it has been found that engineers should be in charge of the operation, and the organization encourages states to employ them. WHO has also held seminars on geographic reconnaissance methods and has demonstrated the necessity for making and using good maps.

From 1959–61, WHO was concerned with the problems of spraying. The campaigns in some states were not so successful as had been hoped. A special sprayer evaluation unit was sent out to various regions of the world to carry out extensive field work on devices and improvements. The information gained from this unit has been disseminated by the organization, and states have been encouraged to use it.

The substance itself is extremely important in spraying, since that effective in one region may not work in another. WHO-supported research on insecticides also involves identification of strains and duration of invection.

WHO supplies a kit to show how much resistance malaria vectors have developed so that another insecticide may be used if there is strong resistance and further spraying with the first would be futile. To help states determine when their substance is no longer producing results, a special insecticides testing unit is sent out.

The spraying campaign is ended when inspection units determine that the area is free of vectors and, at the same time, examine the population. The WHO Expert Committee on Malaria has laid down standards for case detection and surveillance, and, through experimentation, has discovered what kinds of tests are most effective (and easiest) for determining the frequency of new cases as well as how often such tests should be given. Two extensive experiments on frequencies were carried out in India and Ceylon.

Along with eliminating vectors, states also treat people who have contracted the disease. WHO has supported research for inexpensive, easy, and quick ways to accomplish this.

A disease such as malaria cannot be treated completely as a national phenomenon to be eradicated by a program confined to one state. Vectors have to be eliminated on an area basis, and the area of breeding does not always coincide with national borders. Therefore, WHO has encouraged states to cooperate with one another and has supported a large number of regional meetings as well as conferences between states with common borders.

To interest the public, over 100 postal administrations took part in a philatelic campaign under the slogan: "The world united against malaria."

The worldwide attempt to eradicate malaria has resulted in an estimated drop in the number of cases from 250 million in 1955 to 140 million in 1962. The world organization has played an important part in this success. It is clear that the actual campaign has to be financed and carried on by national governments, but the world organization, through its research, support of training institutions, and provision of experts and opportunities to share experience, has been an important element. In the case of malaria, many could be persuaded to undertake campaigns when shown that they would be saving money. It has been estimated, for example, that the economic loss from the disease in Thailand alone runs around $15 million a year, whereas the campaign between 1954 and 1958 cost the country only $500,000.

Campaigns against malaria have proved especially successful. However, the need for a well-prepared and carefully executed program is particularly evident. It has been found that DDT loses its effectiveness, so unless the disease is completely eradicated during the effective period, malaria-carrying mosquitoes will build up an immunity to the insecticide. Careful planning can reduce this danger considerably, and WHO has been able to help countries make necessary preparations and carry out effective programs.

A Positive Definition of Health

As long as international cooperation is directed at disease—checking spread, curing, preventing outbreak—the objectives and goals can be defined with some clarity, and success can be measured in terms of reducing the incidence of disease. Although international cooperation has been able to aid in achieving this goal, and cooperative efforts today include the whole world, the job is far from completed. Much more needs to be done to develop effective programs in research and in poor areas. It is to be expected that WHO, UNICEF, and other international organizations will continue to help achieve these goals.

But the absence of disease is now only a part of WHO's goal. Health is now looked at positively, as a state of complete physical, mental, and social well-being. Responsibility for health is no longer confined to curing and preventing disease, but has expanded to include total environmental hygiene, mental health, education for good health habits, and many other objectives. The goal is to establish an environment that encourages and promotes good health, has people who practice good health habits, and provides adequate facilities for taking care of any difficulties and illnesses that arise.

In the attack on diseases, objectives can be defined and methods used can be determined by scientific data: if a fly carries the disease, then destroy the fly; if penicillin cures the disease, then use penicillin. No such easy determination of objectives and methods is possible when the goal is complete well-being. The range and extent of programs possible is multiplied to such an extent that setting priorities becomes a major problem. Is it more important to wipe out one disease; should more effort be made to educate the people in hygiene; should more hospitals be built; should more doctors and nurses be trained? All are valid programs, but the question is: What should be given priority; where should the limited funds available be channeled? There are no objective answers; opinions differ. Each state has to work out its own program.

What should be the role of the international organization in helping to realize the goal of physical, mental, and social well-being of all people everywhere? If national states—especially the less developed ones—are prevented from undertaking an inclusive and comprehensive program because they lack funds and personnel, what can the international organization do with its very restricted budget? This problem has led the organization to search for projects and programs particularly amenable to international action. This has meant a good deal of experimentation—and a good deal of disagreement among members. It is not possible here to outline all projects undertaken, but some of the more important types will be described briefly to show what kinds of projects are particularly adaptable to international action.

1. *Building national health administrations.* A national health agency is important for a state seeking to improve the health of its nationals. Especially in the less developed countries, initiative must come from the government, and most of the programs and projects are government sponsored. Strong incentives are needed to change centuries-old poor health habits. A health service must survey the health problems of the country, draw up and execute plans, and follow up on projects undertaken. Then, international organizations have an agency with which they can cooperate in the health field.

After the first World War, a number of states appealed to the League for help in setting up national health organizations. In 1929, the League assisted China by taking part in a survey of the country's health needs and drawing up proposals. It also helped states organize or reorganize special services within the national agencies, and WHO has continued to give this type of assistance.

2. *Training programs and facilities, seminars.* One object of international organizations in the nonpolitical field has been to spread resources to affect as many people as possible. One method has been through their educational programs, especially those designed to teach people who, in turn, will teach others.

The programs of international health organizations in this area have taken several forms. Conferences and seminars held from time to time permit health officials to exchange information and experience. This type of program is most successful in dealing with a specific widespread problem, especially where it is confined within one region.

Many states suffer from lack of trained personnel in the field of health. WHO and UNICEF have tried to help fill this gap by assisting in setting up training centers (some of which are servicing a region rather than one country). The international organization has usually helped in drawing up the plans for these centers, has supplied a part of the administrative and teaching staffs, and has sometimes offered fellowships for study abroad. The objective of the international organization is to get the institution started and functioning in such a manner that the state itself can eventually assume responsibility for the total operation.

Most new nations will have to look forward to many years during which the supply of trained personnel falls short of the needs of the country. One way to relieve this situation has been to adopt new standards and types of training. While a doctor, a registered nurse, or a technician requires years of education, such highly trained persons perform many jobs that could be carried out by less trained persons. Therefore, programs have been initiated to train for particular skills. Often, teams of such persons set up under fully trained supervisors are capable of servicing a large area. WHO has helped in developing programs of this nature as a direct response to the needs of many states.

3. *Pilot projects.* Pilot projects have proved especially suited for international action. They have been used to show national administrations how to carry out a specific program and have added to the reservoir of experience that the international organization is able to share with the world.

Pilot projects have been carried on by WHO in almost all aspects of its overall program—environmental hygiene, eradication of disease, control of disease, and others. The object of these programs is to involve local personnel as much as possible and to encourage them to go on with similar projects afterward.

4. *Environmental projects.* These projects have been undertaken often in cooperation with FAO. With the positive concept of health adopted in the

WHO Constitution, the attention of the international organization has been extended beyond the narrower concern with disease in the individual to the individual as a part of a total environment. A state of physical, mental, and social well-being requires a healthy environment. Projects have been undertaken in such fields as sanitation, nutrition, and hygiene education. As WHO itself cannot undertake a comprehensive program in any one country, most of its programs in this area have been pilot projects, seminars, and fellowships to help states develop their own projects.

5. *Studies, research, and dissemination of information.* As has been pointed out above, from the beginning of international health cooperation, organizations have been useful in facilitating the exchange of information and experience and in promoting research. This aspect has continued to develop.

The international organization has encouraged research into areas that for one reason or another have not been given adequate attention by national governments. Recently, a great deal of effort has been directed to ailments particularly prevalent in the newer nations. However, the organization has also attempted to promote research and cooperation in the health problems of the more advanced countries. In keeping with this objective, special attention has been paid to mental health, social casework, alcoholism, juvenile delinquency, the effects of radiation, and nutritional problems of affluent societies.

WHO has been able to devote little money of its own to these objectives, and has confined itself to encouraging specific research in national institutions, to providing fellowships, to publishing and disseminating findings, and to sponsoring conferences and seminars.

6. *Country surveys.* As mentioned, the health needs of the newer nations are enormous. States with a paucity of trained personnel are often unable to assess the extent of the needs, to develop an overall rational program, or to develop specific project plans. In the past, health projects often have been undertaken on the basis of ad hoc considerations, such as a particular administrator's desire to reduce a disease in his own home area or a factory's need for healthier workers. This kind of haphazard planning often leads to failures. As time passed, health administrators in some of these states became concerned with this situation. Wanting to make their programs more effective, they have turned to the world organization for help.

Responding to these demands, WHO has accepted into its program provisions for country surveys. Teams organized by WHO, often including personnel from FAO, UNICEF, and other organizations, in cooperation with indigenous health officials, survey the health needs of a country and help to work out priorities for effective long-range programming.

Such surveys and projected programs are a very complicated matter. To be taken into consideration are such factors as funds and personnel available, relationship of health projects to other developmental goals, and the needs of industry. Much still has to be learned; however, WHO has been making progress. One important aspect of this approach is its usefulness in helping to make outside assistance—national, international, private—more effective. In the past, agencies have initiated isolated programs that often have not been so successful as hoped. An overall plan into which these agencies can fit their projects has a better chance of success.

PROBLEMS OF INTERNATIONAL HEALTH COOPERATION

In common with almost all other international organizations, international health organizations are faced with the ever-persistent problem of lack of funds. Each year, WHO sees a slight budget increase, but it always falls far below what the organization would like to have. This problem was not so acute in the early days of international health cooperation. At that time, the objectives were narrowly defined and the mandates of the organizations limited. As pressures for expanding the functions of the organization have increased, the financial problem has become acute. WHO's very broad mandate, multiple functions, and responsibilities demand an enormous budget for effective fulfillment. However, the budget has not kept pace with the growing functions of, and demands on, the organization.

Lack of funds not only is a problem in itself but also gives rise to serious policy-making difficulties. Somehow, the limited resources have to be spread among the multitude of objectives set for the organization. Somehow, priorities have to be assigned to general areas of concern and, within these, to specific programs and projects. There is no scientific way to make such decisions, and so naturally there are numerous opinions on how and where WHO's money should be spent.[17] Many long hours are spent by the Secretariat and policy-making organs in trying to hammer out programs. Friction is often generated, and it is sometimes hard to reconcile all the different viewpoints and demands.

Attempts to work out a general overall policy for the organization have been made, involving attention to decisions on where international cooperation is most needed and can be most effective. Should the organization spend more time on encouraging research; should it devote more effort to building national health services, to setting up training centers; should it concentrate on eradicating certain widespread and particularly pernicious diseases; or just where should the organization concentrate its efforts?

There has been a tendency recently to move away from planning in terms

---

[17] The same applies to UNICEF and other agencies engaged in health programs. However, this section will concentrate on WHO as the leading organization in the health field.

of single projects toward trying to work out long-term programs. This approach runs into budgetary difficulties; WHO's funds are supplied on a yearly basis. However, the organization has been able to work out a system based on estimates that enables it to undertake some long-range planning.

Some Organizational Problems

WHO's constitution made provision for regional health organizations within the framework of the organization. This arrangement has presented the organization with a number of problems. The idea behind regions would seem to be a sound one: many problems affect one region more than others and therefore lend themselves to regional cooperation; regional offices provide a valuable link between individual countries and the central organizations. The regional offices were thought of primarily as a way to increase the effectiveness of the organization. The center would concentrate on building a fund of technical and scientific knowledge and a roster of available experts. The regions would make the assessments of conditions and needs.

Decentralization demands effective coordination. Unfortunately, this has not been easy to achieve. There has tended to be duplication of efforts. Regions have become jealous of their positions and have demanded more autonomy. WHO has tried to work out satisfactory arrangements, but the patterns adopted have not been wholly successful.

There are problems of coordination not only within WHO but also among the agencies interested in health and related fields. WHO has been involved in the search for means of bringing the Specialized Agencies and the United Nations into a better working relationship and of promoting cooperation with national and voluntary agencies. As WHO's concept of its own areas of responsibility has expanded, so has that of many other organizations. Thus today there is much overlapping, making cooperation among the organizations increasingly important. At the same time, it has been found that many projects undertaken as isolated units do not produce the desired results. An area needs a factory to produce farm equipment, but if the factory is to function efficiently it cannot rely on labor subject to recurring malarial attacks. Just to cure malarial patients will not be effective unless the cause of the disease can be wiped out. And so it goes on indefinitely. Today, the approach is more often in terms of total needs of the environment, thus demanding the cooperation of a large number of agencies—national, international, and voluntary.

WHO has been called on to fit its health programs for the newer nations into the general development programs, when these exist, and to cooperate with other agencies of the United Nations on a regular basis.

Functional or National Emphasis?

In the early years of international health work, states cooperated on a fairly equal basis. With the increase in new nations and the growing concern for development, new patterns of cooperation have emerged, and WHO, with other organizations, has been confronted with a problem of approach.

As a functional organization, part of WHO's mission is helping health officials in all countries to profit from cooperative endeavors, thereby promoting fulfillment of its objective of good health for everyone everywhere. The types of programs fitted to this approach are best accomplished by centralization—by an international organization to promote cooperation. On the other hand, the goal of good health can be reached also by helping each country to build its own effective program. If the limited funds available are to be put to the best possible use, building national health programs involves cooperation with several agencies within a particular country. If this road to world good health is to be followed, coordination and cooperation among various agencies at the national level will be important.

Thus, organizations that originally thought their task one of functional cooperation are now emphasizing cooperation with other agencies to promote development in single states. The split between supporters of the two approaches has caused problems within WHO. Both have been used, and this probably will continue to be so. The function of the Secretariat becomes a different one when the emphasis is on national programs. No longer is it to aid national administrations in their attempts to cooperate. Its main function becomes that of a depository of information, experience, and personnel that can be made available to those in need of assistance.

It is probable that this new approach will continue to be an important one in international health work until discrepancies in conditions around the world cease to be so great. These same discrepancies pressure the wealthier countries to aid their less fortunate neighbors.

However, participating in programs to develop countries has not diminished the need or rationale for continued purely functional cooperation, and many of WHO's programs are directed to this need. It is to be expected that as the newer nations develop their own national health administrations and accumulate experience, these will develop techniques and methods they can then share with some of the more advanced nations so that cooperation will become once again a mutual sharing. For instance, could not experiences in using semitrained personnel aid the United States in some areas that suffer from a perennial lack of fully-trained personnel?

Political Problems

No international health organization has been completely free from political problems. One of the first has been that of membership. Since health problems affect everyone, should not an international health organization be universal in membership? This would seem logical, but has never been so. From the period of the International Office of Public Health to the present, states have been excluded or have refused to participate for political reasons. Austria and Germany were piqued that Paris was chosen as the seat of the office, and for a while they refused to cooperate with the organization. States excluded from the U.N. are excluded from WHO: Red China and others have not been able to join; Spain became a member only after she had become acceptable in the United Nations. For almost ten years, Russia and the Eastern European states, although technically members, refused to co-operate.[18]

Although political differences and wars have tended to affect the attitudes of states toward international health organizations, there is one example of continued health cooperation in spite of political differences. Japan continued to work with the League Health Organization after she had withdrawn from the League itself.

Political, economic, social, and religious ideologies sometimes are a cause of friction within WHO. Population growth has been considered an appropriate area of activity for WHO. Suggesting remedies and solutions has, however, brought criticism from certain groups. For example, a report urging the use of contraceptives gave rise to criticisms from some religious groups. The subject of health insurance has involved the organization in debates on the merits of particular economic and political systems. These and other topics foster the temptation to use WHO as a platform for a particular system.

It is thus difficult for even a health organization to prevent politics and ideologies from intruding. WHO has been able to keep these at a minimum, but must always be on the lookout.

A particularly unpleasant problem has been that of organizing a regional office in the Mideast. WHO, in an attempt to get states in the area to rise above their political differences and to cooperate in the health field, made provision to include the Arab states and Israel in the same region. This move proved impossible to execute. Although Israel was willing, many of the Arab states refused. Finally, it was decided that the regional committee should be divided into two subcommittees: subcommittee A to consist of all Arab states and a few others; subcommittee B to contain Israel and other non-Arab members.[19]

GENERAL EVALUATION

International health cooperation has produced significant, positive results. Cooperation among states to solve specific problems when national action alone is insufficient has been effective. Thus, the spread of epidemics was

---

[18] Charles S. Ascher, "Current Problems in the World Health Organization's Program," *International Organization*, February, 1952, pp. 27–50.

[19] A similar difficulty has plagued other international organizations. For instance, in the International Civil Aviation Organization, Israel attends the European-Mediterranean region, and any communications between her and the Middle East region are taken care of through Paris.

controlled when states, recognizing the inadequacy of national action, agreed to develop an international system based on observance of mutual obligations and application of scientific findings. International standardization of substances has been accomplished through cooperation. Scientific knowledge has been advanced cooperatively by use of international organizations to collect and disseminate information. In these and other areas, the goals of international cooperation have been explicit and narrow, and the use of conventions and organizations has brought them close to fulfillment.

However, it is not always possible to use narrow goals to evaluate success. As the mandates of international health organizations have expanded, the goals have become increasingly removed from what can be attained in the near future. They embody an ideal condition. Even in the more advanced states, the ideal of complete physical, social, and mental well-being is far from realized; while in the less developed areas, only the most rudimentary steps have been taken. The extremely comprehensive and inclusive goals of WHO do not provide us at present with good criteria by which to judge the effectiveness of international cooperation and international health organizations.

WHO has definitely made a contribution. Given its broad mandate and its pitifully inadequate means, its successes are admirable. The broad mandate has caused the organization to search for types of programs particularly suited to an *international* organization. The search will continue, and as health conditions change, the types of programs will also change. While the developing areas' demands and needs have increased pressures on the organization to assign ever larger proportions of its resources to them, WHO has not lost sight of the more advanced nations' needs and of the importance of encouraging and sponsoring cooperation among them.

WHO itself still suffers from organizational problems. Many are related to its regional system and to the need for more coordination with other agencies. At present, much of the effort of many administrators is consumed in problems of coordination rather than in attacking substantive matters. WHO will continue to have problems, but it is expected that it will work out many of these and will be able to develop more efficient ways to encourage cooperation and undertake programs.

INTERNATIONAL CONTROL OF NARCOTICS

One health problem that never has been a part of the mainstream of international health efforts has been that of narcotics. Always handled separately and involving its own patterns of international cooperation, narcotics control has been one of the success stories. The struggle has not always been an easy one, nor is it possible today to write finis to the efforts. The attempts still go on, and so does the use of narcotics.

The impetus for international cooperation came from states that wanted to keep their own areas free from narcotics but were unable to do so on a unilateral basis. As world commerce expanded, so did the flow of drugs among areas. At mid-nineteenth century, there was not general agreement that this was an appropriate object for governmental control. In England, a vociferous group was horrified by the effects of narcotics and concerned about their ever increasing use. These forces campaigned successfully, and the topic became one of the great moral issues of the day. By the beginning of the twentieth century, public opinion in England and other Western states was urging governmental control and for international action. Thus, in 1919, began the attempt to control narcotics by international means.

The object of control has, from the beginning, been restriction of narcotics to scientific and medical purposes. The aim has not been to get rid of all narcotics—possibly an easier objective—but, rather, to prevent their being used by unauthorized persons This meant narcotics would continue to be produced and to enter international trade, but only for legitimate use.

The Problems

Restriction of narcotics has not been easy. Many of the drugs were being produced over a widespread area; many of the raw materials were growing wild in some parts of the world. Simple production methods for some drugs allowed factories to be established with little capital or apparatus.

In some states, drugs represented an important source of income, and whole districts found their livelihoods in growth and production of drugs—a condition that has existed down to the present. Some states were reluctant to deprive their people of this income source and even more unwilling to cut off the foreign exchange derived from export. It was not, therefore, in the interest of all states to bring these substances under control. Even after much of the traffic was internationally controlled, some states were refusing to cooperate since illicit trade brought even better profits than had legitimate trade.

States that did try to cooperate were not always successful in fulfilling their obligations. Production facilities are hard to detect, especially when shrewd promoters deliberately try to hide them. Where the raw material, such as cannabis, grows wild, the task is compounded.

Finally, there is the problem of universality. If only a few states agree to cooperate, the way is open for other states to take advantage of a lucrative market. To be totally successful, every state must participate in the system and be willing and able to carry out the provisions of the agreements—a goal that, unfortunately, has never been attained.

Approaches to a Problem

The system as it has evolved over the last half-century has involved two complementary parts: (1) conventions, which obligate states to limit and control narcotics; (2) international agencies, which have been established to supervise states but cannot operate without full cooperation from states.

Early efforts were confined to narrow objectives and did not involve international machinery. Even with these limited beginnings, states could see that the international approach was valid and of help to them in their own, at times purely selfish, attempts to curb narcotics in their territories—homeland and colony. As states gained confidence in the workability of an international approach, they became more willing to broaden the area assigned to international consideration, and so the system grew.

As states that undertook obligations lived up to them, there grew a confidence that helped prepare states to broaden their obligations. They could be fairly certain their partners in the system would abide by *their* commitments. This type of international trust is conducive to building on modest foundations. The establishment of international supervisory machinery fortifies this feeling of trust.

Methods of Control

The system as it has developed has made use of several methods of control.[20] The general, overall objective of control can be subdivided into three specific targets: (1) control of use; (2) control of traffic; (3) control of production and availability. Each of these will be examined to see what kind of system has been worked out as well as to try to assess its successes and note its difficulties.

Limitation on the Use of Narcotics. Since narcotics use takes place within states, it is within states that action must be initiated to restrict use. At the beginning of this century, some states began to nationally adopt provisions limiting the use of drugs, and were even willing to undertake *international* obligations to assure limitation. But it is easy for states to agree to commit themselves internationally to something they have already adopted in their own legal order, and often the practices of states went beyond anything they were willing to commit themselves to internationally.

The first international action was a conference in Shanghai in 1909. At this time, it was possible to pass only resolutions, not binding conventions, calling on governments to control the use of opium Three years later, in January, 1912, at an international conference in the Hague, the first convention was adopted. States agreed to control certain narcotics; a system of control was to be established by each state. The Hague Convention provided for progressive suppression of opium smoking; use of manufactured narcotics

---

[20] For a general treatment of control, see "Narcotic Drug Control," *International Conciliation,* May, 1948; Leland M. Goodrich, "New Trends in Narcotics Control," *International Conciliation,* November, 1960.

was to be limited to legitimate medicinal purposes, while their production, sale, and use were brought under a system of permits and registration.

States with possessions in the Far East became increasingly concerned by the extent of opium smoking and adopted more demanding obligations for the area. By a 1925 agreement, opium was to become a government monopoly. Even then, opium smoking was not to be completely stopped. It was to be restricted to a few divans, and the number of retail outlets was to be reduced. In 1931, minors were to be prohibited by law from smoking opium, and severe penalties were to be levied against persons inducing them to smoke. Although some states—notably China and the United States—pressed for an outright prohibition on opium smoking, most states were unwilling to go that far. Opium smoking continued to flourish in the Far East, increasing during the Japanese occupation when the Japanese encouraged it. The colonial powers became even more concerned, and most of them announced their intention to outlaw opium smoking at the end of the Japanese occupation. Gradually, all states in the area have adopted laws prohibiting the practice.

The Control of Traffic.   Trying to control narcotics by limiting their use to legitimate purposes is a difficult way to approach the problem. As long as it is permissible to grow raw materials and produce narcotics in unrestricted quantities, and as long as narcotics move freely from area to area, the task of implementing a ban on use is almost hopeless. National governments could and did initiate their own systems for control of production and manufacture and set limitations on imports of narcotics. Control of manufacture did not give rise to many difficult problems in most Western countries. Control of imports did. Most finished narcotics are used in very small dosages, which have over the years become increasingly expensive. The situation encouraged smuggling which, in turn, has led to the development of means to try to stop it. Here was a truly international situation, suited for cooperation. States were having difficulty in stopping drug importing, and wanted help from states that were exporting.

The first step taken was a 1912 agreement by which states were to prohibit export to countries trying to prohibit import. In Geneva in 1925, an international conference hammered out a system of import and export certificates by which they hoped to restrict narcotics trade to legitimate purposes. Under this system, an exporter may export substances covered by the agreement only if he has obtained authorization from his government, and this can be granted only after an import certificate is issued by the government of the importing country.

In order to strengthen this system, provision was made for establishment of an international agency to exercise certain supervisory functions. The Permanent Central Opium Board (PCOB) was to receive from participating states estimates (which were not binding) of amounts of narcotics they needed to import for legitimate purposes, along with statistics covering amounts of narcotics produced and manufactured and stocks on hand. Using this information, the PCOB could watch for excessive accumulations that might be diverted into the illicit traffic and could ask governments for explanations. If a state refused to offer a satisfactory explanation, the Board could call the situation to the attention of contracting states and recommend that no more narcotics be exported to that country until its stocks had been reduced legitimately. The system also covered noncontracting states for which the Board itself established estimates.

Through these provisions, states hoped to keep illicit narcotics out of international commerce. In 1931, the system was reinforced. Governments were to provide the PCOB not only with estimates of their import needs but also with estimates of their total needs, making it possible for the Board to fulfill its supervisory duties more effectively.

Nevertheless the illicit traffic continued. Thus a second line of attack was suggested—cooperation to apprehend and punish illegal traffickers. Here again the results were modest. During international narcotics conferences, suggestions to include provisions on traffickers were invariably met with sufficient opposition to prevent their adoption. Until 1936, international action consisted of recommending that states establish a single authority to supervise control of drugs, and of preparing a model code for administrative control of drug traffic (in 1932). It was agreed that trafficking in narcotics would be considered an extraditable offense; thus those states that ratified the instrument agreed they would send such criminals to countries possessing enough evidence to prosecute them. The convention also provided that the criminal law of all signatories should contain similar provisions for offenses involving narcotics, and it called for cooperation between police authorities of different countries in pursuit and prosecution of offenders. Unfortunately, only a few states ratified this convention.

Besides these attempts to secure binding commitments, international organizations have tried to persuade states to adopt a more severe approach toward traffickers. There have also been efforts—which have failed—to consider traffickers international criminals. Today, most countries have made participation in illicit traffic liable to severe penalties.

The International Police (INTERPOL) has given special attention to the problem of traffickers. Through its network of national offices, it has been able to help countries track down a great number of offenders, and its filing system has proved helpful to narcotic police officers.

The United Nations has assisted local police forces by helping to determine sources of drugs that find their way into illicit traffic. States are requested to send samples of drugs produced in their areas to the United Nations Narcotics Laboratory (established by a General Assembly resolution in 1954). When a state discovers illegal narcotics, it is requested to send a sample to the laboratory, where it is compared with the national samples. If it corresponds to one of these, the country from which the illicit drug has come is notified so that it can take proper measures.

Limitations on Production and Manufacture.   Control of the use and traffic of narcotics has been helpful in the effort to stamp out narcotics, but a third approach has strengthened the system—control of production and manufacture. As long as there is no control over production, attempts to eliminate illegal traffic will be impossible, since sizable quantities are bound to find their way into illegal trade.

The approach has involved conventions obligating states to certain action and international supervisory machinery. One problem in developing an effective system has been that of deciding whether to use quotas or estimates, or to institute an international monopoly. It has been suggested that the needs of the world be assessed and the quantity necessary divided among manufacturing countries. This was unacceptable to most states. Others have proposed establishment of an international monopoly of certain drugs. A number of the key producing countries supported this proposal; however, some of the major consumers, among them the U.S., killed it. The consuming countries objected to international pricing which the producers insisted was necessary to assure adequate returns to them. It seemed that the only kind of a system acceptable to a worthwhile number of states was one based on the use of estimates. After several years of preparatory work, a convention was adopted in 1931, embodying a system of elimination by estimate and establishing a new international drug body—the Drug Supervisory Body (DSB).

Each party reports estimates of its total needs for the drugs covered and the amounts it has in stock. The DSB studies these estimates, making recommendations to governments whose estimates are considered excessive and drawing up estimates for those states that fail to submit their own. On the basis of these estimates, the Body issues a statement of the world's requirements for narcotic drugs.

A licensing system set up for a number of drugs is to be applied nationally to all persons manufacturing, importing, selling and distributing, or exporting. Furthermore, the convention prohibits the export of several drugs in amounts exceeding 5 kilograms to states not ratifying the 1925 or 1931 conventions (setting up the import–export license system).

The system established by the 1931 convention supplements the earlier agreement on traffic, so controls were now applied to all stages between manufacture and ultimate consumption.

However, the system suffers from two important shortcomings: it does not cover all narcotic drugs and does not include all states; among the nonratifying countries have been some major producers. Moreover, the system was unable to withstand the Second World War. In part, responsibility for the breakdown must be attributed to Japanese and German policies of promoting the use of drugs in some areas and of encouraging smuggling. Fortunately, it was possible to reestablish the system soon after the end of hostilities.

Tightening up the System.   Soon after the United Nations was established, it took over responsibility for narcotics control.[21] The Permanent Central Opium Board and the Drug Supervisory Body continued to function. Their members are now chosen by the U.N. and WHO. The Commission on Narcotic Drugs, a functional commission of ECOSOC, was established to study the general status of narcotics control in all countries. This Commission decides what improvements are necessary and prepares new measures for this purpose. It also affords an international forum where any government whose control is inadequate may be publicly called to account. One of the Commission's major concerns has been the attempt to plug up the loopholes in the system.

The fact that not all drugs are covered by the system is a constant source of concern. Provision was made in both the 1925 and 1931 conventions to cover certain types of new drugs, especially new derivatives of substances already covered in those conventions. Nowhere was there provision for the new synthetic drugs with narcotic effects which were coming out of laboratories. By a protocol of 1948, a system for bringing these under international control was established. The protocol authorizes WHO to place under control any new drug, including synthetics, that could not be controlled by provisions of earlier conventions and were found to be either addiction-producing or convertible into an addiction-producing drug.

Another problem has been that of the widespread opium trade. Since the poppy grows wild in many parts of the world and is easy to cultivate, the most effective system of control would be to restrict growing. Attempts to bring growing under international control have usually met with strong resistance. In order to eliminate the trade, a protocol of March, 1953, called for the licensing of poppy farmers in opium-producing countries. This protocol came into force in 1963. Its provisions are now included in the Single Draft Convention.

The number of conventions has also given rise to problems. The early conventions applied only to those states ratifying the instrument. This situation has led to a rather chaotic condition: some states have accepted all; others are parties only to some. Many have felt there was no need for two supervisory bodies; one could operate the system. This could not be done without a new convention, since some states were parties to conventions empowering one body but not to conventions covering the other body. Further, the various regimes applied to specifically enumerated drugs. As some conventions involve stricter control than others for the drugs covered, this has meant that

---

[21] For a good survey of the United Nations and narcotics control, see J. F. Mabileau, "The Fight against Narcotics," *United Nations Review,* February, 1964, pp. 29–34.

some drugs were more controlled than others. Out of concern for this situation came the idea for consolidating existing agreements and the suggestion for the Single Convention on Narcotic Drugs.[22]

The Commission on Narcotic Drugs did the preliminary work on the Convention, preparing three drafts, sending these out to governments for their comments, and revising in light of these comments. In 1961, an international conference was called to draw up the final draft of the convention.[23]

The Single Convention, which came into force in October, 1962, includes with few exceptions the provisions of all previous agreements, and in some areas advances beyond these in an attempt to tighten up the system. Whereas it had been impossible to persuade states to limit production, a first step has been made: only those states already exporting opium may continue to do so. Any state wanting to enter the trade must get permission from ECOSOC. Until this time, anyone could produce and export as long as he abided by the licensing regulations outlined above. This provision is an attempt, albeit small, to keep out new producers.

All narcotics are now to come under international control, and use of many of these for other than scientific and medicinal purposes is explicitly prohibited. The system of a national licensing and recording regime extends to all drugs, not just those manufactured, as previously, and covers the cultivation of most narcotics.

One body has been established and given competence to level an embargo on exports from, as well as imports to, states that have more narcotics on hand than considered necessary and where there is the possibility of diversion into illicit trade. Previously, the PCOB was restricted to recommending an embargo only on imports.

Much research in drugs has been done over the past years, and many new types have been discovered. Many of these new drugs are non-habit-forming, but, unfortunately, none are so effective as some of the habit-forming ones. The conference to draft the convention passed a recommendation urging states to prohibit the use of particularly dangerous drugs if substitutes were available to accomplish the same purpose.

The Single Convention goes far toward eliminating loopholes in the system and providing for more effective control of narcotics. One limitation, as mentioned above, has been the lack of universality. The same problem now faced drafters of the Single Convention. Import requirements of nonparties were estimated and the parties were obligated not to ship narcotics above

---

[22] In other fields—for example, refugees—where they have been several agreements, the U.N. has instigated efforts to combine the commitments where possible into a single convention.

[23] For an analysis of the Single Convention see Adolf Lande, "The Single Convention on Narcotic Drugs," *International Organization*, Autumn, 1962, pp. 776–98.

these levels. There was pressure at the drafting conference to extend the provisions of the new convention in a similar manner. Russia and the Eastern European states objected violently. They felt that no system should be imposed on states that had not been invited to attend the conference or permitted to become a party to the convention (i.e., Communist China). A compromise was reached by permitting a reservation to the section extending the system to states not permitted to become parties.

New Problems and Approaches

In the past, it has been assumed that states undertaking obligations in international conventions will carry them out. Breaking or not living up to international commitments has been considered a willful and usually reprehensible act. So it has been with narcotics agreements.

This type of thinking might have been applicable when most agreements were concluded between states of similar development and orientation or when one state had the means of forcing another to abide by provisions. In recent years, there has had to be a rethinking of this position. Today, international conventions are being entered into by an ever-increasing number of states—states in various stages of development and with different political, economic, and social systems. This has two results. First, interpretations of individual provisions often differ; second, states are not always capable of carrying out commitments they undertake. The first result has not caused trouble in narcotics agreements, but the second has.

The system established for narcotics relies on each state to set up machinery adequate to the task of control within its own territory. This may not always be possible. Some states lack administrative machinery and adequate police forces trained in narcotics work. Some states may want to see illegal traffic reduced but may not know how to cope with large numbers of farmers who rely for their livelihoods on growing the raw material. Or a state may want to wipe out addiction but may have no means or personnel to handle the task of rehabilitation. These and other problems have confronted states that are parties to conventions and sincerely want to abide by their commitments.

It has been found that pointing an accusatory finger at the recalcitrant state may not bring about change. Sometimes, it produces a negative reaction; no one likes to be condemned for something he feels he cannot help. The United Nations and other international organizations have become concerned with this situation and have searched for ways to help.

The Narcotics Drug Commission has prodded states that have not been living up to their obligations under narcotics agreements.[24] A part of technical assistance funds has been earmarked for narcotics assistance since

[24] See Leland M. Goodrich, "New Trends in Narcotics Control," *International Conciliation*, No. 530 (November, 1960), pp. 227–38.

1960. States are reluctant to request help in this area; their development problems are so great that they are apt to consider narcotics control a minor issue, far down on their list of priorities. To encourage states to seek help in narcotics, it was decided that a special portion of the technical assistance budget be allotted for this purpose, and that it be nontransferable.

The principle behind narcotics technical assistance is the same as that behind all international technical assistance programs. The United Nations cannot force any state to take assistance, even when a government's inability to take action leads to increased traffic in narcotics, thus affecting many other states. However, by setting up the program, the United Nations stands ready with its facilities to help any government that applies to it.

The assistance provided has fallen into three categories: experts, fellowships for training abroad, and regional projects (seminars, consultative groups, etc.). Although at first there was little interest in applying for this assistance, requests have increased, and the organization has been able to help a number of countries. Some projects have been undertaken in cooperation with Specialized Agencies—WHO (care and treatment of addicts), FAO (development of crops to replace narcotics raw materials). The International Police Organization has cooperated with the United Nations in a seminar for enforcement officers.

The United Nations has also been concerned with special regional problems. It has been recognized that programs within one country will not always produce the results required unless action is also taken in neighboring countries. Therefore, ECOSOC has passed resolutions calling for cooperation within regions plagued by especially difficult problems, and intercountry projects for technical assistance have been encouraged. In line with this policy, a survey team sent to the Mideast was able to help delineate the problems and to suggest ways by which national governments could cope with them more effectively within their states and in cooperation with their neighbors.

General Evaluation

Over the years since the beginning of this century, a workable system for narcotics control has evolved. Within their own territories, governments have agreed to develop effective control systems. Many states go beyond the agreements in their own practices, but the instruments do represent a basic minimum required for effective world regulation. States also agree to provide an international agency with statistics on their needs, production, and stocks of narcotics to enable this body to carry out supervisory responsibilities. This body has no way of checking the figures, no competence to investigate for itself, nor any way to force states to comply, i.e., the system functions on the principle of voluntarism.

Why does it work? Primarily because the governments of most states have been convinced of the harm of narcotics addiction in terms of drain on manpower and economic losses, and they want to wipe out nonlegitimate uses of drugs. To do this on a unilateral basis has proved extremely difficult; only through worldwide cooperation will the ultimate goal of restriction to scientific and medical purposes be attained. It is therefore in the self-interest of states to cooperate.

But there is still illicit use of narcotics, in some areas increasing rather than decreasing. The system, then, as it is presently functioning, is not 100 percent perfect. One of the most difficult problems is that of mainland China. As long as that state is barred from membership in the system and continues to be a source of much narcotic substance in illicit traffic, difficulties will continue.

This situation can be helped by increasing penalties in areas where dope trafficking is not considered a major crime and by increasing cooperation among enforcement personnel. In both these areas, the Single Convention is not adequate. Some states were unwilling to include comprehensive provisions in the Convention. Continued assistance to countries unable to develop their own effective control systems will help.

There are, however, other problems. New drugs are being discovered all the time. Research results will probably have both a positive and negative effect on addiction: positive in that non-habit-forming drugs that can replace the more harmful ones now used may be discovered; negative in that harmful drugs requiring easily available components and simple preparation may also be discovered. This negative effect will present what appears today to be an almost insurmountable problem.

The problem of rehabilitating the addict needs further attention. In some areas, he is treated as a common criminal, in others as a person suffering from psychological and social problems. Provisions in laws of states reflect this difference. Rehabilitation will continue to be handled within states, but cooperation in research projects and sharing experiences could lead to improved methods.

Although the record of narcotics control is not perfect, much has been accomplished through international cooperation, and it is safe to predict that continued cooperation will lead to more improvements.

Chapter 17

Engineering Social Development

The right of the state to maintain social order and to guide social change within its political boundaries is at the core of domestic jurisdiction. Indeed, throughout the centuries, states have jealously guarded these exclusive prerogatives. Only slowly and cautiously did they concede international responsibility in these areas. Gradually they did concede it nevertheless.

As a matter of fact, recognition of international responsibility for social development has emerged as the result of a peculiar admixture of humanitarian ideals and commercial interests. To be sure, humanitarian ideals provided the initial impetus. Slavery and slave trade were identified as social diseases triggering a campaign in Western Europe, especially Great Britain, for their prohibition. When national legislation was assured it was followed by demands for action on the international scale. In 1841 an international treaty was signed at London by Britain, France, Prussia, Russia, and Austria in which these governments pledged to prevent their subjects from engaging in slave trade. In the following year the Webster-Ashburton Treaty provided for the policing of the West African coast by joint British-American naval squadrons.

Meanwhile the idea of social ills itself had undergone some expansion. Gradually it was extended to cover exploitation of women and children and the abuse of workers. The campaign to implement a program of minimum standards through national legislation, however, faced a more general and certainly a more determined opposition. Merchants and businessmen were reluctant to adopt such standards. They feared that increased expense on safety, health or other welfare benefits for the workers would price them out of the market. They were willing to consider such standards only if they became mandatory for all producers in the market which was by now rapidly expanding from the local to the national and then to the international scale.

Consider the following illustration from United States' history. White phosphorus, used in the manufacture of matches, had harmful effects on the health of the workers. When this was realized a number of state legislatures introduced bills setting minimum safety standards. They met with obstinate opposition. Introducing such measures, it was argued, would involve added expenses which might put the manufacturers to an unfair disadvantage in interstate trade, and in the end, might drive the industry out of any state. These arguments were persuasive and the bills lost. The proponents of minimum standards sought national legislation. Again the argument of competition was presented; this time the anti-bill forces argued that the American industry would not be able to compete in the international market. Again, legislative action was blocked.

Sympathy for the working man—and especially for women and children —was nevertheless expanding. At first interest came from educated people, economists, and professional men. Blocked in domestic political processes, they turned to international cooperation for a remedy. In 1900 the International Association for Labour Legislation was formed. This organization supported studies and passed resolutions calling on states to take action and remedy some of the worst conditions, among these the lack of safeguards in the match industry. Although it had no power of binding or compelling states, its pioneering brought visible results. Official conferences were called; conventions were drawn up, adopted, and sent to the states for approval and ratification. The Association stimulated the following three-step process: (1) groundwork done by "experts"—examining problems, suggesting possible conventions, drawing up careful agenda; (2) conference of "diplomats"—recognized government representatives—at which conventions were adopted; (3) ratification and implementation by individual states.

These were meager beginnings—but they were a start. Then followed World War I, the rapid expansion of the international workers' movement, and above all international organizations dedicated to the realization of minimum standards throughout the world.

INTERNATIONAL LABOR ORGANIZATION[1]

A New Idea

During the years before the first world war, labor movements and organizations, while putting most of their effort into pressuring industry and

[1] The social welfare activities of international organizations are very diffuse. Except for the ILO, these have been spread out among a number of agencies and have often been little

national governments for changes beneficial to the worker, were at the same time conscious of being part of a worldwide movement that was, to be sure, at first confined to the Western world. Many labor leaders knew one another. From these leaders came an idea—an international labor organization devoted to improving working conditions throughout the world. By the end of the first world war, labor's importance in many Western states made it impossible to disregard its voice. When the statesmen met at Versailles to discuss the new world organization, labor was there, prepared to put pressure on the diplomats.[2] It was ready with arguments as to why there should be an international labor organization. The difficulty of raising standards nationally was stressed, and it was pointed out that by raising the standards, particularly by increasing wages, purchasing power would increase. This, in turn, would encourage the expansion of trade, and so, it was argued, the whole world would benefit. But there were those who did not go along with labor's point of view. These were worried that only some states would accept the obligations to improve conditions, and these states would then be at a disadvantage in world trading. Those who objected to most national labor and social legislation also objected to any attempt to do the same thing internationally, deploring such measures as leading to increased government interference into an area in which it had no business. Others objected that conditions throughout the world varied so much that it would be unrealistic to attempt to set standards on a world basis.

Although there was strong opposition to the idea of an international labor organization, some of the statesmen at Versailles supported labor. Not only the fact that the labor leaders were there with plans but also fear of the power of labor were important determinants. The war over, workingmen throughout Europe were demonstrating and striking. The more radical, rejoicing in the victory of the Bolsheviks in Russia, were convinced that it was only a matter of a short time before the whole capitalist structure would be overthrown. These conditions influenced some of the statesmen. The demands of labor could not be easily tossed aside. Concessions would have to be made nationally and internationally if the more leftist of labor factions were to be kept from gaining control of labor movements.

Thus, the first independent international organization concerned with

---

more than halfhearted attempts to do something about social conditions. Today, there is great need for effective international cooperation in this area if the aspirations of the peoples of the world are to be realized. The ILO has been a successful organization which has done a great deal of experimenting in the area of international legislation for improved social and labor conditions and in other approaches to this end. For this reason, this section will devote a large amount of space to the ILO and what might be called the ILO approach. It is believed that a great deal can be gained from this kind of intensive analysis of one organization.

[2] For an account of pressures which labor exerted on the conference at Versailles, see E. J. Phelan, *Yes and Albert Thomas* (New York: Columbia University Press, 1949).

social standards was established at Versailles. Although the International Labor Organization (ILO) was to cooperate with the League, it was to be an independent organization. But ILO was to be more than just another international organization: in its organization and in its approach, it was to be a pioneer.

The Tripartite System

Some labor leaders had been thinking in terms of an international labor union, an organization consisting of representatives of labor; others envisaged an organization similar to traditional ones—delegates to be government representatives, usually with the idea that labor would be given a place on the delegation in an advisory capacity, but voting to be by states. Within the British civil service, an idea was taking shape that represented a new concept:[3] labor and social standards should be the concern of three groups— employers, employees, and governments—so it would be advantageous if all three groups participated in the process of setting international standards. And thus the ILO tripartite organizational arrangement was conceived.

Like most international organizations, ILO follows the conference pattern in its organization: the Annual Conference to which all states send delegates and which formulates general policy; the Governing Body, a smaller group to direct the work of the organization and to supervise the secretariat; and finally the secretariat itself, the International Labor Office.[4] In the two policy-making organs, the principle of tripartism was to apply. Each four-member delegation to the Annual Conference was to be composed of two government representatives, along with one worker and one employer. The Governing Body was to have twelve government delegates, plus six employer's and six worker's delegates. Tripartism has also applied in most committees set up by the organization to deal with specific problems and in most special conferences called by the organization.

In this way, the three groups were to be separately represented. Since the interests of labor and management were thought to be independent of one another and of government, the system was considered to be a reflection of the existing situation in the Western capitalist countries. Government was to have the largest representation, as governments were ultimately responsible for enforcing legislation and, therefore, should not be in a position to be outvoted by the other groups.

Not only was the system thought to be reflective of conditions, but was also adopted as a means to make the work of the organization more effective. If labor and management, it was argued, were brought into the process of "legislating," they would be more apt to be interested in seeing that the

[3] Bernard Beguin, "I.L.O. and the Tripartite System," *International Conciliation*, May, 1959, pp. 408–13.

[4] For a clear description of tripartism, see *ibid.*

conventions adopted by the organization were ratified nationally. They would put pressure on their own governments and would in their bargaining with each other work to achieve this end.

The tripartite formula has not always been easy to apply. One of the problems is the choice of representatives from labor and management: Who should represent these groups? It was left up to national governments to designate the organizations most representative of these groups, while the ILO reserved the right to pass on the individuals selected. Where there is a single large national organization, the solution is simple. However, where there are a number of organizations, there are apt to be problems. In the United States, the existence of two large labor unions—the Council of Industrial Organizations and the American Federation of Labor—presented a problem. The solution was to have these groups alternate in designating the U.S. labor representative. For the employer group, it was decided that the same system should apply: the National Association of Manufacturers and the National Chamber of Commerce were to alternate. When the NAM refused to appoint anyone, the National Chamber of Commerce remained the representative of U.S. employers.[5]

The formula seemed a valid one for Western states in the early postwar years. In these countries, labor and employers were independent of their governments, and their cooperation was necessary if labor standards were to be improved. But the liberal capitalist system was losing ground in some areas of the world. At first, Socialist Russia did not seek membership in the ILO, and thus the organization was spared a decision on the validity of tripartite representation from there until the mid-1930's.

The "corporate state"[6] was the first to present the organization with a serious problem: Could the corporation be considered truly representative of the workers? These were not independent, but were, rather, government controlled. The individual worker had no choice; he had to be a member of the corporation. Should the corporate state, then, be accepted? The Credentials Committee voted to accept the credentials of the worker representative from Italy. Most of the other worker delegates were adamantly opposed to this action, to the very idea that the Italian workers' delegate be permitted to participate in the work of the organization. Although outvoted in the Credentials Committee, they were able to keep the Italian workers' delegate from participating in the conference committees. These committees were set up on the basis of tripartism, with each (government, worker, and em-

---

[5] *Ibid.,* pp. 419–26.

[6] The corporate state was the system espoused by the Italian Fascists, and later—less stressed, however—by Nazi Germany. The idea was that economic policy was to be made by national councils or "corporations," consisting of representatives of labor and management. The system was only imperfectly realized, as it was actually the government which dictated policy in both states.

ployer) conference group's electing its own members to participate. This system provided the workers' delegates an opportunity to exclude the Italians, and they did so.

The next objection came from the employers' group. Russia joined the organization. The credentials of Russian delegates were challenged. This time, it was the employers who put up opposition: In a Socialist state there are no independent employers, these being functionaries of the state entrusted with *administering* businesses for the state under the direction of the government. The debate over Russia has continued down to the present, but has become even more crucial over the years. In 1935, Russia was still only one state—the only Socialist state. Since then, the number of Socialist states has increased. Not only states with almost complete nationalization of industry and business on the Soviet pattern, but other countries in which part of the economy is nationalized, have been joining ILO. Even in states still claiming to have free enterprise systems, the control of government over almost every phase of the economy has been increasing.

The liberal model on which the ILO originally based its tripartite system has now disappeared. This situation has involved the organization in an ongoing debate as well as in the search for an organizational pattern acceptable to all states and reflecting conditions as they now exist. The views of various delegates have been varied. There have been suggestions that the tripartite system, since it no longer conforms to the government-labor-management relationship, should be abandoned; there have been suggestions that the ratio (2–1–1) be altered—some suggesting that governments be given an increased number of representatives. But no suggestion has commanded a majority large enough to secure an amendment to the Constitution. As a result, the old ratio is still used. To each suggested change, opposition has been vehement, often coupled with threats to leave the organization should it be adopted.

Moderation, in the form of maintaining the original formula, has prevailed not so much because the majority of delegates have believed this formula to be the best, but because the majority of delegates has felt that the organization should be maintained and that it can be most effective as a universal organization, i.e., one composed of representatives of all economic and social systems and not just of particular systems.

This has been the position of most government and worker delegates, but the employers continue to work for expulsion of employer delegates from Socialist states. In this situation, to keep Socialist employer delegates out of the ILO committees the employers have tried to apply the same procedure the worker group used in the case of the Italian workers. The employers have not, however, been completely successful. A system that secures at least some representation to Socialist employers has been worked out and is supported by the government and worker groups. All delegates desiring to participate in conference committees may enter their names on a list and attend the meetings, each group to decide which of the delegates will be permitted to vote. Any delegate who feels he has been wrongly excluded by his group may appeal to a special conference board which can increase the voting delegates of any committee by two. Thus, there is now the possibility, realized in almost all cases, for Socialist employer delegates to participate on conference committees. The solution is a compromise and avoids direct confrontation of the issue.

The question as to whether tripartism is still a valid principle remains. A factor which also bears on this problem is the change in the function of ILO. In 1917, those who adopted tripartism were considering the applicability of this system to the international standard-setting process. ILO's primary task was to work out minimum social and labor standards for the world. In order to promote this, it was thought helpful to have represented those national elements actually involved in the process. These were the days when many of the gains for workers were obtained in direct negotiations of labor and management. Today, in most of the world, standards are to a large extent initiated by governments, and, therefore, the importance of having the two other groups represented can be questioned. Moreover, standard-setting is no longer the primary concern of ILO. Today, much of ILO's effort is directed toward assistance to the less developed areas as these struggle to industrialize and modernize. In these areas, ILO has conceived its task as not merely to concentrate on working conditions but to provide assistance in the actual techniques of industry. Hours of work and safe working conditions are still considered important, but so are the methods of production, the skills of management, and the training of workers. When these new concerns are taken into consideration, tripartism is again a useful system. The problems of operating a plant are similar whether it is in a welfare-capitalist system or in a Socialist system.

Although the desire to exclude nonindependent workers' and employers' groups still finds expression within some delegations, newer emphasis on the production process and recognition that even in so-called capitalist systems these groups are no longer so independent of government influence and control as formerly has tended to reduce the vehemence of the argument.

INTERNATIONAL LABOR LEGISLATION

Once the principle of tripartism was accepted, there arose another problem for which the British civil service once again provided a novel solution.[7] The usual prewar procedure for international conventions had been used in "legislating" international labor standards. First an international meeting of concerned individuals studied a problem. When it decided there was a

---

[7] B. Beguin, *op. cit.*, p. 411.

definite need for a convention and that it would be possible to obtain consent from most states, a conference of plenipotentiaries was called to draw up the actual convention to be submitted to states. The ILO General Conference was not the same as a normal conference of plenipotentiaries, and the question arose as to whether it could perform the same function as a conference of governmental representatives. If it could not, would it be necessary that any draft convention agreed on by the General Conference be submitted to and adopted by a special conference before it could be submitted to states for ratification? If this approach were adopted, ILO would become little more than a drafting organization.

To solve the problem, a new approach was adopted. The General Conference accepted the principle that unanimity was not necessary. Measures that received a two-thirds majority would be considered adopted by the organization. Governments, in accepting the ILO Constitution, agreed to submit these measures passed by the Conference to their national parliaments for adoption. Thus, the customary system of convention-making was upset. Instead of the usual adoption by unanimous vote, signature of plenipotentiaries, and ratification by sovereigns, the system involved adoption by the General Conference and submission to parliaments where, it was hoped, the conventions would be adopted as part of the legal system of each state.

Although the goal is to draft conventions, the delegates to the Conference, while recognizing the desirability of international action on a specific problem, have sometimes not been willing to put provisions into convention form. The organization is provided with alternatives to take care of this: the Conference can adopt recommendations or resolutions embodying the standard but not involving the same responsibilities on the part of members as does a convention.

The Process of Drafting—the ILO Method[8]

The ILO was a response to demands for higher standards for workers. As conceived, its original function was development of an international labor code that would cover all aspects of labor—wages, hours, periods of rest, apprenticeship, health and safety, and others. The idea was revolutionary: an international organization to set standards in an area that could be considered within the domestic jurisdiction by almost any criteria.

The organization regarded its task, i.e., the development of an international labor code, as a long-term project, to be built up by piecemeal drafting. Over the years, the ILO has developed a procedure for drafting, and the

[8] For a detailed description and analysis of the drafting process, see: Minta Chou Wang, "The Development of I.L.O. Procedures for Making and Implementing International Labor Conventions between 1945 and 1957" (dissertation, Columbia University, New York). International Labour Office, *The International Labour Code, 1951* (Geneva, 1952), Vol. I, Code, preface.

procedure has been followed for almost all its conventions. The problem has been to draft conventions acceptable to the largest number of states possible without setting the standards so low that there is virtually no benefit to having an international standard. If the standards of the country with the lowest existing standard were accepted, the convention would be no more than an affirmation of existing circumstances and would not represent any improvement on the world level. The objective is to find minimum standards acceptable to many states without setting them too low.

The organization starts with a problem. The problem may come from the secretariat, one of the committees of the ILO, its General Conference, or Governing Body. The problem is usually a very narrow one. It has been difficult, for example, to draft a general minimum hours convention, but it has been possible to set minimum hours for women, children, and for workers in specific industries.

The first step is that of research. Once a problem is suggested, it is important to find out the extent of the problem and conditions in the various states. The secretariat relies on questionnaires to member states and on statistics for compiling this information. Thus, for example, if the organization is concerned with setting maximum hours for coal miners, it will attempt to find out how many hours coal miners are working in each of the member states. States will also be requested to give their opinions as to whether the problem suggested is one for which an international convention would be helpful and useful and, if so, to indicate what they think should be covered by the convention.

Once the information has been gathered and analyzed, a draft convention is drawn up. Most of the drafting takes place within the secretariat, although, sometimes, drafting will be done by special conferences—such as the Maritime Conference. The drafting is actually a long process. The original draft has tried to incorporate many of the suggestions submitted by individual states, but having to take into account the views of many states has resulted in a draft of compromises—compromises decided on by the drafting group within the secretariat or committee. So, the draft is once again sent out to the states to get their opinions. Again, the responses are analyzed and the draft changed to incorporate what seems to be desired by most states. The new draft is again sent out to the states. This final draft is the one that will be considered by the General Conference, and so the secretariat tries to get it to the states far enough in advance of the meeting to give them time for careful consideration.

From the very beginning, when Albert Thomas was Director of ILO, special attention has been given to preparations for the General Conference[9] M. Thomas insisted that the agenda be carefully worked out and that

---

[9] For a vivid and lively account of preparations, see Phelan, *op. cit.*, pp. 71–104.

all documents be prepared and organized in such a way that they were useful to the delegates. This careful attention to the conference has helped ILO to expedite its business and, very important, has helped the delegates to come away with the feeling that they have accomplished something. In some organizations, conferences have been poorly prepared. As a consequence, much time has been devoted to organizational questions, and they end in confusion. As a result, many delegates complain that their time has been wasted.[10] M. Thomas was determined that this would not happen in an ILO General Conference.

For M. Thomas, the primary responsibility of the General Conference was to adopt conventions. Since the body was too large to engage successfully in long debate or to draft its own conventions, the secretariat was to draft the convention in such a way as to present the Conference with a number of alternatives from which it could choose. Where the replies of government indicated difference, alternate articles would be drawn up. Thus, the Conference would have only to choose between alternatives and would not have to engage in new drafting if it disagreed with a particular provision of the convention.

When the secretariat, in analyzing the comments of governments, comes to the conclusion that states may not be willing to embody the standards in a convention, a resolution or recommendation is drawn up to present to the General Conference. Sometimes, the Conference is presented with drafts in two or three forms from which it can choose. In recent years, there has been a tendency to make more use of recommendations and resolutions than conventions.

This procedure attempts to accomplish two things. First, it seeks to find formulas acceptable to the largest number of states possible. This is done by consulting the opinions of governments at every stage in the process. Unfortunately, the number of replies to questionnaires received is often small, which means the drafters often have to use their own judgement in deciding what will be acceptable to states. Second, the procedure is designed to permit the Conference to act, i.e., to minimize the amount of debate and drafting. Some delegates have voiced dissatisfaction at the amount of time required between the time a problem is considered one for the Organization to work on and the time the actual instrument is voted on. The procedure *is* a lengthy one; time has to be given to states to reply to the questionnaires. However, most agree that the length of time is helpful in that it permits governments sufficient opportunity to study the measures and to formulate their own opinions. When the delegates arrive at the Conference, they are not

---

[10] See Charles S. Ascher, *Program-Making in Unesco* (Chicago: Public Administration Service, 1957), pp. 30–34. This account also indicates the importance of such things as good translation service, and comfortable rooms.

faced with proposals they are unprepared to handle—unless, of course, they have not studied the communications from the secretariat.

New Approaches

ILO was the creation of Western leaders, and the convention technique was patterned on the experience of the prewar period. It was assumed that a state in adopting conventions accepted an international commitment within its power to fulfill. If a state did not live up to a commitment it was because, for some reason, it chose not to. This was a natural assumption, since the prewar international conventions contained standards already in force within most of the states that were parties to the instrument. It was thus natural to assume that states were capable of living up to their international commitments. Even when ILO drafted conventions embodying standards above those in effect nationally, it was assumed that states had the means to implement any conventions they accepted. For example, if it was discovered that additional safety measures should be introduced by certain industries, these measures would not be difficult for states to adopt. Furthermore, states were unlikely to adopt conventions that imposed burdens they were unwilling to accept. Thus, it could usually be assumed that if a state adopted a convention it would implement it.

These observations were based on conditions within Western states, i.e., within the industrialized areas where much had already been accomplished nationally in the way of improving conditions of workers. In the early years of ILO, since the majority of members were developed, the assumptions on which the system was based were valid. But as the non-Western, nonindustrialized members increased over the years, there was need for reconsidering the assumptions of the system. These new states, which were in the very early stages of industrialization and in which social legislation was not yet developed, were being asked to accept conventions that often represented extensive advances over national practice. The ILO found that the new states were not living up to their commitments. Often, wanting to be considered equal and worthy members of the world community and desirous of being a part of the movement for better labor and social standards, the governments felt compelled to adopt conventions. The general attitude of the Organization encouraged this position: much time was spent trying to persuade states to adopt conventions, and there was a tendency to measure the success of the ILO in terms of the number of conventions adopted. Thus, there was pressure on states to accept the conventions—a pressure that some of the older states resisted for their own reasons, but one that did seem to effect the newer, less secure states.

Many of these newer states were observed not to be implementing the standards they had adopted. Although there were some within the Organization who were quick to point an accusing finger at these "offenders," there were others who asked the question "why?" Why were these newer states not implementing the agreements in the same way the older states were? The intentions of the states were often good: governments sincerely desired to bring their standards up to the international minimum. However, many states lacked the necessary administrative machinery, were unable to draft appropriate legislation, or were hard put to find the funds necessary. Or, perhaps, the customs of the country were such that it was difficult for the government to effect changes. In other words, the fact that states were not abiding by their obligations often could be attributed to the difficulties of the system in the country, and were not necessarily attributable to a lack of desire on the part of government.

Recognizing this, the ILO looked for ways to make it possible for states to live up to commitments. The approach adopted by the Organization was a twofold one. First was an attempt to make the instruments containing standards more flexible and more adaptable to conditions in developing nations. Second, assistance was offered to states.

It was the original conception of ILO that it would build up a code of binding conventions. A convention involves a definite commitment on the part of states for which they can be held accountable by the international organization. Recommendations and resolutions, on the other hand, are in the nature of suggestions to states and, as such, do not impose binding obligations. They therefore lend themselves more readily to goals, i.e., to setting standards the international organization has agreed are desirable, but which states are not ready to accept as a binding commitment. In recent years, there has been a tendency to make increasing use of these instruments. Today, the labor code as drafted seems to represent the maximum acceptable in convention form in the world taken as one unit. Although there continue to be conventions drafted, these are far fewer than in the earlier days of the Organization.

More use has been made in recent years of regional[11] and industry conferences.[12] Conferences have been called to work out common approaches to problems which affect one region more particularly than others. Instead of having the whole Organization concern itself with an industry that exists in only a few states, a special conference of delegates from these states is called. For some industries, there are regular industrial committees which meet periodically to discuss common problems. For these various partial groupings, resolutions have been found to be the most suitable instrument. One of the purposes of these committees is the same as the

---

[11] The new ILO Constitution, drafted in 1944, makes provision for regional conferences in Article 38.

[12] For a discussion of the work of industrial committees, see John Price, "Industrial Committees of the I.L.O.," *International Labour Review,* January, 1952, pp. 1–43; and *International Labour Code, op. cit.,* pp. cxxi–cxxv.

general purpose of ILO—to set standards. Their use permits standard-setting to be undertaken in specific areas without involving the whole organization, thereby leaving the General Conference free to devote its efforts to problems that are worldwide in scope.

Besides using instruments that put less pressure on states, the ILO has experimented with inserting into the actual instruments provisions which make these more flexible. The regulations concerning conventions contained in the ILO Constitution have made this advisable. Conventions presented to national parliaments must be accepted in the form in which they are received; they may not be amended. This means that if a legislature feels it cannot adopt one provision in a convention, it has no alternative but to reject the whole instrument. ILO has considered this an important provision of the Constitution, and the majority of delegates have been unwilling to have it changed. Since the conventions result from efforts of labor and employer groups as well as governments, governments should not be permitted to change provisions by unilateral action.

However, techniques have now been worked out to give national legislatures more choice than that of merely adopting or rejecting.[13] Conventions have been drawn up that contain a core of provisions considered essential to the convention, i.e., those without which the convention would be of little use. These are mandatory for states to accept. States then must agree to a specified percentage of the remaining provisions, choice being left to each state. Other conventions have contained alternatives for provisions on which there has been disagreement during the drafting procedure. In some, optional clauses are inserted so that states are given the choice of not accepting provisions they do not wish to. Another method has been to include clauses over which there has been disagreement in a nonbinding annex.

From early in the history of ILO, it was recognized that standards would not always be applicable to all states.[14] In 1919, a convention was adopted in which a state was permitted to apply a lower standard by making a declaration to that effect. It was expected that, when possible, states would adopt the convention standards, and that those opting for lower standards would attempt to raise their practices to conform with the international standard when conditions within the state permitted. Although this technique was used early in ILO history, it was used infrequently until after the second world war, i.e., until there was more concern for the difficulties of the newer states.

---

[13] *Ibid.*, Vol. I, preface.

[14] Constitution of the International Labour Organization, Art. 19(3), provides: "In framing any conventions or recommendations of general application the Conference shall have due regard to those countries in which climatic conditions, the imperfect development of industrial organization, or other special circumstances make the industrial conditions substantially different and shall suggest the modes, if any, which it considers may be required to meet the case of such countries."

Whereas in most Western states conditions throughout the country do not vary to any great extent, in only a few scattered cities and industrial centers of many non-Western nations are conditions beginning to be "Western" and "modern," and outside these is a great "hinterland" where life is primitive and hard. It is often possible for states to implement standards in the more "modern" sections of the country, but at present extremely difficult to do so in the "hinterland." A number of conventions take cognizance of this situation and permit states to exempt regions from their application.

Suggestions have been made that conventions contain general principles, but permit each state to work out details to fit its own conditions and needs. No such convention has as yet been adopted, and it is possible to see some difficulties were one to be drawn up. When the convention contains very specific provisions, there is less room for disagreement as to interpretation than when one contains general principles. The idea would probably be more acceptable were it to be realized in the form of recommendations or resolutions—that is, when there is not the binding character of a convention.

The *International Labor Code* has developed by bits and pieces over the last half century. This has meant that some provisions are old, that there are gaps in some areas, and overlapping commitments in others. Also, older conventions have not contained provisions, as those outlined above, taking into account the problems of the non-Western world. For these reasons, there have been suggestions that parts of the Code be revised and brought up to date. The secretariat has attempted to respond to these suggestions, and has done an extensive review of the Code, attempting to discover those parts most in need of revision. It has then sent out questionnaires to the states, soliciting their views. Unfortunately, the replies have been few and have not shown much interest in the project. As a consequence, there has been little revision of the older parts of the Code.

While the ILO has attempted to adapt its standard-setting system to the needs and realities of the newer nations, it has also attempted to keep abreast of developments in the advanced countries. Thus, it has been working on standards for workers in nuclear industries, especially safety provisions, and has been studying the problems presented by increased automation.

Evaluation of ILO Approach

ILO was the first international organization created primarily to set international standards, and it approached this task with enthusiasm and energy. Has it been effective? This is a hard question to answer. It is certainly true that labor standards have improved in every state since 1917, but it is also true that this development cannot be attributed solely to the efforts of the international organization. Often, minimum international standards are accepted by states that already have adopted these nationally. However, the organization has probably induced many improvements. It has been especially effective when it has concerned itself with special groups and special problems. Many of the improved safety regulations and provisions for workers in dangerous industries can be traced to ILO initiative and conventions.

One group for whom the ILO has shown particular concern from early in its history is the merchant sailors. A special committee, the Maritime Conference, was set up to keep their problems under continuing scrutiny. Today, there are more than 25 conventions that cover merchant sailors, and it is highly probable that these have meant a very real improvement in the working conditions of this group.

The maritime conventions cover a wide range of topics, including hours of work (8 hours a day at sea with special provisions for ports and overtime), holidays, provisions for nonprofit employment agencies and for medical examinations, conditions of service, etc. There are even two conventions covering the food of sailors. According to one of these, cooks are required to have certificates of qualification based on examinations that include "a practical test of the candidate's ability to prepare meals" as well as a "test of his knowledge of food values, the drawing up of varied and properly balanced menus and the handling and storage of food on board ship." Recently, a special convention covering stateless refugee seamen was passed, making it possible for seamen to go ashore. Many had been confined to their ships for several years due to lack of proper papers.

One can conclude that the great spectacular gains of labor over the past half-century—gradual reduction of hours, increase in wages, improved social security benefits, etc.—cannot be traced to the efforts of ILO alone. The real contribution of the Organization seems to have been in trying to see that benefits were extended to groups less successful in obtaining improvements through national channels, and in some areas where states had been hesitant to undertake improvements by themselves.

In the early years of the Organization, there was a tendency to count ratifications and to measure the success of the Organization in terms of how many states had adopted how many conventions. That is, there was a tendency to equate the number of adopted conventions with an improvement in conditions. Somehow, it was thought, if we could get more conventions drafted and adopted, the worker would benefit.

Even within the Organization, there were those who soon became dissatisfied with this purely convention approach and sceptical about its efficacy. What help, it was asked, are pension provisions for a worker if he can't find a job? What benefit does the worker receive from minimum wages if he is out of work? The depression helped to turn the ILO's attention away from conventions. It was recognized that provisions could not be legislated in a vacuum, that these were dependent on general social and economic conditions in a country. It was recognized that it was possible to improve the welfare of workers only where social and economic conditions were good.

So there began to be within the Organization a tendency to see labor conditions as an integral part of the whole socio-economic structure of the country and, in turn, a tendency to take a more realistic view of the limitations of the convention method. At the Philadelphia Conference in 1944, this new approach to labor and its problems was given expression in a declaration:

> Confident that the fuller and broader utilisation of the world's productive resources necessary for the achievement of the objectives set forth in this Declaration can be secured by effective international and national action, including measures to expand production and consumption, to avoid severe economic fluctuations, to promote the economic and social advancement of the less developed regions of the world, to assure greater stability in world prices of primary products, and to promote a high and steady volume of international trade, the Conference pledges the full co-operation of the International Labour Organization with such international bodies as may be entrusted with a share of the responsibility for this great task and for the promotion of the health, education and well-being of all peoples.[15]

Surely, ILO continues to work to set minimum world standards and to use conventions for attaining this end, but this is no longer the central and only preoccupation of the Organization.

IMPLEMENTATION OF CONVENTIONS

In the early years, the most difficult problem—as viewed by the ILO—was getting states to adopt conventions. It was thought that if a state made a convention a part of its municipal legal order it would be implemented—an observation which was, to a large extent, valid during the early period of the Organization. However, as has been pointed out, the increased non-Western membership presented the ILO with the reality of a second gap. No longer did acceptance assure implementation; rather, there was often little relationship between legislation and implementation.

The Organization has not been content to consider its job accomplished once it has drafted and passed a convention. To make a reality of its obligation to the worker, it would have to find a way to narrow these gaps.

To narrow the first gap, between international adoption of a standard and national legislation, the Organization has used three techniques: (1) resolutions; (2) informal contacts between secretariat staff and national governments; (3) the national interest groups.

The Organization has passed numerous resolutions calling on states to

---

[15] "Declaration Concerning the Aims and Purposes of the International Labour Organization," Article IV.

adopt ILO conventions as part of their national legislation. The technique is not a particularily effective one, although it does help to keep the issue alive. At times, the Director and others of his staff have been successful in persuading governments to take action. M. Thomas spent much of his time traveling from country to country, talking with government officials (as well as with labor and management groups), and trying to persuade these to initiate efforts to adopt and implement conventions.[16] Again, although one can point to a few successes here and there, the general impact of this approach is not spectacular.

It is the third of these approaches that has met with most success. The tripartite system gave the organization a unique opportunity to mobilize national interest groups. Although it is not possible to gauge the actual effect of these groups on governmental action with any certainty, there does seem to be evidence that national legislation to implement ILO conventions and recommendations has been made a part of the programs of national labor groups, and that the efforts of these have been successful at times in securing passage of the desired legislation.[17]

The second gap—between national legislation and national implementation—has been of particular concern to the organization. Here again, national labor organizations have often supported the efforts of the international organization and have put pressure on their governments. In the following sections, attention will be turned to the international techniques that have been adopted. Here one finds that there are two major approaches to the problem: (1) a system of international supervision; and (2) direct assistance to governments.

International Supervision[18]

Although it was thought that states adopting conventions would implement them, the original architects of ILO realized this might not always hold true and believed that the organization should have some way of supervising states in order to assure compliance with the provisions of conventions. The system as established is based on the assumption that states accepting conventions desire to implement them and will be willing to submit to international supervision and to a mild form of international prodding, should this prove necessary. The system was conceived of as an actual aid to states; states would

---

[16] E. J. Phelan, *op. cit.,* pp. 143–78.

[17] It is interesting to note that other international organizations have attempted to involve national groups in the international work and to use these to put pressure on governments. UNESCO has national commissions, UNICEF and WHO have national committees. These are, however, more advisory and auxiliary in character and have not been drawn into the work of the organizations so intimately as labor and management groups in the ILO.

[18] For a detailed treatment of international supervision, see M. C. Wang, *op. cit.*

want to assure themselves (and also one another) that they were abiding by their international commitments.

The system is based on information supplied by states. States have been asked to supply the international organization with information regarding implementation of conventions. This information is studied and evaluated by an international supervisory body.

In the beginning, the system was applicable only to ratified conventions, and was used only to determine whether national legislation was in conformity with the international instrument. Over the years, the system has been modified. Especially noteworthy are provisions for extending international supervision to actual implementation and administration. Recognizing that legislation can often remain a dead letter on the statute books of a country, the organization has considered it part of its responsibility to extend its supervision beyond mere legislative enactments. The second important modification concerns states covered: whereas only those states that had adopted a convention came under the early supervisory system, today the system has been extended to cover conditions in states that have not adopted conventions and recommendations.

Early in the history of ILO, various groups began to press for extending coverage to nonratifying states. The supervisory procedure itself involves both ratifying and nonratifying states. Why, asked the ratifying states, should we submit to being supervised by states that have not ratified a convention? Since these states have no responsibility vis-à-vis the convention, they should not sit in judgment of states which have undertaken obligations. There was also pressure from some of the nonratifiers to extend the system. We, argued these states, are not always able to ratify conventions (due, for example, to difficulties in a federal system), and must sit and hear ourselves criticized for not adopting conventions. But, these continue, if you examined conditions in our countries, you would find that we often have higher standards than some of the self-righteous ratifiers.

These states were arguing for a more realistic view of the aims of the International Labor Organization. Conventions, these stressed, are only a means and should not be valued as an end in themselves. What the organization should concentrate on is working conditions. If these are good, then a state should not be unduly criticized for not having ratified a convention. The accomplishments in the field of labor conditions should be emphasized, and not merely the adoption of international instruments.

Since pressure came both from among states that traditionally ratified conventions and from those that did not, it was possible to obtain agreement on the principle that the international supervisory system be extended to cover all conventions and recommendations in all states. This new system tends to deemphasize the importance of the conventions themselves and tries to center attention on the provisions and principles contained within the instruments.

Methods of Supervision

The international supervisory system is based on the voluntary cooperation of states, since it must rely on the information submitted by states. The organization has no way of forcing governments to comply with its requests for information, and many states are not very cooperative.

The information is sent to the secretariat, which organizes it and forwards it to a committee of experts for examination. The committee studies the reports. Its observations, along with the original report, are sent to the Governing Body and then to the Annual Conference, where the material is studied by a special committee before being submitted to the conference as a whole. Thus, the supervisory system involves all the major organs of the organization.

The findings are published. On ratified conventions, suggestions are made on how states can better conform to the international standards. For nonratifying states, the convention is regarded as a goal toward which these states are working, and the report contains only an evaluation of the progress toward realizing this goal.

In the original ILO Constitution, there were provisions for putting "teeth" into the international supervisory system. For states that were particularly recalcitrant, economic sanctions were to be applied by the organization. The original constitution also left the way open to use the International Court. Neither of these methods was ever used, and, when the delegates met in Philadelphia to rethink the principles, structure, and organization of the ILO, it was decided not to include these in the new constitution.

That the more extreme methods have not been used does not mean that all states have responded to the criticisms of the organization and have conscientiously made sure they are applying all provisions of all conventions they have accepted. Unfortunately, this has not been the case. Many states are criticized time and time again for the same shortcomings. Why, then, has the organization not used its sanctions? The reason would seem to lie in the realities of international cooperation. States do not like to feel forced to cooperate. Most successful examples of cooperation have been achieved when states voluntarily adopt obligations they consider to their advantage to accept. The same applies to ILO conventions. States accept these for a number of reasons: more developed states in the hope that less advanced ones will follow and thus incur the burden of increased costs, or because of pressures from labor groups at home; less advanced states to secure respectable acceptance in the international community, or other reasons. For whatever reasons, states like to think their action is voluntary vis-à-vis the international community.

Once having accepted the obligation, states have been willing to submit to international supervision, but are less anxious to have this action lead to definite sanctions. Often, states that are criticized vehemently and frequently by an international body respond by taking a defensive attitude or by becoming dissatisfied with the organization. The ILO has considered it more important to promote a positive attitude on the part of states toward ILO than to punish a state for noncompliance with a particular convention. It has often been shown that publication of findings of the organization regarding noncompliance has been sufficient to bring about the necessary changes. When states have resisted pressure—when they have not changed—the organization has been reluctant to employ sanctions that might lead to a negative attitude toward the organization and possibly even withdrawal— which probably would not secure compliance anyway.

It is also to be noted that action of the organization means action voted on by a majority of delegates. Delegates have often been reluctant to vote action because they do not desire to be on the receiving end of such action at some time in the future. As has been pointed out, few states can point to a spotless record as regards conventions, and, therefore, all consider themselves potential targets of sanctions they might initiate.

One further factor has played a role in not using sanctions—fear that use of sanctions would result in a decrease in number of ratifications. If states thought they might be liable to economic sanctions, they might be even more reluctant to undertake international commitments.

Today, the ILO's strongest weapon is publicity, and it has been demonstrated in the past that this often does encourage states to change policies. Most states do not relish having the world know they are not abiding by their international commitments, and would much rather be considered "good" members of the international community. In recent years, there has been a tendency for those evaluating the reports of governments to try to look for reasons why a particular state is not implementing a measure, and to give the reasons in its report.

The procedure outlined above applies to the general supervisory responsibilities of ILO. The organization has also experimented with another form. Many delegates have shown sincere concern for the workers' right of association. This right, it is argued, is basic to the whole concept of ILO. Although ILO has accepted Socialist states, there have been strong complaints voiced by many delegates to any system that denies to the worker the right of free association. Not only has the problem been raised in ILO, but it has also been discussed by ECOSOC, where pressure was exerted to put into operation an international system for assuring this right to workers and others. It was decided that ILO was better equipped to set up a system for investigating, and ILO was called on to cooperate with ECOSOC in doing this.

The Governing Body of ILO has established a Fact-Finding and Conciliation Committee made up of independent experts empowered to receive complaints from government, worker, and employer groups. When the Committee receives a complaint, it communicates with the state against which the complaint has been made and inquires whether this state is willing to have the Committee proceed with an investigation. Only in the case of complaints brought by one state against another when both states have ratified the Convention on Freedom of Association is the Committee given competence to undertake an investigation without prior consent of a state.[19]

There was bitter objection to making the system so dependent on a state's willingness to submit to investigation. In an attempt to satisfy these objections, the Governing Body was given the power to publicize criticisms against governments, in which case the matter does not go to the Fact-Finding Committee.

A number of complaints has been brought to ILO. Most of these were never handled by the Fact-Finding and Conciliation Committee, as the government concerned refused to give its consent. In one case, the state involved—Venezuela—withdrew from the organization.

The system seems to be effective where states basically recognize the right of free association but where certain practices or laws contravene this right. Where there is little importance attached to this right, where there is no general regard for its importance or for upholding it, the system fails. It cannot force states to introduce this right into their legal orders; it can only help those states that recognize the right but have certain policies that seem to deny its exercise to certain groups or in certain circumstances.

A third method of international supervision employed has been that of the intensive investigation. This involves the thorough study of a situation covered by an international convention in order to determine whether a state is actually carrying out its international commitment. The most famous in the field of labor was actually undertaken not by ILO but by an ad hoc committee of ECOSOC in the early 1950's. In both ECOSOC and the ILO, there had been a number of accusations that practices amounting to forced labor existed in certain states. The U.S.A., U.S.S.R. and South Africa became the primary targets for these attacks. The ad hoc committee studied conditions in a large number of states and the allegations made against these. The findings of the committee were the bases of resolutions by both ECOSOC and ILO, calling for compliance with existing conventions on forced labor, ratification by states not having done so, and abolition of the practice generally. Finally, the findings led to the drafting of a new and more comprehensive convention on the subject. The question still remains as to

---

[19] *The I.L.O. in a Changing World* (Geneva: International Labour Office, 1958), pp. 69–70.

whether this investigation resulted in any changes in the practices of states. Unfortunately, the answer to this must be no. States interpreted the report as they saw fit, rejected those parts that indicated existence of such practices as not being a valid interpretation of conditions, and continued to raise complaints of "forced labor" against other states (U.S.S.R.'s attacks on the U.S.A.) that had, in effect, been cleared of all charges. The report was helpful in defining the problem and in analyzing the extent of forced labor in the world, but as a technique for bringing about changes in offending states, it was a failure.

It would seem, from the above outline of attempts through international action to get states to bring their practices into conformity with international minimum standards, that the most effective techniques have relied on the voluntary cooperation of states that want to bring national practices into conformity. Further, it appears that the organization can be most helpful when it does not point an accusing finger at "violators" or make an issue out of offenses. ILO has, to a large extent, avoided passing judgements on participating states and has attempted to offer its supervisory techniques as instruments of genuine assistance. Although this pattern has been generally accepted, some states have attempted to turn meetings of representative bodies into forums for denouncing others. When this occurs, it is not, unfortunately, usually attributable to any concern for the worker—his condition and rights—but rather is prompted by desires to embarrass states for political reasons.

Technical Assistance

The system for international supervision of conventions was, as has been pointed out, based on the assumption that states might need a little prodding now and then to encourage them to bring national practices into line with international obligations. From early in the organization's history, it was realized that this pressure could not always be effective, even when states wanted to comply. ILO has, therefore, undertaken to provide direct assistance to states requesting help.

The first assistance was in the form of legislative drafting. In the early 1930's, some states accepted conventions and wanted to have the provisions elaborated in their own legal system but were unable to draft appropriate legislation. To help these states, the secretariat sent out experts who had knowledge of similar legislation in other countries. This type of assistance was given not only to the newer, less industrialized states, but was also requested by more "advanced" states. For example, the United States government was aided by ILO in drafting its first social security legislation. Another way ILO has helped is by drawing up model statutes which are made available to states on request.

However helpful well-drafted legislation might be, it was soon recognized that legislation alone did not necessarily guarantee that the standards would be realized within a state. Sometimes, it was a matter of inadequate administrative machinery to see that the laws were translated into action; in other cases, the social and economic conditions of the country were such that it was literally impossible to implement the laws to the extent and in the manner envisaged by the drafters. It was recognized that no matter how willing or dedicated to the cause of raising labor standards a government might be, it could not just legislate them into existence when conditions in the country could not support the program. So, gradually, the ILO began to broaden its concept of its responsibility. No longer could it be content with setting standards but must also play its part in helping countries to develop, for only then could the standards be realized. Only when a country had raised itself up, had "developed," would the means be available for raising the standards of workers and for improving their condition.

ILO's first assistance programs were haphazard affairs. The organization examined all government requests for help. When it thought a program was one for which ILO had the means and personnel, it accepted it. This approach led to scattered, isolated projects. Although many of these projects were in themselves successful, many had to be written off as failures because their effect in the total picture was so negligible. A program to speed up production in a steel mill may succeed in producing larger quantities of steel at lower prices per unit, but it is not very valuable if there are not enough industries using the type of steel produced so that much of the added product is stock-piled. Training men for skills may result in an increase in the number of trained men, but is of little use if there are no openings for the skills they have learned. To build a new industrial plant in an area in which there are not enough workers or for which there are no supervisors or managers causes problems.

As time passed, the policy-makers in ILO realized that in order to maximize the benefits from ILO technical assistance activities, projects would have to be conceived of in terms of larger programs. This had led to cooperation with other agencies within the framework of the United Nations Expanded Program of Technical Assistance and also to general planning with development agencies of the countries themselves, where such exist. In doing this, an attempt is made to fit ILO projects into the overall development program of a country.

In assessing its role in promoting development, ILO has emphasized two aspects of the development process—economic and social. It has been pointed out that ILO recognizes the dependence of labor conditions on the general economic situation in a country, and has accepted responsibility for helping countries to improve their economies. In order to accomplish this, ILO has instituted technical assistance projects in such fields as vocational guidance and training, managerial and supervisory training, and productivity projects. That is, it has initiated programs directly concerned with improving the economy of the country, concentrating on the industrial sector.[20]

Recently, technical assistance programs[21] have emphasized production assistance, the idea being that a great deal can be done about increasing the output of various plans. Productivity missions, consisting of one to five experts, have been sent out. One type of mission, the demonstration mission, seeks to demonstrate the applicability of particular productivity improvement techniques. One such mission in Southeast Asia held seminars in each country for top management, senior government officials, and trade union leaders in order to acquaint them with the objectives of the mission and the benefits that can result from application of modern industrial management techniques. Next, executives from a few selected plants were given a short theoretical training course to demonstrate the practical improvements that could be made in productivity. The press and radio were used to arouse the interest of individuals and the public. Some of the results of this mission were actual increases in productivity: in a railway workshop, a 100 percent increase in the output of brake shoes; in a furniture factory, a 65–100 percent increase in two products; in a match factory, a decrease in packing time per batch from 83 to 63 minutes; in a pottery works, a saving of the equivalent of $17,000 in new equipment. Of even longer-term importance, the governments of Burma, Indonesia, Thailand, and others have sought long-term technical assistance in productivity.

Today, about one-half of ILO's technical assistance is in the form of vocational training programs. Much of the money for training programs today comes from the Special Fund. Some of the projects are isolated institutions, individuals are given fellowships, instructors are sent to individual factories, etc. In some states, there has been an attempt to develop an overall program. In Iran, a single accelerated training center was established in 1957, after two years of preparatory work, to give courses in the building trades. By 1959, the instruction in this center was taken over by Iranians; other centers for other trades have been established. Another use of the original center has been for seminars so that officials from other states in the region can benefit from the experience of the Iranians. In 1960, for example, a seminar was attended by 14 specialists from 7 Middle East countries.

One other example of a more coordinated approach has been the program in Central America, started in 1958. An ILO mission was sent to study factors affecting productivity and to draw up a program. The second phase was training in the application of productivity improvement techniques for

---

[20] For a brief summary of ILO programs and projects, see *The I.L.O. in a Changing World, op. cit.,* pp. 84–110.

[21] The following examples have been taken primarily from *ibid.,* pp. 39–61.

selected personnel in economic development agencies of Guatemala, Honduras, Nicaragua, and El Salvador. Professional staffs of local enterprises, government officials, and factory managers were given training either through seminars or demonstration projects in plants. These brought about tangible results. For instance, a shoe factory in Nicaragua produced 120 pairs of shoes a day in February, 1957, 240 in November, and by the following July the output had increased to 300.

In order to spread the experience of the mission, the material used was expanded and edited and finally published to be used by others. In 1959, this program developed into a combined productivity and vocational training project, and fellowships were given to foremen and supervisors for short, intensive courses.

A good deal of the ILO's work in the vocational training field has been directed toward increasing the supply of vocational instructors in the less developed countries. One such is the ILO project in Brazil, in which the ILO has assisted the National Industrial Apprenticeship Service to develop training facilities that have been opened to selected instructor trainees from other Latin-American countries. This type of program also promotes another objective of the organization—the training of people who will train others.

These are but a few examples of the very numerous projects and programs being undertaken by the organization in its attempt to help countries develop themselves economically so that they will be on a better economic footing and will then be able to make sure the workers benefit.[22]

However, ILO has not been satisfied to concentrate only on economic development but has also emphasized the need for social improvements. In 1941, when delegates from a number of states met to consider changing the ILO Constitution to fit the needs of the postwar world, there was general agreement on the importance of humanizing labor. Labor should not be considered a commodity in the industrial process. It was to be one of the objectives of the organization to encourage and secure for labor more respect than it had often had. In most of the industrially advanced states, labor unions have become strong enough to prevent labor's being used as a commodity, and workers have been accorded more respect than in the early days of the industrialization process.

In the developing countries, this is a real problem. Government officials and industrial managers sometimes become so dedicated to the goals of economic development and, at the same time, so frustrated by the lack of sufficient capital that they overlook the needs of the workers. When they do recognize these, they claim there can be no real improvement until there is a

---

[22] For a study of the difficulties of labor technical assistance, see W. J. Hull, "The Growing Pains of International Technical Cooperation," *International Labour Review,* October, 1961.

strong economic base, and to take care of the needs of workers at present would mean a slowing down of the development process. It is better, these argue, to build the economy first; only then will it be possible to divert money to taking care of the needs of the workers.

The problem is perplexing. It is true that to use a large portion of scarce money for workers' benefits would mean taking it from capital, already recognized as inadequate for the needs of the country, and would result in a definite retarding of economic development.

The problem is one often debated in the various organs of ILO as well as in other international organizations concerned with problems of development. It has been the general consensus of ILO that it should not turn its eyes away from the needs of the workers for the sake of faster development, but should, rather, search for ways to promote social development along with economic development. As a country develops, it is confronted with many new social problems that cry for solutions. These should not be overlooked, but some attempt should be made to take care of the most serious of these. As more is understood about the development process, it is increasingly clear that social progress cannot wait until economic development is well along. The lack of social development itself can slow down the process of economic development. Consequently, ILO has encouraged developing states to look at social and economic development as part of the same process.

ILO in its general program and in its technical assistance projects has emphasized the need for social reform, and has stressed the danger of economic development's being considered an end in itself rather than a means to achieving a better life and to raising the standard of living.

In keeping with this objective, the organization has been engaged in a number of technical assistance projects in social security. An expert was sent to Panama to help organize a scheme; in Paraguay, another expert gave advice on actuarial and administration problems; in Peru, advice on plans and financial estimates for new social security schemes was provided. ILO has also been instrumental in promoting health and safety for workers. An expert was sent to Indonesia to advise the labor inspectorate on organization of services and establishment of regulations and standards. When he arrived, he organized a training course for labor inspectors and gave advice in connection with workmen's compensation cases.

The organization tries to encourage developing states to regard the *International Labour Code* as setting goals toward which they should be striving. Where possible, it has encouraged projects which, while promoting the social objectives of ILO, also make a contribution—often indirectly, to be sure—to economic progress as well. Projects such as those which promote better labor–management relations or initiate health inspection systems for plants accomplish this objective.

At the same time, ILO continues to push for general improvements not easily evaluated in terms of their contributions to economic development, but which reflect the objectives of the ILO: "irrespective of race, creed or sex , . . . all human beings have the right to pursue material well-being and spiritual development in conditions of freedom and dignity, economic security and equal opportunity."[23]

REGIONAL APPROACHES

The ILO has been the most active international organization in setting international standards in the general area of labor and social rights. One of the difficulties in recent years is a result of the increase in membership of the organization, primarily from low-standard areas. This has resulted, as mentioned above, in a general retreat from standard-setting. There are fewer new conventions than formerly, and there is the feeling that it may not be possible at present to raise existing standards until the less developed countries have an opportunity to catch up with the more advanced.

Although there would seem to be little prospect for much progress in new worldwide standard-setting, interest has been aroused in the possibility of progressing regionally. The Western European nations have indicated a willingness to establish international social standards applicable to their region. Since the national social standards in most states that are members of the Council of Europe are higher than those existing in many other areas of the world, it has been possible for Europe to adopt standards above those laid down in the instruments that have worldwide applicability.

Standard-setting in Europe has been the result of cooperation within the framework of the Council of Europe. Drawing on the example and experience of ILO, the Council supported the drafting of a European Social Charter by a special tripartite conference. The Charter covers a great many of the subjects contained in the *International Labour Code:* social security, vocational training and rehabilitation for the disabled, medical assistance, assistance to migrants, and others. The Charter is seen as a first step in a process by which standards will be raised in Europe. At present, work has been undertaken on a social security code to be the first of many codes to supplement the Charter's more general provisions with specific binding commitments.

The Council members wanted to institute international supervisory machinery that would serve the same purposes as the ILO system—encouraging states to live up to obligations they have undertaken internationally. There was strong pressure to provide for a tripartite system. This would have involved developing a system outside the general framework of the Council, as the Council is composed of representatives of legislatures. The proposal

---

[23] Article II.a. Declaration concerning the Aims and Purposes of the International Labour Organization.

was turned down. As a consequence, the supervisory agency is composed of regular Council members, and action to be taken is voted on by the whole Council.

OTHER GROUPS SINGLED OUT FOR SPECIAL ACTION

Women

Concern for the rights and protection of women led to early twentieth-century international cooperation. Men became aroused at the exploitation of the "weaker sex," and promoted conferences in an attempt to establish international standards that would remove some of the outstanding hardships. Successes were slight, but by the first world war there were international conventions covering night work and traffic in women.

These beginnings were largely the result of male efforts. As women in many countries began to assert their claim to equality, they became an international interest group, putting pressure on international organizations to take heed of their demands. Although not organized—as labor is—they have had an impact on the international bodies. One indication of this has been the fate of the ECOSOC organ to deal with the rights of women. Originally, ECOSOC established the Commission on the Status of Women as a subcommission of the Human Rights Commission. This was an unsatisfactory arrangement for the women. They demanded and obtained a change: the commission is now one in its own right—not merely a subcommission.

The League of Nations concentrated on trying to eradicate traffic in women and children, and established an advisory committee to study the problem and to encourage cooperation in stopping this traffic.

By the time the United Nations came into existence, there was more pressure for action. There have been two directions to this drive in the interest of women: (1) protection of women; (2) equality for women.

The two approaches have often split women's interest groups into opposing camps. Until rather recently, protectionism has prevailed to a large extent. There was general agreement that women should be given preferential and special treatment as regards in certain areas of human activity—especially in the area of work. They should not be permitted to work on particularly hazardous and strenuous jobs, should be given special consideration before and after childbirth, and so on. Recently, the effort to secure for them equality with men has been gaining momentum. Attention has been directed especially to certain fields: equal pay for equal work, equal opportunities to enter professions and crafts, equal political and civil rights, equal access to political offices, and equal educational opportunities, among others.

Internationally, the achievement of these goals has been sought through conventions, i.e., international standard-setting. There has been an effort to draft conventions that would obligate states to provide for women.

The United Nations Charter recognizes the equality of men and women and provides that there shall not be discrimination against them on the basis of sex. These provisions have not prevented introduction of special measures intended to protect women where, on the basis of women's characteristics as a group, they are considered necessary.

In the postwar years, most international conventions have originated in the Commission on the Status of Women. An example is the 1952 Convention on the Political Rights of Women. This Convention provides that women shall have the right to vote and be elected and hold public office on the basis of equality with men. In the 1958 Convention on the Nationality of Married Women states agree to permit women to choose whether they wish to retain their citizenship on marrying an alien. ECOSOC has also shown its concern by passing a number of resolutions on such subjects as women's status in private law and the traffic in women, and has encouraged abolition of certain ancient laws and customs (e.g., child marriage and bride price, etc.).

The ILO has also concerned itself with women and has recently passed a Convention on Equal Work Performed. In working out the details of this Convention, ILO was assisted by the Commission on the Status of Women.

The movement to guarantee women rights internationally has gained momentum since the second world war, and we may legitimately ask whether the efforts of international organizations have had an impact on this movement. This is not an easy question to answer with any certainty, but some observations can be made. As in the whole area of standard-setting, there are great diversities in the world community. In some areas, women have gained a high degree of equality with men as regards their political, civil, and educational rights, and in employment, at the same time, are protected where their sex makes this advisable. In other areas of the world, women are little better than slaves. It is to be noted that it will not always be possible to raise the standards for women in many areas until the general standards of all within a country improve. Thus, it will be necessary to bear in mind that progress can be measured only with reference to their relative position as a group vis-à-vis men in the same environment.

Many delegations to the United Nations have adopted the custom of including women. As women from less advanced nations have come into contact with those from more advanced—not only through meetings at the United Nations but also under the auspices of various exchange programs—the less advanced have become increasingly aware that women can and do live on the basis of relative equality with men in some cultures.

For some, this has been a real revelation. Returning home, they have often been able to arouse interest among women for a change of attitude toward the role of women in society within their own cultures. The Commission on the Status of Women has encouraged this, and has studied ways to promote these efforts. There does seem to be an awakening of women that is spreading—probably to a large extent due to the ever-increasing contacts between women of less developed areas with conditions in more advanced areas. The conventions, many of which have been adopted by a number of less developed countries, have contributed to the improved status of women. Even some of those states that chose not to adopt these conventions still consider them to be goals for future effort. Thus, while there have been changes, these cannot be considered exclusively attributable to the efforts of the United Nations; many other forces have been operative. But the U.N. with its conventions has helped to set goals and objectives toward which states can strive and are working.

The Commission has recognized the limitations of a purely conventional approach, and has been searching for ways to supplement it. The Commission has sponsored research into the more unsatisfactory conditions of women to discover how widespread certain practices are and how these can best be eliminated. ECOSOC has accepted the principle that technical assistance can be used for projects involving the status of women. Seminars have been held to study problems in some depth. Conferences—many regional—have been called to give an opportunity to leaders among women to share their experiences and problems, and an advisory service has been made available to those countries desiring to implement one of the conventions on women or to undertake a program to improve their status.

Thus, work to improve standards among the world's women has followed in broad outline the ILO experience: conventions have been used with the hope that states will adopt and implement them. The limitations of a purely convention approach have led to attempts to use more direct methods in aiding those states that want to introduce reforms and changes but do not have the means and expertise to do so.

Children

Children have been another group singled out for special international action. As regards children, less has been attempted through the convention approach and more effort has been devoted to direct aid to children. Especially noteworthy have been the programs of UNICEF.[24]

The convention approach has not been completely overlooked. The Commission on Human Rights has considered the rights of children, and the result has been acceptance of a clause within the draft of covenants of hu-

---

[24] See pp. 373–78, 421–22, and 555–56 for a discussion of UNICEF.

man rights dealing with children, and a Declaration on the Rights of the Child, adopted by the General Assembly in 1959.

The Declaration states that "the child needs special safeguards" and that "mankind owes to the child the best it has to give." The child, regardless of whether he is born in or out of wedlock, or regardless of his "race, colour, sex, language, religion, political or other opinion" shall be given the means to develop "physically, mentally, morally, spiritually and socially." His right to special legal protection is claimed along with his right to a name and nationality, to the benefits of social security, adequate nutrition, housing, recreation, and medical services. Free and compulsory education is to be provided. If he is handicapped, he is to have special treatment and is to be protected against "all forms of neglect, cruelty and exploitation." Thus, states have *declared* that they agree children should be given special consideration.

The International Labor Organization has concerned itself for many years with protecting children and young people who are working. Conventions cover such things as minimum age, and set requirements for special health and safety measures for young people under a certain age.

INTERNATIONAL RESPONSIBILITY FOR THE WORLD'S SOCIAL DEVELOPMENT

International organizations that have adopted international standard-setting as an approach to raising social standards have been aware that this approach cannot always be successful without some sort of concrete assistance. So, especially since the end of the second world war, much attention has been given to developing programs to assist states in accomplishing the goals set forth by international instruments. There has been a shift from emphasis on standards to development—social development. The problem is seen as not merely one of legislation but rather as an ongoing, long-term process.

Interested in the concept of social development are not only the international organizations but also a wide variety of voluntary agencies long active in the field. Many of these have, over the years, developed a good understanding of numerous problems associated with social development in several areas of the world, and have been able to develop effective programs.

Both the League and the United Nations recognized that benefits could ensue from drawing these agencies into cooperation with the international organizations. The drafters of the United Nations Charter made special provisions for many of these organizations to have consultative status in ECOSOC. A number of operating agencies—Specialized Agencies, UNICEF, and UNHCR—have developed very close relationships with voluntary agencies concerned with the same problems and groups of people. These arrangements have often worked out to the benefit of both international organizations and the voluntary agencies.

The benefits of cooperative endeavor have been increased as emphasis has shifted away from *standard-setting* to *implementation* of standards and the development process. Government officials may be able to meet, to draft conventions, and to promote their ratification by states, but for the development process to be successful more than government action is necessary—the cooperation of groups within the country must be secured. These can be helpful in interpreting the work of international agencies to the public, in helping to finance projects, and in getting people involved in implementation of programs. International organizations have recognized this and have attempted to gain the cooperation of groups and to assist these in carrying out social development programs.

International Organization and Social Development

International programs and projects to promote social development have been widely diffused among international organizations so that it becomes difficult to give a general description. Many of the activities have been covered in other chapters. Here, an attempt will be made to look at the programs and efforts of the United Nations itself.[25] In many ways, the United Nations has become a dumping ground for programs that do not fit in such categories as health, labor, and children, and there is always the possibility that U.N. programs will overlap with, and duplicate the work being undertaken within, other agencies. Not only are many worldwide organizations concerned with social welfare and development, but regional agencies also have been multiplying in recent years, until today there are some thirty intergovernmental bodies in the field.[26] Such agencies as the Institute of Nutrition of Central America and Panama, the Inter-American Conference on Social Security, the Caribbean Commission, and the Colombo Plan are all concerned to some extent with social development. This situation has led to much confusion and duplication. Many within the United Nations were dissatisfied with the role the organization seemed to be playing, i.e., a catchall for odd projects, and there has been an attempt to give the United Nations a more positive role and to see it develop programs for which a universal organization is most suited. The United Nations has been working to this end, and is attempting to confine its very limited resources to projects in which a *world* organization can make a maximum contribution.

---

[25] The heart of U.N. activity in this field is the Bureau of Social Affairs of the Secretariat. The Bureau is almost like a secretariat of a specialized agency; the Social Commission is like the executive body of the Specialized Agencies, and ECOSOC and the General Assembly would then be the large assemblies.

[26] Martha Branscome, "Intergovernmental Channels," *The Annals* No. 329, May, 1960, p. 37.

The United Nations Emphasis

Community Development Program.   One of the areas in which the U.N. has been concentrating in recent years is community development,[27] which began to be considered an appropriate type of program for the international agency to promote in 1951. Many active in social development work were seeking projects that would involve the people as much as possible. Many were concerned with the unevenness of development: progress was being made in many of the cities, but often the villages had not begun to advance. It was hoped that the concept of community development would be an answer to these concerns.

The world organization had a few examples to which it could turn for guidance: some of the voluntary agencies had had success in carrying out projects; some governments had been undertaking programs. The greatest criticism of these was their isolation and apparent lack of any spreading power. A community might develop very successfully, but this remained an isolated phenomenon. The problem, as seen by the U.N., was to find a way to get more than single projects underway. In order to do this, the U.N. could not rely on setting up its own community development projects. The U.N.'s job, as seen by the organization, was to put the idea across to national governments. If governments of developing states could be persuaded of the importance of such projects and would be willing to undertake programs, then the effort could be successfully expanded beyond isolated projects.

The U.N. Secretariat was asked to study what had already been done in community development work. The report, based on three years of study and analysis, was circulated, and gradually enthusiasm grew. Discussion in the Social Commission aroused delegates from new nations, who, on returning home, were able to interest their governments. Once having generated enthusiasm, the U.N. faced the problem of how best to help governments.

It was decided that the organization should be prepared to offer interested states technical assistance. The typical program involves three aspects: (1) strengthening national services; (2) establishing and supporting demonstration centers; (3) training of personnel.

The services provided are on the national level: help to central governments to develop the necessary expertise to carry on programs. Ideally, the technical assistance operation is carried on by a team. However, the international technical assistance experts have rarely functioned as a team. Governments, which are actually responsible for making requests, often call on

---

[27] Julie Henderson, "Social Problems," *Annual Review of United Nations Affairs, 1962–1963* (Dobbs Ferry, N.Y.: Oceana Publications, Inc., 1964), pp. 68–70. Department of Economic and Social Affairs, *Community Development and National Development* (New York: United Nations, 1963). Department of Economic and Social Affairs, *Community Development and Related Services* (New York: United Nations, 1960).

experts from different countries, who arrive at different times, and are assigned to government departments that have trouble cooperating among themselves.

The idea of community development has not always been well accepted. For example, political considerations kept the concept from being adopted in many Latin-American countries. Dictatorships regarded the concept as threatening. The idea behind community development is to arouse the community to its own capabilities and to help it learn to see and attack problems that stand in the way of economic and social development. Dictatorships fear such independence. Thus, it was only after new governments had succeeded in putting down dictatorships in states such as Venezuela, Colombia, and Bolivia that the community development approach took hold.

Enthusiasm for this approach to development has not been without its critics. Economists have asked whether such things as straightening streets and building community centers could be related to economic development, i.e., whether it was worthwhile at this point to undertake programs that had no direct bearing on the economic development of countries. Some felt that the relationship of community development to national planning should be given further study. When the program was first conceived, the primary emphasis was on local self-help through such devices as community centers. Overall national planning was the subject of heated debate, with only the Eastern European states supporting it. Gradually, states found that community development showed the best results when planned as a part of national development. Another issue raised was that of the relationship of community development to land reform and other institutional reforms.

As programs matured, these and other concerns began to give rise to questions and to the need for a fresh look at the whole concept. A special review board of experts drawn from all over the world was asked to make an evaluation of the total program.

The U.N. has not only tried to get governments interested in undertaking community development programs, but has also tried to influence other international agencies in directing their attention to problems that fit in with this. UNICEF's shift to more emphasis on primary education, WHO's concern for preventive public health and environmental sanitation, FAO's increased interest in educational programs are all in part attributable to the efforts of the United Nations.

Housing. A second major concern of the U.N. in the social field—housing—is of recent origin.[28] The rapid growth of cities in developing nations had made this a challenging problem which bears directly on social welfare. New workers from small communities have major adjustment problems when moved to large urban centers. Crowded quarters made up of

---

[28] Henderson, *op. cit.,* pp. 70–75.

primitive shacks, poor (or no) sanitary conditions, and inadequate water supply compound the difficulty. The new nations themselves have become concerned with housing as urban communities have been expanding and as there has been increased awareness of the seeming connection between poor housing and political instability.

Both ILO and WHO have shown some interest in housing, but neither had placed major emphasis on the problem. It therefore appeared to those concerned with social development programming that this would be an area particularly suited to U.N. action.

The first question raised was whether the limited resources of the organization could be used to produce any meaningful results. Was not, it was asked, the real problem that of financing? Could the U.N. do anything worthwhile that involved only small outlays of money? In investigating this problem, it was found that some capital was available to governments through such agencies as the Inter-American Development Bank, the Alliance for Progress, and the European Development Fund. Therefore, the U.N. felt it might be able to make a contribution.

The U.N. has conceived of its role as involving three aspects: (1) arousing interest; (2) collecting information on and suggestions for effective approaches; (3) providing technical assistance. The interest of governments is sought through discussions in U.N. organs. Information and experience is being gathered by the new Intergovernmental Committee on Housing.[29] The report of the Committee will be distributed to the Committee on Industrial Relations, the regional economic commissions, and the Specialized Agencies. It is expected that these agencies will add their suggestions. Finally, it will be discussed in ECOSOC, which will attempt to work out priorities. As the report goes from place to place, it will not only be enriched by those who receive it and add their comments, but it is expected that it will also arouse the interest of people from various countries, who will then communicate this interest to their own governments.

Technical assistance has already been provided a number of countries, usually in the form of demonstration projects or experts sent out to advise governments.

Population.   The third area of concentration is population. Social development programs depend on reliable data concerning populations and competent interpretation of this data. If international organizations (and national governments) are to use their limited resources effectively, they need to know what social conditions are and what the trends will be. This

---

[29] This Committee was set up by ECOSOC, and a new formula was used. In order to assure that the Committee would be composed of experts, governments were to appoint their delegates in consultation *with* the secretary-general rather than merely consulting him *after* the fact.

kind of information can be obtained from population studies and their analysis.

Although debates in the General Assembly and other U.N. organs have indicated a consensus that the U.N. should engage in population research, there are sharp differences when it comes to a discussion of population policy. Today, there seems to be wide agreement among the developing nations of Africa and Asia that some form of population control is necessary; however, these have not been able to obtain a majority of the organization to support this position.

In 1962, the General Assembly engaged in a large-scale debate on population. At that time, a resolution, which was interpreted as authorizing technical assistance in birth control, was proposed. After long, heated debate, the resolution failed of adoption (34–34 with 32 abstentions). This vote shows more support for the principle than had been evident in previous Assemblies. Although the Assembly refused to adopt the resolution, the organization continues to give assistance in family planning to those few states that request it.[30]

The emphasis of the United Nations' program has been on demographic aspects of population rather than on control of population. Its activities have been of three kinds: (1) improving the capabilities of the newer nations; (2) encouraging data gathering and processing comparable on a worldwide basis; (3) evaluating the data and doing research on particular facets. The organization has been especially concerned with developing the capabilities of the newer nations. Many of these have been engaged in census-taking for a number of years, but have made little use of the data collected. One reason has been the lack of trained personnel. Experts were sent out from the United Nations to investigate the situation in Southeast Asia. They found, for example, that in the Philippines only two people were trained in demography—a girl ready to get her Ph.D. In Indonesia, a department in the university included four economists with advanced training in demography. However, each of these men had to hold six or seven jobs in order to keep ahead of the inflation in the country.[31]

The U.N. approach has been an attempt to see that more people from the developing nations receive training in demography. Fellowships to study abroad have been offered, but these are of limited value. More effective have been the government established regional demographic centers in Santiago, Bombay, and, very recently, Cairo. These are beginning to provide their respective regions with trained demographers. The United Nations has also

---

[30] From 1952–62, the Social Bureau received only half a dozen requests of an operational nature in population matters, and of these only three were requests for help in family planning. See Henderson, *op. cit.,* p. 88.

[31] See *ibid.,* p. 87.

sent out demographic advisers. Governments interested in improving their national programs can seek assistance from the technical assistance program.

Programs and Projects

Administration Building.   An effective social welfare program requires good administration. This is particularly true today. In almost all countries, the government has assumed responsibility for the social welfare of its people. Legislatures can pass good laws and appropriate money, but the program can be a failure if there are not adequate administrative agencies to carry it out. Often, governments have been anxious to initiate programs and have provided administrative agencies, only to find these unable to carry through on programs due to a lack of trained and experienced personnel.

UNRRA in its effort to help with the reconstruction of war-devastated countries put particular emphasis on reestablishing welfare departments and agencies. Once these were functioning, UNRRA's aid could be channeled through them. Here, it was primarily a question of reestablishment, for most of the UNRRA programs were in states that had had these agencies before.

The United Nations has followed UNRRA's example and has stressed the importance of efficient national administration. This approach is in keeping with the general principle underlying United Nations' development policy: the main objective of international organizations should be to assist less developed countries in their own efforts to progress economically and socially. If this is to be realized, it is necessary that states have adequate organizational machinery.

In order to assist states that turn to the United Nations for help in setting up or improving their administrative organizations, the United Nations instituted the Advisory Social Welfare Services, which was to promote national administration building. This has formed an important part of the community development program.

Coordination and Cooperation.   It has already been mentioned that there has been a proliferation of international agencies concerned with social welfare problems. Such a situation is bound to result in duplication and omissions, and cries out for the development of mechanisms and institutions for coordinating efforts in order to maximize effectiveness. Coordination of the policies and activities of the Specialized Agencies was one of the responsibilities of ECOSOC as laid down in Article 58 of the Charter. Although the Charter provides only for the Specialized Agencies, the fact that many voluntary agencies are connected to ECOSOC through their consultative status has been helpful in encouraging these to coordinate their programs with those of the United Nations family.

With the initiation of the U.N. Expanded Program for Technical Assistance, there were provisions for improving cooperation among agencies involved in the program. Not only has the United Nations promoted cooperation on this level but also has tried to encourage a more coordinated approach within countries themselves. States have been encouraged to set up planning councils or committees in their central governments. In 1957–1958, for example, Latin America had practically no central agencies, but by 1962 every country had some sort of commission or council. The U.N. also promotes coordination through its own agents, the Resident Representatives. In some areas, the Resident Representative has been successful in developing an attitude of cooperation among international, national, and voluntary agencies. On the regional level, the economic commissions— whose mandates were extended to cover social development—have been helpful instruments of coordination and cooperation among the states in the region.

The coordination, or balancing, of social and economic aspects of development has also been an objective of the world organization. Countries that are just beginning to pull themselves out of their backward state have tended to allocate most of their resources to economic aspects of development. Social welfare often has been considered a later step in the development process: only after the country, it is argued, has managed to put its economy on a sounder footing will there be the necessary funds for social welfare programs. To allocate money for large-scale social projects at an early stage would only slow down the development process. The United Nations has tried to counter this argument by pointing out that often economic development is not successful without some social progress. ECOSOC and other agencies concerned with social welfare have tried to encourage states to phase economic and social development, pointing out that the two should proceed together, and that economic progress will be swifter and more satisfactory if attention is also given to removing especially harmful social problems. One way to achieve this goal is to have social departments set up in the government and represented on planning boards. Many Latin-American states, Pakistan, Indonesia, the Philippines, and other countries have done this.

The effect of the United Nations in this area is often difficult to pinpoint. Usually, there are no actual programs or projects one can point to as generating certain changes. Governments pick up ideas and are often influenced by their contact with U.N. personnel and their exposure to reports and debates at the United Nations.

The whole area of coordination—actual coordination of agencies and promotion of coordination within states and regions—of economic and social programs would seem to be an area particularly suited to a worldwide international organization. The problems involved are immense, and difficulties are encountered all along the way. Rivalries between agencies, national and international, often succeed in preventing effective cooperation. The

United Nations, however, continues its attempt to work out more effective institutional and informal patterns.

Research and Analysis. Another activity for which a worldwide organization would seem to be particularly suited is research and analysis. As states undertake social and welfare programs, more information is available. An analysis of experiences in different areas can help other countries contemplating similar programs. The United Nations is becoming an international depository for such information, and it has been experimenting with ways to make this more available and useful. Good research is also necessary as a prerequisite for effective social welfare programming. States must be able to locate the most pressing problems and be able to make projections as to the future.

One major study undertaken by the staff of the Bureau of Social Affairs was a worldwide survey of conditions and trends of human fertility.[32] Governments need to know what to expect in the way of population growth as they begin to think in terms of planning for the future.

The Bureau staff was able to estimate the birthrate and gross reproduction rate for more than a hundred countries. For some of these—especially in Africa—no such scientific study had previously been made. The survey provided a comprehensive view of how changes in fertility are related to social, economic, and cultural factors, with interesting results. There seemed to be little correlation between levels of economic and social development and fertility rates. In some areas, the birthrate was found to be between 40 and 50 per 1,000 population; others were in the range of 50 to 60; while some rates fell well below 40. There seemed to be little change in rates where there had been recent gains in health, education, and related fields. Julie Henderson, Director of the Bureau of Social Affairs, has commented on the significance of these findings:

These findings are pertinent in evaluating the hypothesis, commonly stated in discussing population policy, that concentrating efforts in certain social and economic fields will be more effective than birth control programs as a means of moderating fertility and population growth. The findings also imply strongly that fertility in the less developed regions of the world is not so uncontrolled as many writers assert; varying degrees of restraint in reproduction appear to be the rule in these regions.[33]

The United Nations has also sponsored research into problems that seem to be troubling many states. One such study—of social security—related social security programs to levels of income and suggested ways to begin a social security system. To use these findings, states must be able to appraise

---

[32] See *ibid.*, pp. 76–77.
[33] *Ibid.*, p. 77.

current levels of income and measure change—for which they can turn to the United Nations for assistance.

A major project, started in 1960, has been the series, "Planning for Balanced Development." Here, case studies cover states that have not achieved satisfactory integration of social and economic development as well as some—for example, Japan and one of the Indian states—that have been more successful.

Perhaps the most significant undertaking of the U.N. is the *World Social Report.* The *Report* gives an opportunity to study and review social programs and social development throughout the world. Each study, undertaken biannually, surveys functional areas—levels of health, education, housing, income, etc.—and, starting with the 1963 *Report,* analyzes social conditions region by region. This analysis was started as a response to requests from the regional economic commissions.

With the 1963 *Report,* there was an opportunity to review progress over a 10-year period. The conclusion is gloomy; there have been few improvements in the level of living throughout most of the world. Each *World Social Report* does an extensive analysis of a particular topic.

The newest project of Social Affairs was made possible by a generous gift of the Netherlands—an institute to study the interrelationships between economic and social factors in planned development. It has been mentioned above that the U.N. has stressed the need for balanced progress, but up until now, there has been no comprehensive analysis of the links between the two, of the effects of one on the other. The institute will be an originator and catalyst; at present it is not thought of as a permanent institution. It will look into such topics as the effectiveness of various agents of planned development—agricultural extension agents, doctors, teachers, community development workers, and others. This kind of study is badly needed, as there has been, up to the present, no real effort made to develop genuine evaluative criteria by which to judge programs.

The research undertaken by the U.N. has been important in two ways: (1) pinpointing problems and revealing trends; (2) evaluating the effectiveness of programs and projects. Both aspects are necessary for rational planning by the U.N., states, the Specialized Agencies, national governments, and voluntary agencies. It is necessary and important to look for those problems in need of attention, and equally important to be able to select problems helped by assistance. In order to do this, one must know what are the effects of specific programs and projects. Broad comprehensive analysis of effectiveness has been undertaken only recently. Projects had been studied in terms of their narrow goals: Had a village adequate pure water? Had the U.N. been able to cut the cost of housing? Now the question is whether these and other projects have had any impact on the overall social and economic development of a country. Have programs eliminated the problems they have sought to? This is a much more difficult and complex assignment, but one necessary if there is to be real social development in the emerging nations.

Training and Experts.   Providing training facilities, fellowships, and experts has been an accepted kind of technical assistance for almost any type of program. The object is to spread out the effects of international action as far as possible. Thus, institutions that undertake ongoing training are often used.

The use of training institutions in the field of population has already been mentioned. In housing, these have also formed an important part of the U.N. program. Three important regional centers for housing research and training have been aided by the world organization: one for hot-humid Asia and the Far East, in Bandung, Indonesia; one for hot-arid Asia and the Far East, in New Delhi, India; and one for Latin America, in Bogotá, Colombia. The United Nations has cooperated with the government of Turkey and the University of Pennsylvania in establishing a housing and planning school in Turkey.

Related to institutions are the seminars. A great variety of these are held each year to discuss problems and to share experience. It has been found that the most valuable of these are usually undertaken regionally, where it is possible to work through a problem applicable to a few states. A seminar on population in Asia and the Far East, for example, focused on the need to draw realistic conclusions from the close relationship between population problems and economic development. Emphasis was put also on the types of demographic information needed in business and government activities. A close look was given to those areas of data-collecting in which the states in the area were most deficient, and a list of 11 such areas was drawn up. Another seminar in Puerto Rico dealt with training for town and country planning. The discussions ranged from the need to change the outlook of planning boards to the necessity to keep in mind the effects of the atomic age. Of particular help and applicability was the careful consideration given to the study of curricula and prerequisites for planning personnel on different levels of authority.

It is difficult to assess the effectiveness of these and the many similar seminars the U.N. holds—alone and in cooperation with national and international agencies. Most probably, officials and experts do pick up ideas and approaches which they, in turn, make use of when they return home.

The fellowship program is another varied and widespread one. Fellowships are awarded to individuals for a great range of subjects—community development, various aspects of housing, demographic research and training, and others. In granting these, an attempt is made to choose individuals who will be filling positions of responsibility within their own governments when they return home.

Experts are used when governments have particular problems they want to have solved, and when it is thought that someone on the spot, able to analyze the problem and surrounding conditions and suggest and work out effective solutions, would be helpful. It is expected that when a U.N. agency sends out experts governments will assign counterparts who will cooperate with the expert and benefit directly from this association. This ideal has not always been achieved. Sometimes, the adviser ends up taking over the program completely; at other times, the counterpart has no desire to use the adviser to any extent.

In the field of providing training and finding experts, the U.N. can draw on a much wider base than can national agencies which are often confined to selecting personnel from within their own territories and to offering training facilities at home. Even though the U.N. can draw on a wide area for personnel, it is often difficult to find trained and experienced people who are willing and capable of serving in the developing areas. The developing nations would like to have only highly trained personnel. The consensus in the Secretariat seems to be that experts with middle skills can be as effective—if not more so in many cases—as extremely successful technicians. The job has been to convince the developing nations of this.

Another problem is that of the counterpart. First, new nations often lack trained personnel who can benefit sufficiently from their experience with the U.N. expert to be able to take over and run programs initiated by the international organization. Another aspect derives from the political instability of some of these states. Trained counterparts are sometimes dropped from government service when a new political faction takes over.

One advantage the United Nations has over bilateral programs is its ability to call on personnel from all parts of the world. Developing nations often prefer experts from other developing states, as these are often better able to understand conditions and problems than are experts from more advanced areas. The question has been raised as to whether this does not deplete the sending state of much-needed personnel. Apparently, the few who do go out benefit from their experience. For instance, a country such as India which is turning out a rather large number of statisticians often finds it has more in the junior grades than it can use. Appointment in other countries gives these better training, involving more responsibility than they would be able to get at home.

Experts have been used in numerous types of programs, among them housing. In countries undertaking community development programs, one of the problems is that of working out ways to finance low-cost housing. A housing expert sent to Ghana was able to work out a loan scheme that granted credit to families willing to do all the work of building the house except producing the roof, doors, and windows. The plan was in keeping with the principle behind community development—self-help. In 1961, four years after the scheme had been initiated, 15,000 units had been built, and delinquencies on loans were less than .5 per cent.

The pattern worked out for Ghana is now a part of the fund of experience accumulating with the U.N. Future experts and government officials can look to this pattern to see whether in other countries its adoption is feasible. However, seldom can one pattern be taken over without some modifications. The scheme for Ghana is not workable in areas where men work ten hours a day, six days a week. For these areas a contractor is sometimes used to do part of the work, while families improve, finish, and expand the house.

Some indication of the range of projects can be obtained by looking at some of the types of requests the U.N. receives and fills in the area of housing. Experts have been sought to formulate national housing and building programs, to prepare surveys for regional and city development plans, to organize national planning and housing agencies, to plan rammed-earth construction, to plan the financing of housing schemes, to give advice on emergency housing, to help with the designing of housing, to develop building research institutions, and so on. In some cases, the U.N. has been called on to draft master plans for cities—Amman, Asunción, Cairo, Djakarta, Karachi, Kuala, Lumpur, and Rangoon. In Latin America and the Middle East, U.N. experts in rural housing and village planning have been provided to assist UNESCO's Fundamental Education Centers.

Pilot Projects. The United Nations in recent years has been turning down projects in social welfare which other agencies would be equally capable of executing, and has been trying to encourage pilot projects related to the fields of emphasis outlined above.

Pilot projects have been undertaken by the organization in the field of housing—trying to work out and build housing at the lowest costs possible. Usually, the money for materials comes from governments, voluntary agencies, and other funds. The U.N. is responsible for the technical guidance of the project. In Somalia, such cooperation resulted in building model houses at one-quarter of the cost of standard inexpensive models previously built by the city of Mogadishu.

Evaluation of U.N. Efforts

These, then, seem to be some of the directions United Nations social welfare and development work are taking. There has been an attempt to concentrate the very limited resources available on projects that seem to call for action by a world international organization, and in fields in which other agencies are not active. Most of the funds for these projects come from technical assistance budgets, of which the United Nations itself receives only a small proportion. Because of the very limited resources with which it must work and the types of problems with which it is attempting to deal, it is not possible to look for tremendous results. But the United Nations does seem to be working out ways to maximize the effects of its resources.

The field of social welfare is enormous, and progress toward effective, ongoing programs in all countries is small, as is evident from a study of the *World Social Reports*. The United Nations probably will not be able to change this. Only when states themselves have the necessary funds and the desire will this happen. Today, there are numerous agencies assisting governments. Often, these agencies have a difficult time cooperating with one another. Whether the United Nations will be able to improve its coordinating machinery is a question. Here, there is definitely room for improvement. Another area in which there seems to be a need for more effort is the field of evaluation of projects and programs. We still know little about how a program effects the total development process and what its long-term benefits will be. There have been beginnings made in truly evaluative studies, but as yet very few concrete results. Such studies are not possible until enough programs have been completed, a situation we may now be reaching. In both these areas the United Nations is active, but as yet the results are not too encouraging.

Chapter 18

Protecting the Rights of Persons

There have always been exceptions to the exclusive jurisdiction of states over persons within their territories. Accredited representatives of foreign powers, of course, enjoyed special status. So did most consular officials. Both groups, however, were modest in size.

Numerically more significant are resident aliens. For centuries they enjoyed special treatment. This was especially true since the Western penetration of the Ottoman Empire and the colonization of Asia and Africa. European, and to some extent American states, had little confidence in the legal procedures in these areas. They insisted and militarily enforced special treatment for their citizens. Extreme examples of this position were agreements establishing consular courts which, for all practical purposes, excluded Western aliens from local jurisdiction. Although the practice of consular courts began to decline by the end of the nineteenth century, some restraint upon jurisdiction over citizens of other states remained in force.

Exceptions to the exclusive jurisdiction of states over persons within their territories was not restricted to foreigners. During the last centuries we have witnessed a growing tendency to impose international tests even in the relationship of the state toward its own citizens. This tendency may have had a variety of origins. Undoubtedly it received its main impetus from the impact of Nazi Germany. The record of mass exploitation, the brutal violation of the most elementary human rights, in fact, the extermination of millions of people by a Western so-called 'civilized' nation reinforced the demand for some international protection of the most rudimentary rights of man.[1]

---

[1] For an analysis of the prerequisites for effective protection of individual rights, see Peter N. Drost, *Human Rights as Legal Rights* (Leiden: A. W. Sitjhoff, 1951); Arthur N. Holcombe, *Human Rights in the Modern World* (New York: New York University Press, 1948), pp. 120–141.

TRADITIONAL LAW OF STATE RESPONSI-
BILITY FOR ALIEN RIGHTS

The international rules covering aliens are to be found primarily in customary international law. Customary international law consists of those norms generally recognized and implemented by the majority of states. Since there is no convention or authoritative statement of this law acceptable to all states, the task of discovering just what the norms are is difficult. Scholars have sought to discover the law by scrutinizing the practices of states and statements of foreign offices, and by studying decisions of courts, both national and international.[2] The recognized scholars disagree among themselves, so that the student is obliged to weigh the works of these. Often, there is agreement on general principles, but on the more specific provisions of the law there is often a lack of consensus.

While customary international law has recognized the exclusive jurisdiction of a state in its relationship to its own nationals and citizens, it has set limits on the state's jurisdiction as regards aliens. In the past, these limitations were accepted by the majority of states.

In accepting these limits, a state reserves to itself the right to decide whom it shall permit to enter its territory. There is in international law no provision which gives a person the right to enter a state other than that of his own nationality. Therefore, it is perfectly permissible for a state to refuse to allow aliens generally or specific groups and categories of individuals to enter, and to refuse entrance for specific purposes or to limit the period of sojourn to a designated length of time. It is only for those persons who are *permitted* to enter a state legally that the provisions in international law covering aliens become applicable. Once a state does let aliens into its territory, it usually recognizes that its jurisdiction over these persons is not absolute. This does not mean that the alien is totally removed from the jurisdiction of the state of sojourn, or that he can do and act as he pleases, or that he has the same rights he enjoyed in his own state. Only in narrowly specified areas do states generally recognize limitations on their own jurisdiction. For the most part, the alien is obliged to obey the laws in the country of sojourn. States have usually not required aliens to serve in their armed forces or to vote if by doing so the alien would be acting contrary to his obligations to his home state. Thus, United States citizens, who by voting in a foreign election can lose citizenship, would usually be exempt from any obligatory voting laws in a foreign country. Although an alien cannot be forced to serve in the armed

---

[2] See L. Oppenheim, *International Law* (8th ed.) (London: Longmans, 1955), Vol. I, pp. 636–91; C. G. Fenwick, *International Law* (3d ed.) (New York: Appleton-Century Crofts, Inc., 1948), pp. 275–301; J. L. Brierly, *The Law of Nations* (6th ed.) (New York: Oxford University Press, 1963), pp. 276–91.

forces of another state, he can be required to participate in civil defense activities in times of emergency.

An alien retains any personal rights acquired in another state. Thus, a marriage which would not be considered valid were it performed in the state of sojourn is nevertheless recognized if it was undertaken according to the laws of the state of nationality. The same principle is applied to adoption, inheritance, succession, etc.

Although a state can bar any alien from entering its territory, it cannot prohibit him from leaving the country when he wishes, provided the alien has paid his taxes, has no court or other legal proceedings pending, and so on.

The majority of states today have very rigid legislation covering aliens. For instance, states have laws which: prohibit aliens from working except in special circumstances; bar them from engaging in certain businesses; forbid them from owning certain types of property; do not recognize professional degrees earned in other countries; place a high duty on possessions brought in or taken out of the country. These restrictions are recognized as valid in international law. At present, no principle would require a state to treat aliens in the same way as nationals. However, it is usually required that a state not restrict the movement of aliens completely. For instance, if a state does not permit an alien to live in certain areas, buildings, or hotels, there must be some place where he can live. That is, the state cannot make it absolutely impossible for the alien to exist; however, it can make it extremely difficult for him to do so comfortably. Better treatment of aliens is often secured through bilateral and, today, some multilateral agreements, or is extended on the principle of reciprocity.

From the above, it is clear that a state can, in most respects, regulate matters pertaining to aliens; but this right is not absolute. In certain areas, the state is not free to act arbitrarily. States have recognized that they have certain *obligations* to aliens. States have been willing to undertake restrictions on their own freedom of action in order to secure other states' guarantees (in the form of recognized obligations) for their own citizens.

Once an alien has been permitted to enter a country, he can expect that he will be protected in his person and property by the state of sojourn. There seems to be some acceptance of a principle which requires a state to make special provisions for aliens during periods of unrest. An alien, however, cannot expect to have special protection for his property in case of a rebellion or riot. A car left on the street, overturned, and demolished during such a period would not be considered to involve negligence on the part of the state. An individual who goes knowingly out in the streets during a riot and gets hit by a flying rock cannot claim the state should have protected him. On the other hand, if a state has some indication that antiforeign demonstrations are going to take place, and does not take reasonable steps to inform and safe-guard aliens, it can be considered to have been negligent and not to have fulfilled its obligation in international law.

These principles were long considered well established, and most states lived up to their obligations. However, today the situation is not so clear. These laws are being challenged by some of the newer states as rem-nants of the period of Western colonialism and domination. Some states have challenged the position that they should be required to give aliens pro-tection beyond what they are affording their own nationals. They see the requirements to treat aliens differently as arising during a period when the stronger states were able to enforce their will on the weaker, which usually meant the imperial Western nations demanding special treatment for their nationals in colonial and other non-Western areas. The position of these states is that aliens cannot expect special consideration although they can expect the same protection as nationals of the state in which they are sojourning.[3]

A further obligation in customary international law has been generally recognized by states—the obligation to assure aliens justice. This requirement has included guaranteeing to the alien access to regular courts or other tribunals when he considers that his rights have been violated. States have also undertaken to assure that there will be no discrimination during proceed-ings against the alien because of his status as an alien or because of his nationality.

Although there is general recognition of this "denial of justice" principle, there is wide disagreement as to the criteria by which one should judge when justice has been denied. There have been two positions: (1) "justice" to be measured by a minimum standard; (2) "justice" to be measured by standards applicable to nationals of the country of sojourn.

Traditionally, Western states have accepted the first measurement. Euro-pean states have sought to demand for their own citizens considerations often going beyond what nationals of the country expect or receive. Europeans residing in non-Western areas were used to a "higher" standard of justice and to more comfortable accommodations in jail. These Westerns put pressure on their own states to obtain guarantees in the states of sojourn that they would receive treatment more in keeping with that expected at home, or in other Western countries. This concept of a minimum standard of justice has never been clearly defined in terms of objectives and specific criteria or provisions. It is possible to state only that it has been interpreted to mean a minimum standard as judged by general Western norms.

---

[3] S. N. Guha Roy, "Is the Law of Responsibility of States for Injuries to Aliens a Part of Universal International Law?" *American Journal of International Law* October, 1961, pp. 863–92. Pal and Tunkin in *International Law Commission Yearbook*, 1957, Vol. I, pp. 165–66.

The minimum standard was never accepted by the Latin American states, who continued to apply the national standard.[4] Today, the majority of new nations and the Eastern European states support the Latin American position. This leaves only a minority of states promoting the principle of a minimum standard.

The above discussion has indicated that states recognize they have certain obligations to an alien and are prohibited from denying him certain rights. By virtue of these obligations, an individual permitted to travel, reside, or work in a foreign country will expect to enjoy certain rights and, if these are infringed, will expect a just handling of his case. If, however, the state of sojourn does not fulfill its obligations, what recourse is then open to the alien? Although in the past states have generally conformed to the accepted provisions, there have always been cases in which the individual has felt his rights were not adequately protected and observed.

In order to provide recourse in such cases, there has developed within customary international law a special institution—diplomatic protection of nationals abroad. To resort to this, an alien must have exhausted local remedies available to him. In other words, an individual cannot seek diplomatic protection for any wrong he contends has been done him until he has taken his claim before the appropriate administrative or judicial authorities of the "offending" state.

Diplomatic protection is a process involving the home state of the injured alien. This state makes direct representation to the state in which its nationals claims to have been wronged and seeks redress. In order to fit this institution into the framework of customary international law, it was necessary to develop a fiction: a state can be injured in the person of one of its nationals and, as an injured state, can demand compensation from the offending state.

It is clear that in a legal system which only recognizes states as subjects it is not possible to include provisions for individuals to bring claims directly against states. In order to get around this principle and to provide the alien with some recourse, it was claimed that when an individual did not find adequate redress in a state not only the individual, but also his home state were being wronged. Now it was possible, so the logic of this argument goes, to raise the claim from a purely national one (an individual against a state) to an international one (one state against another).

Diplomatic protection continues to be an accepted institution in international relations. Today there is less insistence on the fiction: it is generally accepted that when a state seeks redress for one of its nationals, it does so on

---

[4] For a statement of the Latin American position, see Gomez Robledo in *Yearbook of the International Law Commission*, 1960, pp. 265–69.

behalf of the individual and not because the state somehow feels itself wronged in the person of its national.

Several ways are open to the two states in these cases: (1) the case may be settled by diplomatic means; (2) the two states can agree to submit the case to special arbitration; (3) the case can be brought before a claims commission, where there is one.

Whether a state takes up the claim of its national is left to its own discretion; that is, no provision in international law requires a state to start diplomatic proceedings. A state may decide, for example, that for political or other reasons it does not want to protect a national, in which case the individual has no further recourse once he has exhausted the local remedies available to him. Hence, this system does not afford any absolute guarantee to the individual. There is no international body to which he can appeal his case, nor is the individual permitted to seek the aid of a third state. Thus, it does not seem possible to see in the institution of diplomatic protection any genuine international responsibility since: (1) only the state of nationality may seek redress; (2) there is no requirement that it do so.

Recently, in some instances the principle applied is that the individual himself can take his case to an international tribunal. These are, however, rare and are the result of special arrangements, treaties, or contracts.

1. Peace treaties: At Versailles, special provision was made for minorities of Eastern Europe. The peace treaties contained guarantees for the rights of individuals but without any right for individuals to present their cases to an international body. When, however, Silesia was divided between Poland and Germany, leaving minorities on both sides of the border, the two states agreed to permit representatives of these minorities to present cases before an international body. This agreement applied only to cases involving violations of the specific rights granted in the treaties.
2. Contracts between states and aliens: There has been a growing number of contracts to which states on the one hand and aliens on the other are parties. Most of these recognize the general principles of diplomatic protection as outlined above. A few, however, have included special provisions for an injured party to take his claim to an international body.[5] As examples: Republic of Liberia and African–American Corporation (31 March, 1955); Libya and the Gulf Oil Company (April 8, 1957); Iran–Consortium Agreement of 1920 (September, 1954).

Generally, individuals can expect to enjoy a minimum of rights when they have been permitted to enter a country as aliens, and usually states abide by the general principles discussed above. However, in the last analysis, the

---

[5] Raghubir Chakravarti, *Human Rights and the United Nations* (Calcutta: Progressive Publishers, 1958), pp. 75–78; Myres S. McDougal and Gerhard Bebr, "Human Rights in the United Nations," *American Journal of International Law,* July, 1964, p. 639.

individual must rely on the state of sojourn or his home state to enforce his rights. No international tribunal or agency is permitted to assist him. It is, therefore, difficult to see in the institution of diplomatic protection any genuine assumption of responsibility by the international community for the rights of individuals.

INTERNATIONAL RECOGNITION OF THE UNIVERSALITY OF HUMAN RIGHTS

Having looked at aliens as a category of persons for whom international law has made special provisions in the form of rights to be granted, we turn next to a consideration of human rights in general.[6] It has already been pointed out that states have traditionally considered the rights of their nationals to be within their domestic jurisdiction and, therefore, removed from the competence of international law and organization. In the following section, the extent to which human rights have been internationalized will be examined.

One human right—the right to practice one's own religion—has long been an exception to the general principle that rights of individuals were not of international concern.[7] Europe had been shaken by religious wars, and there were instances of rulers going to the aid of coreligionists who were being persecuted in other states, thus precipitating international war. In 1555, 1648, 1660, 1678, and 1697, treaties were concluded by which the parties agreed to guarantee religious freedom in their territories. Europe's concern for Christian minorities in Turkey led to the extraction of guarantees from the Sublime Porte. A number of the treaties concluded at the Congress of Vienna in 1815 contained clauses providing for religious liberties and minority rights. That states were willing to include provisions for rights in treaties indicates that they did not completely exclude human rights from the concern of international law.

These early treaties did not confer rights directly on the individual. They were agreements whereby the *state* undertook the obligation to grant certain rights. An individual who felt that his rights under the treaty were being violated could try to get redress within the state, but, if this failed, there was no international organization nor any other state to which he could turn for assistance. Thus, while states were willing to undertake certain obligations,

---

[6] For a more complete treatment of human rights and international law and organization, see Chakravarti, *op. cit.;* Holcombe, *op. cit.;* Hirsch Lauterpacht, *International Law and Human Rights* (New York: Frederick A. Praeger, Inc., 1950); Moses Moscowitz, *Human Rights and World Order* (Dobbs Ferry, N.Y.: Oceana Publications, Inc., 1958); James Frederick Green, *The United Nations and Human Rights* (Washington, D.C.: Brookings Institution, 1956).

[7] R. Chakravarti, *op. cit.,* pp. 6–11; M. Moscowitz, *op. cit.,* p. 14.

they were unwilling to establish any machinery for holding themselves accountable.

At the Peace Conference of Paris in 1919, the position of most states conformed to the traditional concept of international law and organization, and the League Covenant did not contain any provision for general human rights. In the peace treaties concluded at the same time, the major powers forced the inclusion of certain guarantees for Eastern European minorities, and the Covenant included provisions for the people in the mandated territories.[8] These were provisions for special groups of persons, and all attempts to extend even minority rights to cover all minorities were rejected. States were unwilling to accept voluntarily any commitments vis-à-vis their subjects. Only when states were forced to accept such obligations—as was the case in Eastern Europe—were these included in the agreements.

In 1919, the statesmen at Paris were still principally liberal in their thinking and attitudes; that is, "human rights" were thought of in terms of noninterference by the state. The state's job was to *interfere* as little as necessary in the affairs of its nationals, leaving them as much freedom as possible. Projected to the international level, this concept of the role of the state vis-à-vis its nationals resulted in retaining for the state the maximum degree of freedom possible. Coupled with this liberal idea of the function of law, the strong hold of nationalism needs to be mentioned. Any attempt to limit a state's freedom of action or any aspect of control was violently rejected as an interference with the sovereignty of the state. Thus, the atmosphere at Paris was not receptive to any general acceptance by states of obligations in the area of human rights, nor to supporting any program giving the League any responsibilities in this field. In human rights, the League Covenant did not represent any advance over pre-World War I conditions. Here and there, states had been forced to accept obligations, but, generally, human rights continued to belong to that sacred realm—domestic jurisdiction of states on which was placed a large sign: International Community Hands Off!

During the interwar period, changes were occurring which were to affect the atmosphere at San Francisco. The idea of the liberal state was losing out to the new welfare state. Nationally, in almost all states, growing acceptance of increased governmental action and responsibility carried over to the field of individual rights. Many realized that rights could not be protected solely by accepting the principle that states should interfere as little as possible; rather, it was recognized that rights often needed direct governmental action if they were to be guaranteed adequately. Also significant for the change in attitude at San Francisco was the shock experienced at the Germans' wanton disre-

[8] Andrew Martin, "Human Rights in the Paris Peace Treaties," *British Yearbook of International Law*, 1947, pp. 392–98.

gard for human rights, since they were considered a highly cultured nation. Here, a state had included in its ideology, as in its practice, ideas considered by many to be impossible in a "civilized" community. Leaving the Germans free to regulate human rights as they wished left the international community helpless when these rights were violated or disregarded. Should there not, asked some, be some way for the international community to guarantee to individuals at least the basic minimum rights necessary for man to live in dignity as man?

The question was raised at San Francisco. But, judging by the provisions finally adopted in the Charter, the time was not yet ripe for states willingly to accept the idea of international guarantees for human rights. However, the very fact that the U.N. Charter includes seven references to human rights does represent a step beyond the League Covenant. There was some hope at San Francisco that an international bill of human rights would be included in the Charter, but the decision was made to postpone the drafting of such a convention. It was recognized that agreement on specific rights would be difficult to work out, and some states (the United States among them) were reluctant to promote the inclusion of rights, realizing that this would increase difficulties in securing ratification. In spite of the fact that action was postponed, the promoters of international guarantees were not discouraged; there was a general feeling that a covenant would be forthcoming soon after the United Nations machinery was in operation.

CHARTER PROVISIONS FOR HUMAN RIGHTS

Of the seven references to human rights contained in the Charter, the two most important are found in Article 1.3 and Article 55.*c* (when coupled with Article 56):

> To achieve international cooperation in solving international problems of an economic, social, cultural, or humanitarian character, and in promoting and encouraging respect for human rights and for fundamental freedoms for all without distinction as to race, sex, language, or religion;
> . . . the United Nations shall promote:
> universal respect for, and observance of, human rights and fundamental freedoms for all without distinction as to race, sex, language, or religion.
> All members pledge themselves to take joint and separate action in cooperation with the Organization for the achievement of the purposes set forth in Article 55.

Examining these two provisions, the nature of the commitments undertaken by the states becomes clear.[9] States have, in actuality, not committed themselves to grant any specific rights to their subjects; they have agreed to

---

[9] See Drost, *op. cit.*, pp. 28–32.

cooperate and to *assist* the United Nations—as an organization—in *its* endeavors to promote respect for human rights. The significance of these provisions lies not in the creation of obligations for states but rather in the fact that an international organization has been given a mandate to deal with general human rights. In 1919 at Paris, the drafters did not foresee that the League should concern itself with rights, while the drafters at San Francisco put the consideration of human rights among the problems to be of concern to the organization, and many looked ahead to the eventual codification of human rights as a part of international law.

Both the General Assembly and ECOSOC are given competence by the Charter to promote human rights. It is interesting to note that in the general provisions for establishing commissions (Article 68) special mention is made of a human rights commission: "The Economic and Social Council shall set up commissions in economic and social fields and for the promotion of human rights, and such other commissions as may be required for the performance of its functions."

Under this Article, a Human Rights Commission was set up by ECOSOC. The task of this Commission was to explore the possibility of promoting international cooperation in the area. It was *not* conceived of as a body to handle individual complaints concerning nonobservance of human rights by states. Such a body would not have been possible within the framework of the United Nations as conceived of by the Charter. The mandate of the organization, as pointed out above, provides for promotion of, not enforcement of, human rights.

Many have not understood the Charter provisions. Thousands of communications, addressed to the United Nations or to the Human Rights Commission, have requested assistance or have asked the organization to consider cases of violations. Members of the United Nations were not united in their opinions of what the organizations should do with these communications, and the problem gave rise to much discussion, during which two points of view dominated: (1) the U.N. should be able to receive and examine these petitions (Latin America, Near East, Asia, Africa); (2) the Charter contained no provision for handling individual petitions (U.S., U.K., Western Europe, U.S.S.R., Eastern Europe).[10] The Commission finally agreed that "it has no power to take any action in regard to any complaints concerning human rights." This represents a valid interpretation of its competence and duties as laid down in the Charter. However, the pressure to do something continued. Some felt that many people had great faith in the United Nations, especially in the newer nations, and if the U.N. completely ignored the problems of these peoples many would lose interest in the organization. Finally, a compromise procedure acceptable to most states was worked out.

---

[10] See pp. 633–35 for a discussion of the right to petition granted under the trusteeship system.

Petitions were to be neither destroyed nor returned, but were to be read by the Secretariat, which was instructed to divide them into two groups: (1) a nonconfidential group containing a brief description of the substance of each communication; (2) confidential group, containing allegations against specific states, notice of these to be sent only to the Commission and the state against which the claims were made. Nothing further was to be done with these complaints. The Commission continues to abide by what it considers to be its mandate under the Charter and to reject any role as guardian of human rights.[11]

It is clear that at San Francisco the delegates refused to support any genuine abrogation of the traditional right of a state to regulate its relationship to its subjects, or to make the United Nations the guardian of rights. At the same time, there was hope that the United Nations would be able to promote human rights, recognition that states needed to cooperate if these rights were to become universal, and confidence that the organization could play a role in this development.

THE UNIVERSAL DECLARATION OF HUMAN RIGHTS

It has been pointed out that the delegates to the San Francisco Conference had discussed the possibility of an international bill of rights, but had finally decided to leave this task to the organization. Hopes were high when the Human Rights Commission settled down to its task. Soon, however, problems arose. In light of these, the United States insisted that the job be divided into two parts: (1) a declaration, to be tackled first and to contain a statement of general principles; (2) a covenant, to contain binding commitments and provisions for implementation of the rights. Although there were objections to this approach, it was finally accepted, and work proceeded on the Declaration. In an amazingly short time, it was possible for the Commission to present a completed draft to ECOSOC. The task was not an easy one. There were various cultural and philosophical interpretations of "rights" to be reconciled, and there was the problem of the "old" vs. the "new" rights, i.e., civil and political rights on the one hand; social, cultural, and economic rights on the other. Should only the old rights be included, as in the traditional bills of rights of Western states, or should the new rights also be included? In light of these problems, how was it possible to reach agreement in such a short time? There are, perhaps, two answers to this question. First, interest in the project was keen—the horrors

---

[11] Although this position has been maintained by the commission as regards petitions, attempts have been made to use the United Nations as an enforcement agency. See below, pp. 582–89, for a discussion of the attempts in the General Assembly and Security Council to persuade the organization to take action against states violating human rights.

of the atrocities in Europe and Asia were still vivid and frightening. Second, the document was to be a *declaration,* and, as such, to have no binding character. It was not difficult for states to support a project that had great appeal and didn't really commit them to anything concrete. Thus, in December, 1948, the Declaration was adopted in the General Assembly by a vote of 48–0, with 8 abstentions.[12] The Declaration was hailed as a major achievement of the U.N. Attention was now turned to the covenant, and the prognosis for equally speedy and successful completion was expressed by many delegates.

The Impact of the Declaration

What is the significance of the Declaration on Human Rights? First, the character as a *declaration* should be stressed. It is a statement of those rights considered to be the basic rights individuals should enjoy. In effect, states are saying: In the Charter, human rights are mentioned with the duty imposed on the organization to promote these. There has not been any agreement as to the content of these rights; now we offer a statement of the content of human rights. States do not, by supporting the Declaration, recognize any obligation to enforce these, nor do they give to the U.N. any power of supervision. The Declaration is merely a statement of what they have been able to agree are "human rights." Legally, therefore, the Declaration does not effect the competence of states to decide for themselves what rights they will grant within their territories.

Although the Declaration has not internationalized human rights, it has made some positive contributions. The very universal character of the document can be cited. For the first time, states from various areas of the globe were able to agree on what human rights are. This is an accomplishment. The Declaration can serve as a yardstick against which the progress of states and peoples in the field of human rights can be assessed. Up to this time, the only measures were those found in Western bills of rights—a situation distasteful to most of the new nations.

The Declaration has not lain idle; it has found many uses. In the United Nations, it has been cited often in regard to issues under discussion. South Africa's policy of apartheid has been attacked as violating the rights of the declaration; Bulgaria, Hungary, and Romania have been criticized for not living up to their commitments regarding rights undertaken in the peace treaties, and the argument has been buttressed by references to the Declaration. Russia's policy toward alien spouses has been denounced in the General Assembly as contrary to the rights in the declaration.[13]

---

[12] Abstaining were: the U.S.S.R., the Ukraine, Byelorussia, Czechoslovakia, Poland, Saudi Arabia, South Africa, and Yugoslavia.

[13] For fuller treatment of these and other human rights "cases" taken up by the United Nations see below, pp. 584–89.

In these instances, the Declaration has been used to reinforce cases; it has not been used as the sole basis of a complaint. When, in the United Nations, action has been taken, it has been justified by claiming that any flagrant violation of human rights impaired the friendly relations among states. The use of a violation of human rights as the basis for U.N. action against a state has met violent objections from states on the grounds that the Declaration does not give legal cause for removing human rights from the area of domestic jurisdiction. Besides being cited in specific cases, the Declaration has been reaffirmed in a number of resolutions of the General Assembly.

The most positive contribution of the declaration has been its use by the newer nations and in regional agreements:

1. The Federal Act of Eritrea includes rights taken directly from the declaration.
2. Trusteeship Agreement between Italy and Somaliland reflects the declaration.
3. The Netherlands–Indonesia Union Statute provides that the Netherlands and Indonesia shall recognize certain fundamental rights and freedoms taken from the declaration.
4. It is mentioned in the European Convention for the Protection of Human Rights.
5. The peace treaty with Japan contains guarantees based on the declaration.
6. The constitutions of the following contain sections incorporating provisions from the declaration: Indonesia, Syria, El Salvador, Haiti, Libya, Jordan, Puerto Rico, Basic Law of West Germany.[14]

Thus, the Declaration has been a useful instrument in many states, not because of any legal force but because it represents a ready-made statement of human rights acceptable to the majority of states. It is possible to foresee that it will continue to exert its influence.

THE STRUGGLE FOR GENERAL INTERNATIONAL GUARANTEES

To many, the Declaration was seen as a beginning only. Now that there was agreement on what human rights are, pressures were exerted: (1) to make the U.N. an effective guardian of these rights—if not for all individuals everywhere, at least in cases where the violations of human rights were flagrant and unquestionable; (2) to push human rights into international law by promoting binding obligations on states and effective means of international implementation or supervision.

Even though the Declaration is not a binding legal instrument, it has been accepted in resolutions of the General Assembly as establishing goals toward

[14] *United Nations Review*, December, 1963, p. 32. See also, McDougal and Bebr, *op. cit.,* pp. 639–40.

which states should strive. What has the United Nations been able to do to promote states' observation of these rights? The efforts of the international organization can be divided into two groups: (1) efforts in the organization to encourage states to bring laws and practices in their territories into accord with the Declaration; (2) attempts to deal with violations of human rights.

A System of Reporting

One of the techniques used in international organizations to encourage states to fulfill obligations is to request or require that they report to the international organization, and that the organization arrange to publish this data. Although, as has been pointed out, there are no binding international commitments in the area of general human rights, a system of reporting has been passed by the General Assembly. That this system has been adopted in spite of the absence of binding obligations is probably due to the general acceptance of guarantees for human rights as important today. Even states that consistently violate them claim they uphold them. "Human rights" are like "democracy": no self-respecting state can be without them. When the mood of the times is such, it becomes almost impossible for a state to vote against provisions for human rights without running into the danger of becoming considered somehow pariah by the rest of the states.

The Secretary-General has been instructed by the General Assembly to collect the reports of states on legal institutions and procedures for the protection and promotion of human rights, and to publish these in a *Human Rights Yearbook*. States are not obligated to submit material, but have been encouraged in resolutions of ECOSOC and the General Assembly to do so. There is no provision for any organ of the U.N. to examine this material, to check on the validity of the statements, to make suggestions, or to take action. Thus, states are free to pick and choose what they wish to submit, and it is highly unlikely that they will choose to provide information that would cast them in a poor light. What, then, is the usefulness of the *Yearbook?* It is valuable as a guide to states that want to improve their procedures for guaranteeing human rights. As the legislative and administrative practices of many states are included, a state can study these and perhaps find methods it can adopt.

Advisory Services

The second program developed to promote the observance of human rights is that of Advisory Services.[15] Set up in the Secretariat and financed by the Technical Assistance Program, this consists of sending qualified advisers to states that request assistance for drafting human rights legislation, for solving particularly troublesome problems in the field, and in organizing

---

[15] R. Higgins, "Technical Assistance for Human Rights," *The World Today*, April, 1963, pp. 174–80.

seminars, usually on a regional basis, to discuss specific human rights problems.

Neither of these two programs involves any form of coercion. This is true. However, to emphasize this is to overlook one of the roles international organizations have been assigned and one in which they have often been successful—that of availability. The United Nations is ready to help any state that applies to it, and has developed programs to make this assistance more effective. Since on the issue of human rights states are usually quite touchy, these might well prefer to turn to an international organization rather than to another state, once they decided to look for assistance (especially as the states most likely to use the service are the new nations and the states with the most experience, the Western states). Unfortunately, the Advisory Service has been requested by but a few states. On the other hand, the seminars (18 have been held) have been well attended.

Turning to the second category of action, the question that needs an answer is: How successful have international organizations (in particular, the U.N.) been in handling cases involving violations of human rights?

South Africa

A number of states have attempted to make the United Nations an effective guardian of human rights by trying to promote action against states considered to have violated human rights. The case continuously before the U.N., and in which the human rights issue has been most emphasized, is that of South Africa. Since the first session of the General Assembly, the case has been on the agenda, and various means have been used in an attempt to persuade South Africa to change its racial policy.

The problem of South Africa has been twofold: (1) South Africa's relation to Indians in her territory—a matter covered by treaty; (2) the general policy of apartheid. To solve these problems, the General Assembly has suggested round table discussions, establishment of a commission, use of the Secretary-General or another individual—i.e., it has tried just about every type of instrument evolved by international organizations to promote the peaceful settlement of disputes. Along with making these suggestions, the General Assembly has set up special commissions to study the problem and has passed a number of resolutions.

Recently, the resolutions passed by the United Nations have become more and more violent in tone.[16] The Western states, while often condemning the policies in South Africa, were, for a time, able to keep the tone of the resolutions mild in the hope that South Africa could be persuaded by the knowledge that the majority of states disapproved of her policies. Since the

---

[16] General Assembly Resolutions 1375 (XIV), 1598 (XV), 1881 (XVIII), and 1978 (XVIII); Security Council Documents S/5761 (June 9, 1964), and S/5773 (June 18, 1964).

non-Western states have obtained the majority of votes in the General Assembly, and as most of these are tremendously sensitive about the issues involved in this case, these have pushed for more condemnatory resolutions—and have succeeded. In 1960, a proposed resolution would have requested states to impose sanctions against South Africa, with the justification that South Africa's racial policy was endangering international peace. It was not considered possible to take action on the basis of a violation of human rights, but, rather, an attempt was made to show that such a flagrant violation would, and did, constitute a danger to world peace. This had to be done in order to bring the proposed action within the Charter.

The effort to initiate economic sanctions against South Africa has continued. A Security Council resolution[17] has called for cessation of the sale and shipment of equipment and materials for manufacturing and maintenance of arms in South Africa. Although the U.S., U.K., and France have opposed general economic sanctions, insisting that milder more persuasive tactics would be more effective, they did not block the establishment by the Security Council of a Committee of Experts to study the feasibility of sanctions.

The report of the Committee indicated that South Africa would be damaged by sanctions *if* these were universally applied over a sustained period of time.[18] Pressure continues to mount and it may be only a question of time before the organization adopts a comprehensive program of economic sanctions.[19]

While the major concern of the organization has been with the general policy of apartheid, cases of individual violation of human rights have been singled out for special attention. For example, a resolution was passed by the General Assembly[20] in 1963 requesting South Africa to "abandon the arbitrary trial now in progress" involving 11 charged with attempting to overthrow the government of South Africa by violence. The resolution called on South Africa to release all political prisoners held for opposition to apartheid. The action of the organization did not have any effect as the accused stood trial anyway.

The United Nations has used almost every means available in trying to get South Africa to change its racial policy. It has persuaded, cajoled, threatened. And the result of all this has been disappointing. It would seem that the effect of this terrific pressure has been to strengthen the forces within the country supporting the policy of apartheid. Many South Africans have come to regard the United Nations as an organization completely unwilling to un-

---

[17] Security Council S/5471. December 4, 1963.

[18] The Committee also pointed out the necessity for mitigating the hardships such measures would cause on the economies of some countries.

[19] For a general treatment of sanctions see the United Nations Charter.

[20] General Assembly Resolution 1881 (XVIII). October 11, 1963.

derstand their position and problems, and they seem to have little respect for the organization.

Voting on the recent resolutions has shown not only an increase in positive votes due to the addition of new members, most of whom support these measures, but has also shown a decrease in the number of abstentions and negative votes among the older members. This change is probably due to two factors—increasing impatience with South Africa and reluctance to incur the ill-favor of the Afro-Asian states. Many states seem to have become extremely annoyed over the South African issue. So much so that some condemn not only the culprit but also states that do not support stronger United Nations' action against South Africa. Since these states are now a majority in the U.N., to alienate them is often considered unpolitic.

Balanced against these pressures to support U.N. action against South Africa has been concern for the effects of such action on interpretation of Article 2.7—the domestic jurisdiction clause. The United States and Western Europe, in particular, have been reluctant to set a precedent by which the organization would be given competence to take action in cases involving human rights. They themselves do not want their problems in this area to be brought before the world organization.

Other Cases of Violations before the U.N.

The South African problem has not been the only case in which an issue has been tied to a violation of human rights in one form or another.

1. *Case Involving Bulgaria, Hungary, and Romania.* In 1949, the General Assembly requested a study of legal proceedings against church leaders in these countries considered to be a violation of the peace treaties signed by the three. The resolutions adopted by the General Assembly expressed deep concern and requested the signatories to cooperate in taking steps called for to ensure that the human rights provisions in the treaties were carried out. The case was taken to the International Court, which handed down an advisory opinion on the legal questions involved. With this, the General Assembly condemned the three for "willful refusal" to fulfill their obligations and to appoint representatives to a treaty commission as called for in the peace treaties. In this case, the charge was not that the three had violated any general human rights provisions in international law or in the Charter but, rather, provisions in peace treaties. U.N. action in these cases did not seem to have any effect on the behavior of the three states.

2. *Case Involving Prisoners of War in Russia and Eastern Europe.* In 1950, it was brought to the attention of the General Assembly that some prisoners of war taken captive during the second world war had still not been returned to their home countries. The Secretary-General was requested to appoint a commission to study the problem. When it submitted its report in 1957, several thousand persons (German, Italian, and Japanese) were claimed to be still in captiv-

ity. Although the commission appealed to Russia and Eastern European states to return these persons, no immediate action was taken. Subsequently, most of these prisoners were repatriated, but it is difficult to attribute this action solely to U.N. concern and efforts.

3. *Case Concerning Soviet Spouses of Foreign Nationals.* In 1947, a decree was passed in the U.S.S.R., prohibiting Russian citizens from marrying non-Russians, and forbidding those who had already married non-Russians from leaving the country. The problem was brought first to the attention of the Commission on the Status of Women, was passed on to ECOSOC, which referred it to the Commission on Human Rights, and was finally debated in the General Assembly itself. In a resolution passed by the General Assembly, Russia was requested to withdraw these measures. For a few of the affected persons, permission to leave the U.S.S.R. was granted; for the majority, there was no relief. For the few lucky ones, action seems to have been prompted by considerations other than the demonstration of concern by the U.N.

4. *Case of the Greek Prisoners.* Ten trade union leaders were sentenced to death in Greece. The case was brought to the attention of the First Committee of the General Assembly, which agreed to request its Chairman to discuss the problem with the Greek delegation. A later resolution of the General Assembly requested the President of the General Assembly to meet with Greek officials. In this case, there was no resolution condemning Greek action or even calling on Greece to change the sentence. Here, the action was a mandate to the officers of the organization to see whether they could help by discussing the problem. The death penalty was subsequently rescinded. In this case, it seems very possible that the action of the U.N. was a contributory factor. Greece felt the pressure of the organization and attempted to adjust her action accordingly.

5. *Case of the Spanish Prisoners.* In 1952, 24 Spaniards were arrested for taking part in a strike and were sentenced to death. The case was brought to the attention of the United Nations, where no specific action was taken. Later, the sentences were rescinded. As in the Greek case, the realization that many states condemned such severe penalities in cases of labor disturbances probably had an effect on the government of this state.

6. *Oatis Case.* In 1951, William Oatis, an American correspondent, was arrested in Prague on charges of espionage and conspiracy. He was held 72 days incommunicado, and was tried without benefit of defense counsel or the right to call witnesses in his defense. The question was raised by the United States in ECOSOC, where a general resolution abhorring arbitrary action against bona fide correspondents was passed. The case was subsequently debated in both the General Assembly and Security Council. Czechoslovakia claimed the affair came under the domestic jurisdiction clause. United Nations action had no effect on the Czech government. Oatis was later (in the post-Stalin era) released, but apparently not due to any action by the organization.

7. *South Vietnam.* In 1963, complaints were brought to the General Assembly concerning the violation of human rights by the government of the Republic of Vietnam against the Buddhist community. A mission was established by the President of the General Assembly to "collect information, conduct on-

the-spot investigations, receive petitions and hear witnesses."[21] The General Assembly never debated the comprehensive document, as the government of South Vietnam changed and it was decided that the complaint was no longer relevant.

From the above outline of some of the more important cases in which human rights issues have been involved, it is clear that the success of the United Nations has varied. In some cases, U.N. action seems to have brought—or contributed to bringing—about the desired effect; in other cases, U.N. action seems to have had little or no impact.

In analyzing the way states voted on these issues, it becomes clear that states have been motivated by political considerations as well as by regard for the actual human rights issues involved. For instance:

Russia: has consistently supported measures against South Africa and on the death penalties cases involving Spain and Greece; has voted against resolutions regarding the peace treaty rights in Bulgaria, Hungary, and Romania; the issue of spouses of Russian citizens; and the Oatis case. In cases when she has opposed U.N. action, she has attacked this as being in violation of the domestic jurisdiction provisions in the Charter. It is clear that this clause was called into use in cases involving Russia herself or her satellites but not in cases involving Western states.

United States: has often been hesitant in condemning South Africa, has voted for action regarding Hungary, Bulgaria, and Romania and Soviet wives, was against taking strong action in the Greek and Spanish prisoner cases, and took a cautious attitude in the Oatis case. The U.S. vote has not been so markedly affected by the East–West divide, although it has tended in that direction. The U.S. seems much more apprehensive of the possibility of having her own minority problems brought before the U.N. and is therefore cautious. However, the fact that she has recently supported action against South Africa indicates that she is not altogether consistent in holding human rights as exclusively within the domestic jurisdiction of a state.

The Role of the United Nations

In general, the record of General Assembly action in human rights cases leads to the conclusion that it has not been particularly effective. Where feelings are strong, such as in the case of South Africa, there is indication that spotlighting the issue in the U.N. may induce an effect opposite to that desired. In some cases, concern leading to raising the issue in the international organization may influence small states to take the desired action in order to keep their record clean and not alienate other states. Strong states, or those with the backing of strong states, do not seem to be affected by U.N. attempts to change conditions.

The question of the legality—in terms of the Charter—of even discussing

---

[21] Quoted from General Assembly Document A/5630, Annex II, in McDougal and Bebr, *op. cit.*, p. 636, footnote 132.

human rights issues has never been completely clarified, so that each time such an issue comes up those who oppose action call the competence of the organization into question. It is unfortunate to have the issues thus involved with one another, as it is often impossible to tell just what is being voted on and why states are voting as they do. Some states—especially Western European and the U.S.—are afraid of the trend to permit the organization to investigate and discuss such cases, but are sometimes persuaded to assent in order not to alienate proponents of the "cause," or because the state involved is "on the other side" in the East–West conflict.

From the above it is clear that, although the U.N. has taken action in cases involving human rights, a general proposition that violations of human rights fall within the mandate of the United Nations has been rejected. Only when human rights can be tied to some other issue, or when enough states are aroused by some allegedly flagrant violation, is the issue brought up, and even then there is bound to be opposition from states on the grounds that the organization lacks competence even to discuss the matter.

Within the U.N. it has been the General Assembly to which states have turned in search of an international guardian, or at least for a vehicle for censoring states that violate the rights of individuals. Although the record of the General Assembly cannot be considered very good, it would seem that states will continue to turn to the General Assembly for support against flagrant disregard for human rights. Which cases will be given consideration by that body and acted on will probably often be decided on the basis of political considerations rather than on any objective evaluation of the seriousness of the human rights issues involved.

Since the United Nations today cannot be considered to be an international guardian of human rights, attention will be turned to an analysis of what would be required if the organization were to perform this service, and to the steps or partial steps already taken in this direction.

For human rights to become internationally enforceable[22] there are two basic requirements: (1) clear enumeration and definition of the rights to be enforced, contained in instruments binding states to implement them; (2) machinery for international supervision and implementation.

STALLED PROGRESS ON AN ENFORCEABLE COVENANT

The Declaration on Human Rights, as already mentioned, was thought of as a preliminary step to the drafting of a binding covenant. Work on the Covenant began in an atmosphere of optimism, based on the ease with which the Declaration had been drafted and accepted by the General Assembly. Unfortunately, this optimism soon proved unfounded.

[22] Drost, *op. cit.*, chap. vi.

From the very beginning, the Human Rights Commission found it difficult to get agreement on many questions, and hopes for the speedy adoption of an international bill of rights began to dim. Today, in 1965, the task is still not completed. Many now are voicing doubts that it will ever become a reality. Others feel that even if the job is completed many states will not be willing to ratify it, and it would then be far from an instrument binding on all states.

Why has the Covenant suffered such a sad fate? The answer to this question seems to lie in a number of factors. One reason the idea of binding commitments on human rights was postponed at San Francisco was that many delegates anticipated difficulties in reaching agreement. The second attempt, which finally decided on a declaration rather than binding obligations, failed for substantially the same reason. States have been able to come to agreement on broad general principles for which they could not be held accountable. Once attention is directed to the enumeration of specific rights that will be binding on states, it immediately becomes difficult to get positive results.

Which Rights?

One of the first tasks of the Human Rights Commission was to decide on the nature of the rights to be included. The Western European States and the United States wanted to limit the Covenant to the traditional rights—i.e., those civil and political rights included in the constitutions of most of those states. The role of the government in guaranteeing these rights is often conceived of as negative and protective: the government shall not interfere in a citizen's right to free speech, assembly, and so on, and shall protect him from interference in the exercise of these by other citizens. Russia, Eastern Europe, and most of the new nations objected to this narrow interpretation of human rights. These states wanted the Covenant to cover all aspects of human rights: man should be guaranteed a "good life," he should enjoy social, economic, and cultural rights. These rights involve a much more active role for government. To translate a living wage, adequate social insurance, education, and the like into "rights" guaranteed by the government involves the state in a much broader way than does securing the "old" rights. A covenant covering the new rights would, in reality, make the welfare state mandatory in international law.

The United States and Western European states did not reject the inclusion of newer rights because they objected to making these "rights," for these states have to a large extent realized much of the ideal of the welfare state at home. But they recognize difficulties in setting up norms by which to judge whether these comprehensive rights are being upheld, and they object to establishing standards which the majority of states, as judged by Western criteria, cannot live up to for many years to come.

Because of the difficulty in obtaining agreement on the rights to be included in the covenant and the difference in the nature of government involvement in implementation of the two sets, the United States representative suggested that the commission draft two covenants—one including the traditional rights and another containing the newer ones. This suggestion was finally adopted. The implication of this move would seem to be that it has already been decided within some governments that the first convention has a chance of being ratified, but not the second. So, again, the prospects for universal acceptance of the product of the Commission seem dim.

The Problem of Implementation Systems

The second complex of problems deals with the implementation machinery. Broadly, there have been six suggestions:[23]

1. Some types of international tribunal to which individuals and groups would be able to take cases against states that had violated rights contained in the covenants (see European Human Rights Court).
2. A commission to exercise general supervision, to examine petitions from individuals or groups, and to attempt to settle controversies by negotiations (see European Human Rights Commission).
3. Ad hoc committees to be set up when the need arose to examine petitions from individuals and to publish the results of the committee's investigation (see ILO Committee on Freedom of Association).
4. A committee to examine complaints brought by one state against another (see minority and mandate provisions of the League of Nations).
5. Implementation to be left completely to states accepting the covenants, with no provision for international supervision or control (see system for non-self-governing territories under the U.N.).
6. A system whereby committees would be set up to analyze and comment on reports submitted by states (see trusteeship system).

Acceptance of any of the first three positions would mean a definite break with the traditional concept of the relationship between international law and the individual. The individual would be guaranteed the rights directly, and would be permitted to petition an international body in cases of violation of these rights.

Suggestions 4 and 5 fit more easily into traditional international law. States agree to accept certain obligations, and if they do not carry out their commitments, other states are able either to complain to the offending state or to draw the attention of an international agency to the alleged violation. In both cases, it is left to diplomacy, good offices, or conciliation to try to work out a settlement between the states; i.e., there is no provision for the confrontation of the individual and the offending state.

---

[23] For an account of various proposals for implementation and the attitude of states toward these, see McDougal and Bebr, *op. cit.,* pp. 629–35.

The problem of implementation still remains. Provisionally, a system involving a fact-finding commission to which states can bring complaints against other states has been adopted by the Third Committee for the Draft Covenant on Civil and Political Rights. For the second set of rights, ECOSOC would be given responsibility for examining reports submitted by states and for making recommendations on the basis of these. New suggestions have been made from time to time—for an attorney general, for a high commissioner, etc. But the basic problem is: Are individuals and groups to be given the right to petition an international agency directly, or will states alone be permitted to take steps when rights of individuals or groups are violated? To permit the individual free access to an international agency would strengthen the system, but would probably be unacceptable to many states, thus precluding universality. A system that does not permit the individual direct participation in an international implementation process does not afford the same level of guarantee, but it has the advantage of being more acceptable to more states.

It has been possible for the Human Rights Commission to draft two covenants. These have, since 1956, been debated in the Third Committee of the General Assembly, which worked over them article by article, and has now forewarded them to the General Assembly for its consideration.[24]

The slow progress has discouraged many. Some delegates have already indicated that their states probably will not ratify the Covenants. The provision against which there is much criticism is that granting the right of self-determination. The United States, among others, has voiced strong objections, and has indicated that if this is included there is little chance that the United States government will ratify. There has been a complete shift in the United States position. Once a strong supporter of the convention approach, the U.S. has turned to complete rejection in advance of any binding instrument. The U.S. position seems to be that any guarantees given by many states—especially Eastern European and some new nations—would be meaningless. Furthermore, there seems to be some feeling that the U.S., in which, on the whole, the citizens enjoy these rights, would be brought before the international body and judged for her shortcomings in this area by states that have a much poorer record. The U.S. is well aware that some of her policies—for example, toward immigrants—and practices— especially toward Negroes—would be considered violations of human rights. These and other considerations have led the U.S. to adopt a position against binding agreements. In order not to reject the objective completely, the U.S. has stressed the importance of seminars, technical assistance, and other means to promote the observance of rights.

---

[24] The progress of the draft Covenants in the United Nations may be followed in the yearly "Issues before the General Assembly," *International Conciliation* (usually published in October).

The U.S. has not been alone in indicating reluctance to undertake international obligations as regards human rights.[25] It also seems doubtful now that the United Kingdom will accept the final Covenants, and Russia has stated a number of times that the inclusion of any international implementation procedure involving individual redress will make the Covenants unacceptable to her. Other states have also shown signs of reluctance. Thus, the hope for a genuine, universal international bill of rights, for which there were high hopes at San Francisco, now seems dashed,[26] and it is questionable whether the Covenants will represent an advance over the Declaration.

When the time for ratification comes and states have to face the possibility of being called to account before an international body for violations of human rights—either in a state-to-state process or through some form of an individual right of petition—how many will subject themselves to this type of procedure? Or, if no supervisory machinery is included, how much more meaningful will the Covenants be than is the existing Declaration?[27]

It is clear that progress toward any genuine international acceptance of human rights as part of international law or within the competence of international organizations has been slow and hesitant. The United Nations has no clear mandate to consider cases of violations of human rights, and its efforts to take jurisdiction have not been very successful. Without a binding agreement containing provisions for some form of international supervision and implementation, there will probably be no change. International efforts, however, are not completely without effect. The organization has been given the authority and means to help these states that request assistance and through its seminars, yearbooks, and other means is keeping the goal of human rights for every individual before states and has been mobilizing world public opinion behind this goal.

REGIONAL APPROACHES TO THE PROTECTION OF HUMAN RIGHTS

In the sections above, the record of human rights in the world community has been examined. International attempts to provide protection have not

---

[25] There are indications that the United States may be changing her position. See Richard B. Bilder, "The International Promotion of Human Rights: A Current Assessment," *American Journal of International Law,* July, 1964, p. 729 and references cited there.

[26] Although there seems to be little support for pushing the covenants on the part of many states, there is an active group trying hard to keep the process moving. Within the Third Committee of the General Assembly, work goes on. Each item is discussed, and there are those who try to keep the Committee from becoming stalled on specific points.

[27] Of course, the Covenants, unlike the Declaration, will involve binding obligations on the part of states, but how meaningful will these be for the individual if there is no system for holding states accountable?

been confined to world attempts; there have also been regional efforts to internationalize human rights.

One of the difficulties encountered in raising rights above the national level has been that of reconciling definitions, objectives, and interpretations. Differences in political, social, economic, cultural, and philosophic develop-ment and backgrounds account for many of these difficulties. Rights such as freedom of speech, of information, and of association may be considered important in a stable political system; but how much freedom can a state grant its citizens when its primary aims are to unite the people, to accustom them to obeying laws, and to promote stability? Should arrangements permit exceptions? Many such difficult questions have to be answered in evolving worldwide rights.

In spite of the lack of progress in the United Nations, some states have joined in guaranteeing individual rights on an international level. Both Western Europe and the Americas have taken steps in this direction. In both of these regions are grouped states with a common heritage of philoso-phy, political ideology, and cultural tradition.[28] It is possible that this, along with the fact that only a few states are involved, has made progress easier. But even then, as will be pointed out, American efforts have not resulted in any real advance over the worldwide accomplishments.

European Experiment

The Western European region has had more success than any other in elevating some human rights above the national level. Under the auspices of the Council of Europe, it was possible for 15 countries to reach agreement on some human rights and fundamental freedoms for which the states have been willing to provide international implementation procedures.[29]

The drafters of the European Convention agreed to limit the rights for which states could be held accountable internationally to the traditional civil and political rights already largely recognized and guaranteed within their territories.[30] Only in a few instances did ratification of the Convention necessitate revisions of, or additions to, existing laws and practices.[31]

---

[28] The obvious exception is inclusion of the U.S. in the American region.

[29] For a treatment of the development of the European system, see Gordon L. Weil, "The Evolution of the European Convention on Human Rights," *American Journal of Interna-tional Law,* October, 1963, pp. 801–28.

[30] The rights originally covered included: the right to life; freedom from inhuman punish-ment and slavery; the right to liberty and security of person and to a fair trial; freedom from conviction under ex post facto laws; the right to respect for private life and to freedom of thought, conscience, and religion; freedom of expression and of peaceful assembly, and to marry and found a family (Articles 2–12). In a protocol completed in 1950, the following rights were added: the right to own property, the right of parents to supervise their chil-dren's education, and the guarantee of free elections.

[31] One example of a law that had to be changed occurred in Austria. In four cases, claims were made that the appeal proceedings in Austrian law denied the defendant proper

Probably more important than the fact that these rights were part of the legal systems of the states involved was the general familiarity of the drafters with one another's legal systems, and their confidence that the rights would be interpreted and implemented in the majority of member states in a similar way.

The approach to internationalizing human rights in Europe has been the same as that being attempted on the world level: an instrument enumerating and defining the rights that states are bound to enforce, and institutions for international implementation. The European states elected to provide international procedures that would permit the individual recourse to an international agency for alleged violations of the rights.

The European Convention does not bestow rights directly on individuals; rather, it retains the form of international conventions. It is an agreement between states in which states obligate themselves to grant the enumerated rights. Thus, it is not an enactment by an international community organ, affecting individuals directly; it becomes effective only in those states that by their usual constitutional procedures ratify and implement the Convention.

Once the rights were agreed on, the problem of implementation had to be faced. What sort of international machinery was to be established? What procedural rights would the individual have? As regards this question, the drafters showed a high degree of ingenuity. They provided for a range of international action and permitted states to accept what they wanted. The process is based on two principles: (1) state to state complaints, (2) individual petitions. The international organization was to have competence to hear complaints brought against a state either by other states or by individuals. The competence of the European organization is, however, not to be confused with a court of appeal. Its primary function is to insure that states are abiding by the obligations they have undertaken in the Convention.

The Process and the Organs.[32]   Two agencies have been created to deal with complaints—the European Human Rights Commission and the Euro-

---

administration of justice as called for in the convention. Before the cases were discussed in the Commission, the Austrian legislature passed laws to bring Austrian procedure into line with the requirements of the Convention. See Weil, *op. cit.,* p. 807; Philippe Comte, "The Application of the European Convention on Human Rights in Municipal Law," *Journal of the International Commission of Jurists,* Summer, 1962.

[32] Egon Schwelb, "On the Operation of the European Convention on Human Rights," *International Organization,* Summer, 1964, pp. 558–85; Gordon Lee Weil, *The European Convention on Human Rights* (Leiden: Sitjhoff, 1963).

The organization for guaranteeing human rights is part of the Council of Europe system. The Convention was drawn up under the Council of Europe, and the organs of the Council are used by the Human Rights Commission and Court. The "legislative" body of the council, the Consultative Assembly, is composed of representatives from the parliaments member states. A smaller body, the Committee of Ministers, is composed of the foreign minister of each member nation. It is this Committee (along with the Secretariat) that is important in the human rights system.

pean Human Rights Court. The process that was written into the Convention is a long and complicated one—no doubt, among other things, to check any tendency on the part of the international organization to act hastily or when emotions and feelings are aroused. By making the process a long one, states have some guarantee that cases will be thoroughly studied and considered before any decision is reached.

Commission on Human Rights. A body to be composed of one member from each ratifying state, elected for a six-year term by the Committee of Ministers of the Council of Europe from a list of three nationals submitted by each state. The Commission is serviced by the Secretariat of the Council of Europe. Petitions are to be sent to the Secretary-General of the Council, who turns them over to the Commission. Petitions may be sent in by states or individuals (including nongovernmental organizations and groups). In the case of individuals, only those petitions against states that have ratified an optional protocol will be processed. The Commission studies the petitions, makes a decision on whether the petition comes within its competence,[33] and informs the defending state accordingly. Most petitions thus far submitted have failed to pass this first step. The reasons most often given for rejection have been that domestic remedies have not been exhausted, the complaint was "manifestly ill-founded," was brought by an individual against a state not bound by the protocol,[34] or the time limit (between the last decision of a domestic court and presentation to the Commission) had been exceeded. Once a petition is accepted as admissible, it is sent to a seven-member subcommission, which hears both sides of the case. The first objective of this subcommission is to effect a friendly settlement between the parties. In other words, it does not "try the case," but brings the parties together and tries to help them work out an agreement; it cannot impose any settlement on the parties. Its second function is to ascertain the facts of the case. If it proves impossible for the subcommission to bring about a settlement, it sends a statement of the facts to the Commission.

The Commission examines this report and looks for any evidence of a breach of the Covenant. The Commission forwards the subcommission's statement of the facts, along with its own opinion as to whether it has found a breach of the Convention, to the Committee of Ministers of the Council of Europe. There are, at this juncture, two possibilities for further action on the case: it can go for a decision to the European Human Rights Court or to the Committee of Ministers. If the case concerns a state that has signed the second optional protocal, the Court hears the case. If the jurisdiction of the

---

[33] The process as first established involved the use of smaller committees of three to screen petitions and make suggestions on their acceptability to the Commission. This was abandoned when the number of petitions (very large when the system was first introduced) decreased to a point where it became possible for the Commission to do all the work itself.

[34] See below for discussion of protocols.

Court has not been accepted, the Committee of Ministers decides by a two-thirds vote what action is to be taken, and sends its decision to the defending state, which, by virtue of its ratification of the Convention, agrees to consider itself bound by the decision of the Committee of Ministers, or of the Court.

European Court of Human Rights. The Court consists of a number of judges equal to that of the member countries of the Council of Europe (at present 17). Judges are elected by the Consultative Assembly of the Council, and sit in their individual capacity, not as representatives of their countries. The judges sit as a chamber of seven to hear a case. The judge who is a national of the country concerned, or a person of its choice, sits ex officio. Cases can be referred to the Court by the Commission, by the government of the state whose national is alleged to be a victim, by the government that has referred the case to the Commission, or by the government against which the complaint has been made. The rulings of the Court contain a statement of reasons and are final. A judge may deliver a dissenting opinion.

This process is certainly a laborious one. However, this is to be expected where there is a definite break with tradition: international law has steered clear of permitting individuals to present cases against a state before an international forum. Exceptions have been made, as mentioned elsewhere, for certain carefully defined groups. The novelty in this Convention is that it covers *all* persons within a state. Therefore, it is not surprising that the machinery established encourages cautious action by the international agency. Members of the Commission have acted in a most conservative manner, and have been guided by a very strict and narrow interpretation of the Covenant. This is particularly evident in the early steps of the process: of the first 713 applications received by the Commission, 710 were never handed over to one of the seven-member subcommissions. It is evident that the Commission has been very careful in applying the criteria of the Convention, accepting only those cases in which there is a clear violation of the instrument.[35]

This very conservative approach may in part be attributed to the attitudes of the Commissioners themselves. Aware of the novelty of the procedure and desirous of evolving an acceptable and workable system, one thing they have wanted to avoid has been denunciation by any state for exceeding their mandate. Thus far, they have been successful. The European states now seem to have confidence in both the Commission and the Court, as evidenced by the increasing number of acceptances of the two optional protocols.

The European system has some interesting precedents which might be studied in evolving a worldwide system. One problem that had to be faced

---

[35] Of the 1,749 petitions filed in the years 1955–62, the commission, by the end of 1962, decided on 1,217. Only 13 were communicated to respondent governments before rejection, and in only 7 cases were petitions declared admissible. E. Schwelb, *op. cit.,* p. 581.

was: What would be the relationship between the individual and the international community? Should there be a break with custom and tradition and the individual be made a subject in international law, or should he continue to be handled as an object? We have seen above that the Convention holds to the traditional form by obligating states instead of bestowing rights directly on individuals. The procedure for implementation shows a similar reluctance to make a genuine break with traditional procedures. The individual is, to be sure, permitted to petition the Commission in his own right; but his right of petition stops there. It is to be recalled that the Commission does not make a binding decision on a case. It sends its decision in the form of a report to the Committee of Ministers or to the Court, and there the final determination is made. The individual cannot take his case either to the Committee of Ministers or to the Court; he cannot even appear before these bodies. Thus, once again, the insidious hold of traditional thinking regarding the relationship between international law and the individual reasserts itself.

As has been pointed out, the Convention drafters did not think it wise to include within the main body of the Convention provisions for compulsory jurisdiction by the Commission, or of the Court in any cases, in petitions brought to it by the individual. The only system dealing with complaints contained in the Convention itself is on a state-to-state basis. That is, it provides for the Commission to consider any case brought to it by another party to the instrument.[36] The extended jurisdiction of the Commission and the acceptance of the Court were not only put in optional protocols, but these protocols also could be accepted for a limited period of time. This provision was included so that states would be encouraged to "try out" the system without having to accept an unlimited obligation. Of course, the drafters hoped that all states would accept the two optional protocols for an unlimited period, but they were reluctant to make this obligatory. At the time of completion of the Convention, many expressed doubts that the optional protocols—especially the one dealing with the Court—would be accepted by many or even by enough states to bring the system into existence.

Fortunately, these doubts have proved unfounded. Article 25 (giving the individual the right to petition the Commission directly) has been adopted by 10 states, and the tendency has been for states that originally accepted this provision for a short period to renew it for longer periods. Article 46 (dealing with jurisdiction of the Court) has been adopted by eight states, two of which (Ireland and Sweden) have accepted its jurisdiction for an unlimited period of time. It would appear, then, that most of the European states do not feel they have anything to fear from participating in the entire system, that the actions and decisions of the international bodies have been such as to develop confidence in the system.

---

[36] The only cases brought by states have been two brought by Greece against Britain as regards Cypriots, and one by Austria against Italy, dealing with the South Tyroleans.

The Commission and the Court have tried to reconcile the stipulation in the Convention prohibiting an individual's taking his case to, or appearing before, the Court with a general regard for justice, including the right of an individual to argue his own case. The first case taken to the Court, the Lawless case,[37] shows how this was affected. When the vote was taken in the Commission on whether the case involved a violation of the Convention, the majority of one voted negatively. By a strict interpretation of Articles 31 and 34 of the Convention, the case should have stopped there. However, it was the opinion of the Commission that, since they were so closely split, Lawless's case should be considered by the Court.[38] When the case was brought to the Court, Ireland objected to the Court's taking jurisdiction on the grounds that the decision of the majority should have been determinant. The Court overruled this objection and proceeded to hear the case.

This action would seem to indicate that unless there is a substantial majority rejecting the indictment, a case will not be stopped from being brought before the Committee of Ministers or the Court.

The second problem the Commission attempted to resolve in its search for a just system was the prohibition on the appearance of individuals before the Court. To many, this appeared to give the state—which was permitted to defend itself—an unfair advantage. Since the Commission would be using its own report in presenting Lawless' case, it decided that Lawless should have an opportunity to comment on the findings in the report, and, accordingly, it sent its report to Lawless. Ireland objected to this action, pointing out that the Convention (Art. 31) clearly stipulated that the findings of the Commission were not to be published. The Court did not sustain the objection; rather, it said that if it should deem it necessary or helpful to consider Lawless' remarks, it would do so. It, therefore, did not turn down entirely the initiative of the Commission.

In both these instances, there is indication that the Commission and the

---

[37] Lawless was arrested on July 11, 1957, and detained without trial in a military detention camp for seven months. This action was taken under an act of 1940 which empowered the Irish government to arrest and detain persons without trial when it considered this necessary to preserve peace and public order, and after it had made a proclamation to that effect. Lawless protested the legality of his detention under the relevant provisions of the Irish Constitution and of Irish law. The high court upheld the cause of detention and rejected Lawless' plea. Lawless next appealed to the Supreme Court, invoking not only the constitution and laws of the Republic, but also the provisions of the European Convention on Human Rights. In November, 1957, the Supreme Court dismissed the appeal. Two days after the announcement of the Supreme Court's rejection, Lawless transmitted an application to the European Commission on Human Rights, alleging that his arrest and detention under the 1940 act without charge or trial violated the convention (Art. 5). A. H. Robertson, "The Lawless Case," *British Yearbook of International Law, 1960*, pp. 343–54: and A. H. Robertson, "Lawless v. The Government of Ireland (Second Phase)," *British Yearbook of International Law, 1961*, pp. 343–54.

[38] Ireland had signed both optional protocols, and so the court had jurisdiction in any case against Ireland referred to it by the commission.

Court are prepared to make every effort, within the confines of the Convention, to assure the individual a fair hearing.

Summary Observations and Conclusions: Why the System Works.
It can be concluded that the European experiment is proving itself. If, then, it has been successful, what are some of the elements in this arrangement which may have contributed to this success?

1. A document limited to a few rights on which states are in agreement and which are already largely a part of the domestic legal order of the majority of states, and with provision for extending these rights when this seems feasible and possible.[39]

2. Careful and cautious attitude of the international body in sticking closely to the Convention when accepting and acting on petitions.

3. Secrecy of proceedings. No publicity is permitted throughout the whole procedure until the Committee of Ministers is satisfied that a state is not abiding by the decision of that body, or until a case is before the Court. There is no open forum for one state to attack another in the Assembly of the Council of Europe (as has been done in the General Assembly). As a result, human rights issues have not been as politicized as in the U.N.

4. The system makes use of peaceful settlement (in the seven-member sub-commissions) before any decision on the merits of the case is made by an international body.

5. A flexible system of implementation, with the inclusion of a minimal implementation system in the obligatory part of the Convention and including a more comprehensive optional system.

6. No sanctions involved. States have shown a real reluctance in the past to take on obligations which, if violated, might result in sanctions. Where there has been provision for such a course of action by an international organization, it has usually proved unsuccessful. It is possible that in the event of habitual disregard of decisions of the Committee of Ministers or the Court, the Committee could expel a state from the Council of Europe, but it is highly unlikely that such action will ever be taken.

7. The Court can decide only on the case before it. It does not have any power of judicial review; i.e., it judges whether in a particular case the Convention rights have been violated by a state, not whether the laws of the state are in accord with the Convention.[40]

8. The system rests on the assumption that states ratifying the Convention are willing and able to abide by the obligations they have undertaken.

9. The members seem to have confidence in one another, and expect that the system will be implemented in a similar manner by all states that are parties to the Convention, so they do not fear they will be attacked by states which are themselves open to criticism.

---

[39] Protocols extending the system to cover additional rights have been adopted by the Council of Europe.

[40] It is to be expected that a state brought before the Court will alter its laws so that they are in accord with the Convention. See above, p. 594 fn. 31.

These, then, seem to be some of the elements that have contributed to the evolution of a workable system of international guarantees for the rights of individuals. Some of these conditions cannot be met on the world level for some time to come. The others should, however, be given careful consideration by those responsible for working out the details of the two Draft Covenants before the United Nations, although their inclusion cannot guarantee that those states presently voicing their doubts on ratification would be persuaded to change their positions. It is this author's opinion that for a long time to come the prospects are dim for worldwide universal acceptance of a genuine rights convention and an adequate implementation system.

Commitments of the Americas

The American states began considering the possibility of developing some form of regional international guarantees for human rights long before the 15 Western European states began drafting their convention.[41]

Like the European region, the American states (with the exception of the United States) form a community with similarities in philosophic, legal, cultural, and political backgrounds. Most have Iberian ancestry, experience with autocratic governments, and a mass of uneducated, poor peasants. The similarities, as in Europe, cannot hide the many differences that exist among these states, and especially the differences between the Latin states and the United States. Since the United States with its very different legal and social system has been included in American international arrangements, the result is a community composed of very dissimilar elements. In spite of the differences that exist, attempts have been made to form a community, one of whose objectives has been the internationalizing of human rights.

In 1945, at the Inter-American Conference at Chapultepec, a resolution to draft a Declaration on the Rights and Duties of Man was passed. The Declaration was adopted at the thirty-first Conference of American States at Bogotá. At the same time, a resolution was adopted, calling for creation of an inter-American court, but it has thus far not come into being.

The American Declaration in its form is similar to the Universal Declaration (U.N.); that is, it is not a binding convention, rather it contains a statement of rights considered important for states to grant their nationals. Unlike the European Convention, the American Declaration includes the "newer" rights—social, economic, cultural—along with the "traditional" rights—civil and political—thus reflecting the tendency of the so-called non-Western states to expand the concept of human rights while, at the same time, making it more difficult to devise effective and acceptable implementation machinery.

---

[41] For a general discussion of the development of the inter-American efforts, see Charles G. Fenwick, *The Organization of American States* (no publisher), 1963, pp. 213–16, 440–50.

The system devised by the American states and accepted by OAS in 1960 created an Inter-American Commission on Human Rights which can make general recommendations to states, prepare studies on human rights problems, and serve as an advisory body to OAS on rights questions. The Human Rights Commission also has been given some competence to deal with individual petitions: it has been empowered to receive reports on alleged violations, bring these to the attention of governments concerned, request information from these governments, and make general recommendations to the governments. This is a much less formal and "legal" procedure than that worked out by the Council of Europe countries, and it does not provide for court proceedings or actual hearings.

The American states have been unable to go much beyond the world community in elevating human rights above the sphere of domestic jurisdiction and in providing the individual with international guarantees that his rights will be observed and respected. Only Europe has been able to make some progress in this direction, and then only as regards those traditional rights about which there was a high degree of consensus before the drafting of the European Convention.

One reason for the difficulty in the American area stems from the role intervention has played in inter-American relations and law. An effective procedure for guaranteeing human rights would involve a form of intervention, and it has thus been rejected by some states, while other states have promoted it as a way to weaken particular systems. It has, that is, been difficult to keep human rights from being politicized.[42]

It would seem that states are not yet ready to accept a system of international guarantees for human rights. There is general recognition that human rights are important, and most profess to guarantee them domestically. However, all states realize that their records are not altogether spotless, and are reluctant to join in a system of implementation that might involve their being held accountable before an international body. Especially is this so if the case is brought by, or backed by, states considered even less exemplary in their systems for assuring rights, or is to be judged by delegates from states well known to consistently disregard human rights.

---

[42] C. Neale Ronning, *Law and Politics in Inter-American Diplomacy* (New York: John Wiley and Sons, Inc., 1963), pp. 63–85.

Chapter 19

Assuring the Rights of Groups

Health, welfare and the political rights of persons have gradually invited worldwide concern. The individual, however, was not the only subnational focus of international cooperation. In fact, it was preceded by efforts to assure the rights of particular groups. Whereas the United Nations was first to propose the idea of international guarantees for international human rights, international provisions for the protection of groups predated the League of Nations.

Perhaps the earliest expressions of international protection of subnational groups relate to religious minorities. Some rulers were forced to offer special guarantees; others cooperated more voluntarily. The Turkish Sultan, for example, was compelled to assure protection to Christian minorities within his empire.[1] On the other hand a number of Catholic monarchs were willing to protect Protestant minorities in the hope that Catholic minorities could remain secure in Protestant lands.[2]

The rapid rise of nationalism in the late 18th and 19th centuries generated a new minority problem. In the multilingual states of Central and Eastern Europe, the dominant group fired by zeal for a cohesive nation-state, often sought to compel the cultural assimilation of the minorities, while the latter fired by their own ethnic devotion sought to hold on to their traditions and customs. The situation became even more explosive when foreign powers intervened in behalf of irredenta groups.

The first attempts in support of national minorities were initiated on the state level; Austria and Turkey issued decrees guaranteeing minorities cer-

---

[1] See above p. 576.

[2] For a good general treatment of international efforts on behalf of minorities, see C. A. Macartney, *National States and National Minorities* (London: Oxford University Press, 1936).

tain rights. In practice these decrees were often not enforced and afforded little protection against the rising nationalist passions of the majority. Austria, one of the great powers of the time, was left to work on her minority problems without outside intervention. Turkey was less fortunate. Under pressure from other European states, the Sultan was forced, in the early 20th century, to accept outside "help" in the implementation of his more tolerant decrees on minorities.

A special case of subnational groups are the refugees. In consequence of wars, revolutions, partitions, and political persecutions millions of people left their homelands and sought resettlement in other countries. The unprecedented proportion of the problem in our century stimulated international concern to assure that these countless homeless people should be given an opportunity to start a new life.

These early attempts to guarantee rights of subnational groups developed as a result of definite problems within the European community. They may have served as early experiments. For in our time nationalism and political persecutions have reached global proportions and present an accute challenge to international cooperation.

MINORITIES, THE PARIS PEACE TREATIES, AND THE LEAGUE

The minorities question was of major concern to those statesmen who met in Paris in 1919 to redraw the map of Europe and to reestablish the peace of the world.[3] The attitude of the majority followed the principle espoused in the prewar era—minority rights should be guaranteed. The danger, as seen at this time, lay in attempts to assimilate minorities to the dominant majority in a state. Such attempts could lead to unrest within the state and to possible conflict between states, and, also for humanitarian reasons, should be avoided. At the same time, this was the period of self-determination: peoples should be permitted to determine to what nation they wished to belong.

If self-determination was a leading principle at Versailles, why were there any minorities at all? The answer to this lies in two directions. First, to carve up Eastern Europe along completely national lines is almost an impossibility. Nationalities in the region are so intertwined, with little pockets of one group surroundd by another and members of one minority sprinkled throughout the area dominated by another group. Either the idea of a state as a rather solid territory had to be replaced by the idea of a state with little pieces here and there (i.e., like the U.S. and Pakistan today), or there would necessarily have been a gigantic relocation of peoples. Second, the principle of self-

---

[3] Julius Stone, *International Guarantees of Minorities* (London: Oxford University Press, 1932), chap. i.

determination did not win complete support. For reasons of strategy, economics, or plain revenge, Europe's Eastern states were so carved out of the collapsed empires that in each one were large minority groups.[4]

Having created a situation considered potentially unstable, the effort was made to reduce the possibility of trouble. The new states and defeated countries were forced by the great powers to guarantee certain enumerated rights to members of minorities within their territories. The rights guaranteed were of two kinds: assurances that minorities would not be discriminated against as regards public employment, exercise of professions, and in industry; and guarantees that members of minorities would retain their separate identity as regards use of language, religion, and in education.

The provisions in the peace treaties could not be changed by unilateral legislation, but could only be modified with the consent of a League Council majority. The effect of these treaties was to internationalize, under the League, concern for ensuring that minorities were enjoying their rights.

Although it had been foreseen in Paris that the League should play a role in the supervision of the treaties, no specific machinery was established either in the treaties themselves or in the League Covenant, so it was left to the League Council to work out its own system, which it then changed from time to time.

It was decided that the minorities might send petitions to the League Secretariat, which would screen the petitions to see that they complied with specifications laid down.[5] The petition was then sent to the government and circulated with the government's reply to all Council members. In order to comply with the provisions of the minorities treaties, which permitted only Council members to bring a complaint before that group, a Council committee studied each petition and decided whether to bring the case to the attention of the Council.

This committee had one definite advantage: it made it unnecessary for states to act on their own in bringing complaints to the Council—a practice which puts one government in the position of acting as accuser, an unpleasant position. In the system evolved, a committee performed this function. This tended to make the practice more palatable. The committee was also reluctant to bring a case before the Council until it had attempted itself to bring about a friendly settlement. If, however, its efforts in this direction failed, the case came before the Council, which also could try to

---

[4] It has been estimated that between 20 and 30 million people remained as minorities in this area. See L. A. Mander, *Foundations of Modern World Society* (Stanford, Calif.: Stanford University Press, 1948), p. 665.

[5] See Raghubir Chakravarti, *Human Rights and the United Nations* (Calcutta: Progressive Publishers, 1958), pp. 16–18; Julius Stone, *op. cit.;* and L. P. Mair, "The League Council and a Minorities Commission," *The Political Quarterly,* July–September, 1930.

persuade the government to alleviate the conditions leading to the petition. The Council also had authority to send any legal questions involved to the Permanent Court.

The League system for guaranteeing minority rights was one of trying to persuade states to live up to their commitments in the treaties; it did not provide for a genuine system for deciding cases or enforcing decisions. It relied on the willingness of states to comply with suggestions from the Council or on their vulnerability to pressure from this body. Although the individual was permitted to petition the League, the decision as to what petitions would be acted on lay with a committee of the Council. If this committee refused to submit a petition to the Council, the petitioner had no recourse unless he was able to interest some other Council member in his case—as usually happened when for political reasons one state was looking for an opportunity to embarrass another state. In general, it can be said that the system did not prove very successful.

One other effort was made by the League to guarantee the rights of minorities—the special regime for Upper Silesia. As in the case of the minorities treaties, this regime was an imposed one—imposed by the great powers on Poland and Germany. The border between Poland and Germany in Upper Silesia proved so difficult to agree on that its final delineation was postponed at Paris. When the decision on the border was made, it left sizable Polish minorities in Germany and German minorities in Poland—and neither state satisfied with the decision.

Both states were forced to undertake obligations similar to those undertaken by Eastern European states in Paris. However, implementation was not entrusted directly to the League, but to a special body located in the area. It was thought that the proximity of the agency to the problem areas and its removal from publicity would enable it to be more effective. In each country were minority offices to which complaints could be brought. If the matter could not be settled at this level, the petition was forwarded to a president. On the whole, the system worked well, as long as Poland and Germany agreed to cooperate with it. However, in 1937, the two states decided to discard the international machinery, and agreed by treaty to handle their own minority problems.

FAILURE OF A SYSTEM

A system such as that devised by the League and dependent on the good intentions of states can work as long as states accept the objectives of the system. If states are generally willing to carry out their obligations, a system of petition, conciliation, and pressure from the world organization can be adequate to take care of any slight infractions and violations which might occur. However, when the very idea of the institution—in this case, the protection of minority rights—is rejected by states, or when states begin to use minorities in other states for their own political purposes, there is little prospect for success. This is what occurred in Europe.

The principle behind the minorities arrangements was not completely accepted by the states subjected to the system. Poland made the strongest objections on the grounds: first, that the system represented an intrusion into what was actually a domestic affair; second, that it put those states having to accept the minorities treaties in an inferior position. This second objection was leveled against the great powers and other European states which, while proclaiming the justice of the system, were completely unwilling to adopt any obligations or international supervision as regarded their own minorities. These new states were embarking on the job of molding and building their own identities, and were often unwilling to accept the idea of permitting groups to maintain a separate identity. Minorities were often criticized for not wanting to integrate and assimilate. Among many of the minorities appeared individuals and groups who reacted to pressure from the dominant group and did not feel they owed any particular loyalty or allegiance to the state.

When the National Socialists seized power in Germany, they were able to take advantage of this discontent. In Eastern European states were groups and colonies of Germanic peoples—many of these in settlements started several centuries ago. The Germans, with their racial ideology and theories of the "master race," were able to appeal to those elements of the Germanic groups who resented the pressures to integrate coming from the dominant majority. The use to which these minorities were put is well known.

At the same time Germany was coming to the defense of "persecuted" minorities in Eastern Europe, claiming that these were not being permitted to enjoy the rights assured them at Paris and objecting to measures introduced to assimilate them, she was making sure that certain of her own groups would not be assimilated to Germans. Germany attempted to isolate the Jews completely and, later, to exterminate them. It is interesting that the German Jews were probably the most assimilated and loyal minority in Central Europe, and that it was Germany's aim, in this case, to "unassimilate" this group.

In both cases, Germany was acting in accordance with the principle accepted at Paris: minorities should be guaranteed their own culture and rights and not be forced to assimilate. It is small wonder that this principle was discredited! After the second world war there was no longer talk of "protecting" minorities or establishing special regimes for them. The experiment was considered to have failed. Most states were now unwilling to promote the cause of the minorities.

Although the League regime was based to a large extent on the principle of preserving the separate identities of minorities within a mixed state, there was one other approach tried—the transfer of populations. In the Balkans, the problem of minorities was "solved" by providing for the return of ethnic groups to the "mother country"—a country often never visited by the returned individuals, many of whom could trace their ancestry in the "foreign" country back several generations. Two such major population switches were effected during the League period—between Greece and Bulgaria, and between Greece and Turkey. Another transfer was agreed to by Hitler and Mussolini—the transfer of the Southern Tyroleans "back" to the Reich—an operation never completed.

The role of the League was a significant one in the first two transfers. The international organization was able to help make the move and reestablishment of these peoples easier and smoother than it might otherwise have been. League representatives supervised the actual transfer of Greeks, Bulgarians, and Turks, and the League was able, once these had arrived in their new homelands, to help them start rebuilding a new life.

As far as many were concerned, these experiments were successful. The states were relieved of a minority problem. But successful only if the individual is forgotten: great numbers of people were uprooted from lands they thought of as their own, and were returned to a "home" they had never known.

Although such transfers involve hardships for individuals, there may be times when this type of a solution may prove to be a satisfactory one. Where there are strong national feelings fed and supported by outside powers, a transfer of the minority may be the only way to put an end to a difficult situation. An example of the problem is Cyprus. There, a Greek majority and a Turkish minority have been unable to work out a satisfactory pattern of coexistence. The situation has been exacerbated by Greece and Turkey, each concerned with its own conationals on the island and, at times, indicating a willingness to interfere physically on their behalf. The result has been unrest, finally erupting into civil war. To some, the Cyprus problem is a clear case for which resettlement is the solution.

Where resettlement seems called for and can be agreed on, the international organization can play a significant role in supervising the actual transfer of peoples and in assisting the new immigrants to resettle should the states involved be unable or unwilling to do so.

The principle this approach attempts to promote and to preserve is that of the uninational state. Since minorities can cause both internal tension and international crises, say the proponents, the best way to promote harmony is to keep the state as free from minorities as possible.

THE UNITED NATIONS AND MINORITIES

Although those meeting at San Francisco declined to institute a minorities system as had been tried under the League, the United Nations has not remained oblivious of the problems of minorities. On December 10, 1948, the General Assembly passed a resolution[6] stating that the United Nations could not remain totally indifferent to the fate of minorities and calling on the Subcommittee on the Prevention of Discrimination and the Protection of Minorities[7] to make a thorough study of minorities and their problems.

The Subcommittee attempted to define and categorize minorities, to make a world survey of their conditions, and to develop some sort of definition of minorities in need of protection. From the very beginning, the Subcommittee met with violent objections to its undertakings. The Subcommittee had interpreted its task as a twofold one: to define the kinds of special protection a minority needs to preserve its cultural identity on the one hand, and an analysis of nondiscriminatory practices necessary to assure minorities participation in the political and economic life of the state on the other hand. The problem was to try to balance the needs of the minority and the needs of the state. Objections centered on any efforts to protect the separate identity of the minority.

In the face of the very impassioned rejection of this dual approach to minorities, the Subcommittee decided to confine its efforts to problems of discrimination—that is, to the "assimilation" approach. Even attempts to define and group minorities according to any criteria have failed. The Subcommittee undertook its task in the hope of producing a system for the protection of minorities, but became completely discouraged by the reaction of many states. It finally was forced to conclude that the problem was insoluble for the time being, and suggested that it be laid aside. Since that time, the primary contribution of the Subcommittee has been its studies of minorities—location, size, types, and evidences of discrimination.

There appears to be tremendous reluctance on the part of much of the United Nations membership to having the organization undertake any action to protect minorities. The emphasis has been on the importance of preventing any discrimination—although without much support for any form of international supervision—and, generally, the objective seems to be to encourage the assimilation of minorities. It is the potentially disruptive aspect of minorities which states fear. Many seem to consider it more important to avoid trouble than to try to work out a system that would be based on the principle of a multigroup state composed of many groups who would preserve their own identity and culture. Rather, it is the homogeneous state that is to take precedence.

---

[6] General Assembly Resolution 217 C (III).

[7] This Subcommittee was established in 1947, and by its very creation shows that a majority of the General Assembly was willing to support some form of consideration of minorities by the organization. For a description of the committee at work, see Inis L. Claude, Jr., "The Nature and Status of the Subcommission on the Prevention of Discrimination and Protection of Minorities," *International Organization,* May, 1951, pp. 300–312.

Many of those emphasizing the need for creating the image of a state as one united people have had unfortunate experiences with minorities. Not only European but also many Latin-American states have had difficult problems to work out with their minorities. Other states are in the process of statebuilding. The cold war, with the fears it arouses, and the so-called need for unity in face of the enemy have increased the appeal of the assimilation approach.

Another factor is the emotional response to discrimination today. Any kind of discrimination is considered an evil; the cry is for equality and equal treatment, not only in the traditional sense of equality before the law but in all ways. This tremendous emphasis on equality makes it difficult to gain support for any measures that, instead of promoting the idea of equality and sameness, justify the preservation of differences. Today, it seems that to be "different" is to be unequal. States want to be considered equal to one another even when there are wide differences that preclude any genuine equality, and internally, for a variety of reasons, stress is on equality, integration, and assimilation.

It has been impossible for the United Nations, in face of the tremendous objection to any measures that would give minorities special rights, to devise any system for protecting the identity of minorities. The emphasis is on human rights to be granted on the basis of equality and nondiscrimination. No one should suffer because he is a member of a minority group. Only states and former colonies are to enjoy the right of self-determination, and any efforts by minorities within states—the South Moloccans or Hyderbadis, for example—have been unsuccessful in the United Nations. Nationalism and equality are the principles to which most states are giving their allegiance today.

The most recent action of the U.N. regarding groups generally has been the passing of a Declaration on discrimination by the General Assembly in 1964. The Declaration calls for equality and nondiscrimination. The emphasis accepted in this Declaration is on the unity of groups within a state. All groups should be treated equally by the government and by other groups within a state.[8] The drafters of the Declaration had no intention of providing minorities with any special rights or privileges to assure these their separate identity.

Now that the Declaration has been passed, work has begun on a convention that would have binding legal character. It will be interesting to follow progress of this effort to see whether it runs into the same kinds of difficulties as did the attempt to draft a binding human rights covenant.[9]

---

[8] The United States and some other states objected to the provisions concerning nongovernment action as necessitating interference by the government in the private affairs of citizens. The objections were turned down by the majority of members of the General Assembly.

[9] See above, pp. 589–93.

PREVENTION AND PUNISHMENT OF GENOCIDE

Although members of the United Nations have been reluctant to guarantee to groups special minority rights and privileges, they were—in the first years of the organization—concerned with the problem of total extermination of groups. That is, while members of the organization have been unwilling to undertake any obligation to recognize a right to political self-determination[10] or cultural identity on the part of groups, there is consensus that the actual physical identity—the very existence—of groups be guaranteed internationally.

Concern for such international guarantees developed as a response to the experiences of certain minorities in Nazi Germany. Hitler was not the first leader to advocate the destruction of a people, but his attempt to eliminate the Jews was supported in modern times by an advanced nation, and was of such proportions and carried out in such a ruthless and efficient manner as to arouse complete revulsion among many in the world.

Genocide, a term invented to fit this crime, was the subject of one of the first resolutions of the General Assembly, calling for a convention to outlaw the practice internationally. The Convention was adopted by the General Assembly by a vote of 55–0 on December 6, 1948.

The Convention has been ratified by 66 states. The principle involved is one that is approved by most states, but still the Convention has failed to secure ratifications from such "civilized" states as the United States and the United Kingdom.

Within the United States, the ratification of this Convention became a major issue. Ratification was attacked by those in the U.S. who opposed using treaties in the field of human rights. Many feared that this would mean giving jurisdiction to the federal government in an area at present reserved to the individual states. The opposition put its case before the public in numerous speeches, articles, and editorials. Some of these gave the impression that U.S. ratification meant giving jurisdiction over U.S. citizens to an international tribunal—an erroneous interpretation of the Convention. Although a special subcommittee of the Senate Committee on Foreign Relations recommended approval, the Committee itself took no action on the convention.

Genocide, defined in the Convention as acts such as killing, causing bodily or mental harm, deliberately inflicting conditions of life, "committed with intent to destroy in whole or in part, a national, ethnical, racial or religious group," is a crime for which individuals are punishable by

---

[10] Except in the case of colonial areas. For a discussion of the right of self-determination, see below, pp. 652–77.

the states in which the crime is committed, unless an international tribunal is established, with jurisdiction over cases of genocide.[11]

The provisions for implementation are very mild as far as the actual involvement of an international organization is concerned. The Convention provides (Art. VIII):

> Any Contracting Party may call upon the competent organs of the United Nations to take such action under the Charter of the United Nations as they consider appropriate for the prevention and suppression of acts of genocide. . . .

Although genocide is now a crime in international treaty law, the United Nations has not been given any genuine responsibility for enforcing the law. Allegations of genocide have been made from time to time and the cases discussed in the General Assembly, but little action has evolved from these debates. One of the most recent assertions of the crime of genocide has been made against the Huti for their treatment of the Watutsi in Rwanda. The division of the Belgian trust territory into two states left minorities in each section. The majority group in Rwanda, the Huti, had been servants and workers for the Watutsi. Once freed, these undertook to wipe out their former masters. The case was brought to the United Nations, where it was debated in the General Assembly.

The drafters of the Convention—whose primary objective was to prevent a recurrence of the Jews' experience under the Nazis—seem to have overlooked the source of the German action. The policy was government sponsored and government directed. Under the Genocide Convention, the German government would have been obligated to punish offenders. Is it to be expected that those members of the government responsible for the policy would instigate proceedings against themselves? There is in the Convention no provision for the suffering minority group to appeal to an international agency, nor does it even make legal the intervention of the United Nations or other states in cases of flagrant violation. To be sure, genocide enjoys the moral condemnation of all nations, but this is small comfort to a minority threatened by a determined dominant group.

The attempt to provide international guarantees to prevent states from totally wiping out groups within their borders has not been so successful as many had hoped. The problem continues to be one of reconciling the desire of groups to enjoy their own identity within a state with the need and pressure for the unity of the state. The principle seems to be accepted that

---

[11] At the time the Convention was drafted, there was optimism concerning the possibility of establishing an international criminal code and court, and the drafters of the Genocide Convention anticipated that this court would have jurisdiction in cases of genocide. The code and the tribunal have not materialized, thus leaving punishment of the crime to each domestic legal order.

states should not go so far as to attempt to wipe out minorities. However, states have been unwilling to undertake binding commitments and to participate in an international system to assure even the physical preservation of minority groups.

REFUGEES

The history of international efforts on behalf of national, ethnic, and religious groups has not been a particularly successful one.[12] However, for one group, the effects of international cooperation have been very different. The story of international efforts on behalf of refugees is one of the brightest chapters in the development of international law and organization.

One of the first problems is to define "refugee." Generally, refugees today are divided into two broad categories: (1) international refugees; (2) national refugees.

International refugees are those persons who, because of persecution or fear of persecution for their religion, politics, culture, or nationality leave the country of their nationality and seek refuge in a foreign state. National refugees are persons whose reasons for leaving an area are generally the same as those of the international refugee, but who seek refuge in a state which recognizes them as nationals. The Volksdeutsche expelled from Eastern Europe after World War II were accepted by Germany (East and West) as Germans. The Muslims fleeing to Pakistan and the Hindus to India were accepted by these states as nationals. The Chinese leaving the mainland are recognized as having the same nationality as the peoples of Hong Kong and Taiwan. East Germans in West Germany and North Koreans in South Korea are national refugees. Generally, the international efforts on behalf of refugees have been confined to international refugees.[13]

Before discussing international refugee law and organization, one further group needs mention: the Displaced Persons. These were people outside their homelands at the end of World War II. Most had been part of the large-scale slave labor projects of the Nazis. The greater part of this group was both willing and able to return to their homelands, i.e., there was no element of persecution involved for most. Therefore, they did not fall into the category of refugees. Some of these persons did eventually become international refugees. Many DP's returning to Russia and to some of the Eastern European states were persecuted on arrival. News of this reached the DP camps in

---

[12] For a general treatment of the development of international refugee law and organization, see Joseph B. Schectman, *The Refugee in the World* (New York: A. S. Barnes & Co., Inc.,). John George Stoessinger, *The Refugee and the World Community* (Minneapolis: The University of Minnesota Press, 1956).

[13] There have been exceptions: League efforts on behalf of Greeks, Bulgarians, and Turks; the work of the United Nations agency in South Korea, etc.

the West and led many of the remaining DP's to seek refugee status. The Western states recognized that now there was the element of persecution and, therefore, that these persons could be considered genuine international refugees.

In the following sections, the term "refugee" is used to refer to "international refugees."

Refugee Law

Refugees form a minority group in any country in which they are found, but the history of their place in international law and organization relates them more to aliens than to minorities. They have been treated as a special kind of alien rather than as a type of minority.

Refugees could, however, not be assimilated completely to aliens, for a characteristic of the alien, on which his international rights and privileges have been based, is his nationality. The whole system of diplomatic protection is premised on the fact that an alien has a home state to which he can turn for protection if his rights are violated and to which he can return. Behind the tradition of alien rights is always the principle of reciprocity: you treat my nationals well, and I will treat yours equally well.

The refugee is, however, an alien without a home state. In some cases, he loses his nationality when he becomes a refugee, thus becoming *de jure* stateless; otherwise, he retains his nationality but ceases to enjoy the protection of his state of nationality, and then is usually considered *de facto* stateless. It is this characteristic of the refugee—his statelessness—that sets him apart from other aliens in international law, and has prompted special consideration and action. A stateless person has no state to which he can return and enjoy full rights of citizenship if he is dissatisfied with his alien status; he is always an alien and in need of special rights if he is to exist normally in most states today.

Unless special provisions are made for him, the refugee is generally subject to laws covering aliens. Alien legislation is often very restrictive, making it difficult for aliens to work, to rent adequate housing, to travel, etc. Improvements in the conditions are usually made on the basis of reciprocity, making the refugee ineligible. Much of this restrictive legislation developed from pressures in a state to protect citizens. When jobs are scarce, why should aliens be hired? When housing is limited, why let aliens rent the more desirable (i.e., often the cheaper) units? Why should aliens receive public assistance or social security benefits when they have not contributed to the accumulation of such funds?

Europe, the center of most refugee populations until recently, had such restrictive legislation during the interwar period, just at the time when the first groups of modern refugees started dribbling across the continent—the

Russians. Unable to accept the new order in their homeland, these were the first refugees for whom the international community showed a concern—a concern that has continued down to today when refugees from Algeria, Pakistan, Angola, from Rwanda, China, and many other areas have received international assistance in one form or another.

Since the early days of the League, international action on behalf of the refugees has had two aspects: (1) drafting and promotion of international agreements by which states obligate themselves to grant refugees rights and to provide them services; (2) development of international organizations or agencies to assist refugees in lands of asylum and to aid in their resettlement or integration. Thus, from the very beginning, the approach to the refugee has been both legal and organizational.

Agreements have contained provisions by which states obligate them-selves to grant the refugees certain rights. The early agreements usually assimilated refugees to other aliens; that is, refugees were to enjoy rights equal to those being enjoyed by aliens. Special provisions were made for problems peculiar to refugees—identity papers, travel documents, and oth-ers. Recently, agreements have contained an increasing number of provisions for refugees to enjoy rights on the same footing as nationals.

These agreements do not confer the rights directly on the refugee.[14] They are international instruments: states undertake obligations that they agree to carry out in their own territories. The refugee cannot appeal to an interna-tional tribunal; his only recourse in law is the court in the country which has offered him asylum.

If the obligations are not enforceable internationally, making them of the same nature as those undertaken in various minority agreements, why has implementation of refugee conventions met with more success than that of the minorities agreements? One answer lies in the way the obligations have been undertaken. In the minorities agreements, the instruments were often forced on states, giving rise to a feeling of resentment and inferiority; while refugee agreements have always been entered into voluntarily by states. Refugees have seldom become a political force regarded as a danger to the state; their numbers are usually small. Thus, they do not seem to constitute the same kind of threat that minorities do.

The cause of the refugee has a strong humanitarian appeal, and has had large nongovernmental support—for example, the Red Cross. It is probably this humanitarian appeal and the fact that early conventions contained minimum obligations that account for states having entered into these agreements willingly and having generally lived up to their commitments.

---

[14] Paul Weiss, "International Protection for Refugees," *American Journal of International Law,* April, 1954, pp. 193–222. Louise W. Holborn, "The Legal Status of Political Refugees, 1920–1936," *American Journal of International Law,* October, 1938, pp. 680–703.

International Refugee Organizations

The second answer to the question of the success of implementation must take into account the role of international organizations. Along with the development of international refugee law has gone that of international refugee organization. The agencies established have not been tribunals or commissions before which refugees or other interested parties could bring complaints against states. They have had two primary responsibilities: (1) to coordinate efforts for relief and resettlement; (2) to afford the refugee legal and political protection and assistance.

Early in the history of the League refugee agency, there was concern for the difficulties the refugee was having in individual states. The international agreements of the time did not adequately provide for his needs. Even these were sometimes not being implemented quite satisfactorily. Under the leadership of Nansen, first League High Commissioner for Refugees, a way was sought to satisfy the needs of the refugees. States were asked whether they would permit a representative of the High Commissioner's Office to assist refugees within their territory. All states with sizable concentrations of refugees agreed to this suggestion, and so developed the tradition of a network of local branches of the international agency. The representatives in the branches, being on the spot, could study the problems peculiar to the refugee in each country.

These representatives had no authority to force governments to do anything. They could merely bring problems to the attention of the proper authorities and suggest solutions. Having studied conditions in the country, the representatives were often able to make suggestions acceptable to the authorities, and, in many instances, the lot of the refugee improved. The representatives were also able to assist the refugee to enjoy the rights to which he was entitled. Often, ignorance of the laws on the part of the refugee or the local officials as well as language difficulties kept refugees from benefiting from provisions made for them. Representatives were sometimes able to remedy this situation.

An attempt was made in 1922 to give the High Commissioner's Office more authority in states. However, only France and Belgium ratified the agreement, so the informal method continued.

The system for helping refugees as developed by the League proved effective. It did not solve all the refugee's problems; it did, however, lead to improvements in conditions in most countries. It succeeded as well as it did because states themselves were willing to grant rights and provide services. But willingness is not always enough. The system of having within the states representatives of the international agency, sensitive to both the problems of the refugees and to conditions within the country, proved itself during this period.

The League agencies did not have funds to assist the refugee to reestablish himself. It was, however, felt by many that the High Commissioner should be concerned with more than the legal problems in lands of asylum, that he should assume an active role in the resettlement of refugees. For this reason, his mandate included the coordination of private and public agencies engaged in giving material and other assistance to refugees. This has continued to be an important aspect of the work of international refugee organizations; and it has often resulted not only in channeling money to groups who might otherwise have received no aid, but also in helping to prevent duplication of efforts. The High Commissioner, with his knowledge of the total refugee problem, is able to help agencies develop more rational programs of assistance to refugees.

Although the end of the League period saw many problems unsolved and many refugees unaided, it was a period when effective patterns, approaches, and methods were initiated and developed. Except for short intervals, these have persisted until the present.

During the war, international refugee work slowed down. States were too concerned with more pressing problems. However, toward the end of the war it became apparent that when they got into Germany the allies would be faced with an enormous problem in the form of millions of Displaced Persons. It was decided that the care and repatriation of these persons would be entrusted to the United Nations Relief and Rehabilitation Administration (UNRRA).[15] The DP did not fit the definition of a refugee used in international law and organization, for these people did not lack a home state to which they could return as they were nationals of allied and associated powers.[16] It was thought at the time that the problem would be that of providing means for sending these people back to their countries and, until this was possible, for caring for them. A large part of these persons needed only this kind of assistance, and were adequately provided for by the organization.

UNRRA represented a new concept in, and approach to, refugee work: UNRRA was to take complete charge of DP's until these could return home. Housing, feeding, medical attention, law and order—all were provided by the international agency. In those countries where it was caring for DP's, UNRRA became almost a state within a state. This was possible for two reasons. First, the allied powers, which had created UNRRA, provided it with adequate funds. Second, the areas with high concentrations of DP's were the ex-enemy states of Germany, Austria, and Italy. These were not in a position to refuse the intrusion of the agency—even in Austria and Italy, where the agreement was made between UNRRA and an indigenous govern-

---

[15] Displaced persons were only a part of UNRRA's postwar operations. For information on its reconstruction activities, see below, Chapter 13.

[16] For a discussion of the term "international refugee" see above, p. 613.

ment,[17] consent was willingly given. If for no other reason, the financial argument was compelling. To care for this number of aliens would have been difficult for these states, dependent as they were on UNRRA to supplement their resources if they were to keep their own peoples alive.

When UNRRA's end neared, the problem of the DP was still far from solved. Within the United Nations, the suggestion for creating a temporary Specialized Agency, the International Refugee Organization (IRO), was accepted.[18] IRO, like UNRRA, was provided with funds adequate to assume full responsibility for the care of the refugees. IRO's mandate called for the agency to repatriate the DP, but also permitted it to look for other solutions—integration in the country of asylum or resettlement in another country. By the time IRO began operations, the majority of DP's remaining in camps were unwilling to return to their homelands in the East. In spite of pressure put on the organization and on the U.N. by Russia and other Eastern European countries,[19] IRO mobilized its efforts to find opportunities for resettlement in other European countries and overseas, and undertook programs for the transportation and settlement of refugees. IRO, a temporary agency, knew it had to look ahead and realized that those DP's who were destined to remain where they were, either from choice or because no other country would take them, could not continue to exist in isolated communities under an international organization. So, gradually, IRO turned over many of its functions to indigenous governments.

It had been hoped that IRO, during its four years of operations, could solve the problem of Europe's DP's, now genuine refugees.[20] However, not only were there numbers of original DP's who could not be resettled, but also new refugees began arriving from Eastern Europe. Many hoped that the life of IRO could be extended, even if on a reduced scale. Resistance, especially from the United States which was unwilling to continue to financially support an operating agency, was too great, and IRO closed its operations.

The majority of members of the United Nations were unwilling to see the United Nations completely divest itself of all responsibility for refugees, and

---

[17] In Germany, agreements were made with the occupation authorities, as no German government existed at the time.

[18] A comprehensive analysis and description of the IRO is found in Louise Holborn, *The International Refugee Organization* (London: Oxford University Press, 1956).

[19] While Russia and many Eastern European states had been members of UNRRA, they refused to join IRO, partially because they did not want to support the organization financially, and partially because they considered those DP's not returning home as traitors, war criminals, etc., and, therefore, unworthy of international assistance. To these states, the only "solution" to the DP problem was repatriation—a solution unacceptable to many Westerners because repatriation often meant death, prison, or banishment for the returnees.

[20] See above, p. 613.

so it was decided to return to the League pattern: a high commissioner with responsibility for the legal and political protection of refugees, and for the coordination of public and private assistance.

The Magna Charta for Refugees

Not only did the United Nations return to the League pattern in organization, but it also renewed efforts to expand international refugee law. As long as the majority of refugees was enjoying the special legal protection of UNRRA and IRO—both had persuaded governments to make special provisions for refugees to work, provided them with the necessary identity and travel documents, etc.—there was little interest in the development of international agreements of the nature drafted in the interwar period. Once IRO's termination was settled, however, there was pressure from the organization itself and from a number of states to improve the status of refugees through international agreements.

In 1951, a conference was called to draw up a new refugee convention to supersede all prior agreements and to improve the status of refugees. The result of these efforts was the Geneva Convention, the "Magna Charta of Refugees."[21] It does go beyond previous agreements, especially by providing many rights equal to those of nationals rather than, as in most prewar instruments, equal to those of aliens generally. The Geneva Convention is the same type of agreement as the earlier ones: rights are not granted refugees directly, but, rather, states undertake obligations. Today, more than 40 states have ratified this agreement, including most Western states (except the United States) and many new nations. The Russians and Eastern Europeans (Yugoslavia is an exception), from which many of the refugees covered have been coming, have not become members and have refused to support the work of the High Commissioner.

The Geneva Convention is similar to prewar instruments in that it does not cover *all* refugees. It singles out groups of refugees for whom its provisions will be operative—in this case: (Art. 1)

> For the purposes of the present Convention, the term "refugee" shall apply to any person who:
> 1) Has been considered a refugee under (past) Arrangement(s) . . .
> 2) As a result of event occurring before 1 January 1951 and owing to well-founded fear of being persecuted for reasons of race, religion, nationality, membership of a particular social group or political opinion, is outside the country of his nationality.

---

[21] Article-by-article commentaries of the Geneva Convention are provided in Nehemiah Robinson, *Convention Relating to the Status of Refugees* (New York: Institute of Jewish Affairs, 1953); C. A. Pompe, *The Convention of 28 July 1951 and the International Protection of Refugees* (mimeographed) (United Nations High Commissioner for Refugees, May, 1958).

The Statute of the United Nations High Commissioner for Refugees (UNHCR) also limits the coverage of the international agency in a similar way, except that it does not completely limit the agency to the time limit established in the Convention. Both instruments exclude persons being helped by other organs and agencies of the United Nations, those who are recognized as having the same nationality as persons in the land of asylum, and criminals whose crimes are extraditable. Ways have been sought to get around these confining restrictions. The Geneva Conference passed a resolution encouraging states to extend the benefits of the Convention to other refugees, and representatives of the UNHCR in the various countries have worked to this end. In the case of the High Commissioner's mandate, a way around the limitation has been found through the use of good offices.

The High Commissioner's Office has felt that it should be the hub of refugee work throughout the world, not merely confined to certain specified groups of refugees. The Office, therefore, requested the General Assembly to permit it to offer its good offices to other groups of refugees. Gradually, it has by this device extended its interest to almost all refugees everywhere.

States seem to be unwilling to undertake convention obligations as regards refugees of the future. They do not want to commit themselves in advance to something that might later become onerous. It has been one of the jobs of the international refugee agency to try to get more extensive coverage for more groups of refugees, if only on an ad hoc and informal basis.

One of the features of the Geneva Convention that distinguishes it from earlier agreements and represents a step forward in protecting the refugee's rights is the very close tie provided between the Convention and the international agency. Whereas the League High Commissioner had undertaken to persuade states to live up to their international commitments on an informal basis, the Geneva Convention contains the following provision: (Art. 35.1)

The Contracting States undertake to co-operate with the office of the United Nations High Commissioner for Refugees, or any other agency of the United Nations which may succeed it, in the exercise of its functions, and shall in particular facilitate its duty of supervising the application of the provisions of this Convention.

. . . the Contracting States undertake to provide them (UNHCR or succeeding agencies) in the appropriate form with information and statistical data requested concerning:

(a) the condition of refugees.
(b) the implementation of the Convention, and
(c) laws, regulations and decrees which are, or may hereafter, be in force relating to refugees.

Thus, states agree to cooperate with the High Commissioner. There is no way to force such cooperation, but the record of states has been a good one. When governments are willing to cooperate, the High Commissioner's Office has been very effective in helping them to provide for refugees.

One program the High Commissioner has developed into a very successful system is that of the legal adviser. The legal adviser has become a sort of consul, offering a type of consular service to the refugee. The legal adviser attempts to see that refugees are enjoying the rights to which they are entitled by domestic and international law within municipal legal systems.

The High Commissioner has also continued the work, begun under the League, of trying through direct contact with the competent authorities to persuade governments to adopt national laws and policies more favorable to refugees. The Office has concentrated especially on areas where the Geneva Convention is inadequate, such as working permission and public assistance.

Today's Efforts and Problems[22]

Today, international organizations, especially the United Nations, continue to promote the cause of refugees, and their efforts have met with a high degree of success. States have shown concern for the very desperate plight of these brave people who, unable to live in their homelands because of persecution or fear of persecution, having given up everything, now need to be helped to build meaningful and satisfying lives in a strange land. States have cooperated in large measure with international officials to obtain this end. Another factor leading to success in this area has been the caliber of men who have been high commissioners: from Nansen, van Heuven Goedhard, to Schnyder, the Office has had outstanding men with a fine sense for diplomacy. They have been able to persuade governments to change policies without arousing resentment to their interference. They have adopted the position that states can best be approached through quiet diplomacy, and have avoided any finger-pointing and denunciating. Their task, as they have interpreted it, has been to aid and to cooperate with states, not to pass judgement on them.

The Office of the High Commissioner has also been successful in helping to make the best use possible of the funds available to various agencies for refugee work. An effort has been made to insure that there are not groups (such as some of the new Eastern European refugees) oversupported, while others (such as the Chinese in Hong Kong) are left with no assistance. The High Commissioner has often been able to arouse interest in refugees whose plight was particularly difficult, and has helped to avoid much duplication of effort.

One of the very successful IRO programs was that of resettlement. This involved preparing the refugees, persuading countries to accept them, ar-

---

[22] James M. Read, "The United Nations and Refugees—Changing Concepts," *International Conciliation*, March, 1962.

ranging and financing transportation, and helping with adjustment in the new homelands. The High Commissioner does not have funds adequate to undertake this kind of program. For this, another international agency, outside the framework of the United Nations, has been established—the Intergovernmental Committee for European Migration (ICEM). The UNHCR and ICEM have worked closely together and have been able to provide resettlement opportunities for many European refugees. They have been especially successful in locating opportunities for the handicapped and others usually ineligible for general resettlement schemes.[23]

The UNHCR and other international agencies can be successful in helping the refugee to reestablish himself only when they receive the cooperation and support of states. Another group of agencies that has been of great help in providing refugees with services, especially individual and personal attention, are the voluntary agencies. These have often worked in close cooperation with the international agencies.

Special Groups of Refugees

Particular groups of refugees have, from time to time, been singled out for special international action, with special international agencies. One such group, as mentioned above, were the DP's. UNRRA's refugee work and IRO were directed primarily at this group of people.[24] Another such group has been the Palestine Arabs.

At the time of the partition of Palestine, many Arabs fled from what then became Israel. Great numbers of these have been concentrated in the Gaza Strip. It was thought, at the time, that the problem was a temporary one, and one that would be solved easily once the Middle East quieted down. To care for these people, the General Assembly voted to establish a temporary agency—the United Nations Relief and Works Agency (UNRWA).

UNRWA, like UNRRA, was to be an operating agency, providing refugees with necessities until they could be repatriated or resettled. As time has passed and the problem has not been solved, the General Assembly has renewed its mandate, and UNRWA has had to continue to provide for the refugees, expanding its operations to include schooling, vocational training, and guidance.

The international agency has been ineffective in providing a satisfactory permanent solution for these refugees. Resettlement in the Arab lands of the area would seem to offer the best possibilities; however, this is impossible because of political factors. Neither Israel nor the Arab states have been

---

[23] ICEM has also assisted in the resettlement of Russian refugees from China.

[24] Both organizations had some authority to help refugees who had fallen within the framework of the prewar conventions, but their major efforts were directed toward helping DP's.

willing to encourage these refugees to settle in their states, and so these continue to live in camps and, as long as the General Assembly renews its mandate, to be cared for by the international agency assisted by voluntary organizations.

An International Status for Refugees?

At times, it is suggested that refugees enjoy an international status.[25] This would not seem to be the case. Refugees enjoy rights not because of international agreements alone; they enjoy rights because states *ratify* these instruments and implement them. The state, as in the case of human rights or minority rights, is the intermediary. The international convention does not bestow rights directly, nor are nonparties to the agreements bound by the provisions.

The international agreements, as has been mentioned, assimilate refugees either to aliens or to nationals for the majority of their rights. This results in differences in the various states. Furthermore, the refugee has no legal recourse if his rights are violated and he cannot find satisfaction in the state. The High Commissioner has no mandate to intervene on behalf of individual refugees, although in a few states he has been permitted to do this. There is no legally constituted international tribunal to settle disputes between states and refugees. Without this, it does not seem possible to consider the status of the refugee international. States, acting as an international community, have shown a genuine concern for refugees, have promoted the development of laws and organizations to assist refugees, and have cooperated with the organizations. They are, however, free to renounce agreements and to demand the withdrawal of the High Commissioner's representatives. There is no way to force a state into continuing to cooperate. This, however, does not diminish the effectiveness of international actions. As long as states are willing to assist the refugee, the system will continue to be a valuable one.

There are still problems. Not all refugees are covered by the Geneva Convention or by the mandate of the High Commissioner. Many states have extended the provisions of the Geneva Convention to cover nonconvention refugees, and the High Commissioner has obtained permission from the General Assembly to extend his good offices to most refugees. These actions have helped, but it is now time that states reconsider the definition of refugees contained in the Convention and Statute of the Office of the High Commissioner.[26] Another problem plaguing the High Commissioner is the lack of funds, especially for pilot projects and projects for groups not being aided by other agencies. At first, the High Commissioner was not permitted to seek

---

[25] See Paul Weiss, *op. cit.*

[26] See above, p. 620.

any funds. This has been changed, and the High Commissioner now has a fund that he administers with a special committee and for which he is permitted to solicit contributions.

These are among the problems which remain and on which the High Commissioner and others are working. There are refugees of long standing for whom no permanent solution has been found, but there is hope for many of these. There continue to be new refugees. Africa today contains the largest numbers of new refugees, many of whom, through the assistance of the High Commissioner, have been helped to resettle.

Refugees have been helped by the action of the international community, but always by only a segment of that community. For states from which refugees are fleeing are, understandably, sometimes unwilling to assist in their resettlement. To these home states, the refugee is often a traitor, a criminal, or the like—a person unworthy of any special treatment. These states are often outspoken in their denunciations of such persons and of the care these people are receiving from other states. This situation will continue: What state will look favorably on the efforts of others to help those who have renounced it?

People will continue to seek refuge as long as human rights are not universally guaranteed and implemented. Were there to be universal guarantees for human rights, with a system for international supervision to assure compliance, the refugee problem would disappear. Perhaps, here and there, an individual would have a valid reason for seeking asylum, but the great numbers who, from time to time, have fled to seek freedom would disappear. Until such a time, the refugee will need assistance if he is to build a new life for himself in an alien environment; and the efforts of the international community will continue to be an important factor in his readjustment.

Chapter 20

Ending the Colonial Era

No less important and certainly politically no less volatile than the aspirations for human rights and well-being and the drive for the protection of special subnational groups is the principle of self-determination. It expands democracy, as it were, to the international scale.

Though it may be a logical extension of Western ideology and in fact has become a Western ideal, the principle of self-determination was advanced most vigorously by Russia in the nineteenth century presumably to foster her imperial designs. During the First World War it became a tool of allied psychological warfare. Finally it was legitimized by President Wilson's fourteen points and the subsequent Treaty of Versailles.

In its original framework this principle applied primarily to Central Europe. It was ostensibly the determining criteria in the establishment of member states to the Austro-Hungarian monarchy, and the *cordon sanitaire* along the Soviet borders. Versailles however significantly extended the range. Determined to seize German and Turkish colonial territories, but precluded by President Wilson's devotion to ideals Britain, France and Italy agreed to administer some of these territories as League of Nation's Mandates. They accepted some international responsibility and pledged to guide some of these ex-enemy territories toward independence.

Once the validity of the principle on a global scale was admitted its appeal could not be restricted to arbitrarily selected areas. It generated not only agitation for independence but widespread demands for international supervision over all colonial administrations. The United Nations Charter reflects the rapidly growing concern, but the ultimate proof of the efficacy of the principle of self-determination is the emergence of some seventy new states since the inception of the organization.

THE LEAGUE MANDATE SYSTEM

During the First World War, the Allies had to face the problem of two crumbling empires: the Austro–Hungarian and Turkish. For the Austro–Hungarian, the principle of self-determination was applied and new states created. For the non-European Turkish empire, the planners of the postwar world were unwilling to apply the same principle. The Arab lands were not considered ready to enjoy independence, nor were the colonies wrested from Germany to be freed.

While these areas were not to be set up as independent states, they were also not to be made colonies in the traditional sense. They were to become "mandated" areas—areas administered by a state under the supervision of the League of Nations.[1]

The system was accepted as a compromise between growing anticolonial feeling and annexationism in the allied countries. Sentiment against further colonization was developing in both England and France, as well as in traditionally anticolonial United States. Emphasis at this time was not so much on complete independence (although England herself had made some promises to this effect in the Middle East) as it was on the idea of looking at colonies as sacred trusts—as areas not to be exploited for the benefit of the mother country but to be developed for the benefit of the "natives." More advanced European states would take responsibility for "civilizing" the "backward" areas. These ideas, not those of self-determination and independence, finally found expression in the mandate system. Even so, there were strong voices in opposition, demanding outright annexation and considering any system of supervision an outright interference in the internal affairs of the mother country. However, the forces for some international supervision were able to get their views accepted, if only in a very mild form.

The mandate system was looked on as an approach to peace. It would stop any further international tension over colonies, and, as the colonies were to be administered for the benefit of those in the colonies, would promote better relations between the colonies and the home states.

One limitation of the system was the area covered: only ex-enemy colonies were to be included. No state would conceive of placing its own colonies under any form of international supervision, no matter how mild. It was hoped by some that the system would promote a new kind of rivalry among colonial powers—a race to improve the mandated areas—and that this would carry over into the administration of nonmandated colonies. So,

---

[1] For a valuable treatment of the whole mandate system see Quincy Wright, *Mandates under the League of Nations* (Chicago: University of Chicago Press, 1930); also, H. Duncan Hall, *Mandates, Dependencies and Trusteeship* (Washington, D.C.: Carnegie Endowment for International Peace, 1948).

generally, there were high hopes for this new concept in colonial relationships.

In order to carry out the function of international supervision, the Mandate Commission, consisting of experts from the administering states and other states, was established in the League of Nations. The Commission had no authority to act directly nor to give orders to colonial administrators; the final decision was always in the hands of the administering state. The Commission could study conditions in the colonies, evaluate, and criticize. In order to perform this function, the Commission relied on reports from the mandatory powers, which were willing to provide comprehensive information and to use a questionnaire worked out by the Commission for this purpose. When the Commission suggested a more comprehensive questionnaire, the colonial powers balked, and it was not used. Members of the Commission, who were to act as independent experts and not as representatives of their respective governments, were often very probing in their questioning of colonial administrators. The Commission, when it finished its examination, prepared a report for the League Council. The Council considered the report, added its own observations, and sent it to the state concerned.

Woodrow Wilson and others had thought in terms of giving individuals and groups in the mandated areas the right to petition the League directly. Such a system was unacceptable to the majority of the League's membership. However, the idea of petitioning was not completely abandoned. Petitions first went to the state involved before being considered by the Commission.

The system represented an admission that colonies were a responsibility to be administered in accord with international standards and under the supervision of an international organization. Although actual administration was left to the colonial powers, important decisions were made by the Commission and were adopted as policy for the area. A Commission action on naturalization of inhabitants illustrates this. The question was whether the administering power had the right to naturalize those in the mandated areas, thereby making them, in effect, actual subjects of the power. The Commission did not object to the naturalization of individuals who so requested this, but did refuse to permit the mandatory the right to naturalize en masse. The League Covenant forbade the administering power from making the mandate areas into armed fortresses and from training the inhabitants for anything other than police and defense. Could the power enroll men in its own armed forces and use these outside the territory? The Commission decided that this could not be done. Decisions such as these made by the Commission were carried out by the administering powers.

The mandate system probably encouraged states to keep their policies in the areas "enlightened"; i.e., to adopt as the standard by which to judge their policies not the benefits to the homeland but, rather, the benefits to the peoples in the areas. The two methods used were the searching questioning of administrators and the focusing of world opinion on the areas.

The arrangement had weaknesses: among these, the denial of the right to petition the League directly, the prohibition on any type of inspection tour by the League body, and the fact that the system consisted primarily of colonials judging themselves and other colonials. Although this last may be considered one of the weaknesses of the League system, it had, at the same time, strengths: the Commission conducted its business usually in a sympathetic atmosphere. The critics, usually administrators themselves, knew and appreciated the difficulties in the colonial areas and were, therefore, usually realistic in their suggestions. The administrators were often willing to listen to suggestions and to try to see that these were carried out in their areas.

The mandate system was one of the most creative innovations of the League Covenant. It recognized that the colonial system, as it flourished around the turn of the century, was not a necessity of organization of states. The system attempted to bring the administration of areas up to international standards in order to promote development of the indigenous populations. It further recognized the usefulness of having the colonial powers submit their policies to international scrutiny as a way to promote more rapid progress.

THE TRUSTEESHIP SYSTEM

By the time the statesmen had come together in San Francisco, there were new ideas in the wind; the idea of "sacred trust" was being strongly challenged. Independence was put forward as the goal by some. However, there were those vehemently opposed to this goal: Britain was the leader of this opposition.[2] Even the majority of those supporting independence were not thinking in terms of the immediate future for most areas. They looked ahead to a period of preparation and development, varying in length according to the readiness of the area, during which the colonial powers would assume responsibility and authority until it was possible for the power to step quietly out of what would be that time be a functioning, orderly, self-sufficient state.

The general principle accepted, then, at San Francisco was that of "trusteeship," with the ultimate goal being independence or self-government. The main support for this had come within the United States from private and nongovernmental organizations which, in the end, were able to influence the official United States position. States were to consider their colonies a sacred

---

[2] Within the United States were those in favor of taking over the Pacific Islands from the Japanese for "strategic reasons," and in opposition to the idea of independence for colonial areas.

trust; not—as in the League days—primarily out of humanitarian concern for the peoples, but in order to prepare these people for a day in the future when they would be able to assume full responsibility for themselves.

This approach, however, was to be, once again, applicable only to ex-enemy territories (from both world wars). States with their own colonial areas were no more willing in 1945 than they had been in 1919 to place their *own* colonies in a system involving international supervision.[3]

The provisions in the U.N. Charter separate the colonies into two groups: the trusteeship areas (Chaps. XII and XIII) and non-self-governing territories (Chap. XI). For the trusteeship areas, a system closely patterned on the League's mandate system is established; while for the territories, the U.N. Charter includes a declaration of principles.

Although the colonial powers resisted any mandate to include their colonies in the system, they did not preclude such action for the future. The Charter contains provisions for "territories voluntarily placed under the system by states responsible for their administration" (Art. 77). Along with these areas to be included on a voluntary basis were also: (1) territories now held under mandate; (2) territories that may be detached from enemy states as a result of the second world war. Thus, the same principle as that applying to the mandate system was adopted: colonies were to be detached from the ex-enemy, and no state was to be permitted to annex these areas outright, but would have to accept certain international standards and goals and submit to a form of international supervision. Although there was hope that the colonial powers would enter into trusteeship agreements for their other colonies, not one such agreement was ever concluded.[4]

One set of colonies caused particular concern—the Italian. The Great Powers, responsible for the future of these, were unable to agree on their disposition, and in the Italian Peace Treaty left this thorny question to the United Nations itself. It was finally decided that Libya should be given her independence,[5] Italian Somaliland should be put under the trusteeship system, and Eritrea should become an autonomous unit federated with Ethiopia.

For Somaliland,[6] Italy was made the administering authority with provi-

---

[3] See below for arrangements concerning colonial areas.

[4] The areas under the system were: Tanganyika, (Britain), Ruanda–Urundi (Belgium), Cameroons (Britain), Cameroons (France), Somaliland (Italy), New Guinea (Australia), Togoland (Britain), Togoland (France), Pacific Islands (U.S.), Western Samoa (New Zealand), Nauru (Australia).

[5] Libya was to become independent not later than January 1, 1952. A United Nations commission was appointed by the General Assembly to assist the Libyans in drawing up a constitution and establishing an independent government.

[6] For an account of the trusteeship system in Somalia, see A. A. Castagno, Jr., "Somalia," *International Conciliation,* March, 1959; and Lawrence S. Finkelstein, *Somaliland under Italian Administration: A Case Study in United Nations Trusteeship* (New York: Woodrow Wilson Foundation, 1955).

sion for more international supervision than was called for in the other trust agreements and with the date for independence stipulated in the agreement. The agreement was drawn up by the General Assembly itself, rather than by the future administering power as was the case for the other areas. In none of the other trust agreements was there included a date for independence. The Italian colonies—less advanced than some of the other colonies—were the only ones that could look ahead to independence at a predetermined time, and this because they had been colonies of a recent ex-enemy!

The trusteeship system drew heavily on the mandate system. It was possible, however, in 1945 for the drafters of the Charter to put more teeth into the new system, to provide for some of the shortcomings of its predecessor. This was particularly true of the means available to the United Nations organ for securing a picture of conditions in the areas. The Mandate Commission had to rely almost exclusively on the reports of the administering power, while the Trusteeship Council has three means for securing information: (1) the annual report submitted by the administering authority; (2) periodic visiting missions; (3) petitions (written and oral) from people in the territories.

The Annual Report

The annual reports of the administering authorities are based to a large extent on the questionnaire adopted by the Trusteeship Council. The questionnaire asks for detailed information on political, economic, social, and educational conditions in the territories. The questions asked are very comprehensive and require the administering state to be much more complete in its report than was the case during the League period.

The reports are gone over carefully by the Trusteeship Council according to a set procedure:

1. An opening statement by the special representative of the administering authority.
2. Questions by Council members to the special representative for further explanation of points in the report.
3. Answers by the special representative to points raised in the second step.
4. General debate, during which Council members make general remarks on conditions in the territory.
5. Draft conclusions and recommendations drawn up by a drafting committee.
6. Discussion of draft and, finally, adoption of report by the Trusteeship Council.

The final report of the Trusteeship Council is sent to the General Assembly, where it is debated and forms the basis of further recommendations by that body.[7]

---

[7] In the case of "strategic areas," the report of the Council goes to the Security Council.

Visiting Missions

The second source of information available to the Council is the visiting mission. Unlike the Mandate Commission, which had to rely on reports, the Trusteeship Council can send out missions to investigate conditions on the spot. Like the Council itself, the visiting mission is composed of persons nominated by administering and nonadministering states (two from each category).

The missions not only look at general conditions and evidences of developments in keeping with U.N. Charter objectives (Art. 76), but also are guided by the criticisms of the Trusteeship Council and the General Assembly in attempting to find out whether there has or has not been progress in the areas of particular concern to these bodies. Thus, the visiting mission sent to Ruanda–Urundi and Tanganyika in 1959 was instructed by the Council to look carefully at, among other things:[8]

1. Electoral process: to see why universal suffrage had not been introduced.
2. Progress toward independence: to see why there had not yet been target dates established.
3. Training of personnel: to note progress toward training more indigenous personnel for administrative responsibilities and in technical fields.

While the mission was in Tanganyika,[9] it chartered a plane and traveled more than 4,000 miles to visit all but one of the eight provinces. Members of the mission talked to all segments of the population: They heard the views of those responsible for local administration, tribal leaders, leaders of labor groups, individuals with special problems, and others. The mission, in its report, indicated it was satisfied that all interested groups had been permitted by the administering authorities to make their views and opinions known to the mission.

This type of free access seems to have been characteristic of the experience of the visiting missions generally.[10] The technique is one that not only gives the Council a much better picture of conditions and a more effective way to establish how much progress is being made in the territories, but is also a good way to prod the administering authorities into more action.

In the 1959 mission report, the Tanganyikan administration was commended for its general policy toward Tanganyika, but was criticized for not having introduced universal suffrage, not having trained enough civil servants, and not having sufficiently expanded the facilities for secondary and higher education for the indigenous peoples. Also, the suggestion was made

---

[8] *United Nations Review,* March, 1960, pp. 26–27.

[9] This was the fifth regular visiting mission sent to that territory.

[10] At times, petitioners indicated that this had not always been the case.

that there was now need to consider drafting a constitution and a citizens' law for the territory. The report, in other words, indicated that the shortcomings pointed out by the Trusteeship Council still existed, and that there were steps which the administering authority could take to remedy these.

After the Council members had an opportunity to study the report of the mission, the special representative from the administering authority, Fletcher-Coke, was given an opportunity to comment on the report. He outlined the steps being planned for the territory, giving special attention to the particular areas criticized by the mission. Council members were then given an opportunity to comment on the report and on the comments of the special representative. During the discussion, much attention was given to the role of the governor of Tanganyika in the Council of Ministers. Some members objected to the system that gave the governor the deciding vote in case of a tie in the Council. Since the Council was, at the time, composed of half white and half Africans, some Trusteeship Council members thought this would result in giving to the governor the deciding vote in too many cases. Fletcher-Coke pointed out that the assumption that the Council of Ministers usually split along racial lines thus giving the whites the majority in most cases, was unfounded. In actuality, he pointed out, the governor rarely was called on to cast the deciding vote, as the Council rarely found itself deadlocked.

After this type of careful searching by the Council, a final report was drawn up. In this case, the Council decided that the administering authority still needed to put more emphasis on training civil servants, on facilities for higher education, and on the development of rural areas, and should consider changing the role of the governor in the Council of Ministers.

The visiting mission seems really to have helped the Council perform its functions more effectively.[11] The system also opened the way for contact between the colonial peoples and the United Nations. During the League days, there was no communication between the people and the mandate Commission; if anyone knew there existed a body interested in them and their problems, it was thought of something way off in Geneva, accessible only through an intermediary—the administering power. For the people in the trusteeship areas, the link has become a more genuine one. Many more have known there was a body trying to look after their interests and willing to consider their grievances. The interested agency is no longer way off, but, rather, periodically among them and willing to examine problems on the spot.

---

[11] The visiting missions and the Trusteeship Council did not, however, always agree on consequences to be drawn from reports. For example, the Council repudiated the conclusions of a part of the 1954 report of the mission to Tanganyika and Ruanda–Urundi. See Thomas R. Adam, "Trusteeship and Non-self-governing Territories," *Annual Review of United Nations Affairs, 1955–1956* (Dobbs Ferry, N.Y.: Oceana Publications, Inc., 1957) pp. 127–29, 130–31.

These regular missions have kept administering authorities on their toes. Not only has the Council used these with good results, but, when it felt that it would be helpful, has sent out special missions to deal with important constitutional problems. Such missions were sent to Western Samoa in 1947, and to French Togoland in 1957. The Togoland mission was actually dispatched by the General Assembly.[12]

Petitions

The third tool available to the Trusteeship Council is the petition. Individuals and groups were given the right by the Charter to petition the organization directly. At San Francisco, the majority supported the position that international supervision of a system whose object it was "to promote the political, economic, social, and educational advancement of . . . inhabitants" and "to encourage respect for human rights and for fundamental freedoms for all without distinction as to race, sex, language, or religion," had to provide a way for these "inhabitants" to present their grievances to the international supervising agency if the system was to be meaningful and effective. The organization was not to rely on the administering authorities' willingness to forward petitions (as in the League system), but was "to accept petitions and examine them in consultation with the administering authority."

During its active years, the Trusteeship Council was presented with a great number of petitions, both written and oral. These varied considerably as to their content and importance, but the Council tried to consider all that were properly submitted.

The year 1953 was a typical one for the Council.[13] During its Twelfth Session, the Council was called on to deal with 395 written petitions, and granted three oral hearings not connected with the written petitions. Of these hearings, two dealt with general conditions in Somalia and the third concerned a land question in Tanganyika. There were also six requests for oral presentations in support of written petitions (two general questions on French Cameroons, and four on Ruanda–Urandi; all were rejected). Numbers of the written communications were not discussed by the Council, as it was decided that these raised questions on which there had been recent action in the form of resolutions. All together, 258 petitions were discussed.

Although petitions were received from all trust territories, only those from Tanganyika will be briefly outlined in order to give some indication of the range of complaints.[14] From that East African state, one oral and six written petitions were considered. The oral petition, presented by Kirilo Japhet on

---

[12] See below, for more specific information on this special commission.

[13] *United Nations Bulletin,* August, 1953, p. 91.

[14] United Nations Trusteeship Council, *Official Records* (12th sess., 1953), Annexes, Agenda Item 5, pp. 93–96.

behalf of the Meru Citizen's Union, related to the Wa–Meru land question. The Council did not act on this, but only took note. On three of the written communications, the Council did not make recommendations. One of these was sent in by a German, asking for reentry into the territory; a second from a chief protested his removal from office; the third was a complaint concerning the procedure followed in electing tribal authorities.

On three petitions, the Council did pass resolutions. One came from a man involved in litigation over charges he had deserted his wife. The Council did not feel that it had any authority to do anything about this, as it was a matter for the courts of the territory. The sultan of one part of Tanganyika claimed he owned certain lands. This complaint was turned over to the Administering Authority. The third was from a man who claimed he had been falsely excluded from the territory on the grounds that he was a German citizen, whereas, the petitioner claimed, he, being from Danzig, could not be considered a German. The Council felt that the question was a complicated one, involving international law, and that it was not competent to make a decision.

In 1959,[15] the Council heard Jalle Bolkain, Magistrate of Kwajalein Atoll, and Amata Kabu of Majuro Atoll, both in the Pacific Islands Trust of the United States. These two men complained that property had been taken away from people on the atolls without their having received just compensation and without their having been able to present their claims to a court of law.

Three Council sessions were devoted to a consideration of this issue. The special representive of the United States was given an opportunity to present his case. At the end of the discussion, the representative reported that the United States administration would be willing to pay a fair rent for the land the United States had taken. It is probable that the petitioners, without the international forum, would have found it much more difficult to get satisfaction from the United States government—they had been trying for over three years without any results.

One source of almost annual petitions was the Ewe. The Ewe is a group of people located in the two Togolands and in British Gold Coast (Ghana). For years, spokesmen of the Ewe had attempted to persuade the Trusteeship Council and the General Assembly to help them to unite in one area. The French and British had attempted to satisfy this desire for unity by establishing a consultative commission elected by the Ewes, but this and other measures did not prove very satisfactory. The problem of the Ewe was complicated by the presence of factions *opposing* the uniting of these people. Petitioners representing both sides were heard at the United Nations. The issue was the source of long debates in both the Trusteeship Council and the General Assembly. With no clear-cut support for either position among the Ewe, the

---

[15] *United Nations Review,* Vol. 2, No. 12 (June, 1960), p. 44.

General Assembly finally decided to back the British suggestion that the issue be put to a plebescite in British Togoland. Asked to decide between union with the Gold Coast Continuance of the trusteeship status, with final determination of status to be made at sometime in the future, the majority selected union.[16]

Petitions have usually come from the indigenous population, although a group from Ruanda–Urundi, for example, did complain of discrimination against Europeans in judicial matters and in admission to restaurants and hotels. The usual petitions are handled quickly by the Council, which relies on the Standing Committee on Petitions to do most of the preliminary screening and to make recommendations. Only the more important ones are debated by the full Council, and sometimes even the General assembly becomes involved.

The system has proved helpful to the Trusteeship Council in the accomplishment of its tasks. The wealth of material contained in petitions has given a clearer picture of actual conditions in territories. Petitioners who appear in New York or before visiting missions are usually asked questions on topics unrelated to the petition itself, that is, they serve as a source of general information. At the same time, the system has helped to insure to individuals and groups attention to grievances which, without the prodding of the international agency, might have gone unheeded.

Independence or Self-Government—The Objective of the System

As mentioned before, the objective of the trusteeship system, as set forth in Article 75 of the U.N. Charter, is to promote "progressive development towards self-government or independence as may be appropriate to the particular circumstances of each territory and its people and the freely expressed wishes of the people concerned."

The system was established not just to assure enlightened administration, but was to supervise progress forward and promote independence or self-government. Emphasis was not to be on *conditions* in the colonies but rather on the *progress* being made toward obtaining the goals set forth.

This aspect of the system has resulted in the most bitter debates in both the Trusteeship Council and the General Assembly. The division has been clear-cut and highly consistent: administering states supported by other colonial powers on one side; ex-colonial and anticolonial states on the other. The struggle has centered mostly on timing. No matter how quickly the administering states progress, it is too slow for the anticolonials; no matter when

---

[16] The outcome of the plebescite, while giving a majority to union with the Gold Coast, showed very different results in the two sections of British Togoland. The North showed a majority for union, while the South cast its votes for continuing under the trusteeship system. The General Assembly made the decision to consider the outcome for the whole territory rather than dividing the area.

the anticolonials consider an area ready for more self-government or independence, it is too soon for the administering states. To be sure, by the time
the Trusteeship Council began its operations, the colonial powers accepted
the idea that most of the colonies would be freed and that they were
responsible for helping these to prepare themselves for independence. However, this acceptance has come too late. By the time there was a genuine
commitment to the idea of trusteeship and development within the colonies,
the pressure for immediate independence had the support of much of world
public opinion, and the desire to be free was mounting in the colonies
themselves. Not even in the face of this rising sentiment could the powers be
persuaded to put their other colonies under the trusteeship system.

On the issue of independence, there has also been a split between the
Trusteeship Council and the General Assembly. The composition of the
Council, half administering and half nonadministering, has tended to make
that organ conservative. On a number of items, the Council has split in
half, so that no action could be taken.

In 1959, when the council was considering sending the visiting mission to
Tanganyika and Ruanda–Urundi,[17] the nonadministering states pushed for
establishing target dates for independence, reasoning that this would help in
working out timetables for constitutional reforms and the formulation of
development plans in the territories. This, in turn, would help the peaceful
evolution of these. The administering states argued that trying to set dates
was not possible. It was better to take a step, evaluate progress, and
proceed. In the Council, there was a tie vote, so no mention of setting dates
was included in the report to the General Assembly.

When the Council's report was debated in the General Assembly, the
question of target dates was raised again. By 1959, the ex-colonials and
anticolonials had increased in the United Nations so that, when they were
agreed on an issue, they could command a majority in the General Assembly.
This is what happened in this case. The Assembly voted (52–15 with 8
abstentions) to request the administering authorities to produce timetables.

The role of the international organization has been especially active
during the period just prior to independence. The Trusteeship Council and
the General Assembly have taken seriously the provision in Article 76 that
the future status of trust territories shall reflect "the freely expressed wishes
of the peoples concerned." The General Assembly has not accepted the word
of the administering state, but has demanded proof that the population has
been given a meaningful choice and has expressed its wishes.

One territory whose final disposition led to much debate was French

---

[17] See above, p. 631, for discussion of this visiting mission. *United Nations Review,*
March, 1960, p. 26.

Togoland.[18] The decision to accept the results of the plebiscite in British Togoland[19] affected the choices open to the French Togolese: in effect, it meant there could be no uniting of the two Togolands as had been desired by some. Soon after this decision, the French granted Togoland a new statute that gave to the Togolese a greater amount of self-government but also tied the territory closely to the French Union. The people were asked to choose between the statute and continuation under the trusteeship system, with the status of the territory to be left to a future decision. The statute received more than 70 per cent of the vote, but the referendum had been boycotted by one of the largest parties.

The new statute led to acrimonious debate in both the Trusteeship Council and the General Assembly. One of the principal objections was that the referendum had not permitted the voters to choose immediate independence; another was that, unlike the British in their Togolese referendum, the French had not sought the aid of the United Nations in drawing up the questions and in making plans for the plebescite.

The General Assembly was unwilling to accept the results of the plebescite as the basis for termination of trusteeship, and voted in 1957 to send a special six-man commission to Togoland to examine the results of the plebescite. The commission, after its trip, made specific suggestions for the modification of the statute, and called for new elections to the Legislative Assembly. During the course of debate on the commission's report, the French indicated their willingness to make the suggested changes and to hold new elections. In the General Assembly, it was decided that the United Nations should be invited to supervise the election (to which France agreed).

After the elections, the General Assembly was satisfied that these had reflected the true wishes of the people, and also that France had made the statute changes necessary to bring it into accord with the recommendations of the organization. At this point, the General Assembly was willing to dissolve the trusteeship agreement with France for this territory.

The international organization had no way to force France to act on its recommendation. However, France realized that the General Assembly would not approve the end of the trusteeship arrangement until she had complied with the wishes of the organization. Therefore, she agreed to accept the changes in the statute and the involvement of the international organization in the elections.

For four years, Togoland had been on the agenda of the General Assembly. The procedure for dealing with it proved successful: France took the initiative, and the General Assembly made suggestions that France, in turn,

---

[18] "Issues before the Thirteenth General Assembly," *International Conciliation,* September, 1958, pp. 93–100.

[19] See above, pp. 631–32.

was willing to carry out. In this way, the difficult situation resulting from the outcome of the first plebiscite could be resolved. It is very possible that the transition from colonial status to new nation would not have proceeded so smoothly without the aid of the United Nations—debate, study commission, and supervision of elections.

The United Nations has similarly played a role in making other acts of self-determination orderly, and reflective of the wishes of the people. A plebiscite in British Cameroons resulted in a division of that area between Nigeria and the newly formed Republic of Cameroun[20] (previously French), and after its plebescite Ruanda–Urundi was divided into two separate states. Whether these divisions are wise from the standpoint of economic and political feasibility can be questioned. What, however, can be concluded is that a genuine effort was made to give the people in the areas a meaningful choice, and that the role of the United Nations was not an insignificant one.

General Evaluation

Although the Trusteeship Council is still a principal organ of the United Nations, it has practically no more work to do; the majority of the trust areas has achieved independence. Those areas left are either small and very underdeveloped (Western Samoa, Nauru) or in the "strategic" category (the United States Trust Islands in the Pacific).[21] One can say that today the U.N. Charter trusteeship system has completed its task.

The record of the Council has been good; it has been able to prod administering powers into moving ahead more rapidly than would probably have been the case had states been left to develop their own policies without international supervision and publicity. It was, however, not possible for the system to fulfill its purpose completely. The system included but a small number of dependent areas. Most colonies were never placed under the system.

The ever-increasing pressure for independence affected the system. The idea behind the system was that the administering states would undertake to prepare the dependent peoples to assume responsibility for running their own states, and then would step out. There is no easy way to establish the point at which the colonial power should step down. The majority of the United Nations has pushed for independence as quickly as possible. They have, in actuality, rejected the idea of a protracted period of preparation. On the other

---

[20] The Cameroun question has subsequently become the issue of a case before the International Court of Justice.

[21] At San Francisco, the United States, influenced by its military advisers, was able to have a special category of trust areas—strategic—included in the Charter. For these areas, the final authority was to be the Security Council and not the General Assembly as for the other trust territories.

hand, the administering authorities would have preferred to wait until the territories had come closer to achieving Western standards of political development before severing the trust relationship. Since it was the majority position that prevailed, the United Nations had a very short period of time during which it could carry out its mandate. In view of this, the record of the system is a good one.

THE UNITED NATIONS AND NON-SELF-GOVERNING TERRITORIES

Whereas the League's concern for colonial peoples was restricted to mandated areas, the trusteeship areas have formed only a minor part of the United Nations' concern for colonies. The "colonial issue" has permeated all the major U.N. organs, has consumed them in untold hours of debate, until few problems today remain free of being related to the colonial issue. The United Nations is itself more than half ex-colonial, so that few states dare to espouse an outright colonial policy. Those statesmen sitting in San Francisco in 1945, hammering out the Charter, would have denounced as incredulous even a partial glimpse of the United Nations today; and many would have been horrified had they been able to foresee what would develop out of the Charter's provisions for colonies. As perhaps no other part of the Charter, the provisions for colonies have undergone a complete reinterpretation and revision.

From the early days of the United Nations, there has been pressure from the ex-colonial members, supported by Russia and Eastern Europe, for action in two directions: (1) to extend the principle of accountability and international supervision of colonial administrations to cover *all* colonies, not just those under the trusteeship system; and (2) to gain recognition and support for making self-determination, usually thought of in terms of independence, into a right to be granted all dependent areas.

The Declaration on Non-Self-Governing Territories

Although it had been impossible to persuade the colonial powers to place their colonies under the trusteeship system, the Charter contains a declaration setting forth principles similar to those for the trust areas but with a very important difference—there was to be no international supervision.

Similar to the Declaration on Human Rights, the Declaration on non-self-governing territories was not to have any legally binding power but, rather, was to be in the form of a statement of principles which the colonial powers, by ratifying the Charter, agreed to follow in *their* administration of dependent areas. The colonial powers did not envisage that the United Nations should supervise, aid them, or interfere in any way. They were—they thought—accepting no obligation or commitments that could be enforced or even discussed in the United Nations; colonies were still a matter within the domestic jurisdiction of the state and not open to any evaluation or criticism by other members of the organization.

Although the colonial powers had successfully blocked attempts to get all colonies into a trusteeship system, the anticolonial forces had not completely lost: getting the Declaration into the Charter was cause for satisfaction. It was to prove an opening wedge through which the anticolonials could push their program.

The Declaration, Chapter XI, is a statement of the principles by which the colonial powers will be guided in the administration of the colonies:

—that the interests of the inhabitants of those territories are paramount;
— (they) accept as a sacred trust the obligation to promote to the utmost the well-being of the inhabitants of these territories;
—to ensure, with due respect for the culture of the peoples concerned, their political, economic, social, and educational advancement, their just treatment, and their protection against abuses;
—to develop self-government, to take due account of the political aspirations of the peoples, and to assist them in the progressive development of their free political institutions, according to the particular circumstances of each territory and its peoples and their varying stages of advancement.

This, as has been pointed out, was included in the U.N. Charter as a *declaration.* As far as the colonial powers were concerned, the only direct obligation to the United Nations in this Chapter of the Charter was contained in Article 73.e:

. . . to transmit regularly to the Secretary-General for information purposes, subject to such limitations as security and constitutional considerations may require, statistical and other information of a technical nature relating to economic, social, and educational conditions in the territories for which they are respectively responsible other than those territories to which Chapters XII and XIII (Trusts) apply.

This seems to imply that the only responsibility given to the United Nations as regards dependent territories is that of collector of information. Such an interpretation has been unacceptable to those forces opposed to the colonial system. They have tried to extend the role of the United Nations in three areas: (1) to make use of information gathered according to Article 73.e; (2) to give the organization responsibility for determining when an area "has attained a full measure of self-government;" (3) to give the organization responsibility for deciding what areas a new member should report on.

Building a New Trusteeship System

Information and Its Use. A careful reading of Article 73.e, quoted above, shows that the drafters of this article did not anticipate that any actual use would be made of the material submitted by the colonial powers. It was to be collected by the Secretary-General "for information purposes." No provision was made for any systematic analysis or evaluation of this material. It almost seemed as though this information was to be filed away somewhere where it could be read by anyone interested.

This interpretation of Article 73.e has been hotly contested by the anticolonial forces in the United Nations. Why, they asked, is there a provision for submission of information if nothing is to be done with it? If states are to report on economic, social, and educational conditions, then it is, they argue, the duty of the organization to analyze this information in order to determine whether the colonial states are administering their areas in accordance with the principles accepted in the Declaration. In order to do this efficiently, so these forces argued, there should be an organ similar to the Trusteeship Council.

Although the administering states objected to this line of argument, they found themselves in a minority and unable to prevent establishment of a committee to examine and discuss the information submitted under Article 73.e. The colonial powers who had refused to extend the competence of the Trusteeship Council to all their colonies now found that they were going to be held accountable for their policies and practices in dependent areas. Their only real alternative was to leave the United Nations, and this they did not want to do.

In comparing the provisions on reporting under the trusteeship system and the system for non-self-governing territories, two significant differences should be noted: (1) "political" conditions are not mentioned in Article 73; (2) "conditions" are to be reported on under Article 73; "advancements" under the trusteeship system.

Over the years, the system for handling this information has been developed and refined:[22]

1946: The General Assembly passed a resolution calling on the Secretary-General to summarize, analyze, and classify the information he received in his annual report.

1947: A resolution calling on the administering powers to include in their reports information on progress of areas toward self-government and participation of local populations in administration of colonies was rejected by the General Assembly. At this time, the colonial powers still could command a majority for their viewpoint on many issues. Their position that nothing in the Charter justified this action was able to get the support of enough states to block the resolution. However, these same powers were unable to block a resolution calling for the establishment of the ad hoc Committee on Information to examine

---

[22] See Benjamin Rivlin, "Self-determination and Dependent Areas," *International Conciliation*, January, 1955, pp. 238–44.

the information and report to the General Assembly. The composition of this Committee was based on the same principle as the Trusteeship Council: one-half administering states, one-half nonadministering.

1948: The mandate of the Committee was renewed for one year. The colonial powers successfully blocked a move to make this a permanent body.

1949: The Committee was extended for three years. Again, a move to give it permanence was defeated.

In this way, machinery for considering reports on non-self-governing territories has become well established. Every three years, the Committee has been renewed for another three-year term. The colonial powers have had to accept its existence, although they have successfully blocked moves to make it permanent.

The Committee on Information does not have the same powers as the Trusteeship Council. It may not hear petitions from individuals or groups within the colonies, and may not send missions to gather information firsthand. Rather, it is confined to studying the reports submitted by the colonial powers and questioning representatives of those states.[23] These limitations have meant that the Committee on Information has never been able to establish the same close contact with the areas and their peoples as has the Trusteeship Council.

Whereas the Trusteeship Council can comment on and make suggestions concerning individual colonies, the Committee is limited by its mandate to making observations and suggestions on functional fields, without singling out individual administrators or colonies. During its first years, the Committee was not permitted to discuss political conditions in the colonies. There was constant pressure to remove this restriction—pressure resisted successfully by the colonial powers for years.[24] Finally, when the Committee's mandate was due for renewal in 1961, it was extended, and included provisions for considering political and constitutional information:[25] another victory for the anticolonial forces.

Article 73, unlike Article 88, does not provide for a questionnaire to channel and organize the information to be submitted. Thus, the colonial powers could avoid reporting on unfavorable aspects if they chose. This was another condition unacceptable to the anticolonials. In 1947, these forces were able to get a resolution, calling for a questionnaire, passed by the General Assembly. Ever since, the administrators have used this in submitting their information.

According to Article 73.e, the information submitted on dependent areas

---

[23] In this respect, the system resembles the League mandate system more closely than the U.N. trusteeship system.

[24] See B. Rivlin, *op. cit.,* pp. 241–43.

[25] "Issues before the Seventeenth General Assembly," *International Conciliation,* September, 1962, p. 61.

should cover "economic, social, and educational" conditions. The colonial powers argued that they could be required to answer questions only on these aspects of their administrations, and were able for many years to resist the inclusion of political questions in even an optional part of the questionnaire.

By 1953, the majority of the General Assembly was sympathetic to a strengthened system of accountability, and a revised form containing questions on political conditions as well as the degree of progress toward self-government was adopted. The anticolonial forces wanted information on rights being enjoyed by people in the colonies. Information on the provisions in laws implementing the principles in the Declaration on Human Rights was demanded in the obligatory section of the questionnaire.

Since the Committee on Information has not been able to hear petitions directly or to send missions, there has been criticism that reliance on the word of the administering authority did not provide the Committee with an opportunity to ascertain a true picture of conditions in the colonies. Some sort of direct contact with the inhabitants was thought desirable by many. The anticolonial forces have not been very successful in trying to obtain this objective: any resolution to extend to the Committee the right to hear petitions or to send missions has been turned down. The most possible has been the adoption of resolutions calling on the colonial powers to consider including colonial peoples as advisers on their delegations to the Committee.

The colonial powers have successfully thwarted attempts to "pack" the Committee on Information and to do away with the principle of equal representation. There have been proposals that more nonadministering states be given representation on the Committee. However, the composition of Committee resembles the Trusteeship Council: half from states administering colonies and half from those without colonies.

As the years have passed, the United Nations has thus strengthened the system for holding colonial powers accountable to the international organization. The addition of new members—most ex-colonials has diminished the strength of the colonial powers in the organization. Another factor has been the changing attitude of the colonial powers and their supporters. Today, the older states usually try to avoid alienating the new nations: support for any issue to be voted on by the General Assembly has to include at least some of these states if it is to pass. The old colonial powers have had to accept this evolution. At times, they have been able to slow down developments, but once a new wrinkle is added to the system of accountability, most of the administering powers have given their full cooperation. In this way, a trusteeship system, once only for those colonies lucky enough to have been colonies of the enemy, has come to cover all dependent areas.

Determination of When an Area Is Self-Governing.   The anticolonial forces have used Article 73 not only to extend the principle of accountability and, in effect, to develop a second trusteeship system, but also to involve the organization in the decision as to when an area has become self-governing. The Declaration applies to those territories "whose people have not yet attained a full measure of self-government." The Charter does not say how or by whom determination as to when an area has attained this status is to be made. The question is an important one, as a state is not obligated to report on areas that have attained self-government.

The colonial powers argued that since there was no specific provision for any organ of the United Nations to make such a determination, each individual state would make its own and so inform the organization. The anticolonial forces would not agree to this interpretation; rather, they asserted that once an area had been reported on, it was the responsibility of the organization itself to apply the Charter—that is, to decide when an area had become self-governing. A third position envisioned shared responsibility in making the determination. For this group—as for the extreme anticolonial forces—a unilateral judgment by the administering authority would not indicate satisfactorily whether self-government had actually been attained. On the other hand, reasoned these, the Charter did not empower the organization to make any such determination; therefore, there should be some way to involve both agencies.

Soon after the United Nations began functioning, the Secretary-General sent out a request to states asking for a list of all those areas for which Article 73 was applicable. Eight states sent in answers, containing the names of 72 areas for which the states agreed to submit information. This satisfied the General Assembly at the time, and there was no criticism of the lists.

In 1947, 12 of the original 72 territories, including a number of French territories, the Panama Canal Zone (U.S.A.), and Malta (U.K.) were not reported on. Immediately, objections were voiced in the General Assembly, and the states not reporting were called on to give their reasons for withholding information. In all areas, claimed the three administrators, there had been constitutional changes resulting in a degree of self-government for the area sufficient to satisfy the requirements in Article 73. This was unacceptable to a number of members of the organization. The issue turned on a definition of self-governing. The colonial powers have recognized as self-governing those areas that manage their own *domestic affairs* even if the mother country remains responsible for *foreign affairs,* the military, and other areas. These states claim those territories are self-governing which have formed a union or are associated with the mother country, when the relationship has been approved by the people in free elections, and the local population has its own organs and institutions for managing its affairs. Many of the ex-colonial and anticolonial states do not like this, claiming it is just a mild form of colonialism, not true self-government. Many do not like to accept anything short of complete independence as fulfilling the Charter's requirement for self-government.

In 1948, the first step was taken to try to bring the organization itself into the process of determining when an area has achieved self-government. The General Assembly passed a resolution welcoming progress toward self-government in many dependent areas, and suggesting that the United Nations should be informed of the constitutional changes that had led the administering power to consider it was no longer bound to submit information on the area.

In 1950, Netherlands ceased to transmit information on Indonesia and supplied the United Nations with the constitutional changes on which it was basing this action. Now a debate arose: Did the organization have to accept the word of Netherlands, or was it free to make its own determination? The General Assembly decided that it could pass on the Dutch report and, accordingly, adopted a resolution in which it noted the independence of Indonesia, followed by its admission to the United Nations, and took further note that a report pursuant to Article 73.e would no longer be necessary. In this case, the General Assembly asserted its right to examine the data provided by the Netherlands and to decide for itself whether it considered the area to be self-governing. By taking this step, the majority in the General Assembly was giving a warning to other administrators: if we do not agree that an area is self-governing, we reserve the right to say so; in which case we do not agree that you have fulfilled your obligations under Chapter XI, and we will expect you to continue to report on the area under question.

Again in 1953, the General Assembly asserted its right to approve—and, by inference, to disapprove—a state's decision, and it agreed to the statement: "(It is in) the competence of the General Assembly to decide whether a non-self-governing territory has or has not attained a full measure of self-government as referred to in Chapter XI."[26] This clause was part of the resolution affirming the new status of Puerto Rico—a resolution which gave only reluctant approval and contained a statement that the people had "in free exercise of their sovereign will, chosen to leave effective control over their foreign affairs and national defense with the United States government." This resolution was actually a success for the more conservative states: the principle that self-government did not necessarily demand complete independence had not been altogether rejected.

By this time, the system for determining when a state may cease to report was well established. The administering state submits its decision with a report on the constitutional changes made in the colony. The Committee on Information studies the material and makes its recommendations, which are then studied by the Fourth Committee prior to coming before the General Assembly. Denmark (for Greenland) and Netherlands (for Netherlands Antilles and Surinam) submitted the requested information to the United

---

[26] General Assembly Resolution 748 (VIII), November 27, 1953.

Nations. In both cases, a form of association between the mother country and the ex-colony was approved in a resolution of the General Assembly. In the Netherlands situation, four years (1951–55) elapsed between the time the information was sent to the organization and the passage of the resolution agreeing to the new status.

Up to the present, with the exception of Southern Rhodesia, the organization has accepted the constitutional changes made by the state as adequate. The colonial states have not recognized that the resolutions adopted are any more than affirmations; that is, they have not conceded that the organization has any legal right to pass judgment on their decisions. The determination is, in the last analysis, the prerogative of the administering state and not of the organization.

In 1954, a resolution of the General Assembly attempted to associate the organization even more closely with the decision by suggesting that the administering state agree to permit a mission to go to areas about to obtain self-government. Such missions were authorized *if* the General Assembly thought it advisable and *if* the administering member agreed. No use has been made of this provision up to the present.

Britain has asserted that the General Assembly has no real authority to participate in the decision to remove an area from the non-self-governing category. Britain has asserted that once she had granted self-government to an area she could not interfere in the affairs of that area—a position rejected by many in the General Assembly.

As "self-governing" is not a clear term, there have been differing ideas among members of the organization as to when an area could be considered to have attained self-government. A few states would like to have self-government equated with independence. The majority of members are not willing to accept this position, and have accepted as self-governing those areas which have voluntarily associated themselves with the former metropole. However, there has been no agreement on just what kinds of association and relationships are to be acceptable as fulfilling the criteria of the Charter. In an attempt to provide itself with a clear statement of just what a self-governing area is, the General Assembly requested the Committee on Information to draw up a definition.

The Committee found that it was unable to arrive at a definition that would be useful, and decided to confine itself to drawing up lists of factors that could be used as criteria in judging whether an area was self-governing.

The Committee drew up three sets of factors: one set applicable to independent states, one to areas which continued their association with the metropolitan area, and one set applicable to self-governing territories that became component parts of federal or unitary states. The Committee stressed that, in its opinion, there was nothing definitive about these factors, that each case had to be studied separately, and that the factors could serve as guides to determine its status. In 1951, provisional lists of factors were presented, and these were adopted, after some revising, by the General Assembly in 1953.

The factors are stated in quite general terms. As an example, those that apply to states which have attained independence include:

A. *International Status*
   1. *International responsibility.* Full responsibility for the acts inherent in the exercise of its external sovereignty and for the corresponding acts in the administration of its internal affairs.
   2. *Eligibility for membership in the United Nations.*
   3. *General international relations.* Power to enter into direct relations of every kind with other governments and with international institutions and to negotiate, sign and ratify international instruments.
   4. *National defense.* Sovereign right to provide for its national defense.
B. *Internal Self-government*
   1. *Form of government.* Complete freedom of the people of the Territory to choose the form of government which they desire.
   2. *Territorial government.* Freedom from control or interference by the government of another state in respect of the internal government . . .
   3. *Economic, social and cultural jurisdiction.* Complete autonomy in respect of economic, social and cultural affairs.[27]

This effort provided the General Assembly and its organs with criteria to help them decide whether the constitutional changes reported for an area by the administering member did, in fact, adequately provide the inhabitants with a full measure of self-government. Since 1953, the lists have been used in this way.

The General Assembly had developed a system for "checking up" on the colonial powers, and these powers had accepted responsibility for seeing that the inhabitants in dependent areas move toward self-government. By the 1950's, most colonial powers accepted the idea that it would not be long before practically all areas were self-governing. For most areas, the colonial powers have been willing to hasten the process. However, the question of timing has caused difficulties.[28] The anticolonial forces want self-government *now*—tomorrow if necessary, but the day after is already too late. The colonial powers take the position that an area should not be given the opportunity to decide whether it wants self-government and what kind of system it wants—independence, association, or union—until it has progressed sufficiently to make a mature decision. This, they contend, takes time, especially in those areas where few of the inhabitants have had any educa-

---

[27] General Assembly Resolution 648 (VII).

[28] See above, pp. 635–39, for a discussion of handling this problem under the trusteeship system.

tion, and fewer still have experience in running a country. Now, these say, we have accepted responsibility for preparing the dependent peoples, but this cannot be accomplished overnight; it takes time to prepare a people who have barely entered the threshold of the modern world to the place where it is possible for them to manage a state. The anticolonials, looking at the history of colonial administration, are unsatisfied with this position. The colonial powers for years did very little to help the inhabitants of these areas to develop self-sufficiency. They have, to be sure, accepted the principle of trusteeship, but reluctantly and too late. Now the time has come to free the colonies whether they are, according to Western standards, adequately prepared or not.

The anticolonial forces have tried to include another element in the system for non-self-governing areas—target dates. There has been pressure within the General Assembly to accept the idea that conditions in each of the colonies should be studied and a date for self-government set.[29] Against this position it has been argued that it is impossible to say how fast areas will progress. The development must proceed slowly; for each step there must be the necessary preparation.

Although the administering states have resisted permitting the United Nations to determine when an area had achieved a full measure of self-government, they have been unable to prevent the organization from assuming a role. Legally, nothing has been changed: the administering states still have to initiate the necessary reforms and prepare for plebiscites and elections; legally they make the final determination as to whether an area is ready to assume responsibility for its own affairs. However, the colonial states could not act in a vacuum. They could—and can—not resist the tremendous pressure from the majority of United Nations members. They have fought or tried to moderate each step the General Assembly has taken to involve itself in the procedure. They have been successful in slowing down the process, but they have not been able to halt it.

All of the above developments regarding non-self-governing territories have been accomplished through resolutions of the General Assembly. They have not involved *legal* obligations. However, to argue only from the legal effect of the General Assembly's decisions would be to overlook the real impact of this action. The colonial powers have submitted to the process, have presented the required information, have helped in drawing up lists of factors, and have been influenced by pressure from the organization.

Transmission of Information by New Members. Under Article 73, members of the United Nations assume a responsibility to transmit information concerning non-self-governing territories. In the foregoing section, the

---

[29] A precedent was set for the idea of target dates in the disposition of the former Italian colonies. The trusteeship agreement with Italy set two years for Libya and ten years for Somaliland.

process for terminating this responsibility has been analyzed. We turn now to the problem of deciding what areas should be included in the system. That is, pact of this action. The colonial powers have submitted to the process, have on which territories should information be submitted to the Secretary-General?

The Secretary-General's letter in 1946 to all members of the new United Nations, requesting each to send to him a list of the areas on which it would be reporting, has been mentioned.[30] When new states were admitted to membership, starting with the 16 in 1955, the same procedure was followed.

The Secretary-General's report to the Eleventh Session stated that he had received negative replies to his inquiry concerning minorities. This gave rise to heated debate. Again, as in the case of the cessation of annual reports on dependent territories, a question of the competence of the organization was involved. Was each new member responsible for deciding whether it controlled areas that were non-self-governing, or was the organization to decide? Some members put forth the position that Chapter XI was a unilateral declaration made by each individual state on accepting the Charter, and to back up their position they pointed out that in 1946 the General Assembly had accepted without question the member's statements of territories.[31] Any effort would be discriminatory, asserted these, as only the new members' replies would be given this treatment, and, besides, this would involve the organization's making judgments on the constitutions of these states, which it was not entitled to do.

Other members of the Fourth Committee objected to considering Chapter XI purely a unilateral declaration. Chapter XI was an integral part of the Charter—a multilateral agreement—and, therefore, the organization had the competence to call on the member nations to fulfill obligations. To support this position, it was pointed out that the General Assembly had agreed to draw up lists of factors to serve as criteria, and had developed a procedure for examining information on constitutional changes to decide whether an area was self-governing or not. Therefore, it was reasoned, there should be no objection to the United Nations using this same criteria to judge whether a new member had non-self-governing areas on which it was obligated to report.

The Fourth Committee was finally able to obtain a majority for the suggestion that an ad hoc committee be set up to examine the replies received from new members by the Secretary-General, and to request them to submit their views on any area whose status appeared questionable to the Committee. The General Assembly did not adopt this proposal. The Fourth Commit-

---

[30] See above, p. 644.
[31] See above, p. 645.

tee made new suggestions in 1957, only to have these rejected by the plenary body.

One reason for the seeming difference in the strength of supporters for introducing a system in the two organs is due to the voting requirements in the Fourth Committee and in the General Assembly. A proposal needs only a simple majority to pass the Committee, but for the General Assembly a two-thirds majority is required. The forces opposed to these measures were able to block action in the General Assembly until 1959.

In 1959, it was possible for the anticolonial forces to command enough support to pass a resolution establishing a six-nation committee to "enumerate the principles which should guide members" in determining whether or not they had an obligation to transmit information on territories.[32]

The committee, composed of three administering (Netherlands, U.K., and U.S.) and three nonadministering (India, Mexico, Morocco) states, was able to agree on twelve principles acceptable to the General Assembly. Although the resolutions on dependent areas of new members were couched in general terms, the real objective had been to force Spain and Portugal to report on their overseas territories. Both states claimed that their overseas possessions were integral parts of the metropolitan area, and that the inhabitants in these had the same voice in formulating public policy as had people in the metropolitan areas. The overseas Europeans enjoyed the same privileges, shared the responsibilities, and were subject to the same duties as those at home; however, very few Africans were accepted as equal to the Europeans. It was this situation that was criticized in the United Nations, where it was asserted that it was not possible to say a colony exercised self-government when the majority of the population was excluded from enjoying the full rights of citizenship.

The pressure, which began to mount in the General Assembly in 1959, was enough to induce Spain to comply and submit information on its overseas possessions, thereby leaving Portugal the primary target. Uprisings in Angola, flights of refugees to neighboring lands, and reports of harsh policies have added to an animosity toward Portugal shared by all anticolonial U.N. members and others. In spite of the general denunciation of Portugal's policy, the particularly irate memebrs were unable, during the Twelfth Session of the General Assembly, to obtain enough votes to pass a resolution calling on the Secretary-General to make a study of conditions in Angola.

The more extreme anticolonial forces have been unsuccessful in their attempt to persuade the General Assembly to adopt a regular procedure for examining the lists of dependents supplied by new members in order to ascertain whether these contain all non-self-governing areas. The attention paid to the problem in various organs of the United Nations seems to have had

---

[32] General Assembly Resolution 1467 (XIV) December 12, 1959.

different results in the attitudes of the two countries for which many states had questions—Spain and Portugal. Spain, whose overseas areas are small, sparsely populated, and not too important to the Spaniard, has reacted to the pressure by deciding to comply with the wishes of the United Nations majority: she reports. Portugal, with many small and two very large colonies considered very important to this little country, has reacted in a very different way: she has refused to submit information. She has been put on the defensive and clearly resents the intrusion of the organization into her affairs.[33] One wonders whether Portugal would have joined the organization if she had had even an inkling of these developments!

The whole question as to whether the organization has the competence to reject the statements of new members on their territories is today an academic one. The only territories, according to the practice and views of the majority of United Nations members, that would fall into this category are those "overseas," i.e., separated from the metropolitan area. There are no more nonmembers of the United Nations that have such territories. Secondly, the fact that Portugal has refused to submit information on her territories has not prevented the organization from considering conditions in these areas. It has not, therefore, been necessary for the organization to have formal reports on territories in order to act.

The first objective of the anticolonial elements in the United Nations—to extend the principle of accountability to all non-self-governing areas—has been, to a large extent, successful. The colonial powers have been unable to hold their position; i.e., that they had agreed, in ratifying the Charter, to regard their colonies as a sacred trust, that they had precluded any close scrutiny of their administrations by the United Nations, and that they alone were competent and responsible for determining when an area was self-governing. The system as it has evolved has had beneficial results for a large number of colonies. The close scrutiny of conditions and of progress toward specified goals, the publication of reports, and the criticisms made has prodded the colonial powers into moving at a rate faster than would probably have been so had they been left to themselves. On the whole, these states have taken their defeat rather gracefully; they have, to be sure, balked at each advance, trying to stop the anticolonial group where possible, or at least to moderate international action.[34] Once a new procedure has passed, they have usually complied, sometimes reluctantly, sometimes only after showing

[33] For a good discussion of Portuguese colonial issue, see Patricia Wohlgemuth, "The Portuguese Territories and the United Nations," *International Conciliation*, November, 1963.

[34] In 1955, when a proposal to expand the scope and power of the committee was discussed, the United Kingdom made it known that if this happened she would withdraw from the U.N. See Thomas R. Adam, "Trusteeship and Non-self-governing Territories," *Annual Review of United Nations Affairs, 1955–1956* (Dobbs Ferry, N.Y.: Oceana Publications, Inc., 1957), p. 118.

their disapproval. Belgium has boycotted the Committee on Information; Britain refused to submit information on political developments and constitutional changes; France has balked. In the end, all have complied; only Portugal has continued to hold out against the tremendous pressures, and she was a latecomer.

Holding states accountable for their administrations, checking progress, and analyzing developments has been only the first part of the anticolonial campaign—a preliminary step to independence, or self-government when independence has not been possible. The second target has been self-determination.

THE DRIVE FOR LIBERATION OF THE COLONIES

During the period of the League of Nations, the question of self-determination was not an issue: it had been all settled in Paris. Within the Western states, voices were beginning to be heard in favor of a change in colonial policy, but these were still weak and unable to exert much influence on policy-makers. There were improvements, to be sure, but no genuine effort to prepare the dependent areas for eventual independence. What was done was the result of a humanitarian concern for people rather than part of a movement to end colonialism. Colonialism to the end of the League period was accepted by most Westerners as a very natural relationship.

But the movement to gain support for the principle of self-determination was growing, and has become today one of the most discussed issues in the United Nations.[35] The pressure has been to transform a principle into a right—a right of peoples to determine for themselves what their future should be. No longer should there be a colonial relationship in which one party is able to dictate the policies of another; every people should decide on its own policies according to its own needs as it sees them, not as some mother country sees them.

When the delegates met in San Francisco, these ideas were in the air, but were strongly opposed by a number of the colonial powers led by Great Britain. The Conservative government in London was still thinking in terms of the British Empire, without which Britain would have been unable to make the record she did in the war. Britain realized that she had relied on her colonies for troops, supplies, and bases; and many a Britisher could not conceive of the future without these colonies. It was, then, not possible to

---

[35] For a general treatment of self-determination, see B. Rivlin, *op. cit.;* Hans Kohn, "The United Nations and National Self-determination," *Review of Politics,* October, 1958, pp. 526–45; Clyde Eagleton, "Excesses of Self-determination," *Foreign Affairs,* July, 1953, pp. 592–604.

incorporate a right of self-determination within the Charter with this strong opposition. It was also impossible to keep out the principle of self-determination.

The Reinterpretation of the Charter

In the first article of the U.N. Charter, self-determination is mentioned: "(The Purposes of the United Nations are:)
2. To develop friendly relations among nations based on respect for the principle of equal rights and self-determination of peoples . . ."

It is clear that self-determination as here called for is not a *right* of peoples, but is a *principle* by which the parties should be guided in their relations with one another. It would seem to be more of a negative idea: states should not—as the Germans and Japanese had recently done—subject peoples to an alien rule against their wishes. From the wording of this article, it would appear that the drafters were thinking more in terms of future efforts at colonization than in terms of independence for existing colonies.

The anticolonial group was unsatisfied with this interpretation. To have any meaning, self-determination must apply to colonial areas. In 1958, they were able to secure support for a resolution containing provisions for the organization: ". . . to study ways and means which would ensure the right of peoples and nations to self-determination." The resolution reflects the thinking that self-determination should be a right of peoples, not merely a principle to guide state behavior. The colonial powers objected violently to this "reinterpretation" of the Charter: the organization had been given no mandate even to discuss colonial issues, except where conditions would bring these under another provision of the Charter. The relations between the mother country and her colonies is a matter within the domestic jurisdiction of a state and, as such, comes under the meaning of Article 2.7 (the clause prohibiting the United Nations from intervening in "matters which are essentially within the domestic jurisdiction of any state"). They had, their argument continued, not agreed to subject their colonial relationships to the scrutiny of the organization. However, the protests of the colonial powers have been in vain. Colonial problems are today not "essentially" domestic problems but are, rather, international problems for whose solution international cooperation is appropriate.

One indication that self-determination has become accepted by many as a substantive right is its inclusion, in 1955, in both Draft Covenants on Human Rights. Many Western states—especially the U.S., U.K., France, and Australia—have objected violently to including self-determination among the basic human rights. The Covenants are enumerations of rights that states will obligate themselves to guarantee each individual within their territories. Self-determination has meaning only when applied to groups of people and does not, therefore, actually fit in with the other rights in the Covenants.

Furthermore, to grant the rights of self-determination would leave the door open for anarchy. These were some of the arguments put forth by this group. In spite of strong statements by the opposition, including a clear assertion that inclusion of self-determination as a right would almost preclude any chance of obtaining the United States' ratification, the Third Committee adopted the provisions, thereby really putting a damper on any hope for a genuine international bill of rights.[36]

The movement to elevate self-determination to a substantive right has raised a number of questions, most of which have not been adequately answered in a consistent way. Unless the term "self-determination" has a content on which the majority of states agree, acceptance of it as a legal right in international law is problematical.

Who Shall Be Free?

The first question that needs to be raised is, *who* has the right of self-determination? Article 1 mentions the self-determination of *peoples,* but does not define "peoples." Therefore, it has been possible to disagree. Since the anticolonial forces have been most interested in using the concept as a wedge by which they could justify bringing colonial problems to the organization, it is natural that their interpretation of the term should emphasize colonial peoples. The majority of members of the United Nations have reserved "colonial" for "traditional" colonies—overseas areas separated from the metropolitan area by water and peopled by a racial group different from that in the mother country. The Russians and Eastern Europeans have been especially anxious to have the idea of differences in race—particularly as defined by skin color—included in the definition. The status of the colonial peoples is, in this use of the concept, different from that of the mother country: there is a ruler and ruled relationship in terms of populations. This use of "peoples" for whom self-determination applies thus includes primarily those areas under the trusteeship system or covered by the Declaration on Non-self-governing Territories.

This interpretation has been contested by some of the Western states as being too narrow. Belgians have taken the position that restricting the use of "peoples" to colonial areas is too narrow. Is not, they argue, any group that is uncomfortable within a state, or any state whose freedom of action and policy-making is narrowly restricted by another state, just as entitled to exercise the right of self-determination as the colonial areas? The Belgians resented the often acrimonious and violent criticisms leveled at their administration of the Congo before its independence, especially from Russia when Russia's policies toward groups within its own and the Eastern European states were just as reprehensible. Belgium's extreme position—use of the

---

[36] For a discussion of these efforts see above, pp. 589–93.

term to cover all groups everywhere—has had little support within the United Nations. However, the United States, the United Kingdom, and others have attempted to broaden the concept of peoples to include the Eastern European states, but have, generally, been unable to elicit much support for this position. If we are to judge by the use of the term by the majority of members, it must be concluded that "peoples" is confined to colonial areas in the traditional sense.

For those supporting the first position, once an area has exercised its right to self-determination, the right no longer applies to the peoples within the area; it can still be used by the area as a whole when threatened with any form of "neo-colonialism." This has been important for the new nations. Once independence is attained, insistence on the principle of self-determination is replaced in speeches by "territorial integrity" and "sovereign equality." These become the focus. The new states are faced with the job of building new nations, often out of very different groups that had been united under the banner of independence and political freedom. Once the country attains independence, the unity often vanishes. It is, therefore, understandable that the leaders of these nations resist making self-determination a right to be granted groups *within* states. Attempts by the Naga, the Pathans, and the Amboinese to find a sympathetic response in the United Nations for their desires for self-determination were absolutely fruitless. The majority of the members agreed with India, Pakistan, and Indonesia that Article 2.7 applied: this was a matter of domestic jurisdiction, and, therefore, it was not permissible for the organization to help in any way.[37]

When Is an Area Free

A second question that has caused trouble is: When has an area exercised its right of self-determination? Is it necessary that an area have attained complete independence before it is possible to assert that self-determination has been exercised? Many of the ex-colonial areas and the Soviet Union would like to answer this question in the positive. As long as any aspect of an area's policy is determined by an outside state, it should be considered still eligible to exercise its right. It has been very difficult to support this position by using the United Nations Charter. There is no justification for claiming

---

[37] It is interesting to note in this context that the Western European states had come under heavy criticism for dividing Africa without due consideration to tribal divisions, resulting in administrative areas containing a number of very different tribes and in tribes being split between areas. Once independence has been achieved, the Africans, asserting "territorial integrity" have not rectified the situation, which has resulted in a number of disputes. The only cases in which any effort was made to give to the peoples within the area—not just the area as a whole—a choice of what political unit they desired to join were the trusteeships of the Cameroons and Togoland. Some of the other unsettled disputes that plague intra-African relations are between Kenya and Somaliland, Ethiopia and Somaliland, Morocco and most of her neighbors.

preference for independence. Self-government is stated as an alternative to independence in Article 76.1 (trusteeship provisions), and it is mentioned alone in Article 73.b (provisions for non-self-governing territories) as a goal for dependent areas. Its coupling with independence precludes any interpretation that would make the two the same. Therefore, since the Charter presents the alternatives, it has been difficult for the extreme anticolonial forces to gain majority support for the view that only self-determination resulting in independence is acceptable.

Another forceful argument confronting the extremists is the nature of some of the areas. It is conceivable that an India, a Nigeria, an Indonesia—or even a Burundi or a Jamaica—might become states. But what of a Nauru, a Timor, a Fiji—tiny specks on the globe for which complete independence would seem impractical? In some of the smaller areas, the leaders have weighed the advantages and disadvantages of independence and have decided there were other, more important considerations, often economic. To sacrifice control over foreign affairs and defense—which, after all, a little area hardly can control for itself—in return for association which assures economic aid and perhaps an outlet for an expanding population (as in Puerto Rico) has seemed the wiser choice.

As has been pointed out in discussion of the cessation of reports under Chapter XI, a number of areas on which the General Assembly was asked to approve the colonial powers' action did not opt for independence but, rather, selected association or union with the metropolitan area. This set a precedent to which the colonial powers could refer for support of their position that self-determination could result in self-government with some relationship to the metropolitan area. This position has usually been supported by a majority of the United Nations membership.

The Role of the United Nations in the Process

A third question that has arisen is: How is a people to exercise its right to self-determination? Here, there has been no development of a procedure or unanimity of practice. Only rarely has the United Nations been associated with the process. In the case of the trusteeship areas, the role of the United Nations has often been an active one.[38] The organization has been called on to help supervise plebiscites for many of these territories. In the non-self-governing territories, United Nations action has been of a different nature. In some areas, direct agreement between the administering state and the territory has resulted in a procedure acceptable to both parties. Ghana, Nigeria, French Sahara, and other colonies became independent with very little notice being taken by the United Nations. In other cases, the organization did become involved. The U.N. was called on to take action by, or on

---

[38] See above, pp. 635–38.

behalf of, those areas which were not able to work out an agreement with the mother country. In such cases, three courses of action have been open to the United Nations: (1) to take no action; (2) to pass a resolution calling on the administering power to attempt a solution with the area; (3) to send some sort of mission or conciliatory body to help the parties reach a settlement.

The choice among the three courses has not been determined by any objective criteria but, rather, by a number of factors such as strength of the mother country, ability of the dependent area to get support of powerful groups in the United Nations, and whether there was fighting or not. Each case as it came up has been handled as an individual one, and the course of action taken has been determined by what was feasible in terms of getting a majority of the members to support it.

Since there was no procedure and no special organ to handle problems of independence in the colonies, and the Committee on Information could make only general recommendations, the only avenue was to bring the issue into one of the main political bodies—the Security Council or General Assembly. Since the early days of the organization, there has hardly been a session of the General Assembly in which some area seeking freedom has not been the subject of debate, often acrimonious and bitter. The Security Council gets seized of the problem if and when it can be shown that a situation is endangering the peace.

In the following section, brief sketches of two issues will be presented to show how the organization has been involved and what the effects of United Nations action seem to have been.

Indonesia.[39]   One issue on the agenda for many sessions was that of Indonesia. Soon after the Japanese left the Netherlands East Indies and the Dutch returned to reestablish their control over the islands, there were difficulties, and fighting broke out. Australia and India brought the situation to the attention of the Security Council in July, 1947, on the grounds that peace was threatened. The Council decided it had jurisdiction, and called on both sides to cease hostilities.

A cease-fire was agreed to, but fighting was not completely halted. The Security Council then requested the consuls in Batavia to study the situation and report to the Council. These men were, then, to act as a sort of international commission of inquiry to study the effects of the cease-fire agreement and note violations. To help settle the political dispute, the Council offered its good offices through a committee of three. The Good Offices Committee spent many long hours trying to find common ground between Netherlands and Indonesia.

---

[39] Alastair Taylor, *Indonesian Independence and the United Nations* (Ithaca, N.Y.: Cornell University Press, 1960); William Henderson, *Pacific Settlement of Disputes: The Indonesian Question, 1946–1949* (New York: Woodrow Wilson Foundation, 1954).

The Committee was able to help the sides reach a truce agreement, signed on January 17, 1948. The truce did not last long; in December, it was denounced by Netherlands. Fighting broke out again. The Security Council immediately called for a cease-fire and requested the Dutch to release the political prisoners she was holding. Twice more, it made its call to the Netherlands, and on January 1, 1949, recommended establishment of a federal, independent Indonesia. On the same day it voted to replace the Good Offices Committee by the United Nations Commission on Indonesia.

The Dutch, in March, notified the Council that they were ready to comply with Council resolutions, were releasing the political prisoners, and suggested a round table conference at The Hague. The Dutch had by now accepted independence as the only possible status for Indonesia and were ready to work out the details.

The Commission was directed by the Council to work out with the two parties arrangements for cessation of hostilities and details for the round table conference, which finally met from August to November. The result of these meetings was the Charter on the Transfer of Sovereignty by which Netherlands transferred complete sovereignty to the republic. The only area on which it was not possible to get agreement was New Guinea, to be settled at a later date.

The Charter was ratified by the Dutch and Indonesians and recognized in a resolution of the General Assembly. The Commission continued to function, observing the implementation of the Charter and the transfer of sovereignty until April 6, 1951.

For almost four years, the United Nations had been dealing with the problem of Indonesia. It had used a variety of instruments—resolutions, fact-finding committee, good offices committee, conferences, etc.—in an attempt to help the two sides reach an agreement. It is very possible that the same solution—i.e., an independent Indonesia—would have been reached without the assistance of the United Nations. However, it seems extremely likely that a great deal more blood would have been shed, and feelings would have been even more hostile than they were. The Indonesian leaders were unwilling to accept anything short of complete independence; the Dutch, at first, would not agree to this. However, the Dutch were also unwilling to lose everything for Indonesia: they were debilitated and were suffering severe economic difficulties as a result of the Second World War. Within the Netherlands, feeling was growing that the Indies were more a liability than an asset and would continue to be. The United States was also extremely influential in bringing about the change in Dutch policy. The Netherlands was threatened with withdrawal of Marshall Plan aid if they continued to refuse to grant the Indonesians their independence.

The process of negotiating was made easier by the presence of the international commission: concessions, instead of involving a loss of face, can be turned into an attempt to conform with the wishes of the international community, and are, therefore, often easier to make. It would seem that this happened at many points during the long, arduous process. It can be concluded, then, that the international organization did perform an important role in bringing about a solution to this problem.

The Charter on the Transfer of Sovereignty and its implementation settled the main issue: Indonesia became independent. However, one problem was left—that of New Guinea. It had been decided during the round table conference that West Irian (formerly called West New Guinea) should not be considered a part of Indonesia in working out a general political settlement, but that the final disposition of this area should be subject to direct negotiations between the new Republic and the Netherlands to begin within a year of the transfer of sovereignty.

Negotiations did begin on schedule but proved fruitless, and, in 1954, the Netherlands refused to continue participating. The Indonesians brought the issue to the United Nations; so, once again, the colonial issue between the Indonesians and the Netherlands was put on the agenda. This time the General Assembly was to become involved.

This area, although administered by the Dutch as an integral part of their East Indies, is very different from the other islands and is extremely primitive. The Dutch position was that the people should exercise their own right of self-determination and that they—the Dutch—were preparing them to do this. For the Indonesians, West Irian had been a part of the Empire and should be a part of the new Indonesia.

A draft resolution calling on the parties to reenter negotiations and report progress failed to secure the necessary two-thirds vote in the Ninth Session of the General Assembly. At the Tenth Session, a resolution expressing the concern of the organization and the hope that negotiations would be resumed was passed. At the Eleventh Session, the question again appeared on the agenda. As the plea for resuming negotiations had had no effect, another resolution was introduced, suggesting a good offices commission, but was not adopted. The anticolonial forces were unwilling to let the matter drop, and 21 African and Asian states requested that West Irian be included on the agenda for the Twelveth Session. The only resolution passed at that Session was one calling on the two parties to try to find a solution. Finally, in August, 1961, the two parties did agree to begin negotiations again.

It is impossible to judge whether the action of the United Nations was influential in bringing about the final settlement. In this case, there was no active participation—no commissions, no resolutions containing substantive suggestions—only a resolution calling on the parties to cooperate. The Dutch may have been influenced by this pressure but they were more concerned about the prospect of an armed encounter with the Indonesians—a very real possibility.

No agreement resulted from this round of talks. In 1961, it was the Dutch who appealed to the United Nations. In 1960, the Declaration on the Granting of Independence to Colonial Peoples had been passed, and the Dutch made use of this in a proposed resolution. "[R]ecognizing the paramount importance of respect for the principle of self-determination," the Dutch suggested a commission to look into conditions in the territory and into the possibility of a plebescite, to be supervised by the United Nations, "to register the wishes of the population." Several Asian and African states were incensed: this was a misuse of the Declaration. It did not take into account the existence of Indonesia. Several resolutions were presented to the General Assembly, but none secured the necessary votes.

In December, 1961, the situation worsened: President Sukarno was ready for war, and actually began to drop paratroopers and to send infiltrators by boat. Neither side actually wanted a full-scale military engagement. Negotiations were resumed, with a United Nations official there to help. Finally, in August, 1962, a settlement was reached. The agreement involved a virtual capitulation on the part of the Dutch in face of the resolve to use force on the part of the Indonesians.

The 1960 Dutch proposal had contained a suggestion for international administration of the area. Although the resolution was not adopted at the time, the idea of international administration was retained as a real possibility and appears in the final solution. To provide for a smooth transitional period, the two states agreed on a period of United Nations administration. Early in the fall of 1962, administration was handed over by the Dutch to the United Nations Temporary Executive Authority (UNTEA), which, in turn, handed over full responsibility to the Indonesians in May, 1963.[40]

The UNTEA, financed by the Dutch and Indonesians, was an actual administration with absolute authority during its existence. The Secretary-General provided it with the security forces it deemed necessary. When the UNTEA turned over authority and withdrew, it left behind technical assistance personnel to help with the economic development of the country. As a result of this procedure, the transfer of authority from the Dutch to the Indonesians was a smooth one. During the short period of UNTEA, several projects were undertaken which will continue, and a number of local persons trained for administrative jobs.

Thus, finally has ended the long, weary, and, at times, bloody and bitter struggle of the Indonesians for independence—for the exercise of their "right" of self-determination. "Their" objective was achieved, even to forcing the Dutch out of West Irian.

---

[40] See Paul W. van der Veur, "The United Nations in West Irian: a Critique," *International Organization*, Winter, 1964, pp. 53–74.

This case illustrates U.N. application of the term "self-determination" to a colonial area. The Indonesian leadership, under Sukarno, regarded self-determination as a right to be exercised by the Dutch Indies as *One Unit*. He received support for this position from the other Asian and African states. Resolutions passed in the General Assembly treated Indonesia as a whole and finally sanctioned Indonesian administration of West Irian. Never was any opportunity to exercise self-determination given to those areas of Indonesia unwilling to accept control by Djakarta. The only concession to these areas, strongly advanced and supported by the Dutch, was the original stipulation that Indonesia be a federal republic. And even this was dissolved by the central government, necessitating the use of force in some areas. Any outside support for the cause of dissatisfied areas was looked on by the central Indonesian leadership, supported by non-Western areas, as a malicious attempt to divide and weaken the country.

In the case of settlement for West Irian, a similar use of self-determination was made. The only reason for associating the Island to Indonesia was the fact that it had been administered as a part of the East Indies by the Dutch. There existed no close economic or political ties and no ethnic similarity, and geographically it would make more sense were this area joined to the other parts of the island (now divided as part colony and part trusteeship of Australia). And yet, the area has been turned over to Indonesia. Here, a fiction has been applied to make this action more palatable: West Irian has not been made an integral part of Indonesia; rather, it was to be given, in 1969, the opportunity to exercise *its* right of self-determination under United Nations' supervision. The Indonesians feared that were the West Irians to be "developed" by the Dutch, they would be able to compare conditions in their territory with those in Indonesia itself and would decide against union. The Indonesian claim that under the Dutch the West Irians would be continuing in a colonial relationship, and that the Indonesians should have responsibility for the West Irians, thus eliminating colonialism in the area (according to the definition acceptable to many non-Western states), does not seem to be a valid one. Not only will pressure be put on the West Irians—probably more than just verbal persuasion and propaganda— to join the Indonesians,[41] but the West Irians will probably not develop so quickly as was possible under the Dutch, the economic difficulties in Indonesia not permitting it. To be sure, it is not possible to over- look the fact that the Dutch did little for the Island until recently.

In attempting to assess the role and influence of the United Nations in the Indonesian case, it is possible to conclude that the outcome would not have

---

[41] Since West Irian has been turned over to be administered by Indonesia, Sukarno has indicated that there is now no need for a plebiscite since the outcome is already certain, i.e., union with Indonesia.

been very different had the organization not become involved. The pro-Indonesian forces were powerful, the Dutch were weak and ready to give in rather than attempt to continue large-scale military operations that—as became clear in both the initial Indonesian and the later West Irian conflicts—would most probably have ended in defeat. The organization, however, was able to assist the two parties in their search for agreement once both sides indicated willingness to compromise, although the Dutch were forced to retreat much further than the Indonesians.

Algeria. One of the most bitter colonial issues before the United Nations has been that of the future of Algeria. From its Tenth Session until independence was proclaimed by President de Gaulle on July 3, 1962, the problem was being considered by the General Assembly. At times, the Security Council was also seized of the issue. The issue became an extremely complicated one, so intertwined with French domestic problems that it is possible here only to attempt an outline of the major developments within the United Nations relating to the problem, and to try to assess the importance of United Nations' action.

During the interwar period, Algerian nationalism began to grow and to become more insistent; the first postwar uprising took place on May 8, 1945, the day after the German surrender. This, however, was only a brief demonstration, and order was quickly restored. For the next nine years, Algeria was quiet, but this was deceiving. Under the surface, the Algerians were intensifying their drive for supporters and fomenting anti-French feeling. In 1954, fighting broke out and continued until agreement was reached in 1962.

The Security Council was seized of the situation in January, 1955, on the initiative of Saudi Arabia. No action was taken. In July of the same year, 14 African and Asian states attempted to have the question included on the agenda of the Assembly's Tenth Session. The General Committee turned down the request—a decision later reversed by the General Assembly itself. France's objections were violent; this was a matter within the domestic jurisdiction of France and, as such, covered by the prohibitive clause in Article 2.7. And France walked out, refusing to attend meetings of the General Assembly or its main committees. In November, a resolution was passed, ending consideration of Algeria.

France had successfully bucked the anticolonial forces. At this time (1955), there were not enough African and Asian members to obtain support for a discussion of the issue. Because many states were more concerned about France—trying not to alienate her—than about the Algerians, a General Assembly majority to discuss the problem could not be obtained.

In 1956, a group of Asian and African states attempted to have the case considered by the Security Council. By a vote of 7 to 2 with 2 abstentions, France's claim of domestic jurisdiction was upheld. Having failed in the

Security Council, the anticolonial forces turned to the General Assembly, where the case was discussed. Numerous resolutions, proposing independence, exercise of the right of self-determination, and direct negotiations between Algerians and French, were rejected in the First Committee. The final result of General Assembly action was a mild resolution expressing the hope that a peaceful solution could be found.

The Twelfth Session had before it a draft resolution of 22 Asian and African states, pointing out that nothing had been accomplished toward carrying out the resolution of the previous session. Again, the First Committee was called on to discuss a resolution (presented by 17 Asian and African states) recognizing the Algerian people's right to exercise self-determination. A milder resolution was submitted by five Latin-American states, Italy, and Spain, and various amendments were made to the first resolution, removing the phrase "self-determination." However, none of these was able to secure enough votes in the First Committee. When the General Assembly met, another resolution, sponsored by 15 states from various regions, was finally adopted. The Assembly expressed its concern, took note of the offers of good offices by the King of Morocco and the President of Tunisia, and hoped that talks would begin.

At its Thirteenth Session, no resolution on Algeria was adopted. Up to this time, no resolution recognizing a right of the Algerians to self-determination was acceptable to the majority of the U.N.; only resolutions that, in effect, called on France to work out a solution were passed. The French objected not only to having the principle of self-determination asserted, but also to any resolution that would have indicated the Algerians should be equal partners in the discussions and to any recognition of the FLN as an official spokesman for the Algerian people. During the thirteenth session, it was clear that support for acceptance of the FLN was growing among the members.

During 1960, there seemed to be more hope for a settlement of the problem: President de Gaulle had proclaimed the right of the Algerian people to self-determination. The African and Asian states renewed their attempts to get through the General Assembly a resolution calling for negotiations between the two sides, even revising it to make it more palatable to the French, but again the resolution failed to pass. France objected, as usual, to any resolution and made it clear she was convinced that U.N. action at this time would hinder settlement. De Gaulle's agreement to meet with representatives of the Provisional Government of the Algerian Republic (GPRA) influenced some votes. For the first time since the insurrection had started, there would be official, face-to-face talks, and some states felt that U.N. action might have an adverse effect on the negotiations.

In 1960, it seemed as though a turning point in the Algerian struggle had been reached. Although the talks had not been successful, that they had been held at all was significant. It is, however, not possible to give the action of the

United Nations any credit for this change in French attitude. The next year, 1961, saw more talks between French and Algerians. It also saw the first resolution on Algeria passed in the General Assembly since 1957. The resolution called for "guarantees to ensure . . . self-determination" and recognized the United Nations' "responsibility to contribute," without stipulating what the organization's contribution should be. It was this problem that still split the members: Asians, Africans (except some of the French African group), and Eastern European states on one side were demanding active U.N. participation in a referendum. On the other side, the Western European states, Latin America, and French Africa south of the Sahara (except Mali) were rejecting any real participation by the organization. In the following year, Algeria was free.

The debates on Algeria were conducted in an atmosphere of hostility from the beginning. Resolutions were passed, but these were never more than calls to France to continue working for a settlement. France herself boycotted the Assembly during much of the debate. To the end, the French refused to recognize the organization's competence to even discuss her relations with Algeria: this was her affair, and for the United Nations to interfere was in direct violation of the Charter. This attitude on the part of France made her unreceptive to suggestions made by the organization. Instead of encouraging the French to reach a settlement, U.N. action tended to antagonize her. Those seeking a right of self-determination never could command a two-thirds majority in the General Assembly. The United States and Western European states, unwilling to alienate France any more than necessary, sought moderation, and the resolutions proposed by this group were very mild and without any hint of a denunciation of French policy. This type of resolution was unacceptable to the anticolonial forces, with the result that the General Assembly became deadlocked and passed no resolutions for a time.

France's eventual change of policy and willingness to negotiate were the result of forces inside France and of some pressure from her allies. When negotiations were begun, international mediators did not help the two parties. The role of the United Nations here was less direct than in Indonesia. A few resolutions had been passed, but these contained only suggestions to France. The outcome of this dispute was the same as the Indonesian—independence for the colonial area. But in Algeria, the cost in lives was much higher than in Indonesia, where the international organization had been able to take a more active role.

The United Nations was "used" by many Asian and African states as a forum for denunciation of France. Most of these states did not seem to have been motivated so much by any desire to work out a way to help the French and Algerians as by a desire to see colonialism ended in the area. Their slogan was Algeria for the Algerians on Algerian terms. This attitude on the one side and the French attitude on the other—with France's allies reluctant to go too far for fear of alienating her—made it impossible for the more moderate forces to help develop an atmosphere in which the United Nations, as an organization, could evolve means for helping France to work through the problem. Many of the moderate forces were motivated more by desires to keep France placated without at the same time alienating the anti-French forces. There seemed to have been few states able to take a dispassionate, objective view.

The two brief studies reveal the kind of role the United Nations has been able to play in cases involving colonial areas' exercise of the principle of self-determination and the struggle to liberate the colonies. The General Assembly has been a forum to which the anticolonial factions could come and raise the issue—could put pressure on the colonial powers. At times the anti-colonial forces powers were influenced by this pressure, sometimes they were not. It can be concluded that this pressure has had the general effect of making the colonial powers aware that they could not hold on to the colonies for long, and, in the case of many areas, to think in terms of granting self-government or independence. However, stress from political organs concerning specific colonies—especially those that the metropole, for one reason or another, was unwilling to see separated from it—has sometimes led to an intensification of hostility. The United Nations as an organization can be most helpful in cases where there is already a willingness to cooperate, or at least to come to some sort of agreement.

From studying these and other cases, the United Nations' use of the term "self-determination" becomes clear. To a majority of the members, self-determination is to be exercised, generally, by a colonial area as a whole. Groups and factions within former colonies are not recognized as having this right. One exception to this was the case of Palestine, where the colonial area was divided and the split recognized by the organization. Israel's determination and her ability to defeat the Arabs in the field so that she herself was able to take control of the area were the crucial factors. In other words, the issue was decided by force. Also, the United States and Russia were both supporting the plan for a separate Jewish state and were able to command the necessary majorities in both the General Assembly and Security Council. The idea of the "colonial unit" was not well established until the ex-colonial membership in the organization increased in later years.

The United Nations Charter makes no provision for an orderly process for assisting in the birth of new nations, and it has usually been difficult to gain support for United Nations action when it was not possible to point to a situation in which international peace was threatened. In the cases of Morocco and Tunisia, efforts to persuade the organization to act—even to pass resolutions—were, for the most part, futile. This has led to the observation that colonial peoples who want independence have a better chance of having their case considered by the United Nations if they engage in large-scale violence. The Charter was conceived at a time when the majority of states still thought in terms of colonial empires and were unwilling to recognize colonial issues as international issues. It has, therefore, been difficult to use the Charter to obtain a hearing for colonial areas. Cases that have received consideration have been those in which some other problem—one within the provisions of the Charter—was involved.

CULMINATION OF THE DRIVE—THE DECLARA-TION ON THE GRANTING OF INDEPENDENCE TO COLONIAL COUNTRIES AND PEOPLES

The attack on the colonial system has gone through a third phase—turning a principle into a right. It has been shown above that a supervisory system had been set up in the Charter (the trusteeship system) and extended to cover most colonial areas, and that there had been pressure within the United Nations, at times resulting in action by the organization, to help colonies liberate themselves.

As the United Nations membership has become composed of more ex-colonials, the goal of independence has been put forth with ever-increasing vehemence. However, the forces behind this movement have had difficulty in getting around the provisions of the Charter, where self-determination is put forth as a "principle" and not as a "right."[42] This has meant that the Charter could not be used to justify having the organization take a hand in liberating the colonies on the sole basis of the self-determination clauses. This, as pointed out above, has meant that only those colonies which used force or threatened the peace could gain United Nations' support.

When states failed in attempts to use the Charter provisions to gain recognition for asserting self-determination as a right, it was decided to draft a special declaration. This Declaration was not to have any legal force, but was to be regarded as an expression of the majority of members and was to serve as a guideline for states in the same way the Declaration on Human Rights has served. The anticolonial forces hoped this Declaration could serve as the basis for involving the organization more actively in the liberation movement.

Several moves made in the organization preceded the Declaration. A resolution the anticolonial forces were able to get passed called for a comprehensive study of the situation and progress in the colonial areas. In 1960, the report (over 3,000 pages) was studied by the General Assembly. A resolution was passed that took note of progress in *some* colonies, but emphasized that "a substantial number of territories still remain . . . and that in the great majority . . . the achievements fall short of the needs of

---

[42] See above, pp. 652–54.

the inhabitants." It is interesting to note that at the same session the report of the Special Committee of Six, setting forth principles to be used by new states in considering territories reported on under Chapter XI, was also considered.[43] Seventeen new members were admitted to the United Nations during that session, thus strengthening the anticolonial forces.

At the Fifteenth Session, Russia presented a Draft Declaration on the Granting of Independence to Colonial Countries and Peoples, containing a call for the immediate cessation of all colonial relationships. At the same time, 45 Asian and African states got together and prepared their own draft, which was a little less radical than that of the Russians. After lively debate, the draft was passed 89–0 with 9 abstentions on December 14, 1960.[44] This was really the end of the colonial powers' influence on colonial issues in the United Nations. They had not even attempted to stop the resolution, did not even vote against it. Colonial relationships were no longer acceptable. The system had been dying for 15 years, but this marked the last knell.

The Declaration proclaims, in no uncertain terms, self-determination as a right.

The General Assembly declares that:

2) All peoples have a right to self-determination, by virtue of that right they freely determine their political status and freely pursue their economic, social and cultural development.

3) Inadequacy of political, economic, social, or educational preparedness should never be a pretext for delaying independence.

4) . . . [All peoples have a right] to exercise peacefully and freely their right to complete independence, and the integrity of their national territory shall be respected.

5) Immediate steps shall be taken, in trust and non-self-governing territories or all other territories which have not yet attained independence, to transfer all powers to the peoples of these territories, without any conditions or reservations, in accordance with their freely expressed will and desire . . . in order to enable them to enjoy complete independence and freedom

6) Any attempt aimed at the partial or total disruption of the national unity and the territorial integrity of a country is incompatible with the purposes and principles of the Charter of the United Nations

7) All states shall observe . . . the provisions of the Charter . . . the Universal Declaration of Human Rights and the present Declaration on the bases of equality, non-interference in the internal affairs of all states and respect for the sovereign rights of all peoples and their territorial integrity.

---

[43] See above, p. 647.

[44] General Assembly Resolution 1514 (XV), December 14, 1960. Abstaining were: Australia, Belgium, Dominican Republic, France, Portugal, Spain, South Africa, U.K., and U.S.

In this Declaration, the position of the anticolonial forces is clearly defined. Self-determination is declared a right to be exercised by a "colony" as a whole; it is not a right of groups or factions within an area. Once it has been exercised—by implication, this is accomplished when an area has attained independence—then the principles of sovereign equality and territorial integrity are to be religiously observed.

The colonial powers had been emphasizing the change in their own policies toward their remaining dependencies. They had pointed to their increased budgetary provisions, to the ever-growing number of the populations in schools at all levels, to the new posts being filled by local people in the administrations of the areas, and to the new political activity—broadened suffrage and new legislatures with ever-increasing responsibility. At the same time, they pointed out that those areas still remaining under some form of colonial control presented complex, difficult, and individual problems that had to be solved. Many were small specks, lacking trained personnel, short of natural resources, and economically unviable, or they were areas of mixed populations. These problems, asserted the colonial powers, were being given careful consideration and ways to handle them were being sought. But this was a matter of time, and until the colony was really ready to take care of itself, it was better off under the tutelage of experienced colonial administrations.

This position, had it been held 15 years ago, might have been acceptable to the majority of colonial peoples. But by the time the colonial powers, with some exceptions (Portugal, in particular), had become genuinely committed to a policy of development, the anticolonial forces were no longer satisfied with this approach. Not only was there resentment toward long years of harsh, or at least unenlightened, administration, but there was also rejection of any form of relationship that was paternalistic or smacked of neo-colonialism. Complete acceptance and equality were now demanded.

The Declaration seems also to reject self-government that falls short of independence. Association and union with the metropole are not mentioned. For many anticolonial forces, the only acceptable way for colonial peoples to attain respect and equality is by severing all political ties: they do not seem to trust any form of union or association, since these are never free of elements of discrimination, of paternalism, of inequality.

A number of states had reservations about the Declaration, but, with the exception of eight abstainers, all voted for it. Those who voted reluctantly seemed to realize that a large majority would be secured and did not want to be counted among the diehard colonials. Some states were careful to point out that the Declaration was not a binding instrument.

There is no doubt that adoption of the Declaration is a landmark in development of the United Nations' colonial policy. It is now clear that there is no moderating the pressure for U.N. action to see the last remnants of colonialism disappear. The Declaration has been mentioned in a great number of resolutions demanding immediate independence for colonial areas.

New Machinery for Supervision and Action[45]

The anticolonials were not content to stop with a Declaration; they wanted special machinery for its implementation. At the Fifteenth Session, Special Committee of 17 (subsequently enlarged to 24) was set up. Until cil and the Committee on Information. For this new Committee, the principle was completely abandoned, and in the Committee as originally constituted were three administering states (Australia, U.K., and U.S.) and fourteen nonadministering (Italy, U.S.S.R., Poland, Yugoslavia, two South American, and eight Asian and African states). No longer could the moderate forces in the organ tone down the actions of the anticolonial group; they were now definitely in a minority, and their position remained unchanged when the Committee was later increased to 24 members.

This new Special Committee on the implementation of the Declaration eclipses the other two colonial organs of the United Nations; these two now do little more than examine the reports submitted to them by administering states. In 1961, the Committee on Information did not even submit proposed resolutions to the General Assembly.

From the beginning of its operations, the Special Committee has issued strongly worded, extremely anticolonial reports and resolutions. Unlike the Committee on Information, it can make recommendations on individual territories, and has taken advantage of this provision to address administering powers directly with criticisms of conditions and suggestions for action. The Special Committee also has authority to receive and to discuss petitions, and has been flooded with so many that it has had to develop a system of priorities. It has been unable to keep up with all the demands made on it. The Committee decided at an early meeting that a thorough study should be made of all colonial areas, so that it would have a basis on which to make recommendations. In order to accomplish this, the Committee has sent out missions to examine conditions on the spot—a privilege never enjoyed by the Committee on Information. Needless to say, the recommendations have almost always called for immediate independence.

The Committee has tended toward extreme positions. Its criticisms have been unrestrained, its demands absolute. One example of this was the Committee's recommendation that the Assembly "declare solemnly that any

---

[45] This section is included here to show the impact of the Declaration on the effectiveness of the organization in dealing with colonial questions. This new system includes both supervisory machinery and a way to facilitate the process of "liberation," and, as such, is related to the sections on these topics above.

attempt to annex" the African protectorates, "or to encroach upon their territorial integrity in any way will be regarded as an act of aggression violating the United Nations' Charter."[46]

The question arises whether the effects of the efforts of the Special Committee will help solve the remaining colonial problems. It is possible that the incessant and violent criticisms will hasten the process of independence, if only by completely alienating the administering states to such an extent that they divest themselves of their responsibility with disgust. However, it seems very doubtful that the Committee will make a very valuable contribution to a friendly solution to the existing problems.

In the territories themselves, high hopes have been raised for the United Nations to solve all problems, and unrealistic requests, which the United Nations is often unable to fulfill, are being made. In the end, the net result may easily be disillusionment with the organization.

Southern Rhodesia.   The Special Committee has not been content to study areas recognized as non-self-governing, but has included areas where the claim of self-government has been made. One such area is Southern Rhodesia. In 1923, Southern Rhodesia was granted self-government by the United Kingdom, a status in actuality enjoyed by the white settlers alone. In the 1950's, the British government proposed, and in 1953 effected, a federation of Northern and Southern Rhodesia and Nyasaland on the basis of economic rationality. The federation was strongly supported by the white settlers, who, by the constitution, were to be in control; it was equally strongly opposed by the African nationalist leaders, who were increasing in strength and influence. The demonstrable objections of the Africans prompted the British to undertake a comprehensive study that resulted in constitutional changes calling for, among other things, token African representation in Parliament. The retention of most control by white settlers did little to satisfy the African nationalists.[47]

The Special Committee studied the situation and decided that according to the principles adopted at the Fifteenth Session Southern Rhodesia was not a self-governing territory, and the Committee urged that the General Assembly discuss the issue, which it did over the objections of the United Kingdom and other Western states. It agreed with the Committee that Southern Rhodesia was a non-self-governing territory.

The U.K. has continued its position of not honoring the organization's decision on the status of the area. Britain answers U.N. calls to make certain changes by pointing out that she cannot interfere in the affairs of an area that

---

[46] As quoted in "Issues before the Seventeenth General Assembly," *International Conciliation*, No. 539 (September, 1962), p. 67.

[47] See "The Federation of Rhodesia and Nyasaland: The Future of a Dilemma," *Africa Today Pamphlets*, No. 4, 1959.

is self-governing.[48] In spite of the British assertions, the organization continues to pass resolutions, such as that of November 6, 1963,[49] in which the members:

2) express deep regret that the United Kingdom government had not implemented the various resolutions of the General Assembly on Southern Rhodesia;

3) call upon the United Kingdom not to accede to the request of the present minority government of Southern Rhodesia for independence until majority rule based on universal adult suffrage was established in the territory;

4) again invite the United Kingdom government to hold a constitutional conference in which representatives of all political parties of the territory would take part . . .

6) decide to keep the question of Southern Rhodesia on the agenda of the 18th Session.

Resolutions such as the above have been able to command large majorities when presented in the General Assembly. This particular one passed 73–2 (Portugal, South Africa), with 19 abstentions (*inter alios:* France, Italy, Turkey, U.S., Belgium, Canada; the U.K. delegation did not participate in the voting).

This indicates that the organization majority considers the U.N. is competent and has the authority to make decisions regarding the status of an area, even when there is opposition from the state which has been, or is, responsible for the area.[50]

The Special Committee of 24 will continue its pressure for independence, and the General Assembly will probably approve most of its work. It would seem possible to suggest that once the Committee has thoroughly examined conditions in the areas agreed to be non-self-governing, it will turn its attention to areas whose status as self-governing was approved by the General Assembly during an earlier era—for instance, Puerto Rico and Surinam. For today, in 1965, it appears that the drive to end colonialism will not stop until every colonial area is independent.

INDEPENDENCE NOW; WHAT NEXT?

It seems evident that United Nations action has helped hasten the process of breaking up the colonial system. In recent years, dependent areas have not

---

[48] For a clear statement of the U.K. position, see "Southern Rhodesia," *United Nations Review,* April, 1964, pp. 16–17.

[49] General Assembly Resolution 1889 (XVIII).

[50] See above, pp. 655–56, for a discussion of the situation in the General Assembly on this point during an earlier period.

attained independence as a result of a successful revolt, as did the United States, or because they have shown themselves eminently capable of handling their own affairs, as Canada or Australia. The majority have been freed before they could—as judged by almost any objective standard—administer themselves or before they had sound economies. Colonies were freed that had no more than a handful of college technical institute graduates or even high school trained persons, and whose people had never served in any responsible post in an administrative structure—governmental or business. And yet, these areas have been granted independence and have been accepted as full members of the United Nations on the basis of sovereign equality.

There has been a tendency among leaders of the colonial peoples to regard independence as an end, as a goal in itself, and these have, during the last days of the colonial relationship, often concentrated their attention so thoroughly on independence that they have not prepared adequately for the day *after* independence. In some recently proclaimed states, the situation has been compounded by a flight of foreign personnel, as in the Congo, or by difficult problems associated with the transfer of authority, as in Rwanda, Burundi, and West Irian. In these areas, a vacuum has been created.

ONUC's Civilian Operations in the Congo[51]

Belgium's sudden promise of independence, followed by the outbreak of mutinies, first in Thysville and Léopoldville and later spreading to other areas, caused panic among a number of the white civilians, who began to flee in all directions. Soon it became evident that the Congo was headed for disaster, not only as a result of political forces, but also due to the imminent collapse of all public services. Communications systems were almost completely broken down; many farms were not being worked; there was fear that schools would be pitifully short of teachers when they reopened after the summer vacation; hospitals were understaffed, or not staffed at all; the country started sliding toward bankruptcy. These and other equally serious problems needed immediate attention.

Before independence was proclaimed, agreements had been reached for U.N. technical assistance in the Congo; however, at the time the agreements were drawn up, there had been no thought of the mass exodus of almost all trained personnel from the area. A Consultative Group was formed, composed of high-ranking specialists in various fields. It was to advise the Congo government on planning of social and economic programs, and was to train Congolese to take over responsibility at various levels.

---

[51] The following is based principally on *The U.N. in the Congo* (Carnegie Endowment for International Peace, 1962), pp. 63–75; King Gordon, and *The Role of the United Nations in the Congo* (The Hammarskjöld Forums) (Dobbs Ferry, N.Y.: Oceana Publications, Inc., 1963), pp. 43–52.

The Consultative Group was directly responsible to the Chief of Civilian Operations who, in turn, was responsible to the U.N. Special Representative in the Congo. This arrangement had definite advantages over the usual organizational pattern for technical assistance programs. Whereas the high-ranking representatives of the various agencies are usually responsible to the headquarters of their own agencies, the Consultative Group was responsible to a center in the field. This made the coordination and integration of projects much easier and smoother.

The first problem was to get the services back in operation. Since there were few Congolese replacements for the 1,723 foreign technicians and professionals[52] who left the country, it was necessary to recruit foreign experts to fill the jobs. Shipping channels were dredged and railroads began to function again. The immediate threat of a shortage of food was alleviated by UNICEF and FAO. The excellent air network built by the Belgians could continue operations with ITU and WMO personnel brought in to maintain it. Not only were these various teams operating the facilities, but they were also training Congolese to take over. Here they ran into real difficulty: few Congolese had had the secondary education necessary as background for courses in such complicated fields as electronics and meteorology.

The mass exodus in 1960 left the Congo in sore need of medically trained personnel; almost all doctors had fled, and there was not one Congolese doctor in the whole territory. WHO was able to supply a small staff of doctors, but hardly enough to meet even the minimum requirements if epidemics were to be avoided. The Secretary-General made an appeal that brought a quick response from the Red Cross, making it possible to keep hospitals operating. Large-scale vaccination campaigns were undertaken in three provinces—in one, only after smallpox had already broken out, taking the lives of many.

These measures were only stopgap. Once the teams of doctors and medical personnel had been organized for hospital and public health work, it was necessary to look ahead to putting medical services on a more permanent footing. This necessitated a reorganization of the central and provincial health departments as well as the training of Congolese professional and technical staffs. Sixty-one Congolese were sent abroad on fellowships to take an accelerated, three-year course to qualify them as doctors; later in the year another fifty-one left for study. Only a few students could be sent abroad; so, with an eye to the future, ONUC provided six professors and a technician for the medical school at Lovanium University in Léopoldville.

Training programs were also set up or strengthened in other fields. By the end of 1962, there were about 1,200 Congolese in programs in the Congo itself. There were 463 students enrolled in the National School of Law and

---

[52] Out of a total of 1,966. K. Gordon, *op. cit.*, p. 65.

Administration, an institution established in 1961 by the Congolese government, ONUC, and the Ford Foundation. Another 400 were studying to be police commissioners and officers at the new Léopoldville Police School. Most of the programs at these and other centers have had to be intensive, crash programs—for instance, three-month training programs in agricultural machinery have been established to get the machinery back in use as quickly as possible. A school of mines was organized to turn out sorely needed mine personnel.

When the mutinies broke out in July, 1960, most of the teachers in the Congo were on vacation. Many fled, and it was impossible to estimate just how many would be available when the fall term opened. Fortunately, the situation was better than many had anticipated; the presence of United Nations forces had encouraged a number to return. However, ONUC did recruit about seventy French-speaking teachers.

The problem went deeper than merely trying to replace those teachers who had left. The whole organization was in need of overhauling. ONUC provided 16 advisers to assist in reorganizing the school system, revising programs and methods, and also to help establish teacher-training programs.

One of the worst problems was that of the secondary schools. Almost all the teachers had been Europeans, of whom many had fled; but more serious was the low number of pupils enrolled. Room had to be made and teachers found to educate many more if the Congo was to produce its own technicians and professional personnel. One big step in this direction was the opening, in 1962, of the Pedagogical Institute in Léopoldville, staffed entirely by ONUC.

Thus, in almost every field, ONUC was providing personnel to replace the Europeans and at the same time was laying the groundwork for the Congolese to take over themselves. But still one problem had to be worked out if all this spadework was to bear fruit: the economy of the country had to be put on a sound footing. At the time of independence, the Congo had a potentially rich economy, but independence and the subsequent disorder threatened to upset the whole economy. Capital had been leaving the country at an alarming rate since 1958; foreign exchange reserves had declined; the secession of Katanga had lost the government about half its revenue; political disturbances had put a stop to economic activity, especially agricultural and mining, in many areas of the country. These ever-worsening conditions were made more acute by the lack of trained economists, financial experts, and bankers. The Congolese government was introducing programs—such as an increase in salaries of civil servants—that further weakened the economy.

Trying to straighten out the economy became a prime objective of ONUC. A monetary council was established under a United Nations expert. The council put controls on foreign trade and currency. United Nations funds have been used to help relieve the foreign exchange situation. United Nations personnel, at the request of President Kasavubu, also helped draw up the budget and gave advice on customs, taxation, and other matters. These measures could only prevent disaster. The basic problems were too severe to be solved by such action. It was suggested that an advisory unit of experts from IMF, the Bank, and the United Nations be created to help the government "determine import priorities, allocate import quotas, supervise the flow of imports, impose stiff fiscal and foreign exchange controls and prevent smuggling."[53] As the political situation in the Congo improved, it was possible to ameliorate some of the worst economic problems.

The United Nations Civilian Operation in the Congo was the largest international project since UNRRA[54]—the largest United Nations undertaking to date. The operation was fraught with difficulties from the beginning. Political unrest and fighting made it necessary to shut down projects temporarily. The economic crises and periods of tension between the United Nations and the Congo government made long-term planning impossible until the Adoula government came to power and resumed a more friendly attitude toward ONUC. Special emergencies arose, demanding immediate attention: outbreaks of epidemics; famine among 350,000 Baluba refugees in South Kasai; influx of refugees from Angola (close to 120,000), from Ruanda-Urundi (50,000), Baluba in Elisabethville (80,000); a currency crisis in Kivu. In all these emergencies, ONUC proved itself capable and was able to provide necessary aid.

By the end of 1961, conditions in the Congo had become stable enough for ONUC Civilian Operations to begin looking like a normal technical assistance program, although it was still much larger than those in other countries. The program has not been able to solve all the pressing and complex problems of the new Congo. It has, however, averted major crises that could have meant the loss of many lives and the complete cessation of services—communication, education, health, administration and finance—in the country, and it has helped the Congolese work out long-term projects and plans designed to help the Congo become a self-sufficient nation.

The civilian operations would have been impossible without the military operations. For logistics and often for protection, the military was called on to help the civilian department. The two formed an important unity during the blackest days of the Congo, and the two together were an important factor in bringing about order in the area. The existence of the U.N. forces not only

---

[53] "Issues before the Seventeenth General Assembly," *International Conciliation,* No. 539 (September, 1962), p. 51.

[54] UNRRA predated the U.N.

made it possible for the civilian operations to function, but also their very presence encouraged many of the foreigners who had fled in panic during the first days of independence to return and to resume their work.

The United Nations proved itself in this undertaking, not only in the operation of many services itself, but also in the coordination of activities of many agencies. The organization, with top personnel on the spot, was able to analyze problems and to appeal to various agencies to help, thus acting as a catalyst. National, private, and international agencies responded and were immediately fitted into the overall program. The Chief of Civilian Operations, with responsibility for all projects, eliminated much duplication, and was able to make the best possible use of resources available, a condition often lacking in regular technical assistance programs. It is not possible to judge whether the program will be successful in its ultimate objective in the near future. The needs of the Congo are still great, the lack of trained personnel still serious, and many of the political problems still unresolved. The country does, however, have a much better chance of achieving its goals than would have been the case without United Nations assistance.

Other International Efforts

Although the Congo Civilian Operation has been the largest of its kind, the United Nations has attempted to help other countries over the difficult period of adjustment to independence. New nations have received aid from the regular Technical Assistance Program, which, as a result of the great increase in number of these states, has become more and more oriented toward their needs.

The operations of the United Nations in West Irian has already been discussed.[55] In this case, the United Nations assumed responsibility for the administration of an area. Although West Irian did not become a new state but, rather, attained a new status, the United Nations was able to help effect a smooth transition and transfer of authority from a colonial power (Netherlands) to a new nation (Indonesia).

When Belgium's trust territory, Ruanda–Urundi, obtained independence, the result was chaos. Although both the United Nations and the Belgians had searched for a way to keep the two sections of the small, economically poor, and densely populated area together, they separated into two states. Feelings were bitter on both sides of the border. The withdrawal of Belgian troops presented problems. In order to help maintain order, the Secretary-General was authorized in 1961 to spend $2 million to continue essential services in the two new states.

Belgian assistance continued after her withdrawal but was insufficient. In order to assess the needs of the new countries, a team of United Nations

---

[55] See above, pp. 659–62.

experts was sent out. The team was also to help organize the administration and work out details for an economic union of the two states as well as to plan for a comprehensive technical assistance program.

In the case of Ruanda–Urundi, there was not the same mass exodus of Europeans nor the same protracted instability and fighting (although there was wholesale slaughter of minority groups) as in the Congo. There were definitely problems, and the United Nations was able to help.

At independence, many of the colonies are overly sensitive regarding any kind of help that might be interpreted as a form of colonialism. The colonial forces, civilian and military, that had been providing order and the necessary services in colonies are often resented by the new state, and, as a consequence, many leave the country before there are adequate local replacements. Who is to fill the resulting vacuum? If another country were to offer its services, this would be interpreted by the ex-colony and by the anticolonial forces as an attempt by the state to force the new nation into a new colonial relationship. These have been shown that the United Nations is able to step in without arousing fears of new colonialism. It has also been shown that it has been possible for the United Nations to recruit capable experts, to interest national and private agencies, and to coordinate the efforts of these and of the various Specialized Agencies. The United Nations has demonstrated its ability to step in and operate existing services, to act quickly and effectively in emergencies, and to help the new governments to plan for the future.

Although there are few areas remaining in a colonial status, some of these will undoubtedly go through a difficult period when they become independent. It is to be hoped that the United Nations will be able to proffer these peoples the same kind of assistance it has the Congolese. The biggest problem will be, most probably, that of financing the operation. Civilian operation has depended on the voluntary contributions of members. Whether the members will again provide the amount of money necessary is a question.

Although the record of the United Nations in new nations has been good, it has been given major responsibility in only a few states. Most areas attaining independence receive some technical assistance, but this is usually very limited, and the United Nations has not become a major factor in the transition from colonial status to new nation.

APPENDIX

Appendix

THE UNITED NATIONS SYSTEM

The "United Nations" comprises on the one hand the core organization established by the Charter of the United Nations and the Statute of the International Court of Justice (reproduced below). It consists of six main organs, whose composition and functions are summarized in the following paragraphs: the General Assembly, the Security Council, the Economic and Social Council, the Trusteeship Council, the Secretariat and the International Court.

In addition, a group of "specialized agencies" are affiliated with the U.N., though they are autonomous, constituted by separate charters and with separately determined memberships.

The interrelationships of these bodies are described in the organizational chart on page 19.

General Assembly

The General Assembly, in which each member is represented equally, is the keystone of the United Nations. It has the sweeping power to discuss and made recommendations on any questions within the scope of the Charter, except that it may not consider a dispute or situation currently before the Security Council. The General Assembly is also responsible for studies and recommendations to promote international cooperation in all fields—political, legal, economic, social, cultural, educational, health, and human rights. It is the highest administrative authority of the United Nations, receiving and considering reports from all other organs, approving the budget, and supervising the work of the Secretariat. It may itself discuss and recommend action to maintain peace and security, or may call dangerous situations to the attention of the Security Council. It elects the other (major) organs of the

681

United Nations. On recommendation of the Security Council, it likewise admits new members and appoints the Secretary-General.

Security Council

The Security Council of eleven members, including the five permanent members (United States, U.S.S.R., Britain, France, and China), has the "primary responsibility for the maintenance of international peace and security." In executing this task, it acts for all members of the United Nations and is accountable to no other body. It is organized to function continuously. The Council may consider any dispute or situation that threatens the peace, recommend measures to settle issues peacefully, or order use of various forceful measures to halt violence and prevent aggression. It may also propose plans for the regulation of armaments. A Military Staff Committee, consisting of the chiefs of staff of the five permanent members, is responsible to the Security Council. The Council was thus conceived as a small body, capable of swift, independent, and effective action in dealing with international crises.

Economic and Social Council

The Economic and Social Council, composed of 18 members elected by the General Assembly, initiates studies and recommends action with respect to international economic, social, cultural, and similar nonpolitical matters, and is also responsible for implementing the Charter's provisions in regard to human rights. Creation of the Council as a major organ in contrast to the perfunctory role originally assigned to it at Dumbarton Oaks was in direct response to widespread demand that economic and social cooperation be considered vital functions of the United Nations. In this regard, the organization of the United Nations represents a great advance over the League of Nations, which had no separate major body responsible for such matters.

Responsible to the Economic and Social Council are a group of regional economic commissions (for Europe, Asia and the Far East, Latin America, and Africa) and several functional commissions (social, human rights, population, statistical, status of women, narcotic drugs, and international commodity trade). Also reporting to ECOSCO are a number of operating agencies, created to carry out united programs of social and economic assistance: the United Nations Children's Fund, the Special Fund, the High Commissioner for Refugees, and a peculiar interagency coordinating instrument—the Technical Assistance Board. The activities of these bodies are discussed in later chapters. The Economic and Social Council is itself accountable to the General Assembly.

Trusteeship Council

The Trusteeship Council consists of an equal number of those states that administer trust territories and those that do not. Under the authority of the

General Assembly, it supervises the execution of special agreements safe-guarding the welfare, human rights, and development toward self-government of the inhabitants of territories placed under trusteeship of the United Nations. Only territories voluntarily brought under the system by the controlling state are subject to the Council's authority; but once this is accomplished, the Council calls for and reviews reports from the administering authority, accepts and examines petitions from the inhabitants or others concerned with conditions in the territory, and sends visiting missions to inspect the territories at firsthand. The Council's powers are considerably more extensive than those of its forerunner, the Permanent Mandates Commission of the League of Nations.

Secretariat

The Secretariat of the United Nations, headed by the Secretary-General, serves as the staff for all the other organs, putting their decisions into effect, arranging for their meetings, and collecting information needed for their consideration. It is an international civil service, responsible only to the United Nations, with special privileges and immunities to safeguard its international character and independence from external authorities.

Court of Justice

The International Court of Justice is the principal judicial organ of the United Nations, functioning under a separate statute but forming an integral part of the organization. The 15 judges are elected by the General Assembly and the Security Council. All member states of the United Nations are automatically parties to the statute and under obligation to comply with the decision of the court in any case brought before it to which they are parties. The court may also be asked for advisory opinions on legal questions by the General Assembly or the Security Council.

Specialized Agencies

In addition to the United Nations organization proper, 12 intergovernmental specialized agencies, functioning under their own constitutions, carry out separate programs of international action in their respective fields. They are, however, related to the United Nations by formal agreements providing that they submit reports and, in some cases, budgets to the Economic and Social Council for its consideration and approval. They agree to consider recommendations made to them by the United Nations and, in particular, to assist the regular organs of the U.N. in carrying out decisions related to the maintenance of peace and security. Most of the specialized agencies are also organizationally involved with the U.N. as participants in the United Nations Expanded Program of Technical Assistance.

Three of these agencies are public international unions that existed prior to creation of the United Nations, but their constitutions are slightly changed in order to bring about their integration with the United Nations system. These are: Universal Postal Union (UPU), established 1875; International Telecommunications Union (ITU), originally established 1865; International Labor Organization (ILO), established 1919.

The other specialized agencies, newly organized during or after the second World War, are:

Food and Agriculture Organization (FAO), 1944.
International Monetary Fund, 1944.
International Bank for Reconstruction and Development, 1944.
United Nations Educational, Scientific, and Cultural Organization (UNESCO), 1945.
World Health Organization (WHO), 1946.
International Civil Aviation Organization (ICAO), 1947.
World Meteorological Organization (WMO), 1950.
International Finance Corporation (IFC), 1956.
Intergovernmental Maritime Consultative Organization (IMCO), 1958.

Another specialized agency, the International Refugee Organization ceased operations at the end of 1951.

The International Atomic Energy Agency (IAEA), established in 1957, has a working relationship with the United Nations, although it is not formally designated a specialized agency.

The charter for an international trade organization has been signed, but has failed of enough ratifications to bring the organization into operation. However, the U.N.-sponsored Conference on Trade and Development, held in 1964, has proposed a new organization that will be related to the U.N. and, among other functions, will administer the General Agreement on Tariffs and Trade adopted in lieu of the ITO.

Nongovernmental Organizations

A novel feature of the United Nations system is the semiofficial status accorded nongovernmental organizations. Several international associations representing labor, business, farm, religion, and other private interests have been accredited to the Economic and Social Council, and are entitled to send observers to its sessions, present communications to it, consult with its committees, and even propose items for the council's agenda. On invitation, their representatives may speak before the council. These organizations, in category A, include:

International Chamber of Commerce.
International Confederation of Free Trade Unions.
International Cooperative Alliance.
International Federation of Agricultural Producers.
International Federation of Christian Trade Unions.
International Organization of Employers.

Inter-Parliamentary Union.
World Federation of Trade Unions.
World Federation of United Nations Associations.
World Veterans Federation.

A much wider group of private organizations has been given B status, and may appoint observers but cannot communicate directly with or appear before the Economic and Social Council. Similar relationships exist with several of the specialized agencies. This arrangement, in effect, brings the main agencies of professional and public opinion within the scope of the United Nations system and recognizes the importance of maintaining direct contact between the "people" and international institutions.

Membership

Membership in the United Nations organization proper has been extended to 115 states as noted on the list which follows.

One, Indonesia, has formally withdrawn, leaving 114 as of March 15, 1965.

Certain states as noted below have at various times surrendered separate membership as a result of merging with others.

China, though continuously recognized as a member state has been represented only by the Nationalist Government controlling since 1949 only the area of Taiwan (Formosa). The People's Republic (Communist), governing the Chinese mainland, has been excluded from participation, while claiming to be the only appropriate representative for all of China (a claim likewise made by the Nationalist Government).

Each specialized agency determines its own members separately from the U.N. itself. This sometimes results in a much more restricted membership. (Most Communist states have refrained from joining the International Bank and the International Monetary Fund, for instance.) Occasionally, as in the case of Switzerland, a state which is not a U.N. member, has become a member of some of the affiliated organizations.

ROSTER OF THE UNITED NATIONS

(as of March 15, 1965)

MEMBER	DATE OF ADMISSION
Afghanistan	19 November 1946
Albania	14 December 1955
Algeria	8 October 1962
*Argentina	24 October 1945
*Australia	1 November 1945
Austria	14 December 1955
Belgium	27 December 1945

SOURCE: United Nations Office of Public Information
* Original member. (There are 51 in all.)

MEMBER   DATE OF ADMISSION

*Bolivia	14 November 1945
*Brazil	24 October 1945
Bulgaria	14 December 1955
Burma	19 April 1948
Burundi	18 September 1962
*Byelorussian SSR	24 October 1945
Cambodia	14 December 1955
Cameroon	20 September 1960
*Canada	9 November 1945
Central African Republic	20 September 1960
Ceylon	14 December 1955
Chad	20 September 1960
*Chile	24 October 1945
*China	24 October 1945
*Colombia	5 November 1945
Congo (Brazzaville)	20 September 1960
Congo (Democratic Republic of)	20 September 1960
*Costa Rica	2 November 1945
*Cuba	24 October 1945
Cyprus	20 September 1960
*Czechoslovakia	24 October 1945
Dahomey	20 September 1960
*Demark	24 October 1945
*Dominican Republic	24 October 1945
*Ecuador	21 December 1945
*El Salvador	24 October 1945
*Ethiopia	13 November 1945
Finland	14 December 1955
*France	24 October 1945
Gabon	20 September 1960
Ghana	8 March 1957
*Greece	25 October 1945
*Guatemala	21 November 1945
Guinea	12 December 1958
*Haiti	24 October 1945
*Honduras	17 December 1945
Hungary	14 December 1955
Iceland	19 November 1946
*India	30 October 1945
*Iran	24 October 1945
*Iraq	21 December 1945
Ireland	14 December 1955
Israel	11 May 1949
Italy	14 December 1955
Ivory Coast	20 September 1960
Jamaica	18 September 1962
Japan	18 December 1956
Jordan	14 December 1955
Kenya	16 December 1963
Kuwait	14 May 1963

MEMBER	DATE OF ADMISSION
Laos	14 December 1955
*Lebanon	24 October 1945
*Liberia	2 November 1945
Libya	14 December 1955
*Luxembourg	24 October 1945
Madagascar	20 September 1960
Malawi	1 December 1964
Malaysia	See Note No. 1
Mali	28 September 1960
Malta	1 December 1964
Mauritania	27 October 1961
*Mexico	7 November 1945
Mongolia	27 October 1961
Morocco	12 November 1956
Nepal	14 December 1955
*Netherlands	10 December 1945
*New Zealand	24 October 1945
*Nicaragua	24 October 1945
Niger	20 September 1960
Nigeria	7 October 1960
*Norway	27 November 1945
Pakistan	30 September 1947
*Panama	13 November 1945
*Paraguay	24 October 1945
*Peru	31 October 1945
*Philippines	24 October 1945
*Poland	24 October 1945
Portugal	14 December 1955
Romania	14 December 1955
Rwanda	18 September 1962
*Saudi Arabia	24 October 1945
Senegal	28 September 1960
Sierra Leone	27 September 1961
Somalia	20 September 1960
*South Africa	7 November 1945
Spain	14 December 1955
Sudan	12 November 1956
Sweden	19 November 1946
*Syria	24 October 1945
Thailand	16 December 1946
Togo	20 September 1960
Trinidad and Tobago	18 September 1962
Tunisia	12 November 1956
*Turkey	24 October 1945
Uganda	25 October 1962
*Ukrainian SSR	24 October 1945

Note No. 1—On 16 September 1963, the Federation of Malaya (which was admitted on 17 September 1957) became known as Malaysia after being joined by Singapore, North Borneo (Sabah) and Sarawak.

MEMBER	DATE OF ADMISSION
*USSR	24 October 1945
*United Arab Republic	24 October 1945
*United Kingdom	24 October 1945
United Republic of Tanzania	See Note No. 2
*United States	24 October 1945
Upper Volta	20 September 1960
*Uruguay	18 December 1945
*Venezuela	15 November 1945
Yemen	30 September 1947
*Yugoslavia	24 October 1945
Zambia	1 December 1964

Note No. 2—Tanganyika was admitted to membership on 14 December 1961 and the state of Zanzibar was admitted on 16 December 1963. On April 26, 1964, both states decided to unite as one sovereign state under the name of the United Republic of Tanganyika and Zanzibar. Later in the year, on 2 November, the name was changed to the United Republic of Tanzania.

Note No. 3—Indonesia, which was admitted to United Nations membership on 28 September 1950 withdrew with effect from 1 March 1965.

CHARTER OF THE UNITED NATIONS

WE THE PEOPLES
OF THE UNITED NATIONS
DETERMINED

to save succeeding generations from the scourge of war, which twice in our lifetime has brought untold sorrow to mankind, and

to reaffirm faith in fundamental human rights, in the dignity and worth of the human person, in the equal rights of men and women and of nations large and small, and

to establish conditions under which justice and respect for the obligations arising from treaties and other sources of international law can be maintained, and

to promote social progress and better standards of life in larger freedom.

AND FOR THESE ENDS

to practice tolerance and live together in peace with one another as good neighbors, and

to unite our strength to maintain international peace and security, and

to ensure, by the acceptance of principles and the institution of methods, that armed force shall not be used, save in the common interest, and

to employ international machinery for the promotion of the economic and social advancement of all peoples,

HAVE RESOLVED TO
COMBINE OUR EFFORTS TO
ACCOMPLISH THESE AIMS

Accordingly, our respective Governments, through representatives assembled in the city of San Francisco, who have exhibited their full powers found to be in good and due form, have agreed to the present Charter of the United Nations and do hereby estbablish an international organization to be known as the United Nations.

CHAPTER I
PURPOSES AND PRINCIPLES

Article 1

The Purposes of the United Nations are:

1. To maintain international peace and security, and to that end: to take effective collective measures for the prevention and removal of threats to the peace, and for the suppression of acts of aggression or other breaches of the peace, and to bring about by peaceful means, and in conformity with the principles of justice and international law, adjustment or settlement of international disputes or situations which might lead to a breach of the peace;

2. To develop friendly relations among nations based on respect for the principle of equal rights and self-determination of peoples, and to take other appropriate measures to strengthen universal peace;

3. To achieve international cooperation in solving international problems of an economic, social, cultural, or humanitarian character, and in promoting and encouraging respect for human rights and for fundamental freedoms for all without distinction as to race, sex, language, or religion; and

4. To be a center for harmonizing the actions of nations in the attainment of these common ends.

Article 2

The Organization and its Members, in pursuit of the Purposes stated in Article 1, shall act in accordance with the following Principles.

1. The Organization is based on the principle of the sovereign equality of all its Members.

2. All Members, in order to ensure to all of them the rights and benefits re-

sulting from membership, shall fulfill in good faith the obligations assumed by them in accordance with the present Charter.

3. All Members shall settle their international disputes by peaceful means in such a manner that international peace and security, and justice, are not endangered.

4. All Members shall refrain in their international relations from the threat or use of force against the territorial integrity or political independence of any state, or in any other manner inconsistent with the Purposes of the United Nations.

5. All Members shall give the United Nations every assistance in any action it takes in accordance with the present Charter, and shall refrain from giving assistance to any state against which the United Nations is taking preventive or enforcement action.

6. The Organization shall ensure that states which are not Members of the United Nations act in accordance with these Principles so far as may be necessary for the maintenance of international peace and security.

7. Nothing contained in the present Charter shall authorize the United Nations to intervene in matters which are essentially within the domestic jurisdiction of any state or shall require the Members to submit such matters to settlement under the present Charter; but this principle shall not prejudice the application of enforcement measures under Chapter VII.

CHAPTER II
MEMBERSHIP

Article 3

The original Members of the United Nations shall be the states which, having participated in the United Nations Conference on International Organization at San Francisco, or having previously signed the Declaration by United Na-

tions of January 1, 1942, sign the present Charter and ratify it in accordance with Article 110.

Article 4

1. Membership in the United Nations is open to all other peace-loving states which accept the obligations contained in the present Charter and, in the judgment of the Organization, are able and willing to carry out these obligations.

2. The admission of any such state to membership in the United Nations will be effected by a decision of the General Assembly upon the recommendation of the Security Council.

Article 5

A Member of the United Nations against which preventive or enforcement action has been taken by the Security Council may be suspended from the exercise of the rights and privileges of membership by the General Assembly upon the recommendation of the Security Council. The exercise of these rights and privileges may be restored by the Security Council.

Article 6

A Member of the United Nations which has persistently violated the Principles contained in the present Charter may be expelled from the Organization by the General Assembly upon the recommendation of the Security Council.

CHAPTER III
ORGANS

Article 7

1. There are established as the principal organs of the United Nations: a General Assembly, a Security Council, an Economic and Social Council, a Trusteeship Council, an International Court of Justice, and a Secretariat.

2. Such subsidiary organs as may be found necessary may be established in accordance with the present Charter.

Article 8

The United Nations shall place no restrictions on the eligibility of men and women to participate in any capacity and under conditions of equality in its principal and subsidiary organs.

CHAPTER IV

THE GENERAL ASSEMBLY

Composition

Article 9

1. The General Assembly shall consist of all the Members of the United Nations.

2. Each Member shall have not more than five representatives in the General Assembly.

Functions and Powers

Article 10

The General Assembly may discuss any questions or any matters within the scope of the present Charter or relating to the powers and functions of any organs provided for in the present Charter, and, except as provided in Article 12, may make recommendations to the Members of the United Nations or to the Security Council or to both on any such questions or matters.

Article 11

1. The General Assembly may consider the general principles of cooperation in the maintenance of international peace and security, including the principles governing disarmament and the regulation of armaments, and may make recommendations with regard to such principles to the Members or to the Security Council or to both.

2. The General Assembly may discuss any questions relating to the maintenance of international peace and security brought before it by any Member of the United Nations, or by the Security Council, or by a state which is not a Member of the United Nations in accordance with Article 35, paragraph 2, and, except as provided in Article 12, may make recommendations with regard to any such questions to the state or states concerned or to the Security Council or to both. Any such question on which action is necessary shall be referred to the Security Council by the General Assembly either before or after discussion.

3. The General Assembly may call the attention of the Security Council to situations which are likely to endanger international peace and security.

4. The powers of the General Assembly set forth in this Article shall not limit the general scope of Article 10.

Article 12

1. While the Security Council is exercising in respect of any dispute or situation the functions assigned to it in the present Charter, the General Assembly shall not make any recommendation with regard to that dispute or situation unless the Security Council so requests.

2. The Security-General, with the consent of the Security Council, shall notify the General Assembly at each session of any matters relative to the maintenance of international peace and security which are being dealt with by the Security Council and shall similarly notify the General Assembly, or the Members of the United Nations if the General Assembly is not in session, immediately the Security Council ceases to deal with such matters.

Article 13

1. The General Assembly shall initiate studies and make recommendations for the purpose of:

a. promoting international cooperation in the political field and encouraging the progressive development of international law and its codification;

b. promoting international cooperation in the economic, social, cultural, educational, and health fields, and assisting in the realization of human rights and fundamental freedoms for all without distinction as to race, sex, language, or religion.

2. The further responsibilities, functions and powers of the General Assembly with respect to matters mentioned in paragraph 1(b) above are set forth in Chapters IX and X.

Article 14

Subject to the provisions of Article 12, the General Assembly may recommend measures for the peaceful adjustment of any situation, regardless of origin, which it deems likely to impair the general welfare or friendly relations among nations, including situations resulting from a violation of the provisions of the present Charter setting forth the Purposes and Principles of the United Nations.

Article 15

1. The General Assembly shall receive and consider annual and special reports from the Security Council; these reports shall include an account of the measures that the Security Council has decided upon or taken to maintain international peace and security.

2. The General Assembly shall receive and consider reports from the other organs of the United Nations.

Article 16

The General Assembly shall perform such functions with respect to the international trusteeship system as are assigned to it under Chapters XII and XIII, including the approval of the trusteeship agreements for areas not designated as strategic.

Article 17

1. The General Assembly shall consider and approve the budget of the Organization.

2. The expenses of the Organization shall be borne by the Members as apportioned by the General Assembly.

3. The General Assembly shall consider and approve any financial and budgetary arrangements with specialized agencies referred to in Article 57 and shall examine the administrative budgets of such specialized agencies with a view to making recommendations to the agencies concerned.

Voting

Article 18

1. Each member of the General Assembly shall have one vote.

2. Decisions of the General Assembly on important questions shall be made by a two-thirds majority of the members present and voting. These questions shall include: recommendations with respect to the maintenance of international peace and security, the election of the non-permanent members of the Security Council, the election of the members of the Economic and Social Council, the election of members of the Trusteeship Council in accordance with paragraph 1(c) of Article 86, the admission of new Members of the United Nations, the suspension of the rights and privileges of membership, the expulsion of Members, questions relating to the operation of the trusteeship system, and budgetary questions.

3. Decisions on other questions, including the determination of additional categories of questions to be decided by a two-thirds majority, shall be made by a majority of the members present and voting.

Article 19

A Member of the United Nations which is in arrears in the payment of its financial contributions to the Organization shall have no vote in the General Assembly if the amount of its arrears equals or exceeds the amount of the contributions due from it for the preceding two full years. The General Assembly may, nevertheless, permit such a Member to vote if it is satisfied that the failure to pay is due to conditions beyond the control of the Member.

Procedure

Article 20

The General Assembly shall meet in regular annual sessions and in such special sessions as occasion may require. Special sessions shall be convoked by the Secretary-General at the request of the Security Council or of a majority of the Members of the United Nations.

Article 21

The General Assembly shall adopt its own rules of procedure. It shall elect its President for each session.

Article 22

The General Assembly may establish such subsidiary organs as is deems necessary for the performance of its functions.

CHAPTER V
THE SECURITY COUNCIL

Composition

Article 23

1. The Security Council shall consist of eleven Members of the United Nations. The Republic of China, France, the Union of Soviet Socialist Republics, the United Kingdom of Great Britain and Northern Ireland, and the United States of America shall be permanent members of the Security Council. The General Assembly shall elect six other Members of the United Nations to be non-permanent members of the Security Council, due regard being specially paid, in the first instance to the contribution of Members of the United Nations to the maintenance of international peace and security and to the other purposes of the Organization, and also to equitable geographical distribution.

2. The non-permanent members of the Security Council shall be elected for a term of two years. In the first election of the non-permanent members, however, three shall be chosen for a term of one year. A retiring member shall not be eligible for immediate re-election.

3. Each member of the Security Council shall have one representative.

Functions and Powers

Article 24

1. In order to ensure prompt and effective action by the United Nations, its Members confer on the Security Council primary responsibility for the maintenance of international peace and security, and agree that in carrying out its duties under this responsibility the Security Council acts on their behalf.

2. In discharging these duties the Security Council shall act in accordance with the Purposes and Principles of the United Nations. The specific powers granted to the Security Council for the discharge of these duties are laid down in Chapters VI, VII, VIII, and XII.

3. The Security Council shall submit annual and, when necessary, special reports to the General Assembly for its consideration.

Article 25

The Members of the United Nations agree to accept and carry out the decisions of the Security Council in accordance with the present Charter.

Article 26

In order to promote the establishment and maintenance of international peace and security with the least diversion for armaments of the world's human and economic resources, the Security Council shall be responsible for formulating, with the assistance of the Military Staff Committee referred to in Article 47, plans to be submitted to the Members of the United Nations for the establishment of a system for the regulation of armaments.

Voting

Article 27

1. Each member of the Security Council shall have one vote.

2. Decisions of the Security Council on procedural matters shall be made by an affirmative vote of seven members.

3. Decisions of the Security Council on all other matters shall be made by an affirmative vote of seven members including the concurring votes of the permanent members; provided that, in decisions under Chapter VI, and under paragraph 3 of Article 52, a party to a dispute shall abstain from voting.

Procedure

Article 28

1. The Security Council shall be so organized as to be able to function continuously. Each member of the Security Council shall for this purpose be represented at all times at the seat of the Organization.

2. The Security Council shall hold periodic meetings at which each of its members may, if it so desires, be represented by a member of the government or by some other specially designated representative.

3. The Security Council may hold meetings at such places other than the seat of the Organization as in its judgment will best facilitate its work.

Article 29

The Security Council may establish such subsidiary organs as it deems necessary for the performance of its functions.

Article 30

The Security Council shall adopt its own rules of procedure, including the method of selecting its President.

Article 31

Any Member of the United Nations which is not a member of the Security Council may participate, without vote, in the discussion of any question brought before the Security Council whenever the latter considers that the interests of that Member are specially affected.

Article 32

Any Member of the United Nations which is not a member of the Security Council or any state which is not a Member of the United Nations, if it is a party to a dispute under consideration by the Security Council, shall be invited to participate, without vote, in the discussion relating to the dispute. The Security Council shall lay down such conditions as it deems just for the participation of a state which is not a Member of the United Nations.

CHAPTER VI
PACIFIC SETTLEMENT OF DISPUTES

Article 33

1. The parties to any dispute, the continuance of which is likely to endanger the maintenance of international peace and security, shall, first of all, seek a solution by negotiation, enquiry, mediation, conciliation, arbitration, judicial settlement, resort to regional agencies or arrangements, or other peaceful means of their own choice.

2. The Security Council shall, when it deems necessary, call upon the parties to settle their dispute by such means.

Article 34

The Security Council may investigate any dispute, or any situation which might lead to international friction or give rise to a dispute, in order to determine whether the continuance of the dispute or situation is likely to endanger the maintenance of international peace and security.

Article 35

1. Any Member of the United Nations may bring any dispute, or any situation of the nature referred to in Article 34, to the attention of the Security Council or of the General Assembly.

2. A state which is not a Member of the United Nations may bring to the attention of the Security Council or of the General Assembly any dispute to which it is a party if it accepts in advance, for the purposes of the dispute, the obligations of pacific settlement provided in the present Charter.

3. The procedures of the General Assembly in respect of matters brought to its attention under this Article will be subject to the provisions of Articles 11 and 12.

Article 36

1. The Security Council may, at any stage of a dispute of the nature referred to in Article 33 or of a situation of like nature, recommend appropriate procedures or methods of adjustment.

2. The Security council should take into consideration any procedures for the settlement of the dispute which have already been adopted by the parties.

3. In making recommendations under this Article the Security Council should also take into consideration that legal disputes should as a general rule be referred by the parties to the International Court of Justice in accordance with the provisions of the Statute of the Court.

Article 37

1. Should the parties to a dispute of the nature referred to in Article 33 fail to settle it by the means indicated in that Article, they shall refer it to the Security Council.

2. If the Security Council deems that the continuance of the dispute is in fact likely to endanger the maintenance of international peace and security, it shall decide whether to take action under Article 36 or to recommend such terms of settlement as it may consider appropriate.

Article 38

Without prejudice to the provisions of Articles 33 to 37, the Security Council may, if all the parties to any dispute so request, make recommendations to the parties with a view to a pacific settlement of the dispute.

CHAPTER VII

ACTION WITH RESPECT TO THREATS TO THE PEACE, BREACHES OF THE PEACE, AND ACTS OF AGGRESSION

Article 39

The Security Council shall determine the existence of any threat to the peace, breach of the peace, or act of aggression and shall make recommendations, or decide what measures shall be taken in accordance with Articles 41 and 42, to maintain or restore international peace and security.

Article 40

In order to prevent an aggravation of the situation, the Security Council may, before making the recommendations or deciding upon the measures provided for in Article 39, call upon the parties concerned to comply with such provisional measures as it deems necessary or desirable. Such provisional measures shall be without prejudice to the rights, claims, or position of the parties concerned. The Security Council shall duly take account of failure to comply with such provisional measures.

Article 41

The Security Council may decide what measures not involving the use of armed force are to be employed to give effect to its decisions, and it may call upon the Members of the United Nations to apply such measures. These may include complete or partial interruption of economic relations and of rail, sea, air, postal, telegraphic, radio, and other means of communication, and the severance of diplomatic relations.

Article 42

Should the Security Council consider that measures provided for in Article 41 would be inadequate or have proved to be inadequate, it may take such action by air, sea, or land forces as may be necessary to maintain or restore international peace and security. Such action may include demonstrations, blockade, and other operations by air, sea, or land forces of Members of the United Nations.

Article 43

1. All Members of the United Nations, in order to contribute to the maintenance of international peace and security, undertake to make available to the Security Council, on its call and in accordance with a special agreement or agreements, armed forces, assistance, and facilities, including rights of passage, necessary for the purpose of maintaining international peace and security.

2. Such agreement or agreements shall govern the numbers and types of forces, their degree of readiness and general location, and the nature of the facilities and assistance to be provided.

3. The agreement or agreements shall be negotiated as soon as possible on the initiative of the Security Council. They shall be concluded between the Security Council and Members or between the Security Council and groups of Members and shall be subject to ratification by the signatory states in accordance with their respective constitutional processes.

Article 44

When the Security Council has decided to use force it shall, before calling

upon a Member not represented on it to provide armed forces in fulfillment of the obligations assumed under Article 43, invite that Member, if the Member so desires, to participate in the decisions of the Security Council concerning the employment of contingents of that Member's armed forces.

Article 45

In order to enable the United Nations to take urgent military measures, Members shall hold immediately available national air-force contingents for combined international enforcement action. The strength and degree of readiness of these contingents and plans for their combined action shall be determined, within the limits laid down in the special agreement or agreements referred to in Article 43, by the Security Council with the assistance of the Military Staff Committee.

Article 46

Plans for the application of armed force shall be made by the Security Council with the assistance of the Military Staff Committee.

Article 47

1. There shall be established a Military Staff Committee to advise and assist the Security Council on all questions relating to the Security Council's military requirements for the maintenance of international peace and security, the employment and command of forces placed at its disposal, the regulation of armaments, and possible disarmament.

2. The Military Staff Committee shall consist of the Chiefs of Staff of the permanent members of the Security Council or their representatives. Any Member of the United Nations not permanently represented on the Committee shall be invited by the Committee to be associated with it when the efficient discharge of the Committee's responsibilities requires the participation of that Member in its work.

3. The Military Staff Committee shall be responsible under the Security Council

for the strategic direction of any armed forces placed at the disposal of the Security Council. Questions relating to the command of such forces shall be worked out subsequently.

4. The Military Staff Committee, with the authorization of the Security Council and after consultation with appropriate regional agencies, may establish regional subcommittees.

Article 48

1. The action required to carry out the decisions of the Security Council for the maintenance of international peace and security shall be taken by all the Members of the United Nations or by some of them, as the Security Council may determine.

2. Such decisions shall be carried out by the Members of the United Nations directly and through their action in the appropriate international agencies of which they are members.

Article 49

The Members of the United Nations shall join in affording mutual assistance in carrying out the measures decided upon by the security Council.

Article 50

If preventive or enforcement measures against any state are taken by the Security Council, any other state, whether a Member of the United Nations or not, which finds itself confronted with special economic problems arising from the carrying out of those measures shall have the right to consult the Security Council with regard to a solution of those problems.

Article 51

Nothing in the present Charter shall impair the inherent right of individual or collective self-defense if an armed attack occurs against a Member of the United Nations, until the Security Council has taken measures necessary to maintain international peace and security. Measures taken by Members in the exercise of this right of self-defense shall be immediately reported to the Security Council and shall not in any way affect the authority and responsibility of the Security Council under the present Charter to take at any time such action as it deems necessary in order to maintain or restore international peace and security.

CHAPTER VIII
REGIONAL ARRANGEMENTS

Article 52

1. Nothing in the present Charter precludes the existence of regional arrangements or agencies for dealing with such matters relating to the maintenance of international peace and security as are appropriate for regional action, provided that such arrangements or agencies and their activities are consistent with the Purposes and Principles of the United Nations.

2. The Members of the United Nations entering into such arrangements or constituting such agencies shall make every effort to achieve pacific settlement of local disputes through such regional arrangements or by such regional agencies before referring them to the Security Council.

3. The Security Council shall encourage the development of pacific settlement of local disputes through such regional arrangements or by such regional agencies either on the initiative of the states concerned or by reference from the Security Council.

4. This Article in no way impairs the application of Articles 34 and 35.

Article 53

1. The Security Council shall, where appropriate, utilize such regional arrangements or agencies for enforcement action under its authority. But no enforcement action shall be taken under regional arrangements or by regional agencies without the authorization of the Security Council, with the exception of

measures against any enemy state, as defined in paragraph 2 of this Article, provided for pursuant to Article 107 or in regional arrangements directed against renewal of aggressive policy on the part of any such state, until such time as the Organization may, on request of the Governments concerned, be charged with the responsibility for preventing further aggression by such a state.

2. The term enemy state as used in paragraph 1 of this Article applies to any state which during the Second World War has been an enemy of any signatory of the present Charter.

Article 54

The Security Council shall at all times be kept fully informed of activities undertaken or in contemplation under regional arrangements or by regional agencies for the maintenance of international peace and security.

CHAPTER IX

INTERNATIONAL ECONOMIC AND SOCIAL COOPERATION

Article 55

With a view to the creation of conditions of stability and well-being which are necessary for peaceful and friendly relations among nations based on respect for the principle of equal rights and self-determination of peoples, the United Nations shall promote:

a. higher standards of living, full employment, and conditions of economic and social progress and development;

b. solutions of international economic, social, health, and related problems; and international cultural and educational cooperation; and

c. universal respect for, and observance of, human rights and fundamental freedoms for all without distinction as to race, sex, language, or religion.

Article 56

All Members pledge themselves to take joint and separate action in cooperation with the Organization for the achievement of the purposes set forth in Article 55.

Article 57

1. The various specialized agencies, established by intergovernmental agreement and having wide international responsibilities, as defined in their basic instruments, in economic, social, cultural, educational, health, and related fields, shall be brought into relationship with the United Nations in accordance with the provisions of Article 63.

2. Such agencies thus brought into relationship with the United Nations are hereinafter referred to as specialized agencies.

Article 58

The Organization shall make recommendations for the coordination of the policies and activities of the specialized agencies.

Article 59

The Organization shall, where appropriate, initiate negotiations among the states concerned for the creation of any new specialized agencies required for the accomplishment of the purposes set forth in Article 55.

Article 60

Responsibility for the discharge of the functions of the Organization set forth in this Chapter shall be vested in the General Assembly and, under the authority of the General Assembly, in the Economic and Social Council, which shall have for the purpose the powers set forth in Chapter X.

CHAPTER X

THE ECONOMIC AND SOCIAL COUNCIL

Composition

Article 61

1. The Economic and Social Council shall consist of eighteen Members of the

United Nations elected by the General Assembly.

2. Subject to the provisions of paragraph 3, six members of the Economic and Social Council shall be elected each year for a term of three years. A retiring member shall be eligible for immediate re-election.

3. At the first election, eighteen members of the Economic and Social Council shall be chosen. The term of office of six members so chosen shall expire at the end of one year, and of six other members at the end of two years, in accordance with arrangements made by the General Assembly.

4. Each member of the Economic and Social Council shall have one representative.

Functions and Powers
Article 62

1. The Economic and Social Council may make or initiate studies and reports with respect to international economic, social, cultural, educational, health, and related matters and may make recommendations with respect to any such matters to the General Assembly, to the Members of the United Nations, and to the specialized agencies concerned.

2. It may make recommendations for the purpose of promoting respect for, and observance of, human rights and fundamental freedoms for all.

3. It may prepare draft conventions for submission to the General Assembly, with respect to matters falling within its competence.

4. It may call, in accordance with the rules prescribed by the United Nations, international conferences on matters falling within its competence.

Article 63

1. The Economic and Social Council may enter into agreements with any of the agencies referred to in Article 57, defining the terms on which the agency concerned shall be brought into relationship with the United Nations. Such agreements shall be subject to approval by the General Assembly.

2. It may coordinate the activities of the specialized agencies through consultation with and recommendations to such agencies and through recommendations the General Assembly and to the Members of the United Nations.

Article 64

1. The Economic and Social Council may take appropriate steps to obtain regular reports from the specialized agencies. It may make arrangements with the Members of the United Nations and with the specialized agencies to obtain reports on the steps taken to give effect to its own recommendations and to recommendations on matters falling within its competence made by the General Assembly.

2. It may communicate its observations on these reports to the General Assembly.

Article 65

The Economic and Social Council may furnish information to the Security Council and shall assist the Security Council upon its request.

Article 66

1. The Economic and Social Council shall perform such functions as fall within its competence in connection with the carrying out of the recommendations of the General Assembly.

2. It may, with the approval of the General Assembly, perform services at the request of Members of the United Nations and at the request of specialized agencies.

3. It shall perform such other functions as are specified elsewhere in the present Charter or as may be assigned to it by the General Assembly.

Voting

Article 67

1. Each member of the Economic and Social Council shall have one vote.

2. Decisions of the Economic and Social Council shall be made by a majority of the members present and voting.

Procedure

Article 68

The Economic and Social Council shall set up commissions in economic and social fields and for the promotion of human rights, and such other commissions as may be required for the performance of its functions.

Article 69

The Economic and Social Council shall invite any Member of the United Nations to participate, without vote, in its deliberations on any matter of particular concern to that Member.

Article 70

The Economic and Social Council may make arrangements for representatives of the specialized agencies to participate, without vote, in its deliberations and in those of the commissions established by it, and for its representatives to participate in the deliberations of the specialized agencies.

Article 71

The Economic and Social Council may make suitable arrangements for consultation with non-governmental organizations which are concerned with matters within its competence. Such arrangements may be made with international organizations and, where appropriate, with national organizations after consultation with the Member of the United Nations concerned.

Article 72

1. The Economic and Social Council shall adopt its own rules of procedure, including the method of selecting its President.

2. The Economic and Social Council shall meet as required in accordance with its rules, which shall include provision for the convening of meetings on the request of a majority of its members.

CHAPTER XI
DECLARATION REGARDING NON-SELF-GOVERNING TERRITORIES

Article 73

Members of the United Nations which have or assume responsibilities for the administration of territories whose peoples have not yet attained a full measure of self-government recognize the principle that the interests of the inhabitants of these territories are paramount, and accept as a sacred trust the obligation to promote to the utmost, within the system of international peace and security established by the present Charter, the well-being of the inhabitants of these territories, and, to this end:

a. to ensure, with due respect for the culture of the peoples concerned, their political, economic, social, and educational advancement, their just treatment, and their protection against abuses;

b. to develop self-government, to take due account of the political aspirations of the peoples, and to assist them in the progressive development of their free political institutions, according to the particular circumstances of each territory and its peoples and their varying stages of advancement;

c. to further international peace and security;

d. to promote constructive measures of development, to encourage research, and to cooperate with one another and, when and where appropriate, with specialized international bodies with a view to the practical achievement of the social, economic, and scientific purposes set forth in this Article; and

e. to transmit regularly to the Secretary-General for information purposes, subject to such limitation as security and constitutional considerations may require, statistical and other information of a technical nature relating to economic, social, and educational conditions in the territories for which they are respectively responsible other than those territories to which Chapter XII and XIII apply.

Article 74

Members of the United Nations also agree that their policy in respect of the territories to which this Chapter applies, no less than in respect of their metropolitan areas, must be based on the general principle of good-neighborliness, due account being taken of the interests and well-being of the rest of the world, in social, economic, and commercial matters.

CHAPTER XII
INTERNATIONAL TRUSTEESHIP SYSTEM

Article 75

The United Nations shall establish under its authority an international trusteeship system for the administration and supervision of such territories as may be placed thereunder by subsequent individual agreements. These territories are hereinafter referred to as trust territories.

Article 76

The basic objectives of the trusteeship system, in accordance with the Purposes of the United Nations laid down in Article 1 of the present Charter, shall be:

a. to further international peace and security;

b. to promote the political, economic, social, and educational advancement of the inhabitants of the trust territories, and their progressive development towards self-government or independence as may be appropriate to the particular circumstances of each territory and its peoples and the freely expressed wishes of the peoples concerned, and as may be provided by the terms of each trusteeship agreement;

c. to encourage respect for human rights and for fundamental freedoms for all without distinction as to race, sex, language, or religion, and to encourage recognition of the interdependence of the peoples of the world; and

d. to ensure equal treatment in social, economic, and commercial matters for all Members of the United Nations and their nationals, and also equal treatment for the latter in the administration of justice, without prejudice to the attainment of the foregoing objectives and subject to the provisions of Article 80.

Article 77

1. The trusteeship system shall apply to such territories in the following categories as may be placed thereunder by means of trusteeship agreements:

a. territories now held under mandate;

b. territories which may be detached from enemy states as a result of the Seond World War; and

c. territories voluntarily placed under the system by states responsible for their administration.

2. It will be a matter for subsequent agreement as to which territories in the foregoing categories will be brought under the trusteeship system and upon what terms.

Article 78

The trusteeship system shall not apply to territories which have become Members of the United Nations, relationship among which shall be based on respect for the principle of sovereign equality.

Article 79

The terms of trusteeship for each territory to be placed under the trusteeship system, including any alteration or amendment, shall be agreed upon by the states directly concerned, including the mandatory power in the case of territories held under mandate by a Member of the United Nations, and shall be approved as provided for in Articles 83 and 85.

Articles 80

1. Except as may be agreed upon in individual trusteeship agreements, made under Articles 77, 79, and 81, placing each territory under the trusteeship system, and until such agreements have been concluded, nothing in this Chapter shall be construed in or of itself to alter in any manner the rights whatsoever of any states or any peoples or the terms of existing international instruments to which Members of the United Nations may respectively be parties.

2. Paragraph 1 of this Article shall not be interpreted as giving grounds for delay or postponement of the negotiation and conclusion of agreements for placing mandated and other territories under the trusteeship system as provided for in Article 77.

Article 81

The trusteeship agreement shall in each case include the terms under which the trust territory will be administered and designate the authority which will exerise the administration of the trust territory. Such authority, hereinafter called the administering authority, may be one or more states or the Organization itself.

Article 82

There may be designated, in any trusteeship agreement, a strategic area or areas which may include part or all of the trust territory to which the agreement applies, without prejudice to any special agreement or agreements made under Article 43.

Article 83

1. All functions of the United Nations relating to strategic areas, including the approval of the terms of the trusteeship agreements and of their alteration or amendment, shall be exercised by the Security Council.

2. The basic objectives set forth in Article 76 shall be applicable to the people of each strategic area.

3. The Security Council shall, subject to the provisions of the trusteeship agreements and without prejudice to security considerations, avail itself of the assistance of the Trusteeship Council to perform those functions of the United Nations under the trusteeship system relating to political, economic, social, and educational matters in the strategic areas.

Article 84

It shall be the duty of the administering authority to ensure that the trust territory shall play its part in the maintenance of international peace and security. To this end the administering authority may make use of volunteer forces, facilities, and assistance from the trust territory in carrying out the obligations towards the Security Council undertaken in this regard by the administering authority, as well as for local defense and the maintenance of law and order within the trust territory.

Article 85

1. The functions of the United Nations with regard to trusteeship agreements for all areas not designated as strategic, including the approval of the terms of the trusteeship agreements and of their alteration or amendment, shall be exercised by the General Assembly.

2. The Trusteeship Council, operating under the authority of the General Assembly, shall assist the General Assembly in carrying out these functions.

CHAPTER XIII
THE TRUSTEESHIP COUNCIL

Composition

Article 86

1. The Trusteeship Council shall consist of the following Members of the United Nations:

    a. those Members administering trust territories;

b. such of those Members mentioned by name in Article 23 as are not administering trust territories; and

c. as many other Members elected for three-year terms by the General Assembly as may be necessary to ensure that the total number of members of the Trusteeship Council is equally divided between those Members of the United Nations which administer trust territories and those which do not.

2. Each member of the Trusteeship Council shall designate one specially qualified person to represent it therein.

Functions and Powers

Article 87

The General Assembly and, under its authority, the Trusteeship Council, in carrying out their functions, may:

a. consider reports submitted by the administering authority;

b. accept petitions and examine them in consultation with the administering authority;

c. provide for periodic visits to the respective trust territories at times agreed upon with the administering authority; and

d. take these and other actions in conformity with the terms of the trusteeship agreements.

Article 88

The Trusteeship Council shall formulate a questionnaire on the political, economic, social, and educational advancement of the inhabitants of each trust territory, and the administering authority for each trust territory within the competence of the General Assembly shall make an annual report to the General Assembly upon the basis of such questionnaire.

Voting

Article 89

1. Each member of the Trusteeship Council shall have one vote.

2. Decisions of the Trusteeship Council shall be made by a majority of the members present and voting.

Procedure

Article 90

1. The Trusteeship Council shall adopt its own rules of procedure, including the method of selecting its President.

2. The Trusteeship Council shall meet as required in accordance with its rules, which shall include provision for the convening of meetings on the request of a majority of its members.

Article 91

The Trusteeship Council shall, when appropriate, avail itself of the assistance of the Economic and Social Council and of the specialized agencies in regard to matters with which they are respectively concerned.

CHAPTER XIV

THE INTERNATIONAL COURT OF JUSTICE

Article 92

The International Court of Justice shall be the principal judicial organ of the United Nations. It shall function in accordance with the annexed Statute, which is based upon the Statute of the Permanent Court of International Justice and forms an integral part of the present Charter.

Article 93

1. All Members of the United Nations are *ipso facto* parties to the Statute of the International Court of Justice.

2. A state which is not a Member of the United Nations may become a party to the Statute of the International Court of Justice on conditions to be determined in each case by the General Assembly upon the recommendation of the Security Council.

Article 94

1. Each Member of the United Nations undertakes to comply with the de-

cision of the International Court of Justice in any case to which it is a party.

2. If any party to a case fails to perform the obligations incumbent upon it under a judgment rendered by the Court, the other party may have recourse to the Security Council, which may, if it deems necessary, make recommendations or decide upon measures to be taken to give effect to the judgment.

Article 95

Nothing in the present Charter shall prevent Members of the United Nations from entrusting the solution of their differences to other tribunals by virtue of agreements already in existence or which may be concluded in the future.

Article 96

1. The General Assembly or the Security Council may request the International Court of Justice to give an advisory opinion on any legal question.

2. Other organs of the United Nations and specialized agencies, which may at any time be so authorized by the General Assembly, may also request advisory opinions of the Court on legal questions arising within the scope of their activities.

CHAPTER XV
THE SECRETARIAT
Article 97

The Secretariat shall comprise a Secretary-General and such staff as the Organization may require. The Secretary-General shall be appointed by the General Assembly upon the recommendation of the Security Council. He shall be the chief administrative officer of the Organization.

Article 98

The Secretary-General shall act in that capacity in all meetings of the General Assembly, of the Security Council, of the Economic and Social Council, and of the Trusteeship Council, and shall perform such other functions as are entrusted to him by these organs. The Secretary-General shall make an annual report to the General Assembly on the work of the Organization.

Article 99

The Secretary-General may bring to the attention of the Security Council any matter which in his opinion may threaten the maintenance of international peace and security.

Article 100

1. In the performance of their duties the Secretary-General and the staff shall not seek or receive instructions from any government or from any other authority external to the Organization. They shall refrain from any action which might reflect on their position as international officials responsible only to the Organization.

2. Each Member of the United Nations undertakes to respect the exclusively international character of the responsibilities of the Secretary-General and the staff and not to seek to influence them in the discharge of their responsibilities.

Article 101

1. The staff shall be appointed by the Secretary-General under regulations established by the General Assembly.

2. Appropriate staffs shall be permanently assigned to the Economic and Social Council, the Trusteeship Council, and, as required, to other organs of the United Nations. These staffs shall form a part of the Secretariat.

3. The paramount consideration in the employment of the staff and in the determination of the conditions of service shall be the necessity of securing the highest standards of efficiency, competence, and integrity. Due regard shall be paid to the importance of recruiting the staff on as wide a geographical basis as possible.

CHAPTER XVI

MICELLANEOUS PROVISIONS

Article 102

1. Every treaty and every international agreement entered into by any Member of the United Nations after the present Charter comes into force shall as soon as possible be registered with the Secretariat and published by it.

2. No party to any such treaty or international agreement which has not been registered in accordance with the provisions of paragraph 1 of this Article may invoke that treaty or agreement before any organ of the United Nations.

Article 103

In the event of a conflict between the obligations of the Members of the United Nations under the present Charter and their obligations under any other international agreement, their obligations under the present Charter shall prevail.

Article 104

The Organization shall enjoy in the territory of each of its Members such legal capacity as may be necessary for the exercise of its functions and the fulfillment of its purposes.

Article 105

1. The Organization shall enjoy in the territory of each of its Members such privileges and immunities as are necessary for the fulfillment of its purposes.

2. Representatives of the Members of the United Nations and officials of the Organization shall similarly enjoy such privileges and immunities as are necessary for the independent exercise of their functions in connection with the Organization.

3. The General Assembly may make recommendations with a view to determining the details of the application of paragraphs 1 and 2 of this Article or may propose conventions to the Members of the United Nations for this purpose.

CHAPTER XVII

TRANSITIONAL SECURITY ARRANGEMENTS

Article 106

Pending the coming into force of such special agreements referred to in Article 43 as in the opinion of the Security Council enable it to begin the exercise of its responsibilities under Article 42, the parties to the Four-Nation Declaration, signed at Moscow, October 30, 1943, and France, shall, in accordance with the provisions of paragraph 5 of that Declaration, consult with one another and as occasion requires with other Members of the United Nations with a view to such joint action on behalf of the Organization as may be necessary for the purpose of maintaining international peace and security.

Article 107

Nothing in the present Charter shall invalidate or preclude action, in relation to any state which during the Second World War has been an enemy of any signatory to the present Charter, taken or authorized as a result of that war by the Governments having responsibility for such action.

CHAPTER XVIII

AMENDMENTS

Article 108

Amendments to the present Charter shall come into force for all Members of the United Nations when they have been adopted by a vote of two thirds of the members of the General Assembly and ratified in accordance with their respective constitutional processes by two thirds of the Members of the United Nations, including all the permanent members of the Security Council.

Article 109

1. A General Conference of the Members of the United Nations for the purpose of reviewing the present Charter may be held at a date and place to be

fixed by a two-thirds vote of the members of the General Assembly and by a vote of any seven members of the Security Council. Each Member of the United Nations shall have one vote in the conference.

2. Any alteration of the present Charter recommended by a two-thirds vote of the conference shall take effect when ratified in accordance with their respective constitutional processes by two thirds of the Members of the United Nations including all the permanent members of the Security Council.

3. If such a conference has not been held before the tenth annual session of the General Assembly following the coming into force of the present Charter, the proposal to call such a conference shall be placed on the agenda of that session of the General Assembly, and the conference shall be held if so decided by a majority vote of the members of the Genral Assembly and by a vote of any seven members of the Security Council.

CHAPTER XIX
RATIFICATION AND SIGNATURE
Article 110

1. The present Charter shall be ratified by the signatory states in accordance with their respective constitutional processes.

2. The ratifications shall be deposited with the Government of the United States of America, which shall notify all the signatory states of each deposit as well as the Secretary-General of the Organization when he has been appointed.

3. The present Charter shall come into force upon the deposit of ratifications by the Republic of China, France, the Union of Soviet Socialist Republics, the United Kingdom of Great Britain and Northern Ireland, and the United States of America, and by a majority of the other signatory states. A protocol of the ratifications deposited shall thereupon be drawn up by the Government of the United States of America which shall communicate copies thereof to all the signatory states.

4. The states signatory to the present Charter which ratify it after it has come into force will become original Members of the United Nations on the date of the deposit of their respective ratifications.

Article 111

The present Charter, of which the Chinese, French, Russian, English, and Spanish texts are equally authentic, shall remain deposited in the archives of the Government of the United States of America. Duly certified copies thereof shall be transmitted by that Government to the Governments of the other signatory states.

IN FAITH WHEREOF the representatives of the Governments of the United Nations have signed the present Charter.

DONE at the city of San Francisco the twenty-sixth day of June, one thousand nine hundred and forty-five.

INDEX

Index

Note: Italic page numbers indicate that references are found in footnotes.

This book has been set on the Linotype in 11 and 10 point Garamond #3, leaded 1 point. Tabular material is in Mono Modern #8. Part numbers and titles are in 12 point Garamond #3. Chapter numbers are in 12 point Garamond #3 and 24 point Garamond #248; chapter titles are in 18 point Garamond #248. The size of the type page is 27 by 44½ picas.